EXCAVATIONS AT THE MOLA DI MONTE GELATO

A ROMAN AND MEDIEVAL SETTLEMENT
IN SOUTH ETRURIA

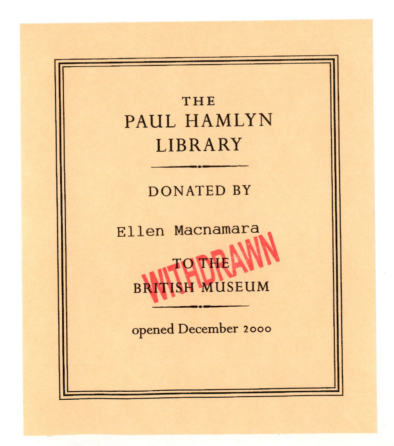

This volume has been published with the help of a very substantial subvention from the Trustees of the British Museum, as well as with grants from the M. Aylwin Cotton Foundation and King Alfred's College, Winchester.

EXCAVATIONS AT THE MOLA DI MONTE GELATO

A ROMAN AND MEDIEVAL SETTLEMENT
IN SOUTH ETRURIA

T.W. Potter and A.C. King

with

L. Allason-Jones, P. Arthur, D.M. Bailey, F. Fedeli Bernardini, A. Claridge, J. Conheeney,
J. DeLaine, C.M. Gilliver, O. Gilkes, J. Giorgi, R.P.J. Jackson, F. Marazzi, J. Osborne,
H. Patterson, J. Price, P. Roberts and D. Wilkinson

and

C. Cartwright, J. Cook, I.C. Freestone, R. Hobbs, K. Matthews, O. Murray,
P. Parsons, B. West, D. Williams and R.J.A. Wilson

with drawings principally by

R.D. Andrews, S. Ashley, S. Cann, S. Gibson and T.W. Potter

principal photographs by

K. Warren

ARCHAEOLOGICAL MONOGRAPHS OF THE
BRITISH SCHOOL AT ROME
No. 11

Published by the British School at Rome London,
in association with
THE BRITISH MUSEUM

1997

ISBN 0 904152 31 6

Cover illustration: The mill and waterfalls on the river Treia at the Mola di Monte Gelato *(Photograph: Kate Warren)*

Typeset by Cristal, via degli Orti di Galba 24-26, 00152 Rome, Italy
and printed by Tipograf S.r.l., via Costantino Morin 26/A, 00195 Rome, Italy
Cover design by Silvia Stucky

This volume is dedicated to the memory of Molly Cotton,
an inspirational mentor during my early exploration
of southern Etruria

Contents

viii

List of Tables

PREFACE

The excavations here reported form part of a long-standing investigation into the archaeology and history of the central part of the Ager Faliscus. It originated as a field survey, conducted by John Ward-Perkins and the British School at Rome in the 1950s, and by myself, for the School, in the later 1960s. In conjunction with this, I have in addition initiated a number of excavations in the area, aimed at setting in a sharper focus the results of the field survey. The present project forms part of this broader investigation, and the research design will be reviewed in the first chapter. Here it is necessary to make only three general points.

The first is to emphasize that most of these excavations arose from questions posed by study of the field-survey data. Conclusions derived from surface collections can be extremely informative, as Ward-Perkins demonstrated so magisterially in his work on the Ager Veientanus (Kahane, Murray-Threipland and Ward-Perkins 1968); but they also need testing and refining by the application of sophisticated techniques of excavation, as the Monte Gelato investigations have clearly demonstrated. The reading of the evidence acquired from surface inspection (set out in Chapter Two) in no way prepared one for the remarkable picture that emerged from our trenches, nor for the subtle nuances of the chronological sequence.

Secondly, it is pertinent to add that the site was to yield a range of artefacts that was by any standard exceptional. This turned what might have been a relatively small-scale enquiry (as was initially intended) into a major project, leading to a substantial publication. The wealth of sculpture, inscriptions, and objects in metal, bone, glass, pottery and other materials, together with critically important assemblages of animal, bird and fish bones, which poured forth on almost a daily basis, indeed remains an enduring memory. They allow for a much more sophisticated interpretation of the site's changing nature and status than is usually possible and, in turn, raise intriguing questions about the depositional factors that lie behind so rich a pattern of survival. These we are scarcely able to answer (and they are seldom addressed in classical archaeology, despite their prominence in prehistoric studies); but this is clearly an aspect of our results which merits further research.

Finally, it is pleasant to be able to record that, while the publication is largely in English, and produced in British institutions, the project as a whole was emphatically Anglo-Italian. This extended well beyond the composition of the team of archaeologists and specialists. Relations with the local community were close, and I recall with particular pleasure the visits of groups of children, organized by local schools. Their interest in the archaeology may have been nearly equalled by their fascination with the idiosyncratic Italian in which they were not infrequently addressed; but we very much welcomed these educational initiatives which, together with growth of true collaborative projects, represent a most welcome trend over recent years. We trust that this volume, together with the many discussions that have also appeared in Italian, will be seen as a further contribution to our understanding of the archaeology of a region with an especially rich and rewarding patrimony.

T.W. Potter

ACKNOWLEDGEMENTS

Monte Gelato was an extraordinarily pleasant and happy excavation, due in large measure to a first-class and highly dedicated team. Many began their archaeological careers as students of Dr King at King Alfred's College, Winchester, and have subsequently taken full-time employment in British archaeological units. For them, Monte Gelato was truly a 'busman's holiday', and we owe them a special debt of thanks for their loyalty to the project, which brought them back to the site year after year. We cannot, alas, mention all who worked with us – the list is far too long – but we would like to express our warmest gratitude to Oliver Gilkes, our chief supervisor throughout the project; to Robin Brunner-Ellis, Crispin Jarman, Nicki King, Sally Martin and David Wilkinson who also supervised; and to Martin Brown, Simone DeTurris, David Forster, Alan and Jane French, Douglas Hird, Tony Hurley, Federico Marazzi and Alex Turner, who were the most conspicuously long-term excavators. It is most striking that virtually all who were with us at the start of the project in 1986 were still digging at Monte Gelato in the last season of 1990.

We also gladly acknowledge Dr Simon James of the British Museum, who was the main site planner throughout the excavation, and thus deeply involved with interpreting a complex site; Mr Danny Andrews, ARIBA, who carried out the survey of the valley and the mill; and Dr Kate Gilliver, who ran the Finds Department with enormous efficiency, and who also coordinated the specialist study season at the British School at Rome in 1991.

The field team was accommodated in a *palestra* at Campagnano di Roma, and we are most grateful to the *Comune* and then mayor, Sig. Filippo Lorenzetti, for all manner of help, not least the provision of evening meals for some of the seasons: we were delighted and honoured when the *Comune* of Campagnano awarded the British School at Rome, as principal sponsor of the project in Italy, a gold medal. To the British School itself we are especially indebted. Here was accommodated the main post-excavation team, drawn principally from staff of the British Museum. These comprised Kate Warren (Photographic Division) who, between 1988 and 1990, did all the studio photography, as well as the majority of the photographs on site (and who gratefully acknowledges the loan of much equipment by Bronica Ltd); Sandra Smith (1988), Penny Fisher (1989) and Loretta Hogan and Denise Ling (1990), of the Museum's Conservation Department, who conserved the entire collection and, in 1990, joined the vessels from the huge second-century dump in a fish-pond (cf. Figs 216 and 217); and Janice Conheeney, who, as a museum assistant in my department, in 1988 organized the storage of the collections, before beginning an independent study of the human remains. The achievements of the British Museum staff will be obvious in the pages of this volume, and we are particularly grateful to them; and, too, to their respective Keepers for providing special leave, especially Dr Andrew Oddy, head of Conservation at the British Museum.

We also offer our sincere thanks to our principal illustrators, Stephen Ashley and Sally Cann. They carried out their excellent work at the British School, and rose to the challenge of drawing an extraordinarily diverse range of objects with commitment and great skill. All who worked in the School are extremely indebted to successive Directors, Professor Graeme Barker and Professor Richard Hodges, for their support; and especially to the then Assistant Director, Amanda Claridge, for aiding the project in every possible way, both academically and logistically. We would also like to acknowledge with warmth and affection the work of the School's staff, who so very unassumingly and yet so efficiently ease the path of those involved with projects like the one here described.

Likewise, the Italian authorities did everything they could to ensure that the excavation ran smoothly and without hindrance. I personally owe a deep and profound debt of gratitude to the former Superintendent of Antiquities for southern Etruria, Prof. Paola Pelagatti, for her support over many years; and now to her successor, Dott. G. Scichilone, for his warm encouragement. We also owe much to Dott.ssa Bruna Amendolea, of the office of the *Assessore della Cultura*, particularly in her attempts to improve the *mise-en-valeur* of the site. But our warmest thanks must be reserved for the region's inspector, Dott.ssa Clementina Sforzini, who has been unflagging in her efforts to help the project. Both by her work on the site and behind the scenes, she has been a true friend of the excavation, and we most genuinely appreciate it.

Our sponsoring bodies have been numerous. The British School has been more than generous in allocating funds and logistic support, while our biggest patron has been the British Museum, which provided financial help (and, as described above, much more) throughout, including the study season. We gladly thank the Trustees; the former Director, Sir David Wilson; the present Director, Dr Robert Anderson; and the Keepers of the various departments concerned (Prehistory and Roman Britain; Greek and Roman Antiquities; Medieval and Later Antiquities; the Research Laboratory and the Department of Conservation). I owe a very real personal debt of gratitude to the former Keeper of my own department, Dr Ian Longworth, for his unswerving support and encouragement; without it, the Monte Gelato excavation could hardly have happened. Likewise I owe a very deep debt of gratitude to Kate Down who, with the assistance of Judith Cash, both of my department, undertook the onerous task of preparing the typescript, not least a daunting array of tables, with astounding good cheer.

We were particularly delighted to receive a grant from the M. Alywin Cotton Foundation towards the costs of this volume, and take great pleasure in dedicating it to the memory of Molly Cotton; this is in tribute to her contribution to the work in South Etruria, and especially her guidance during my Ager Faliscus field survey in the later 1960s (in which she from time to time participated).

We are also extremely grateful to the British Academy, the Society of Antiquaries of London, King Alfred's College, Winchester, the Society for the Promotion of Roman Studies, and the Craven Fund of the University of Oxford, for their financial contribution to the project, which was conducted at a total cost of £51,000. Many individuals, far too numerous to name in their entirety, have also been free and generous in their help. We particularly thank the specialists who have contributed to this volume, not least scientists from the British Museum's Research Laboratory, who have examined problematic material; and would like to make special mention of those whose names do not necessarily feature in the text, but who have given us advice and help: Janet Ambers, Sheridan Bowman, Piero Brunetti, Andrew Burnett, Lucos Cozza, Paolo Delogu, Vincenzo Fiocchi Nicolai, Riccardo Francovich, Sheila Gibson, Karen Hughes, Catherine Johns, Enzo Litta, John Lloyd, Federico Marazzi, Lidia Paroli, Nicholas Purcell, Joyce Reynolds, Valerie Scott, Andrew Wallace-Hadrill, Susan Walker and Chris Wickham. Nor can we forget the friendly officials of the *Parco suburbano della valle Treja*; Giancarlo, the kindly proprietor of the much frequented Monte Gelato bar; and the contribution of my own family, especially my wife Sandra, who did a huge amount to aid the project, both in terms of organization (especially the travel arrangements) and in deeply valued moral support. Likewise, I owe much to my readers, especially Neil Christie (himself a Monte Gelato digger), who subjected the excavation text to ruthless scrutiny, to its great advantage; and to Gill Clark who, as the British School's Publications Manager, has made a decisive contribution to this volume, in an editorial role.

Finally, I would like to pay special tribute to the co-director of the project, Anthony King. It was he who directed work on site, and supervised the arrangements in Campagnano, and he brought to the project an enviable degree of archaeological expertise, and a very real flair for interpreting the evidence in the ground. He was also responsible for assembling the first-rate team. His many other duties have meant that he was unable to do as much for this volume as we had hoped, so that the report and illustrations of the excavations were largely drafted by myself; however, it is very much the fruit of extended discussion, and represents our joint views. We both, I fancy, enjoyed the project to the full but, without his talent and commitment, it would have been a shadow of what it was to become.

T.W. Potter

Chapter One

INTRODUCTION: THE NATURE OF THE PROBLEM

The Mola di Monte Gelato lies in the pleasantly wooded valley of the river Treia, about 34 km north from the heart of Rome. Until the creation in the early 1980s of a suburban park, extending down the Treia valley from the Mola to Mazzano and Calcata, this was a relatively remote and isolated spot. Yet its setting is known to millions, as a backdrop to the countless films that have been made there over the past 40 years or so. Attracted by charming waterfalls and the rustic remains of a medieval mill, bridge and tower, cinematic and television directors are still drawn to the Mola di Monte Gelato. So too, these days, are numerous weekend visitors, largely from Rome, who make the now easy drive from the city, up the Via Veientana, the modernized *superstrada* that has partly replaced and partly improved the Via Cassia. The city of Rome and its hinterland are thus integrated in a way unthinkable even twenty years ago, but a phenomenon which, as this volume will show, can be closely paralleled in

the past. Indeed, the history of the Mola is in many respects a mirror of the changing fortunes of Rome itself.

The hill known as Monte Gelato lies in fact some 1,100 m to the east of the Mola (Fig. 1). For convenience, we have tended to call the site at the Mola 'Monte Gelato', and indeed wonder whether it is the seductive and creamy-cold texture of the waterfalls which provides an origin for the toponym. That, however, is speculation. What is not in doubt is that the place has an intriguing history, and a very rich archaeology, as the ensuing pages will attempt to show. But first we must set out something of the background to the project, not least to demonstrate how it fits into a relatively coherent and logical campaign of research into the archaeology of this region (Figs 2 and 3).

The Mola di Monte Gelato is situated in the southern part of the Ager Faliscus. This effectively corresponds with the drainage basin of the river

Fig. 1. The Mola di Monte Gelato in 1970, looking southeast across the terrace of the main site towards the mill and adjacent tower. *(TWP)*

1

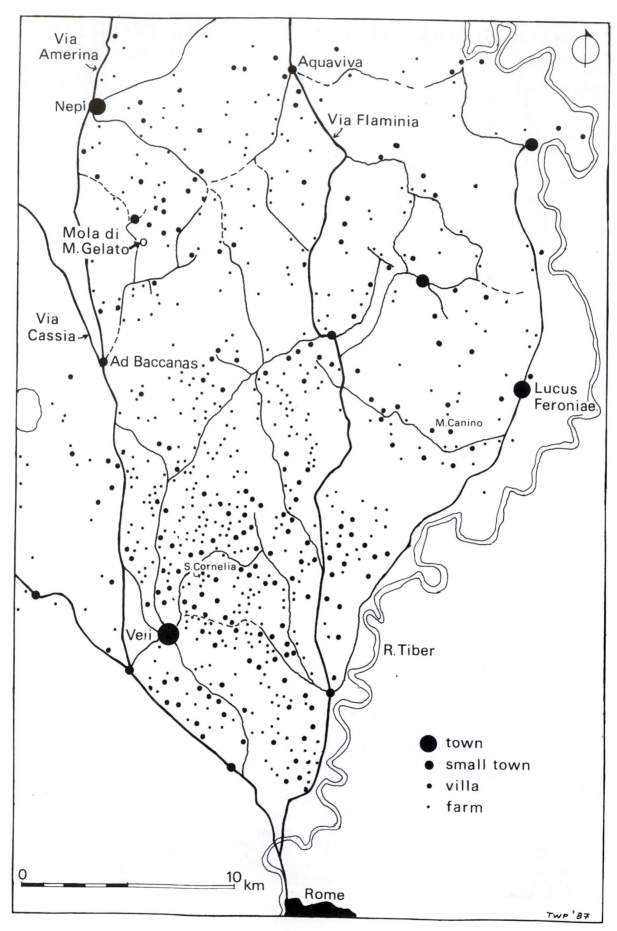

Fig. 2. South Etruria in the early Imperial period. *(TWP)*

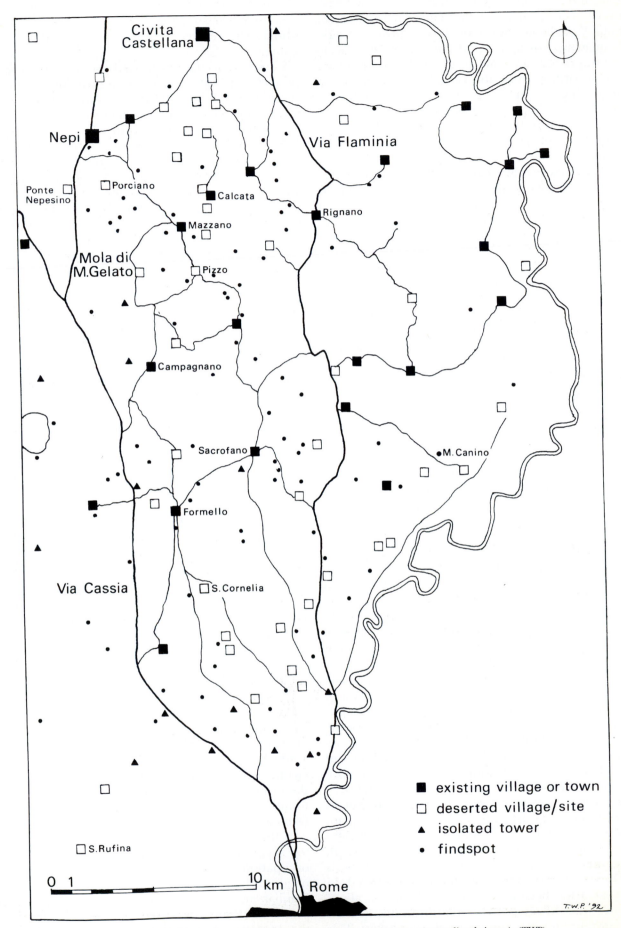

Fig. 3. South Etruria in the medieval period. (Lines are roads in use in medieval times.) *(TWP)*

Treia, and its tributaries, which flows in a northeast-erly direction, entering the Tiber to the east of Civita Castellana, more or less opposite Poggio Sommavilla. It is a favoured and fertile land, occu-pied in pre-Roman times by the Faliscans, a people who, according to Strabo (v. 2.9), 'spoke a special and distinct language all of their own'. Although culturally close to the Etruscans, the Faliscan lan-guage appears to have been most akin to Latin, and it may be that the Latins and the Faliscans shared common roots.

The Faliscan region has been long studied. Fun-damental was the work of Adolfo Cozza and Angelo Pasqui, together with Gian Francesco Gamurrini and Raniero Mengarelli, in the late nineteenth cen-tury, so splendidly presented by Cozza's grandson, Professor Lucos Cozza (1972: 429-30; 1981), in the relevant volumes of the *Carta archeologica d'Italia*. Similarly important are the studies of the great his-torian, Giuseppe Tomassetti (1913, republished with further commentary in 1979), with their de-tailed documentary and topographical discussions. All modern scholars are indebted to these pioneer-ing works.

Hardly less influential was Thomas Ashby, Dir-ector of the British School at Rome between 1906 and 1925, whose studies of the Campagna (Ashby 1927; 1986) 'will always remain a treasured posses-sion of any lover of the Roman countryside' (Ward-Perkins 1970: x). It was Ashby who properly estab-lished a British tradition of topographical studies in the environs of Rome, a mantle that was brilliantly assumed by John Ward-Perkins when he was Dir-ector of the British School, between 1946 and 1974. Of the South Etruria field survey, which he initi-ated and directed, it is hardly necessary to write. Its unique importance in the history of landscape studies is universally recognized, so much so that field survey is now a dominant theme of contempor-ary investigations. Even though methodologies have become ever more sophisticated, the value of the work in South Etruria – conducted as it was at a time when so many sites were in the process of being destroyed – remains. It is a point vividly made by survey in 1989 of the sector to the southwest of Campagnano di Roma, which painted a sorry pic-ture of an archaeologically devastated landscape (King 1993). Whilst not all of the Roman Cam-pagna has suffered in this way, the timeliness of Ward-Perkins's intervention is nevertheless obvi-ous, as he himself clearly recognized (1955: 44).

My own involvement with the region began in 1966, when I was asked to survey some 200 square kilometres of the central and southern Ager Falis-cus. These results, although available in typescript, have never been published in detail. This is because, when the manuscript was prepared in 1980-81, I was becoming increasingly uneasy about the accuracy of my pottery identifications, which I thought, upon reflection, to be overconfident. This is why there is currently a project underway to re-examine (and computerize) the collections, with a view to reassessing the South Etruria survey as a whole. The results, we can be sure, will be intri-guing.

Ward-Perkins always stressed the need to develop pottery chronologies by excavation of promising sites revealed by the survey. Thus we were to devote five seasons of work to the deeply-stratified bronze age and iron age site beside the river Treia at Narce, just a few kilometres downstream from the Mola di Monte Gelato. Discovered in the autumn of 1966, the site clearly had the potential to illumin-ate a crucial period of Faliscan pre- and proto-his-tory. It was a complex and difficult site, but did indeed provide an important corpus of material, including faunal and floral assemblages, spanning the period between the latter part of the second millennium BC and about 250 BC (Potter 1976). Considerable light was shed upon the evolution of stock and arable economies. In the fourth and third centuries BC the site was used for tile manu-facture, exploiting exposures of Pliocene clay which underlie the volcanics. This industrial tradi-tion continued elsewhere along the Treia valley in Roman and medieval times, not least at the Mola di Monte Gelato, where Roman pottery wasters and an early medieval pottery kiln were discovered in the present excavations. Indeed, the question of local pottery manufacture in the Roman period has been greatly illuminated by Peña's study of a num-ber of the kiln sites in the region (Peña 1987), which indicates widespread and relatively intensive rural production.

The other main direction of post-survey excava-tions in the Ager Faliscus has focused upon the transition from the dispersed pattern of rural set-tlement in the Roman period to the fortified and nucleated towns and villages (*castelli*) which domin-ated the medieval landscape. It had been long recognized that the documentary sources imply that these medieval sites were, in the main, cre-ations of the tenth and eleventh centuries AD, which, as Toubert (1973) demonstrated, were often undertaken for economic reasons. Closer to Rome, in the Ager Veientanus, farming based on rural 'villas' carried on well into medieval times, as histor-ical and archaeological research has shown (Kahane, Murray Threipland and Ward-Perkins 1968; Wickham 1978; 1979). It is a point most vividly made by the excavations at Santa Cornelia, the primary centre of the *domusculta* of *Capracorum*, founded *c*. 774-6, by Pope Hadrian I (Christie and Daniels 1991).

In the Ager Faliscus there seemed to be reasons for suggesting a rather earlier trend towards the occupation of defensible positions. The arguments need not be rehearsed again in detail, for they are familiar and in some respects flawed. They were proposed (Potter 1975) partly because forum ware, the lead-glazed pottery produced from the late eighth century in Rome, was conspicuously rare on the late Roman 'villas' (unlike the Ager Veientanus), but did occur on some of the defended medieval sites. Moreover, the Ager Faliscus had become, from the time of the Lombard invasion of 568, something of a frontier zone. Sutri, for instance, fell to the Lombards and was retaken soon after, in 592-3, and hostilities are frequently mentioned in the letters of Gregory the Great. Later, in the eighth century there was conflict between Rome and the Lombard king, Liutprand, as well as with local nobles like Duke Toto of Nepi. It did not seem implausible to correlate the archaeological and historical evidence, and to infer an earlier phase of medieval *castelli* than in some other regions.

Two excavations were made to test the point, one in 1971 at Mazzano Romano (Potter 1972) and the other in 1982 at Ponte Nepesino (Cameron *et al.* 1984), a now deserted promontory site, overlooking the Via Amerina, to the south of Nepi. Both yielded forum ware, in association with masonry structures (at Mazzano) and wooden buildings (at Ponte Nepesino); but radiocarbon dates from Ponte Nepesino suggested that occupation was unlikely to have begun before the later ninth century. There thus remained what seemed to be an archaeological gap between the apparent demise of the late Roman 'villas' – somewhere in the sixth century, to judge from surface finds – and the emergence of the medieval *castelli*, three to four centuries later.

The time was clearly ripe to examine the question from a different angle, by choosing a well-stratified Roman rural site, where there might be some possibility of occupation continuing into medieval times. The Mola di Monte Gelato was a prime candidate. Here was what appeared to be a large Roman villa, overlooking the Treia valley, and its waterfalls, with surface indications of both late Roman and medieval occupation. Moreover, nearby was a deserted medieval *castello*, known as Castellaccio, a juxtaposition that is not uncommon in the Ager Faliscus (Potter 1975; 1979: 165-7). It seemed to raise the possibility that there might have been movement from one to other, an intriguing thought that merited investigation.

Tomassetti (1882; 1913: 109-10) had long before recognized the potential importance of the site at the Mola. He identified it with the *castrum Capracorum* referred to in a bull of 1053, with its lands, vineyards and mill, together with a church of Saint John *que dicitur Latregia* (= Treia), 27 miles from Rome. He noted that the name *Capracorum* is preserved as *Crepacore*, one of the *quarti della tenuta Montegelato* (Tomassetti 1882: 147), also observing that it is half Greek and half Latin – a fascinating observation given that our excavations were to demonstrate the presence of Greek speakers at the site in Roman times. Moreover, he discussed in a summary fashion the results of excavations carried out between 1875 and 1877 by a Signor Giorgi, on

behalf of the *principe* Del Drago. Tomassetti must have seen some of this work on a visit to Mazzano in 1876 '*per dirigere alcune scavazioni di antichità*' (1882: 146). He recorded how Giorgi was spurred on by the discovery of very many fragments of marble, and found a '*cappella cristiana presso i piloni di un ponte romano diruto (sul Treia), con un piccolo sotteraneo (lunga m. 4×3,50)*'. There was a Latin cross in iron, and near the church a Christian burial with large tiles, gold earrings and glass *balsamarii*. There were in addition '*due torri cadute, un altro sepolcreto formato di loculi scavati nel tufo, donde la contrada trasse il nome di Scifelle (altro quarto di Montegelato)* [500 m to the south of the Mola]; *una vena d'acqua eccellente presso la collina e innumerevoli avanzi di stoviglie più o meno rozze*'.

Tomassetti (1877; 1882) also referred to an ancient Roman road, a *diverticolo della Cassia*, and inscriptions from nearby Monte Caio (below, Fig. 8: *CIL* XI 3207, 3228). Further light on these is shed by the archival research of Fiocchi Nicolai (1988: 235-7), who has published the transcription of three further inscriptions, made by the *guardiascavi* on the 21 December 1877. They are early Christian tombstones, one dated to AD 361, and a second, of *Iohannes* and others, to AD 407. The third, of Calvisius Mesalinus, is not dated, but is presumably of the same general period.

We will show below that Tomassetti was almost certainly correct in his correlation of the bull of 1053 with the site at the Mola di Monte Gelato; it is very plausibly identified as *castrum Capracorum*. We cannot convincingly locate all the features mentioned in his description, but there is a sufficient correlation between our results and those of Giorgi, as described by Tomassetti, to suggest that we were digging in the same place. The *piccolo sotteraneo*, in particular, eludes us (unless it is the rock-cut cave to the west of the church, although the dimensions do not match), as do the two collapsed towers (although it is clear that Tomassetti was describing a wide area, since he mentioned the zone known as Scifelle, which lies well to the south of the Mola). But the church, the paved road and the burials have all been relocated during our work.

The name *Capracorum* immediately links the site with the *domusculta* founded about 776 by Pope Hadrian I (772-95). The *Liber Pontificalis* states:

> The same most holy Pope [Hadrian I] created and founded four papal estates, of which one is called Capracorum, in the territory of Veii, about 15 miles out of Rome. Of this estate, the original farm of Capracorum together with several other farms adjoining it, was his own property, inherited from his family; and to it he added a number of other estates, giving just compensation for each to the persons from whom he bought them. This *domusculta* of Capracorum, with its *massae* [lands], *fundi* [farms], *casales* [farm buildings], vineyards, olive groves, watermills and all else appertaining to it, be established under apostolic privilege and with the sanction of solemn penalties, that it should for all

time continue to be applied to the use of our brothers
in Christ, the poor; and that the wheat and barley
grown each year in its fields should be carefully collected and stored apart in the granary of our holy
church. The wine, too, and the vegetables grown each
year in the domains and fields of the aforesaid *domusculta*, should similarly be diligently collected and stored
separately in the storehouse of our holy church. And of
the pigs which should each year be fattened in the *casales* in the said *domusculta*, one hundred head should be
slaughtered and stored in the same storehouse.

(*Liber Pontificalis* (Duchesne) I, 501-2)

Once thought of as a continuous tract of land, it
is now clear that the *domuscultae, Capracorum* included, consisted of a series of farms, with their own
separate estates (Wickham 1978: 174). Moreover,
their purpose, whilst overtly to feed the poor of
Rome, had a political significance as well. Rome in
the eighth century was a city under threat – from
the Lombards (Liutprand had taken Sutri and its
territory in 728-9) and from nobles like Duke Toto
of Nepi, who in 768 was able to install his brother
as anti-pope. The *domuscultae* were thus additionally
intended to assert papal authority in the countryside around Rome (Christie 1991b).

We referred above to the site of Santa Cornelia,
which excavation and documentary evidence
together show was unquestionably the estate-centre
of the *domusculta* of *Capracorum*. Although nothing
is heard of the *domuscultae* after the mid-ninth century, it is clear on archaeological evidence that
Santa Cornelia continued in occupation, and probably between 1026 and 1035 it was converted into a
monastery. Tomassetti conjectured that the estate-
centre passed from Santa Cornelia to the Mola di
Monte Gelato although, in the absence of any evidence to show that the *domusculta* continued to
exist after 846, this must remain in question – especially as no suitable buildings were identified in the
present excavations. It is to these that we must now
turn.

As chance would have it, attention had already
been focused upon the Mola when, in 1983, widening of the road-cutting that leads down to the river
Treia from the north brought to light burials, early
medieval interlace sculpture, and Roman and medieval walls. The paved Roman road was also visible.
These discoveries were recorded by the Superintendency inspector for the area, Dott.ssa Clementina
Sforzini, and further damage was prevented. When
our own programme of work was finally launched,
in September 1986, this was clearly the place at
which to begin.

The results were immediately fruitful (Fig. 4).
Cleaning of the side of the modern road-cutting
revealed part of a small early Imperial bath-house,
with later structures above. A trench was therefore
excavated on the east side of the road-cutting, and
came down upon the remains of two superimposed
churches, with associated burials. It was an auspi-

cious start, and over the following four years a substantial area of the gently sloping ground to the
north and east of the church was investigated. The
preservation of structures and stratigraphy was very
variable. The hillside had been terraced into at
least three levels in Roman times, and structures
and deposits on the lower terrace, immediately
beside the modern road, had survived very well.
The buildings on the upper terrace had suffered a
fair amount of damage from ploughing, although
there were intact deposits over most of the floors
except within the church, where only one small
area of floor remained. The top terrace, on the
other hand, had been severely affected by modern
agriculture, and only features that were deeply
recessed into the bedrock were preserved. Even
some *selce* blocks from the road paving had been
pulled out by the plough, although covered by as
much as 1.5 m of colluvium; further up the hillside
a scatter of blocks on the surface shows that it must
have been destroyed more or less completely.

This in itself amply illustrates the destructive
effect of modern agriculture. However, we were in
1989 to meet the man who claimed to have first
ploughed the site in the early 1950s, as part of the
Ente Maremma scheme. He spoke of walls (including one in what was evidently *opus reticulatum*)
which were then standing to a height of 2.0 m, as
well as numerous large tufo blocks, of the sort utilized in the early medieval complex, to the southeast of the church. He also referred to a white
marble statue, lacking only an arm. These structures
were duly levelled. Furthermore, in 1976, as
records in the Villa Giulia show, vine trenches were
cut over much of the area. These penetrated to a
depth of 1.4 m, with immensely destructive results.
Thus, when we came to excavate in the central part
of the site (below, Fig. 11, Trench H), and beside
some still-standing masonry, in close proximity to a
low cliff (Fig. 4, Trench K), we found that virtually
no stratigraphy survived. It is clear therefore that
much of the better-preserved parts of the main site
have been examined, and that, while there is
doubtless much more to be discovered, it would
seem that the most fruitful areas have now been
explored. Indeed, on the east side of the site,
where a track now runs across the area and up the
hill, bedrock outcrops at a number of points: whatever there may have been there has long since disappeared.

We call the site to the east of the modern road
the 'main site' to distinguish it from work undertaken elsewhere in the valley. One focus of attention arose by chance rather than by design. In the
spring of 1989, a local *azienda agricola* acquired the
land on the south and west sides of the modern
road, opposite the main excavation. This was covered
with scrub, and comprised a low ridge, running
parallel with the modern road, and flattish terrain,
the old flood plain, extending down to the river
Treia. The whole area was then systematically

MOLA DI MONTE GELATO 1986 - 1990

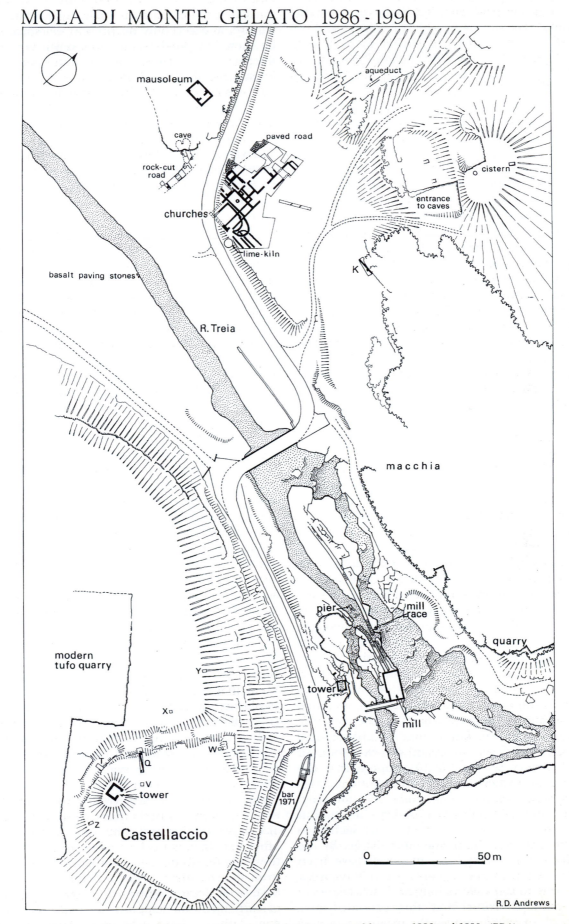

Fig. 4. The site and its known archaeological features, surveyed between 1986 and 1990. *(RDA)*

bulldozed and ploughed, and a deep drainage ditch was also cut. When word finally got out, the bulldozing was stopped, and we were asked to assess the damage to what proved to be a rich archaeological area. Immediately conspicuous was a brick-built mausoleum or temple-tomb of early Imperial date, on the crest of the ridge. This we surveyed and partially excavated in 1989 and 1990, and were able to show that it was the sole surviving feature on that part of the ridge. Also revealed was a rock-cut early medieval cave habitation, set into the ridge below the mausoleum. We investigated the entrance to the cave: we acquired dating evidence and identified a number of other features. Finally we examined the area below the cave, and uncovered some poorly-preserved Roman wall-footings, and a remarkable road-cutting, which reached a depth of nearly 4.0 m. It was clearly the precursor of the paved Roman road, and was filled with rich dumps of Roman-period refuse.

In addition to these excavations, a new survey of the valley was made, by Richard Andrews, who also prepared detailed drawings of the still-standing mill, bridge and adjoining tower. This was an important work of record, since plans were afoot to restore these buildings, thereby inevitably changing their appearance. The mill machinery, which was still operating in the 1950s, is very well preserved (cf. Figs 127 and 128), and we are delighted to include in this volume Dott.ssa Fedeli's study of the documentary and architectural evidence relating to the mill. To date, work has only been carried out on restoring the tower, but the plan is to have a small site museum, with information panels.

The final element of the project was to survey and acquire dating evidence from the castle site of Castellaccio. This had become extremely overgrown over the previous 25 years, but the remains of a tower were still visible, as well as a rock-cut ditch along the northwest side of the site. In 1990, therefore, seven small trenches were excavated, five on the castle itself and two on the flattish ground beyond the ditch. Although the density of trees precluded the recovery of building plans, both walls and an adequate collection of sherds were found, indicating that the site was first occupied (some prehistoric material apart) in the eleventh-twelfth centuries AD. Given that occupation had effectively ceased on the main site by about AD 1100, it is very reasonable to suppose that the castle was the successor of the valley-bottom settlement. If so, it was not apparently held for long. There is little material that post-dates the twelfth century, and the quantities of refuse are such as to imply that the population was never large. By the late thirteenth century, they may well have been moved to Mazzano, leaving only the mill complex as testimony to the valley's long and rich history.

It is perhaps ironic that this extended programme of investigation into the origins of *incastellamento* in the Ager Faliscus should weaken, if not destroy, the original proposition: the medieval nucleated settlements do seem to be mainly a late feature, and certainly on present evidence cannot be shown to pre-date the later ninth century. Yet the period between the late sixth and ninth centuries still remains archaeologically shadowy and elusive, even at a site like the Mola di Monte Gelato with its abundance of evidence. We shall show below that there is little stratigraphical evidence for activity on the site after a major collapse of roofs and walls, dated on good coin evidence to the mid-sixth century AD, at any rate before *c.* AD 800, and we certainly cannot assert that there was continuity of occupation between the later sixth and later eighth centuries.

It is the purpose of this volume, therefore, to present these findings in appropriate detail, as a contribution to an ongoing and stimulating debate. Its production was greatly facilitated by a study season in 1991, when a dozen specialists gathered at the British School to examine and catalogue the finds. This provided a forum for a fruitful dialogue and exchange of views, from which this volume has benefited greatly – as it has from the opportunity to present the findings at conferences in Siena, Rome, London and Nottingham and in many other public lectures.

Meanwhile, further work continues. In 1991 a team headed by Dr Simon Stoddart and Dr Caroline Malone then of the University of Bristol (now of the University of Cambridge), and with my general involvement, working in close collaboration with the Superintendency of Antiquities and other Italian archaeologists, began a programme of excavations within the old centre of the nearby town of Nepi. It is a place with a distinguished history, extending back into the pre-Etruscan period. Nepi and Sutri are together described by Livy (vi. 21.4) as '*loca opposita Etruria et velut claustra inde portaeque*', referring to a revolt by these cities in 386 BC, and a Latin colony was sent to Nepi in either 383 or 373 BC. Later a Roman *municipium*, it is described as a *frourion* (fortress) by Procopius (*De Bello Gothico* iv. 35), alluding to its strategic role on the Via Amerina in the sixth century AD. This role it maintained throughout medieval times. Duke Toto, as we have seen, was an aggressive leader in the eighth century, and the Borgia fortress (which overlies the still-standing Roman gate to the town) remained an imposing symbol of Nepi's military importance until recent times.

The excavations at Nepi (which are receiving very notable support from the *comune*) offer the prospect of complementing and calibrating the results from other excavations in the region, not least those at the Mola di Monte Gelato. Already rich sequences from the seventh century BC to Republican times have been discovered by the cathedral, and dumps of early medieval sculpture, of the same type and date as those found at Monte Gelato, bear witness to a doubtless splendid Carolingian *duomo*, the predecessor of the present Romanesque building. Here, if anywhere in the Ager Faliscus, we may expect archaeological work to cast further light upon the so-called 'Dark Ages', and provide the basis for a comparison between the rural sequence garnered from our work at the Mola di Monte Gelato and at a nearby urban counterpart. It is a logical sequel to the investigation here reported, and it is more than encouraging that the vitality which has, I think, attended the programme of survey and excavation in this part of Etruria is hardly abated. That is surely a tribute to the distinguished scholars, Italian and British, who long ago set an archaeological agenda for us to follow today.

Chapter Two

THE SETTING

GEOLOGY AND GEOMORPHOLOGY

The site rests on the volcanic deposits of the Pleistocene period. These constitute the landscape of the entire South Etruria region, and have had a profound influence on the pattern of human settlement and economy. The generally soft tufos laid down as an indirect or direct result of volcanic action have formed fairly level plateaux, which in due course have been deeply cut by river systems. Locally, the river Treia, although relatively small, has created a deep, steep-sided canyon system, with a number of superbly secure locations for defended settlements. Security was a prime consideration at various periods of the region's history, notably in the Faliscan period and at the time of medieval *incastellamento*. Pre-Roman centres, such as Narce, and medieval villages, like Mazzano Romano and Calcata, amply illustrate this in the Treia valley, as does the medieval site of Castellaccio at the Mola di Monte Gelato itself.

The river Treia runs in a palaeovalley cut into the *tufo leucitico del Fosso Treia*, which can be seen in the cliff face below the waterfall (Alvarez 1972: 165). Overlying this is the *tufo stratificati varicolori di Sacrofano*, a fairly soft tufo into which the palaeovalley is also cut, and which forms the sides of the valley in various places. Subsequently, a lava flowed down the palaeovalley. This is the hard *piperno di Mazzano*, a grey to bluish grey highly welded and resistant tufo of pyroclastic origin, with inclusions of collapsed *scoriae* (Mattias and Ventriglia 1968; 1970: 360-1; Gancarz 1970: 13-15). It derived from the Monti Sabatini (Alvarez 1972; 1973), and forms the hard shelf on which the main site was positioned. Some deep features, such as the limekiln (below, Fig. 64), were cut into the *piperno*. However, most rested upon, or were dug into, a soft, yellow-brown tufaceous deposit, that had formed over the bedrock. In places this appeared to cover artificially cut surfaces in the bedrock, implying a period of formation not long before the first occupation of the main site in Augustan times. It may well be the result of downslope erosion, brought about by agricultural activity over the previous millennium. Some was certainly water-lain, probably during the heavy rainstorms that are a feature of the region.

One other volcanic deposit is represented in the study area, namely a ridge of *tufo rosso a scorie neri*, which underlies the mausoleum or temple-tomb. This is a low density, soft reddish-brown tufo with buff and black *scoriae*, 0.15-0.2 m in diameter (Mattias and Ventriglia 1970: 348-9). It is easily excavated, and housed at least one cave habitation in medieval times (Fig. 4).

THE SITE

When first explored in the 1960s, the Mola di Monte Gelato was still relatively remote. Approached only by a *strada bianca*, it was very much a country preserve, in sharp contrast with today. However, the vegetation was much less dense (Fig. 1), and signs of antiquity were abundant. These were recorded initially by John Ward-Perkins, and supplemented by later visits. Hitherto unpublished, the field observations are cited here in a manuscript first drafted in 1972, since they shed interesting light on what was achieved by the South Etruria survey team, especially when it can be matched against the excavated record.

D7 (835737-8) An important multi-period complex at the Mola di Monte Gelato.

Pre-Roman:
A. A scatter of archaic tile and pottery on the low hill overlooking the Mola on the north side.
   Brown coarse-ware, with fingerprinted cordons, red burnished sherd, internal-slip ware.
B. A cuniculus-shaped tunnel, cut into the base of the cliff on the south side of the Mola, may also be pre-Roman in date. The tunnel extends for about 12.0 m, and is apparently unfinished. There are no traces of vertical shafts.

Roman:
C. The remains of a substantial Roman villa (*c.* 100 × 150 m), on the north side of the Mola. It is built on a low natural platform, which slopes down to within 30 m of the river. The remains of a *tufelli*-faced wall survive in the face of a low cliff at the north end of the platform. There are also traces of *opus quadratum* walling still *in situ*. The villa is situated near the point where paved Roman road crosses the river Treia. This road enters the valley of the Mola from the south and, after crossing the river, heads northwest, on the line taken by the modern road to the Via Cassia – Mazzano road. A section of *selce*-paved road, 6.0 m wide, is visible in the section of the modern road cutting. Other remains include tufo blocks and much tile, tufo *opus reticulatum*, various marbles (white Italian, *Africano, cipollino, corallina breccia*), white and basalt tesserae, red-painted wall-plaster, window-glass and fine glass. There is also a tufo moulding [cf. Fig. 161, below], and a quarry in the cliffs [cf. Fig. 22, below]. These quarries appear to have been producing

long tufo blocks, suitable for *opus quadratum*; but their date is uncertain. Ward-Perkins additionally recorded a tufo channel, probably from a water duct; and a tufo altar with traces of an inscription. He also mentioned post-Roman architectural remains, including a marble spiral colonnette and a marble slab with interlace.

Black glaze (three – all very abraded, and perhaps derived from site A); *terra sigillata* (eleven), African red slip ware (fifteen), second century AD, late second century AD, mid-late third century AD, mid-fourth century AD or later (as dated by John Hayes in 1968).

Colour coat, Hayes Form 197 (4), sherds with cogged decoration, flanged bowls, lamp fragment.

Medieval:
D. [Detailed records were also made of Castellaccio, the mill and the adjacent tower, which it is unnecessary to repeat here, as they are described in Chapter Three.]

The excavated evidence apart, there is little to add to the above account. Not noted were the caves in the northern part of the valley, nor the cisterns and aqueduct channel on the crest of the hill above; the latter may well not have been visible. The creation of the park in 1982 has resulted in some changes, especially the provision of car parks and the planting of trees (and of course a deluge of visitors). The unfortunate bulldozing of the area to the west of the main site has also greatly changed the appearance of the landscape.

THE PAVED ROMAN ROAD

The road referred to above was surveyed in 1967-68, and recorded in some detail. It proved to be one of the better-preserved Roman roads of the Ager Faliscus, a country route that ran more or less parallel with the Via Amerina (Fig. 5). Briefly noticed by Tomassetti (1882; 1913) and by Martinori (1930: 208), it still retained many stretches of paving and there were few points where its course could not be established with certainty. The function of the road is also clear; if the large number of villas and farms along its route provides any guide, then it must have come into use primarily as a service road for these sites. Indeed, the fact that it is the southern section that is paved would tend to suggest that the produce of these estates was intended principally for the markets of Rome.

The road originated as an unpaved track, which left the Via Amerina at Casale l'Umiltà (Fig. 5), a short distance to the south of Nepi. It then headed southeastwards, across the two plateaux divided by the Fosso di Ronci, and down into the valley of the Fosso Stramazzo. The paved road appears to have started within a large settlement (E21), which straddles the Fosso Stramazzo. The size of this site suggests that it may have been a *vicus*. The first section of intact paving, destroyed about 1970, lay in the side of a modern cutting for the Via Cassia – Mazzano road, some 200 m west of site E21. It was 1.9 m wide, with polygonal blocks set in make-up.

Beneath was the bedrock, in which deep ruts could be seen, belonging to an unpaved predecessor. This was precisely the sequence identified by excavation in 1970-71 of another stretch of paved road at Vallelunga, 3.5 km to the south (Potter 1979: 107; see below); here there were three pairs of ruts under the paved surface. It may be, therefore, that the rock-cut road excavated at the Mola di Monte Gelato relates to this early phase of road.

After the Fosso Stramazzo, the paved road (and doubtless its precursor) climbed the ridge to the south of the Mazzano road in a still prominent cutting, some 10.0 m wide. Its immediate destination was the crossing of the river Treia at the Mola di Monte Gelato where, according to Tomassetti (1882: 147), there was a bridge. The road then headed out of the valley, swinging first southwestwards to avoid the hill on which the medieval castle of Castellaccio stands, before turning back to take a more or less straight line south. Through the woods to the south of the Mola a good deal of paving still survived, but once out of the *macchia*, the surface had been destroyed and only the occasional block was to be found. Its general direction is nevertheless quite clear, as it headed down to a minor stream that drains into the Treia, the Fosso Sarnacchiola.

At this point, in the Valle del Pero, there was in effect a T-junction (Figs 5 and 6): while the main road turned west and then south, a branch road headed off towards the east. We shall describe this branch road first. Two features made its line immediately obvious. Initially, there was a long stretch of paving, resting upon an *agger*, immediately below site D5. Then, some 600 m east of the T-junction, the road entered a long cutting through a north-south ridge in the Valle del Pero. This cutting itself formed another junction, upon which no fewer than four ancient roads converged. The paved road immediately headed south, climbing out of the cutting and entering a substantial villa site, D10. The arrangement of levels was such as to suggest two constructional phases, with the cutting as the primary feature and the building of the paved road as a secondary stage. The paving itself was very clear at D10, showing that the road then struck southeastwards down the ridge. At 843716, close to sites M18 and M19, there was another long stretch of paving, 2.2 m wide, and the road apparently terminated at a substantial villa site (M21), covered (in 1968) by a derelict farm. We should not, however, exclude the possibility that the paved road once continued, for the terrain beyond M21 was heavily wooded and difficult to explore. There was certainly a seemingly old track which headed down to Campagnano, and a Roman origin is by no means improbable.

The branch road evidently acted as the focus for a radial network of communications, serving the dispersed sites of this area. The main road, on the other hand, was clearly designed to link up with the

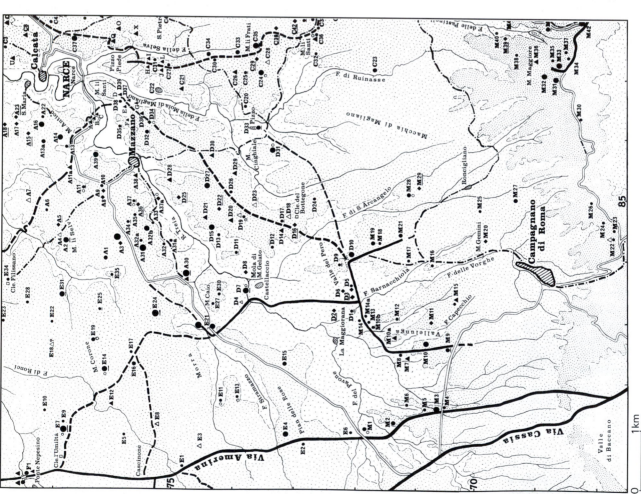

AGER FALISCUS FIELD SURVEY

- ◆ Pre-Roman site
- ◆ Pre-Roman site with some Roman material
  A24◆
- ▲ Pre-Roman tomb or cemetery
- ● Roman villa or farm
- • Minor Roman site
- ◉ Roman site with some pre-Roman material
- △ Roman tomb(s)
- ⊘ Deserted Medieval village
- ○ Minor Medieval site
- + Church
- ▬▬▬ Paved Roman road
- ▬ ▬ ▬ Unpaved pre-Roman or Roman track
- –·–·– Medieval road

LAND HEIGHTS:

▨ above 300 m.   ▦ 300-200 m.   ▢ 200-150 m.

T▲ Faliscan cemetery from Pasqui & Cozza 1894

Fig. 5. The southwestern area of the Ager Faliscus, with data from field survey between 1966 and 1971. Part of a larger map, drawn in 1972. *(TWP)*

nearest trunk road, the Via Amerina. Its course was established at several points. It could first be seen just west of the Fosso Sarnacchiola, with paving set into a prominent shelf; then at Vallelunga (Fig. 7), where there was also a clearly marked ford across the stream, and subsequently at the Fosso Capecchio: here a cuniculus 87.5 m long facilitated the crossing of the stream. It then turned south down a ridge, its course marked by the occasional scatter of *selce* blocks (for example, at M10). These extended as far as the modern Via Cassia to Campagnano road. This area to the south was not surveyed in the 1960s, and when examined in 1989 (King 1993) proved to have been severely damaged by modern agriculture. However, it seems very probable that it swung southwestwards to join the Via Amerina, and thus the main trunk-road system down to Rome.

As noted above, the road was investigated by excavation in 1970 and 1971 when a stretch was uncovered during building work at the car racing track at Vallelunga (site M106). In 1970, only the visible remains were examined, but the following year the paving stones were lifted, under the supervision of Sig. A. Bracci, assisted by Miranda Buchanan and Graeme Barker, as I was unable to be present. This exposed completely the earlier wheel ruts visible in Figure 7. There were three pairs of

ruts, and another at the edge of the excavated area (Potter 1979: fig. 31). Some 50 m away was a building, 13.0 m wide, recessed into the bedrock. Foundation trenches were recorded at both ends, as well as a central partition, resting on a low sill. No masonry survived *in situ* (although there were tufo blocks in the vicinity) and it may be that this was largely a timber structure. More probably, however, the blocks had been robbed out. In the fill over the floor were sherds of the second-first centuries BC, including black glaze, closely paralleled by the assemblage from near Sutri, published by Duncan (1965). Duncan's forms 7, 9, 20 and 38B, and a loom weight, Duncan form A131, were all represented in the finds from Vallelunga.

There can be no doubt that at least some of the ruts formed while the adjacent building was in occupation. The paved road, on the other hand, is certainly later, and may not have been laid much before the end of the first century AD; it is a matter considered in more detail in discussing the same road at Monte Gelato in the next chapter. It varied in width between 2.25 and 2.3 m, and on each side was a low kerb, made of carefully faced but otherwise irregular pieces of basalt, 0.1 m high. There were also two stones in the kerb with rounded profiles, which projected 0.25 m above the paving; placed precisely 20 Roman feet apart, they may

Fig. 6. Cuttings marking the T-junction of the Roman paved road in the Valle del Pero, to the south of Monte Gelato: see Figure 5. Looking southeast. *(AMS)*

Fig. 7. The Roman paved road at Vallelunga (Fig. 5, site M10), under excavation in 1970.
Note the earlier ruts. *(TWP)*

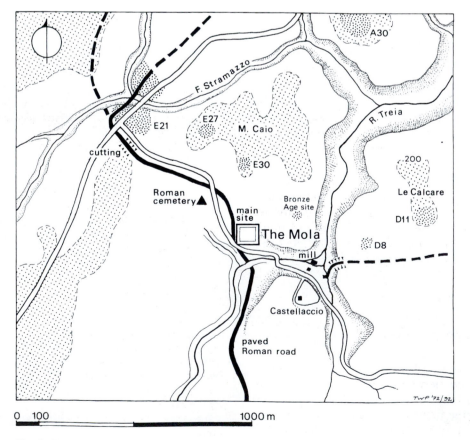

Fig. 8. The Mola di Monte Gelato in its local setting, showing ancient sites, roads and tracks
(dotted) identified mainly between 1966 and 1971. *(TWP)*

have been distance markers. Similar stones appear on some main highways, with a nearby example on the Via Amerina just to the north of the Settevene – Campagnano road (Frederiksen and Ward-Perkins 1957: 76 and pl. xviia).

The paving was neatly constructed with large polygonal blocks of *selce*, some over a metre in length. They were set into tufaceous make-up, so that the surface was 0.4 m above the bedrock. Parallel with the southeast side of the road was a retaining wall of long tufo blocks, some over 1.0 m in length, and 0.6 m high and 0.45 m wide: contemporaneity with the construction of the road is demonstrated by chips of *selce* in the foundation deposits. The blocks may well have derived from the adjacent Republican building.

The quality of the building work at Vallelunga requires emphasis, since it is in some contrast with that at Monte Gelato (below, Figs 17 and 18). There were no kerbstones at Monte Gelato, and the arrangement of the paving-stones was generally much more haphazard. However, it will be shown that some or all of the surface was relaid in late Roman and/or in early medieval times, albeit to an inferior standard. This was evidently not the case at Vallelunga, although this does not necessarily mean that it was abandoned. A recent study of the Via Flaminia at Malborghetto has clearly demonstrated its continued use in early medieval times (Bosman 1993), and durably made country roads like that at Vallelunga would have served for many centuries with minimal maintenance. The stretch at Monte Gelato, on the other hand, will have seen particularly heavy wear, running through a settlement, and its downhill course will have exacerbated this.

There is, however, an additional possibility, namely that the Vallelunga stretch did go out of use, and that the branch road replaced it as the main route to the south, heading down through the area where Campagnano was to grow up (Figs 3 and 5). There is some support for this in that three of five sites along its route yielded African red slip ware of the fifth and sixth centuries, whereas only one of seven sites along the Vallelunga section produced pottery of comparable date. The matter might have been clinched by the recovery of medieval pottery from the sites along the branch road, but none was identified, and the question can only be left open.

FIELD SURVEY IN THE VICINITY OF THE MOLA DI MONTE GELATO (FIGS 5 AND 8)

The following notes, prepared in 1972, describe the sites examined between 1966 and 1971 in the area shown on Figure 8. Some had also been looked at in earlier British School at Rome exploration, led by John Ward-Perkins in the late 1950s. In addition, a bronze age site, with a diameter of *c.* 30 m, was observed to the north of the Mola in 1990, and a recently looted Roman cemetery, with rock-cut tombs, was seen in the same year. The latter lies to the northwest of the main site, but was too overgrown to permit a proper record. It should also be noted that Peña (1987) has made a detailed study of the Roman pottery-producing centre at site A31 (Fig. 5), to the west of Mazzano.

A30 (838-9747)
An important site on the Ponte Maglianella ridge. At the west end there is a cemetery, which has been the focus of clandestine excavations (area A). Towards the east end is a building nucleus (area B), measuring about 100 × 70 m. There is a large dump of building rubble, including tufo blocks, *selce* lava fragments, a corner stone with a moulding in tufo, other architectural fragments and much tile and dolia. Other finds include white Italian marble, *opus spicatum* bricks, fragments of fine glass, and an inscribed tile base. There are also fragments of archaic tile.
Area A: painted Italo-Corinthian sherd (one), pre-Roman coarse-ware.
Area B: BG (9 – 4 misfired to a reddish colour); these include typical third-century BC pieces (including a stamp), as well as sherds more likely to be second or first century; also TS (two); ARS (five), two late second century AD; sherd with cogged decoration; Hayes 197; rouletted beaker; colour coat; lamp fragment; flanged forms; base in a brown burnished fabric, with a stamped reticulate motif.

D8 (838737)
A scatter of archaic tile and pottery on a low hillock.
Pre-Roman coarse-ware, fragment of a spindle-whorl.

D11 (841739)
A scatter of material, including archaic and later tile, dolia and pottery, ploughed out from a knoll on Le Calcare (the name meaning limekilns).
TS (three); ARS, second half second century AD (one).

E21 (828-9744-5)
A large and important site, which extends over both sides of the Fosso Stramazzo. To the south of the stream, there is an underground cistern and a scatter of tile and pottery on the hilltop. The main part of the site lies, however, on more level ground on the north side of the stream, beside the point where a minor tributary enters from the north. The importance of the site is underlined by the fact that the paved Roman road begins within the settlement. Its exact status – a village or a very large villa – is, however, unclear. There is a funerary inscription lettered in a style characteristic of the second or third centuries AD (Reynolds 1966: 65), and other remains include tufo blocks, much tile, Italian marble, *opus spicatum* brick, painted wall-plaster, basalt tesserae, window-glass and fine glass, and a fragment of bronze.
BG of the second or first centuries BC; TS (fourteen); ARS: most sherds are second or third centuries AD in date, but some are fourth and fifth centuries AD.
Colour coat, fine beakers, Hayes 197, sherds with cogged decoration, flanged forms.

E27 (833743)
A scatter of tile and pottery on the west slopes of Monte Caio.
ARS, mid third-mid fourth centuries AD (two), Hayes 197 (two).

E30 (834742)
A thin scatter of tile and pottery on the southern slopes
of Monte Caio.
TS (one).
Tomassetti (1877: 263) recorded two sepulchral inscrip-
tions from Monte Caio (*CIL* XI 3207, 3228).

These notes serve mainly to illustrate the rich
archaeological inheritance of this part of the Ager
Faliscus, at any rate as it survived in the 1960s. The
Mola di Monte Gelato was but one of many sites in
the region, and not a place of special consequence.
There were numerous other Roman villas around,
some apparently large and luxurious, and while
few, if any, manifest signs of early medieval occupation, this may be no more than a reflection of the
difficulties at the time of the survey in recognizing
the pottery (which was not identified in the surface
collections from the Mola di Monte Gelato).

Chapter Three

THE EXCAVATIONS

INTRODUCTION

As outlined in Chapter One, the excavations were spread over five seasons, which took place every September between 1986 and 1990 (Figs 9 and 10). Once it was established that there was a heavy overburden of plough-soil, considerable use was made of a mechanical excavator. This enabled the strippage of a comparatively large area, about 1,500 square metres in all. The site was backfilled yearly, to discourage vandalism and illicit *sondages*. Remarkably, there was very little of either, despite the accessibility of the site and a great deal of public interest.

For recording purposes, the site was divided into a number of areas, each of which was given a letter (Fig. 11). The contexts, 1,378 of which were allocated, were then listed by these areas, as A1, B1 etc. A full list is retained in the archive, but the original site references are used throughout the volume; the only exception is the burials, where it proved more convenient to renumber them in sequence (although here too the original references are cited, and are carried onto some of the drawings). The catalogue numbers cited in this section refer to the different categories of material (for example, small finds, ironwork, sculpture) described and discussed in Chapter Four.

The importance of the results was such that we gave high priority to publishing interim reports, nine of which were produced, mainly for Italian journals and conference proceedings. These were principally about the site, but did include articles about the freed-people tomb inscription (Gilliver 1990), and the inscribed Greek 'stork-vase' (Murray *et al.* 1991). Whilst a quite proper procedure, this does have the disadvantage of presenting interpretations which ultimately may turn out to be dubious or wrong when the evidence is assessed in its entirety. Thus initial attempts to postulate a degree of continuity between late Roman and early medieval times must now be treated with scepticism and, in all probability, rejected outright. Likewise, a structure that from the outset we regarded as a latrine (and is so labelled on many published plans) is, in reality, quite certainly a fish-pond, built to ornament an elegant Augustan complex. Similarly, DeLaine's work on the 'mausoleum' suggests that it is better termed a temple-tomb, while the features that we long considered to be oil-vats are in fact most probably water cisterns.

These matters are debated in the sections that follow; but they require emphasis here since some of the preliminary conclusions have already passed into the wider literature (for example, Christie 1991a: 356), as more or less established fact. Such certainty is rarely possible, and we have tried to examine a range of interpretations, before favouring one or the other. Erroneous readings of the data doubtless remain; but we hope that there is a sufficiency of detail in the ensuing analysis for these, in due course, to emerge.

THE EARLY IMPERIAL ROMAN COMPLEX (PHASES 1 AND 2) (FIGS 12 AND 13)

The evidence to be set out below will show how in Augustan times an elegant ornamental courtyard complex was laid out, facing a road. This was apparently not a working farm, although there could have been such a place nearby. It might have been a sacred site, although no temple was found; but it is more probable that the investigated early Imperial remains were above all decorative in purpose, and resembled in many respects Varro's villa near Casinum (*De Re Rustica* iii. 5.8).

Subsequently, in phase 2, a paved road, bathhouse, cisterns and a mausoleum (or temple-tomb) were added to the complex, all probably in the first half of the second century. Pottery was manufactured in the vicinity, and at least two of the potters were Greek. There was also wine production, the wine being transported in locally made amphorae. The majority of the buildings then seems to have been pulled down in the late second or early third century when, in all likelihood, the place was abandoned until around the mid-fourth century, in phase 3.

THE ROADS

Two roads were uncovered during the excavations. One was part of the well-known paved country route down to the Via Amerina or Via Cassia, described above in Chapter Two; the other was of earlier construction and hitherto unknown. It is referred to throughout the text as the 'rock-cut road', since this was the principal feature of its construction.

The rock-cut road (Figs 9, 14-16)

This was initially identified in the side of a modern drainage ditch, cut in 1989 at the eastern edge of the flood plain of the river Treia and at the foot of the rock scarp along the western side of the modern road. The scarp is some 2.5 m in height at this point, and steeply inclined, although it slopes away to nothing a short distance to the south. There must, therefore, have been a reason for taking this particu-

17

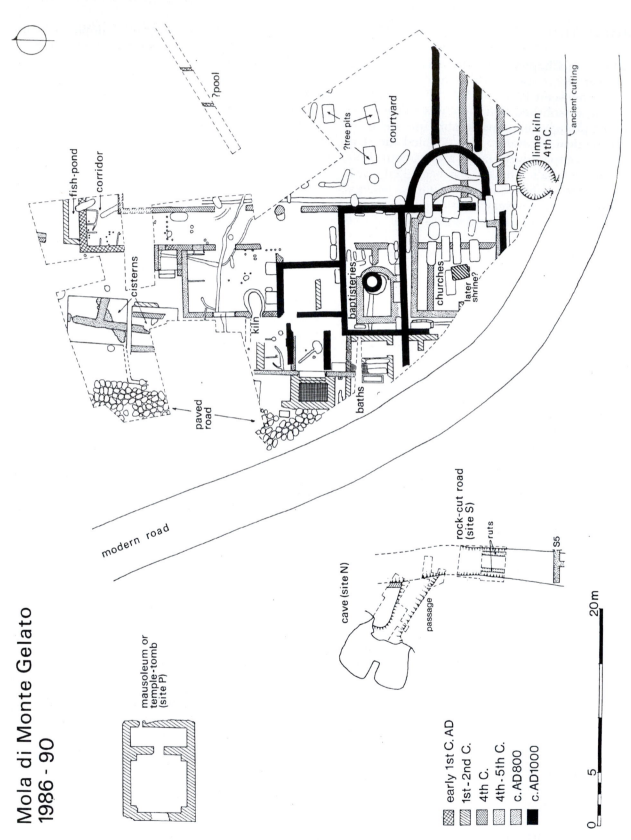

Fig. 9. General plan of the main site. (TWP)

Mola di Monte Gelato
1986 - 90

mausoleum or
temple-tomb
(site P)

cave (site N)

passage

rock-cut road
(site S)

ruts

S5

early 1st C. AD
1st - 2nd C.
4th C.
4th - 5th C.
c. AD800
c. AD1000

0   5   20m

?pool

fish-pond
corridor

cisterns

paved
road

kiln

baths

?tree pits

courtyard

baptisteries

churches

later
shrine?

lime kiln
4th C.

ancient cutting

modern road

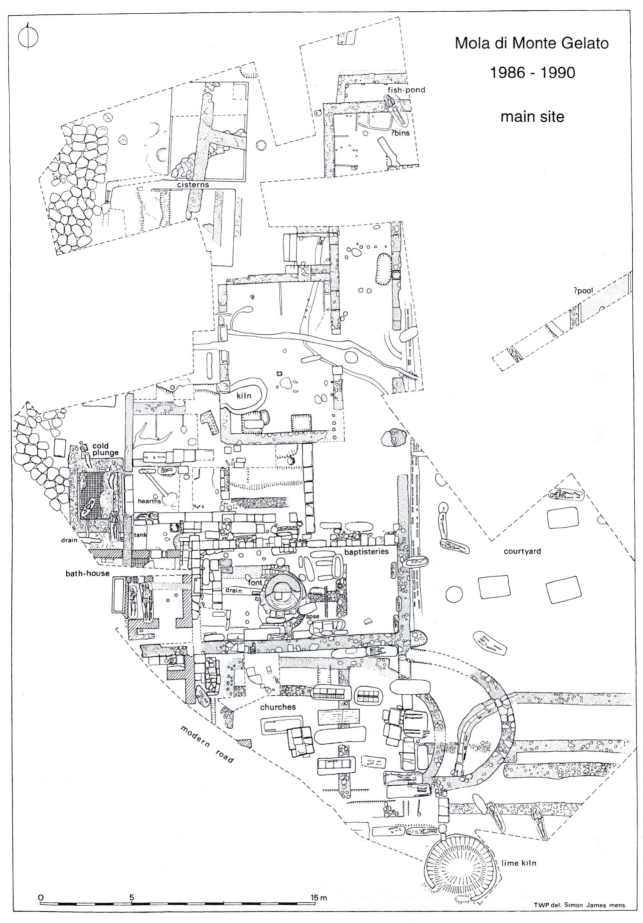

Mola di Monte Gelato
1986 - 1990

main site

fish-pond

?bins

cisterns

?pool

kiln

cold
plunge

hearths

drain

tank

baptisteries

courtyard

bath-house

font

drain

apse

churches

modern   road

lime kiln

0   5   15 m

TWP del. Simon James mens.

Fig. 10. Detailed plan of the main site, all phases. *(TWP)*

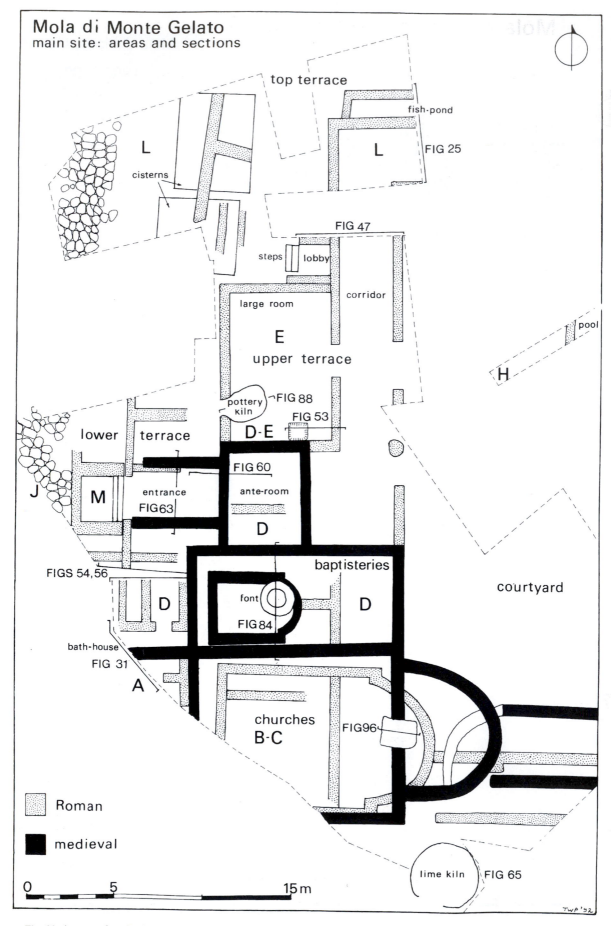

Fig. 11. Areas and main descriptors of the main site. For sites N, P and S see Figure 9; for site K see Figure 38. *(TWP)*

Mola di Monte Gelato 1986-90: phases

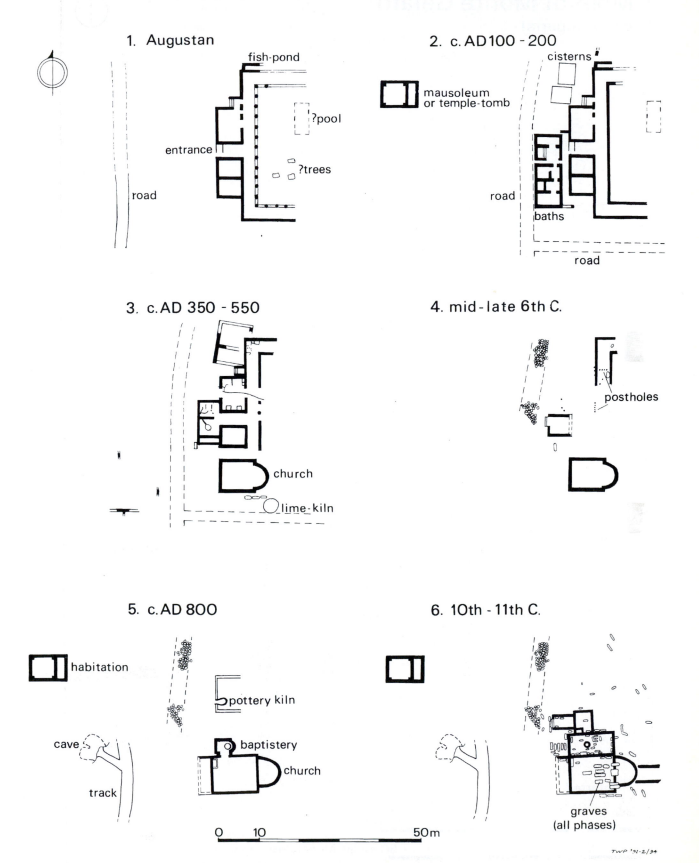

1. Augustan

fish-pond

?pool

entrance

?trees

road

2. c. AD 100 - 200

cisterns

mausoleum or temple-tomb

road

baths

road

3. c. AD 350 - 550

church

lime-kiln

4. mid-late 6th C.

postholes

5. c. AD 800

habitation

pottery kiln

cave

baptistery

church

track

0   10   50m

6. 10th - 11th C.

graves (all phases)

TWP '91-2/94

Fig. 12. Principal phases on the main site, excluding site K. *(TWP)*

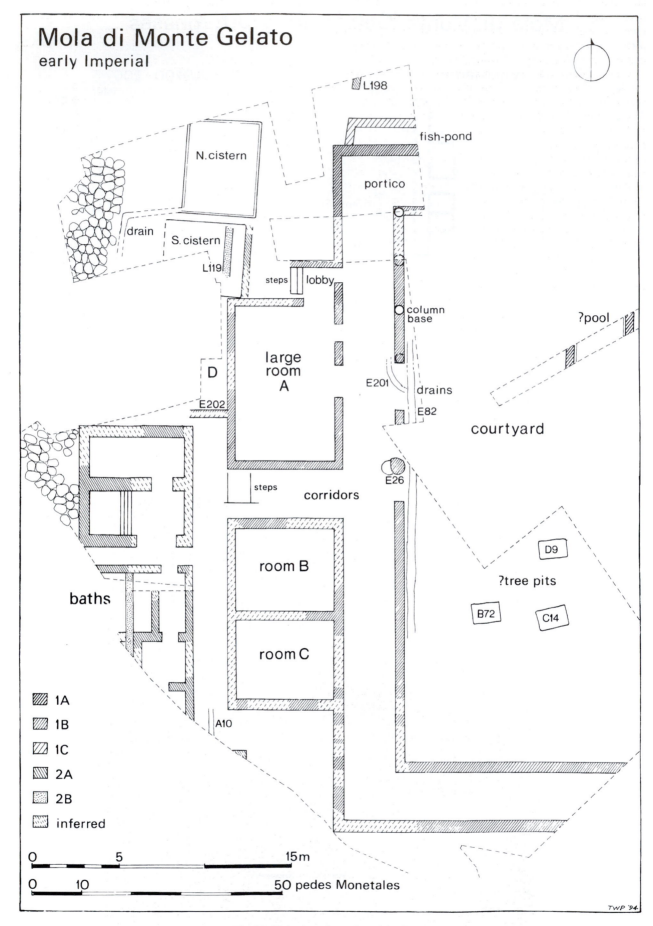

Fig. 13. Main site: phases 1 and 2. *(TWP)*

lar route, rather than the easier terrain later followed by the paved road. This must surely reside in the fact that an alignment parallel with that of the façade of the courtyard complex was considered of prime importance, despite the inconvenience of cutting through the scarp.

A trench was cut across the road where it intersected with the face of the scarp. A length of 2.3 m was exposed completely, and a further 2.3 m down to the basal silts (Fig. 15). The total depth of the incision into the bedrock was 3.5 m, and its width at the top was 2.65 m. The sides, however, tapered gradually, so that at the bottom of the cutting the width was reduced to 1.95 m. Two very pronounced wheel-ruts were scored into the bedrock. Between 0.3 and 0.35 m in depth, and some 1.4 m apart (measured from centre to centre), there were clear wheel-scuffing marks along the edges: they had evidently formed through the heavy passage of traffic, rather than being cut features, and had in fact been filled in with *selce* cobbles, presumably in an attempt to slow further down-cutting (Fig. 16).

As noted in Chapter Two, wheel-ruts were a conspicuous feature of the precursor to the paved road at Vallelunga (the onward continuation of the paved road at Monte Gelato). There were three pairs, with widths of 1.38, 1.4 and 1.5 m (Potter 1979: 107-8, where, however, the drawn scale is incorrect). These are a little on the wide side for a vehicle, but allowance must be made for the tendency of tufo, normally a soft rock, to wear very rapidly. By way of comparison, Ward-Perkins (1961: 19) recorded an average figure of 1.24 m at the northeast gate of Veii, and Chevallier (1976: 89) suggested 1.3 m as a standard axle-width in antiquity, and 1.45 m in the Middle Ages. The measurements at Monte Gelato and Vallelunga are therefore not significantly outside the range.

Rock-cut road, site S

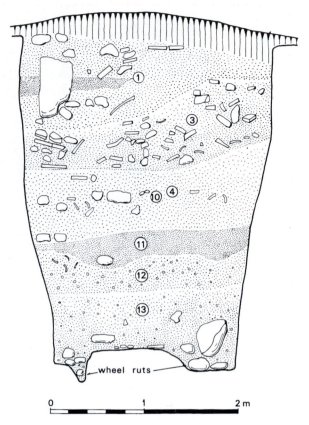

Fig. 14. Deposits in the rock-cut road; for description of the layers, see text. *(TWP)*

Fig. 15. North section of the rock-cut road, excavated in steps. *(KW)*

Fig. 16. The ruts at the base of the rock-cut road, with the cobble fill partly removed. *(KW)*

The line of the road was established in all for a distance of 16.0 m, sufficient to confirm its north-south orientation. To the south it presumably headed across the flood plain to a bridge across the river Treia, while to the north it skirted the eastern side of the low ridge (below, Fig. 89) where later a mausoleum or temple-tomb was to be built. It then climbed the hill in the cutting which today carries the modern road.

Although the style of the road, with its great depth, is manifestly Etrusco-Faliscan, it does not seem to have been the result of successive lowerings of the surface, as the soft rock became too rutted for use: the sides were smoothly cut, with no traces of the earlier working levels customary with such roads (Frederiksen and Ward-Perkins 1957: 186). Given that its orientation is precisely that of the adjacent Augustan complex, along the cardinal points, it may well be that both were part of a unitary design, with the rock-cut road passage as a feature of that layout. Archaic in style, it harks back to older traditions, the signs of which are still so conspicuous in the surrounding countryside, not least around the former Faliscan centre at Narce (Potter 1976: pl. IIb).

It is not easy to say when the road went out of use. The bottom metre was filled with silts and sands of waterlaid appearance (Fig. 14, units 12 and 13), but contained no datable material. Above was a series of dumps with much second- and early third-century pottery, building materials, slag and a number of small finds. These included bone needles and pins (cat. 112, 115, 119, 123), some fine glass, and part of a jet bracelet (cat. 147). The deposit in many respects resembles others, described below, filling the feature interpreted as a fish-pond, and also a cistern. However,

some well-stratified sherds indicate that the dumps cannot have been made before the fifth century AD (cf. below), so that this section of the road cutting at least must have been a prominent feature for much of the Roman period. Doubtless it served as a convenient short cut from the main site down to the valley bottom.

The paved road (Figs 9, 17-18)

Two areas of this road, the overall course of which was described in the previous chapter, were uncovered. It took a much easier line that diverged from the north-south orientation of the rock-cut road, and its onward route up the hillside could be seen as a gently curving hollow way, littered with *selce* paving-stones (Fig. 4). It is not clear at which point it descended onto the flood plain of the river Treia, but a scatter of paving-stones on the far side of the river may indicate the position of the crossing. There is, however, no trace of the bridge referred to by Tomassetti (1882: 147).

The surviving paving was rather irregular and haphazard, and not at all like the neat work revealed further south at Vallelunga (Fig. 7). There were no kerbstones, and only in the northern part of Trench L was there the semblance of a properly laid edge (Fig. 18). There was, however, an *a cappuccina* roadside drain along part of this stretch (Fig. 17 and below, Fig. 23,b), fed from a nearby cistern. The drain was not traced further south, and almost certainly relates to the bath-house, constructed *c.* AD 100.

With a width of *c.* 3.2 m, the road was both wider and different in character from the sections examined at the Fossa Stramazzo and Vallelunga (cf. Chapter Two). This is explained by the fact that the blocks were partly or wholly

Fig. 17. The drain on the east side of the paved road: see Figure 23b. *(KW)*

Fig. 18. The road in the northern part of site L, sealed beneath colluvium. *(KW)*

re-laid, possibly both in late Roman and medieval times. This was very evident in the section adjoining the bath-house, where the blocks overlapped the footing of the demolished *piscina*, and sealed a third-century coin (cat. 6). There was also pottery of the late eighth and early ninth centuries in some deposits below the paving, confirming the re-laying of at least part of the road. This renders extremely difficult the dating of the original construction, for which there is little real evidence. One deposit beneath the paving (M104) did yield sherds broadly assignable to *c.* AD 100, and the alignment of the northern stretch with the cisterns, and the southern part with the bath-house, may be an indication of a general contemporaneity. Moreover, this would not be inconsistent with the finds from beneath the road at Vallelunga, and recalls the sequence of road surfaces at Podere Sant'Angelo, on the country route between the Via Flaminia and the Monti Sabatini (Kahane, Murray Threipland and Ward-Perkins 1968: 127): here the paving was laid at some point after the mid-first century AD, and may have used *selce* from the nearby quarry at Monte Maggiore, the focus of a considerable number of well-appointed villas, occupied throughout Imperial times (Potter 1979: 135-6).

The building of this paved stretch of road at Monte Gelato may have been part of a general attempt to upgrade a much frequented route from the rich farmland of the central Ager Faliscus down to the trunk roads that led to Rome. It was lined with substantial sites, the owners of which presumably paid for the work – for example, T. Humanius Stabilio, who in the first century AD built a road bridge at his own expense in the adjoining Ager Veientanus (Guzzo 1970). Certainly the new section of road at Monte Gelato must have been altogether more practicable than its rock-cut predecessor, and forms one of a number of signs of change in the nature of the site around the beginning of the second century AD.

THE COURTYARD (FIG. 13)

The gently sloping hillside to the east of the roads was terraced into three levels (Fig. 19). The lowest, and smallest, lay immediately beside the paved road, and was cut to a depth of some 2.0 m, to accommodate a small bath-house, probably built around the beginning of the second century AD. Above lay an extensive main, or upper, terrace, while to the north was a third, or top, terrace. There may have been still higher terraces beyond the excavated area, and there

were certainly structures on the crest of the hill above the valley (Fig. 4). These include a rock-cut channel, probably part of an aqueduct (Fig. 20), and also cisterns (Fig. 4), and it is easy to imagine that the entire northern hillslopes were eventually built up. It is all the more unfortunate that plough damage in this area has been so severe.

The main upper terrace was occupied by a large courtyard, bounded by a portico. The whole of the west side of the courtyard was uncovered, as well as parts of the north and south ranges. The eastern side was not located, but there is adequate space for a square arrangement, as suggested below for phases 3 and 4 (Fig. 38). Alternatively, if the pool in the courtyard lay centrally, a rectangular layout is implied.

It is quite evident that the courtyard was set out in *pedes Monetales* (hereafter *p.M.*). Thus the portico corridor measured 2.96 m internally, or 10 *p.M.*, while the length of the north-south portico is very close to 110 *p.M.* (32.85 m = 110.9 *p.M.*). Likewise, the two surviving column bases are 20 *p.M.* from centre to centre, suggesting that columns were placed at intervals of 10 *p.M.* Other instances of Roman mensuration will be cited below. There is, of course, nothing surprising in this, for careful surveying was a commonplace in early Imperial times (see, for example, Duncan-Jones 1980); but it is an illustration of the attention that was lavished upon the layout of the complex.

The interior of the courtyard was only explored in part, and most extensively in the southwestern corner. Ploughing had removed any trace there may once have been of a surface, and features were notably sparse. However, there were three closely grouped and evenly spaced rectangular pits (B72, C14, D9) (Fig. 13), each measuring *c.* 1.7 × 1.2 m (that is, close to 6×4 *p.M.*). As they survived, all were fairly shallow, with depths ranging from 0.1 to 0.25 m; but ploughing had bitten deeply into the subsoil, so that they must originally have been much deeper. Their fills were of soft tufaceous earth, containing a few small fragments of pottery: those sherds from pit C14 were tentatively assigned a date in the late Republican-early Imperial period, indicating that the pits (which are surely of the same period) should be contemporary with the courtyard.

The grouping of the pits suggests that there was probably another in the unexcavated northwest corner, making a cluster of four in all. Their function is more problematic, for they were clearly not intended for refuse. However, their context does provide an important clue. As will be seen, the courtyard was embellished with a pool, a marble *labrum* and

Schematic section, M, E and L

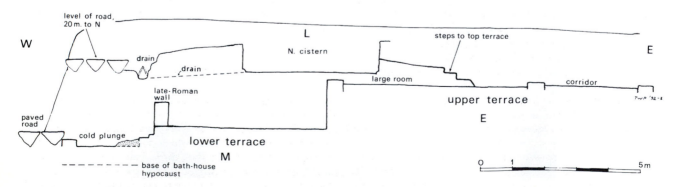

Fig. 19. Section showing the relative levels in different parts of the site. *(TWP)*

Fig. 20. The rock-cut aqueduct channel on the ridge to the north of the main site, looking south. *(KW)*

statuary, indicating a place of some elegance. It would therefore be entirely consistent with this picture were the pits to have contained trees or shrubs, as part of an ornamental garden. This would certainly have befitted the beautiful setting, adjacent to the river Treia with its attractive sequence of waterfalls, and is in harmony with the apparent absence of functional, agricultural buildings on the site at this time.

The laying out of a garden is hardly surprising, in the light of the evidence of the Vesuvian region (Jashemski 1979; MacDougall and Jashemski 1981). At the San Marco villa at Stabia, to cite but one instance, trees flanked a pool in a courtyard surrounded by a portico (De Vos and De Vos 1982: 323; Mielsch 1987: 168), and recent botanical studies have amply illustrated the wide range of species that might be grown in such gardens (Mastroroberto 1990). Groves of trees were also planted in the Latian temple complexes, in Hellenistic tradition (Caroll-Spillecke 1992; Coarelli 1993). At Gabii the pits were 1.5-1.6 m across in the first phase, and 1.2-1.3 m across in a second replanting, figures comparable with the Monte Gelato examples. While the three pits hardly constitute a grove, clumps of trees in the courtyard seem an entirely reasonable interpretation.

The pool referred to above was identified in a narrow exploratory trench (H) in the northern part of the courtyard (Figs 11 and 13). Modern ploughing and vine-trenching (to a depth of 1.4 m) has had a ruinous effect upon the archaeological deposits, but the very bottom of the feature did survive (Fig. 21). This comprised a grey *cocciopesto* floor with much wear in the centre; piercing it was a circular hole 0.28 m in diameter which, if not a later feature, may

have been for drainage. It was flanked by walls, 0.5 m in width, made of rubble and mortar, lined with pale yellow tufo blocks on the inside. A quarter-round moulding sealed the junction between the walls and the floor on both sides.

The internal width of the pool was 2.9 m (9.79 *p.M.*), and it was probably intended to have been 10 *p.M.* across. Although its north-south dimensions were not established, it was a substantial feature. That it was decorative, rather than functional, in purpose is, however, a matter of inference, based upon its position within the courtyard, and the items of sculpture referred to above. Likewise, there was no direct dating evidence for the construction of the pool, although there was late Roman pottery in the silty and loamy fills above it, which mark its disuse. It does not, however, lie in an obviously measured position in *p.M.* within the courtyard, and may not therefore have been part of the initial design. On the other hand, there is no real reason to doubt that it belongs within the first main phase of the site's history.

THE PORTICO (PHASE 1A)

Little that was original remained of the phase 1 portico. This is due to the fact that it was later converted into an enclosed corridor, and only two column bases survived. One lay in the northwest corner, where traces of curvature in the footing left little doubt that there had been an emplacement for a column resting on a very low stylobate (Fig. 13). The other was 20 *p.M.* (centre to centre) to the south, and was much clearer. A circular base, 0.4 m in diameter, was

Fig. 21. Site H: the base of an *opus signinum* pool in the courtyard. *(KW)*

edged with small orange *tufelli*, set in grey-white mortar; this was cemented onto a block of grey tufo, 0.5 m square. The base stood only 60 mm above the adjacent *cocciopesto* floor of the portico, an additional indication of the low height of the stylobate. There may also have been another column base still further to the south, where there were two successive, roughly circular, pads of grey mortar (Fig. 13; D26). However, these do not fit the mensuration in Roman feet, and are more likely to belong to a later door emplacement.

The original back wall of the portico survived only in the northwest corner (cf. below, Fig. 42). Standing to a height of between 0.6 and 0.75 m, it owed its preservation to the fact that it had been recessed into the tufo that underlies the top terrace. The wall was made of *opus reticulatum*, with *tufelli* that averaged 0.1 × 0.1 m in size, cut from a hard brownish tufo. This is not unlike the leucitic tufo which was quarried from the cliffs below the waterfalls (Figs 4 and 22) and, in all probability, they were manufactured locally. There was also a very small section of *opus reticulatum* a short distance to the south, adjoining the lobby (below, Fig. 40,b). Although complicated by the later blocking of a door, this stretch appeared to terminate with tufo quoins. If so, this is a pointer to the work being of Augustan date (Blake 1947: 274; Lugli 1957: 506), with the farm at Monte Forco in the Ager Capenas providing a good local parallel (Jones 1963: 150). The relatively large size of the *tufelli* is also consistent with this date, and is in harmony with the ceramic record from the site (Roberts, this volume), which effectively begins with material of the Augustan period, especially *terra sigillata*. While none was stratified in primary

contexts, there is little real difficulty in regarding the first phase of the courtyard complex as a creation of the early decades of the first century AD.

The floor of the portico survived only as a *cocciopesto* surface, laid on a variable amount of make-up (Fig. 23,a). Even though it was to remain in use for four to five centuries, there were few signs of repairs or replacement, and it must be seriously doubted whether the existing floor was the original one. Indeed, the evidence from adjoining rooms is for a white tessellated surface in this period, and it would be surprising if this had not extended into the portico. The inside walls of the portico were certainly rendered in plaster, to judge from a small surviving section, painted in now very faded red, against the base of the *opus reticulatum* opposite the lobby. One drain of the period was identified, being a U-shaped gully that debouched into the courtyard from the western portico (Fig. 23,a, E201). This presumably marks one of the entrances through the portico, and indeed lies opposite a doorway into a room in the western range.

THE WESTERN RANGE

There were several rooms adjoining the western portico. They are denominated as phase 1B in Figure 13, to reflect the fact that the surviving walls were largely rebuilt in the late Roman period. However, there was a sufficiency of *opus reticulatum tufelli* from fallen sections of wall (particularly from the lower terrace) to suggest that these later footings

Fig. 22. Tufo quarry in 1970 for *opus quadratum* blocks; cf. Figure 4 for location. *(TWP)*

mainly followed lines established at the beginning of phase 1. This conclusion finds support from the fact that Roman feet were used to measure out many of the main elements.

Almost exactly central to the range was a corridor, 10 *p.M.* wide, leading from the portico down to the lower terrace and the road. Very eroded wide steps were cut down into the subsoil at the western end of the corridor (see below, Fig. 60), although these appeared to have been placed only in the northern part, thus leaving a passage at the level of the upper terrace. This is puzzling, but the explanation may be that it led to structures laid out at that level, which were later destroyed when the lower terrace and bath-house were inserted. Alternatively, and more probably, it provided passage to some ornamental feature, such as a garden, which occupied the area between the façade and the road.

To the north of the corridor was room A, which we have tended to describe as the 'large room' (Fig. 13). This measured internally 5.8 × 8.65 m (19.59 × 29.22 *p.M.*), which is sufficiently close to 20 × 30 *p.M.* to imply that these were the intended figures. There seem to have been two entrances onto the portico in this period, as well as a small lobby or vestibule to the north. This lobby provided access both to the portico and, via a flight of rock-cut steps, to the top terrace. A small fragment of white mosaic survived *in situ*, set in pale mortar upon the bedrock (into which the lobby and the north end of the large room had been recessed). There were also many white tesserae, of similar size and appearance, incorporated into a secondary drain in the large room (cf. phase 3, below). This was surely also floored in mosaic,

although the resemblance between this tessellated surface and that in the later bath-house may suggest that the work could belong to the late first or early second centuries, rather than to the Augustan period. However, whatever the date, there was apparently extensive use of mosaic, matching other indications of an elegantly laid-out complex.

There were two further rooms, B and C, to the south of the corridor. Of almost equal size, they were also 20 *p.M.* internally, although the total internal length, 9.65 m (32.6 *p.M.*) is a little more than that of room A. This may be explained by the fact that the overall arrangement of the west range allows for very nearly identical spacing between (a) the north wall of the lobby and the north end of the portico and (b) the south wall of room C and the south end of the portico. In other words (and best seen on the phase plan, Figure 12,1), the rooms of the western range projected centrally, leaving virtually symmetrical empty spaces in the northwest and southwest corners. It can hardly be doubted that this was intentional, especially as the façade fronted onto the road. Given that the stylobate and colonnade opposite the east end of the corridor, between the façade and the courtyard, were completely rebuilt in the late Roman period, obliterating the earlier layout, it is reasonable to conclude that the original arrangement was that of a relatively formal and prestigious entrance. Against this is a lack of really substantial foundations for such a structure; but, with so much subsequent architectural intervention, it would be optimistic to pretend that unequivocal evidence would survive (and, indeed, the area was not completely investigated).

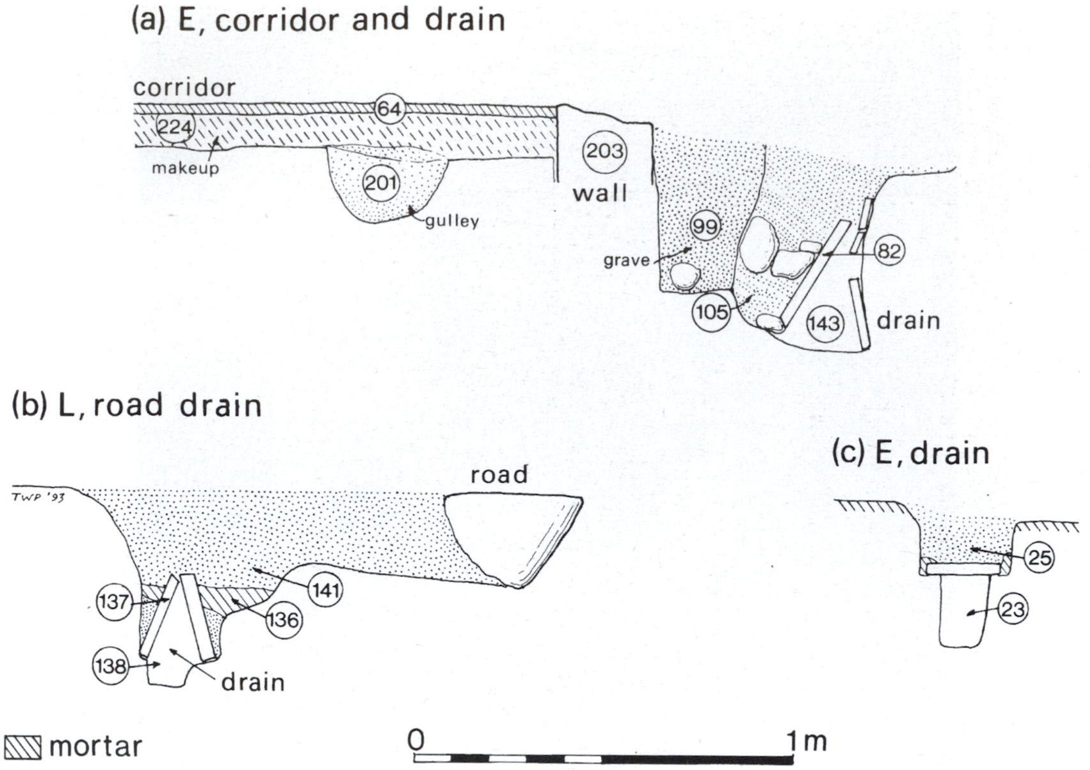

(a) E, corridor and drain

(b) L, road drain

(c) E, drain

Fig. 23. Sections across drains:

(a) E64: *cocciopesto* floor. E224: mortary make-up. E201: gully for drain with yellow-brown sandy silt fill; first century AD. E99: brown loam fill. Drain along edge of courtyard: E82: tiles. E143: silts within drain, with mid-Imperial pottery. E105: fill of grey-brown soil, with tufo packing, and second- to early third-century pottery.
(b) L141: grey-brown silt, with a ?fifth-/sixth-century coin, and mid to late Imperial pottery. L136: yellow-grey mortar capping. L137: tiles (averaging 0.19 x 0.22 m). L138: grey-brown fill, with second- to early third-century pottery.
(c) E25 (also E26, E76, E78): brown-black silt, with fifth-/sixth-century pottery. E23: rock-cut drain, with tile cover, sealed by mortar. *(TWP)*

THE NORTHERN RANGE: THE FISH-POND (FIGS 24 AND 25, AND BELOW, FIG. 41)

The only phase 1 structure to be identified on the north side of the portico was a rectangular feature, built up against the back wall of the corridor. Although only a part was uncovered, it was at least 3.5 m in length, measured internally, and between 0.95 and 1.0 m in width. The walls were solidly constructed, varying in width from 0.46 to 0.56 m; and the structure was recessed into the bedrock to a maximum depth of 1.6 m below the highest surviving point of the surrounding walls. These extended to the base of the feature on the north and west sides, but below the *opus reticulatum* wall to the south it was the tufo that formed the side. The tufo had been cut as a gentle slope which descended towards a relatively flat bottom, although with a slight downward slope to the east. There was no evidence for any sort of lining, although the tufo would have been relatively impermeable.

The masonry belongs to more than one phase. The original build was in well-cut blocks up to 0.5 m in length, and with course heights of 0.12 m. As Figure 40,c, below, makes very clear, the upper part of the west wall had, however, been rebuilt in much smaller and less regular blocks, with variable courses of 60-100 mm. Similar repairs had been carried out on the north wall and, at its eastern end, it had been completely refaced over its whole height in a crude style that distinctly recalls *opus incertum* (below, Fig. 40,d).

One notable feature of the walling is the heavy and careful application of mortar to the joins, doubtless with the intention of making them watertight. This is explained by the fact that four *tubuli* fed into the structure, two at the west end and two along the north side. They were 0.14 m in diameter, with a bore of 90 mm, and were angled downwards, showing that they carried water into the feature. The trenches by which they had been inserted into the subsoil to the west and north were not visible, and the layout of these conduits could not, therefore, be established; but they could have formed part of an underground system of aqueducts, with the rock-cut channel on the crest of the hill to the north (Figs 4 and 20) perhaps being part of it.

The walls butted against the *opus reticulatum* wall of the corridor, and thus post-date it; they are accordingly denominated as phase 1C on Figure 13. However, there were sherds of Augustan type in the foundation trench, and the walls cannot be very far separated in time, despite their different construction. The repairs must also all belong within the first century AD, since the primary silt, which formed after the latest rebuild (Fig. 23, unit L184), contained pottery of the late first or early second centuries. This was a dark grey-brown deposit, some 0.15 m deep, and with relatively few finds: it is the sort of sediment that might well have accumulated at the base of a water-filled feature.

The primary silt was in turn covered by two successive dumps, L165 and L105. Although separated only by a thin and discontinuous lens of what appeared to be white plas-

Fig. 24. The fish-pond looking west; note the pipes. To the left: the northwest corner of the portico. *(KW)*

L, east section

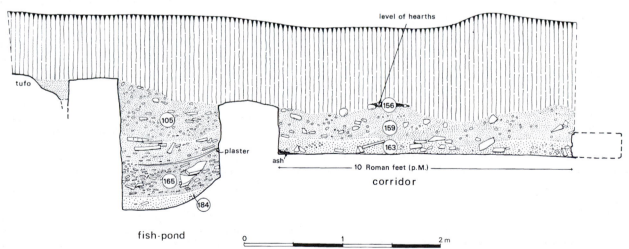

Fig. 25. Section across the fish-pond and portico corridor:

Fills in fish-pond: 105: upper fill, late second century. 165: lower fill, early second century. 184: primary silt, dark grey-brown colour, late first- to early second-century pottery.

Layers over corridor: 156: interpolated hearth from just to the west; a related nearby hearth yielded fifth- to sixth-century pottery. 159 (= 157): rubble, wall fragments with tile, *opus reticulatum*, statue of Venus, and pottery of early to mid fifth century. 163: red-brown silt, with little rubble and few finds; at the base, some ash on the floor. *(TWP)*

ter, the finds suggest that the lower (L165) belongs to the early second century and the upper to the later second century. It is extremely curious that the intervening deposit should be so ephemeral, and it may be that the dumps were in fact contemporaneous, but derived from different sources of refuse. On the other hand, despite the difficulty in excavation of distinguishing precisely between the two deposits, joins were limited to sherds from just two lamps and one colour-coated vessel. A much greater degree of mixing should be expected were the dumps made at the same time, and it is perhaps best to take the evidence at face value and regard the deposits as the result of two separate actions, which took place some 50-70 years apart (see Roberts, this volume, for the dating evidence).

Where this rubbish was generated is unclear, for the adjoining courtyard complex seems an unlikely source. Most probably it came from buildings higher up the hillside to the north, although a slightly more distant origin is not impossible. Interestingly, the dumps included a significant number of wasters (the 'stork-vase' (Figs 239-42, below) amongst them), and wine amphorae of local origin (type P105: Arthur, this volume). The wasters are closely paralleled by finds from a site with pottery kilns just 2.0 km to the northeast (Fig. 5, A31 – Peña 1987: site 9) and certainly imply another production centre. This was quite probably at the Mola di Monte Gelato itself, where later, pottery of early medieval date was also to be manufactured (see below).

The range and quantity of the pottery was remarkable (cf. below, Figs 216 and 217). There were over 400 vessels in the two deposits, varying in size from small drinking cups to large flagons and amphorae, and in quality from elegant green-glazed dishes to kitchen-wares. A few were complete, with just some slight damage, but many could be largely restored. This was also the case with the glass vessels, many fine examples of which were found (Price, this volume). The pottery and glass together provide a further argument for suggesting that the material in the deposits had not been transported over any great distance.

The other finds are listed in Table 1, which reveals some interesting differences between the two groups. Common to both are some fine items of jewellery, and a remarkable array of bone needles and pins. Also noteworthy are many elements from a bone fan (cat. 100), a rare and luxurious object. The later deposit (L105), however, does in addition include a substantial proportion of building materials. Apart from many fragments of roof tile, there are pieces of box flue (one largely complete), a fragment of white mosaic floor and much *opus sectile*, as well as a large part of a marble *labrum* (below, Fig. 144), and the complete neck of an ornamental crater (below, Fig. 146), also in marble. Here is unambiguous testimony of the pulling down of buildings, and the breaking up of elegant decorative furnishings. These must surely relate to the adjoining courtyard complex, and the significance of this will be considered further below. There were also the remains of two articulated skeletons of dogs, both working animals who had sustained some injuries (King, this volume).

Two other points about the contents of the deposits require emphasis. One is the presence of a few graffiti (below, Fig. 140) in both Latin and Greek. They derive from the later second-century dump, except for the 'stork-vase' (Murray *et al.* 1991, and this volume), signed by Abaskantos and Epinikos, which came from the early second-century layer. This is the cup of a drinking club and, being a very cracked waster, must have been made locally: together with the graffiti, it is compelling evidence for the presence of Greeks at Monte Gelato. They were presumably slaves although, as Murray has shown (Murray *et al.* 1991), of a highly literate and educated kind, as the motto on the cup makes clear.

The other significant conclusion derives from a study of the organic remains. Despite sieving 55 litres of soil, plant remains were disappointingly sparse; however, the animal bones more than compensate for this. Apart from normal domestic species, and a number of chickens, these include edible dormice; toads (one from the primary silts); fourteen fish bones (see below); and a large number of bird bones, of which those of a tawny owl, jays, thrushes, blackbirds and chaffinches could be readily recognized. There were also tentatively identified bones of ducks, and two oyster valves.

Table 1. Small finds from the fish-pond (catalogue numbers in parentheses).

	early second century (L165)	later second century/early third century (L105)
copper alloy	Aucissa brooch (3)	bracelet (8), two needles (18, 19), box fitting (28), two strips (42, 44)
lead		?net weight (49)
bone	three needles (17, 108, 111), strip inlay (135)	fan (100), handle (102), inlay (103), four needles (106, 109, 110, 114), fourteen pins (116-18, 120-2, 124-5, 128-33)
glass	melon bead (138)	two glass counters (142, 143)
stone		weight (149)
iron	key (1), six nails	key (2), hook/hinge staple (4), T-clamp (5), three pieces of binding (8-10), stud (11), 22 nails
marble sculpture		*labrum* (4), complete neck of crater (5)
building materials	much tile	much tile, including many pieces of box flue, fragment of mosaic (limestone), 124 pieces of marble veneer

Thrushes, blackbirds and chaffinches are of course common garden birds; but tawny owls and jays require a secluded woodland environment, where they can find adequate protection. This allows for the intriguing possibility that there may have been an aviary, perhaps in the adjacent courtyard. The raising of birds, especially fieldfares (a thrush, *Turdus pilaris*), for the table was a profitable business (Varro, *De Re Rustica* iii. 2.15; Toynbee 1973: 277-8); but they were additionally kept for pleasure. Varro has provided a detailed description of the aviary in his villa near Casinum (*De Re Rustica* iii. 5.8-17). He kept chiefly songsters, such as nightingales and blackbirds, which lived amongst the colonnade of a portico and in trees planted in a courtyard. There were also ponds for fish and ducks, making an ambience that so vividly recalls the description of the above pages as to be remarkable. Indeed, one might wonder whether the stork on the 'stork-vase' – although convincingly linked by Murray (Murray *et al.* 1991: 102) with the name of a pottery vessel (*pelargos*) – could not also be an allusion to an aviary on the site.

This in turn brings up the question of the function of a building that, from the moment of its discovery, we regarded as a latrine. This interpretation depended essentially upon its long rectangular plan, and the provision of water pipes to flush out the tank. Against such a view are: (a) the absence of a floor, even though the *opus reticulatum* wall stands to a height of 0.75 m above the corridor; (b) the absence of any lavatory seat emplacements in the back wall, which rises still higher; (c) the lack of any deposits, especially in the primary silts, which resemble an accumulation of human waste. Moreover, the plans of latrines in Italian villas are usually of much more conventionally proportioned rooms, rather than long, narrow structures (cf., for example, Rossiter 1978).

The true purpose of the structure was only realized, however, at a relatively late stage in the preparation of this report. Both the literary and the archaeological sources indicate that tanks or ponds provided with vessels such as amphorae or *tubuli* were used to house fish; the vessels created places for the fish to breed, and Higginbotham (1991; forthcoming), who has produced an authoritative survey of the subject, illustrates a fish-pond with eels swimming in and out of *tubuli* arranged almost exactly like the Monte Gelato example (Higginbotham 1991: fig. 104). This in itself would be suggestive enough, but confirmation that the structure was indeed an eel pond came with the identification of a vertebra of *Anguilla anguilla* (and also two fish spines) from the lower fill. Shad was represented in the upper layers, but this is more likely to be food refuse (there were eleven fish bones, mostly unidentifiable), than an indication of the pond's inhabitants.

Fish-ponds were probably not uncommon in the Roman Campagna (Thomas and Wilson 1994: 164-7), and certainly could be a profitable enterprise. Eels were particularly popular from the first century BC, and were raised in enormous quantities, fetching high prices (e.g. Pliny, *Naturalis Historia* ix. 170-1). But, as Pliny also informed us, they were also kept as pets, and even decorated with jewellery, an ornamental role I have already alluded to in discussing Varro's villa near Casinum. Varro told us that he had 'two oblong fish-ponds, not very wide, facing the colonnades' (*De Re Rustica* iii. 5.12), a description which fits the Monte Gelato example very closely. Certainly the modest dimensions of the pond would appear to rule out commercial production of eels, and it is best seen as a harmonious ornamental addition to an elegant porticoed courtyard, with trees, a nymphaeum (below, Fig. 142), statues, a fountain (below, Fig. 144), pools and an aviary.

THE SOUTHERN RANGE AND SIDE ROAD

Only a limited area was investigated beyond the south portico, since outcrops of bedrock indicated that little could have survived. Moreover, a large late Roman limekiln had cut away any earlier features. There would have been space for a series of rooms for there is a 6.0 m gap between the portico and a steep-sided and certainly ancient cutting into the bedrock. This cutting, which still carries the modern road, follows an alignment that is parallel with the south portico (Fig. 12,2), and may be contemporary with it; but there is no direct evidence for its date, and the overall layout of the Augustan complex (Fig. 12,1) rather suggests that this remained vacant ground at this time (and quite possibly later).

PHASE 1: THE OTHER FINDS

No refuse deposits of the first century AD were encountered in the excavations, and the small quantities of pottery of this date all occurred in residual contexts (Roberts, this volume). This is further confirmation of the non-functional aspect of the investigated area at this time, although the second-century finds from the deposits in the fish-pond must imply that there was a substantial villa nearby. No traces of buildings were discovered in the very thick *macchia* overlooking the waterfalls, although there is one possible ancient footing exposed in the surface of the track that runs along the southeastern side of the river Treia. However, the most obvious possibility must be the area to the north of the courtyard complex, where the ground rises gradually to the ridges that surround the valley. While the vestiges of only one footing, perhaps of this period, were identified (see below, Fig. 41, L198), there is ample space here for a considerable range of buildings, although little is likely to have survived the effects of modern ploughing.

It is the sculpture, architectural elements and inscriptions which otherwise shed most light on the site at this period. They are discussed in detail in the catalogues, but a few summary words will be appropriate here. Mention has already been made of the marble crater and *labrum* (usually, but not always, associated with the *caldarium* of a bathhouse). To these may be added the lower half of a nymph, reused in a late Roman floor; a weathered male head (?Ganymede) from a medieval context; and a statue of Venus, two-thirds life-size, from a late Roman fill over the portico corridor (Claridge, this volume). An early Imperial date would not be inappropriate for any of them. The identifiable architectural fragments are not numerous, but include an architrave, two sections of a cornice and a block with a decorative moulding, all again quite possibly of early first-century AD date. A pilaster capital was also found, with a parallel of the late Republican-early Augustan period; it may derive from a small temple or funerary monument (DeLaine, this volume). In short, these finds certainly do not contradict an Augustan date for the complex, and amply support the notion of a graciously embellished place.

The assumption here is that all these items were part of the phase 1 complex, and not later introductions to the site, as often happened (for example, Santa Rufina: Reynolds 1991: 301; Santa Cornelia: Reynolds 1991: 137). The inscriptions are more problematic, especially the important tomb monument of four freed-people, including C. Valerius Faustus, cattle merchant and *magister* of the *Augustales* at Veii

(Gilliver 1990; this volume). Almost certainly Augustan in date, it was found in a late Roman limekiln, but had survived incineration (Figs 135 and 136). Faustus's spouse would appear to have been a lady called Hilara, with an extremely rare *nomen*, Aesconius. This may indicate a family relationship with an Augustan veteran equestrian officer, Aesconius Capella, who was a *duumvir* of Veii (Gilliver 1990). All the other inscriptions are also funerary, except for that on a fragment of local *peperino*, also from the lime-kiln. It reads *fa*]CIVND[*um curavit* on one line, and]S.ET.HILA[on the next, and Purcell (1988a: 286) has suggested that it records the work of *curatores fani* or *magistri pagi* or *vici*, in late Republican or Augustan times.

There was a substantial village-like settlement at the Fosso Stramazzo (Fig. 8, E21), less than a kilometre to the north, from which the inscription could derive. Alternatively, it may indeed be from the Mola di Monte Gelato itself although, as will be seen in the discussion, below, a context is not easy to identify. For the funerary inscriptions there are, however, good local contexts. There is the second-century mausoleum or temple-tomb on the ridge opposite the main site (cf. DeLaine, this volume), and a Roman cemetery, ravaged by the *clandestini*, some 200 m to the northwest, by the paved road. Tomassetti (1877) records sepulchral inscriptions from Monte Caio (Fig. 8), including one of the *praetor* Q. Petronius Urbanus (*CIL* XI 3207; see also 3228), and there is a further funerary text from the Fosso Stramazzo site (Reynolds 1966: 65, no. 18). There is no real need, therefore, to invoke the cemeteries of Rome as the source of these inscriptions, and an origin in the vicinity of the Mola di Monte Gelato is entirely plausible. If so, the strong onomastic links with Veii and Rome that the inscriptions record is of considerable interest. One, for example, bears the name Herennia (below, Fig. 139), which recalls M. Herennius Picens, consul in AD 1 and patron of Veii (*CIL* XI 3797). Settlement in the towns and countryside of South Etruria by people from Rome was a well-defined phenomenon from Augustan times onwards (Potter 1991: 176-7; Purcell 1983: 161, 166), and would help to explain the apparent urban connections of the complex at the Mola di Monte Gelato.

THE PHASE 2 DRAINS

From the late first or early second centuries AD there were significant modifications to the complex. Some were minor, like the provision of an *a cappuccina* tile drain (E82) along part of the west side of the courtyard (Figs 13 and 23,a). This cut across the phase 1 drain (E201) from the portico, and contained second-century pottery in its fill. It was recessed into the natural subsoil to a depth of 0.5 m, and flowed from north to south. Although the full extent did not survive at either end, its sealed nature means that it was not intended as an eaves-drip. The idea may have been to carry away, down hill, storm water, although it would appear to have become rapidly choked with silt.

One other drain (A10) of this period lay on the lower terrace (Fig. 13), parallel with the east wall of the bath-house (cf. below). Only a short length was exposed, due to the overlay of later features; but it was 0.22 m wide and cut 0.42 m into the bedrock. Presumably it once held a terracotta or lead pipe. There were a few sherds of early Imperial date in its fill, and there is no reason to doubt its association with the bath-house.

ROOM D

It is also possible that a room (D) was added to the west of the large room (A) in phase 2, at the level of the upper terrace. In the limited area that was excavated, there was a *cocciopesto* floor, at the edge of a shallow foundation trench (E202), running east-west and parallel with the southern edge of the upper terrace (Fig. 13). In the late Roman period there was a door threshold in the western wall of the large room, but this was clearly a late insertion. However, it is possible that this represents a replacing of a much earlier doorway.

THE CISTERNS (FIG. 26)

In the northwest area of the excavation were two adjacent cisterns. Both showed the same broad alignment, although this differed slightly from that of the main complex, instead following that of the paved road. There is no very obvious reason for this, unless it was dictated by a higher ridge of bedrock between the cisterns and the northwest corner of the courtyard.

Plough damage had been severe, and had removed all traces of the wall around the north cistern. What remained was a rectangular tank, 5.46 × 4.24 m, and with a maximum surviving depth (at the north end) of 0.9 m. There seems to be no real correspondence with *p.M.* here (18.44 × 14.32), unless there was a general intention to make it 20 × 15 *p.M.* The floor was made up of a somewhat coarse *cocciopesto*, with clear signs of differential wear. There was a well-made quarter-round moulding around the base of the walls, which were lined with whitish *opus signinum*. This had been applied in two stages, an initial coarse mixture and then a smooth surface, giving a total thickness of 20 mm. There had been difficulties in the coating of the tufo, however, and in places nails had been driven into the rock, to aid the keying. This was not entirely successful, and the west face had partly fallen away. Much of what remained had also become detached on that side, giving the impression of a job that was poorly done (cf. Vitruvius viii. 6.14, on the lining of cisterns).

The base of the adjoining south cistern was 0.3 m (perhaps, therefore, one *p.M.*) higher, and much less well preserved. No superstructure survived, and part of the floor had been ploughed away. There was a gap of 0.46 m between the two cisterns, and the overall internal dimensions of the south cistern were *c.* 4.5 × 4.2 m, so that it was smaller and squarer in shape. Traces could be seen of a wall footing, 0.4 m wide, along the east side, but it consisted of no more than tufo rubble set in a bluish grey mortar. It was not, however, precisely aligned with the north cistern, a disparity of layout which seems somewhat curious. Possibly they represent two separate periods of construction.

Neither cistern was completely excavated, and the manner in which they were fed is unclear. A drain was, however, identified in the southwestern corner of the north cistern. It consisted of a U-shaped cut into the bedrock, down to just below the base of the cistern, and headed towards the paved road; there were traces of what appeared to be a mortar capping. The channel then debouched into an *a cappuccina* drain, running along the east side of the paved road (Fig. 23,b).

The whole channel of the cistern drain was not fully excavated, and the feature is not easy to understand in detail. It seems a rather crude device for draining the cistern and,

Fig. 26. The north cistern, and later Roman footings, looking southwest. The scant remains
of the south cistern are on the left. *(KW)*

given that the channel was apparently cut through the *opus signinum* lining, must be regarded as a secondary construction. This in turn raises the question of function. We have tended to regard these features as water cisterns, whilst recognizing that they might also have served as vats for the separation of oil or the fermentation of wine. It could indeed be that a complex of presses lies just outside the excavated area, to the north. However, given the proximity of the bath-house (DeLaine, below), which lies at a much lower level (Fig. 19), it does seem much more plausible to regard them as cisterns, constructed specifically to service the baths.

There is no direct evidence with which to date the building of the cisterns, although they were manifestly inserted into the Augustan complex and aligned on the paved road. They are thus most probably to be assigned to phase 2 which, to judge from the evidence of the bath-house, may have begun *c.* AD 100. Subsequently, a wall-footing (Fig. 13, L119) was built on the floor of the eastern part of the south cistern. Whether this represents a modification of the cistern or belongs to a period after its abandonment is, however, uncertain, in the absence of proper stratification (cf. Fig. 39).

The backfilling of the north cistern, where there was a good depth of deposits, appears to have taken place rapidly. There was a very thin layer of grey-brown silt on the floor, not more than 20 mm thick, and then a dump of loose rubbly fill, 0.4 m deep. Above this was a layer with less rubble and more colluvium, but with a sufficiently homogeneous character to suggest that it was not a natural accumulation. This conclusion is supported by the finds, which indicate

that the backfilling took place in the late second or early third century. This is close in time to the final dump in the fish-pond, and also the date of virtually all of the refuse in the rock-cut road: the Severan period, therefore, would seem to mark something of a watershed in the site's history.

The other finds from the north cistern include some pieces of bronze and lead sheet (cat. 26, 27, 87), an iron hook (cat. 3) and two iron rings (cat. 6, 7). There was also much wall-plaster, all of it very fragmented, but with some traces of faded painted decoration. Recognizable were yellow and white flowers and green vegetation, while other pieces bore purple and red paint. Tile and lumps of mortar also occurred in significant proportions, and a tufo cornice of late Republican or early Imperial date (below, Fig. 161) had been thrown into the upper fill, where it had come to rest diagonally, along a tip line. Another section of this cornice was recorded as a surface find in 1970.

THE BATH-HOUSE (FIGS 27 AND 28), by J. DeLaine

On the western edge of the main site, next to the paved Roman road, were discovered the remains of a small bath building, the heated part of which came to light during the widening of the modern road in 1983 (Fig. 29) and was investigated during the first two seasons of excavation (DeLaine in Potter and King 1988: 263-6). This was followed by the

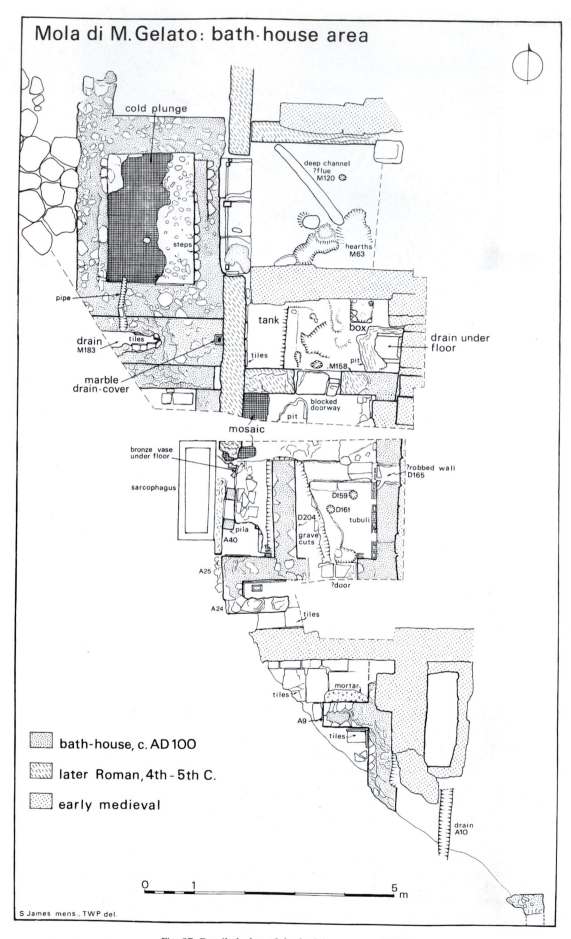

Fig. 27. Detailed plan of the bath-house area. *(TWP)*

bath-house: reconstructed plan

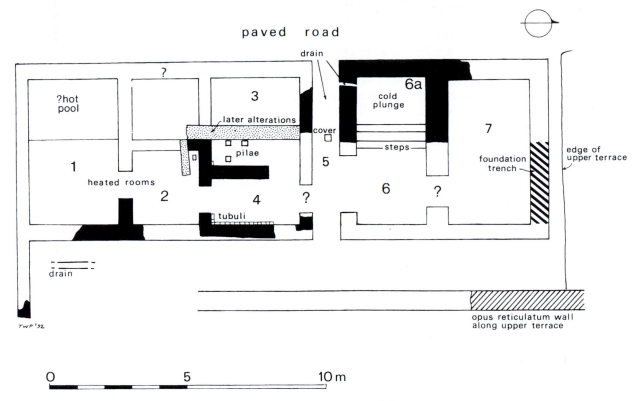

paved road

- drain
- ?hot pool
- 3
- 6a
- cold plunge
- later alterations
- cover
- 7
- pilae
- 5
- steps
- foundation trench
- edge of upper terrace
- 1
- heated rooms
- 2
- 4
- ?
- 6
- ?
- tubuli
- drain
- opus reticulatum wall along upper terrace

TWP '92

0   5   10 m

Fig. 28. Bath-house plan. *(TWP)*

Fig. 29. The southern part of the bath-house and later features. The section to the left is drawn in Figure 54. *(TWP)*

discovery of the cold section during the 1990 excavation season (Fig. 30). Unfortunately the southwest corner of the building appears to have disappeared during the construction of the modern road, while much of the northeastern section was deliberately demolished in Antiquity to make way for later Roman and early medieval structures. It is not, therefore, possible to recover the complete plan of the baths, although the main lines are clear. The bath building appears to have consisted of a simple rectangular block, approximately 6.5 × 19.3 m, containing at least seven rooms. There were four (or possibly five) heated rooms in the southern half, separated by a narrow corridor from an unheated room with a cold plunge pool and with one large or two smaller rooms to the north of the pool.

Heated areas (rooms 1 to 4) (Figs 27 and 28)

Rooms 1 and 2

Only the northeast corner of room 1 remains, although the line of the south wall of the room can be inferred from the short section of wall appearing in the modern road cutting. This appears to form the southern limit of the bath block. Both the northwest and southeast corners of room 2 are preserved, defining a room c. 2.5 m square. There is no evidence to indicate whether or not there was a further room to the west of room 2.

The surviving walls of the two rooms have a maximum height of 0.5 m and enclose the hypocaust space. Both floor and walls of the hypocaust preserve extensive traces of a tile lining, formed predominantly from reused roof tiles of minimum dimensions 0.48 × 0.69 × 0.025 m with their flanges removed, but including a few standard *bipedales* (Figs 29 and 31). One jamb of an opening between the two hypocausts is preserved, which may indicate that there was also a door between the two rooms at this point. No *tubuli* from the wall heating remain in place, although there is a single *tubulus* mortared vertically into the sub-floor in the northwest corner of room 2. It is hard to see how this *tubulus* may have functioned in relation to the bath, since it is too far from the wall to have been part of the heating system and could not have acted as a drain for a pool as it had no outlet at the base. It is more likely to be related to a later use of the area which involved building a rough wall which sits on the hypocaust sub-floor and runs parallel to the north wall of room 2. The northeast corner of the room remained concealed by a baulk, but there appears to have been a doorway into room 4 in the centre of the north wall.

Room 3

Although part of the north and east walls remains to a maximum height of nearly 1.0 m above the sub-floor of the hypocaust, the original arrangement of the room is rather obscured by later phases, including late Roman walls and early medieval burials. There appears to have been a door into room 4 at the north end of the east wall, but the south wall has been truncated and the jamb does not survive. Both walls are of concrete construction, but the upper part of the north wall appears to incorporate a tufo ashlar block which is difficult to interpret. It is unlikely to have functioned as a threshold, as the top of the block is 0.2 to 0.4 m higher than the floor levels of the rooms on either side, while the use of

solid tufo door jambs in an otherwise brick-faced concrete construction has few parallels.

In the eastern section of the room, part of the hypocaust remains intact (Fig. 32). Tiles line the floor and walls of the hypocaust as in rooms 1 and 2, with those on the wall appearing to support the inner edge of the wall tubes, one of which remains in place in the southeast corner of the room. The hypocaust *pilae*, 0.39 m high, are composed of eight courses of *bessales* of average dimensions 0.2 × 0.2 × 0.034 m. The *pilae* are covered by standard *bipedales* which support the floor of the room. As well as the floor packing, which remains over most of the east end of the room, small areas of white mosaic, with tesserae averaging 10 mm square, survive in places at an average height of 0.71 m above the hypocaust sub-floor. The hypocaust appears to have continued under the doorway to room 4.

Room 4

This room, only c. 1.6 m wide, appears to form a heated passage linking rooms 2 and 3. The north wall has been much altered in the late Roman period by the cutting through and later blocking of a doorway, but sufficient of the Roman structure survives to suggest that there was originally no opening between this and room 6. The floor of the room is reasonably well preserved, being broken through to the hypocaust space only in the opening between rooms 3 and 4. A row of *tubuli* extending below floor level remains along the southern half of the east wall and as far as the opening to room 2.

All the visible walls of these heated rooms are of brick-faced concrete with a tufo rubble core, except for the tufo ashlar block mentioned above. The bricks are predominantly regular triangles of average length along the face of 0.26 m within the range 0.23-0.28 m, and of average thickness either 33 mm in the range 30-35 mm, or 38 mm in the range 38-40 mm, suggesting that they were cut from a mixture of *bessales* and *bipedales*. The horizontal mortar joints are irregular but mostly fall within the range 20-24 mm, although they can be as wide as 30 mm. The modulus of five rows of brick and five of mortar averages 0.29 m. The bricks are yellow to salmon-pink in colour and of a uniform consistency.

The Cold Rooms (Rooms 5-7) (Figs 27 and 28)

Room 5

This is a narrow space, 0.95 m wide, defined by the north wall of room 3 and the south side of the pool room 6a. There does not appear to have been a wall to the west, which would suggest that this room formed an entrance passage from the Roman road which ran along the west side of the bath block. A large drain of *a cappuccina* type runs under the floor of the room, in an east-west direction, into which runs a rough drain from the pool (Fig. 33). Only the tufo rubble and mortar packing of the floor remains, except at the east end where a white marble drain cover connecting with the drain survives, set into what may be a later concrete floor some 0.24 m above the level of the mosaic floors in the heated rooms. The same large drain reappears further to the east, on a line with the outer east wall of the heated rooms. This whole area east of the corridor and the pool was greatly altered in later phases, so that it is no longer possible to tell whether the corridor also continued straight across, or whether this area formed part of room 6. In either case there must have been a doorway in the east wall corresponding to that in the west.

Fig. 30. The plunge bath (Fig. 28, no. 6a) looking south, with to the left late Roman walls and the entrance to the baptistery complex. *(KW*

Section in modern road cutting, A

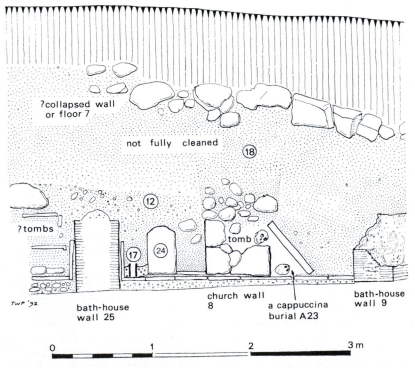

Fig. 31. Section of the southern part of the bath-house, overlain by the churches, and with burial no. 26 (A23).
7: tufo blocks and lumps probably from the latest floor of the church (or its wall). 18: darkish fill; traces of a demolition or robber trench down to the church wall, 8, are indicated by a discrete cluster of tufo lumps. 12: layer with building material and human bones. 17 (=19): loose grey layer with fifth- to sixth-century pottery. 24: wall built of roughly-shaped blocks and lumps of tufo, resting on a thin layer of soil; beside it is a *tubulus* set in mortar. *(TWP)*

Fig. 32. The bath-house, second baptistery west wall, and overlying deposits (Figs 54 and 72).
In the foreground, the sarcophagus of burial no. 61. *(TWP)*

Fig. 33. The bath-house drain (Fig. 28, no. 5) looking east. *(KW)*

Room 6a

The cold plunge pool (Fig. 30), which measures 1.78 × 2.6 m, is one of the best preserved parts of the bath block. The white mosaic floor is in good condition (and is made with small tesserae averaging 8.0 mm square), although the eastern side is concealed by later rubble concrete. The north, south and west sides, defined by a wall 0.6 m thick of tufo rubble concrete faced with tufo blocks, survive to only a few centimetres above the floor of the pool, except in the northwest corner. On the east the wall forms two steps, the lower complete step being 0.24 m wide and 0.31 m high; the risers are also faced with tufo blocks. The outer east edge of the pool is concealed by the later threshold block, but it is clear from the shallowness of the resulting pool that there must have been a stepped ledge dividing it from the rest of room 6, a common method of constructing such pools.

Rooms 6 and 7

Very few traces of these rooms were preserved. The east wall of room 6 was completely obliterated by a later concrete floor, and it can only be assumed that it followed the line of the hot rooms. A rough and shallow concrete foundation, which continues the line of the west boundary of the pool northwards, is the only surviving structure relating to room 7 and even this may be a later addition as there appears to be a join at this point. A trench for another shallow foundation runs parallel to the edge of the upper terrace and close to it, and this presumably denotes the northern boundary of room 7. It is also possible that the later Roman walls which start at the northeast corner of the bath-house – one running north-south cutting room 7 in two, and the other east-west continuing the line of the north wall of the pool – reflect the arrangement of the earlier structure.

DISCUSSION

Although the basic linear arrangement of this small bath building, with unheated rooms to the north and heated rooms to the south, is clear, a number of features require further comment. From its location at the end of a series of heated rooms, it can be assumed that room 1 was the *caldarium* and a hot pool can be restored on the west, or, less probably, on the south. The poor state of preservation of the remaining three or four heated rooms makes it difficult to identify the function of each or to determine the circulation pattern, although the wall heating in room 4 precludes this being a *tepidarium* in the strictest sense (Rebuffat 1991: 7). This would make room 3 the only possible candidate for a *tepidarium*, with access from room 5, as well as suggesting that room 2 functioned as a *sudatio*. Since no evidence was found on the east side for the *praefurnia* of the heated rooms, these are most likely to be sought to the west of rooms 1 and 2. Room 6 is clearly a *frigidarium*, with a cold plunge pool, and this would suggest that the ill-defined room 7 to the north, if belonging to the bath at all, might have acted as an *apodyterium*. The corridor room 5 appears to have allowed access to the baths from the road as well as from an area between the upper terrace of the complex and the

east side of the block; it is no longer possible to determine whether there was also access into rooms 6 or 7 from the east.

With the exception of the area around Vesuvius buried in the eruption of AD 79, baths belonging to rural villas in Italy have been little studied and parallels are few. On the whole, the early examples gathered by Fabbricotti (1976) have at most two heated rooms, as have the late Republican-early Imperial examples from *villae rusticae* at Scansano, near Grosseto (Del Chiaro 1989; 1990), and Petraro, near Stabiae (De Caro 1987). It appears that the multiplication of heated rooms in otherwise unpretentious rural bath-houses should be seen as a later phenomenon, one which presumably follows the better-documented development of elaborate public and urban bath buildings under the influence of the Imperial *thermae* (cf. DeLaine 1992). The same has been suggested for the appearance of bath-houses as independent structures in rural villas rather than integral parts of the *pars urbana* (Rossiter 1978: 37); the small third-century bath-house of the villa at Crocicchie is a case in point (Potter and Dunbabin 1979).

In the absence of any datable finds relating to the construction phase, the bath can only be dated broadly on the basis of its plan and the type of construction. Its independent structure, the increased number of heated rooms, and the incorporation from the start of a cold plunge, together suggest a *terminus post quem* for the Monte Gelato bath towards the end of the first century AD. The use of brick-faced concrete for the heated areas, and the cutting of the facing bricks into triangles, would also suggest a date not before the later part of the first century and more probably in the second; the quality of the brickwork should preclude a date after the middle of the third century. The use of tiles to line the walls as well as the floors of hypocausts has a number of parallels, for example the late first- to early second-century baths at Massaciuccoli (Levi 1935: 218-19, figs 3-5), but is unlikely to have any value as a chronological indicator.

The location of the Monte Gelato bath-house, next to the *diverticulum* and with access from it as well as presumably from the rest of the complex on the terrace above, must raise the question of what clientele the building was intended to serve. Nothing is known about the provision of baths for rural workers, including small tenant farmers and day labourers, who would have had no such facilities at home. With baths becoming an increasingly fundamental part of daily life for urban dwellers under the Empire, it would be surprising if the rural population had recourse only to the public baths in the nearest town or *vicus* on market-days and holidays. One possibility is that public baths were sometimes provided by rural villas. This seems to be the context of two very similar inscriptions from rural areas, one from near Ficulea (*CIL* XIV 4015), and the other from near Bologna (*CIL* XI 1 712), which advertize refined or commodious urban-style baths – '*more urbico*' – on private estates. Too few mid-Imperial villas with baths have been fully excavated and published to allow us to identify with any certainty those which might have served a wider clientele than the villa owners and *familia*, but it could be plausibly suggested that those like Monte Gelato, with more developed facilities in a separate bath block and access to a public road, should be high on the list of potential candidates.

THE TEMPLE-TOMB OR MAUSOLEUM (FIGS 34-7), by J. DeLaine

Remains of a rectangular structure, *c.* 6.8 m wide and 10.6 m long, with walls of brick-faced concrete, were identified and partially excavated on the top of a small ridge on the west side of the Roman and modern roads. The ridge is about 6.0 m above the roads, so that the building would have been particularly prominent. It is divided into two unequal parts, with a small chamber facing almost due east, overlooking the road, and a larger one, cut into the hillside behind.

The main chamber is almost square and has reinforcing piers 0.56 m square in each corner, suggesting it was originally roofed with a cross-vault. The smaller chamber, 1.73 m wide, was reached from the main chamber through a narrow doorway 0.88 m wide. An area of possibly medieval rebuild in the centre of the rear (west) wall of the main chamber may indicate the location of an original access door, but further excavation would be necessary to confirm this. Excavations in both chambers failed to uncover any trace of a built floor, although the presence of a slightly projecting brick course forming a narrow ledge on the south wall of the smaller chamber at the same level as the sill of the door may suggest that an original floor at that level was removed at some later period. The natural tufo in the main chamber is 0.42 m lower than the door sill and shows signs of levelling in addition to a number of ruts and irregular depressions, relating to later use of the structure in early medieval times.

The walls, 0.71 m thick, survive to a maximum height of 1.0 m. They have no separate foundations but sit directly on the natural tufo. In the main chamber the underlying tufo appears to have been cut back at the rear (west) to create an artificial platform and levelled to form a uniform bedding for the walls. The internal face of the walls in the smaller chamber follows the irregularities of the underlying tufo. A rough drain passes through the foot of the south wall of the main chamber. A layer of mortar and tufo rubble, extending for up to 0.24 m beyond the outer wall of the smaller chamber, was used to level the irregularities in the natural tufo, and the outer face of the wall above it rests on a levelling course of *bipedales* of dimensions in the range 0.56-0.6 m long and 40-45 mm thick.

All the walls are of brick-faced concrete construction with a core of irregular *tufa caementa*. The bricks are mainly light yellow to pale salmon-pink in colour, with noticeable inclusions of red and black angular fragments and some small nodules of darker orange-red terracotta. Where visible in the top of the wall the bricks are mainly neat triangles with

Fig. 34. The mausoleum or temple-tomb, looking southwest. *(KW)*

Fig. 35. Excavated southeast quadrant of the mausoleum. *(KW)*

some irregular trapezoidal pieces. Brick measurements were taken from the exposed interior faces of the walls only. A *bessalis* of sides 0.197 m and 36 mm thick was used in the door jamb, and some of the facing pieces appear also to be cut from *bessales* of uniform thickness within the range 30-38 mm. These are combined in the facing with thinner bricks (18-30 mm thick), which may be cut from roof tiles, and with bricks of variable thickness generally within the range 38-46 mm but with some up to 60 mm thick, presumably cut from *bipedales* or *sesquipedales*. The mortar joints are variable within the range 9-30 mm, with most falling within the range 13-21 mm and having a median of 17 mm. The modulus of five courses of brick and five of mortar ranges from 0.27 to 0.305 m. The strong, hard mortar consists of a grey, rounded fine aggregate in a fairly clean white matrix.

On the outer face of the west wall of the building, at the highest point of the surviving structure, traces remain of a decorative brick moulding consisting of a half-round 42-6 mm thick over a deep fillet 60 mm tall, the total height of the moulding being 0.12 m. The half-round mouldings appear to be formed from *bipedales* 0.590-0.595 m long, cut in four to produce rectangles 0.14 m wide. It is possible that bricks with a bevelled edge found in the fill of the rock-cut road, and perhaps the fragments of brick columns and capitals/bases found elsewhere on the main site, are also to be related to this structure.

Discussion

Despite the fact that little more than the plan of the building survives, it is clear that the remains are

to be identified as the substructures of a small temple or temple-tomb on a high podium, which can probably be restored as prostyle and either tetrastyle or distyle *in antis*, reached by a set of frontal steps across the full width of the pronaos.

Although brick-faced concrete tombs enjoyed a particular vogue in Rome and its hinterland during the second and early third centuries AD (Blake and Bishop 1973: 117-38), few examples of true temple-tombs, distinguished by a separate pronaos, survive. In addition, the distinction between temple and temple-tomb is not an easy one, as can be seen from the various interpretations given to structures such as Sant'Urbano alla Caffarella, the so-called 'Tomb of Annia Regilla' or 'Temple of Deus Ridiculus' (Kammerer-Grothaus 1974: 154-87), the 'tempietto' forming part of the Villa dei Sette Bassi (Lupu 1937: 179-83), and the structure from the Villa del Torraccio di Torrenova reconstructed in the Museo delle Terme (Quilici 1974: 583-7; Pensabene 1985), which form the closest parallels to the building under consideration. In the absence of evidence for either arcosolia or columbarium niches, the existence of a lower chamber or chambers within the podium of the building is inconclusive: as appears to have been the case with the so-called 'Tomb of Annia Regilla', the vaulted chambers in the podium may have functioned only as substructures, the actual tomb chamber being the

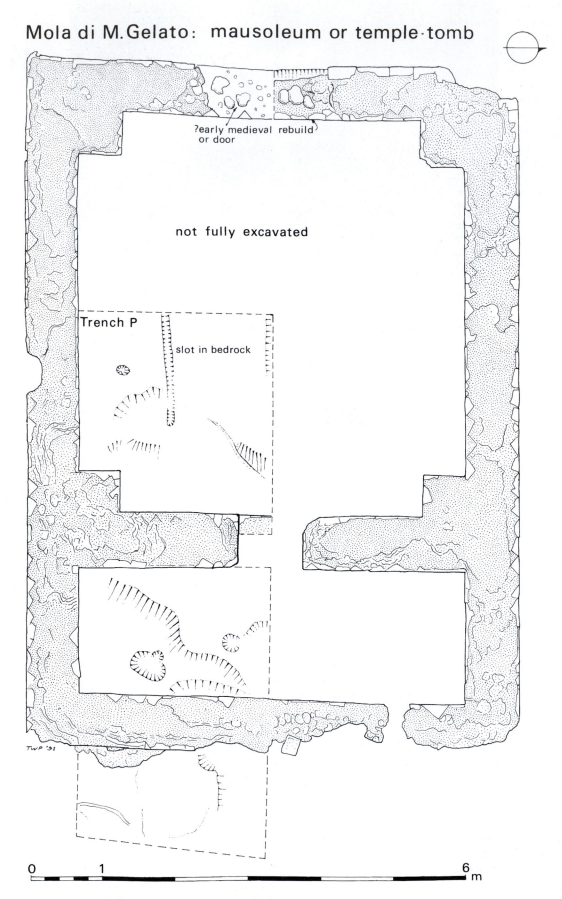

Fig. 36. Plan of the mausoleum or temple-tomb. *(TWP)*

cella above. The location of the structure parallel to and overlooking the road, and its eastern orientation, are also ambiguous. It should also be borne in mind that there is not necessarily any relation between this structure and the villa and baths on the opposite side of the road.

In the absence of any clear archaeological evidence, only general indications of the date of the structure can be given on stylistic grounds. Most of the parallels cited above are thought to be Hadrianic to Antonine in date, and the use of brick facing even within the podium chambers would tend to suggest a date later rather than earlier in this period, certainly closer to Rome.

DISCUSSION OF PHASES 1 AND 2

The analysis of the first two phases of the site's history reveals a place of some pretensions, with a population of presumed urban origin, especially Veii and Rome, and sophisticated taste. As originally envisaged in the Augustan period, it was provided with relatively grand architecture, accompanied by some handsome sculpture, ornamental trees, an aviary, a fish-pond for eels, and a pool. It was, in short, a place built to grace a lovely setting.

While the excavations were in progress, we were reluctant to describe the site as a villa, although this was the preferred interpretation at the outset of the investigation. The misgivings arose partly through the discovery of the inscription in the limekiln which Purcell (1988a: 286) thought might refer to the work of *curatores* of a *fanum* or magistrates of a *pagus* or *vicus*. But they also stemmed from the failure to identify any traces of a residential area or a *pars rustica*. As excavation and study proceeded, the notion that the original site was a religious complex gained ground (although no temple was found in the main complex), as did the idea that it may have been a *vicus*.

These uncertainties would now seem to be resolved. There seem to be an insufficiency of buildings for it to have been a *vicus*, and the *fanum* hypothesis is likewise difficult to sustain. On the other hand, the identification of the Augustan complex as part of a villa gains credence in the light of the remarkably close analogy drawn above with Varro's Casinum villa, and with some features of the Vesuvian gardens. The presence of a Campanian-style country house, with luxurious elements like the keeping of songbirds and eels, would be entirely appropriate in a place with attractive waterfalls and much natural woodland along the valley slopes. There may indeed have been no attached farm at this time, as would appear to be the case with the contemporary villa of the Volusii at Lucus Feroniae (Moretti and Moretti 1977).

Who then was its owner? Here we must stress again the epigraphic links with Veii and Rome (Gil-

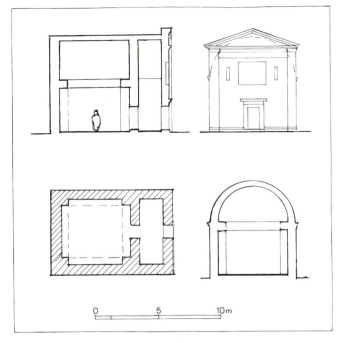

Fig. 37. A possible reconstruction of the mausoleum or temple-tomb. *(SG)*

liver 1990; this volume), which surely hint at a wealthy *dominus* mainly based in either, or both, places. Indeed, one is bound to wonder whether the recovery of the Augustan tomb monument of C. Valerius Faustus, a *mercator bovarius* and a *magister Augustales* at Veii, does not by extraordinary chance reveal the owner of the place. Cattle merchants were prosperous people, to judge from the ancient sources (Gilliver 1990: 195 n. 9): to take one example, C. Caecilius Isodorus, *libertus*, left 3,600 pairs of oxen, 257,000 other cattle, and also 60 million sesterces in cash when he died in 8 BC (Pliny, *Historia Naturalis* xxxiii. 135). Faustus, an important public official, was also doubtless a wealthy man. Naturally, it is very speculative to suggest this correlation; but the fact that most of this very large funerary monument was found suggests that it cannot have been brought far, and we have shown that the area was a focus for tombs. At the very least, the possibility should not be ignored.

Around the Trajanic or Hadrianic period (and the fragility of the dating evidence requires emphasis), there are manifest signs of change. The original phase 1 entrance was blocked by a bath-house, a new paved road was constructed, and for the first time significant quantities of rubbish were being generated, albeit much of it of high quality. Later a temple-tomb of some elegance was built on the ridge overlooking the main complex and, to judge from the absence of any features in the surrounding bedrock, stood in isolation. We may reasonably infer that Monte Gelato remained a favoured place in the Antonine period, whose inhabitants ate much pork, young and tender chickens, and delic-

was probably a delapidated Roman building, and eventually the floor became buried beneath refuse. Subsequently, as the section (Fig. 47) clearly shows, this was engulfed by fallen wall (including *opus reticulatum*) and rubble, in the latter part of the sixth century, or later.

STRUCTURES OVER THE CISTERNS

The pottery from the north cistern leaves little doubt that it was filled in in the late second or early third century (although see below). There must have been extensive demolition at the time, for the fill included many fragments of wall-plaster, mostly very small, but bearing traces of purple, yellow, green and red paint: some appeared to show yellow and white flowers, with green stems. There was also a fragment of a tufo cornice, probably of late Republican or early Imperial date, from the top fill (below, Fig. 161).

The much shallower south cistern, only the base of which survived, is likely to have been filled in at this time too (as was the nearby fish-pond). Indeed, it may already have seen some modification for on its eastern side were the vestiges of a footing (Fig. 39, L119), 0.43 m wide, on the same alignment as that of the cistern wall. It survived only as lumps of tufo, set in a poor mortar, and there was a spread of mortar to the west. No onward continuation of the wall was noted outside the cistern (although plough damage had been severe), and, as already noted in the previous section, it may therefore be part of a modification or refurbishment in phase 2. Alternatively, it may belong to a later structure, all other elements of which have been destroyed.

Quite certainly later than the cisterns is a complex of wall-footings, again preserved only within them (Figs 26 and 48). These take a quite different alignment from that of the cisterns or main Roman buildings, quite possibly because of variations in the level of the bedrock, which rises to a prominent (and very plough-damaged) hump between the eastern and western sides of site L. Stratigraphically, the earliest footing was a crudely built mass of bluish grey tufo lumps (including some broken-up pieces of masonry blocks), laid out in a northeast-southwest direction across the bottom of the north cistern (Fig. 39, L152). Bonded with some mortar, this would seem to be an inelegant attempt to lend stability to the footings that were built across it. Indeed the base of the wall L126 partially lay on fill, rather than on the cistern floor; 0.51 m in width, it comprised roughly-shaped pieces of tufo, together with fragments of tile, set in a grey-buff mortar. Coursing was negligible, as with the footing for wall L150, which was laid out across the foundation (L152), at a somewhat approximate right angle to L126, heading east.

Traces of wall L126 were apparent on the floor of the southern cistern, and a large post-hole (E212) could mark the onward continuation of wall L150. However, the rest of the building had been largely destroyed. The only hint may

be a two-phase foundation (L198), where one wall had been added to another, to the north of the fish-pond. As with the foundations built across the cistern, this was aligned slightly to the east of north, in contrast to the other Roman buildings. All may therefore have belonged to the same structure, although its overall plan must remain conjectural.

Dating evidence is not abundant. The only clues are provided by a possibly fourth-century coin (cat. 31), not more closely datable, and two pieces of fourth-century glass (cat. 83, 85). All were in the upper fill of the cistern, adjacent to the walls, but a direct association cannot be asserted. Otherwise, the only other late Roman material was a small group of sherds (L146) from the top fill of the cistern in the northeastern corner. They belong to the fifth-sixth centuries, and may have been deposited in an area of subsidence.

One other feature requires mention. This is a shallow, flat-bottomed trench, 0.4-0.5 m in width, running in a north-south direction, and cut into the floor of the southern cistern (Fig. 39, L107). On the base were traces of what may have been impressions of wooden posts, quite closely spaced. The trench proved to be on the same alignment as a large possible post-hole (L130, although this yielded only Republican pottery), and, 9.0 m to the south, with another post-socket (M6), 0.15 m in diameter, and only 0.1 m deep. It is possible, then, that there was a wooden fence, bordering the road, along the top and upper terraces.

THE LOBBY

The so-called lobby, or vestibule, which gave access to the top terrace, underwent a series of major changes in the later Roman period. Originally floored in white mosaic, this was largely broken up, and a drain (E144) was laid north-south across the room (Figs 39, 47, 49). Its northern limits are unknown, but to the south it took a line across the large room, out through the doorway and across the corridor into the courtyard. The lobby drain consisted of a gully, 0.3 m wide, containing a *tubulus*, 0.11 m in diameter; one length of *tubulus* was preserved in situ (Fig. 50), but the rest had been subsequently stripped out. The drain was then filled in with earth and debris (including many fragments of tesserae from the mosaic floor), and sealed with concrete. Given that the lobby was recessed into the tufo, its purpose must have been to reduce the build-up of water behind the north wall of the room.

Covering the drain was a tile floor, a small part of which survived intact (Fig. 51). It included two complete tiles, one 0.39 m square, the other 0.42 m square, and many smaller fragments. A wall 0.43 m in width (E61) was built across the southern entrance and the drain, leaving a narrow doorway, 0.66 m in width. It butted against the corridor wall (E30) to the east, and against the rock-cut wall (E206) to the west. The construction utilized an irregular combination of pieces of tufo blocks and fragments of tile, set in a grey mor-

Fig. 40. Masonry styles. (a) *Opus reticulatum*, Augustan, site L. Scale division: 0.5 m. (b) Wall E30, west side of corridor, *opus reticulatum* and *tufelli* quoins, Augustan. Scale divisions: 0.1 m. (c) Fish-pond, west face, original masonry (?Augustan) and upper repair. Scale divisions: 0.5 m. (d) Fish-pond, north face, latest repair. Scale divisions: 0.5 m. (e) Mausoleum, west wall, probably Antonine. Scale division: 0.5 m. (f) Bath-house, wall A9, probably early second century. Scale divisions: 0.1 m. (g) Blocked doorway (E81) in west side of corridor wall (E30). *Tufelli* type A, fourth century. Scale divisions: 0.5 m. (h) Northeast corner of corridor, wall L196. *Tufelli* type B. Fourth century. Scale division: 0.5 m. (i) North wall (E62) of lobby. *Tufelli* type B. Fourth century. Scale division: 0.5 m. (j) Wall M40, beneath baptistery entrance wall. *Tufelli* type B. Fourth century. (k) Wall M22, on lower terrace. Fourth century +. Scale divisions: 0.1 m. (l) North wall (E22) of large room. *Tufelli* type C. Fourth century +. Scale divisions: 0.5 m. *(KW/TWP)*

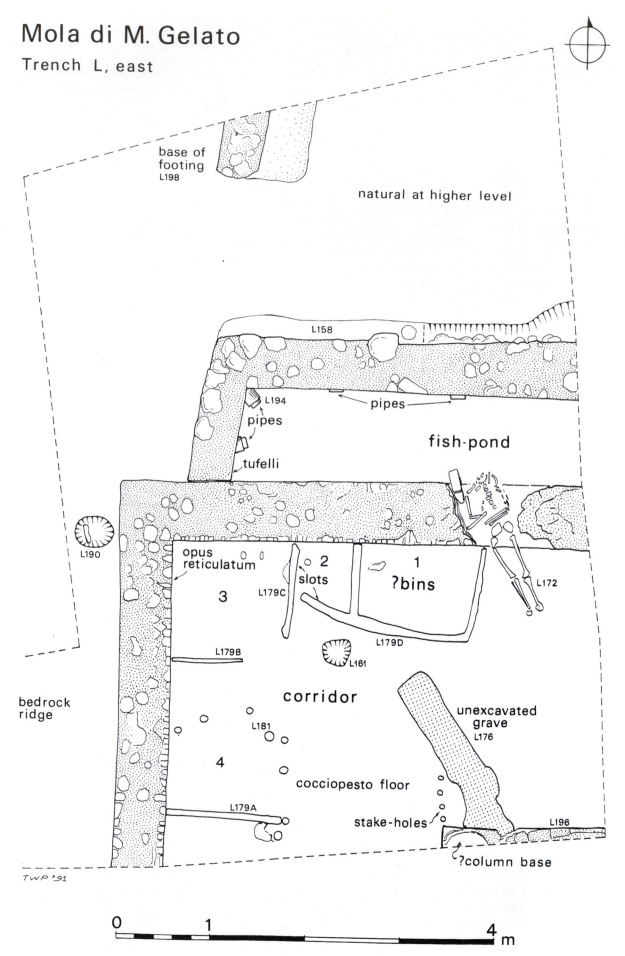

Mola di M. Gelato
Trench L, east

base of
footing
L198

natural at higher level

L158

L194

pipes

pipes

fish-pond

tufelli

L190

opus
reticulatum

2
slots

1
?bins

L172

3

L179C

L179D

L179B

L161

corridor

unexcavated
grave
L176

bedrock
ridge

L181

4

cocciopesto floor

stake-holes

L179A

L196

?column base

TWP '91

0   1   4 m

Fig. 41. Features in the northwest corner of the corridor around the courtyard. *(TWP)*

Fig. 42. The northeast corner of the corridor, with the fish-pond beyond, looking northwest. Also visible are the grooves for late Roman bins and a medieval grave: cf. Figure 44. *(KW)*

Fig. 43. As Figure 42, showing the holes for horizontal timbers of the bins cut into the reticulate walls. *(KW)*

Fig. 44. Fill with fifth- and early sixth-century pottery over the corridor in site L; the ranging pole rests on hearths. *(KW)*

Fig. 45. The western corridor and the large room (left) at the end of excavation, looking north. *(KW)*

Fig. 46. View looking southwest across site E, with the lobby (right) and the large room (left). In the foreground is the corridor, pit E159 and post-holes and stake-holes of late Roman date. *(KW)*

tar, an uncharacteristically shoddy piece of work for this site. It must have stood, however, to some height, since two contiguous post-holes (E177, C178) would appear to have supported scaffolding.

The north wall of this phase was totally obliterated by a later rebuild, described below. Nothing can therefore be said of its position or character. There was, however, some stratified datable pottery. The tile floor sealed sherds of the first-second centuries, while the fill of the gully for the drain contained pottery broadly describable as mid-Imperial. Whether these are contemporary or residual is not clear, for building-work at this time is contradictory to the general

impression of widespread demolition in the Severan period, followed by little or no occupation. It is an enigma that is not really resolved.

A post-hole (Figs 47 and 50 (E155)) was subsequently cut through the drain, making a large hole in the pipe. With a maximum diameter of 0.18 m, and a depth of 0.3 m, it held a fairly substantial post, and was matched by a second post-hole (E161), 0.17 m in diameter and 0.45 m in depth, a short distance to the west (Fig. 49). Both were in close proximity to wall E62, built along the north side of the lobby, and may have held scaffold posts. The wall (Fig. 49) rested on a conspicuous offset (E93), 0.4 m high, which projected

E, north section

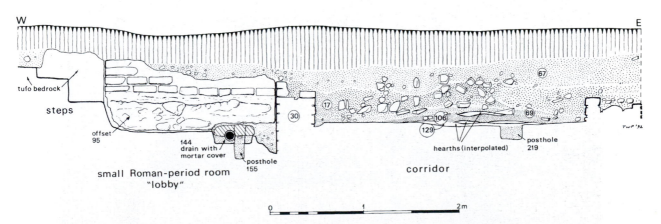

Fig. 47. Section across the lobby and corridor.

For the features in the lobby, see text. Layers over corridor: 67: grey-brown silty loam. 17: a layer of rubble, including *opus reticulatum* and wall-plaster, presumably collapse from wall 30. 69: dark grey silt with late Roman pottery. 106: dark grey-brown silt, with sixth-century pottery, underlying a hearth. 129: red-brown layers of hearths, with fifth- to sixth-century pottery. 219: post-hole with dark brown fill. *(TWP)*

Fig. 48. Late Roman walls built into the north and south cisterns, looking north. Note the modern plough grooves under the ranging pole. *(KW)*

Fig. 49. The lobby looking east. *(KW)*

Fig. 50. The pipe, cut by a post-hole (E155), in drain E144 in the lobby, looking north. *(KW)*

Fig. 51. The tile floor covering the drain in the lobby, with the large room beyond, where a wooden partition (E115) is visible running under the ranging pole. Looking southwest. *(KW)*

some 0.3 m beyond the line of the wall; it was roughly built with lumps of orange tufo, set in a grey-white concrete. Above was the wall itself, with fairly regular *tufelli* (type B), also in orange tufo and with courses of 80 mm. The offset partially blocked the lowest rock-cut step, and is thus clearly later. The wall, on the other hand, was built flush with the northern end of the stairway, showing that it must have continued in use.

The doorway in the corridor wall was blocked up, also using orange *tufelli* in a grey-white mortar, and with courses of 80 mm. This is likely, therefore, to be contemporary with the north wall of the lobby, E62. In addition, the door in the south wall was filled in with tufo lumps, tile and greyish mortar, and a second wall (E22) built against it, as the north wall of the adjoining large room. The construction consisted of somewhat irregular, roughly faced *tufelli* (type C) in a yellow tufo, with course heights of 0.13 m, and a width of 0.47 m.

Although the masonry style of the north and south walls of the lobby differ, they would appear on stratigraphical grounds to have been built at the same time. It may be, therefore, that it was the availability of materials that dictated the form of construction: reuse of older masonry was, after all, a commonplace of the period. This does not, however, explain the doubling of the width of the south wall of the lobby, which is not repeated elsewhere in the large room that adjoins it. The answer may well be that the inner wall, E61, was partially demolished to make an offset that matched that on the north wall: these offsets would then have provided supports for a wooden floor, as their common level also implies.

No doorway into the large room or the corridor was found but, with a raised wooden floor, these would have been at a level that would have been destroyed by ploughing. Indeed, it is the absence of a door threshold that increases the likelihood of a floor of planks, raised some 0.4 m above the earlier floor surfaces. The fill over the tile floor, but beneath the level of the offsets, yielded two coins of AD 353-8 (cat. 14, 15), and pottery of broadly similar date. A mid to late fourth-century date is thus implied for the construction. In the latest fill were sherds of the fifth-sixth centuries, although again with no associated floors.

THE LARGE ROOM (A)

Whilst this room always retained its plan as a substantial enclosed space (measuring 5.7 × 8.18 m in its final phase), the walls underwent considerable modification. This may have been of a rather piecemeal nature, however, since fallen sections of *opus reticulatum* (in places with *tufelli* additions) in the lower terrace to the southwest indicate that some of the original masonry did remain into late Roman times. The details of the walls are as follows (Fig. 39).

North wall (E22)

As described above, this was rebuilt, probably in the mid to late fourth century, in irregular *tufelli*, apparently in front of the original wall, although at floor level (Fig. 40,1). Little trace remained of the first wall, since this end of the room had been recessed into the bedrock; this was badly damaged by ploughing over the higher shelf where the original wall had stood. Towards the east end, the tufo had been shaped into a masonry block, 0.46 m in width (E206); but nothing else survived.

West wall

This was poorly preserved, and consequently difficult to divide into phases. The northerly section (E46) was cut out of bedrock, on the top of which were traces of tile and mortar, which gave the appearance of a rebuild of an earlier footing, 0.46 m in width. A drainage channel, running westwards from drain E54, had later been cut through it. The wall adjoined a threshold (E47) of grey tufo, 2.18 m in length; the blocks had been recessed so as to leave a rim on three sides, and there were two sockets for the doors to swing on. This would appear to have been inserted, since it overlay drain E23 (itself quite a late feature, as will be shown). The central part of the threshold had subsequently been cut away.

To the south of the threshold, the wall continued as a footing 0.47 m in width, with two courses, 80 mm high, of *tufelli*, and a course of tile. It thus resembles wall M22, on the lower terrace (below, Fig. 55), which is of fourth-century date. It terminated in a block of upstanding bedrock, 0.65 m in width, so that it projected to the west, where wall E202 continued that line. There was mortar and tile on top, and it seems probable that this was the jamb for a doorway that provided access to the lower terrace. In the fill over the terrace, immediately to the west of the large room and close to this doorway, there was a fallen section of masonry with an opening for a door (or possibly a window). The opening was at least 0.7 m in height, and the wall was built with irregular *tufelli*, with course heights of 80-100 mm, together with pieces of tile (Fig. 52). Its appearance is thus somewhat different from the neater construction seen in the footings of the wall to the north of the jamb, described above.

After a gap of 1.0 m, suitable for such a door, the wall (E3) continued as a rock-cut foundation, with some mortar and tile on top. This was a rather wider foundation, 0.55 m across, and was of one build with the south wall, D74.

South wall (D74)

The footing was built of tufo lumps and mortar, 0.55-0.6 m across, and, together with E3, would appear to be relatively early in the sequence. Its foundations were fairly shallow, with a depth of 0.2-0.3 m. Indeed, the east end of the wall, together with the southern end of the east wall (E7), had disappeared completely. That this is not due to modern agriculture is clear from the fact that a line of six small postholes (D113) ran down the west side of wall E7 and across the foundations of D74. Averaging 0.15 m in diameter, they were mostly rather shallow (Fig. 53 shows the shallowest), and were probably therefore cut from a higher level, which had been destroyed by ploughing.

East wall

A small section of the east wall, opposite the lobby, retained its original *opus reticulatum* construction with traces of red-painted plaster (Fig. 40,b); but the rest of the wall was constructed in different techniques, representing subsequent rebuilds. The neatest masonry lay on either side of a tufo threshold block (E81), in the northeast section of the wall (Fig. 40,g). The block measured 1.02 × 0.46 × 0.29 m, and was flanked by carefully cut *tufelli*, with course heights of 80 mm. Four courses were preserved, two being at foundation level. The doorway was subsequently blocked, although only a layer of grey-white mortar survived as evidence of this.

Fig. 52. The upper and lower terraces, showing the fallen door (or window). Left: pit E180 (fill: E179) at the south end of the large room, and the early medieval pottery kiln. *(KW)*

Almost exactly in the centre of the wall (taking wall E61 as the original northern limit) was a second entrance, 1.8 m in width. This was opposite a still wider entrance from the courtyard, and these spacious dimensions may well imply that they were intended to allow access to carts (which, on the evidence of the ruts in the rock-cut road, had axle widths of about 1.2 m), or large animals like horses and cows. Indeed, given the absence of threshold blocks in either case, these may have been arched entrances, without a permanent door. Both features seem to be original, since there were no traces of earlier foundations although, given their shallowness, one cannot be certain.

The entrance had, however, undergone modifications, for the southern jamb, a concrete block, 0.58 × 0.5 m, and a tufo block beyond, were both very clearly later insertions, overlying drain E149. Further to the south, little of the wall (E7) remained, apart from some mortar, and it then petered out completely, to be replaced by the line of posts referred to above (D113).

The interior of the large room

A number of white tesserae, incorporated in later features, shows that the room probably was once paved with a mosaic: subsequently it was provided with a *cocciopesto* floor. In the northern part, this was laid directly on bedrock and, in places, had worn completely away. To the south, where the bedrock sloped down, there was a variable amount of make-up, incorporating pottery of the later second to early third century (E130). Overlying this were at least two phases of flooring, albeit of a rather patchy nature. However, close to the south wall, there was a clear sequence (Fig. 53). Three pits had been cut into the bedrock, all being dug subsequent

to the construction of the wall (Fig. 39). Two adjoined the wall, and were carefully made with an almost square plan. Pit E180 measured 1.13 × 1.18 m, and was 0.98 m in depth; pit D76 measured 1.19 × 1.28 m, and was 0.8 m in depth. They both were filled with a brown tufaceous soil, somewhat darker at the bottom, and contained considerable quantities of tile and other building material. Pit E180 (fill: E179) also yielded a glass jug of late first- to mid second-century date (cat. 26), smashed upon the floor, and much other glass of a similar period, as well as some pottery of the fifth century. The sherds from pit D76 appeared somewhat later, and probably belong to the earlier part of the sixth century.

Both these pits were sealed by the second phase of *cocciopesto* flooring, grey in colour (Fig. 53). There was some make-up, and over pit D76 this included the statue of a nymph (below, Fig. 142), which had been placed upside-down, so as to utilize the flat surface of her base. This work must have taken place, on ceramic evidence, in the sixth century. Later, pit E184 was cut through the floor and part of pit E180. Measuring 0.9 × 0.7 m, and 0.69 m in depth, it yielded some late Roman material in the upper fill, and was certainly prior to the early medieval pottery kiln, built in the late eighth or early ninth century.

Near to these pits was a hearth (E193), surrounded by a cluster of post-holes. One of these, E191, was particularly well made, being carefully packed around with a square arrangement of tiles; the post-pipe was especially clear, 0.12 m square and 0.27 m deep. The other post-holes were smaller, ranging in diameter from 0.1 to 0.16 m, and in depth from 0.13 to 0.21 m; one had tile packing. Evidently there was some sort of wooden structure around the hearth, although interpreting its nature from these vestiges is not possible. However, it is worth noting that there was bronze-

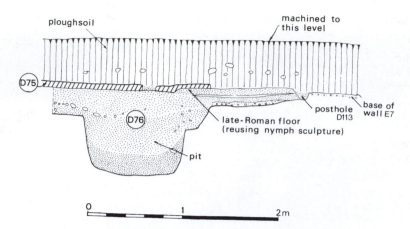

Fig. 53. Section across a late Roman pit, D76, and the southeast end of the large room.
D75: grey *cocciopesto* floor, with some layers of makeup. D113: one of a line of post-holes cutting the wall footing. E7: mortar base of east wall of large room. D76: pit with brown tufaceous fill, darker at the bottom; much building material and sherds of the sixth century. *(TWP)*

casting waste (cat. 41) in the overlying fill, and also a lead ingot (cat. 90). Metalworking is probable, and it may be that the two pits, E180 and D76, were connected with this. They would certainly have been capable of holding water, being rock-cut, although other functions such as storage cannot be ruled out. Indeed, it is not impossible that the glass from pit E180 was intended for recycling.

In the northern part of the room there were some other features, including two drains. The earlier (E144, E149) is the same as that already discussed in connection with the lobby. There was a section of collared pipe, of the same type as that found in the lobby, and also white mosaic tesserae in the fill. It was clearly built before the reconstruction of the north end of the east wall (E7), but cannot be dated closely.

Cutting across the earlier drain was drain E23. This ran east-west across the large room, and out through the main entrance into the courtyard. It comprised a rock-cut trench, some 0.2 m deep, and sealed by a tile and concrete cover (Fig. 23,c). This lay at the base of a larger channel, of variable width, which appears to have functioned as an open drain. A shallower drain (E54) fed into it from the north, and there was also another narrow channel which headed westwards through wall E46.

Drain E23 was evidently laid out prior to the construction of the wide threshold (E47) in the west wall, and also cut across the *a cappuccina* drain (D11; Fig. 23,a, E143) bordering the courtyard. It relates, therefore, to the last main period of use of the large room, and its fill contained sherds of the fifth-sixth centuries, confirming its late date.

There were also wooden features in the northern part of the room. A slot (E115) that ran southwards for 1.85 m from the north wall, must surely have held some sort of timber partition. It was 80 mm in width, and 0.11 m in depth and, perhaps coincidentally, was aligned with a stake-hole to the south of the late drain (E23), and the possible metalworking hearth. In addition, in the northeast corner of the room was an arrangement of slots, averaging 0.11 m in width and 0.12 m in depth. Together they form two rectangular boxes, measuring overall 1.4 × 0.4 m (E73). They are thus not dissimilar to the supposed wooden bins in the northwestern part of the corridor, although more regularly laid out, and may indeed have been for storage. However, they are just as readily explained as the foundations for animal feeding troughs, especially if the partition was for a stall. This would also make sense of the considerable provision of drains, and of the worn nature of the floor in this

part of the room. In short, we might suggest that here was a stable (or perhaps a byre for cows), to which there was easy access through the wide entrance from the corridor. Indeed, Amanda Claridge noted that all the many pieces of marble veneer from the room were covered with some sort of concretion, perhaps deriving from urine.

As a whole, therefore, the room appears to have been adapted as a stable in the northern part, and a workshop area to the south. This also provides a context for a number of iron tools, found both in the room and just to the south. These included a pruning or reaping hook and a linch pin (cat. 23, 25) from within the room, and a metalworking hammer and two axe-adzes (probably for woodworking) from just outside (cf. cat. 12-17); there was also a bronze harness mount (cat. 25). Coin evidence indicates a sixth-century date for these objects. Here would seem to be ample evidence to sustain the functional interpretation advanced above.

Chronology

On the evidence already set out, the large room saw modifications to the north wall in the second half of the fourth century, and repairs to the floor in the south part of the room in the sixth century. Deposits on the floor yielded two coins of fourth- to fifth-century type (cat. 34, 35), a lamp (cat. 59) of *c.* AD 450-550, and pottery of late fourth- to mid sixth-century type (e.g. cat. 163, 171). Occupation, albeit increasingly squalid, must have continued to at least the mid-sixth century. Still later may be the line of posts (D113) cut across the totally demolished wall-footings in the southeast corner; for these, however, direct dating evidence is wholly lacking.

THE LOWER TERRACE

The stratigraphy over the lower terrace was deep, and largely undisturbed by modern intervention. It was, however, extremely complicated, and not every question can be satisfactorily resolved, partly because of the overlay of later foundations, but also because it was never possible to expose the whole complex either in one operation, or completely. Nevertheless, the overall sequence is clear, and mirrors a change from a bath-house, to rooms serving agricultural/industrial purposes and, ultimately, to ecclesiastical structures.

The abandonment and destruction of the bath-house

In common with the entire site, from the bath-house there was virtually no pottery and only five coins which can be dated to the period between *c.* AD 225 and 325. As stressed earlier, with so few rubbish deposits, this may not be significant; but, on the face of it, there was a considerable scaling down in activity for most of the third century, and the bath-house is likely to have gone out of use during this period. The detailed evidence is as follows (cf. Fig. 28 for the room numbers).

Room 1

The hypocaust had been removed to the sub-floor level, over which was late fourth- to mid sixth-century pottery (cat. 156).

Room 2

Prior to the removal of the hypocaust, there were some alterations, including the insertion of a roughly built length of wall of tufo and mortar (Fig. 27; A24), possibly as a floor support. A further stretch of wall (Fig. 27 and below, Fig. 54; A40), was also inserted, and ran northwards through the hypocaust in room 3. It was made up of tile and mortar, and faced in places with tile. The hypocaust was then stripped out to sub-floor level, on which was a fourth-century lamp (cat. 54), and fifth- to sixth-century coarse-ware (cat. 162, 178a).

Room 3

A *tubulus* was inserted as an additional floor support, apparently after the deposition of a coin (cat. 10) perhaps of third- or fourth-century date. Part of the upper floor of the hypocaust was then dug away and, in the fill between the *pilae*, were coins of AD 330-5 and 353-8 (cat. 12, 13). There was also a copper-alloy vase of fourth- to fifth-century type (cat. 15), laid on its side in earth by a *pila*, and well under the floor. Although lacking a handle, and slightly damaged, this handsome object (below, Fig. 170) must still have been of value, and was surely concealed rather than being a casual loss.

Room 4

The hypocaust remained intact (but without a mosaic, a fragment of which survived in room 3). A wall-trench perhaps for a sill-beam (Fig. 27, D165) contained a coin probably of the fourth century (cat. 28), and there was another coin of fourth- to fifth-century date (cat. 41) from the room.

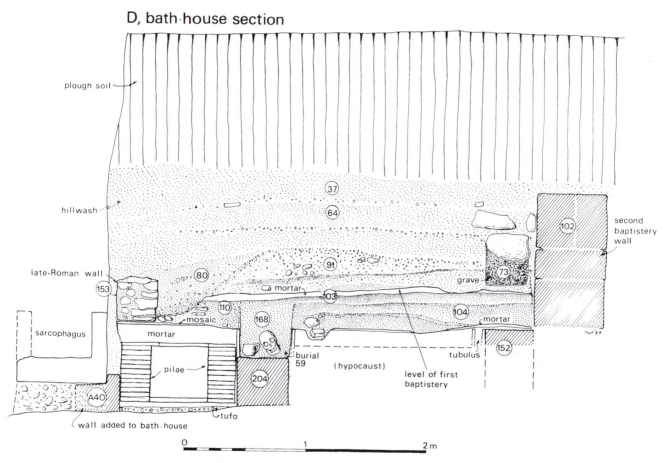

Fig. 54. Deposits over the bath-house, as in Figure 32.

37: hillwash. 64: dark brown hillwash with sixteenth-century pottery. 73: burial with a few very mixed bones. 80: a probable robber trench cut down to the late Roman wall; brown-grey silt fill, and sherds of the eleventh century; it would appear to pre-date the cutting of burial no. 73, but this may not be a correct reading of the sequence. 91: brown-yellow tufaceous fill with a grey silt lens in the middle: this might represent a turf-line. Some ninth- to tenth-century pottery. 103: surface of whitish mortar, of the same appearance as that used in the floor of the first baptistery which is on the same level. 104: layers of grey soil with ash and burnt orange clay; within the deposit were areas of tread; fifth- to sixth-century pottery. 110: soil and rubble beneath 103. 168: burial no. 59, of the late sixth to early seventh centuries, cutting the late Roman deposits, and sealed by the first baptistery surface. 153: late Roman wall on the bath-house mosaic; = M184/22, to the north. 152, 204: bath-house walls. A40: wall (or feature) of broken tile and mortar; a later Roman insertion, but not closely datable. *(TWP)*

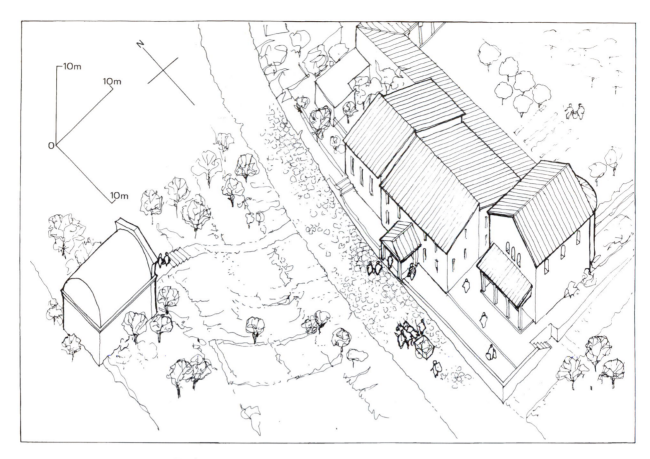

Fig. 70. Reconstruction of part of the late Roman complex. *(SG)*

was expanding, rather than contracting. This was quite possibly as a result of the construction of the church, which may plausibly be seen as an incentive towards enlarging the settlement.

That occupation continued unbroken well into the sixth century is implicit from the finds. There are 24 coins of the late Roman period, four definitely of sixth-century date (three of Justinian I and one of Totila). However, few fine-ware vessels reached the site after about AD 500, although several amphorae of late fifth- to sixth-century type were found. Features in wood, especially partitions and also individual post-holes, often of uncertain purpose, are represented in most areas. While no major structural elements were built in timber, at any rate at ground level, the use of wood was clearly extensive, in marked contrast with the buildings of the early Imperial period. The overriding impression is of a relatively basic existence, perhaps not far removed from subsistence level, for the majority of the population.

There are signs, indeed, that some parts of the building complex may have become ruinous even in the earlier part of the fifth century. Fallen masonry was associated with pottery of this date in the northern part of the corridor, and the deposit was overlain by hearths, probably of the sixth century, and cut by at least one post-hole. Here, therefore, is a clear sign of decay, followed by occupation

of a very run-down kind. The main period of wall-collapse took place, however, around the middle of the sixth century. It is best illustrated by the fallen roof and walls over the north part of the lower terrace, and the collapsed roof in the corridor to the south of the large room. But there was also fallen masonry in the corridor to the east of the large room, overlying deposits with sixth-century pottery, and heavy ploughing may have removed similar layers elsewhere. Only in the workshop on the lower terrace were there no signs of collapsed walls or roof.

There is a temptation to attribute large areas of fallen masonry to a natural disaster such as an earthquake, especially in a region prone to such phenomena. One might recall that tremors of the Tuscania earthquake of 6 February 1971 were felt quite strongly in the Mazzano area, and that Rome has a long history of seismic activity. However, no earthquake is recorded for the mid-sixth century in central Italy (Guidoboni 1989), and there is an absence of tell-tale signs, such as lesions in the walls and floors, at Monte Gelato. Moreover, the areas of wall-collapse do not form a continuous blanket such as occur at, for example, the villa of Patti Marina in Sicily (Voza 1989). We should therefore reject the idea that an earthquake caused the collapse of the buildings at Monte Gelato, and suggest instead that natural decay was entirely responsible.

It is, however, impossible to say how far the church survived these processes, but, with a falling population around, it is unlikely that even this spiritual base could have persisted. As we shall see, when a new church was constructed *c.* AD 800, it was an entirely new building that was erected.

THE SUB-ROMAN PERIOD (PHASE 4)

It is extremely hard to know what happened to the inhabitants of the site at Monte Gelato in the period immediately after the mid-sixth century. There are a few signs of activity, but of so vestigial a kind as to suggest more or less total abandonment. The evidence, such as it is, may be summarized as follows.

(1) A burial (no. 59; below, Fig. 94) contained a vessel of the late sixth or early seventh century (cat. 187), and a radiocarbon date from the bones yielded a calibrated range of AD 565-635 (one sigma: BM-2862).

(2) The collapsed masonry and tile filling the northerly room of the lower terrace was levelled to form a rough *battuto*, in which were visible two probable post-holes (Fig. 71). This surface cannot, however, be closely dated, and could belong to the period of the *domusculta*.

(3) The line of post-holes, D113 (Fig. 39), in the southeast corner of the large room, described in the previous section, clearly belongs to a period when the walls existed as no more than footings.

Yet they perpetuate the line of the Roman walls along the east side of the room, indicating a measure of continuity, although their relative shallowness suggests that they were cut from a higher level. They should belong, therefore, to the period after the mid-sixth century.

(4) The partition (Fig. 39, E225) in the corridor may, likewise, be a very late feature, cut from a higher level.

(5) As noted in the previous section, the workshop on the lower terrace yielded no fallen building rubble, and the south wall (Fig. 27, M158; Fig. 59) was reconstructed in very crude masonry. A lamp (cat. 60), possibly of the seventh or eighth century, was also found in the deposits over the late Roman levels. It is therefore conceivable that occupation may have continued in this room for a time.

(6) In the well-dated stratigraphical sequences (Figs 54, 56, 63, 72), there are no indications of a hiatus between the late Roman and early medieval deposits, such as a turf line. However, the very absence of layers which could belong to the seventh or eighth centuries may in itself be an argument for abandonment, even though one might expect some accumulation of silt on a hillside site.

To these observations must be added the fact that, burial no. 59 and the lamp apart, no pottery of the seventh or early to mid eighth centuries was identified, despite a search made in the light of typologies established for this period by the Crypta Balbi excavations in Rome (for example, Paroli 1992a; Romei 1992; Patterson, this volume). Unless

Fig. 71. Trodden surface with post-holes over the northern part of the lower terrace; the top of the late Roman wall (M22) is visible to the right. *(KW)*

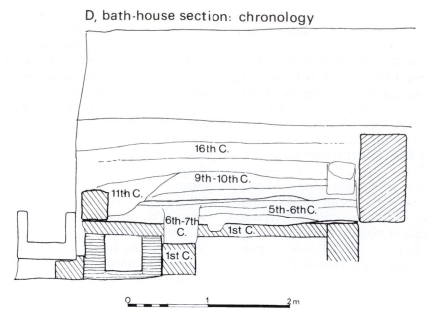

Fig. 72. Chronology of the section in Figures 32 and 54. *(TWP)*

the population at Monte Gelato was by now so destitute that even coarse pottery was beyond its means, it is hard to avoid the conclusion that the site was little, if at all, frequented. This would be a more satisfactory inference if one had any idea where the people might have gone – ironically, since this is one of the questions that the excavation hoped to resolve. But the only alternative is to propose a model where a diminutive population eked out a miserable existence amongst the ruins. For this, as we have seen, there is some very slight structural evidence, but hardly sufficient to make any real case.

THE EARLY MEDIEVAL COMPLEX

INTRODUCTION

Excavation of the main site in the valley bottom brought to light an extensive early medieval settlement. It comprised (1) a church and baptistery, built about AD 800 (our phase 5), and rebuilt and extended about AD 1000 (phase 6); (2) a considerable cemetery, which yielded a minimum of 243 individuals; (3) a pottery production site, albeit of a single kiln, of the late eighth to early/mid ninth centuries; (4) at least one cave habitation, together with others perhaps used for storage; and (5) reuse of the Roman mausoleum, possibly for animals. The Roman road was also repaved, and the existing mill, which is certainly of medieval date, most probably had one or more precursors, given the exceptionally advantageous configuration of the river at this point.

The sculptural finds show that the phase 5 church, of *c.* AD 800, was decorated to the best stand-

ards of the day, and there are other indications that this was a 'high-status' place in this period, with close connections with Rome. It does not seem, however, to have been a nucleated, village-type settlement, and the church probably served a largely dispersed rural community. This role may have been enhanced in the late tenth and early eleventh centuries, when the baptistery was greatly enlarged, the church partially or wholly rebuilt, and other structures added. If so, considerations were by now entirely parochial, and practices, such as the baptismal rite, deeply rooted in tradition. A significant proportion of individuals was probably related, and study of the human remains suggests that this was a hard-working, peasant population. Likewise, the remodelled ecclesiastical buildings would appear to have been plainly constructed, and apparently without internal embellishment.

The ecclesiastical complex was subsequently demolished in a very thorough way, and the main site abandoned. The evidence of the pottery places this around AD 1100, and later material is virtually absent; there is, for example, not a single sherd of archaic maiolica. Only some burials, cut into the ruins, at the base of what may have been a shrine or monument (attributed to phase 7) show that the place was not immediately forgotten. However, by this time occupation had probably begun on the castle site of Castellaccio, built on a hill overlooking the mill complex at the southern end of the valley. The style of the masonry of the mill suggests that this may have been constructed in the twelfth century and, on the evidence of limited trenching, this was also the main period of settlement of Castellaccio (although there is later pottery). It seems entirely reasonable to infer that the population served by the ecclesiastical complex at the Mola di Monte Gelato was moved to Castellaccio, as part of the well-attested phenomenon of *incastellamento* or *accentramento*.

The evidence to support these conclusions is set out in detail in the sections that follow. As with any archaeological interpretation, there are weaknesses and ambiguities in the data, which we shall attempt to identify. Moreover, it is inevitably coloured by Tomassetti's correlation, discussed in Chapter One, between the Mola di Monte Gelato and the *castrum Capracorum* of a bull of 1053, '*cum terris, vineis ... et molaria sua cum ecclesia sancti Iohannis que dicitur Latregia ... positam territorio Vegetano miliario ab urbe Rome plus minus vicesimo septimo*', and with a document of 1128 which describes the church of Saint John as *diruta*.

The likelihood of this correlation is everywhere supported by the evidence assembled in this volume, whether archaeological, art historical (Osborne, this volume), or documentary. Where we must disagree with Tomassetti is in supposing that the estate-centre of the *domusculta* of *Capracorum*, founded by Pope Hadrian I in *c.* 774-6, was shifted from Santa Cornelia, near Veii, to the Mola di Monte Gelato, when Santa Cornelia became a monastery in the early eleventh century. Instead, we shall suggest that our site was part of Hadrian's original foundation, one of a series of farms within the *domusculta* (Wickham 1978: 174), which in this case came eventually to acquire the name of the whole estate. This may in itself be a measure of the relative importance of the foundation at the Mola di Monte Gelato.

The excavations at Santa Cornelia, now fully published (Christie and Daniels 1991), enormously illuminate the archaeology and history of the *domusculta*, and provide important comparative material. Interestingly, our expectation that Monte Gelato would yield a nucleated farm, resembling that at Santa Cornelia, proved to be wholly in error. The ecclesiastical element apart, the two sites were quite differently organized, and the huddle of buildings, many reused from Roman times, around the ninth-century church of Santo Stefano, near Anguillara, provides a closer parallel (Van de Noort and Whitehouse 1992). The histories of Santa Cornelia and the Mola di Monte Gelato would seem, however, to be closely linked. Although for various reasons the *domuscultae* did not apparently survive for long – the last reference to that of *Capracorum* is in 846, when men from the estate worked on the building of the Leonine Wall around the Vatican – both Santa Cornelia and Monte Gelato continued in occupation. However, at Santa Cornelia, although a campanile was added to the church *c.* 875-900, the so-called administrative quarter was burnt down (or so it would seem) in the same period, and lacks evidence of replacement. By the early eleventh century, when a new church was constructed, the site was probably in an advanced state of decay (Christie and Daniels 1991: 186-7). Only with the founda-

tion of a monastery, in *c.* 1035-41, did its fortunes properly for a time revive.

The site at the Mola di Monte Gelato may, likewise, have entered a period of decline after the collapse of the *domusculta*, although there is no specific evidence for this. But it is striking that, as at Santa Cornelia, there was extensive rebuilding of the ecclesiastical complex around AD 1000. It is not impossible that the two events were related, given the similar history of the two sites, and the references in the papal bulls of 1053 and 1128 (if correctly linked with our site) suggest an active and prosperous agricultural community.

There are manifest dangers in approaching archaeological evidence with so conscious a historical model in mind, and this we clearly recognize. On the other hand, it would be foolish wholly to ignore the broader documentary and archaeological background, when it seems to be of such demonstrable relevance. But first the material findings require careful examination, and it is to these that we must now turn.

THE SECOND CHURCH (FIGS 66 AND 73)

The early medieval church was on a slightly different orientation from that of its late Roman predecessor, being aligned more or less exactly east-west. Prior to its construction, the Roman church was razed to its lowest footings, almost obliterating the wall lines in places, especially to the south. As a result it is impossible to say whether the older church was still standing and in use, since its floor and associated levels had been entirely cleared away. Given the lack of diagnostic seventh- and eighth-century material from the site, it may well have been in ruins, unless maintained by a dispersed community, which left little refuse around the church.

The new church was substantially larger than its predecessor. It had a deep apse to the east, internally 4.7 m in length, which was separated from the nave by a cross-wall. The nave measured 10.5 × 8.75 m internally, and was thus relatively squat in plan. There was, however, what we have interpreted as a narthex, or porch, to the west, which was at least 2.8 m in length. Neither the west nor south walls of the narthex survived, so it is impossible to work out its full dimensions; but it would have given a more balanced shape to the building. Yet this interpretation may not be correct. At Santa Cornelia there was no porch, but what may have been a large walled atrium or forecourt in front of the first church (Christie and Daniels 1991: 183 and figs 32 and 33). The nave here was also very squat in plan, measuring internally 13.5 × 14.5 m, and the church at Santo Stefano, near Anguillara, where there may also have been an atrium, is also comparable (Van de Noort and Whitehouse 1992) (Table 2). It is therefore feasible to postulate a similar arrangement at Monte Gelato although, given the way that the ground slopes down to the road in front of the church, a narthex would seem to be the more likely explanation (Fig. 73).

The walls of the church were quite substantial, averaging 0.7 m in width. The foundations were, however, of variable depth. Those of the apse and the south wall were especially shallow, and part of the apse footings had been completely

THE ENTRANCE

Adjoining the west side of the ante-room was a rectangular structure, measuring internally 4.8 × 2.7 m. The north and south walls were made up of large blocks of tufo, up to 1.5 × 0.6 m in size. The south wall was the more neatly built, and stood two courses high to a height of 0.95 m (Figs 62 and 63). The north wall was more shoddily constructed, with blocks of variable width, although the inner face was quite tidily aligned. It partly rested on a Roman wall, just as the southern wall was founded on the Roman floor, with some fill to level it up. The blocks of the western wall had been removed, but it would seem that the Roman threshold was retained in use in this period. The floor then sloped gently upwards towards the east, being well preserved at this point (Fig. 63). In the more easterly part of the room, however, no trace of the floor remained, and it had presumably been dug away; the area was subsequently filled in with tips of tufaceous material (Fig. 60, unit 218). No threshold for a doorway between the entrance and the ante-room was discovered, but this too had probably been removed.

Whether this room served any function other than as a back entrance to the ecclesiastical complex is uncertain. Some burials (below, Fig. 94, nos. 76 and 77) were later introduced into it, and there were multiple interments in a grave, no. 75, cut into the south wall after its partial demolition. Dating evidence was, however, sparse. It is nevertheless reasonably certain that the entrance was constructed at the same time as the second baptistery and the ante-room, around AD 1000, and was demolished a century or so later.

THE EXTERIOR OF THE ENTRANCE AND THE PAVED ROAD

Outside the entrance the Roman levels were sealed by a series of tips. These were not easy to differentiate, but they contained vast quantities of very small sherds of *acroma depurata*, as well as much ash, derived from the pottery kiln of the late eighth to mid-ninth centuries. There was also a number of tufo slabs, which may represent an attempt to provide some rough paving of what must have frequently become a muddy, downslope area.

It is also clear that the road was repaved at this time. This is evident not only from the haphazard arrangement of the *selce* blocks (in marked contrast to the neat work of predecessors of the classical period), but also from the pottery in the make-up. These included many waster sherds from the kiln, thus establishing a firm *terminus post quem*. There is nothing surprising in this. Recent work at Malborghetto has shown how the paving of the Via Flaminia was maintained into the Middle Ages (Bosman 1993) and the same is probably true of the Via Appia (Quilici Gigli 1990). At the Mola di Monte Gelato, the ascent up the hill to the north is relatively steep, about 1 in 7, and it would thus have been effectively impassable for wheeled vehicles during the wet autumn and winter months, without a proper surface. By this time, the old Roman road was nearly a millennium old, and was probably in a poor state. Re-laying of the paving-stones may well have been deemed expedient, probably as part of the building operations in the late tenth or early eleventh century.

Some burials were introduced into the area outside the entrance (below, Fig. 94, nos. 78-81), but were stratigraphically quite late. All were simple graves, with the exception of no. 79, which was a built structure, immediately outside the door.

THE POTTERY KILN (FIGS 87 AND 88)

In the southwest part of the former Roman 'large room' was a simple pottery kiln. It had a single oval chamber, 1.95 × 1.3 m in size internally, and was recessed into the *cocciopesto* floor and overlying deposits, to a depth of at least 0.3 m. There was a flue, properly termed a fire tunnel, cut through a Roman wall to the west and, beyond, a stoking area on the sloping ground covering the lower terrace.

The kiln was provided with a substantial fired clay lining, baked to a reddish orange colour, and containing tile and stone inclusions. It was between 0.2 and 0.4 m thick, and had been given one major relining of the interior and some later patching. Within the chamber was a series of black and grey ashy fills, separated by layers of brown loam. If each deposit of ash represents a separate firing, then together they register the final two episodes of use of the kiln.

There was no evidence for supports for a raised floor, either of a permanent or a temporary nature. Nor were there any fragments of fire-bars in the fill. Temporary kiln furniture may have been used, and removed completely; alternatively, resort may have been made to a floor made up of inverted pottery vessels (themselves usually wasters: Swan 1984: fig. II ii; 114), since there were sherds, albeit of small size, in the deposits.

Kilns of this single-chamber, single-flue type normally had a permanent clay dome, with an exhaust vent at the top. The flue served as a furnace, the heat being drawn upwards through the load, while the gases escaped through the vents (Swan 1984: 114). Such kilns were widespread in the ancient world, and clearly worked very efficiently.

That this was a pottery kiln is not in doubt, since there were vast spreads of ash and small waster sherds all over the adjacent slopes to the west, and also on the ground to the south. So numerous were the wasters, and so extensive the deposits, that a not inconsiderable scale of production is implied, albeit using only a single kiln. The wares mainly comprised vessels for domestic use, although some of the larger ones could have been used for transport. Patterson (this volume) dates them to the late eighth to mid-ninth centuries (or possibly a little later), on the basis of comparable examples from the Crypta Balbi in Rome. Not only does this further underline the close links between the city and its farms at this time, but it suggests that the official purpose of the kiln may have been to supply pots for transporting the produce of the *domusculta* to Rome. Yet it is also easy to imagine how a consignment of vessels for domestic use might have been slipped onto a cart of agricultural produce, and sold off privately. Pottery production, utilizing the excellent local clays, was of long standing in this region, including Monte Gelato and its environs (Peña 1987), and ceramics are still made today, especially around Civita Castellana. This could well have been a factor in placing one of the centres of the *domusculta* of *Capracorum* at this site, but it was also an incentive to private enterprise.

Kilns of comparable date are so far not documented in Italy. Circular stone-built pottery kilns with raised floors, and belonging to the seventh century, have been found at Otranto in Apulia (Arthur *et al.* 1992), and would seem to represent a more elaborate scale of production; but, as Patterson shows (this volume), little is known about pottery manufacture of the early medieval period in the Rome area, or elsewhere in the peninsula. It may well have been quite organized. The related tile industry certainly continued under papal encouragement, as brick stamps (including some of Pope Hadrian I) attest. Manufacture also took place in monasteries and in some Lombard centres (Paroli

Fig. 87. The late eighth- to mid-ninth-century pottery kiln, looking east, in the southwest corner of the large Roman room. *(KW)*

early medieval pottery kiln

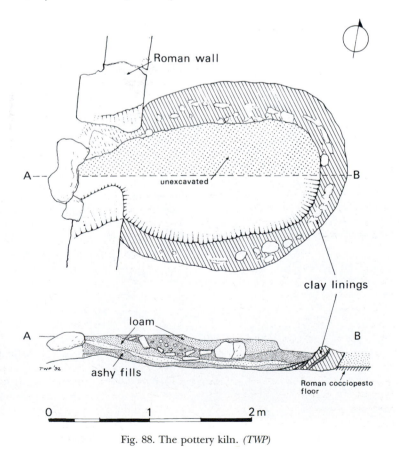

Fig. 88. The pottery kiln. *(TWP)*

1991; Arthur and Whitehouse 1983). But the small pottery kiln at Monte Gelato so far stands alone as a record of a modest rural industry, perhaps started with papal support, but which may have developed private sidelines. The silver *denarius* of Hadrian III (AD 884-5) from burial 43 (D135) in the baptistery may indeed be a hint of some commercial success.

It should be added that, although no traces of unequivocal workshop activity were found around the kiln, the ruinous area of the Roman 'large room' may well have provided such a space. The early medieval floor did not survive, and no features of the period were identified; but the ample dimensions of the room, some of whose walls may still have been standing, would have been most suitable for a workshop – a continuity of function from late Roman times which is striking, if, one must suppose, coincidental.

THE CAVES

The cave, site N

Amongst the features brought to light by bulldozing work on the southwest side of the modern road in 1989, was a rock-cut cave. It had been hollowed out of the tufo face at the head of the long spur that borders the modern road (Figs 9 and 89), and was immediately recognizable as a typical component of medieval sites in the Roman Campagna. Although the dangerous state of the roof precluded investigation within the cave, the entrance was partially excavated.

Internally, the cave measured about 6.0 × 5.0 m, a not inconsiderable floor area (Fig. 90). It was partially divided into two equally-sized rooms by an unexcavated wall of rock, which originally extended nearly half way across the cave. In the more northerly room was a shaft in the ceiling, now choked with soil and vegetation; it measured *c.* 1.2 × 0.7 m, and presumably served as a chimney. Other rock-cut features frequently encountered in medieval cave habitations of this sort, such as beds, benches, niches and mangers, were in this case not visible; but there was a deep accumulation of debris and soil over the floor, which would have concealed most elements of this sort. Cave houses are easy to construct in the soft volcanic tufo, and the tradition of carving furniture out of the rock was of great longevity, as so many Etruscan tombs – to name the most obvious example – clearly show.

The excavations in the entrance showed that the cave was provided with a rock-cut passage, leading up from the early Imperial Roman rock-cut road (site S, above). The road had survived as a hollow way, heading down the slope towards the river, and would have provided a convenient route up and down a cliff some 3.5 m in height. The passage was not fully exposed, but was a minimum of 1.5 m in width, and cut nearly 1.0 m deep into the bedrock, with fairly straight sides. It had also been dug through a Roman wall of *tufelli* and tiles, built along the top of the older road, and there was a post-hole, 0.55 m in diameter but only 0.2 m deep, at the mouth. This may have been for a gate. At the entrance to the cave, the north side of the passage had been cut back at the base, forming a rectangular recess, 0.15 m high. There was also a square socket at the centre. The equivalent area on the south side of the entrance was not investigated, but there can be little doubt that these were housings for a

Fig. 89. The cave habitation, looking northwest. *(KW)*

Cave, site N

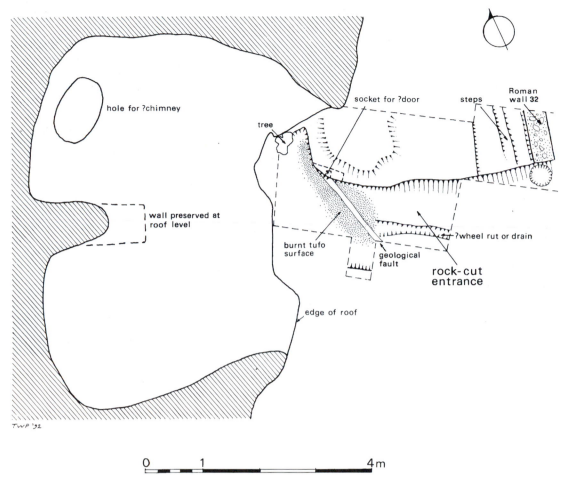

hole for ?chimney

socket for ?door

steps

Roman
wall 32

tree

wall preserved at
roof level

burnt tufo
surface

geological
fault

?wheel rut or drain

rock-cut
entrance

edge of roof

TWP '92

0   1   4 m

Fig. 90. Cave habitation cut into the ridge to the west of the main site. *(TWP)*

door, probably with a wooden sill beam across the passage. The rest of the façade was presumably filled in with wood or other building materials, perhaps with windows on either side of the door, for which there was ample space. Cave storage rooms with simple façades of this sort abound to this day in local villages of medieval origin, like Mazzano and Calcata, and many were undoubtedly once lived in.

Along the centre of the entrance passage was a rock-cut drain, 0.2 m wide and 0.1 m deep, and there was also a diagonal fissure, of natural origin. This latter area had been the focus of an intense fire, which had burnt the tufo to a deep hue of red. This can hardly have been a fireplace, although the localized nature of the burning shows that the conflagration was carefully controlled; it may relate to the abandonment of the cave. Above this was a fine silt wash, and then dumps of pulverulent, tufaceous soil, together with lumps of tufo, fragments of tile and *selce*, as well as a certain amount of pottery.

An examination of the sherds by Helen Patterson indicated that only one was typical of the ninth century, while the rest belonged to the tenth and eleventh centuries. These must therefore mark the abandonment of the cave, and should imply that its main period of use belonged to the ninth and tenth centuries. It is possible that occupation extended well into the eleventh century, since sherds of this period occurred throughout the fill, but the precise period of abandonment must remain uncertain.

Other caves

The dense vegetation along the sides of the spur, where the cave described above was located, precluded the identification of other rock-cut dwellings in this area. Their existence certainly cannot be ruled out. Moreover, other caves are to be found in the upper hillslopes, some 60 m to the northeast of the main site (Fig. 4). These were not investigated in detail, but the main features were quite clear. There was a long entrance, some 20.0 m in extent, with well-cut straight sides. This gave access to a rectangular chamber, again carefully shaped (Fig. 91). It was 9.0 m long, 4.5 m wide and, although the floor was covered with fill, at least 2.4 m high. From it led a smaller chamber, measuring 4.0 × 3.5 m, and of the same height as the main cave.

No excavation was carried out, and there were insufficient surface finds to provide an indication of their date. However, there must be a very high chance that they were cut during the early medieval period. Their large size, and the quality of the work, argue for an organized effort of construction, and they are wholly atypical of medieval rock-cut dwellings. They would, however, have been ideal for the storage of produce, and it is tempting to suppose that they were made for this purpose during the period of the *domusculta* of *Capracorum*. It is certainly the most plausible context, and helps to explain why no other storage building was identified in the excavations.

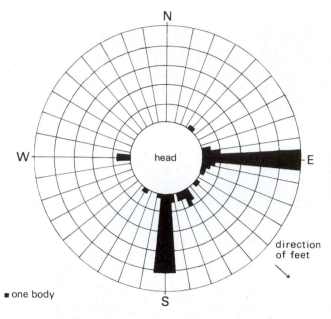

Fig. 103. Orientation of the skeletons. *(TWP)*

Certain or possible grave-goods were found in ten tombs (Table 5). Of immediate interest is the fact that two with fourth-century coins, burials nos. 26 and 60, have osteological traits suggesting that the two individuals were related (Conheeney, below). Only one other tomb (no. 11) contained a Roman coin (and that in the fill, where it may have been introduced accidentally); thus it would seem that the inclusion of the coins with the bones (one was in the mouth) in burials 26 and 60 can hardly be fortuitous. The coins must have been many centuries old when buried and, being of bronze, of no value; but they hint at the continuation of an old pagan practice which was perhaps traditional in this family.

A silver *denarius* of AD 884-5 was placed with a child in burial 43, and a finger-ring, perhaps of sixth-century date, with a disarticulated female in burial 26. Otherwise gravegoods were confined to two pots, a glass vessel (and many fragments) and, much less certainly, an iron knife. The date ranges are listed in the table; it is notable that the range for the vessel from burial 59 is matched by a radiocarbon assessment of cal. AD 565-635 (one sigma), suggesting that the vessel was not old when it was placed in the grave.

The grave finds recall Tomassetti's record of a Christian burial, with large tiles, gold earrings and *balsamarii* of glass (Tomassetti 1882: 146). It was apparently situated outside the church, and should therefore belong with the more elaborate burials recorded in the present excavations. Indeed, there is a clear relationship between these built tombs and the occurrence of grave-goods, suggesting that even a simple pottery vessel (or its contents) was a mark of status. As Table 5 shows, men, women and children were distinguished in this way. It was not, therefore, a clerical hierarchy that was being singled out, but rather members of particular families, whose status was further enhanced by being buried in or close to the church.

tistery, and at its most chaotic in the area to the west of the baptistery, where there may have been a narthex. For those buried *sub divo*, outside the buildings, in most cases alignment hardly mattered: here are further hints that these were the graves of individuals who were towards the bottom of whatever social hierarchy may have existed.

We have already referred to the few individuals who faced the west (burials 7, (?)12, 75). Two are 'high status' graves, and the argument that these were priests facing their flock has its attractions (Rahtz 1977). But burial 7 is that of a woman, ruling out that explanation in this case, and it is perhaps more likely that these were simply mistakes.

POSITION OF BODY

The bodies were generally interred supine, but in a variety of postures, listed in Table 4. The level of disturbance is such that the figures cannot be pressed at all hard for the sample is far too small. The most prevalent practice was to bury the individual with arms folded across the body, and straight legs, in a Christian manner. However, there is a considerable range of variations, and certainly no standard procedure. It may be that these different positions did have some meaning (or, less probably, chronological implications); but no pattern emerges from this fairly small group.

COFFINS AND GRAVE-GOODS

Nails were found in twelve graves, but were only numerous in three, all important burials in the church nave: nos. 2 (fourteen nails), 8 (sixteen nails) and 12 (sixteen nails). There were three from the disturbed grave no. 7, but the remaining tombs yielded only one, or, in one case, two nails; it is hard to suppose that there were coffins in these graves. Fragments of lead were also found in twelve tombs, and might in some instances have been coffin fittings, although only a piece from burial no. 2 appeared convincing.

OTHER SPATIAL CONSIDERATIONS

Although discussed in detail by Conheeney, below, it is worth stressing here that the burials in the baptistery were almost all of infants and children. They were also found in other parts of the site, often in disturbed contexts; but the concentration in the baptistery and the neat organization of these graves imply that special factors were operating. At first sight, it might appear that these were children who had yet to be baptized: but the age range is against this, since there is a wide span (Table 6).

It is notable, too, that the baptistery includes a number of more elaborate tombs, one with a silver *denarius* of Pope Hadrian III (AD 884-5), a rare issue and the only medieval coin from the excavations. Moreover, two of the graves (nos. 36 and 39) had been subsequently emptied of their bones, like many of those within the nave of the church. The implication is that the child burials within the baptistery may reflect higher social ranking within the community, as with those in the church. Interestingly, there is some evidence to suggest that a similar practice may have been followed at Santa Cornelia, particularly after the baptistery had gone out of use (Christie and Daniels 1991: 198). The analogy is particularly apt since, at Monte Gelato too, some of the child interments in the area of the baptistery clearly post-dated the demolition of the building (for example, Fig. 94, nos. 28, 31, 97). Evidently, the site of the baptistery retained a symbolic importance, as did the church, if the monument base (Figs 76 and 77) marking its site is any guide.

Table 4. Body positions.

arm positions	
both straight	six (two males, four infants)
right across body, left straight	four (one male, one female, one juvenile, one infant)
left across body, right straight	one (infant)
both folded across body	twelve (six males, four females, one juvenile, one infant)
left arm folded across body, right arm pointing to right shoulder	two (females)
both arms flexed	two (infants)
	TOTAL: 27

leg positions	
broadly straight	31
flexed	three (infants)

Table 5. Burials with grave-goods (certain or possible).

no.	type	location	sex	age	object	date of object
11	a cappuccina	church	adult infant	<22 yr 1.5-2.5 yr	coin (in fill) base of glass vessel	fourth century ?
12	elaborate	church	-	-	glass fragments	?
24	ossuary	church	M M M F F juvenile juvenile juvenile juvenile	c. 50 yr 30-40 yr 17-25 yr adult adult 20-4 yr 10-15 yr 5-10 yr 5-10yr	glass flask	?sixth to eighth centuries
26 (1)	a cappuccina	church narthex	juvenile adult	12-13 yr adult	coin glass fragments	fourth century
26 (2)	bag of bones	church narthex	F	25-35 yr	finger-ring	?sixth century
43	tile-covered grave	baptistery	juvenile	6-8 yr	coin, iron boss	AD 884-5
59	tile-lined	baptistery ?narthex	M M	17-25 yr 33-45 yr	pottery cup	later sixth to early seventh centuries
60	simple	baptistery ?narthex	juvenile F	7-9 yr 17-25 yr	coin glass fragments	fourth century
101	simple	courtyard	-	-	iron knife	?
106	rock-cut	south of church	F	17-25 yr	pottery vessel glass fragments	later fifth to early sixth centuries

Note: glass fragments were also found in burials nos. 2, 7, 8, 10, 39, 55, 77, 81, 93, 95 and 99, but whether these are coincidental or broken grave-goods is unclear.

Table 6. Approximate ages at death of children buried in the baptistery.

years	0	<1	1-2	2-4	3-4	4-5	6-8	8-9
number of individuals	1	3	2	4	5	1	2	1

THE PHASING

The phasing of the cemetery has been referred to little in the preceding discussion. This reflects the fact that, in many areas of the site, it was difficult or impossible to arrive at a satisfactory verdict, certainly within any very close limits. Few graves could be dated stratigraphically, and relative sequences were not easy to establish. Nevertheless, some general observations can be made.

The earliest datable grave is probably no. 106, one of three rock-cut examples just outside, and parallel with, the south walls of the churches. No. 106 contained a pottery vessel datable to the second half of the fifth century (cat. 186); if not old when it was buried, which seems unlikely, it ought to be a good indication of the date of the grave. On the other hand, no other burial is demonstrably of this period, and it seems certain that the excavated area was not the focus of a late Roman cemetery.

A Roman cemetery has been located by *clandestini*, some 200 m to the northwest of the main site (Fig. 8). It is extremely overgrown, but contains rock-cut tombs, associated with Roman pottery. It is not, however, clear what its chronological limits may have been. Excavations in 1877 did, however, yield three early Christian tombstones. Two can be dated, one to AD 361 and the other to AD 407 (Fiocchi Nicolai 1988: 235-7). The exact provenance of these finds is unknown, but it was these investigations which yielded a Christian church which we assume, but without corroborative evidence, to be the same as that excavated by us. It is, of course, possible that these tombstones had been brought from some other location but, without knowing more of their context, that must remain uncertain. All that can safely be said is that there was an early Christian cemetery in the vicinity of our main excavations.

As we have seen above, the late Roman church cannot be dated closely. The probability is that it was constructed in the early fifth century, to serve this rural community and surrounding sites. If this is the case, it does not, however, appear immediately to have been the centre for burials. Apart from burial 106 (see above), there were human remains incorporated into a sixth-century deposit (no. 69), and burial 59 is dated both by a pottery vessel and by a radiocarbon date to the late sixth or early seventh century; but no other interments can be assigned with certainty to this phase. There are certainly insufficient grounds for suggesting a late Roman cemetery church.

Indeed, it seems fairly clear that the main period of the cemetery belongs to the three centuries between about AD 800 and 1100. With a minimum total of only 243 individuals in all, this implies a fairly small community, perhaps as few as 30, at the roughest of guesses. There may, of course, have been peaks and troughs in the size of the population over this period, and there is some evidence to suggest that more burials belong to the tenth and eleventh centuries or later, than to the ninth century. This is certainly the case in the deeply stratified deposits to the west of the baptistery. At least 32 individuals were buried here and, while many of these graves were heavily disturbed, it is none the less clear that the majority occurred in fairly late contexts (Fig. 54).

Within the baptistery, no burials can be associated with confidence with the early baptistery, except for burial no. 43. This partly underlay the wall of the later baptistery, and contained a coin of AD 884-5. There were, however, sherds of the late ninth and/or tenth centuries in the fill of burial 33, probable tenth-century sherds in burial 32 and possible eleventh-century material in no. 46. Other burials, as pointed out above, post-date the demolition of the building. It

may be, therefore, that the majority of these interments should be assigned to a late period in the site's history.

Within the church, the ossuary (burial 24) was sealed by a small surviving area of the latest flooring of the second church; it should thus pre-date the late tenth century (as the associated glass vessels also imply). Beneath the floor of the ossuary were bones of a juvenile and two infants (no. 23), which must again be relatively early in the sequence. Likewise, there were disarticulated bones of an adult, a juvenile and an infant (nos. 21 and 22) in the adjoining make-up for the second church floor; whether these represent disturbed *in situ* burials, or bones brought in from elsewhere during the building work is open to question.

Another relatively early burial is no. 26, an *a cappuccina* grave placed against the second church wall in the narthex (Figs 31 and 104). The sequence of interments is complex, and the grave cuts were difficult to identify; but, stratigraphically, this burial (which lies at a depth of 0.72 m below the floor of the ossuary (no. 24)) is likely to be contemporary with the first phase of the second, that is the early medieval, church. As we have seen, two late Roman objects, a coin and a finger-ring, were associated with these burials, and *a cappuccina* graves are a recognized late Roman tradition. It follows that the other *a cappuccina* burials within the church nave should be of similarly early date, together with the three 'elaborate' graves (nos. 2, 12 and 13). The only real difficulty is posed by burials 7 and 8 (C23, C55), which seem to have been cut through both church apses (Figs 66 and 94). However, this part of the site had been severely damaged by the plough, and little reliance can be placed upon apparent stratigraphical relationships in this area. It may well be that they were in fact built into the structure of the first early medieval church and perhaps destroyed during the refurbishment of the church and baptistery in the late tenth or early eleventh century.

The fills of three of these graves did yield datable pottery. No. 12 contained a sherd possibly of the tenth century in the lower fill, and another of the eleventh or twelfth century in the upper fill. No. 13 produced a late tenth-century sherd, and no. 17 material of the late tenth or eleventh century. However, each of these burials seems to have been emptied of the bones when the church was pulled down and it is therefore probable that this pottery relates to that phase, rather than the primary period of interment.

Unlike the baptistery, most burials within the church are therefore likely to belong to the first early medieval period, namely the ninth-tenth centuries. The main exceptions are nos. 18, 19, and 20 which were tucked into the northeast corner of the nave, parallel with the north wall. On stratigraphical grounds, these should be late interments, and no. 18 did indeed yield a sherd of tenth-century date. There were also the bones of three infants, one juvenile, five females and five adults in plough-disturbed deposits over the church; these must also represent burials of the last period of the building or, perhaps, graves dug subsequent to its demolition.

Outside these areas, it is more difficult to determine the date of the burials. The group nos. 102, 103 and 104, to the southeast of the church, would seem to be quite late, on stratigraphical grounds. Interestingly, two skeletons (nos. 102 and 103) exhibit osteological characteristics which suggest that they were related. Likewise, the burials between the entrance and the road (nos. 78-81) were inserted into deposits containing wasters from the late eighth- to mid ninth-century kiln, providing a firm *terminus post quem*; these also include a family group (no. 79). Otherwise, there is

Fig. 104. Left: the *a cappuccina* burial no. 26 (A23); right: the northeast corner of bath-house room 1
(wall A9). Cf. Figures 27, 28, 31 and 66. *(TWP)*

only a subjective impression that this seemingly random series of interments, mostly in shallow graves, belongs mainly to the later phases of the graveyard.

The final period (phase 7) of the cemetery is of some interest. As already noted, a number of graves appear to have been emptied of their bones, seven in the nave of the church and two in the baptistery. In at least three cases, the grave structure was then replaced, suggesting continued veneration of the site. This is supported by the fact that burials continued to be made after the demolition of the church and baptistery. This is evident from the fact that some were cut through the wall footings, and adds support to the identification of the rectangular footing in the church nave (Figs 76 and 77) as the base of some sort of memorial or shrine, erected when the ecclesiastical complex was taken down. The site, although largely abandoned, did not lose its sanctity for the local populace: some 600 years of Christian burial and tradition was not easily forgotten. In all probability, it was only when Castellaccio was finally abandoned, probably by the late thirteenth century, that veneration lapsed and the church and baptistery dwindled into folk memory.

CATALOGUE OF BURIALS

In the following catalogue, for ease of reference the graves have been renumbered (cf. Fig. 94). The original site references are, however, used on the other plans, and are also included here. It should also be noted that it was not always possible to draw plans of all the skeletons *in situ*. This was because, once found, it was necessary to excavate and lift a skeleton within the day, due to the threat of vandalism. This was particularly the case in the baptistery, where there was a very high density of burials.

The suggested phasing, itself very approximate, is as follows – phase 3: late Roman; phase 4: late sixth-seventh centuries; phase 5: late eighth to late ninth centuries; phase 6: tenth-eleventh centuries; phase 7: twelfth century or later.

THE CHURCH (FIGS 66 AND 94)

Burial 1 (B15). Rectangular west-east grave, 2.18 × 0.8 m; depth 0.86 m. It cut the second church cross-wall, but the bones had been largely removed; a few adult bones remained. Phase 6.

Burial 2 (C57). Fig. 96. A complex and important tomb which probably underlay the altar. It comprised a rectangular pit of *c.* 1.4 × 1.9 m, with a depth of 1.08 m. Two primary inhumations of an adult and a female (C57, C58), west-east, were found at the bottom, and had not been disturbed. The tomb had a vault in or above it, the mortar remnants of which had partially collapsed into the tomb, when it had half filled with soil; some retained impressions of wood. There were further disarticulated burials, including a male and an adult (C2, C26, C43, C47, C48), above this. At the west end were blocks of tufo which covered that end of the tomb; built into this was the decorated screen with the Cross and the Agnus Dei (cat. 1). Six strips of lead were found (cat. 71, 72, 74), possibly from coffin fittings, and there was a total of fourteen iron nails. There were also three pieces of glass, one handle and two bases, all from lamps (cat. 145b, 148, 149). The primary burial, C57, yielded a radiocarbon date of 1480 ± 45 BP (BM-2861), which calibrates to AD 545-630 (one sigma). Phase 5/6.

Burial 3 (C25). Sub-rectangular north-south grave, 1.35 × 0.58 m; depth 0.25 m. Set beside the second church cross-wall in the apse of the first, late Roman church, it had a large block of tufo in the fill, but no articulated bones; there were a few adult bones in the fill. Phase 6.

side. Oriented north-south, it had been already emptied of its contents. 2.0 × 0.7 m; internal depth: 0.4 m; total height: 0.6 m; wall width: 0.1 m. ?Phase 4/5.

Burial 62 (A5). Disarticulated adult bones in the fill over the bath-house. Phase 7.

Burial 63 (A12). Disarticulated bones of two adults and one juvenile in the hillwash over the bath-house. Phase 6.

Burial 64 (A35). Highly disturbed adult bones in destruction deposits over the bath-house. ?Phase 5 (or later).

Burial 65 (A2). Bones from disturbed burials over the bath-house, including the remains of two adults and one juvenile. Phase 7.

Burial 66 (A21). Bones of a juvenile in the fill over the bath-house. Phase 5/6.

Other burials in this area

There were a number of other very disturbed skeletons in the upper fills. These were so mixed that they have not been put on the plan. They comprise D64, D73, D80, and included an infant, a juvenile and three adults.

ANTE-ROOM TO THE NORTH OF THE BAPTISTERY (FIGS 78 AND 94)

Burial 67 (D275). A built tomb, west-east, against the north wall of the baptistery. It had quite neatly made walls of tufo blocks, two courses wide on the north side. No interment was found, except for a later grave (burial 68), and a few other infant bones. 1.24+ (full length not established) × 0.5 m. One iron nail was found. Phase 5/6.

Burial 68 (D283). A west-east oval grave containing the body of an infant, cut into burial 67 (which may have been emptied at the time). The body rested upon a floor of marble, and was extended with flexed arms. A piece of lead was found (cat. 92). 0.74 × 0.26 m. Phase 6.

Burial 69 (D52). A rib bone, possibly from a juvenile, in the tile collapse associated with mid-sixth-century coins (phase 3). Although very inadequate evidence, this may be an indicator that burials were being made in the area in this period. Phase 3.

Burial 70 (D51). Adult bones in an occupation deposit. Phase 5+.

Burial 71 (D268). Fig. 80. A rectangular slab of grey-blue tufo, 1.44 × 0.6 m, associated with other large blocks of tufo. Although these were not lifted, it seems probable that they represent some sort of tomb structure. Phase 6.

Unstratified burials

There was just one disturbed burial in the plough-soil, D6 (unidentified).

THE SPACE BETWEEN THE BAPTISTERY, ANTE-ROOM AND ENTRANCE (FIG. 94)

Burial 72 (D296). The disarticulated remains of a female and a young juvenile. Osteological study suggests that the two were related. ?Phase 7.

Burial 73 (D286) A structure of tufo blocks somewhat resembling those of burial 71 (although without an obvious grave slab). It seems likely that this too is a grave structure, although it was not further investigated. Phase 6.

Burial 74 (M76). A collection mainly of skulls and long bones placed with no ceremony into gaps between tufo blocks in this corner. They included two males, one female and an adult. Phase 6/7.

THE ENTRANCE TO THE ANTE-ROOM (FIG. 94)

Burial 75 (M61, Sk. 5 and 5a). Two partially articulated male skeletons oriented east-west, with heads to the east. They appear to represent successive burials, the earlier with arms across the chest. There were also bones of another male, a female and two adults. The grave cut was not really clear, but the tomb was c. 1.5 m long, and overlay the south wall of the entrance. Phase 6/7.

Burial 76 (M69, Sk. 4). A west-east grave close to the north wall of the entrance, with two infant inhumations, one much disturbed. The heads are to the west. Shallow grave pit, c. 1.1 × 0.4 m. Phase 6/7.

Burial 77 (M72, Sk. 6). Poorly preserved west-east infant burial near no. 76, much damaged by later activity. Head to the west. It included a fragment of glass (cat. 107). c. 0.71 × 0.32 m. Phase 6/7.

THE AREA BETWEEN THE ENTRANCE AND THE PAVED ROAD (FIG. 94)

Burial 78 (M33, Sk. 1) Fig. 108. A shallow northwest-southeast grave beside the road, containing the skeleton of a male with the head towards the north. The left arm was folded across the stomach and the right arm pointed towards the right shoulder. There was no very clear grave pit, and the body was in a layer of debris from the early medieval kiln. c. 1.7 × 0.5 m. Phase 5/6.

Burial 79 (M112, Sk. 8 and 9). Fig. 109. A north-south grave by the southwest corner of the entrance. It was lined with tufo blocks, and with a tile at the north end, and pieces of tile to form a floor. It contained two successive burials, one female and one male: the bones of the earlier (the male) had been pushed on one side to make way for the later burial. Both heads were to the north, and the arms of the later skeleton were folded across the chest. Osteological study suggests that the two were related. 1.6 × 0.65 m; depth 0.3 m. Phase 6.

Burial 80 (M18, Sk. 3). A north-south grave close to the door threshold, containing a female skeleton with the head to the north, and the arms folded across the torso. c. 1.8 × 0.6 m, depth 0.4 m. Phase 6.

Burial 81 (M16, M88, Sk. 2). A northeast-southwest grave close to the road, with a disturbed skeleton with the head to the northeast. c. 1.2 × 0.35 m. Phase 6.

OVER ROMAN ROOMS TO THE NORTH OF THE CHURCH COMPLEX (FIG. 94)

Burial 82 (E4). Badly disturbed west-east grave beyond the north wall of the ante-room. 1.0 × 0.45 m. Phase 5/6.

Burial 83 (E57). Grave-shaped pit, west-east (approximately), 1.1 × 0.38 m. No bones were found, however. Phase not certain.

Burial 84 (E39, E40). Infant burial, probably north-south. c. 0.4 × 0.22 m. ?Phase 5/6.

Fig. 108. Burial no. 78 (M18), an adult female, buried in a simple grave by the road. *(KW)*

Burial 85 (L172). A northwest-southeast grave, cutting a Roman wall (Fig. 41). It contained the skeleton of a male with the head to the northwest, and arms folded across the torso. There were also some infant bones. *c.* 2.25 × 0.75 m. One iron nail was found. Phase 6/7.

Burial 86 (L176). A northwest-southeast grave, with a sharply rectangular plan. *c.* 1.4 × 0.35 m. Traces of human bone were seen, but it was not excavated. Phase 6/7.

BURIALS IN THE COURTYARD (FIG. 94)

Burial 87 (E99). An oval southwest-northeast grave, containing an infant, with a lining of irregular humps of tufo, and pieces of tile. The skull was to the southwest. 1.08 × 0.5 m. Phase 3 or later.

Burial 88. (H16). A northwest-southeast grave, containing the burial of an infant, with the head to the northwest. 1.0+ (full length not established) × 0.4 m. This grave included one iron nail. Phase 6/7.

Burial 89 (H21). A northwest-southeast grave, parallel with and of similar size to burial 88. Not excavated, but a few adult bones were recorded. Phase 6/7.

Burial 90 (D36). A west-east burial; width 0.45 m, full length not established.

Burial 91 (D84). The west end only of a grave. ?Northeast-southwest. Phase 5/6.

Burial 92 (D18). The north end only of a north-south grave of a female, the rest being cut away by burial 93. The skull lay to the north, and the arms were folded across the chest. Width 0.42 m. Phase 6.

Burial 93 (D5). A north-south burial of a female, with the head (which is missing) to the north. The arms were folded across the chest. One piece of lead was found (cat. 70) and a piece of fourth-century glass (cat. 77). Cuts burial 92. 1.78 × 0.48 m. Phase 6.

Fig. 109. Burial no. 79 (M112), a stone-lined grave with successive interments of a male and female, who were probably related. *(KW)*

Burial 94 (D32). A northwest-southeast burial of a female, with the head to the northwest. The torso is badly crushed. Cuts burial 93. 1.65 × 0.45 m. Phase 6.

Burial 95 (D4, D34). A complex series of west-east infant graves along the exterior of the north wall of the second baptistery. D4 was oriented with the head to the west. Width 0.7 m. Length not properly established. A fragment of glass (cat. 140i) was found. Phase 6/7.

Burial 96 (D90). A poorly defined west-east grave, extending west from burial 95. Dimensions not properly established. Phase 6.

Burial 97 (D78). A west-east infant grave, cutting across the east wall of the second baptistery. The skeleton was oriented with the head (which is missing) to the west. 1.2 × 0.55 m (grave proper 1.1 × 0.32 m); depth 0.42 m. Phase 7.

Burial 98 (B2). Plough-damaged burial of an adult, possibly with a west-east orientation. Phase 6.

Burial 99 (B4). Disturbed northwest-southeast graves, containing some articulated and some disarticulated bones. These include a male burial, with the head to the northwest, and bones of two other males, and five adults. Included was a fragment of glass (cat. 126d). 2.0×0.4 m. Phase 6.

Burial 100 (D63). A west-east burial of a female, with the head at the west. The arms were folded across the chest. 1.8 × 0.48 m. Phase 5/6.

Burial 101 (D69). The edge of what is possibly a west-east grave. Unexcavated. An iron knife was found here (cat. 32). ?Phase 5/6.

Human bones in the topsoil over the courtyard

There were two significant clusters, D9 and D21; one adult was identified.

BURIALS TO THE SOUTH AND SOUTHEAST OF THE CHURCH (FIG. 94)

Burial 102 (C29). A northwest-southeast grave of a male, with the skull to the northwest, and with the arms across the torso. There were also some disarticulated bones. 1.85 × 0.5 m. Cuts Roman wall C34. Phase 6/7.

Burial 103 (C160). A northwest-southeast grave of a female, with the skull at the northwest end. The arms were folded across the chest, with the right arm pointing to the right shoulder. 1.7 × 0.42 m. Cuts Roman wall C34. Phase 6/7.

Burial 104 (C39). Infant burial, northwest-southeast. The grave dimensions were not properly established, but it cut Roman wall C34. Phase 6/7.

Burial 105 (B24). A west-east rock-cut grave, sealed by a tufo slab, containing two adults, one a male and one a female, and two infants, with the heads at the west. The male had his arms folded across his stomach. 1.8 × 0.5 m; depth 0.45 m. ?Phase 3.

Burial 106 (B26). A west-east rock-cut tomb. There were some *in situ* bones of a female in the east end of the grave, indicating that the head had been at the west. There was also a complete pottery vessel, of fifth-century date (cat. 186), and two pieces of glass (cat. 117, 129). The other bones may well have been deliberately removed, as with some burials within the church (which is immediately adjacent). 1.9 × 0.5 m; depth 0.5 m. Phase 3/4.

Burial 107 (A16). The eastern part of a west-east rock-cut grave, the rest having been destroyed by the modern road. It had been emptied completely prior to the excavation. Depth 0.6 m. ?Phase 3.

THE HUMAN BONE, by Janice Conheeney

INTRODUCTION

A minimum of 243 individuals was represented in the human bone. This total includes remains from *in situ* burials, from disturbed burials, and from disturbed and fragmentary deposits of disarticulated bone. The *in situ* burials contained remains of 159 individuals, and it is these that form the basis for this report.

In some ways the analysis has been disappointing, as the fragmentary nature of the remains has meant that much information normally contained in the skeleton has been lost. However, some very interesting patterns emerged in the spatial organization of the burials, which may allow inferences about the social attitudes of the people burying their dead at this site. At the present time little has been published in a comparable way, although many important sites in Italy have yielded human remains. Monte Gelato cannot, therefore, be set into a wider context and has been analysed in isolation.

Composition of the sample

The sample was recovered from ten areas of the site: (1) the church; (2) the baptistery; (3) the possible narthex to the west of the baptistery; (4) the ante-room to the north of the baptistery; (5) the space between the baptistery, ante-room and entrance; (6) the entrance to the ante-room; (7) the area between the entrance and the paved road; (8) over the Roman rooms to the north of the church complex; (9) the courtyard; and (10) to the south of the church.

One hundred and seven burials containing the 159 bodies included in this analysis were excavated within these areas. The number of individuals recovered from burials in each area and the phasing of these burials is given in Table 7 (whilst Table 8 gives additional details of age, sex and condition). The ten groups of bodies as defined by these areas were analysed separately, in order to investigate any spatial differences in the type of person buried. With regard to phasing, it was decided to include all the burials together. This decision was felt to be justified as the majority of burials came from phase 6e. Any further subdivision would have meant that the group sample size would have been so small as to be without meaning. In any case of pathology or possible genetic relationship, where phasing could have a particular importance, the phasing of the body involved was checked.

A further thirteen contexts contained evidence of disturbed burials. These remains produced a minimum body count of 26 individuals. However, they are not included in the analysis as they cannot be phased. This is not a great loss, as the majority of individuals in this category were represented by very small amounts of bone (Table 9), and so would have provided very little additional information.

Table 7. Individuals per area and phasing.

area	no.	phasing
church	51	principally phase 6, some 5/6 and two x 6/7
baptistery	24	principally phase 6, some 5/6 and 6/7
northern or open ground west of baptistery	32	mostly 6/7, some 6 and 5/6, one possible 4/5
ante-room north of baptistery	4	5/6 and 5+
space between baptistery, ante-room and entrance	6	7?
entrance to antechamber	8	6/7
area between entrance and paved road	5	5/6
over Roman rooms to north of church complex	3	5/6, 6/7
courtyard	18	principally 6, some 6/7, one x 5/6, one x 7
south of church	8	6/7 and 6
total	159	

Thirty-seven contexts held disarticulated human bone. These deposits were composed of a minimum of 58 individuals (Table 10).

Representativeness of sample

Since most of the graves date to the early medieval period, the skeletons recovered should give a fair representation of those buried in each area. The baptistery, the ante-room, the space between the baptistery, ante-room and entrance, the entrance to the antechamber and the area over the Roman rooms were excavated in full, so all burials contained there should have been recovered (except in one area of the baptistery: Fig. 78). Most of the narthex and the area between the entrance and road was excavated, and about three-quarters of the church. The courtyard and the area to the south of the church are likely to be the least representative, as little of these areas was uncovered, and the proportion that the excavated part forms of the whole area is not known. This means that for the majority of the ten areas any introduced bias to the sample should be restricted to the, effectively, random disturbance and destruction of some burials in the years between the cessation of burial at the site and recovery today. The 'secondary' bias unavoidable at the majority of sites, where due to practical restrictions only certain areas of a burial sample can be excavated, has been avoided here, with the exception of the courtyard and the area to the south of the church.

It should be stressed, however, that the sample, although now established as 'potentially well representative', in fact only includes those people who were selected for burial within the complex by whatever criteria were operating amongst those living at the site at the time. The sample does not represent the contemporary early medieval population as a whole; merely a predetermined fraction of it. This need not be as negative as it at first appears, as the analysis undertaken here will establish what type of person that fraction was composed of, and so allow conjecture on the selection criteria that may have been in operation.

Limitations to the analysis

The scope of the analysis was limited by four factors: the size of sample; the fragmentary nature of much of the remains; the time span over which stages of the work were completed; and the lack of comparative data.

Although the total sample size is reasonable, the sample size of each of the ten groups, when considered separately, is too small for any statistical analysis. However, given the lack of detailed human bone data available for Italian sites at the present time, it was still considered worthwhile to conduct a detailed analysis, even if this could only be couched in general terms. The majority of the data recorded has been included in the tables and appendix, as too often such data are confined to inaccessible archive reports.

The disturbed and fragmentary nature of many of the remains means that approximately a third of the contexts containing human bone could not be included in the analysis. The fragmentary condition of many individuals is also of consequence as this could have affected many areas of the analysis. Besides limiting the demographic and metrical information retrievable, surprisingly little evidence of pathological change was present. This could be due to the high level of fragmentation and the small proportion present of many of the skeletons.

The cleaning and recording of the material took place in Rome over a period of eleven weeks between 1989 and 1991. The limited time available meant that there had to be restrictions on the amount of information recorded: for example, a selected range of non-metric traits was scored for rather than including all possible traits. Moreover, the analysis of human bone has progressed in the five years [at the time of writing] since the project began, and certain categories of information which the author would wish to record now were not then obvious – for example, calculation of prevalence rates for certain types of pathology. It should also be noted that it was not possible to gain a second opinion on any of the pathology, nor were radiographic facilities available. These would have helped to confirm some of the pathology, and X-rays would have allowed examination for the presence of Harris lines in those individuals exhibiting conditions also associated with stunted growth.

Finally, the lack of comparative material is a particular problem, as the significance of the burials recovered from Monte Gelato will have to be considered in isolation for the time being. This means that unusual features of the Monte Gelato sample relative to elsewhere in Italy will not be apparent until other sites are published in a comparable way.

Table 8. Gender, age and preservation data for _in situ_ burials.

CHURCH

BURIAL	CONTEXT	SEX	AGE	AGE GROUP	% PRESENT	CONDITION
1	B15	3	adult	7	2	2
2	C57	3	>22	7	40	3
	C58	4	>24	7	45	2
	C2	1,3	2x adult	7,7	40,40	3,3
3	C25	3	25-35	4	1	2
4	B53	inf	<5	1	5	2
5	C42	juv, 3	5-10, adult	2,7	5,1	3,3
6	C47	inf	3-4	1	2	1
7	C23	5	25-35	4	40	2
8	C46	3, 2x inf	>17, 0-6mths, 4-5	7,1,1	40,2,5	3,3,3
9	C32	3	adult	7	5	3
10	B21	no bones				
11	B32(B49)	inf, 3	1.5-2.5, <22	1,3	30,20	3,3
12	B16	stone context				
13	B29	no bones				
14	B34	?	?	?	2	3
15	B42	?	?	?	5	3
16	B66	3	adult	7	5	3
17	B60	inf	0-1	1	10	2
18	B8	1,2,juv	25-35,30-40,10-15	4,5,2	85,30,35	1,2,2
	B22	3,3,juv	25-35,17-25,<15	4,3,2	15,10,10	3,3,3
19	?					
20	?					
21	D96	inf,juv	?,<15	1,2	1,5	3,3
22	D108	3	adult	7	10	3
23	D123	2x inf,3	0-5,0,adult	1,1,7	10,50,50	3,3,3
24	D107	1,1,1,5,5,3, 4x juv	30-40,c50,17-25,2x adult,20-24, 10-15, 2x 5-10,?	4,6,3,7,7,3,2, 2,2,2	c50	2
25	D173	2x inf,3	3-9mths,2-3,adult	1,1,7	5,5,5	3,3,3
26	A23	juv,3	12-13,adult	2,7	50,30	2,3
	A3	inf	3-4	1	20	2
	A9	not bone				
	A28	5	25-35	4	70	1
	A4	inf	2-3	1	50	2

BAPTISTERY

BURIAL	CONTEXT	SEX	AGE	AGE GROUP	% PRESENT	CONDITION
27	D43	inf	1,5-2	1	95	1
28	D15	inf	12-18mths	1	95	1
29	D31	inf	3-3.5	1	95	1
30	D231	inf	0-5	1	50	3
31	D233	no bones				
32	D224	inf	4-5	1	90	2
33	D226	inf	6-9mths	1	75	2
34	D222	inf	2-4	1	95	2
35	D237	no bones				
36	D239	no bones				
37	D229	juv,2 inf	8-9,3-4,3.5-4.5	2,1,1	95,95,30	1,1,1
38	D54	inf	0-6mths	1	75	2
39	D57	no bones				
40	D214	3x inf	0-6mths,2.5-4.5,1.5-4.5	1,1,1	60,60,40	2,2,2
41	D132	inf	2-4	1	85	1
42	D140	3	adult	7	20	2
43	D135	juv	6-8	2	95	1
44	D86	inf	?	1	5	3
45	D287	no bones				

BURIAL	CONTEXT	SEX	AGE	AGE GROUP	% PRESENT	CONDITION
46	D282	inf	0	1	80	2
47	D212	inf	3.5-4.5	1	95	1
48	D303	no bones				
49	D332	no bones				
50	D281	inf	3-4	1	10	3
51	D270	no bones				
52	B40	inf	<5	1	5	2
53	D293	juv,3	6-8,adult	2,7	95,5	1,3

NARTHEX OR OPEN GROUND TO WEST OF BAPTISTERY

BURIAL	CONTEXT	SEX	AGE	AGE GROUP	% PRESENT	CONDITION
54	D289,D291	2,2	17-25,17-25	3,3	30,20	2,2
55	D92	5x inf,4,1,2,5	3x 0-6mths,0.5-1.5,3-4, 25-35,20-40,50,40-50	1,1,1,1,1,4,4, 6,6	scraps	2
56	D91	juv,4,5	10-18,>19,33-45	2,3,5	20,30,30	2,2,2
57	D95	juv,inf	6.5-7.5,3.5-4	2,1	95,60	1,2
58	D133	3,2x juv	17-25,<19,?	3,2,2	5,2,2	3,3,3
59	D168	1,1	17-25,33-45	3,5	80,30	3,3
60	A13,A34	juv,5	7-9,17-25	2,3	10,90	2,1
61	no bones					
62	A5	3	adult	7	1	3
63	A12	juv,3,3	<15,>15,>18	2,3,3	5,10,10	3,3,3
64	A35	3	adult	7	2	3
65	A2	juv,3,3	<15,2x adult	2,7,7	15,20,50	3,3,3
66	A21	juv	6-10	2	10	2

ANTE-ROOM

BURIAL	CONTEXT	SEX	AGE	AGE GROUP	% PRESENT	CONDITION
67	D275	inf	3-7	1	1	3
68	D284	inf	1.5-2.5	1	95	1
69	D52	juv?	?	2?	1	3
70	D51	3	>15	adult	5	3
71	D268	no bones				

SPACE BETWEEN BAPTISTERY, ANTE-ROOM AND ENTRANCE

BURIAL	CONTEXT	SEX	AGE	AGE GROUP	% PRESENT	CONDITION
72	D296	juv,5	4-8,21-25	2,3	60,90	2,2
73	D286	no bones				
74	M76	1,1,5,3	17-25,3x adult	3,7,7,7	scraps	3

ENTRANCE TO ANTE-ROOM

BURIAL	CONTEXT	SEX	AGE	AGE GROUP	% PRESENT	CONDITION
75	M61	2,2,2,4,3,3	17-25,2x 25-35,17-21, 15-21,17-25	3,4,4,3,3,3	c50	2
76	M70	inf	1.5-2.5	1	95	1
77	M72	inf	6-12mths	1	40	2

AREA BETWEEN ENTRANCE AND PAVED ROAD

BURIAL	CONTEXT	SEX	AGE	AGE GROUP	% PRESENT	CONDITION
78	M33	1	>45	6	90	1
79	M112	5,1	33-45,25-35	5,4	95,30	1,1
80	M18	5	25-35	4	90	1
81	M16,M88	5	25-35	4	20	1
82	E4	no bones				

OVER ROMAN ROOMS

BURIAL	CONTEXT	SEX	AGE	AGE GROUP	% PRESENT	CONDITION
83	E57	no bones				
84	E39,E40	inf	0	1	40	2
85	L172	inf,1	0,25-35	1,4	5,65	3,3
86	l176	no bone				

COURTYARD						
BURIAL	CONTEXT	SEX	AGE	AGE GROUP	% PRESENT	CONDITION
87	E99	inf	0.5-1.5	1	80	1
88	H28	inf	4-5	1	70	1
89	H21	3	adult	7	1	3
90	D36	no bones				
91	D84	no bones				
92	D18	4	>45	6	30	1
93	D5	5	35-45	5	80	1
94	D32	5	45-50	6	50	3
95	D4,D34	inf	0	1	30	2
96	D90	no bones				
97	D78	inf	4-5	1	95	1
98	B2	3	adult	7	15	3
99	B4	1	25-35	4	30	2
	B4A	2,1,juv,3	22-25,adult,juv,adult	4,7,2,7	75,30,2,10	1,3,3,3
	B4B	3,3,3	>25,>18,>15	4,3,3	20,10,5	2,2,2
100	D63	5	25-30	4	95	1
101	D69	no bones				

SOUTH OF CHURCH						
BURIAL	CONTEXT	SEX	AGE	AGE GROUP	% PRESENT	CONDITION
102	C29	1	25-35	4	95	1
103	C160	5	25-30	4	95	1
104	C39	inf	6-9mths	1	20	3
105	B24	2x inf,5,1	2-3,6-12mths,25-35, 17-25	1,1,4,3	60,30,95,95	1,3,1,1
106	B26	5	17-25	3	30	3
107	A16	no bones				

Table 9. Gender, age and preservation data for burials not *in situ*.

AREA	CONTEXT	SEX	AGE	AGE GROUP	% PRESENT	CONDITION
Church	B1	inf,4,3,3	2.5-3.5,22-25,2x adult	1,3,7,7	10,40,10,10	3,3,3,3
Church	C1	5,3,4,3,2x inf, juv	25-35,adult,2x 17-25, 2x 0-6mths,10	4,7,3,3,1,1,2	35,10,5,10,15 5,10	3,3,3,3,3,3,3
Church	C3	4	17-25	3	20	2
Church	C27	4	>25	7	30	2
Church	D94	3	adult	7	1	2
Baptistery	D33	inf,juv	5,12-17	1,2	10,5	3,3
Baptistery	D38	juv,3	5-10,adult	2,7	10,2	3,3
Narthex	D64	juv	?	2	1	3
Narthex	D73	inf,3	?,adult	1,7	5,10	3,3
Narthex	D80	3,3	<25,adult	3,7	1,10	3,3
Ante-room	D6	?	?	?	2	3
Courtyard	D9	?	?	?	2	3
Courtyard	D21	3	adult	7	10	3

Table 10. Gender, age and preservation data for residual human remains.

CONTEXT	SEX	AGE	AGE GROUP	% PRESENT	CONDITION
B12	juv,3,3	<15,adult, elderly	2,7,8	10,10,10	3,3,3
B28	inf,3	2-4,adult	1,7	5,2	3,3
B36	inf	2-4	1	20	3
B49	2x juv,5	7-15,6-10,22-30	2,2,4	20,70,30	3,3,3
B54	3	>19	7	15	2
B73	inf	0-6mths	1	5	2
B80	inf,3	?,?	1,7	5,5	3,3
CD1	>6x3	>6x adult	>6x7	scraps	3
D1	spoil:- could be any number, counting as one adult				
D2	4	33-45	5	30	2
D3	?	?	?	2	3
D45	3,3,1	>16,>17,>17	7,7,7	5,5,5	2,1,1
D61	3	adult	7	5	3
D73	1	17-25	3	50	2
D80	inf,juv,4	0-6mths,5-15,40-50	1,2,5	10,5,10	3,3,3
D125	1	>25	7	75	1
D73/125	3	>22	7	20	2
D125	3	adult	7	1	3
D192	3	adult	7	1	3
D219	inf,3	<5, adult	1,7	20,20	3,3
D220	inf,3	?,adult	1,7	5,1	3,3
D244	inf,3	<1,adult	1,7	5,1	3,3
D301	inf,3	c1,adult	1,7	10,1	3,3
D316	3	adult	7	1	3
E19	3	14-22	3	15	3
E23	3	adult	7	20	3
E49	3	adult	7	1	3
E67	3	adult	7	5	3
H29	3	>15	7	1	3
L163	3	adult	7	2	3
M1	4	>25	7	5	3
M3	3	adult	7	1	3
M10	3	adult	7	5	3
M14	3	adult	7	1	3
M64	3	adult	7	5	3
M106	juv,2x adult	?,?,?	2,7,7	scraps	3,3,3
R1	3	adult	7	1	3

METHODS

Preservation of remains (Appendix)

Preservation was recorded by the surviving skeletal elements, and by the condition of the bone on a scale of good, average or poor. The percentage of the skeleton present was estimated.

Dentiton was catalogued on the standard chart of Brothwell (1981: 53). In addition to tooth and alveolar bone presence or absence, the chart records the health status of each tooth.

Separation of multiple burials

Generally it was quite simple to separate the remains of several individuals by comparing size, stage of development or age, condition, colour and so on, and confirming by check-

ing articulation. In the case of large deposits of disarticulated bone, which were not included in the final analysis beyond a body count, the remains were treated in the same way as an animal bone sample, with no attempt to reconstruct the individuals. Anything of note on each bone was recorded separately, and the minimum number of individuals present was established by the number of the most frequent bone present.

Age estimation

At any point where age is discussed in this report the estimates given are of developmental or relative age and not of absolute, chronological age. This must always be the case when age estimates are obtained by comparing the degree of skeletal development of one individual to standards for expected skeletal development by a given age as derived from a larger sample. Given the controversy surrounding ageing techniques, the preferred method of age estimation would have been to arrange all the individuals into a series of advancing age from the youngest person present to the oldest. Demographic statements would then be made based on proportions of this series, rather than by referring to individuals as of a definite age. Unfortunately, time restrictions did not permit this, and the usual age groupings have been retained.

Individuals who are still developing provide the most accurate age estimates (Bass 1987: 12), particularly in the most active phases of dental eruption before about ten years of age (Ubelaker 1989: 63-4). After about 25 years of age, when maturity is reached and development ceases, age estimates are based mainly on the progress of degenerative processes, the rate of which tends to be far more variable between individuals and therefore more unreliable. Consequently, infants, juveniles and adolescents are considered in year by year detail in parts of the report, whereas adults are considered in groups of ten year intervals, and in many cases have been simply classed as adult.

A variety of ageing methods was employed for the infants and subadults, applying the principle that it was better to arrive at an age estimate based on as diverse a basis as possible. This avoids errors that may arise when using only one category of development, due to potential inter-individual variability in the rate of that category. This included assessment of the development of the dentition (Schour and Massler 1944), the length of the diaphysis (Johnston 1962; Sundick 1978), stage of epiphyseal fusion, and appearance and fusion of other elements (Salter 1984).

Adults, that is those individuals with a complete dentition and all epiphyses fused, were also subjected to a combination of methods, following the advice of Lovejoy, Meindl and Mensforth (1985). Dental attrition was assessed by comparison with Brothwell's (1981: 71-2) chart of wear stage by age. Although this would not be applicable to a sample which had experienced a soft diet, and therefore little tooth wear, previous studies (Moore and Corbett 1973; Tattersall 1968) have already demonstrated that people of this period were exposed to quite a coarse diet, producing the wear required for this method. Of course, the degree of this wear could still vary between samples, causing some error in the evaluation. It would have been preferable to calibrate the adult dental wear from wear on more reliably aged immature individuals as described by Miles (1978); unfortunately, time did not allow. Age-related changes to the pubic symphysis in the few cases where this was possible were evaluated using the McKern and Stewart method (1957) for males, and the Gilbert and McKern method (1973) for females. Advance of cranial suture obliteration with age was not included, as it is extremely variable between individuals, and therefore notoriously unreliable.

Sex estimation

Estimation of sex was based largely on the dimorphic characteristics of the skull and pelvis, with most weight given to the pelvis. Five grades were assigned: female, probably female, indeterminate, probably male, and male. These are denominated as 1-5 on Tables 8-10.

Skull dimorphism was assessed following Ascadi and Nemeskeri (1970), Ferembach, Schwidetzky and Stloukal (1980) and Brothwell (1981: 90-8).

Observations were made on the pelvis following the Phenice system (1969), and further suggestions by Ascadi and Nemeskeri (1970). The measurements suggested by Ferem-bach, Schwidetzky and Stloukal (1980) were not implemented as they proved to be unrepeatable on this sample. Scarring of the pelvis due to parturition has been demonstrated as unreliable as a guide to sex (Kelley 1979; M. Cox pers. comm.), and so has been excluded from the analysis. Sacral dimorphism was judged with reference to Brothwell (1981: 61).

Where morphological characteristics were ambiguous, metrical data were used as a sexing tool. Only those individuals who, through incomplete data sets, could not be included in the later analysis to establish the degree of dimorphism in this sample could be sexed in this way. Otherwise, to include individuals sexed by metrical information would have created a circular argument.

It is generally accepted that immature individuals cannot be reliably sexed. Ubelaker (1989: 52-3) has suggested that rates of developmental progress differ between males and females, and could possibly be used for sexing. This is not possible here as a subsequent part of the analysis indicated that there was stunted growth in adolescents relative to developmental age in this sample; the developmental data are, therefore, unreliable for sexing purposes. The canine has been shown to be dimorphic even in deciduous dentitions in some cases (Rosing 1983), and dental development is least affected by any impediment to growth. In this case, only the permanent canine was used as this is more reliable, and is in place by 11-12 years. The mesiodistal and bucco-lingual diameters were taken following the definitions by Hillson (1986: 233) and plotted against each other to observe any grouping.

Metrical data

Forty-five cranial and 46 post-cranial measurements were recorded for each individual when the relevant skeletal elements were in sufficiently good condition. They were taken following the conventions laid out in Brothwell (1981: 77-87) and Bass (1987). Any skeletal landmarks referred to in the text follow the definitions given in those works or in that of McMinn and Hutchings (1977). More measurements were taken than are used in this analysis, but this was necessary for future comparisons with samples from other sites as the skeletal metric data for Italy grow.

Stature was calculated from the length of the long bones, using the regression formulae of Trotter and Glesser (1952; 1958). Indices calculated were restricted to the cranial index and the meric and cnemic indices (Brothwell 1981: 87); these are the most commonly quoted indices in reports, and are some of the most useful in describing the physique of the individual.

Evidence for stunting of growth in immature individuals was tested for by comparing estimates of age by diaphysis length to age estimates derived by developmental observations (either tooth development or sequence of fusing, as described above). Corroborating evidence was also gathered by comparing this data to those individuals suffering from hypoplasia, cribra orbitalia or cribra femoralis, or cranial hyperostosis. An explanation of this relationship is given below. Only immature individuals were included, as it has been demonstrated that, after periods of childhood stunting, there is often a rapid growth spurt and the adult section of the population will present no evidence of reduced stature (Clegg 1978; Harrison et al. 1983).

Metrical data were also used to examine the degree of dimorphism present in the humerus, femur and palate, by plotting head diameter against epicondylar width, and length against breadth respectively. Limb asymmetry of the upper and lower arms and legs was noted to investigate the possibility of handedness in the sample.

Non-metric data

Non-pathological variability of specific traits was recorded in order to test for a genetic component to the distribution of burials. In the long term, this will also allow comparison to other sites in order to comment on the 'genetic distance'. Twenty cranial and 22 post-cranial traits (Berry and Berry 1967; Finnegan 1978) were scored as present, absent or data missing. This is a rather restricted number of traits, but included the most commonly used, and the most useful. Occurrences of the traits were plotted on to plans of the burials and particular attention was given to those clusters of individuals presenting more than one trait in common. The data were also examined for patterns of recurring traits, following the study by Saunders (1989) on occupationally related skeletal modification.

Dental pathology

Caries prevalence was recorded by location on a particular tooth. Abcess and ante-mortem loss were recorded by tooth. Calculus, alveolar recession and periodontal disease were recorded on a severity scale of 0-3. The grading for calculus was after Brothwell (1981: 155) and Ramfjord, Kerr and Ash (1966). The normal position of the alveolar crest was taken to be 2.0 mm below the cemento-enamel junction (Barker 1975). Alveolar recession was recorded if this distance had increased. Periodontal disease was recorded as 0 for healthy alveolar; 1 for slight pitting of the crest around the tooth as a possible indicator of inflammation of the soft tissue; 2 for definite remodelling of the bone, particularly of the interdental septa; 3 for severe disease and the presence of infrabony pockets (Conheeney, forthcoming a). The distinction was made between alveolar recession and periodontal disease as it is accepted that some recession may be due to continual eruption of the teeth, even in cases where there appears to be little wear on the occlusal surface (Whittaker et al. 1990).

Dental non-metric traits, including third molar agenesis, malocclusion, crowding of teeth and general pathology were also recorded.

Skeletal pathology

Each individual was examined for evidence of pathology. Osteoarthritis was only diagnosed when the criteria put forward by Rogers et al. (1987) were met. Location of vertebral osteophytes was, unfortunately, only recorded by the areas cervical, thoracic and lumbar and severity, as were Schmorl's nodes and intervertebral disc disease. If carrying out the study today, it would be preferable to record location by specific vertebrae and position on each vertebra. Infections and other pathology were assigned to a most probable cause, following the definitions laid down in standard reference works (Steinbock 1976; Ortner and Putschar 1981; Rogers and Waldron 1989). The levels to which prevalence rates were calculated are included in the relevant analysis section, as the degree of detail of this varies with the type of pathology and skeletal element. The prevalence data is of value in this study as the majority of burials took place over a period of about 300 years. This is a tighter chronological denominator than at some sites (Waldron 1991).

PRESERVATION OF REMAINS (TABLES 11 AND 12)

The macroscopic condition of the bone varies between areas. No microscopic survey was carried out. Survival of the skeleton as a unit tended towards a small proportion of the body being present (Table 11). The total number of bodies in Table 11 is 134 rather than 159, the true total, because several multiple burials were summarized as one entry or body. Considering the total percentage column and row, the remains show a definite skew to poor condition and to poor survival. Forty-four per cent of bone was in poor condition, 30.6 per cent moderate and only 25.4 per cent good. At sites where there are no unusual conditions of preservation, a roughly normal distribution with most bone in the moderate category could be expected. At Monte Gelato 69.5 per cent of skeletons had less than 50 per cent present and 35.1 per cent had less than ten per cent present. Again, in a normal distribution, only 50 per cent of skeletons should be less than 50 per cent represented, and there should not be over 35 per cent of bodies in the smallest category. This would seem to indicate poor preservation for the site as a whole. This is important, and should be noted, as it affects the amount of information available at several stages of the analysis. The poor condition is in part due to the tufaceous soil of the site, which tends to acidity and erodes the bone. That so little of many skeletons survived is probably due to three factors. Firstly, during excavation it was found that several tombs had been cleared intentionally in Antiquity; secondly, graves near to the ground surface were badly damaged and disturbed due to deep ploughing; thirdly, if the majority of bone was already in a poor condition, smaller bones would suffer particularly badly and may disintegrate and be lost.

It is harder to explain why the condition varies between areas. In the church, narthex, ante-room and the area over the Roman rooms, the majority of bone was in poor condition. Other areas were more mixed, except for the baptistery and area between the entrance and road, which were in moderate/good and good condition respectively. Only two bodies were recovered from the latter area, so the good condition of both could be an artifice of the small sample size. The baptistery contained mainly infant burials, and it is generally accepted that small infant bones are fragile and have a lesser chance of survival than robust adult bones. However, there was relatively little intercutting of these graves, unlike adjoining areas.

This phenomenon of variable preservation is more apparent when the cells of the 'areas totalled' section of Table 11 are split into their component parts of male, female, juvenile and infant (Table 12). The pattern that would be expected if age and sex were responsible for differential preservation is for fragile, easily damaged infants to fall into the upper left-hand corner of the table; relatively robust males into the lower right-hand corner; and females and juveniles to be spread in between. Instead, the infants form the majority of those in the 'good' category, and of those in the 'over 90 per cent present' category. Also, there are equal numbers of males and females in the 'good' category, and four females compared with two males with over 90 per cent of the body surviving. Whilst caution is necessary as the figures involved are so small, this would seem to rule out age and sex as the major factors affecting condition and survival of the remains. Much more significant is the fact that burials close to the church, the baptistery apart, were frequently disturbed to introduce new interments.

The relative rates of survival of elements of the skeleton were much as expected. In Table 11 the percentage of predicted numbers gives the number present of a particular

Table 11. Preservation of remains.

	<10	<20	<30	<40	<50	<60	<70	<80	<90	<100	total
CHURCH											
poor	17	2	2	4	2						27
mod.	4	1	2	1	4						12
good	1						1		1		3
total	22	3	4	5	6	0	1	0	1	0	42
BAPTISTERY											
poor	3				1						4
mod.	1	1		1		2		3	1	1	10
good			1						1	8	10
total	4	1	1	1	1	2	0	3	2	9	24
NARTHEX											
poor	8	2	1		1			1			13
mod.	3	1	2		1	1					8
good									1	1	2
total	11	3	3	0	2	1	0	1	1	1	*23
ANTE-ROOM											
poor	3										3
mod.											0
good										1	1
total	3	0	0	0	0	0	0	0	0	1	4
SPACE BETWEEN ANTE-ROOM, BAPTISTERY AND ENTRANCE											
poor	1										1
mod.						1		1			2
good											0
total	1	0	0	0	0	1	0	1	0	0	3
ENTRANCE TO ANTECHAMBER											
poor											0
mod.				1	1						2
good										1	1
total	0	0	0	1	1	0	0	0	0	1	3
AREA BETWEEN ENTRANCE AND ROAD											
poor											0
mod.											0
good		1	1						2	1	5
total	0	1	1	0	0	0	0	0	2	1	5
OVER ROMAN ROOMS NORTH OF CHURCH											
poor	1						1				2
mod.				1							1
good											0
total	1	0	0	1	0	0	1	0	0	0	3
COURTYARD											
poor	3	1	1		1						6
mod.	2	1	2								5
good			1				1	3		2	7
total	5	2	4	0	1	0	1	3	0	2	18
SOUTH OF CHURCH											
poor		1	2								3
mod.											0
good						1				4	5
total	0	1	2	0	0	1	0	0	0	4	8
AREAS TOTALLED											
poor	36	6	6	4	5	0	1	1	0	0	59
mod.	10	5	7	4	5	4	0	4	1	1	41
good	1	1	3	0	0	1	2	3	5	18	34
total	47	12	16	8	10	5	3	8	6	19	**134

KEY:
* nine short of 51 as Burial 24 ten individuals summarized for condition as 1. Burial 55 summarized, Burial 74, Burial 75
** not to true total of burials as several multiple burials summarized as one

Table 12. Preservation of remains split by age and sex for all areas.
Burials nos. 24, 55, 74 and 75 have not been included as they are multiple burials summarized for preservation and condition.)

	<10	<20	<30	<40	<50	<60	<70	<80	<90	<100	total
poor — inf/juv	10	7 1		1 2			2				
poor — ♂/♀			2		1 1		1	1	1		
poor — indet.	18	4		1	3	2					
moderate — inf/juv	3	2 1		1 1	3	1 1	1 3	1	3	1	
moderate — ♂/♀			3		1 2	1				1	
moderate — indet.	3	3									
good — inf/juv	1			1			1	1	1	8	4
good — ♂/♀		1		1	1			1 1	1 3	1 2	4

Key to split:-

inf.	juv.
♂	♀
indeter-	minate

element as a percentage of the number of that element if all individuals were complete (following Mays 1991a; 1991b). Looking at the 'total' column, the percentage of an element recovered appears to be related to its size and possibly to its appearance. Small bones such as the carpals fall below five per cent recovery and the patella, which is not so small but is perhaps not so easily distinguishable as a bone, has around ten per cent recovery. The poor representation of smaller bones, such as those of the hand and foot, relative to larger bones, should be noted, as this could compromise the pathological data. Attribution of cause for much pathology depends on its distribution throughout the body, so, if sections of the skeleton are consistently absent, some pathologies could be missed. When the data are broken down by area in the body of the table, it is apparent that the level of recovery of each element conforms to the varying preservation present in the areas, whilst retaining the overall pattern. This means that the varying levels of preservation of skeletons in each area is not caused by any unusual recovery rates of particular elements. (The catalogue of skeletal parts present for each individual is given below, in the Appendix.)

DEMOGRAPHY

Eighty-three adults, 23 juveniles and 51 infants were recovered from the intact burials (where infants are defined as nought to five years and juveniles as six to fifteen years). Of the adults, 24 were male or possibly male; 23 were female or possibly female; and 36 were of indeterminate sex. The high number for whom sex could not be determined was due to the fragmentary nature of much of the remains. Of these indeterminates, 82.9 per cent were composed of bone in poor condition, and all of them had less than 50 per cent of the skeleton present; 60 per cent had less than ten per cent (Table 8).

Sex composition

The sex ratio over the whole site was practically equal, with 25 males and 23 females (1.09:1). With a few exceptions, namely the baptistery, ante-room, entrance to the ante-room and over the Roman rooms, this was reflected by most of the areas of the site (Table 13). It should be borne in mind that very small numbers are involved, so that a difference of one between the sexes, in areas of the site with few burials, can have a disproportionate effect on the ratios. However, a possible explanation of the exceptions could be seen when the sex composition was broken down by area (Table 14).

The baptistery contained two adults out of 24 skeletons and the ante-room one adult amongst four skeletons; all were of indeterminate sex. Rather than being something unusual in the sex composition, something unusual had affected the age structure across the site and, therefore, indirectly affected the sex composition. This is examined in the next stage of analysis, dealing with age. The area over the Roman rooms yielded only three skeletons, two of which were infants and one a male – hence the apparent male skew to the ratio in Table 13, when it was, in reality, the age structure that was more influential again. The only ratio which cannot be explained away easily is that for the entrance to the ante-room. Here three out of eight burials were male, and there was one female and two infants. It is very difficult to say whether this may have a true cause connected in some way to the location within the site complex, or whether it is an artificial phenomenon associated with the small sample size.

If it is accepted that the sex ratio is approximately equal for all areas of the site where adult burials take place, two inferences are possible. Firstly, neither sex was being reared to adulthood at the expense of the other sex. Secondly,

males and females were treated similarly in death. For example, if the church was the preferential place for burial, both sexes were present in almost equal numbers. Burial no. 2, which may have been beneath the altar, contained a female and an adult of indeterminate sex as the primary burials, and a male and second indeterminate in the complex of burials on top of the primary ones. This seeming equality of treatment was also borne out by looking at the burials which had grave-goods. Burial no. 24, also within the church, and with a glass beaker, contained three males, two females and one indeterminate. Burial no. 26, likewise within the church, had a bronze ring and was a female. Burial no. 59 held two males with a cup between their heads. Burial no. 106, south of the church, contained a female with a complete pottery vessel. The combination of these two inferences makes it tempting to suggest an egalitarian society with regard to sex. However, this data, extracted as it is from burials, need not necessarily mean that the sexes were treated equally in life. A woman may have few rights in many societies but be accorded an élite burial because of the status or wealth of her husband.

One other small point of note is that amongst all the areas of adult burials shown in Table 14, with the exception of the entrance to the ante-room, more bodies were assigned to a positive sex than to a possible sex category. This could suggest that there was marked dimorphism in this sample. This is explored further below.

Age composition

The predicted death curve for a pre-modern society is given in Figure 110. Deaths would be high in those less than one year old, falling off through infancy with a trough in later childhood and adolescence, and then gradually climbing again with increasing age (Clegg 1978: 182). The age structure across the whole site by ten-year groupings is presented in Table 15. This roughly conforms to the predicted curve (the six to fifteen years group is fairly high because of the under tens rather than the older children), except that the number in each age category decreases with increasing age, rather than increasing again after young adults. This can be ignored, as it is a function of the inadequacy of the most commonly used ageing techniques for dry skeletons. At present, the usefulness of these methods tails off rapidly after the age of 45, and they are often not reliable before that age; hence the 18.5 per cent classified only as 'adult' in Table 15. For the same reason the average age of death for the site has not been calculated as this is fairly meaningless, although it is quoted in many reports.

Table 13. Sex ratios by area (combining possible and definite of each sex).

	♂	♀	Ratio (♂ : ♀)
church	6	5	1.2 : 1
baptistery	0	0	-
narthex	6	5	1.2 : 1
ante-room	0	0	-
space between baptistery and ante-room	2	2	1 : 1
entrance to ante-room	3	1	3 : 1
area between entrance and road	2	3	1 : 1.5
over Roman rooms	1	0	1 : 0
courtyard	3	4	1 : 1.3
south of church	2	3	1 : 1.5
TOTAL	25	23	1.09 : 1

Table 14. Sex composition by area.

KEY: 1 = male; 2 = possibly male; 3 = indeterminate; 4 = possibly female; 5 = female; juv. = juvenile (6-15 years); inf. = infant (0-5 years). Burials nos. 14 and 15 have been excluded as no details are available.

(a) numbers in each area

	1	2	3	4	5	juv.	inf.	total
church	5	1	16	1	4	9	13	49
baptistery	0	0	2	0	0	3	19	24
narthex	3	3	7	2	3	8	6	32
ante-room	0	0	1	0	0	1	2	4
space between baptistery and ante-room	2	0	1	0	2	1	0	6
entrance to ante-room	0	3	2	1	0	0	2	8
area between entrance and paved road	2	0	0	0	3	0	0	5
over Roman rooms to west	1	0	0	0	0	0	2	3
courtyard	2	1	6	1	3	1	4	18
south of church	2	0	0	0	3	0	3	8
TOTAL	17	8	35	5	18	23	51	157

(b) numbers expressed as percentages of the total number per area

	total number	1	2	3	4	5	juv.	inf.	total
church	49	10.2	2.0	32.7	2.0	8.2	18.4	26.5	100
baptistery	24	0	0	8.3	0	0	12.5	79.2	100
narthex	32	9.4	9.4	21.9	6.3	9.4	25.0	18.8	100.2
ante-room	4	0	0	25.0	0	0	25.0	50.0	100
space between baptistery and ante-room	6	33.3	0	16.7	0	33.3	16.7	0	100
entrance to ante-room	8	0	37.5	25.0	12.5	0	0	25.0	100
area between entrance and paved road	5	40.0	0	0	0	60.0	0	0	100
over Roman rooms to north	3	33.3	0	0	0	0	0	66.7	100
courtyard	18	11.1	5.6	33.3	5.6	16.7	5.6	22.2	100.1
south of church	8	25.0	0	0	0	37.5	0	37.5	100
	157								

Whilst the age structure for the site as a whole was very much as expected, more unusual patterns were apparent when age composition was considered by area (Table 16). The baptistery, ante-room and the area over the Roman rooms are composed almost completely of under fifteen year olds: 22 out of 24 burials for the baptistery; three out of four for the ante-room; and two out of three for the area over the Roman rooms. This is even more apparent when the cumulative totals of the number dead by each age group, for each area, are considered (Table 17).Of those in the baptistery, 79.2 per cent were dead by the age of five, and 91.7 per cent by fifteen years of age. In the ante-room, 50 per cent were dead by five years, and 75 per cent by fifteen years of age. Over the Roman rooms, 66.7 per cent were dead by five years, but there were no further deaths until the 25-35 age group. The phenomenon is therefore most marked in the baptistery area. To some extent, the figures for burials over the Roman rooms could be disregarded as the product of chance, as there are so few burials in that area. The ante-room is more difficult to explain away in this fashion and, without a doubt, some factor seems to be preferentially selecting infants for burial in the baptist-

ery. This may be related to the recent christening of the infants, or perhaps their unbaptized status, and might also apply to the ante-room next door to the baptistery.

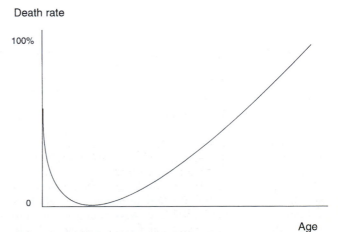

Fig. 110. Death-rate curve, after Clegg (1978).

Table 15. Number in each age group as a percentage of total of whole site (excluding burials nos. 14 and 15).

age	no.	%
0-5	51	32.5
6-15	23	14.6
16-25	22	14.0
26-35	20	12.7
36-45	5	3.8
>45	6	3.8
adult	29	18.5
total	157	100%

teen, the deaths conformed to a tripartite pattern common in other samples (Brothwell 1981; Manchester 1983). Of the immature deaths, 70.4 per cent occurred before the age of five, and 23.9 per cent before one year.

Considering the total figures in Table 18, the large number of deaths, seventeen, before one year of age was probably because of the high immediately postnatal risk to the baby of infection and complications. There was then a trough between one and two years with only four deaths present. Age two to three showed an increase to twelve deaths, age three to four maintained this level with eleven deaths, then the rate falls again to six deaths in age four to five. Although the figures must not be pressed too far, given the small numbers involved, the most likely explanation of

Table 16. Age composition by area.

area	0-5	5-15	16-25			26-35			36-45			>45			adult		
			♂	♀	I	♂	♀	I	♂	♀	I	♂	♀	I	♂	♀	I
church	13	9	0	1	3	1	2	2	2	0	0	1	0	0	1	3	11
baptistery	19	3													0	0	2
narthex	6	8	3	1	4	1	1	0	1	1	0	1	1	0	0	1	3
ante-room	2	1													0	0	1
space between baptistery, ante-room and entrance	0	1	1	1	0										1	1	1
entrance to ante-room	2	0	1	1	2	2	0	0	0	0	0	0	0	0	0	0	0
area between entrance and paved road	0	0	0	0	0	1	2	0	0	1	0	1	0	0	0	0	0
over Roman rooms	2	0	0	0	0	1	0	0									
courtyard	4	1	1	0	1	1	1	2	0	1	0	0	2	0	1	0	3
south of church	3	0	1	1	0	1	2	0									
totals	51	23	7	5	10	8	8	4	3	3	0	3	3	0	3	5	21
totals when areas are combined	51	23	22			20			6			6			29		

Table 17. Cumulative percentage in each age group in each area.

area	by 5	by 15	by 25	by 35	by 45	>45	adult
church	26.5	44.9	53.1	63.3	67.3	69.4	30.0
baptistery	79.2	91.7					8.3
narthex	18.8	43.8	68.8	75.0	81.3	87.5	12.5
ante-room	50.0	75.0					25.0
space between baptistery, ante-room and entrance	0	16.7	50.0				50.0
entrance to ante-room	25.0	25.0	75.0	100.0			0
area between entrance and paved road	0	0	0	60.0	80.0	100.0	0
over Roman rooms	66.7	66.7	66.7	100.0			0
courtyard	22.2	27.8	38.9	61.4	66.7	77.8	22.2
south of church	37.5	37.5	62.5	100.0			

When deaths occurring before 25 years of age, that is, before adulthood, were examined year by year (Table 18), a series of clusters of deaths could be seen. The cluster at 21 years in several of the areas is artificial, as the average age of those placed in the age group 17-25 by tooth wear was used in the plot, creating the false impression that all these individuals were 21 years of age. Ages younger than this group, where tooth eruption could assign ages more finely, could be more reliably considered. Below the age of seven-

this rise between two and four years is the cessation of breast-feeding with the associated nutritional and environmental stress. This stress would be in the form of poor diet after weaning, or illness brought on by insanitary feeding methods. Indeed, the diet described by Wickham (1981: 94) for the early medieval rural population of corn, oil and wine, supplemented by small amounts of beans and fruit, would not appear to be very suited to the needs of a child immediately post-weaning. Iron deficiency due to nutritional stress, or to chronic diarrhoea, causes bony changes which could also support this suggestion. This is examined in the pathology section, below.

In the deaths between five and fifteen years, there was an unusual, slight cluster between twelve and thirteen years. There are no obvious reasons for this; but the most likely explanations are either pathology which targets the early teens, or increased stress at the onset of puberty, tipping the balance between life and death. The first cause may be apparent in the pathology, but only if it was of a type which caused bony changes. There would have to be extremely arduous conditions for the second cause to be possible, but it could be evidenced by signs of nutritional deficiency. Both were tested for in the pathology section below.

When the age and sex composition were considered together (Table 16), there was a very even split between the sexes in all age groups in the total row. To a slightly lesser degree, this held for all the areas with adult burials. This is very interesting as it would appear that childbirth, the most important factor in early female death, had little influence here.

PHYSIQUE

The raw data for this section are presented in Tables 19 and 20. The mean measurements are not presented in the text as the usefulness of this practice seems questionable.

Stature

The statures calculated for all those adults with the required long bones are presented in Table 21. Reading across the stature estimates for each individual, the arm bones appear to produce somewhat greater statures in some cases than the leg bones. This is interesting, as during the recording, it was noted that lower arm measurements tended to underestimate the age of children by one or two years, relative to dental development. Dental development is the most accurate of ageing techniques as it is least affected by nutritional and other hardships. Presumably, then, this deficit in arm length was being caught up by adulthood and in some cases even surpassed. A genetic cause rather than environmental would seem most likely, as other child limb measurements were not affected.

The stature values were plotted for each area. The smallest and tallest males both occurred in the area south of the church at 1.66 m and 1.82 m respectively, although the tall male appeared to be unusual for the site. The females ranged from 1.55 m in height in burials to the south of the church to 1.6 m in those in the courtyard. The average stature for each area is given in Table 22. The male figures were not very different from the modern male average stature of 1.74 m. However, the females of all areas were well below the modern female average of 1.66 m. This deficit in height could explain the dimorphism evident in the sample. Nutritional deficiency can result in reduced stature, and marked sexual dimorphism in a sample can also indicate the presence of nutritional hardship, because much of the female's energy goes into reproduction, thus causing the female to be more compromised in height (T. Molleson, pers. comm.).

None of the areas contained strikingly tall or short individuals compared to the others. In several sites in London,

(St Mary Graces – Waldron, forthcoming; St Mary Spital – Conheeney, forthcoming b) probable privileged burials were within the normal range of statures expected for the period, but all tended to fall towards the top of the range. Other areas of burials would produce a wider spread. This did not appear to be the case at Monte Gelato; if the church, for example, was an area of preferential burial, then data for stature did not reveal any difference from other areas of the site.

Indices

The cranial, meric and cnemic indices were calculated for all individuals for whom the required measurements were recordable. This proved to be an extremely limited number. Therefore, although site areas were considered separately initially, further division into age and sex was not practical.

Cranial shape
The shape of the skull, as determined by its length relative to breadth, is described by the cranial index (Brothwell 1981: 87). The closer this approaches to 100 per cent, the rounder the skull anterioposteriorly (brachycranial), rather than being long and narrow (dolichocranial). The skulls were assigned to categories using the ranges for each cranial type set out by Wells (1982) and the results are presented in Table 23.

The numbers involved were so small as to be virtually meaningless. Long, narrow skulls were most frequent with three skulls, followed by mesocranial with two. The least frequent type was rounded skulls, represented by just one individual. This differs completely from pooled data from medieval sites in Britain, which show that brachycranial skulls were the most frequent type (Brothwell 1972).

Meric index
The meric index reflects the anterioposterior flattening of the femur in the region just inferior to the sub trochanter. As values for the index decrease from 100 per cent, they indicate increased flattening. Right and left femurs were analysed separately to test for differences according to side, and the values were assigned a category according to those set out by Wells (1982).

The marked tendency for the site as a whole (and for all areas taken individually except over the Roman rooms) was for eumeric femurs on both sides, with 76.2 per cent of right femurs eumeric and 81.3 per cent of left (Table 24).

Various explanations for this flattening of the femur have been advanced, although so far no definitive cause has been agreed. Generally, it is accepted that there is a remodelling of the femur in order to cope with stresses imposed on the neck in the most mechanically economic way (Brothwell 1981: 88-9). The suggested sources of these stresses have ranged through vigorous activity over rough ground, strain on the immature femur, calcium deficiency or nutritional stress or, in later life, as being linked in some way to arthritis (Cameron 1934; Buxton 1938; Lovejoy, Burstein and Heiple 1976). Dawes and Magilton (1980) have suggested that in extreme cases of rickets, the meric index may be affected, with individuals presenting a high degree of flattening. In less extreme cases, individuals may still have a tendency towards eurycnemia of the tibia. The roundedness of most femurs at Monte Gelato, therefore, could be taken to indicate a freedom from any of these conditions, if any

Table 18. Age composition of those < 25 years per area.

Church

0	1	2	3	4	5	6	7	8	9	10	11	12	13	14	15	16	17	18	19	20	21	22	23	24	25
	xx	xx	xx	xx				xxx		xxx		xxx								x	xx	x			

Baptistery

0	1	2	3	4	5	6	7	8	9	10	11	12	13	14	15	16	17	18	19	20	21	22	23	24	25
	xx	xxx	xxx	xx	x		xx	x																	

Narthex

0	1	2	3	4	5	6	7	8	9	10	11	12	13	14	15	16	17	18	19	20	21	22	23	24	25
	x	x	xx	xx			x	xx				xx	xx	x							xxxx				

Ante-room

0	1	2	3	4	5	6	7	8	9	10	11	12	13	14	15	16	17	18	19	20	21	22	23	24	25
		x			x								x												

Space between baptistery & ante-room

0	1	2	3	4	5	6	7	8	9	10	11	12	13	14	15	16	17	18	19	20	21	22	23	24	25
						x															x		x		

Entrance to ante-room

0	1	2	3	4	5	6	7	8	9	10	11	12	13	14	15	16	17	18	19	20	21	22	23	24	25
	x	x																x	x		xx				

Courtyard

South of church

TOTALS

Table 19. Adult skull measurements.

sex	burial	context	L	B	H	PBH	NH	NB	GB	J	G1	G2	LB	GL	FL	FB	TFH	GH	S1	S2	S3
5	7	C23																			
3	18	B8a																			
3		B8b																			
5	26	A28	173.5	130.5	129.0	88.2	51.0	/	86.0	/	44.8	39.2	94.5	87.3	32.8	26.9	/	69.5	122.0	120.0	116.0
2	54	D289																	128.0	98.0	
2	54	D291																			
5	56	D91																			
1	59	D168																			
5	60	A34	169.5	126.0	124.5	88.0	48.3	23.9	88.2	123.5	43.2	40.3	100.5	97.4	36.0	29.3	107.4	65.9	116.0	112.0	106.0
5	72	D296																			
5	81	M16																			
1	85	L173																			
4	92	D18																			
5	94	D32																			
1	99	B4																			
1,3	99	B4A																			
5	100	D63	178.5	132.5	131.0	94.0	51.9	24.1	91.4	/	43.4	40.1	98.0	86.5	36.3	28.3	117.6	72.8	122.0	128.0	115.0
1	102	C29a	192.5	138.0	130.5	127.5	49.5	/		/	58.7	/	104.5	99.4	38.0	31.7	123.8	70.4	117.0	128.0	122.0
5	103	C160	/	/	/	/	49.4	25.6	101.4	91.0	49.4	38.0	/	/	/	/	108.2	66.3			/
	105	B24																			
5	79	112(8)	180.0	141.0	125.0	123.5	50.0	24.0	118.7	87.9	52.5	38.5	96.5	92.0	37.2	30.6	114.3	65.1	127.0	121.0	113.0
1	79	112(9)	178.0	144.5	127.5	126.0	47.7	20.6	124.0	89.5	47.8	42.2	90.5	87.5	/	/	107.4	63.2	120.0	115.0	/

sex	burial	context	S1'	S2'	S3'	DA	DC	BQ	SC	09L	U	B'	ROrB	LOrbB	ROL	LOL	HI	GoGo	ML	WI	RCrH
5	7	C23															26.0				
3	18	B8a																			
3		B8b																			
5	26	A28	108.3	108.9	96.3	40.0	19.8	206.5	10.3	71.5	482.5	88.5	35.9	34.2	34.9	36.0	29.0	101.4	94.0	114.5	56.52
2	54	D289	106.4	90.5													29.7	102.2	98.0		
2	54	D291																			
5	56	D91															28.9	96.9			
1	59	D168															25.8	91.5	100.1	127.1	72.0
5	60	A34	102.1	100.7	88.3	49.0	22.8	196.0	10.3	70.0	482.0	89.7	37.2	39.8	34.3	33.9	26.2	92.6	98.0	117.0	54.7
5	72	D296															30.5		93.5	118.0	57.0
5	81	M16																			
1	85	L173																			
4	92	D18															29.0	96.6			62.5
5	94	D32																			
1	99	B4															30.9	45.1	98.5	111.7	69.5
1,3	99	B4A																			

sex	burial	context																			
5	100	D63	105.9	115.3	92.7	46.5	23.7	232.0	7.9	75.4	493.0	96.3	36.0	/	32.5	/	30.2	86.3	104.5	115.5	62.0
1	102	C29a	111.1	115.4	99.8		22.6	/	/	/	/		39.5	/	31.0	/	29.9	113.2	120.0	/	66.0
5	103	C160	/	/	/	46.0	22.6	/	/	/	/	90.6	39.5	37.9	32.2	34.8	27.8	89.8	/	124.5	/
	105	B24	109.9	110.2	91.7	45.0	22.6	305.0	/	/	520.0	95.8	33.8	34.9	33.9	33.4	31.5	94.8	103.5	/	70.0
5	79	112(8)	103.9	108.0	/	40.0	22.0	298.0	/	/	/	96.7	34.4	36.0	30.0	29.5	27.1	89.6	95.0	/	62.0
	79	112(9)															26.0	107.5	/	/	64.0

sex	burial	context	LCrH	RM1/2	LM1/2	RRB'	LRB'	RM2	LM2	ZZ	UCBL	UCMD	LCBL	LCMD
5	7	C23								40.5	7.8	7.2		
3	18	B8a									8.3	7.7	7.7	6.4
3		B8b	57.0	28.1	26.9	34.6		18.2	17.5				7.9	6.5
5	26	A28		25.5	26.9	32.2	31.6	17.2	15.8		7.0	6.4	6.3	5.5
2	54	D289				37.4	36.6			45.8	8.0	7.2		
2	54	D291				32.3	31.1				8.6	7.0	9.0	7.1
5	56	D91	55.5	46.5	47.7					43.9				
1	59	D168	56.0	22.4		29.6	28.5	15.9	16.3		9.0	7.8	8.2	6.8
5	60	A34	62.0	28.2	28.1	28.2	29.6	13.7	13.9		7.9	7.4	7.5	6.2
5	72	D296									8.2	7.7		
5	81	M16									7.0	8.1	6.7	7.1
1	85	L173		27.0	27.4		33.4	15.4	14.1		8.7	7.3	8.9	7.6
4	92	D18		49.9	47.7	29.9	30.2				6.8	6.8	6.8	6.3
1	94	D32		20.0	21.0			12.4	13.6		7.2	6.4		
1	99	B4									1		7.7	7.1
1,3	99	B4A		30.0	28.3	31.9	32.0	17.4	17.4				7.7	
5	100	D63	62.5	30.6	28.9	29.6	30.7	17.6	16.1		7.9	6.9	7.4	6.3
1	102	C29a	65.5	26.8	23.7	30.4	26.5	14.8	14.9		8.8	8.0	/	7.0
5	103	C160	61.5	26.0	/	25.2	35.1	13.0	13.8		7.4	7.2	7.5	6.3
	105	B24	72.0	30.8	33.4	34.7	31.9	18.7	16.9		8.0	6.6	7.4	6.6
5	79	112(8)	61.5	27.8	27.3	32.0	31.9	19.0	18.6		8.8	7.8	/	6.7
1	79	112(9)	/	24.2	24.3	29.9	31.9	18.7	19.9		9.4	8.0	8.6	7.2

Table 20. Adult postcranial measurements.

burial	context	RFdl	LFHd	RFE	LFE	RHHd	LHHd	Atld	RScB	LScB	RCLL	LCLL	SB	SL	Sbdy	RHuL	LHuL	RHuC	LH
2	C57																		
2	C58		43.8																
18	B81	45.6	45.2	/	84.5	46.1	45.9	/	28.0		136.5	139.0			119.0	303.5	301.0	62.0	64.0
26	A28	46.8	42.8	/	67.8	40.5	38.9	70.5	/			134.5			/	302.0	297.5	58.0	57.5
54	D291			70.0	69.5	48.8		79.0	27.0	27.8						329.0	/	79.0	/
56	D91(2)	/	38.3						25.7	/									52.0
59	D168	46.1¹	41.8²	67.6														67.0	61.5
60	A34	42.1	40.9		/	42.3		70.5	24.2	24.3	125.5	132.0	115.0	113.5		292.0	296.0	55.0	54.0
72	D296(1)	43.9	44.2		/	43.9			26.8	25.4						30.1	/	57.0	/
78	M33																		
80	M18/81	39.3	39.9	68.5	70.0		37.4			24.5		141.0	121.0	108.0			287.5	64.0	64.0
85	L173	46.8																67.0	/
92	D18	/	/	/	/						120.0								
93	D5	42.6	42.1	75.0	72.6	39.0	39.5	/	26.0	25.6		137.0				29.9	300.0	60.0	58.0
94	D32	42.9	42.9	/	75.9	40.1	41.0	/	24.4	24.8						297.0	290.0	56.0	57.0
99	B4	/		/	79.9	/	/	88.0	/	25.6									
99	B4A	49.4	/	81.7		46.4	48.8		/		150.5	153.5				316.0	313.0	66.5	64.5
99	B4B		44.6				38.7												
100	D63	43.7	44.3	70.5	72.1	40.7	43.3	/	24.6	25.6	141.0	120.0	120.0	99.0	/	311.5	305.0	61.5	61.5
102	C29(I)	51.1	/	85.6	84.3	49.2		/	28.2	29.8	153.0	161.0	125.0	115.5	/	332.0	327.0	65.5	65.0
	C29(II)						41.9												
103	C160	39.6	40.9	66.5	66.8	37.9	/	/	22.6	22.6		131.0	121.0	/	/	287.5	294.0	58.0	57.0
105	B24	44.4	40.4	68.7	70.6	41.0	40.4	/	23.1	24.4	/	143.0	121.0	129.5	52.2		303.0	55.5	54.0
	B24(II)	50.8	51.3	/	77.9	/	47.0									/	341.0	61.0	57.5
79	M112(8)	41.2	39.0	72.8	72.0	38.0	38.6	/	/	25.6	131.0	131.0	106.0	104.0	/	291.0	287.5	59.0	59.0

burial	context	RRaLi	LRaLi	RUL	LUL	RFeL1	LFeL1	RFeL2	LFeL2	RFeD1	LFdD1	RFeD2	LFeD2	RFeD3	LFeD3	RFeD4	LFeD4	RTiL1	LTiL1	RTiL2
2	C57									25.0		32.8								
2	C58									30.3	27.2	31.4	32.5	28.6	28.0	26.7	25.8			
18	B81	244.5	247.5	266.0	266.0	422.0	421.0	418.0	417.0	25.4	26.4	30.4	29.9		29.6		27.8		335.0	339.0
26	A28	/	/	240.0	243.5	/	436.0	/	436.0	/	24.4	30.4	26.1	/	25.7	/	26.2	/	377.0	/
54	D291					/	422.0	/	417.0										350.5	/
56	D91(2)				236.0															
59	D168	237.0		/						22.8	29.5²	29.4	27.4²							
60	A34	226.5	221.5		241.5	410.5	411.0	407.5	406.5	31.2¹	23.9	32.8¹	26.2	24.9	25.1	24.8	25.5			
72	D296(1)	225.0	/	/						24.8	23.5	26.2	32.7							
78	M33									23.2		30.6						364.0	364.0	358.0
80	M18/81	229.5	225.0	247.0	244.0	418.0	417.5	416.0	415.0	25.5	24.5	27.3	28.7	27.0	26.5	26.3	26.0			

85	L173									24.8	/	31.3	/					383.0	/	379.0
92	D18																			
93	D5	214.0	215.0	/	/	414.0	414.0	409.0	/	23.1	24.2	28.1	26.9	25.6	24.3	24.6	24.3	329.0	/	324.0
94	D32									26.3	25.9	28.7	28.9					339.0	341.0	335.0
99	B4																			
99	B4A																	362.5	357.5	356.0
99	B4B																			
100	D63	230.0	224.0	250.5	241.5	428.5	435.0	425.0	432.5	26.5	26.0	28.6	29.3	28.3	28.3	27.7	27.7	358.5	361.0	355.5
102	C29(I)	237.5	240.0	257.0	258.0	431.0	/	424.5	/	29.9	26.5	28.0	26.6	25.1	27.3	26.1	26.2	338.0	341.0	338.0
	C29(II)																			
103	C160	219.0	221.0	237.5	241.0	409.0	/	407.0	/	25.6	28.8	24.6	24.4	24.1	24.9	28.5	26.4	353.0	355.0	349.0
105	B24	/	233.0	/	/	413.5	420.5	410.5	418.5	27.0	28.8	26.4	26.1	28.0	29.8	25.9	26.3	352.0	361.5	345.5
	B24(II)	/	/	/	/	/	473.5	/	470.0	26.7	27.6	27.3	27.7	/	29.4	/	26.2	413.0	/	408.0
79	M112(8)	/	/	/	/	424.5	427.0	424.0	423.0	24.6	22.6	28.6	29.0	27.6	26.2	23.7	24.7	342.0	340.0	335.5

burial	context	LTiL2	RTiD1	LTiD1	RTiD2	LTiD2	RFiL1	LFil1	RFeC	LFeC	RPatL	LPatL	RPatB	LPatB	RC	LC	RT	LT
2	C57		35.0	35.8	24.5	22.4												
2	C58			30.0		24.3			89.0	87.0								
18	B81	370.5	/	35.0	/	26.8	/	/	/	/	44.4	/	48.0	/	86.0	85.5	60.0	64.0
26	A28	347.0	29.7	31.0	22.7	21.9	/	/	/	/	/	44.4	/	/	/	73.0	56.0	56.5
54	D291																	
56	D91(2)																	
59	D168		/	33.2	/	25.9												
60	A34	/	27.3	28.7	21.5	20.1	/	/										
72	D296(1)	/	/	/	/	/												
78	M33	360.0	30.5	31.8	24.0	25.6	353.0	354.0							82.8	81.0	60.0	60.4
80	M18/81	/	/	30.7	/	22.4	/	/										
85	L173	/	32.4	31.9	25.4	25.7	363.0	/			45.8	/	47.3	/	/	78.7	/	59.3
92	D18																	
93	D5	/	28.6	27.0	23.9	23.1	/	318.0			36.2	37.7	39.8	39.1	/	/	52.0	52.1
94	D32	335.0	30.6	30.8	22.5	22.5	330.0	328.0			38.0	39.7	39.7	40.0	52.3	53.3	74.5	71.2
99	B4										43.3	42.9	43.7	43.2	/	/	/	/
99	B4A	354.0	35.2	34.2	24.7	24.7	352.5	348.5							80.5	80.5	/	62.0
99	B4B														/	/	59.0	/
100	D63	358.0	29.6	29.3	24.1	24.7	/	345.5			41.0	41.4	43.4	44.0	51.0	51.5	74.0	74.5
102	C29(I)	336.0	31.5	30.7	24.6	24.1	334.0	331.0	/	/	47.7	48.1	43.4	/	76.5	/	61.0	59.5
	C29(II)																	
103	C160	349.0	27.4	25.7	21.3	20.3	/	/			/	/	/	/	70.5	70.8	48.9	48.0
105	B24	356.5	32.8	32.3	24.3	23.0	/	/							81.0	80.5	55.0	56.0
	B24(II)	/	34.2	32.3	26.5	26.4	/	/			42.1	43.5	44.4	44.2	89.0	90.0	66.5	65.5
79	M112(8)	336.0	31.0	29.8	22.1	22.8	327.0	/							72.9	72.8	51.2	50.2

Table 21. Stature.

burial	context	area	R fem.	L fem.	R tib.	L tib.	R hum.	L hum.	R rad.	L rad.	R uln.	L uln.
4 2	C58	church	158.3	158.1		158.7						
1 18	B8 (1)	church		166.7		173.2	166.0	165.1	172.3	173.4	175.6	175.6
3 26	A28	church										
2 54	D291	narthex or open ground to west of baptistery					173.2					
5 56	D91 (2)	narthex or open ground to west of baptistery										158.5
1 59	D168	narthex or open ground to west of baptistery							169.2			
5 60	A34	narthex or open ground to west of baptistery	155.6	155.6			156.1	157.4	162.5	160.2		161.1
5 72	D296 (1)	space between baptistery, ant-room and entrance					159.1		161.6			
1 78	M33	area between entrance and paved road			170.0	170.0						
5 79	M112 (8)	area between entrance and paved road	159.1	159.6	160.7	160.1	155.7	154.7				
5 80	M18/81	area between entrance and paved road	157.3	157.3			154.7	154.7	164.0	161.6	163.2	161.9
1 85	L173	over Roman rooms			174.6							
4 92	D18	courtyard					158.4	158.8				
5 93	D5	courtyard	156.4	156.4	156.9		157.8	155.4	156.4	156.8		
5 94	D32	courtyard			159.8	160.4						
2 99	B4A	courtyard			169.8	168.6	169.4	168.6				
5 100	D63	courtyard	160.1	161.5	165.6	166.2	162.8	160.5	164.0	161.1	164.9	161.1
1 102	C29 (1)	south of church	165.5		163.7	164.5	174.0	172.6	169.6	170.4	172.2	172.6
5 103	C160	south of church	155.1		163.9	164.5	154.7	156.8	158.7	159.7	167.5	160.7
5 105	B24	south of church	156.4	158.1	163.6	166.5		159.8		165.4		
1	B24 (11)	south of church		175.5	181.9			176.6				

Table 22. Average stature by area.

area	no. of ♂	average ♂ stature	no. of ♀	average ♀ stature
church	1	166.7	1	158.3
baptistery	0	-	0	-
narthex	2	171.2	2	157.1
ante-room	0	-	0	-
space between baptistery, ante-room and entrance	0	-	1	159.1
entrance to antechamber	0	-	0	-
area between entrance and road	1	170.0	2	158.2
over Roman rooms	1	174.6	0	-
courtyard	1	169.8	4	158.7
south of church	2	170.5	2	155.8

Table 23. Cranial index.

	range	dolichocranial	mesocranial	brachycranial
church	75.2		1	
narthex	74.3	1		
area between entrance and road	78.3-80.9		1	1
courtyard	74.2	1		
south of church	71.7	1		

Table 24. Meric index.

burial	context	R femur				L femur			
		AP	ML	index	interpretation	AP	ML	index	interpretation
CHURCH									
2	3 C57	25.0	32.8	76.2	platymeric	-	-	-	
2	4 C58	30.3	31.4	96.5	eumeric	27.2	32.5	83.7	platymeric
7	5 C23	22.8	25.0	91.2	eumeric	20.6	23.3	88.4	eumeric
8	3 C46	-	-	-		-	-	-	
18	8 (1)	25.4	30.4	83.6	platymeric	26.4	29.9	88.3	eumeric
18	8 (11)	29.8	30.7	97.1	eumeric	-	-	-	
18	3 B22	-	-	-		-	-	-	
23	3 D123	25.3	27.3	92.7	eumeric	-	-	-	
26	5 A28	-	-	-		24.4	26.1	93.5	eumeric
NARTHEX									
56	D91 (2)	22.8	29.4	77.6	platymeric	-	-	-	
59	1 D168	31.2	32.8 (1)	95.1	eumeric	29.5	27.4 (2)	107.7	eumeric
60	5 A34	24.8	26.2	94.7	eumeric	23.9	26.2	91.2	eumeric
SPACE BETWEEN BAPTISTERY AND ENTRANCE									
72	5 D296 (1)	23.2	30.6	75.8	platymeric	23.5	32.7	71.9	hyperplatymeric
AREA BETWEEN ENTRANCE AND ROAD									
80	5 M18/81	25.5	27.3	93.4	eumeric	24.5	28.7	85.4	eumeric
OVER ROMAN ROOMS									
85	1 L173	24.8	31.3	79.2	platymeric	-	-	-	
COURTYARD									
93	5 D5	23.1	28.1	82.2	platymeric	24.2	26.9	90.0	eumeric
94	5 D32	26.3	28.7	91.6	eumeric	25.9	28.9	89.6	eumeric
100	5 D63	26.5	28.6	92.7	eumeric	26.0	29.3	88.7	eumeric
SOUTH OF CHURCH									
102	1 C29 (1)	29.9	28.0	106.8	eumeric	26.5	26.6	99.6	eumeric
103	5 C160	25.6	24.6	104.1	eumeric	28.8	24.4	118.0	eumeric
105	5 B24	27.0	26.4	102.2	eumeric	28.8	26.1	110.3	eumeric
105	1 B24 (11)	26.7	27.3	97.8	eumeric	27.6	21.7	99.6	eumeric
106	5 B26	25.3	27.3	92.7	eumeric	-	-	-	
AREA BETWEEN ENTRANCE AND ROAD									
79	5 M112 (8)	24.6	28.6	86.0	eumeric	22.6	29.0	77.9	platymeric

Table 25. Meric index by area.

	R femur				L femur				how many cases differ between sides
	range	hyp	plat	eum	range	hyp	plat	eum	
church	76.2-97.1		2	4	83.7-93.5		1	3	2/3
narthex	77.6-95.1		1	2	91.2-107.7			2	0
space between baptistery, ante-room and entrance	75.8		1		71.9	1			1/1
area between entrance and road	86.0-93.4			2	77.9-85.4		1	1	1/2
over Roman rooms	79.2		1						-
courtyard	82.2-92.7			3	88.7-90.0			3	0
south of church	92.7-106.8			5	99.6-118.0			4	0
totals		0	5	16		1	2	13	
KEY: hyp = hyperplatymeric; plat = platymeric; eum = eumeric									

Table 26. Cnemic index.

burial	context	R tibia				L tibia			
		AP	ML	index	interpretation	AP	ML	index	interpretation
CHURCH									
2	3 C57	35.0	24.5	70.0	eurycnemic	35.8	22.4	62.6	platycnemic
2	4 C58	-	-	-		30.0	24.3	81.0	eurycnemic
7	5 C23	23.8	19.6	82.4	eurycnemic	25.1	19.3	76.9	eurycnemic
8	3 C46	38.0	26.4	69.5	mesocnemic	36.6	25.5	69.7	mesocnemic
18	B8 (1)	-	-	-		35.0	26.8	76.6	eurycnemic
18	3 B22	32.2	24.1	74.8	eurycnemic	-	-	-	
26	5 A28	29.7	22.7	76.4	eurycnemic	31.0	21.9	70.6	eurycnemic
NARTHEX									
59	1 D168	-	-	-		33.2	25.9	77.1	eurycnemic
60	5 A34	27.3	21.5	78.8	eurycnemic	28.7	20.1	70.0	eurycnemic
AREA BETWEEN ENTRANCE AND ROAD									
78	1 M33	30.5	24.0	78.7	eurycnemic	31.8	25.6	80.5	eurycnemic
79	5 M112 (8)	31.0	22.1	71.3	eurycnemic	29.8	22.8	76.5	eurycnemic
80	5 M18/81	-	-	-		30.7	22.4	73.0	eurycnemic
OVER ROMAN ROOMS									
85	1 L 173	32.4	25.4	78.4	eurycnemic	31.9	25.7	80.6	eurycnemic
COURTYARD									
93	5 D5	28.6	23.9	83.6	eurycnemic	27.0	23.1	85.6	eurycnemic
94	5 D32	30.6	22.5	73.5	eurycnemic	30.8	22.5	73.1	eurycnemic
99	3 B4B	35.2	24.7	70.2	eurycnemic	34.2	24.7	72.2	eurycnemic
100	5 D63	29.6	24.1	81.4	eurycnemic	29.3	24.7	84.3	eurycnemic
SOUTH OF CHURCH									
102	1 C29 (1)	31.5	24.6	78.1	eurycnemic	30.7	24.1	78.5	eurycnemic
103	5 C160	27.4	21.3	77.7	eurycnemic	25.7	20.3	79.0	eurycnemic
105	5 B24	32.8	24.3	74.1	eurycnemic	32.3	23.0	71.2	eurycnemic
105	1 B24 (11)	34.2	26.5	77.5	eurycnemic	32.3	26.4	81.7	eurycnemic

Table 27. Cnemic index by area.

	R tibia					L tibia					how many cases differ between sides
	range	hyp	plat	meso	eur	range	hyp	plat	meso	eur	
church	69.5-82.4			1	4	62.6-81.0		1	1	3	1/4
narthex	78.8				1	70.0-77.1				2	0
area between entrance and road	71.3-78.7				2	73.0-80.5				3	0
over Roman rooms	78.4				1	80.6				1	0
courtyard	70.2-83.6				4	72.2-85.6				4	0
south of church	74.1-78.1				4	71.2-81.7				4	0
totals				1	16			1	1	17	
KEY: hyp = hyperplatymeric; plat = platymeric; meso = mesocnemic; eur = eurycnemic											

of these explanations are accepted. However, until a larger body of comparative material is available it is difficult to comment on the meaning or significance of this index.

Where both left and right femurs survived there was often a difference in the category of index between sides. This may indicate a lack of stability in the index between sides (below, Table 28).

One interesting point is that comparison of the actual values for the index for each individual showed that three of the five individuals in the area south of the church had exceptionally high index values for the sample (Table 25). These were two females from burials 103 and 105 and a male from burial no. 102. The possibility of a familial link is examined in the spatial analysis section below.

Cnemic index

The cnemic index reflects the degree of mediolateral flattening of the tibia in the region of the nutrient foramen. As the index decreases away from 100 per cent, the degree of flattening of the bone increases. Individuals were assigned to categories of the index as set out by Wells (1982).

The most common tibia type was eurycnemic, with 94.1 per cent of right and 89.5 per cent of left tibiae eurycnemic for the site as a whole (Table 26). Again, many explanations of this index have been put forward, but its meaning remains as unclear as the meric index. There was much less difference in the index between sides, with only one pair differing (below, Table 28). Whatever was causing this category of index in the tibiae, therefore appears to have been much more constant between sides than was the cause of the meric index amongst the femurs. Values for the three unusual individuals in the area south of the church appear no different from the others (Table 27). This would tend to support the idea that the femurs were affected by a quite separate factor from that influencing the tibiae.

Limb asymmetry or sidedness

It has been suggested that the dominant side in use, that is in most cases the right arm and left leg, are frequently found to be the larger side in a sample. Whether this is the result of preferential usage, or is in fact determined in the foetus, has been discussed by Mays (1991a; 1991b). The humerus head diameter and length, combined radius and ulna length, femoral head diameter and length, and the tibia length, were examined for signs of this tendency.

The arm measurements showed very little pattern, with the right greater in thirteen cases and the left also greater in thirteen cases (Table 28). A possible explanation of this was supplied by the leg-bone measurements, where four cases were identical between left and right, while in a further five cases there was very little difference. This would seem to suggest that the people in this sample were not favouring either limb over the other.

Sexual dimorphism

The existence of dimorphism in the sample has already been shown by the clear division in stature range. It was further investigated by looking at regions of the body known to differ in average size between the sexes. This included the length and breadth of the palate, the length and breadth of the skull, the dimensions of the canine, and the femoral head diameter against epicondylar width (Figs 111-15).

As expected, each of these plots demonstrated the presence of dimorphism; but, interestingly, the different body parts exhibit this to varying degrees. The cranial and palatal dimensions are difficult to comment on as so few male individuals possessed the required data; but in each case (Figs 111 and 112) the males were distinct from the females at the greater end of the axes. The canine was more

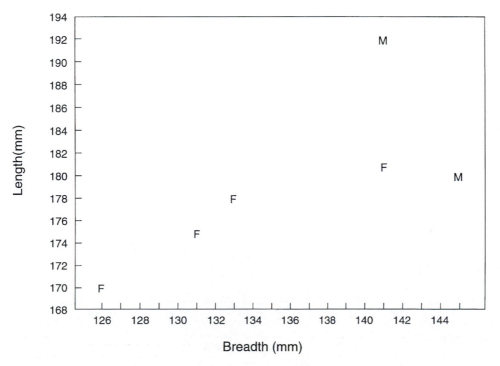

Fig. 111. Cranial dimorphism.

Table 28. Sidedness in different areas.

	right greater	left greater	same	no. in sample
HUMERUS HEAD				
church	2			2
area between entrance and road		1		1
courtyard		4		4
south of church	1			1
HUMERUS LENGTH				
church	2			2
narthex		1		1
area between entrance and road	1			1
courtyard	3	1		4
south of church	1	1		2
RADIUS AND ULNA				
church		2		2
narthex	1			1
area between entrance and road	1			1
courtyard	1	1		2
south of church		2		2
FEMUR HEAD				
church	1	1		2 (but very little in it)
narthex	2			2
space between baptistery, ante-room and entrance		1		1
space between entrance and road	1	1		2
courtyard	1	1	1	3 (right one is almost equal)
south of church	1	2		3
FEMUR LENGTH				
church	1			1
narthex		1		1 (but practically same)
area between entrance and road	1	1		2 (right very little in it)
courtyard		1	1	2
south of church		1		1
TIBIA AND FIBULA				
space between entrance and road	1	1		2 (L is virtually same)
courtyard	1	1	1	3
south of church		2	1	3
TOTAL	23	27	4	54

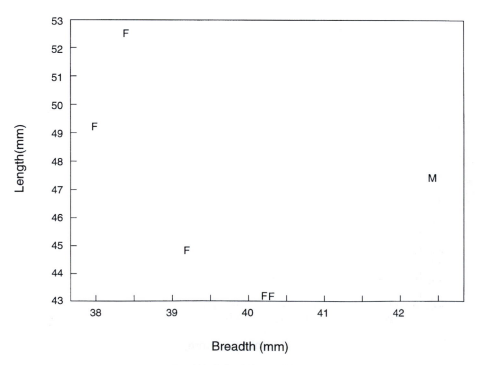

Fig. 112. Palatal dimorphism.

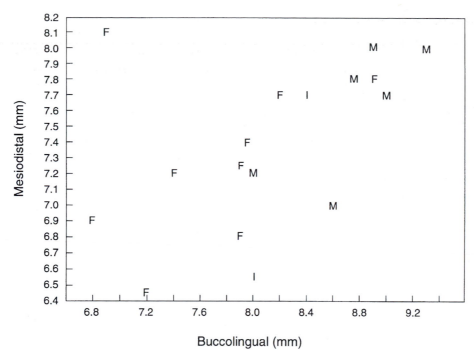

Fig. 113. Dimorphism of upper canine.

informative as more males could be included in the plots. This was very interesting as the division between the sexes was much less distinct for the upper canine (Fig. 113) than for the lower canine (Fig. 114). The most marked split of all was in the plot for the femoral dimensions (Fig. 115), although it is possible that this has an exaggerated appearance because of the scarcity of males. As more Italian sites become available for comparison, it will be possible to see if this is a characteristic of the populations of the period or whether the dimorphism was particularly strong at Monte Gelato.

Certainly from the few individuals that it was possible to include here, with the exception of the upper canine, there was unexpectedly little overlap between the sexes. It seems likely, therefore, that some other factor was acting on the living population to affect their growth potential, and that this factor appears to have had a worse effect on the females than the males. The most likely would be nutritional hardship, compounded by the energy requirements of childbirth. It will have to remain as supposition but, if the tentative suggestion concerning late weaning around two and a half to three and a half years was correct, this may

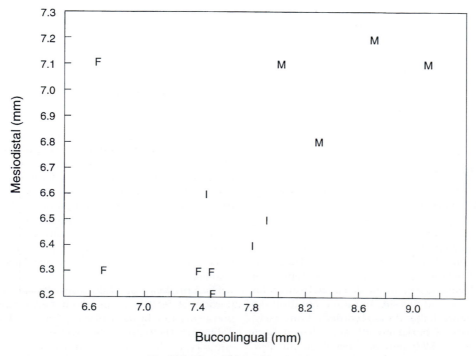

Fig. 114. Dimorphism of lower canine.

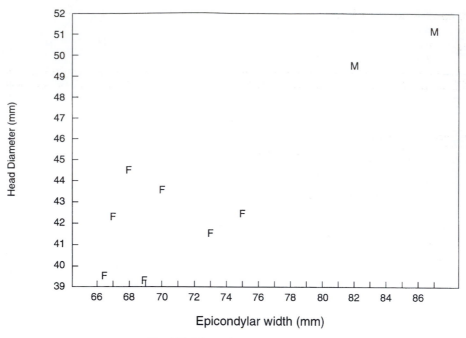

Fig. 115. Dimorphism of the femur.

well support this theory. Mothers would breast-feed longer to cut down demands on other food supplies and possibly to increase the spacing of pregnancies.

DENTAL PATHOLOGY

Deciduous or mixed dentitions were excluded from the following calculations of prevalence. In many parts of this analysis the sample size is so small that the inclusion of one individual may result in a 25 per cent prevalence rate. Working with this sample size appears unreliable on first consideration. However, if only four individuals are present in an area and one has a dental complaint, it is probably reasonable to assume that the complaint is fairly common in that population. Care is necessary not to overinterpret the data; but the evidence is still worth examining. The teeth present for each individual are listed in Table 29.

Wear data has not been included in the analysis. The sample showed evidence of wear at a rate which was roughly in accordance with that set out by Brothwell (1981: 71-2), and this is to be expected for this period.

Congenital complaints

The individuals who presented possible congenital conditions are listed in Table 30. There was only one case of crowding, normally quite a common complaint, and this affected the anterior teeth. It appears to be associated with rotation of the same teeth. In all there were eight individuals with teeth rotated out of the normal tooth row. There was quite a number of malformed teeth. Both lower canines of burial no. 54 had enamel extension down the roots (this was a very common trait at this site, but it was not until the later part of the fieldwork that it was recorded). Conversely, all four third molars of burial no. 81 were shaped from cementum, with just 1.0-2.0 mm of enamel on the tips. Burial no. 105, an infant, had a very oddly shaped upper left

canine, peg-shaped but with three equal cusps, and only a short stubby root about half normal length. There were five other peg teeth amongst four individuals and one taurodontic tooth. Peg teeth are fairly infrequent phenomena in most samples (Mays 1991a; 1991b). Six people had overbite, two markedly so. These were the possibly related individuals in the double burial (79) between the entrance and the road. They also had a palatal torus in common, and a very odd tooth row which raised up the lower anterior teeth in a curve. Two other individuals from burials 26 and 60 have very similar looking, unusual, teeth with short stumpty roots. They also have slender skeletons, whilst the majority from the site appear quite stocky and robust. In addition, burial no. 26 had a three cusped lower left premolar. The possibility of any of the congenital conditions reflecting familial relationships, including these apparent ones, is tested in the spatial analysis below.

Acquired pathology

Caries

Only three children from the whole site suffered from caries. Burial no. 68 was unusual, having two occlusal caries on the lower first molar. This was probably due to the cusp form, and/or little wear, allowing food to get trapped in the fissures. Burials 28 and 72 were more usual in suffering from interproximal caries. Burial no. 28 had only one, but burial no. 72 had four, ranging from slight to moderate severity. This child was buried with a female with notably poor dental health, and it is tempting to suppose that the two could be related and that she may have passed on weak enamel.

The prevalence of adult caries was calculated as the proportion of teeth present which had carious lesions. The prevalence rate by particular tooth for each area is shown in Table 31. Teeth from the baptistery, the ante-room, the entrance to the ante-room and the area over the Roman rooms had no adult caries. These were all areas, however,

Table 29. Teeth catalogue, maxilla.

(a) adults

individual	8	7	6	5	4	3	2	1	1	2	3	4	5	6	7	8
MAXILLA																
AREA BETWEEN ENTRANCE AND ROAD																
79 M112 sk. 8	NP	Y	Y	Y	Y	Y	/	Y	N	Y	Y	Y	Y	Y	Y	NP
79 M112 sk. 9	Y	Y	Y	Y	Y	Y	Y	Y	Y	Y	Y	Y	Y	Y	Y	Y
CHURCH																
7 C23	NP	Y	Y	Y	Y	Y	-	-	-	-	Y	Y	Y	Y	Y	Y
	9	9	9	9	Y	9	9	9	9	9	9	9	9	9	9	9
18 B8 (1)	-	-	-	-	Y	Y			Y		Y	Y		Y	Y	Y
18 B22 (1)	-	-	-	-	-	-	-	-	-	-	-	-	-	-	-	-
18 B22 (11)	-	-	N	N	Y	/	/	/	/	/	/	Y	N	N	-	-
26 A28	N	Y	Y	Y	Y	Y	NP	N	Y	Y	Y	Y	Y	Y	Y	Y
NARTHEX																
54 D289			Y	Y	Y	Y	NP	/	/	/	/	/	/	Y		
54 D291	9	9	9	9	9	9	9	9	9	9	9	9	9	9	9	9
56 D91 (3)	9	9	9	9	9	9	9	9	9	9	9	9	9	9	9	9
59 D168	-	-	Y	Y	Y	Y	Y	Y	Y	Y	Y	Y	Y	Y	-	Y
60 A34	NP	Y	Y	Y	Y	Y	Y	Y	Y	Y	Y	Y	Y	Y	Y	Y
SPACE BETWEEN ANTE-ROOM, BAPTISTERY AND ENTRANCE																
72 D296 (1)	Y	Y	N	/	Y	Y	Y	Y	-	Y	Y	Y	Y	Y	Y	Y
AREA BETWEEN ENTRANCE AND ROAD																
81 M16	Y	Y	Y	Y	Y	Y	/	Y	Y	Y	Y	/	Y	Y	Y	Y
OVER ROMAN ROOMS																
85 L173	Y	Y	Y	Y	Y	Y	Y		Y					Y	Y	Y
COURTYARD																
92 D18	NP	Y	Y	Y	Y	Y	Y	?	Y	Y	Y	Y	Y		Y	
94 D32				Y	Y	Y		.		Y	Y	Y				
99 B4												Y		Y	Y	Y
(99 B4 a)																
99 B4 A	Y	Y	Y	Y	/	/	/	/								
100 D63		Y	Y	Y	Y	Y	Y	Y	Y	Y	Y	Y	Y	Y		
SOUTH OF CHURCH																
102 C29	9	N	N	N	/	Y	Y	Y	/	/	/	Y	-	-	-	9
103 C60	Y	Y	Y	Y	Y	Y	Y	Y	/	/	Y	Y	Y	Y	Y	Y
105 B24 (1)	Y	?	Y	Y	Y	Y	?	Y	Y	Y	?	Y	Y	Y	?	Y
105 B24 (11)	-	Y	Y	Y	/	Y	/	/	Y	Y	Y	Y	Y	Y	Y	/
106 B26	-	-	N	Y	Y	Y	-	-	-	Y	Y	Y	Y	-	-	?
MANDIBLE																
AREA BETWEEN ENTRANCE AND ROAD																
79 M112 sk. 8	Y	Y	Y	Y	Y	Y	/	/	/	Y	Y	Y	Y	Y	Y	?
M112 sk. 9	Y	Y	Y	Y	Y	Y	Y	Y	Y	Y	Y	Y	Y	Y	Y	Y
CHURCH																
7 C23	NP	-	-	N	/	Y	Y	-	-	-	-	Y	N	Y	Y	NP
	9	9	9	9	9	9	9	9	9	9	9	9	9	9	9	9
18 B8 (1)	Y	-	-	-	-	Y			Y		Y		Y		Y	Y
18 B22 (1)	-	N	Y	Y	Y	Y	/	/	/	/	Y	Y	Y	N	-	-
18 B22 (11)	/	Y	/	-	-	-	-	-	-	-	-	-	-	-	-	-
26 A28	Y	Y	Y	Y	Y	Y	Y	N	N	Y	Y	Y	Y	Y	Y	N
NARTHEX																

individual	8	7	6	5	4	3	2	1	1	2	3	4	5	6	7	8
54 D289	9	9	9	9	9	9	9	9	9	9	9	9	9	9	9	9
54 D289	Y	Y	Y	Y	Y	Y	Y	Y	Y	Y	Y	Y	Y	Y	Y	Y
56 D91 (3)	NP	Y	N	N	Y	/	N	N	N	N	/	/	/	N	N	NP
59 D168	Y	Y	Y	Y	-	Y	Y	Y	Y	Y	Y	Y	Y	Y	Y	Y
60 A34	NP	Y	Y	Y	Y	Y	Y	Y	Y	Y	Y	Y	Y	Y	Y	NP
SPACE BETWEEN ANTE-ROOM, BAPTISTERY AND ENTRANCE																
72 D296 (1)	Y	Y	N	Y	Y	/	/	/	/	/	/	/	N	N	N	Y
AREA BETWEEN ENTRANCE AND ROAD																
81 M16	Y	Y	Y	/	Y	Y	Y	Y	Y	Y	Y	Y	Y	Y	Y	Y
OVER ROMAN ROOMS																
85 L173		Y	Y	Y	Y	Y	Y			Y	Y	Y	Y	Y	Y	Y
COURTYARD																
92 D18	Y	?	N	Y	Y	Y	Y	Y	?	Y	Y	Y	Y	Y	Y	NP
94 D32	9	N	N	Y	/	/	Y	-	-	Y	/	Y	Y	N	N	9
99 B4			Y	Y	Y	Y	Y	Y	Y	Y	Y	Y	Y			
(99 B4 a)				Y	Y			Y		Y	Y	Y				
99 B4 A	Y	Y	Y	/	/	Y	/	/	/	/	/	/	/	/	Y	Y
100 D63	Y	Y	Y	Y	Y	Y	Y	Y	Y	Y	Y	Y	N	Y	Y	Y
SOUTH OF CHURCH																
102 C29	9	N	N	Y	Y	Y	Y	Y	Y	Y	Y	Y	Y	Y	N	9
103 C60	Y	Y	Y	Y	Y	Y	Y	Y	Y	Y	Y	Y	Y	Y	Y	Y
105 B24 (1)	Y	Y	Y	Y	Y	Y	Y	Y	Y	Y	Y	Y	Y	Y	Y	Y
105 B24 (11)	Y	Y	Y	Y	Y	Y	Y	/	/	/	Y	Y	Y	Y	Y	-
106 B26	-	-	Y	/	Y	-	-	/	Y	Y	Y	Y	Y	Y	Y	-

(b) infants

individual	5	4	3	2	1	1	2	3	4	5	
MAXILLA											
18 B8(III)		-		-							perm
	-	Y	-	Y	-	Y	-	-	-	-	
27 D43	O		O					O		O	
	Y	Y	Y	Y	Y	Y	Y	Y	Y	Y	
28 D15	V							V23		V	
	Y	Y	/	Y	Y	Y	Y	/	Y	Y	
29 D31				-	-						jaw not lost
	Y	Y	/	Y	Y	/	/	/	Y	Y	
32 D224 V 16											V 26
	Y	Y	Y	Y	Y	/	Y	/	Y	Y	
33 D226	V		V	V	O	O	V	V	V	V	
	55		53	52	51	61	62	63	64	65	
	-	-	-	-	-	-	-	-	-	-	
34 D222 V 16											V 26
	Y	Y	Y	Y	Y	Y	Y	Y	Y	Y	
37 D229 V 17 16				0			0				V 26 27 mixed
	Y	Y		12	11	/	22		Y	Y	
37 D229(11) V 16											V 26
	Y	Y	Y	Y	Y	Y	Y	Y	Y	Y	
37 D229(1)					Y	Y	Y	Y	Y		
38 D54	V							V			
	Y		Y	Y	Y		Y				
41 D132 V 16											V 26
	Y	Y	Y	/	Y	/	THY	Y	Y	Y	
43 D135 O 16	Y	Y	/	Y	Y	Y	/	Y	Y	Y	26 O

individual	5	4	3	2	1	1	2	3	4	5	
47 D212	Y	Y	Y	V 12	V 11	Y V 21	V 22	Y	Y	Y	V 26
53 D293 V 17 16	Y	O 14 Y	V 13	12		21		V 23	Y	Y	26 V Mixed. 27
57 D95 16	y	/	/	/	/	/	/	/	/	Y	26
57 D95 II	Y	Y	/	Y	/	/	Y	Y	Y	Y	V 26
60 A13											
66 A21											
68 D284 V 16	Y O	Y	/	Y	Y	Y	/	/	Y	Y O	V 26
72 D296(11) 16						21		24 V Y	25 V Y	26	V 27 Mixed
76 M70 16 V	Y O	Y	Y O	Y	Y	Y 21 V	Y	Y O	Y	Y O	26 V
77 M72	55 Y	54 Y	53 Y								
97 D78 O 16	Y	Y	Y	/	/	/	/	Y	Y	Y	O 26
105 B24 (III)							Y	Y	Y	Y	

MANDIBLE

individual	5	4	3	2	1	1	2	3	4	5	
18 B8(III)	-	-	-	-	-	-	-	-	-	-	
27 D43	O Y	Y	O Y	Y	Y	Y	Y	O Y	Y	O Y	
28 D15 46 V	V Y	Y	V Y	Y	Y	Y	Y	V Y	Y	V Y	36 V
29 D31 46 V	Y	Y	Y	Y	/	/	/	Y	Y	Y	36 V
32 D224 47 46 V V	Y	Y	Y	Y	Y	/	Y	Y	Y	Y	36 37 V V
33 D226 46 V -	Y V	Y V	Y V	Y V	Y V			Y V	Y V	Y V	36 - V
34 D222 46 V	Y	Y	Y	Y	Y	/	/	Y	Y	Y	36 V
37 D229 V 47 46	Y	Y	/ 43	42 O	41	91	32 O	Y 33 V	Y	Y	36 37 V
37 D229(11)	-	Y	Y	Y	Y	Y	/	Y	Y	Y	
37 D229(1) 46 V	Y	Y	Y	Y	Y	/	Y	Y	Y	Y	
38 D54	V Y	V Y		V Y	V Y	V Y			V Y	V Y	
41 D132 46 V	Y	Y	Y	Y V 42	V 41	Y	/	Y	Y	Y	36 37 V V
43 D135 O 46	Y	Y	Y	Y	Y	Y	Y	Y	Y	Y	36 O

individual	5	4	3	2	1	1	2	3	4	5	
47 D212　46 V	Y -	Y	Y	Y	Y	Y	Y	Y	Y	Y	36 V
53 D293 47 46 V	Y		V 43	42		31	32	33 V	Y	Y	36 37 V Mixed
57 D95 (I) 46	/	/	/	/	/	31 O	/	/	Y	Y	36 Mixed
57 D95 II	Y	Y	Y	Y	Y	Y	Y	/	Y	Y	
60 A13　48 V	Y 47 V 46	/	/	/	/						Mixed
66 A21		Y V/O	Y	Y	Y	Y	Y V/O				
68 D284　V 46	Y O	Y	/	Y	/	Y	Y	/	Y	Y O	V 36
72 D296(a) 46	Y	Y 44 V		42 V	41 V				Y	Y	
76 M70　46 V	Y O	Y	Y O	Y	Y	Y	Y	Y O	Y	Y O	36 V
77 M72											
97 D78　O 46	Y	Y	/	/	/	/	/	/	Y	Y	36 O
105 B24 (III)		N	N	N	N	N	N	N	Y	Y	

with very few adults. This fact, combined with the low prevalence of childhood caries in general, suggests that caries was a disease associated with ageing, and the prolonged exposure to carious agents that greater age would mean, rather than a feature of the population itself, or of the diet. If either of the latter circumstances were the cause of caries, the children would also have been affected.

In all of the areas yielding teeth with caries, the incisors were not affected. Apart from one canine from a burial in the church, caries were restricted to teeth posterior to the premolars, which would agree with modern incidence patterns. The maxilla appeared to be slightly worse affected than the mandible, and people buried within the church were slightly worse affected than those in other areas. On the whole, however, there were few noteworthy differences between the areas, either in prevalence rates or in areas of the mouth affected.

The sites on the tooth attacked by caries, and the frequencies, are set out in Table 32. Of all caries, 44 per cent were cervical, and just over a quarter, 26 per cent, were interproximal. The real rate of cervical caries was higher than this, as many were also interproximal and only scored in that category. The most likely explanation of this type of caries would be natural sugars in the food, combined with poor hygiene, and soft, pulpy food as a secondary factor. Sugars released from food, if not cleaned away, will sit in the saliva around the neck of the tooth just above the gum. This area is therefore most at risk from caries. The interproximal area is also at risk when soft, pappy food becomes

trapped in gaps between the teeth. This attracts and feeds cariogenic bacteria which may result in caries formation. The relatively low rate of occlusal caries was produced by only three individuals, two of whom were the double burial (79) between the entrance and the road. This low prevalence would be due to tooth wear which would flatten out the fissures in the complex cusped posterior teeth, where occlusal caries would be most likely to occur. Only twelve per cent of all caries were gross, meaning that caries was not a severe problem at this site. This was confirmed by the low number of abcesses, only six for the whole sample. Whether this was because the diet was generally healthy, and took a long time to cause caries, or because people were dying early is impossible to demonstrate.

Abcesses

The prevalence rate was calculated by the number of abcesses as a proportion of the surviving tooth sockets (Table 33). As noted in the previous section, the prevalence of abcesses was very low for the whole site, and they were attested in only three areas: the space between the ante-room, baptistery and entrance; the area between the entrance and road; and the courtyard. Again, the maxilla appeared to be slightly worse affected than the mandible. This would follow, as caries attacked the maxilla to a greater extent than the mandible, and the most common cause of abcess is apical infection following exposure of the pulp cavity due to caries or excessive wear. Alternatively, the difference could

Table 30. Dental non metric.

indiv.	tooth rotⁿ	over-bite	pal torus	crowding	fenⁿ	peg.	PE	chip
79 M112 sk. 9	13, 31, 32, 41-42	very	slight	Ant. mand. very	17, 16, 13, 26, 27, 18			
79 M112 sk. 8		raised/ curved ant. teeth	✓		16, 17, 26, 27, 36, 37, 46, 47			
7 C23	28					28	26, 36	36 ling ant. cusp
18 B8 (1)						14, 27		
26 A28	14, 24					(12 NP) 22		
54 D291	0	✓	0	0	0	0	0	32
56 D91(3)								44
59 D168	43						46, 36	
60 A34		✓			14, 26, 34			
72 D296 (1)							25, 26	
81 M16							36, 46	38, 11
92 D18	13	✓				48		15, 16, 25
94 D32							14, 15 24, 35	
99 B4a					26-28			turned into 36
100 D63	43, 33, 12	✓			14, 18, 22			22
102 C29							11	
103 C60	42				33, 43			
105 B24 (1)								14
105 B26	34				14, 24			14

KEY: tooth rotⁿ = tooth rotation; pal torus = palatal torus; fenⁿ = fenestration; PE = pulp exposure

INFANT AND JUVENILE DATA

individual	incisor form
18 B8 (111)	groove on permanent incisors
27 A43	deep groove of wear on 51, none on other incisors
68 D284	55 and 65 something similar to Carabelli's cusp
105 B24 (11)	very old canine – fully circular and three similar size cusps. Root only formed to c. ½ length and still open. Polish wear – peg tooth probably but has three cusps

---

NOTES TO TABLE 30

26 A28	21 not developed. 23 position has lump lingually and over it – could be unerupted 23 but no x-ray.
	12 is very peg-like. 21 and canines normal. Both lower canines very small, almost peg-like.
	All teeth very short roots and skeleton as whole slender – very similar to A3. 34 almost 3 cusped.
54 D291	Both lower canines enamel extends down roots and heavy ridges on crown.
59 D168	Fold in lingual upper 1st incisors.
60 A34	Very short and stumpy roots and very slight skeleton.
81 M16	All four 3rd molars shaped from cementum with 1-2 mm of enamel on top.
85 L173	M2 and M3 have the very elongated cusp form.
102 C29	Calculus deposit so solid has made block of teeth and goes onto occlusal surfaces – could it be endocrinal problem? As well as resorbed sockets, there is alveolar resorption all round remaining teeth but especially severe in left side mandible where all from I to M probably held by tissue only as only just in place now. So wobbly – difficulty eating – could he have died from fever? Gets progressively worse from I to M. Also maxilla looks affected but alveolar is damaged.

---

be a function of the thinner bone in the walls of the maxilla compared with that in the mandible. Only those abcesses which penetrated the alveolar were scored, in the absence of an X-ray programme to detect those contained inside the alveolar. Given the greater fragility of the maxilla, more abcesses may successfully perforate the wall than in the thick plate of the mandible. Anterior teeth were not affected; this corresponds with the caries pattern, suggesting that the observed difference is accurate (despite the lack of X-ray analysis). The high rate in the space area is deceptive, as it is caused by three abcesses, all in the same female, burial no. 72. This was the female buried with the child with very unusual caried dentition.

Ante-mortem loss

The prevalence rate was calculated by the number of teeth lost ante-mortem as a proportion of all the possible sockets present. The rates for each tooth are given in Table 34. The two main causes of ante-mortem tooth-loss are caries or periodontal disease. Given the generally low incidence of severe caries (or abcesses), periodontal disease appeared the more likely cause. In any case, as all three conditions progress with age, it is likely that a relationship will be apparent between them. Four areas yielded individuals with affected maxilliae: the church; the space between the entrance, ante-room and baptistery; the area between the entrance and the road; and the area to the south of the

Table 33. Abcess prevalence by area.

MAXILLA	8	7	6	5	4	3	2	1	1	2	3	4	5	6	7	8
space between baptistery, ante-room and entrance			1/1	1/1								1/1				
area between entrance and road			1/3													
courtyard				1/2												

MANDIBLE	8	7	6	5	4	3	2	1	1	2	3	4	5	6	7	8
space between baptistery, ante-room and entrance																
area between entrance and road			1/5	1/5											1/3	
courtyard																

MAXILLA	8	7	6	5	4	3	2	1	1	2	3	4	5	6	7	8
space between baptistery, ante-room and entrance			100	100								100				
area between entrance and road			33.3													
courtyard				50.0												

MANDIBLE	8	7	6	5	4	3	2	1	1	2	3	4	5	6	7	8
space between baptistery, ante-room and entrance																
area between entrance and road			20.0	20.0											33.3	
courtyard																

Table 34. Ante-mortem loss prevalence by area.

MAXILLA (fractions)

	8	7	6	5	4	3	2	1	1	2	3	4	5	6	7	8
church	1/2		1/3	1/3					1/2				1/3	1/3		
space between entrance, baptistery and road			1/1											1/1		
area between entrance and road									1/3							
south of church		1/3	2/4	1/4									1/4	2/4	1/3	

MANDIBLE (fractions)

	8	7	6	5	4	3	2	1	1	2	3	4	5	6	7	8
church	1/3	1/3	1/3	1/3				1/2	1/2				1/3	1/3	1/3	
space between entrance, baptistery and road		1/1	1/1	1/1				1/3						1/1		
narthex		1/4	1/4				1/4	1/4	1/4	1/4		1/4		1/4		
south of church		1/5	1/5									1/5	1/5		1/5	
courtyard		1/5	2/4	1/5									1/5	2/4	1/5	

MAXILLA (percentages)

	8	7	6	5	4	3	2	1	1	2	3	4	5	6	7	8
church	50.0		33.3	33.3					50.0				33.3	33.3		
space between entrance, baptistery and road			100											100		
area between entrance and road									33.3							
south of church		33.3	50.0	25.0									25.0	50.0	33.3	

MANDIBLE (percentages)

	8	7	6	5	4	3	2	1	1	2	3	4	5	6	7	8
church	33.3	33.3	33.3	25.0				50.0	50.0				25.0	33.3	33.3	33.3
space between entrance, baptistery and road		100	100	100										100		
narthex			25.0				25.0	25.0	25.0	25.0				25.0	25.0	
south of church		20.0	20.0									20.0	20.0		25.0	
courtyard		20.0	50.0	20.0									20.0	50.0	20.0	

Table 35. Prevalence of unerupted teeth by area.

MAXILLA	8	7	6	5	4	3	2	1	1	2	3	4	5	6	7	8
church							1/2									1/2
narthex							1/3									1/2
area between entrance and road	1/3															1/3
courtyard	1/3															2/3

MANDIBLE	8	7	6	5	4	3	2	1	1	2	3	4	5	6	7	8
church	1/4															1/4
narthex	2/4															2/4
area between entrance and road																
courtyard	1/3															

MAXILLA	8	7	6	5	4	3	2	1	1	2	3	4	5	6	7	8
church							50.0									50.0
narthex							33.3									50.0
area between entrance and road	33.3															33.3
courtyard	33.3															66.6

MANDIBLE	8	7	6	5	4	3	2	1	1	2	3	4	5	6	7	8
church	25.0															25.0
narthex	50.0															50.0
area between entrance and road																
courtyard	33.3															

Table 36. Calculus prevalence rates by area.

	total no. that can be scored for this condition	grade 1		grade 2		grade 3	
		no. of sufferers	as a % of total	no. of sufferers	as a % of total	no. of sufferers	as a % of total
MAXILLA							
church	4	2	50.0	2	50.0		
narthex	4	2	50.0	1	25.0		
space between entrance, baptistery and ante-room	1	1	100.0				
area between entrance and road	3			3	100.0		
over Roman rooms	1			1	100.0		
courtyard	5	2	40.0	2	40.0	1	20.0
south of church	5	3	60.0	1	20.0	1	20.0
total	23	10	(43.5%)	10	(43.5%)	2	(8.7%)
MANDIBLE							
church	5	2	40.0	2	40.0		
narthex	4			3	75.0		
space between entrance, baptistery and ante-room	1	1	100.0				
area between entrance and road	3			3	100.0		
over Roman rooms	1			1	100.0		
courtyard	6	2	33.3	1	16.7	3	50.0
south of church	5	3	60.0	1	20.0	1	20.0
total	25	8	(32.0%)	11	(44.0%)	4	(16.0%)

Table 37. Periodontal disease prevalence by area.

	total no. that can be scored for this condition	grade 1		grade 2		grade 3	
		no. of sufferers	as a % of total	no. of sufferers	as a % of total	no. of sufferers	as a % of total
MAXILLA							
church	2					1	50.0
narthex	2						
space between entrance, baptistery and ante-room	1			1	100.0		
area between entrance and road	3					1	33.3
over Roman rooms	1						
courtyard	4	1	25.0	2	25.0	1	25.0
south of church	3			1	33.3		
total	16	1	(6.3%)	4	(25.0%)	3	(18.8%)
MANDIBLE							
church	3					1	33.3
narthex	4	1	25.0			2	50.0
space between entrance, baptistery and ante-room	1						
area between entrance and road	3	1	33.3	1	100.0	1	33.3
over Roman rooms	1						
courtyard	3			1	33.3	2	66.6
south of church	3			1	33.3		
total	18	2	(11.1%)	3	(16.7%)	6	(33.3%)

Table 38. Alveolar recession prevalence rates by area.

	total no. that can be scored	grade 1		grade 2		grade 3	
		no. of sufferers	as a % of total	no. of sufferers	as a % of total	no. of sufferers	as a % of total
MAXILLA							
church	3					2	66.6
narthex	1						
space between entrance, baptistery and ante-room	1			1	100.0		
area between entrance and road	3			1	33.3	1	33.3
over Roman rooms	1						
courtyard	3	1	33.3	1	33.3		
south of church	4	1	25.0				
total	16	2	(12.5%)	3	(18.8%)	3	(18.8%)
MANDIBLE							
church	3					2	66.6
narthex	3	1	33.3				
space between entrance, baptistery and road	1			1	100.0		
area between entrance and road	3	1	33.3	1	33.3	1	33.3
over Roman rooms	1						
courtyard	3	1	33.3			1	33.3
south of church	4	1	25.0			1	25.0
total	17	4	(23.5%)	2	(11.8%)	5	(29.4%)

Table 39. Hypoplasia prevalence rate by area.
(There were also three infant cases, two in the baptistery and one in the narthex.)

	total no. that can be scored for this condition.	grade 1		grade 2		grade 3	
		no. of sufferers	as a % of total	no. of sufferers	as a % of total	no. of sufferers	as a % of total
MAXILLA							
church	3						
narthex	2	1	50.0				
space between entrance, baptistery and ante-room	1						
area between entrance and road	2	1	50.0				
over Roman rooms	1						
courtyard	4			1	25.0		
south of church	4			1	25.0		
total	17	2	(11.8%)	2	(11.8%)	0	0
MANDIBLE							
church	4	1	25.0				
narthex	3	1	33.3				
space between entrance, baptistery and ante-room	1						
area between entrance and road	3	2	66.6				
over Roman rooms	1						
courtyard	4			1	25.0		
south of church	4	1	25.0	1	25.0		
total	20	5	(25.0%)	2	(10.0%)	0	0

Hypoplasia.

The prevalence of hypoplasia is given in Table 39. The mandible was again more severely affected, which is difficult to explain: an individual would be affected in upper and lower dentitions, if suffering from true hypoplasia. Perhaps a congenital defect was imitating the appearance of hypoplasia.

This condition is an interruption of the normal development of the tooth enamel, usually attributed to bouts of childhood illness (Hillson 1986: 127-40; Johnston and Zimmer 1989). The surprising factor is that 23.6 per cent of adult maxillary dentitions were affected, and 35 per cent of the mandibular ones. By contrast, only around thirteen per cent of child dentitions were affected. It is possible that children were sometimes dying before or during the severe disease episodes that would cause the condition, whereas adults with the condition represented those children who had survived the disease. The only conclusion that can be inferred from the data was that about 23 per cent, or roughly one quarter of the adults with surviving dentition, had undergone serious episodes of illness during childhood. (The lower figure is used because of the possibility of overestimation in the mandible.)

SKELETAL PATHOLOGY

Congenital pathology

Vertebral defects

Defects around the junction of the lumbar and sacral vertebrae are common because of the instability of this region (Ortner and Putschar 1981; Waldron, forthcoming). Monte Gelato was no exception to this (Table 40).

A male of 25-35 years from the area south of the church (burial no. 102) had an imperfectly closed sacral canal on the dorsal surface. The level of closure can vary, but is normally fused over from the level of the first and fifth bodies. This case does not qualify as true spina bifida occulta, as the canal was not completely open. Modern frequencies for this complaint are not well known, because the sufferer would probably be unaware of the condition and so would not present at the doctor's surgery. The same probably applies to all the vertebral defects discussed here.

Occasionally the fifth lumbar vertebra has a sacral appearance, or the first sacral vertebra has the appearance of a lumbar vertebra. Burial no. 59, a male of 17-25 years in the narthex, had the former condition, and a female of 25-30 years in the courtyard (burial no. 100) had the latter (with both first and second sacral vertebrae affected).

Various oddities of vertebral form occur which cannot be readily classified. Burial no. 105 from south of the church, a 17-25 year old male, was one such case. The lower articular facets of his fourth lumbar vertebra were crumpled, and the upper facets of the fifth matched and fitted with these.

Other pathology

Two individuals had unusual congenital defects (Table 40). Burial no. 56 in the narthex had the styloid process missing from the left ulna. Burial no. 102 from south of the church had a double facet on the left radius distal facet. The facets were very smooth with no sign of osteoarthritis or trauma.

It is interesting that, with the exception of burial no. 100 from the courtyard, all the congenital defects came from individuals buried in the narthex or from the area south of the church. A familial relationship between these burials is tested for in the spatial analysis section below.

Acquired pathology

Degenerative defects

In common with most archaeological samples, degenerative defects, along with dental disease, were the most frequent pathology. Prevalence rates were calculated as the number of individuals suffering from the complaint as a proportion of the number of individuals in an area of the site.

Osteoarthritis was only scored for those individuals who satisfied the criteria laid down by Rogers *et al.* (1987). The frequencies are given in Table 41. The four areas composed mainly of children (the baptistery, the ante-room, the entrance to the ante-room and the area over the Roman rooms) recorded no sign of the condition, as would be expected since it is associated with ageing. The prevalences in the other areas also closely reflected the age composition of the sample. The church, with 44.9 per cent dead by fifteen years, had only two per cent with indications of the complaint. Similarly, the narthex, with 45.2 per cent dead by a similar age, had no sufferers. The area between the entrance and the road had the highest proportion of sufferers, at twenty per cent, but contained nobody who had died before the age of 25 years. More females than males were affected, but this could simply be due to the small figures available.

The most commonly affected parts of the skeleton were the acetabulum and femur head, the lumbar vertebrae, the cervical vertebrae, and the wrist and foot bones. In modern populations the large weight-bearing joints are most fre-

Table 40. Congenital defects.

1. INCOMPLETE CLOSURE OF SACRAL CANAL				
south of church	burial no. 102	♂	25-35 years	open to bottom of second segment from top
2. SACRILIZATION/LUMBARIZATION				
narthex	burial no. 59	♂	17-25 years	fifth lumbar sacralized
courtyard	burial no. 100	♀	25-30 years	first and second sacral lumbars with intact spines and marked depression between
3. VERTEBRAL ODDITIES				
south of church	burial no. 105	♂	17-25 years	fourth lumbar lower articular facets crumpled and fifth's upper match
4. ANY OTHER				
narthex	burial no. 56	♀	33-45 years	left ulna styloid process missing
south of church	burial no. 102	♂	25-35 years	left radius distal facet 'double-faceted' but still very smooth

quently affected in clinical populations (Ortner and Putschar 1981). In archaeological samples, however, it is not uncommon to find the signs in smaller joints (Mays 1991a; 1991b). Osseous indicators of the disease are symptomatic of the deterioration of the cartilage between the joint articular surfaces, to such an extent that bone articulates with bone, in some cases producing a polished surface or eburnation. It may be extremely painful when it has progressed this far. The difference between modern and archaeological distribution of the condition is probably because the disease would be most troublesome and debilitating in the large joints, and therefore these are most frequently presented for attention, whereas the archaeological samples are possibly identifying cases which may never come to the attention of a modern clinician. The affected individuals would have felt some pain and lack of mobility of the joint. The female in burial no. 79 with severe osteoarthritis of the hip might have been a candidate for hip replacement today. The other cases varied in severity.

The majority of people in a modern population are affected by vertebral osteophytes by about 45 years of age (Bass 1987: 18-21), and there has been much debate as to the extent of stress-related occupational factors on this age-related phenomenon (Ortner and Putschar 1981). The relative frequencies of osteophytes in the different areas at Monte Gelato again reflected the age composition of the samples in the same way as osteoarthritis, but not quite so obviously (Table 41). This was probably because osteophytosis is a far more common condition and would affect a greater age-range of people. Females were more affected than males in every area except that to the south of the church. If the condition is related to physical stress, this could mean that the females were working harder manually than the males, relative to their physique and strength. The areas of the skeleton most affected were the vertebrae and foot bones. The condition of the vertebrae could be predicted, but that of the foot bones was more unexpected. Changes of this type are often attributed to frequent mobility over rough ground, as in the case of an agricultural worker. What is most interesting is that this distribution was also true for the burials in the church. Despite the fact that these graves are the most elaborate on the site, the evidence of the osteophytes would seem to indicate that at least some of those buried in the church were engaged in similar activities to those buried elsewhere.

The prevalence of intervertebral disc disease in the different areas of the site was much more similar to the rates for osteoarthritis (Table 41), and again probably age-dictated. Males and females were equally affected, suggesting that the variation between the sexes apparent for osteophytosis was genuine. The most obvious indication of this disease is erosion and deposition of bone on the body end plates of the vertebrae, as a result of degeneration of the disc. The sufferers would probably have experienced stiffening and lessening mobility of the joints.

Ossification of the ligamentum flavum again corresponded to the age compositon of the various areas. The thoracic vertebrae were mostly affected and some lumbar vertebrae. This is similar in most samples. This would have had no great effect on the living person.

The distribution of bony exostoses and entheses elsewhere in the body was also recorded. Various workers have tried to relate these changes to occupational stress (Saunders 1989). In this sample, hand and foot phalanges were widely affected in all the adult burial areas of the site, including the church (Table 42). This may mean active use of the hands and feet. The next most frequently involved

Table 41. Frequency of osteoarthritis (OA), osteophytes (OP), intervertebral disc disease (IVD) and ossification of ligamentum flavum (LF).

	OA					OP					IVD					LF				
	J	♂	♀	?	total	J	♂	♀	?	total	J	♂	♀	?	total	J	♂	♀	?	total
church	0	0	0	1	2.0%	0	1	3	3	17.1%	0	1	0	0	2.0%	0	0	1	0	2.0%
narthex					0	0	0	2	0	6.5%					0	0	0	1	0	3.2%
space between baptistery, ante-room and entrance					0	0	0	1	0	16.7%					0	0	0	0	0	0
area between entrance and road	0	0	1	0	2.00%	0	2	3	0	100%	0	1	1	0	40.0%	0	0	2	0	40.0%
courtyard	0	0	2	0	11.1%	0	2	4	1	38.9%	0	1	0	0	5.6%	0	2	0	1	16.7%
south of church	0	1	0	0	12.5%	0	1	1	0	25.0%	0	0	1	0	12.5%	0	1	1	0	25.0%

NOTES: The total for the church uses 41 as the total buried there rather than 51 as in Table 7 as the ten people from the ossuary have been excluded.
Locations most affected are:
OA – acetabulum and femoral head, lumbar vertebrae, cervical vertebrae, wrist and feet bones. OP – vertebrae and feet bones. IVD – mainly cervical and lumbar. LF – mostly thoracic, some lumbar.

Table 42. Entheses.

B1 B15	raised on phalange (only phal)
79 M112 sk. 8	fourth metatarsal, proximal hand phalange base, phal. flex, grade 2 on R and L ulnae, R first rib
2 C58	see OP sheet as very advanced
7 C23	L foot phalange (though not on tarsals) though R calcaneum superior facet rough and pitted
8 C46	fourth R metatarsal and metacarpal R and L calcaneum posterior and inferior and R and L talus; tibiae and fibulas proximal ends
18 B8 (1)	L humerus medial distal, R humerus deltoid, R radius
24 D107 (ossuary)	R femur ossified ligament half way down shaft
26 A28	finger phalanges (though note that the skeleton is slight and the feet are not robust)
65 A2	very marked linea aspera and L tibial insertions
78 M33	calcaneum
92 D18	hand phalanges
93 D5	phalanges; both lateral clavicles
94 D32	raised on hand phalanges
100 D63	R and L humeral lateral epicondyles
102 C29	both tibiae marked soleal lines and on inferior surface of clavicles

bone was the humerus, possibly suggesting strenuous physical activity of some sort. The majority of skeletons was robust and stocky, with well-marked muscle attachment sites. A small number was noticeably slender and slight. This included burials 63 and 65 from the narthex and burial no. 94 in the courtyard. Burial no. 63 was particularly interesting as it contained two individuals: a mature adult who was very small and slender, with no muscle markings; and a second adult of more average build, but with non-craggy feet bones (unlike the majority), and no raised flanges on the hand phalanges.

Trauma

The fractures present in the sample are described in Table 43. The most striking feature of the list is that all affect the ribs, and the majority were well healed (although some were slightly misaligned, and one may have had some infection). This suggests that the people frequently received blows of some sort to the trunk. Only adults were affected, but this included males and females equally, so, whatever the cause, both sexes were exposed to it. The good level of alignment does not mean that the rib cage was necessarily bound in some way, as the intact ribs would have braced the fractured ones. The low level of infection means either that the wounds did not penetrate the surface; or, that they were kept clean; or had occurred a long while before death and any infection had had a chance to clear. The most striking case was an elderly male buried next to the road (burial no. 78) whose entire rib cage was crushed. The ribs were fractured in a line near their necks, and on their shafts near to the sternal end. Somewhat surprisingly, the man had survived, and the ribs had healed well, although misaligned and with much ossification of the connecting soft tissue. The man's breathing must have been impaired to some extent by this unnatural rigidity of the rib cage, and he was extremely fortunate not to have sustained fatal internal injuries to organs such as his spleen.

The only other type of trauma in this sample was Schmorl's nodes. Schmorl's nodes are interpreted as the result of herniation of the intervertebral disc into the end plate of the vertebral body due to overlifting by a young person. At Monte Gelato the highest prevalence of this condition was in the burials in the courtyard, where over a fifth of the sample was affected (Table 43). There was one case from the church and one from the narthex. The most commonly affected vertebrae were the lower thoracic and the lumbar, which is usual as these bear the most weight.

Table 43. Trauma.

area	burial	sex	age	location	frequency of individuals with fracture
FRACTURES					
church	18	♂	22-35	rib band - healed well	2/51 – 3.9%
church	24	?	adult	rib neck - healed, misaligned	
narthex	56	♀	33-45	ribs both sides, bony spurs	1/31 – 3.2%
area between entrance and road	78	♂	adult (elderly)	crushed rib cage, healed but misaligned and massive ossification of connecting soft tissue	1/5 – 20.0%
courtyard	93	♀	33-45	2nd and 3rd R ribs and a L rib well–healed though possibly some infection	1/18 – 5.6%
SCHMORL'S NODES					
church				T5 inferior surface	1/51 – 2.0%
narthex				inferior surface L1 or 2	1/31 – 3.2%
courtyard				lower thor.; lumbar	4/18 – 22.2%

Table 45. Infant age estimation.

individual	epiphyseal union	diaphysis length	dental
8 B 8 (III)	10-15	> 5	12 yrs ± 30 mths
26 A4	< 7	2-3	-
27 D43	1-3	1.5-2.5	18 yrs ± 6 mths
28 D15	> 1	1-1.5	1 yr - 18 mths
29 D31	1-5	2.5-3.5	3 yrs ± 12 mths
32 D224	< 5	3.5-5.5	4 - 5
33 D226	tiny	0.5-1	6-9 mths ± 3 mths
34 D222	0-5	2.5-3.5	3 yrs ± 12 mths
37 D229	5-10	c. 9	6-10
37 D229 (II)	0-5	4-5	-
37 D229 (I)	0-5	3-4	3-4
38 D54	0-5	0-0.5	0 ± 2 mths
40 D214A	near birth	newborn-0.5	-
40 D214B	2.5-4.5	0-5	-
40 D214C	0-5	1.5-2.5	-
41 D132	0-5	2.5-3.5	3 yrs ± 12 mths
43 D135	c 7	6-10	7 yrs ± 2 yrs (* small compared to dental and fusion)
46 D282	0	foetal-newborn (nearest to newborn)	-
47 D212	0-5	3.5-4.5	3-4
53 D293	5-10	6-8	6-10
57 D95 I	7-15	c. 6.5	6.5-7.5
57 D95 II	3-7	3.5-4	4 yrs ± 12 mths
60 A13	> 7	-	7 yrs ± 24 mths
66 A21	< 10	-	8 yrs ± 2 yrs
68 D284	c. 5	1.5-2.5	1.5-2.5
72 D296a	c. 5	-	4-8
76 M70	1.5-2.5	1-5	2 yrs ± 8 mths
77 M72	c. 1	0.5-1.5	9 mths ± 3 mths
87 E99	0-3	0.5-1.5	-
88 H28	0-5	4-5	-
95 D34	< 3	0	-
97 D78	3-8	4-5	5 yrs ± 16 mths
105 B24 (III)	< 3	c. 2.5	2-4

Table 46. Pitting or infection.

individual	area	sex	age	
18 B(1)	church	♂	25-35	L 1st metatarsal head; R 1st metatarsal and proximal phalange on plantar surfaces; 2nd unaffected; 5th base slightly pitted; pitting over L calcaneum, talus and navicular, cuboid and 1st cuneiform
54 D291	narthex	♂	17-25	possible infection of proximal 1st phalange of foot; possible trauma or infection as very pitted and spicules of bone; possibly just very strong flex
94 D32	courtyard	♀	45-50	raised roughening and pitting on femur heads

female and child both with very poor dentitions. Given the rarity of caries in children in this sample, it is reasonable to assume that a child with severe caries, in a burial with an adult with exceptionally bad dental health, was probably related to that adult. They could have had weak enamel or an inherited metabolic disorder. Burial no. 79 contained a female and a younger male. These two shared so many unusual characteristics that they were almost definitely related. Both had an oddly shaped line of occlusion; occlusal caries when these were the least common type of caries in the sample; a palatal torus each – a quite unusual trait in any case, and the only two found in this sample; the same pattern with regard to the parietal foramen; and similar skulls. These two cases would clearly seem to indicate that members of families were being buried together in the same grave. Likewise, burials 26 and 60 each contained an adult with very similar teeth of very odd appearance, being exceptionally short rooted and stumpy. These were the only two cases in the sample, and so similar as to suggest some relationship. In addition, the two individuals had very slight and slender post-cranial skeletons when virtually all other skeletons recovered from the site were fairly stocky and robust. It therefore seems quite probable that these two were related in some way. This was interesting, as burial no. 26 was in the church and burial no. 60 in the narthex. If the two were related, this means related burials were taking place both in the same grave and separated in different parts of the site.

Age and sex
Apart from the clustering of infant graves in the baptistery, very little patterning was apparent when age and sex data were added to the site plan.

Indices
The cranial index could be calculated for very few individuals. When plotted on the site plan, these few data produced no pattern at all.

The cnemic index was similarly unhelpful. The meric index, however, revealed a cluster of extremely high values of the index in the area south of the church in burials 102, 103 and 105.

Non-metric traits
The only traits of all those recorded for the skull and the post crania (Table 50) that produced any clustering were the supraorbital foramen and parietal foramen. These are fairly common traits and so, perhaps, should not be accorded too much weight. However, there were few cases as a whole at the site, and those that did occur appear to be in clusters, possibly suggesting related burials. Burials 54, 57, 60 and 79 all had supraorbital foramen and were all in close proximity, although there were other graves between them. There was also a cluster of infants very close together in the baptistery with this type of foramen: burials 32, 33 and 41 and, slightly further away, burial no. 29. Two of the adjacent graves with high meric indices, 102 and 103, also had parietal foramen in common.

Dental non-metric traits
The dental traits are particularly interesting as they are thought to be more strongly genetically controlled than skeletal traits, and there were two unusual characteristics present here. This would suggest possible family relationships even though the burials presenting them were scat-

Table 47. Osteochondritis dissecans.

individual	area	sex	age		
42 D140	baptistery	indet.	adult	L foot proximal 1st phalange – centre of base diameter 3 x 1.5 mm	4.2%
26 A28	church	♀	25-35	L and R 1st proximal phalange foot	2.0%
54 D291	narthex	♂	17-25	R glenoid fossa	
60 A34	narthex	♀	17-35	L glenoid fossa, both femoral medial condyles; tibia medial condyle; phals 6/20 had pits in head, 1/20 in head and base, 1/20 in base; very gracile hands and skeleton	6.5%
100 D63		♀	25-30	R glenoid fossa 3 x 1.5 mm	5.6%

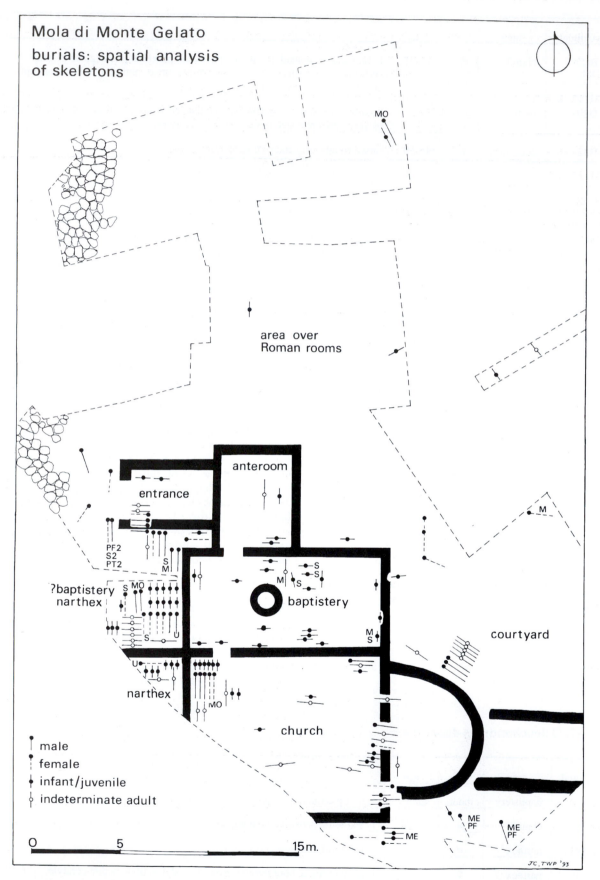

Fig. 116. Distribution of skeletons by age and sex. The letters refer as follows: M, metopic; ME, meric index; MO, oddly formed molar; PF, parietal foramen; PT, palatal torus; S, supraorbital foramen; U, unerupted lateral incisors. *(TWP)*

Table 48. Miscellaneous pathology and observations.

42 D140	patellae, hands and feet and bits of rib only surviving – precisely bits missed in excavation – were graves being emptied on purpose
44 D86	infant has foramen in form of slit *c*. 3 mm above auditory meatus
79 M112 sk. 8 & 9	very similar wear patterns except 8 slightly older probably due to similar cusp patts; think related – anterior teeth have raised occlusal line, they have same parietal foramen pattern, skull shape, cusp form similar, sagittal suture in 9 depressed along length, 8 depressed rear 2/3
79 M112 sk. 9	18 erupted distally
79 M112 sk. 8	elderly female – possible osteoporosis of proximal humeri and femurs – has OA as well
26 A 28	green stain all around phalange probably of L4th metacarpal – matches colour of stain on thoracic vertebra – not on base or head of phalange – could be from a ring finger
27 D43	frontal bone reaches a point where metopic suture would have been on this 2 yr old
43 D135	noted odd found no hypoplasia when such severe cribra orbitalia and cribra femoralis; this applied generally not just to this one
	N.B. lower arm bones consistently gave age 1 yr lower than all other estimates
53 D293	*c*. 8 yrs yet no sagittal suture and no sign of it; bregma asymetric towards left but lambda central; ectocranially double ridge running along where sagittal suture should be
54 D291	thoracic spines twisted to L; probably occurred am as C 3-7 more developed on L and twisted; slightly narrowed lumbar spine
55 D92	omitted as the four adults and five infants were too jumbled to catalogue; no non metric to link elsewhere
59 X D168	5th L vertebra sacralized fully at back, partially on front
60 A34	L superior articular facet of atlas trying to split into double; very very slight ossification of ligamentum flavum, spreading articular facets and odontoid peg – but on whole far healthier spine than majority, i.e. not labourer??
63 A12	adult > 15; very small and slender and no muscle markings adult > 18 more average build but feet not craggy like majority and hand phals no raised flanges
65 A2	indivdual 1 very marked linea aspera and muscle insertion on back L tibia and bones robust individual 2 very slender, even toes not gnarled
94 D32	despite raised finger flanges rest of skeleton quite dainty and no OA
95 D34	could this be twins stillborn? as two infants of very similar appearance – indeed practically indistinguishable, foetal to newborn; also rib and long bone fragment of an adult
99 B4	double L occipital condyle; quite slight for a ♂
100 D63	very bent sacrum – this is sometimes attributed to rickets although this is debatable; foramen of Huschke both sides; large bony 'polyp' in nasal cavity 38 mm AP, 12 mm across and 25 mm top to bottom; smooth surface with striations, flat bottomed with a few pits; has pushed nasal bones to side (and parts of ethmoid); hard up against maxillary bone at side and joining into bone at top of cavity; see plate; slight depression at lambda: L arm markedly shorter than R though L does not appear wilted in any way just shorter; all ribs oddly bowed – could possibly be rickets like sacrum; 1st two bodies of sacrum lumbarized with intact spines and marked depression in artic surf between the two; all bones have bright pink hue, very unusual, only skeleton like this at Monte Gelato
103 C60	very noticeably healthy – even no osteophytes etc. on spine odd; that mandible affected with hypoplasia yet maxilla not, yet the two definitely fit together

Table 49. Frequency of multiple burials per area.

area	no. of multiple burials	total burials	empty burials	total with bones	multiples as % of those with bones
church	10*	26	4	22	45.5
baptistery	2¶	27	8	19	10.5
narthex/open ground	9	13	1	12	75.0
ante-room north of baptistery	0	5	1	4	0
space between baptistery, ante-room and entrance	2	3	1	2	100.0
entrance to ante-room	1	3	0	3	33.3
area between entrance and paved road	1	4	0	4	25.0
over Roman rooms to north of church complex	poss. 1§	5	3	2	33.3
courtyard	2	15	4	11	18.2
south of church	1	6	1	5	20.0
total	29	107	23	84	

*Burial 8
¶ Burial 53 omitted as percentage of bones present suggests one principal body and scraps of others not true multiple burial – i.e. only those with similar percentages of bone per individual are include
§ L172 possibly a single adult burial but possibly including an infant

tered across the site. Burial no. 26 in the church and burial no. 58 in the narthex had unerupted lateral incisors. Burials 24, 59 and 85 had an unusual molar form; elongated and narrowed as though stretched out. These three burials came from the church, the narthex and the area over the Roman rooms respectively.

SUMMARY

There were 107 relatively intact burials which provided parts of 159 skeletons. The great majority of these burials belongs to the period between c. AD 800 and 1100. There were also 26 individuals from disturbed, unphased burials, and at least 58 individuals represented by disarticulated bone. The analysis reported here is restricted to the undisturbed, phased burials. The sample has been considered in isolation because of the lack of comparative material.

The bone tended to be in poor condition and often only a small proportion of the skeleton survived. Thus, 40.4 per cent of bone was classed as poor and only 25.4 per cent as good. 35.1 per cent of skeletons were less than ten per cent complete and 69.5 per cent had less than 50 per cent of the skeleton. The condition varied between areas; however, the bones from the baptistery and the area between the entrance and the road were in relatively good condition.

Of the 157 individuals from relatively intact burials, 83 were adults, 23 juvenile and 51 infants; infants are classed as nought to five years, and juveniles as six to fifteen years. Of the adults, 25 were male, 23 female and 35 of indeterminate sex. The sex ratio of male to female was therefore 1.09:1, and this equality was true of all areas of the site where adults were not in the minority. This suggests that neither sex was being reared to adulthood at the expense of the other sex, and that males and females were being treated equally in death. This includes the interior of the church. However, it must be remembered that this was treatment in death, and the idea of an egalitarian society in life cannot necessarily be extrapolated from this evidence. A woman may be buried in a way dictated by the wealth of her partner, rather than in a style reflecting her own status.

There was much more differentiation of burials across the site when age was considered rather than sex. Of those in the baptistery, 79.2 per cent were dead by five years of age and 91.7 per cent by fifteen (there was one adult burial in the baptistery). There was a similar composition in the ante-room, and in the area over the Roman rooms (though less marked). Here, however, the sample size was very small. The baptistery appears to have been reserved for infant burials, and it may be that this area held those individuals who had died before baptism.

The infant deaths followed a tripartite pattern, with 23.9 per cent of deaths in those aged less than 25 years occurring before one year and 70.4 per cent before five years. The peak of deaths before one year was probably due to the immediate postnatal risk of infection or complications. A second lesser peak, between two and a half and three and a half years, may reflect a late age for weaning, and the nutritional stress that weaning could cause if the diet available was unsuitable. The theory of late

Table 50. Cranial non metric.

individual	metopic	coronal	sagittal	lamboid	sphenoid	other	pariet for	sup orb
79 M112 sk. 9	0	✓	✓	✓		temporal	symmetrical; left stronger; 1 each	symmetrical,1 each
79 M112 sk. 8	0	✓	✓	✓			both, left slightly stronger	very slight both sides
18 B8 (1)		✓						
24 D107 ossuary	1 adult	also very misshapen molar – very similar to one found in D168 – also D168 similar folds in canine as loose canine in D107						
29 D31	✓							infant
32 D224				✓				infant
33 D226	½ metop							infant
41 D132	✓							infant
54 D289	✓	0	0	0		possibly an inca	0	R and L
57 D95 11				✓				infant
59 D168	0	none						
60 A34	0	✓	0	✓				R
72 D296 (1)	0			✓				
81 M16				✓				
100 D63	✓	✓		✓				
102 C29	0	✓ multiple on lateral ⅓s	0	✓ multiple on lower ½s		1 right squamous	1 each side	
103 C60	0	0	0	0		0	1 each side	9

individual	mylo hyoid groove	calc doub/abs	talus double	atlas pb lb hum SA	stern A
79 M112 sk. 9	both sides				
79 M112 sk. 8	both sides				
2 C58		R	R (triple)		
7 C23	L				
8 C48			L		
18 B8 (1)		both			
18 B22 (1)	both				
54 D291	both			L atlas	
56 D91 (3)	both				
59 D168		both			
72 D296 (1)		both		L atlas R db fac	
78 M33		both			
80 M81					✓
81 M16	both				
92 D18	both				
93 D5		R			
99 B4				✓ lat br	
99 B4A		R			
100 D63		R, L almost		atlas db fac	both pats very slight vastus
102 C29	both				
103 C60	both				
104 B24 (1)		both			
105 B24 (11)		both		Atlas db fac both/SA both	very slight vastus notch both sides

KEY TO TRAITS: parietal for – parietal foramen; sup orb – supra orbital foramen; calc doub/abs – calcaneus facet double or absent; talus double – talus facet double; atlas pb lb – atlas posterior bridge or lateral bridge; hum SA – humerus septal aperture; stern A – sternal aperture lat br – lateral bridge; db fac – double facet; pats – patellae

weaning was to some extent supported by evidence of possible nutritional hardship amongst the adult females. There would also be an increased risk of infection from contaminated feeding utensils.

There was also a slight increase in deaths around twelve to thirteen years. A possible explanation is that the onset of puberty, and the stresses imposed by this on the body, were sufficient to tip the balance between life and death. This would suggest that conditions were very arduous indeed. Although tenuous, this argument is supported, to some extent, by the evidence for nutritional deficiencies.

Amongst the adults, there was an even split between the sexes in all age groups, suggesting that death by childbirth did not have a great effect on the sample.

In terms of physique, there was a lack of length of the lower arm in infants compared with the rest of the long-bone lengths (although this was caught up by adulthood). This may be a local phenomenon; future studies will clarify this. There was pronounced dimorphism in stature, where there was no overlap between male and female ranges. The male range was 1.66-1.82 m (the tallest man was unusually tall for this site). The female range was 1.55-1.6 m. The male range was similar to that of modern males, where the average is about 1.74 m. The females from all areas of the site fell well below the modern female average of 1.66 m. This may be due to nutritional hardship, as this can produce stunting in a group. As females are particularly susceptible to deficiencies because of the direction of so much of their energy into childbirth, they may be more prone to stunting and therefore pronounced stunting results.

Occasionally, an area of a particular site may contain individuals who are all at or close to the maximum stature within the stature range for the site; in conjunction with other evidence, this may indicate burials of elevated status. There was no such evidence at Monte Gelato.

The most common skull shape was long and narrow; but there were so few that could be assessed that this is probably not reliable. Most femurs were eumeric, meaning that they were rounded rather than flattened: 76.2 per cent of right femurs and 81.3 per cent of left were in this category of the index. The tendency for rounding rather than flattening was even more pronounced in the tibiae, where 94.1 per cent of right and 89.5 per cent of left tibiae were eurycnemic. Whatever the cause of this phenomenon, it was more constant in the tibia than the femur, as there were more differing values of the meric index between sides in the femur than there were for the cnemic index in the tibia.

There was virtually no sidedness between the arms and even less difference in size between the right and left leg. This could mean that the people were not favouring either limb over the other in everyday activities.

Parts of the skeleton were dimorphic in the same way as stature. The most dimorphic measurements were those of the lower canine and the femur, and seemed so distinct that there was probably more than a simple genetic cause. The most likely candidate would be nutritional deficiencies.

Only three children suffered from caries. One of these was probably related to the female with which it was buried, as she had exceptionally bad dental health. The most common type of caries amongst the children was interproximal. Occlusal caries were rare because of the wear, even on young dentitions, at this site. As only three children were affected, it is suggested that in this sample caries attack was either a disease of ageing, rather than a result of diet, or a genetic characteristic of the sample. This may indicate that there were many elderly people amongst the burials that ageing techniques are, at present, incapable of identifying.

Amongst the adults, 44 per cent of caries were cervical and 26 per cent interproximal (some of which would be cervical). Occlusal caries were rare. Only twelve per cent were gross, suggesting that caries was not a severe problem. This is confirmed by the low number of abcesses, only six throughout the sample. It suggests that the diet was generally a healthy one. However, natural sugars, combined with poor hygiene, would cause the cervical caries, and some proportion of soft, pulpy food would cause attack in the interproximal area.

Ante-mortem loss of teeth was generally more severe in the mandibles than in the maxilliae. This followed the pattern of periodontal disease, rather than that of the caries, again suggesting that caries was not a major problem in this sample. Similarly, there were almost twice as many cases of severe calculus deposits in the mandibles than the maxilliae. This would also correspond with the prevalence of periodontal disease, given the interrelationship of these two conditions. A third of those individuals suffering from periodontal disease were severe cases. This indicates that this was a major problem for the population and the principal reason for tooth-loss, rather than caries. This would also support the suggestion that a substantial proportion of the sample was elderly, as this is very much a disease which progresses with age. However, a substantial proportion was unaffected. As this is not attributable to good hygiene (as the caries prevalence demonstrates), there must have been a good, textured diet, which would require mastication and would thus stimulate the gums and keep them healthy. Individuals buried in the church appeared to suffer more heavily from both caries, periodontal disease and alveolar recession (another age-related condition), suggesting, perhaps, that there was a greater proportion of elderly people buried here than in other areas.

Hypoplasia on the teeth showed that approximately a quarter of the adults had probably undergone bouts of serious childhood illness.

Along with dental disease, degenerative changes to the skeleton were the most common pathology. There were signs of osteoarthritis which were largely age-related. Osteophytes on the vertebrae and elsewhere were more widespread, but still followed the ageing pattern to some extent. Females were more affected by osteophytes than males. If it is accepted that their development may be partly stress-related, this could suggest that the females were working physically harder than the males, relative to their physique and strength. The vertebrae and foot bones were most affected. The changes to the feet may indicate repetitive mobility over rough ground. Findings were similar for all parts of the site, suggesting that there was no overall division of physical labour between the sexes, nor any indication of different status from one area to another.

The great majority of skeletons were of stocky, robust individuals, with well-marked muscle insertions particularly on the humerus and hands. This may be the result of hard, physical work. Only three skeletons were slender or slight, two in the narthex and one in the courtyard.

All fractures present involved the ribs, and only adults were affected. It is impossible to say whether these presumed blows to the torso were the result of accidents or of violence. However, the prevalence was equal between males and females, and there was no evidence for parry fractures, the most common fracture received in violence. Accidental cause seems, therefore, most likely. Schmorl's nodes, perhaps indicative of carrying heavy loads from an early age, were most common in skeletons found in the courtyard.

Signs of nutritional deficiency were most apparent in infants, as could be predicted because of the difficulties associated with weaning and with childhood illness. Very few teenagers, the other group which could be expected to present cribra orbitalia, exhibited signs of nutritional deficiency, although there was a small peak in deaths around this age. The lack of stunting in small children suggests that an effort was made to provide for children; this, however, may not have extended past puberty, since there were a number of teenager deaths. Moreover, the surviving females were stunted compared to the males, due to the additional stress of childbearing.

Nearly all cases of infection involved the feet, again pointing to frequent walking over rough ground. There were five cases of osteochondritis dissecans, which would, however, have had little effect on the individual.

The analysis of non-metric dental and skeletal traits, and of age, sex and physical characteristics, demonstrates that some individuals may have been related. Some were buried in the same grave or in graves in close proximity, but others were found in quite different parts of the cemetery.

INTERPRETATION

The people buried at Monte Gelato were generally robust and physically active, probably from an early age. The role of the site as an early medieval farm is borne out by the higher prevalence of infection and degenerative changes to the feet than any other part of the skeleton, excluding the vertebrae. Although not exclusively pointing to this same conclusion, the restriction of traumatic injury to the ribs would support a physical activity where blows to the torso would be received frequently.

It was probably a hard life, principally because of poor or limited diet and sickness. Almost a quarter of adults presented signs of having suffered severe bouts of disease in childhood. Many infants died at what could be a late weaning age, around two and a half to three and a half years, and another batch died at around the start of puberty. If this second batch was not due to some disease, which targeted this age group, and they did die solely from inadequate nutrition, conditions must have been very hard indeed. Those females who did survive to adulthood were of reduced stature compared to the males, probably because of the additional demands imposed by childbirth. If the suggestion of late weaning is correct, it suggests that they were attempting to prolong the gap between children as long as possible.

In osteological terms, it seems to have been an egalitarian society, for no groups of skeletons were found with characteristics that could be interpreted as indicative of higher status. Practically all the skeletons had a similar physique, suggesting that everybody had to work physically for a living. The same was true between the sexes; males and females were equally robust, and suffered similar degenerative disease. Both therefore presumably participated in the physical work. Interestingly, the 'high-status' graves contained both males and females. This may suggest that 'higher status' was enjoyed equally by men and women. Certainly, both sexes survived equally into adulthood, indicating that neither sex was reared at the expense of the other.

Any division that there was in burial organization seems to have been dictated more by the age of the person than by differing lifestyles or sex. The baptistery was reserved almost exclusively for the burial of young children and, to some extent, this was also true of the ante-room next door. The other areas were more mixed, but there was a slight hint, from the dental evidence, that the church may have held a greater proportion of older people than other areas. Periodontal disease, a disease of advancing age, was more of a problem than caries, and the caries themselves appear to have required a long onset, perhaps confirming that a large proportion of the sample was elderly.

There was also a distinction in burial practice between the baptistery and the rest of the site, with the majority of infant burials in the baptistery being single interments, whilst elsewhere children were buried together or with adults. It seems most likely that children who qualified for burial in the baptistery were viewed or treated differently for some reason. It has been suggested elsewhere that the reason may be that they died before being baptized. Elsewhere, burial seems to have quite often been in family groups. There also appears to have been an element of interrelation across the site which would not be altogether unexpected in a small, isolated community such as Monte Gelato probably was.

All the interpretation advanced here must be viewed with considerable caution as the sample was very fragmentary, and sample size was often very small, once spatial or other divisions were taken into account. The suggestions that are made are those that best fit the evidence; but the evidence itself is not particularly strong in some aspects. When more data for Italian sites become available, it may be possible to confirm or refute some of these ideas.

Acknowledgements
I am very grateful to Dr Tony Waldron for his comments on this paper, and to Mrs Kate Down for her painstaking work in organizing the tables.

EXCAVATIONS AT CASTELLACCIO, 1990, by David Wilkinson

THE SITE

Castellaccio (literally 'nasty castle') lies some 250 m to the southeast of the main excavation area, occupying a now heavily-wooded bluff on the west side of the river Treia (Figs 4 and 117). The present-day tree cover means that all sense is lost of what must have once been a series of commanding views over the mill, the ecclesiastical complex and the surrounding countryside. On top of the bluff, a sub-triangular area of *c.* 0.25 ha is defined to the west and northwest by a wide rock-cut ditch, with traces of a curtain wall on its inner edge. The ground beyond the ditch remains relatively flat. In contrast, the ditch appears as little more than a narrow terrace to the south, where the ground falls away quite sharply, and is apparently absent from the very steep and rocky eastern side. It is difficult to define any entrances precisely, though one may have existed at the northern corner of the enclosure. There is a gap through the rock terraces at this point, but the slope here is very steep, and would have required steps or other structures to create a usable route. Otherwise, the most prominent feature of

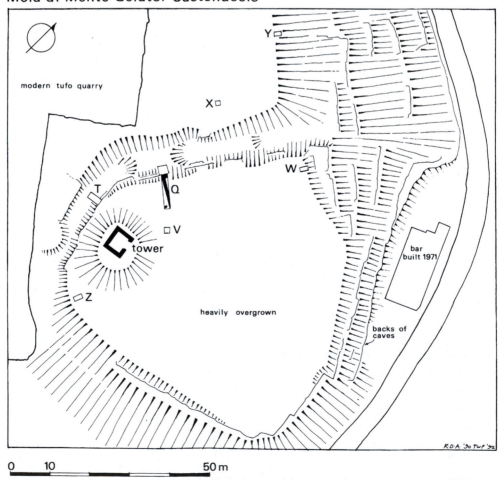

Fig. 117. Plan of the trenches at Castellaccio. *(RDA/TWP)*

APPENDIX: SKELETAL COMPONENTS

For key, see page 180

SKELETAL COMPONENTS

	church	baptistery	narthex	ante-room	space	entrance	area between entrance and road	over Roman rooms	courtyard	south of church	total
1	50	23	28	3	6	8	5	3	18	8	152
2	30	19	14	1	6	5	5	2	9	7	98
3	11	17	15	1	4	8	4	2	8	6	76
4	188	225	161	14	33	94	85	23	115	125	1052
5	10	74	38	1	7	14	22	5	44	19	264
6	98	120	81	12	13	15	32	1	83	52	507
7	46	38	39	5	5	6	15	0	40	20	214
8	8	7	8	0	2	2	3	0	6	5	41
9	0	1	0	0	0	0	0	0	0	1	2
10	10	14	8	1	2	6	2	1	8	4	56
11	11	16	6	1	2	2	3	2	7	3	53
12	6	16	13	1	2	5	2	1	7	4	57
13	12	17	13	1	2	3	3	1	8	5	65
14	18	18	13	1	2	13	3	2	8	8	86
15	16	17	11	1	4	4	3	0	9	5	70
16	11	15	11	1	2	8	4	1	10	6	69
17	12	10	12	1	3	6	3	1	11	5	64
18	15	14	13	1	3	5	4	2	10	5	72
19	13	11	10	1	2	4	3	1	13	7	65
20	7	5	5	0	2	1	1	2	19	11	53
21	12	5	3	0	0	0	2	2	11	10	45
22	44	81	25	9	5	12	6	3	37	15	237
23	32	11	12	0	5	7	10	2	16	13	108
24	62	87	34	13	13	38	21	0	88	42	398
25	7	0	0	0	0	0	0	7	0	0	14
26	13	17	8	1	4	2	4	1	10	6	66
27	13	17	12	1	1	7	3	1	9	6	70
28	26	17	17	1	5	9	3	1	10	7	96
29	25	16	12	1	6	7	3	2	12	7	91
30	4	1	1	0	1	0	1	1	4	2	15
31	6	2	1	0	0	0	0	1	4	2	16
32	21	17	11	2	8	5	3	1	8	5	81
33	17	14	8	1	6	9	3	1	6	6	71
34	14	9	6	1	5	6	3	1	8	6	59
35	14	11	6	1	2	5	2	1	8	5	55
36	41	16	5	1	3	9	11	1	29	24	140
37	38	14	4	1	2	7	11	1	28	25	131
38	41	49	26	9	8	19	10	0	39	17	218
39	37	10	17	0	3	1	13	0	20	24	125
40	40	21	10	9	1	15	15	0	43	35	189
41	3	5	2	0	0	0	2	0	7	2	21
42	74	128	115	11	9	40	29	7	83	34	530
43	63	96	21	11	8	29	30	5	67	40	370
44	6	5	3	0	1	1	3	0	5	2	26

PREDICTED NUMBERS OF EACH SKELETAL ELEMENT

	church	baptistery	narthex	ante-room	space	entrance	area between entrance and road	over Roman rooms	courtyard	south of church	total
1	50	23	28	3	6	8	5	3	18	8	152
2	50	23	28	3	6	8	5	3	18	8	152
3	50	23	28	3	6	8	5	3	18	8	152
4	/	/	/	/	/	/	/	/	/	/	/
5	350	161	175	21	42	56	35	21	126	56	1064
6	600	276	336	36	72	96	60	36	216	96	1824
7	250	115	140	15	30	40	25	15	90	40	760
8	50	23	28	3	6	8	5	3	18	8	152
9	50	23	28	3	6	8	5	3	18	8	152
10	50	23	28	3	6	8	5	3	18	8	152
11	50	23	28	3	6	8	5	3	18	8	152
12	50	23	28	3	6	8	5	3	18	8	152
14	50	23	28	3	6	8	5	3	18	8	152
15	50	23	28	3	6	8	5	3	18	8	152
16	50	23	28	3	6	8	5	3	18	8	152
17	50	23	28	3	6	8	5	3	18	8	152
18	50	23	28	3	6	8	5	3	18	8	152
19	50	23	28	3	6	8	5	3	18	8	152
20	400	184	224	24	48	64	40	24	144	64	1216
21	400	184	224	24	48	64	40	24	144	64	1216
22	250	115	140	15	30	40	25	15	90	40	760
23	250	115	140	15	30	40	25	15	90	40	760
24	1400	644	784	84	168	224	140	84	504	224	4256
25	1400	644	784	84	168	224	140	84	504	224	4256
26	50	23	28	3	6	8	5	3	18	8	152
27	50	23	28	3	6	8	5	3	18	8	152
28	50	23	28	3	6	8	5	3	18	8	152
29	50	23	28	3	6	8	5	3	18	8	152
30	50	23	28	3	6	8	5	3	18	8	152
31	50	23	28	3	6	8	5	3	18	8	152
32	50	23	28	3	6	8	5	3	18	8	152
33	50	23	28	3	6	8	5	3	18	8	152
34	50	23	28	3	6	8	5	3	18	8	152
35	50	23	28	3	6	8	5	3	18	8	152
36	350	161	196	21	42	56	35	21	126	56	1064
37	350	161	196	21	42	56	35	21	126	56	1064
38	250	115	140	15	30	40	25	15	90	40	760
39	250	115	140	15	30	40	25	15	90	40	760
40	1400	644	784	84	128	224	140	84	504	224	4256
41	1400	644	784	84	128	224	140	84	504	224	4256
42	600	276	336	36	72	96	60	36	216	96	1824
43	600	276	336	36	72	96	60	36	216	96	1824
44	50	23	28	3	6	8	5	3	18	8	152

COMPONENTS PRESENT AS PERCENTAGE OF PREDICTED NUMBERS

	church	baptistery	nrthex	ante-room	space	entrance	area between entrance and road	over Roman rooms	courtyard	south of church	total
1	/	/	/	/	/	/	/	/	/	/	/
2	60.0	82.6	50.0	33.3	100	62.5	100	66.7	50.0	87.5	64.5
3	22.0	73.9	53.6	33.3	66.7	100	80.0	66.7	44.4	75.0	50.0
4	/	/	/	/	/	/	/	/	/	/	/
5	11.4	46.0	21.7	4.8	16.7	25.0	62.9	23.8	34.9	33.9	24.8
6	16.3	43.5	24.1	33.3	18.1	15.6	53.3	2.8	38.4	54.2	27.8
7	18.4	33.0	27.9	33.3	16.7	15.0	60.0	0	44.4	50.0	28.2
8	16.0	30.4	28.6	0	33.3	25.0	60.0	0	33.3	62.5	27.0
9	0	4.3	0	0	0	0	0	0	0	12.5	1.3
10	20.0	60.9	28.6	33.3	33.3	75.0	40.0	33.3	44.4	50.0	36.8
11	22.0	69.6	21.4	33.3	33.3	25.0	60.0	66.7	38.9	37.5	34.9
12	12.0	69.6	46.4	33.3	33.3	62.5	40.0	33.3	38.9	50.0	37.3
13	24.0	73.9	46.4	33.3	33.3	37.5	60.0	33.3	44.4	62.5	42.8
14	36.0	78.3	46.4	33.3	33.3	162.5	60.0	66.7	44.4	100	56.6
15	32.0	73.9	39.3	33.3	66.7	50.0	60.0	0	50.0	62.5	46.1
16	22.0	65.2	39.3	33.3	33.3	100	80.0	33.3	55.6	75.0	45.4
17	24.0	43.5	42.9	33.3	50.0	75.0	60.0	33.3	61.1	62.5	42.1
18	30.0	60.9	46.4	33.3	50.0	62.5	80.0	66.7	55.6	62.5	47.4
19	26.0	47.8	35.7	33.3	66.7	50.0	60.0	33.3	72.2	87.5	42.8
20	1.7	2.7	2.2	0	4.2	1.6	2.5	8.3	13.2	17.2	4.4
21	3.0	2.7	1.3	0	0	0	5.0	8/3	7.6	15.6	3.7
22	17.6	70.4	17.9	60.0	16.7	30.0	24.0	20.0	41.1	37.5	31.2
23	12.8	9.6	8.6	0	16.7	17.5	40.0	13.3	17.8	32.5	14.2
24	4.9	13.5	4.3	15.5	7.7	17.0	15.0	0	17.5	18.8	9.4
25	/	/	/	/	/	/	/	/	/	/	/
26	26.0	73.9	28.6	33.3	66.7	25.0	80.0	33.3	55.6	75.0	43.4
27	26.0	73.9	42.9	33.3	16.7	87.5	60.0	33.3	50.0	75.0	46.1
28	52.0	73.9	60.7	33.3	83.3	112.5	60.0	33.3	55.6	87.5	63.2
29	50.0	69.6	42.9	33.3	100	87.5	60.0	66.7	66.7	87.5	59.9
30	8.0	4.3	3.6	0	16.7	0	20.0	33.3	22.2	25.0	9.9
31	12.0	8.7	3.6	0	0	0	0	33.3	22.2	25.0	10.5
32	42.0	73.9	39.3	66.7	133.3	62.5	60.0	33.3	44.4	62.5	53.3
33	34.0	60.9	28.6	33.3	100	112.5	60.0	33.3	33.3	75.0	46.7
34	28.0	39.1	21.4	33.3	83.3	75.0	60.0	33.3	44.4	75.0	38.8
35	28.0	47.8	21.4	33.3	33.3	62.5	40.0	33.3	44.4	62.5	36.2
36	11.7	9.9	2.6	4.8	7.1	16.1	31.4	4.8	23.0	42.9	13.2
37	10.9	8.7	2.0	4.8	4.8	12.5	31.4	4.8	22.2	44.6	12.3
38	16.4	42.6	18.6	60.0	26.7	47.5	40.0	0	43.3	42.5	28.7
39	14.8	8.7	12.1	0	10.0	2.5	52.0	0	22.2	60.0	16.4
40	3.1	4.0	1.5	10.7	0.6	6.7	12.1	0	9.9	16.5	4.9
41	/	/	/	/	/	/	/	/	/	/	/
42	12.3	46.4	34.2	30.6	12.5	41.7	48.3	19.4	38.4	35.4	29.1
43	10.5	34.8	6.3	30.6	11.1	30.2	50.0	13.9	31.0	41.7	20.3
44	12.0	21.7	10.7	0	16.7	12.5	60.0	0	27.8	25.0	17.1

SKELETAL COMPONENTS PRESENT

CHURCH

burial	context	1	2	3	4	5	6	7	8	9	10	11	12	13	14	15	16	17	18	19	20	21	22
1	B15	1																					22
2	C57	1																		1			
	C58	1				1																	
3	C2	2					1				1						1		1				2
	C25	2			1																		
4	B53	1							1						1								
5	C42	2										1									1		
6	C47	1																					
7	C23	1	1	1	14		6	5											1	1			
8	C46	3	3	1	6		1	1								1		1	1				1
9	C32	1				1							1		1								3
10	B21	no bones																					
11	B32(B49)	2	2	1	1							1			1								
12	B16	stone context					6					1											
13	B29	no bones																					
14	B34	1																					
15	B42	1	1																				
16	B66	1	1																1				
17	B60	1	1																				
18	B8	3	3		21	4	12	5	1		1	1	1	2	1	2	1	1	1	2	3	3	6
	B22	3	3	2	11		3											2					2
19	?																	1					
20	?																						
21	D96																						
22	D108	3	3		37	19	1	1			1			1	2		1	1		1	3	1	1
23	D123	10	7	3	5	1	43	24	4		4	5	2	6	8	10	5	3		1			
24	D107	3			36	7	1		4		1				1				6	4		6	16
25	D173	2			5		12	5	1		1	1	1	2	1	1	1	1	2	2		1	6
26	A23	1	2		26						1	1			1	1	1	1	1				
	A3	not bone	1																				
	A9								1														
	A28	1		1																		1	
	A4	1	1																				
27	D43	1	1	1	24	7	12	5			1	1	1	1	1	1	1	1	1	1			7

CHURCH CONTINUED

burial	context	23	24	25	26	27	28	29	30	31	32	33	34	35	36	37	38	39	40	41	42	43	44
1	B15																						
2	C57	1	2				1	1			1	1	1	1	4	1	4	2	1				
	C58	1		1	1		1	1			1	1				1	1	2	1				
	C2						2	2						2							2		
3	C25							1															
4	B53																						
5	C42																					1	
6	C47																8		1				
7	C23				1	1	1	1		1	1	1	1	1	1	2		1		1	1		
8	C46		1			1	1	1			1	1			5	3		2					
9	C32					1	1	1	1		1	1			2								
10	B21	no bones				1	1								1	1					4	5	
11	B32 (B49)																						
12	B16	stone context																					
13	B29	no bones																					
14	B34						1				1												
15	B42						1				1												
16	B66																						
17	B60																						
18	B8	10	15		1	1	2	1	1		1	3	2	3	6	5	6	9	16	1	8	10	1
	B22	2	1		1		2	3		1	2	1			1	5	3	5	3		1		
19	?																						
20	?																						
21	D96																						
22	D108				1	2	1	1	1				1		1		1	1	1		1		
23	D123					1	1		1												7		
24	D107	11	34				7														24	25	3
25	D173	4	11		4	1	1	5		3	8	4	6	6	17	15	14	10	15		1	1	1
26	A23				1	1	1	1		1	1	1	1		1	5	4	5	1		13	12	
	A3	not bone			1			1															
	A9	3			1	1	1	1			1	1	1										
	A28			6	1	1	1	1			1	1	1		2					1			
	A4													1							11	9	1
27	D43																						

BAPTISTERY

burial	context	1	2	3	4	5	6	7	8	9	10	11	12	13	14	15	16	17	18	19	20	21	22
28	D15	1	1	1	21	6	12	5	1		1	1	1	1	1	1	1	1	1	1			6
29	D31	1	1	1	11	5	12	5			1	1	1	1	1	1	1	1	1	1			5
30	D231	1	1	1	4	3																	
31	D233	no bones																					
32	D224	1	1	1	23	6	2	1	1		1	1	1	1	1	1	1	1	1	1			6
33	D226	1	1	1	18	3	12	5															1
34	D222	1	1	1	20		12		1		1	1	1	1	1	1	1	1	1	1	1		7
35	D237	no bones																					
36	D239	no bones																					
37	D229	3	3	3	48	8	7	1			1	3	2	3	3	3	2		2		1	1	10
38	D54	3	1	1	12	2	12	2			1	1	1	1	1	1	1		1				9
39	D57	no bones																					
40	D214	3	3	2	16	15	19	4	2		3	3	3	2	3	2	1	1	2	1	1	1	13
41	D132	1	1	1		2															2	2	4
42	D140	1				1																	
43	D135	1	1	1	22	7	12	5	1				1	1	1	1	1	1	1	1			8
44	D86	no bones																					
45	D287	1	1	1	20	4	9	5	1	1	1	1	1	1	1	1	1	1	1	1			2
46	D282	1	1	1		6	12				1	1		1	1	1	1		1	1			3
47	D212	1	1																				
48	D303	no bones																					
49	D332	mine says none																					
50	D281	1	1														1						
51	D270	no bones																					
52	B40	1	1																				2
53	D293	2	1	1	14	6	7	5	1		1	1	1	1	1	1	1	1	1	1	1	1	5

BAPTISTERY CONTINUED

burial	context	23	24	25	26	27	28	29	30	31	32	33	34	35	36	37	38	39	40	41	42	43	44
28	D15		5		1	1	1	1			1		1	1	2	2	6		1		11	11	44
29	D31		9		1	1	1	1			1	1	1	1	2						11	11	1
30	D231				1	1	1	1			1		1		1						2	1	
31	D233																						
32	D224		9		1	1	1	1			1	1	1	1	2	3	2	3	4		9	11	
33	D226		2		1	1	1	1			1	1	1	1	1	1	6	1			1	2	
34	D222				1	1	1	1			1	1	1	1	2	4	6		4		11	11	
35	D237																						
36	D239																						
37	D229	4	13		3	3	3	3			3	2	4	3	7	4	7		3		10	11	2
38	D54		8		1	1	1	1			1	1	1	1	2	3				5	10	5	
39	D57																						
40	D214		14		3	2	2	2			2	2			2	1	1		1		23	18	1
41	D132				1	1	1	1			1	1									2	4	
42	D140	2	6		1	1	1	1		1											1	1	10
43	D135		7		1	1	1	1			1	1	2	2	7	2	4		4		11	10	1
44	D86																						
45	D287																						
46	D282		6		1	1	1	1			1	1	1	1		1	9		1		7	8	
47	D212		6		1	1	1	1			1	1									10	11	
48	D303																						
49	D332										1						1						
50	D281					1																	
51	D270																						
52	B40				1	2	1						2	2	3	2	4						
53	D293	5	8		1	2	1	1			1	1	3	2	3		7		8		11	11	1

NARTHEX

burial	context	1	2	3	4	5	6	7	8	9	10	11	12	13	14	15	16	17	18	19	20	21	22
54	D289,D291	2	1	1	22	7	8	4	2		1	1	1	1	1	1	1	1	1	1	1		3
55	D92	9	5	4	32	11	13	8	1		2	1	5	5	3	2	4	3	4	2		2	7
56	D91	3		1	2		17	10	2		2	2	3	2	3	2	2	2	3	1			
57	D95	2	2	2	27	11	18	5			2		2	1	2	2	2	2	1	1			
58	D133																						
59	D168	2	2		34	2	4	5	1		2	1	2	1	1	2	1	1	2	2	4		1
60	A13,A34		1	2	33	6	16	7	2		1	1	1	1	1	1	1	2	1	2		2	5
61	no bones																						
62	A5	1																					
63	A12	3		1	3		3							1	2								
64	A35					1										1							3
65	A2	3	1	1	2		1				1												
66	A21	6		1	6		1											1		1			

NARTHEX CONTINUED

burial	context	23	24	25	26	27	28	29	30	31	32	33	34	35	36	37	38	39	40	41	42	43	44
54	D289,D291		2		1	1												2	2	1			
55	D92	2	5			3	6	5			4	2	3	3	2	1		2			8	8	1
56	D91		6			2	2	1			1	2	1				6				7	4	
57	D95				2	2	2	2			2												1
58	D133																						
59	D168				1	2	2	2			1	2	1	1	2	2	6	3	2		3	6	
60	A13,A34	4	20		2	2	1	2	1		1	1	1	2				1					
61	no bones																						
62	A5																						
63	A12		1								1				1	1	4	4					
64	A35						1			1	1	1											
65	A2																10	5	6	1	2	2	
66	A21	6					3														9		

ANTE-ROOM

burial	context	1	2	3	4	5	6	7	8	9	10	11	12	13	14	15	16	17	18	19	20	21	22
67	D275	1						1															
68	D284	1	1	1	14		12	4			1	1	1	1	1	1	1	1	1	1			9
69	D52																						
70	D51	1				1																	
71	D268	no bones																					

ANTE-ROOM CONTINUED

burial	context	23	24	25	26	27	28	29	30	31	32	33	34	35	36	37	38	39	40	41	42	43	44
67	D275	1																					
68	D284	1	12		1	1	1	1			1	1	1	1	1	1	9		9	1	11	11	
69	D52	1																					
70	D51										1		1										
71	D268																						

SPACE BETWEEN BAPTISTERY AND ANTE-ROOM AND ENTRANCE

burial	context	1	2	3	4	5	6	7	8	9	10	11	12	13	14	15	16	17	18	19	20	21	22
72	D296	2	2	2	28	7	13	5	2		2	2	1	1	1	2	2	2	2	2	2		5
73	D286	no bones																					
74	M76	4	4	2	5								1	1	1	2		1	1				

SPACE BETWEEN BAPTISTERY AND ANTEROOM AND ENTRANCE CONTINUED

burial	context	23	24	25	26	27	28	29	30	31	32	33	34	35	36	37	38	39	40	41	42	43	44
72	D296	5	13		2	1	2	2	1		2	2	2	1	3	2	7	3	1		9	8	1
73	D286																						
74	M76				2		3	4			6	4	3	1			1						

ENTRANCE TO ANTECHAMBER

burial	context	1	2	3	4	5	6	7	8	9	10	11	12	13	14	15	16	17	18	19	20	21	22
75	M61	6	3	6	74	6	1	1	1		4	1	3	1	11	2	6	4	3	2	1		2
76	M70		1	1	20	7	12	5			1		1	1	1	1	1	1	1	1			
77	M72	1	1	1		1	2		1		1	1	1	1	1	1	1	1	1	1			10

ENTRANCE TO ANTECHAMBER CONTINUED

burial	context	23	24	25	26	27	28	29	30	31	32	33	34	35	36	37	38	39	40	41	42	43	44
75	M61	7	25		1	6	7	5			4	7	5	4	9	7	9	1	9		23	12	1
76	M70		13		1	1	1	1			1	1	1	1			10		6	2	10	10	
77	M72						1	1				1									7	7	

AREA BETWEEN ENTRANCE AND PAVED ROAD

burial	context	1	2	3	4	5	6	7	8	9	10	11	12	13	14	15	16	17	18	19	20	21	22
78	M33	2	1	1		7	12	5	1		1	1	1	1	1	1	1	1	1	1	1		
79	M112	5	2	2	56	11	11	5			1	1		1	1	1	2	1	2	1			
80	M18	5	1	1			9	5	1		1	1		1		1	1	1	1	1			
81	M16,M88	1	1		29	4																	

AREA BETWEEN ENTRANCE AND PAVED ROAD CONTINUED

burial	context	23	24	25	26	27	28	29	30	31	32	33	34	35	36	37	38	39	40	41	42	43	44
78	M33	5	16		1	1	1	1	1		1	1	1	1	6	5	5	5	8		12	12	1
79	M112	5	5		2	1	1	1			1	1	1	1	5	4	5	4	7	2	9	10	1
80	M18				1	1	1	1			1	1	1			4		4			8	8	1
81	M16,M88																						

OVER ROMAN ROOMS

burial	context	1	2	3	4	5	6	7	8	9	10	11	12	13	14	15	16	17	18	19	20	21	22
82	E4	no bones																						
83	E57	no bones																						
84	E39,E40	2	1	1	23	5	1				1	1	1	1	1		1	1	1				
85	L172	1	1	1							1	1	1	1	1		1	1	1	1	2	2	
86	L176	no bones																						

OVER ROMAN ROOMS CONTINUED

burial	context	23	24	25	26	27	28	29	30	31	32	33	34	35	36	37	38	39	40	41	42	43	44
82	E4							1															
83	E57							1							1						3	5	
84	E39,E40				1	1	1		1	1	1	1	1	1							4		
85	L172	2		7												1							
86	L176																						

COURTYARD

burial	context	1	2	3	4	5	6	7	8	9	10	11	12	13	14	15	16	17	18	19	20	21	22
87	E99	1	2	1	4	5	6																
88	H28	1	1			6	9	4			1	1			1	1	1	1	1	1			10
89	H21	1				6	8	5	1		1	1	1	1	1	1	1	1	1	1			6
90	D36	no bones																					
91	D84	no bones																					
92	D18	1	1	1	23	6	10	5															1
93	D5	1	1		5	5	12																5
94	D32	1	1	1	13																		
95	D4,D34	no bones																					
96	D90	1																					8
97	D78	1	1	1	14	7	12	7															
98	B2	1	1	1																			3
99	B4	4	1		20	4	2	4															
	B4A	3	1		11	1	12	1															4
	B4B					1	6																
100	D63	1	1		29	7	12	5															1
101	D69	no bones																					

COURTYARD CONTINUED

burial	context	23	24	25	26	27	28	29	30	31	32	33	34	35	36	37	38	39	40	41	42	43	44
87	E99		5		1	1	1	1			1	1	1	1			4						
88	H28		13		1	1	1	1													11	11	
89	H21																1				11	9	
90	D36																						
91	D84																						
92	D18	5	11		1	1	1	1	1		1	1	1	1	4	6	5	4	1		9	10	1
93	D5	5	20		1	1	1	1	1	1	1	1	1	1	7	7	4	5	4			6	1
94	D32	3	8		1			1		1			1	1					9		1		
95	D4,D34																						
96	D90		9		1	1	1	1	1	1	1	1	1	1	2	2	9	2	8		11	12	1
97	D78				1	1	1														11	1	
98	B2	3	11		1		1																
99	B4	3	2		2		2	2			3	1	1	1	3	2	4	2	6	2	11	6	
	B4A							2					2	1	3	4	5	2	3	5	6		
	B4B							1							5		2	2	1				
100	D63	5	9		1	1	1		1	1		1	1	1	5	7	5	5	11		12	12	1
101	D69																						

SOUTH OF CHURCH

burial	context	1	2	3	4	5	6	7	8	9	10	11	12	13	14	15	16	17	18	19	20	21	22
102	C29	1	1	1	16	7	12	5	1		1	1	1	1	1	1	1	1	1	1	5	5	5
103	C160	1	1	1	30	3	12	5	1		1	1	1	1	1	1	1	1	1	1	2		1
104	C39	1	1		1		1					1		1	1		1			1			
105	B24	4	1		6	1	6								1				1				
-			1	1	28	6	12	5	1	1	1		1	1	1	1	1	1	1	1	2	3	5
-			1	1	23	2	9	5	1		1		1	1	1	1	1	1	1	1	2	2	4
106	B26	1	1	1	16				1					1	1		1			1			

SOUTH OF CHURCH CONTINUED

burial	context	23	24	25	26	27	28	29	30	31	32	33	34	35	36	37	38	39	40	41	42	43	44
102	C29	5	17		1	1	1	1	1	1	1	1	1	1	6	6	4	5	14	1	11	10	1
103	C160	1	6		1	1	1	1					1	1	4	5	2	4	4		3	9	1
104	C39		1																		1	1	
105	B24		1		1	1	1	1			1	1	1	1							6	9	
-		3	10		1	1	1	1		1	1	1	1		7	7	5	5	8		9	10	5
-		4	7		1	1	1	1			1	1	1		7	7	5	5	8		4		4
106	B26				1	1	1	1		2	1	1	1				1	5	1			1	

KEY: 1) number of individuals; 2) skull; 3) mandible; 4) teeth; 5) cervical vertebrae; 6) thoracic vertebrae; 7) lumbar vertebrae; 8) sacrum; 9) coccyx; 10) right clavicle; 11) left clavicle; 12) right scapula; 13) left scapula; 14) right humerus; 15) left humerus; 16) right ulna; 17) left ulna; 18) right radius; 19) left radius; 20) right carpals; 21) left carpals; 22) right metacarpals; 23) left metacarpals; 24) right phalanges; 25) left phalanges; 26) right innominate; 27) left innominate; 28) right femur; 29) left femur; 30) right patella; 31) left patella; 32) right tibia; 33) left tibia; 34) right fibula; 35) left fibula; 36) right tarsals; 37) left tarsals; 38) right metatarsals; 39) left metatarsals; 40) right phalanges; 41) left phalanges; 42) right ribs; 43) left ribs; 44) sternum.

the site is the ruined stone tower just inside the western ditch (Figs 118 and 119).

Two sides of the hill have suffered some damage in more recent times: from a tufo quarry on the west, and from landscaping for the modern road and bar on the east, where some traces of the backs of caves, of unknown date, still remain. In general, however, the topography suggests that the modern cuttings have encroached little, if at all, onto the medieval site.

EXCAVATION STRATEGY

Extensive excavation on the heavily-wooded Castellaccio site was neither practical nor desirable: tree felling could not be countenanced within a park and nature reserve. It was therefore only possible to excavate small trenches within natural clearings, and the aims of the excavation had to be limited accordingly. Broadly speaking, data were sought on the character and, particularly, the dating of the settlement; it was, however, appreciated from the outset that any data being retrieved from such limited excavation would always have to be interpreted with caution.

Seven trenches were excavated on the site during the three week season in 1990. The main trench Q, measured 10.0 × 1.5-2.0 m, and was sited in a natural clearing where the remains of a perimeter wall were visible on the inner edge of the ditch. The trench was intended to examine the curtain wall, and any structures built up against it. Other smaller trenches also took advantage of small clearings: V was positioned so as to examine the interior of the settlement close to the tower, W and Z the periphery of the site. Trench T was laid out to provide a section across the ditch, while X and Y tested for occupation on the flat area beyond the north ditch (Fig. 117).

THE RESULTS

The area beyond the northwest side of the main enclosure

Trench Y
Size: 2.0 × 1.0 m. Orientation: northeast-southwest. Position: 18.0 m northwest of the main enclosure, on the edge of the scarp.

The tufo bedrock, which was irregular, fissured and degraded, was encountered at 2.18 m below ground level. Above the tufo was a compact, dark brown, tufo-flecked loam (Y4), 0.6 m deep; it contained four sherds of pre-Roman coarse-ware, not more closely datable. This was overlaid by 0.5 m of a very similar deposit (Y3), slightly lighter in colour, but containing 27 sherds of pre-Roman coarse-ware (? bronze age). The remaining stratification consisted of clean, yellow sand (Y2: 0.9-1.0 m deep), covered by loose brown loam and leaf litter (Y1: 0.1-0.3 m deep).

Trench X
Size: 1.0 × 1.0 m. Orientation: northeast-southwest. Position: 6.0 m northwest of the main enclosure, on level ground.

Tufo bedrock lay 0.8 m below ground level, and was covered by one deposit only, a loose grey-brown loam with sparse tufo fragments. No finds were recovered from this trench.

Trench T and the enclosure ditch

The ditch on the west side of the enclosure remains to this day a substantial feature. It varies in size from 5.0 to 12.0 m in width, and is cut deeply into the natural rock. However, neither the actual depth nor the complete profile of the ditch could be ascertained.

Trench T
Size: 1.5 × 3.5 m. Orientation: east-west. Position: within and across the enclosure ditch, at a point opposite the tower.

The trench was excavated to a depth of 1.4 m from the present (relatively flat) ditch bottom. The ditch is thus at least 3.0 m deep, but may well be considerably deeper, given that the side of the ditch as seen in the excavated trench section remained vertical, with no sign of it bottoming-out. The fills, T6 to T1 in order of deposition, proved to be a series of layers of tufo rubble, 0.2 m to 0.4 m deep, in a matrix of either fine loam (T6, T5, T2) or white, decayed mortar (T3). The rubble comprised pieces of brown tufo including, in the case of T3, some fairly large squared blocks, up to 0.3 × 0.44 m. Occasional pieces of dark tufo and *selce* were also present. The white mortar layer additionally contained fragments of a harder, coarse grey mortar.

Two anomalies were noted within the ditch sequence. Firstly, the rubble fills were interrupted by layer T4, a loam, 0.34 m deep, with fine grit and small tufo fragments (pieces larger than 10 × 10 mm were very rare). Secondly, at the top of the sequence, the rubble layer T3 appeared to have been cut away towards the middle of the ditch, and the resultant hole filled by another rubble deposit, T2. The upper surface formed by these two layers sloped only slightly towards the ditch centre, and was relatively flat. Finally, the sequence was completed by T1, a humic, brown loam up to 0.38 m deep.

A few sherds were recovered from layers T4 and T5, ranging in date from the twelfth to the late thirteenth or early fourteenth centuries. Whilst little can be made from what may well be – given the type of context – redeposited material, a piece of archaic maiolica from layer T5 gives a *terminus post quem* of the late thirteenth to early fourteenth centuries for these fills.

Trenches Q, V, W and Z – the curtain wall and the interior of the enclosure

Trench Q
Size: 10.0 × 1.5-2.0 m. Orientation: northwest-southeast. Position: north of the tower, at right angles to and across the perimeter wall.

The first phase of the curtain wall
Excavation of the ditch in Trench Q consisted only of the clearance of vegetation and topsoil, and the excavation of a small amount of rubble. This revealed part of the inner rock-cut edge of the ditch which rose steeply to the foot of a 2.2 m wide ashlar wall foundation, Q15 (Fig. 120). It was faced in neatly-squared tufo blocks, which averaged 0.45-0.5 m in width, and 0.3 m in height. The blocks were tightly fitted, with no visible mortar between the joints. A coarse white mortar was, however, used in the wall core, which consisted of rough tufo fragments of all sizes up to 0.4 × 0.28 m. Wall Q15 survived to a maximum height of 1.36 m on the outer face.

The lowest layer, which butted against wall Q15, was a clean yellow-brown loam containing very sparse tufo frag-

Fig. 118. Castellaccio seen from the west, in the 1960's, across a modern tufo quarry
(JBWP)

Fig. 119. Castellaccio, the tower in 1970. *(TWP)*

Fig. 120. Castellaccio, Trench Q; the first phase of curtain wall. *(KW)*

ments (Q21). On the south side of wall Q4 (which, being later, was left *in situ*, effectively dividing the trench diagonally: Fig. 121), the tufo bedrock was overlain by Q9/10: this was a layer similar and probably equivalent to Q21, and contained two sherds of either Roman or medieval coarse-ware. Within Q9/10 were thin layers of small tufo rubble, beneath which was a deposit of dark grey-brown loam which also butted against wall Q15. The total depth of these deposits was 0.9 m.

The second phase of the curtain wall
A metre in front of wall Q15, and on the same line, was a later perimeter wall, Q3, with a foundation in rough tufo fragments up to 0.32 × 0.2 × 0.2 m high, set in hard, coarse grey mortar with small black inclusions (Fig. 122). Above this two courses survived of the inside face, made up of roughly-shaped tufo blocks up to 0.6 × 0.35 × 0.5 m in height, and set in the same mortar. Much of the wall core and all of the outer face had been robbed or had fallen, so that the original width of Q3 could not be determined. A shallow layer of fine, light yellow-brown loam (Q18) overlay wall Q15 and butted against wall Q3.

The internal walls
Layers Q18 and Q9/10 were cut by a 0.3 m deep foundation trench, Q11, which was only 50-80 mm wider than the wall, Q4, which was constructed within it. Wall Q4 followed a northeast/southwest alignment, being roughly at right angles to, and butting up against, the curtain wall Q3. A length of 7.4 m was revealed, consisting of four courses of roughly-shaped tufo pieces up to 0.4 × 0.3 × 0.25 m, standing to a total height of 0.75 m, and 0.43-0.51 m in width (Fig. 121). These tufo pieces were laid in two lines within a loose, grey mortar but with no true wall core, although some smaller tufo fragments were packed in between. The upper two courses were more clearly faced than those below, which were largely within the foundation trench; these lower courses were also offset by *c.* 0.1 m at the east end of the wall. The fill of the foundation trench was a friable dark

grey-brown loam, which contained a single residual sherd of pre-Roman coarse-ware (probably iron age).

On the north side of wall Q4 was a deep layer of large tufo rubble up to 0.35 × 0.26 m, set in a matrix of soil and grey mortar. Many of the tufo pieces were roughly dressed. To the south of Q4, and again butting the wall, was a fine, light-brown silty loam (Q2), with sparse tufo fragments up to 40-80 mm. This layer, which was only 0.1-0.15 m deep, was cut by the vertical-sided foundation trench (Q23) for the stub of another wall, Q8. The wall was of identical construction to Q4, and survived to the same height. It emerged from the south section of the trench, running for only 0.64 m at approximately right angles to wall Q4. The fill of the foundation trench was a loose mid-brown loam (Q22).

A layer of dark grey-brown loam (Q1) covered the entire trench. This layer contained a few small fragments of tufo and tile, and fourteen sherds, of which the earliest were two fragments of sparse glaze, one late eleventh- or twelfth-century, and the other twelfth-century. The remaining sherds were as follows: seven medieval coarse-wares and domestic ware – probably twelfth to thirteenth/fourteenth centuries; two probable *ceramica laziale* – thirteenth century; one archaic maiolica – fourteenth century; one maiolica – late fifteenth century onwards; one yellow glaze – sixteenth-seventeenth centuries.

Trench V
Size: 1.5 × 1.5 m. Orientation: northwest-southwest. Position: 12.0 m northeast of tower.

The hard, clean surface of the tufo bedrock was reached at a depth of 0.7-0.9 m. The deeper part of the trench consisted of a shallow cut, V5, across the northwest half of the trench, of which only a right-angled corner was seen, on a north-south/east-west orientation; it measured 1.0 × 0.8 m. This cut had vertical sides and was filled by fine sandy loam (V4) with sparse tufo fragments up to 30 by 50 mm. It contained a single fragment of medieval coarse-ware, *c.* twelfth century.

Fig. 121. Castellaccio, Trench Q. View looking northwest towards the curtain wall and
ditch; in the foreground internal walls Q4 (right) and Q8 (left). *(KW)*

In the east corner of the trench was a second right-angled cut, 0.2 m deep, into the bedrock (V8). It followed the same orientation as V5, while the near-vertical sides fell in two stages to a narrow step and then to a rounded bottom. The fill was similar to V4, but contained several irregular fragments of *selce* up to 0.13 × 0.08 m. No pattern could be observed in their placement.

Overlying the fills of both cuts was a compact, yellow-brown fine sandy loam with sparse small tufo fragments (V3). This layer was 0.2 m deep, and covered the whole trench; it contained the following pottery sherds: three probable *ceramica laziale* (thirteenth century); five medieval coarse-ware and eleven medieval domestic ware (all twelfth, thirteenth or fourteenth centuries). The layer above V3 was a mid grey-brown loam, 0.18-0.25 m deep, containing tufo rubble of various sizes, including some squared blocks, averaging 0.3 × 0.3 × 0.15 m, as well as fragments of fine, white mortar with tiny dark inclusions. It contained the following pottery fragments: two medieval coarse-ware and fourteen medieval domestic ware (all twelfth, threenth or fourteenth centuries); one archaic maiolica (late thirteenth to early fourteenth centuries) and one lead-glazed kitchen-ware (late fourteenth to fifteenth-sixteenth centuries).

The uppermost layer in the trench was a mid-brown loam, 0.25-0.3 m deep, containing small tufo fragments and roots; it contained no finds.

Trench W
Size: 2.0 × 1.0 m (reduced to 1.0 × 1.0 m because of tree roots). Orientation: northeast-southwest. Position: north corner of the enclosure, on the inside edge of the ditch.

A very compact yellow sandy soil (W2) was the lowest context excavated in this trench. It was not the natural subsoil, as it contained the following pottery sherds: two probable Roman domestic ware; ten coarse-ware (not medieval); one probable *ceramica laziale* (thirteenth century). Cut into W2 was a small sub-circular post-hole, which was steep-sided, 0.22 m in diameter and 0.14 m deep. It was filled by loose brown loam, containing a single sherd of Roman coarse-ware, and overlain by an identical layer, which was 0.3-0.45 m deep, and again yielded a single Roman coarse-ware sherd.

Trench Z
Size: 2.0 × 1.0 m. Orientation: northeast-southwest. Position: south of tower, on the edge of scarp.

Fig. 122. Castellaccio, Trench Q. The second phase of curtain wall, seen from the ditch. *(KW)*

The irregular, hard clean surface of the natural tufo lay at a depth of 1.17 m below ground level. In the south corner of the trench was a single post-hole, which was 0.22 m in diameter, 0.24 m in depth, and had regular, near-vertical sides sloping to a rounded bottom; it was filled with a very friable, light yellow-brown tufo rubble. Above was a very compact yellow-brown tufo rubble with charcoal flecks (Z7). This layer, which was 0.2 m in depth, was relatively rich in finds, including tile fragments, animal bone and a total of 56 sherds. There comprised 33 medieval domestic wares (one possibly eleventh century, while the others could be of the eleventh, twelfth or thirteenth centuries); thirteen sparse glaze (first half of twelfth century) and ten pieces of medieval coarse-ware (c. twelfth century). This was cut by Z6, a shallow sub-circular scoop, 0.68 m wide and 0.12 m deep. It was filled with a fairly compact yellow-brown rubble, consisting of small fragments of travertine. It contained a single sherd of medieval coarse-ware of the twelfth century. This was sealed by a very hard-packed tufo rubble floor, 0.51 m in depth, which was itself covered by a second similar floor of smaller rubble, 0.28 m deep. This yielded two sherds of medieval domestic ware (twelfth, thirteenth, fourteenth centuries) and two sherds of medieval coarse-ware (c.

twelfth century). Finally, a thin lens of grey-white mortar with minute black inclusions overlay these floors, although only at the north end of the trench.

The tower (Figs 117 and 119)

The surviving structure of the tower rises some 10.0 m above a distinct mound, much of which is undoubtedly made up of rubble fallen from the walls. The building measures 6.0 by 5.0 m externally, has walls 0.75 m thick and is oriented north-south/east-west. The lower half of the tower is very roughly faced, using mainly pieces of fairly hard, dark tufo, but also some *selce*; these range from 0.15 × 0.07 m to 0.2 × 0.09 m, and are set in a good-quality grey to off-white mortar with coarse tufo inclusions. Some of the *selce* fragments are smooth on one side and may have been taken from the paving blocks of the nearby Roman road. The wall core is constructed of similar material to the faces, but also contains some softer, brown tufo.

The upper half of the tower is built in the same mortar as the lower section but, with very few exceptions, using a softer brown tufo. The individual stones are generally larger, up to 0.25 by 0.1 m high, and the impression is of a partial rebuild of the structure. The height of the surviving stone-work, and the placement of the putlog holes, indicate that there must have been several storeys, and the location of the tower on the highest point of the hill suggests that sur-veillance of the surrounding landscape was its major role. In this, it contrasts with the setting of nearby villages like Maz-zano Romano and Calcata, which were built on spurs in the Treia valley, well below the level of the countryside around. Unlike Castellaccio, they were thus invisible from a distance (cf. Potter 1979: 157).

DISCUSSION

Prehistoric and Roman occupation

The discovery of sherds of bronze age or iron age date at Castellaccio is not in itself surprising. It occupies a high, easily defended hill, with a large area available for settlement. As such, it resembles some of the other pre-Roman centres of the Ager Faliscus, such as Narce, Nepi or Torre dell'Isola (Frederiksen and Ward-Perkins 1957: 92-3), so many of which were reoccupied in medieval times.

It is not, however, clear how extensive the pre-Roman settlement at Castellaccio may have been. The small and undiagnostic sherds came principally from Trench Y, where they were found within the upper of two loam layers, which together were 1.1 m in depth. This seems a very substantial de-posit to have survived on the very edge of the ridge, but it was sealed by a further 1.0 m of clean sand. The two well-mixed loam layers could be inter-preted as cultivated soils (explaining the abraded nature of the sherds), and the sand layer as a wind-blown deposit which formed after agriculture had ceased; but it is difficult to see how either could have formed to such a depth unless they had built up against some feature, such as a wall, which was either not revealed by excavation, or has since been destroyed. In short, there are traces of a buried pre-historic landscape at Castellaccio; but its nature and significance is currently elusive.

Roman finds at Castellaccio were limited to a few sherds of coarse-ware from Trench W and a poss-ible sherd from Trench Q. It is also noteworthy that no Roman building materials were found in the excavations, and that the only Roman material reused in the tower was basalt, presumably robbed from the road below. The evidence points there-fore to little or no use of the site during the Roman period.

The medieval origins of Castellaccio

Any discussion of the origins of Castellaccio, when derived from such a small body of data, requires an approach tempered with caution. Above all, the possibility must always be borne in mind that earl-ier material exists, but was not recovered. That said, some tentative conclusions can still be drawn.

No medieval pottery which could be dated earlier than the eleventh century was found. Forum ware, which could indicate activity in the tenth century or before, was conspicuous by its absence, as was any of the *ceramica acroma* from the late eighth-/early ninth-century pottery kiln found on the main excavation. If we compare this with the way that small quantities of prehistoric and Roman pot-tery *did* find their way into the excavated medieval contexts at Castellaccio, it seems reasonable to attach some weight to the negative evidence for occupation before the eleventh century. Indeed, the earliest pottery which can be dated with confid-ence consisted of sparse glazed ware of the first half of the twelfth century. A total of fifteen sherds was found, almost all from layer Z7, where they were associated with charcoal and animal bone (cf. King, this volume). Also from Z7 were 33 sherds of medieval domestic ware and ten sherds of medieval coarse-ware, none of which would be out of place in a twelfth-century context, although one frag-ment could be of the eleventh century.

The limited evidence for wooden structures is mainly associated with the early medieval pottery described above. This applies particularly to a post-hole, cut into the bedrock in Trench Z, and sealed by layer Z7. If we accept that the most likely *ter-minus post quem* for the deposition of Z7 is the first half of the twelfth century, then the post-hole must have been cut before this. Furthermore, provided the post-hole represents something durable (and not, say, just a scaffolding post), we should allow a sufficient period for the use, and decay or destruc-tion, of a wooden structure. The evidence from Trench Z can be supplemented by that from Trench V, where the right-angled corners of two cuts in the bedrock, V5 and V8, were found. The latter contained fragments of *selce*, perhaps the remains of packing for wooden posts, while V5 produced a single fragment of twelfth-century coarse-ware.

None of the foregoing could be described as compelling evidence, but it does suggest the prob-ability that wooden structures were being built on the site in the later eleventh or early twelfth cen-tury. Given that occupation ceased about AD 1100 on the site in the valley, it is more than reasonable to suppose a transfer of the population from there to Castellaccio. Equally, the case for identifying Cas-tellaccio with the *castrum Capracorum* of the bull of 1053, as discussed in the introduction to this vol-ume, finds not insignificant archaeological sup-port. Whilst it would be desirable to have more diagnostic eleventh-century pottery from the castle site, the findings of the very modest investigation tend to sustain rather than refute this correlation with the documentary evidence.

The ditch and the extramural area

Although the cross-section (Trench T) could not be fully excavated, it is clear that the ditch was a substantial feature, 5.0 to 12.0 m wide and over 3.0 m deep. It would be difficult, then, to ascribe it anything other than a defensive purpose, and the vertical inner face is also consistent with this interpretation. The ditch would also be the logical source for much of the stone used in building Castellaccio (although the main site must also have been a useful quarry), so that it may, to some extent, have grown with the settlement. Of the fills which were excavated, the lowest to contain datable sherds, T5, formed during or after the late thirteenth to early fourteenth centuries. The nature of the fills shows them to be a mixture of rubble and masonry from the curtain wall, with one deep loam layer, T4, representing a gap in the process. In its current form, the ditch is noticeably flat-bottomed, giving rise to the suggestion that it may later have served as a track, perhaps when the hilltop was being used for agriculture. If the ditch was so used, this might explain the infilling of a cut in layer T3 to create a level surface.

Two trenches (X and Y) excavated outside the ditch disclosed no traces of medieval occupation, and the extramural terrain is very flat, showing none of the tell-tale humps and platforms which are evident in the enclosed area. Settlement would appear never to have expanded beyond the defences, a conclusion that is consistent with a settlement occupied for a relatively short period by a small population.

The curtain wall

The first phase of the curtain wall (Q15) cannot be independently dated as no diagnostic material was recovered from the foundation deposits. A broad clue may be found, however, in the type of stonework, which is characterized by the neatness of the tightly-fitted ashlars on the inner face, with courses 0.3 m high. The recurrence of this unit of measurement, which is probably a medieval foot, and more or less corresponds to the Roman foot (0.297 m), has already been noted in Lazio, and the phenomenon has been discussed by Andrews (1978). His study has suggested that the change to masonry cut to this module occurred at around AD 1100-50, while both the lengths of the blocks in the Castellaccio example and the neatness of the work would place it between his periods 1 and 2 in the Viterbo sequence. This would suggest a date in the late eleventh or early twelfth century (Andrews 1978: 396-400). However, while such comparisons are worthwhile, it is necessary to be cautious: masonry styles can be highly regional in character, and Monte Gelato lies towards the southern edge of the area which Andrews has discussed. The curtain wall, it should be added, was built directly onto the tufo bedrock, so that some prior clearance of the site must have taken place. The deposits which overlay the bedrock, and butted against the wall, included small tufo fragments and may well relate to the

construction of the wall. No trace was found of any structures against the inside of the first phase of the curtain wall, and the presence of a thick loam layer would also indicate that the space was kept open.

The construction of a second phase of curtain wall (Q3), which uses Q15 as a foundation, also cannot be dated. The construction technique is altogether cruder, and more varied, and it is not really possible to fit it within the sequence proposed by Andrews. Perhaps the only useful observation which can be made is that the first phase wall had been reduced to a few courses, suggesting either a period of decay or, more probably, a major collapse.

Internal structures

A single, rough tufo wall, Q4, to which another, Q8, was later added at right angles, was built against the second phase curtain wall. The presence of structures against the inside of the curtain wall is a commonplace in medieval hilltop villages, for example at nearby Castel Porciano (Mallett and Whitehouse 1967), and needs little comment. No floor levels were found in association with these walls, but wooden floors could have existed, perhaps at first-floor level, leaving a dirt-floored room below. It is unfortunate that the lack of material recovered from Trench Q meant that the structure cannot be dated. Indeed, the only datable building activity within the settlement was identified in Trench Z, where there was a dump of the twelfth century, covered by two hard-packed tufo floor surfaces.

The stone tower is another common feature of medieval hilltop villages of the region. The difficulty at Castellaccio is to establish the date of the tower when, in the absence of other archaeological data, we are again left with only the style of the masonry. This comprises small tufo fragments, somewhere between *tufelli* (small, neat tufo blocks) and *selcetti*-type work. A similar building technique was employed for the defensive tower (below, Fig. 126) in the valley below. Andrews (1978: 406) discussed the possible chronologies of both *tufelli* and *selcetti*-type work, but it is evident that in the state of current knowledge they can only be regarded as very broad clues: that the tower was built somewhere between 1150 and 1250 is most likely, but a date outside this range cannot be excluded.

The end of the settlement

The evidence discussed above suggests that a walled settlement, built at least partly in stone, existed by the first half of the twelfth century, with the tower, or at least the phase of the tower that is now visible, being built somewhat later. Occupation was never, however, heavy or prolonged. Pottery which dates to between the thirteenth-fourteenth centuries and the fifteenth-sixteenth centuries was recovered from destruction layers in the ditch, as well as near the tower. Post-medieval pottery, on the other hand, was found only in the topsoil, and then in very small quantities. On balance, then, Castellaccio probably had a relatively short life, and is likely to have been abandoned by the late thirteenth century. Whether the population was transferred to Mazzano Romano is a matter of conjecture: but it remains the most plausible possibility, especially as the mill, traditionally worked by the people of Mazzano, remained in use.

LA TORRE O SIA NOVA MOLA: IL MULINO DI MONTEGELATO (FIG. 123), di Franca Fedeli Bernardini

Il marchese Urbano del Drago Biscia Gentili, antico feudatario di Mazzano, il 9 ottobre 1830 scrive al Tesoriere Generale dello Stato Pontificio, Mario Mattei, per attivare gratuitamente un nuovo mulino nella tenuta di Montegelato, fatta salva l'osservanza delle leggi sul Dazio del Macinato. Tale mulino 'privativo', in contrasto con le disposizioni di Pio VII, per le facoltà accordate da Leone XII nel 1827 si giustificherebbe, nelle parole del 'barone', con l'antico diritto statutario[1] di costruire mulini, con l'assenza di mole 'camerali' cui farebbe concorrenza e di altre fabbriche cui toglierebbe l'acqua, e soprattutto con la necessità di farina della capitale. A partire dall'autorizzazione del 30 ottobre concessa dal Pubblico Erario, per quanto di propria competenza, il 18 novembre il Presidente della Comarca si rivolge alla Sacra Congregazione delle Acque 'che deve giudicare la libera defluenza' e predisporre un'idonea ispezione sul fiume. Inizia in tal modo un lungo e complesso iter burocratico per ottenere l'autorizzazione definitiva dalla Sacra

Congregazione delle Acque che emette infine apposito decreto il giorno 19 maggio dell'anno successivo.[2]

LA TENUTA DI MONTEGELATO A MAZZANO

Elisabetta Pucci, vedova del marchese d'Elci che aveva acquistato Montegelato dai conti Gallo nel 1813,[3] dopo aver affittato la tenuta ad Arcangelo Sansoni, dal 30 settembre 1827 al 30 settembre 1830, ed avergli rinnovato l'affitto per un altro anno,[4] inizia contestualmente le pratiche, per la vendita o la cessione enfiteutica, seguite dai patteggiamenti con Urbano del Drago,[5] che culminano con l'atto di compravendita il 29 marzo 1837.[6]

Tale tenuta di 240 rubbie si situa in una posizione territorialmente strategica al confine dei distretti di Roma e di Viterbo, tra il territorio dei comuni di Campagnano, Mazzano, Calcata, presso l'antica strada 'comunitativa' detta Logajo che entra nel territorio di Nepi ed incrocia la strada di Campagnano. Il marchese tesse in tal modo una politica di accorpamento e di espansione territoriale attorno ai tre principali nuclei iniziali di possidenza: frammenti di pascolo e di bosco ceduo proprio in località Montegelato, l'antica 'molina' in contrada Le Ripe e la tenuta di Ronciglianello (Figs 124 and 125).[7]

L'intento di sfruttare al massimo le potenzialità del territorio e della tenuta che vuole acquistare[8] è del resto evidenziato, oltre che dall'acquisizione della privativa sui mulini del paese, dalla creazione di un mulino, da affittare dietro corresponsione in denaro contante, e dal progetto di edificazione di una ferriera presso le cascate.

Con la costruzione di tali strutture, che sfruttano la forza motrice generata dalla caduta dell'acqua, il barone intende ribadire e rafforzare i centri delle possidenze passate e future. Inoltre la presenza nella tenuta di una antica calcara,[9] sfruttata almeno

---

[1] Archivio di Stato di Roma (ASR), Archivio del Drago (ADD), fascc. 12-13-14, n. 289: lo statuto è del 1536. La copia conservata in ASR, Statuti, Mazzano 652 è del 1542; cfr. libro V, cap. XXXXI; cfr. inoltre ASR, Camerale II-Molini, b. 26, fasc. 315 (1806). Si ringraziano la dott.ssa M. Pieretti che sta riordinando l'Archivio della famiglia Del Drago per l'indispensabile aiuto fornito nella consultazione dei materiali inediti, gli architetti A. Rebecchini e F. Avarini per ricerche, confronti e consigli, il dott. G. Guaita per indicazioni sulle cave e sulle rocce utilizzate per materiale da costruzione, e la dott.ssa C. Sforzini.

[2] ASR, Sacra Congregazione delle Acque (SCA), b. 138, fasc. 397.

[3] ASR, Congregazione del Buon Governo (CBG), S. II, b. 2319.

[4] ASR, ADD, Cass. Azz. 56, 373, 374.

[5] ASR, ADD, Cass. Azz. 58, p. 90 del 24/6/1831; riprese nel 1833, pp. 103-4.

[6] ASR, CBG, b. 2319.

[7] ASR, Brogliardo del Catasto Gregoriano, Comarca 50, 1819. Montegelato: ppcc: 563, 564; Le Ripe: ppcc: 448, 449, 450, 459, 460; AAD, Cass. Azz. 58, fasc. 51: la tenuta di Montegelato 'confinante nei suoi lati con la tenuta di Roncigliano grande spettante alli Monaci di S. Paolo, di Ronciglianello spettante all'Ill.mo Sr Marchese del Drago, con il territorio di Nepi e con li Beni del Beneficio della Madonna' (1789).

[8] 1679: scudi 230 (ASR, ADD, Cass. Azz. 57, n. 145); 1706-8: scudi 396:04 (ASR, Camerale III, Comuni, b. 1321); 1708-9: scudi 154:15 (ASR Camerale III, Comuni, b. 1321); 1709-10: scudi 205:45 (ASR Camerale III, Comuni, b. 1321); 1710: scudi 132:40 (ASR Camerale III, Comuni, b. 1321); 1714: scudi 197:10 (ASR Camerale III, Comuni, b. 1321); 1743: scudi 242:33 (ASR, ADD, Cass. Azz. 56, pos. 59, n. 8); 1779: scudi 375 (ASR, CBG, S. II, b. 2319); 1785-90: scudi 375 (ASR, CBG, S. II, b. 2319); 1805 ricavo dichiarato all'atto di vendita a Antonio Ciai per 14591:25 scudi di scudi 450.95; proprietà di rubbie 133.3 'solita a affittarsi un anno per l'altro scudi 450' (ASR, CBG, S. II, b. 2319); 1827-30 scudi 325 annui (ASR, ADD, Cass. Azz. 56, n. 374).

[9] La comunità affitta la tenuta, nel 1679, con la calcara per 230 scudi (ASE, ADD, Cass. Azz. 57, n. 40) 'fatto obbligo a mantenere li stradoni', a concedere il passo e il pascolo al bestiame, a permettere di cesare 'spallette e spallettoni', nonché cavare calce che necessitasse ai priori. Nell'affitto per scudi 242:33:24 del 1743 la comunità si riserva la calcara di calce (ASR, ADD, Cass. Azz. 56, pos. 59, n. 8); la tenuta è affittata per il quinquennio 1785-90 per 375 scudi l'anno 'che non possa esser Padrone ... detta Pietra da calce, ne della Cava della Pietra d o Peperino, ma queste restino a favore della Com tà' (ASR, CBG, S. II, b. 2319).

Fig. 123. The mill and waterfalls, looking southwest. *(KW)*

dal XVII secolo, di cave di peperino e di tufo giustificano pienamente l'acquisizione. Entrato in possesso della tenuta, il tentativo immediato di liberarla dagli antichi usi civici e consuetudinari, e di recintarla, porta il marchese a scontrarsi, subito,[10] con la Comunità di Mazzano per tentare, poi, un faticoso compromesso con la stessa frutto di due transazioni nel 1841 e nel 1843.[11] Il barone che, con l'entrata in funzione del mulino, paga tramite l'"Esattore Giovanni Cesarone scudi dieci quali sono per il canone della torre di Monte Gelato e questi per il primo anno maturato a tutto Aprile 1832',[12] con la transazione del 1843 ottiene dalla Comunità l'abbuono della corrisposta dovuta 'per cagione della mola di Mte Gelato dietro il libero

pascolo del bestiame. Se infine intende ristringere tutte le dette Tenute in detto caso l'annua corrisposta come sopra ceduta di Scudi dieci tornerà a beneficio della Comunità'.

LA COSTRUZIONE DEL MULINO (FIG. 126)

Il barone inizia la costruzione del mulino a partire da preesistenze: una vecchia torretta ed una torre sulla penisola formata dai due rami del Treja, identificabili probabilmente con i 'fienili' di Montegelato danneggiati dai 'terrazzani' di Mazzano nel 1808.[13] La prima torre segue le sorti della tenuta agricola e si ritrova menzionata come 'casa diroca-

[10] ASR, CBG, S. II, b. 2319.
[11] ASR, CBG, S. II, b. 2319.
[12] ASR, ADD, Cass. Azz. 55.
[13] ASR, ADD, Cass. Azz. 58, n. 40.

I MATERIALI IMPIEGATI

L'ipotesi, non suffragata da grafici esistenti, di preesistenze medioevali si fonda, oltre che sulla critica delle fonti, sull'esame dei materiali con cui le 'Torri' vengono costruite provenienti, quasi tutti, dalle vicine cave di peperino di Montegelato e di tufo di Castellaccio.

La torretta, appoggiata sulla viva roccia tagliata dalla cava, viene realizzata con 'selcetti' di tufo e peperino locali, mentre la volta in pietra da taglio è realizzata in tufo biancastro di provenienza non identificata con certezza. L'edificio antistante il mulino è costruito nella bella pietra tufacea di Castellaccio, mentre le volte del mulino stesso sono realizzate con materiale tufaceo non immediatamente identificabile per le intonacature e rasature successive. Sicuramente gli scheggioni di pietra delle pareti del mulino sono della cava di peperino locale, come originariamente era la copertura a lastroni del mulino e della torretta antistante.

L'analisi dei materiali sembrerebbe evidenziare con costanza la presenza di volte costruite in ottima pietra da taglio tufacea impostate su paramenti di diverso tipo.

Due gruppi di elementi fanno propendere per una stratificazione storica di tali strutture: i caratteri costruttivi difformi e coesistenti, le diverse tecniche e i materiali (selcetti regolari con stilature di giunti; decorazioni floreali e conci perfettamente tagliati; scheggioni rozzamente lavorati e materiali di spoglio impiegati nei lavori sicuramente ottocenteschi) e gli elementi archivistici (lavori alle torri, estrazione di pietre alle torri, carenza di spese di trasporto per materiale lapideo).

Se non si hanno dubbi sull'antichità della torretta, l'assenza del mulino nella cartografia del primo ottocento può generare incertezze sull'antichità della struttura. Il piano seminterrato detto 'carcerario', che conteneva l'ingranaggio, è coperto da volta a botte in tufo che si restringe in corrispondenza del corpo antistante. La presunta contemporaneità delle due volte realizzate in tufo, al di là dei restauri resi necessari dall'alluvione del 1861,[52] fa apparire probabile una più antica utilizzazione a mulino della parte bassa dell'edificio.

Inoltre se si esamina la muratura della rifolta triangolare questa è realizzata in blocchi di tufo simili a quelli del bel paramento murario, restaurata con l'aggiunta di speroni più tardi, quasi sicuramente ottocenteschi.

Il primo intervento del marchese si limiterebbe pertanto al restauro del paramento, del tetto e della rifolta, alla costruzione del ponte di legno, delle scale in muratura e dell'ingranaggio. Meno convincente appare l'ipotesi di una costruzione interamente ottocentesca dell'antistante corpo e del mulino, realizzato con una 'struttura a scheletro' di ottimo paramento e tamponamento a scheggioni. Avvalorando tale ipotesi si avrebbe una realizzazione ricca di suggestioni mediate da *revival* stilistici; le tecniche di costruzione nell'ottocento per edifici utilitaristici tuttavia non sembrano in genere presupporre simili e raffinati trattamenti del paramento. Il ruolo dell'architetto Poletti, a giudicare dalle registrazioni delle spese e dagli altri documenti d'archivio, si limiterebbe a rilevazioni dell'area e a una visita al cantiere soprattutto a lavori ultimati.[53]

L'ambigua descrizione del Coppi (1847: 30) che visita la zona attorno al 1814, meglio riferibile a Montegelato che non al possedimento della Maggiorana, menziona 'una antica torre sopra quel mulino' della Comunità tra ruderi di antiche fabbriche che erano visibili nella zona di Montegelato fino a qualche decennio fa. La presenza dell'antistante mulino diruto potrebbe giustificare del resto la somma di 10 scudi che il barone deve pagare alla Comunità dal momento dell'avvio dell'attività, per l'uso privativo che intende farne dopo il restauro intrapreso. Reinterpretando pertanto i dati a disposizione, il corpo antistante almeno e la rifolta sembrerebbero coevi e, per quanto detto, non anteriori alla fine del XII secolo.

L'atto del 1154 in cui la badessa Agnese del monastero di San Biagio di Nepi loca per tre generazioni a Gregorio de Senebaldo romano '*molendinum unum ante dirutum, sed a te voluntate nostra raedificatum in plano de Mazzano. Ipsum tibi, concedo cum rotalibus eius et omnibus suis utilitatibus, a tribus lateribus cuius Treia currit, a quarto est molaria antiqua; sic tamen ut liceat mihi meisque successimis domum ibi edificare et animalia quecumque abebimus ille habere ...*', sembra attestare l'esistenza di un vecchio mulino a Montegelato, ricordato un secolo prima e restaurato attorno al 1150 (Hartmann 1895–1901: v. III, p. 30, doc. 183). Il mulino quale appare oggi, con la retrostante torre, simile a quello della Maggiorana, sembra infine tipologicamente affine ad un gruppo di mulini romani 'a torre' (mola di San Sisto Vecchio e moletta dei Frangipane al Circo Massimo) risalenti alla prima metà del secolo XIII, ma molto rimaneggiati successivamente (Bianchi 1989).

---

[52] ASR, ADD, Cass. Azz. 61, pos. 123, n. 1: rapporto dell'agrimensore Luigi Sarmienti del 12 febbraio 1862 sui danni dell'alluvione dell'anno precedente. 'Caduta una parte della volta del Carcerario, è stato trasportato dall'acqua il ponticello di materiale, all'imboccatura del canale, al muro della mola apparisce qualche lesione, lo sperone esistente nell'angolo ove sorte l'acqua del ritricine, in parte è caduto, ed il restante scatenato, oltre altri danni di minore conto.'

[53] ASR, ADD, Cass. Azz. 59, n. 45: esiti dal 23 ottobre al 6 maggio 1831-32 'per spedizione con l'architetto'.

Chapter Four

THE FINDS

INTRODUCTION

The richness and variety of the artefact record will have become apparent in earlier pages. The finds do not, however, in the main derive from rubbish pits or middens of a sort commonly encountered on Roman sites in northern Europe. Rather, they come from dumps in features, especially the fish-pond, the north cistern and the rock-cut road. The late Roman limekiln also yielded important discoveries, while some Roman inscriptions and sculpture were incorporated into later buildings. Likewise, some of the Carolingian decorative stone elements were built into the remodelled church and baptistery of *c.* AD 1000, and survived the subsequent demolition. The graves also produced a few significant items, while the collapsed walls and roofs of the mid-sixth century contained a good deal of material, not least some well-preserved iron tools. Surprisingly, there were no signs of later scavenging in these deposits, very possibly a reflection of the sanctity of the site, at any rate from the late Roman period.

There were episodes of stratigraphical build-up (other than make-up levels), notably in the late Roman period. Moreover, discarded wasters and ash deposits from the early medieval kiln created extensive tips. However, the quantity of refuse was relatively small, a point underlined by the paucity of plant remains and, given the size of the excavated area, animal bones. The implication is that there was a system of rubbish disposal rather unlike that of, for example, Roman Britain, where objects usually proliferate in such layers.

Questions of this sort, concerning the deposition and survival of artefacts and other material, are of some importance. Monte Gelato appears at first sight somewhat unusual in its wealth of finds, but it must be stressed that the majority derives from dumps in a few contexts, rather than through casual loss. This does not account for the exceptional preservation of the objects, many of which are substantially complete, if found in fragments; but this does suggest that this was rubbish generated close to the place of deposition, and ought to relate to the lives of the occupants of the site.

THE INSCRIPTIONS,[54] by C.M. Gilliver

TEXTS AND COMMENTARY

1. [D   ]   M
   [   ]ME ET
   [   ]FAVST
   [CO^]NIVGI
   [   ]BENE
   [   ]TIBVS FE

Figs 132 and 133. A tombstone of the *D(is) M(anibus)* type. Letter size: 22-9 mm. Small Find no. (SF) 37. Reused as a support for the grave slab in burial 12.

It probably commemorates two people, as is shown by the plural ending in line 6, which with the end of line 5 may be restored as *bene merentibus*. The name of the builder would probably have been included in line 5 and since there is no space for the *tria nomina* of a citizen, Reynolds (1988: 284-5) has suggested that the builder may have been of low status, possibly a slave. The identity of the pair mentioned in lines 2 and 3, and the person to whom the tombstone was set up, is unknown.

2. [F]ACIVND[   ]
   [   ]VS•ET•HILA[R   ]

Fig. 134. An inscription on a fairly rough block of local nenfro, 0.285 m high, and broken at both ends. Letters: l1 - 90 mm; l2 - 72 mm. SF 165. Found in the late Roman limekiln.

The inscription is dated to the late Republic or early Empire by the simple letterforms, use of shading, and the content. The first line has been restored by Purcell (1988a: 285-6) as *faciendum curaverunt*, or a variation thereof, the plural form because of the two individuals mentioned in the second line. Purcell has restored the name of the second as Hilario in the light of inscription cat. 3, and suggested that the use of *cognomina* only indicates slave status or freedmen with a common *praenomen* and *nomen*. In the light of the other epigraphic evidence from the site, this argument is plausible. The inscription may record the dedication of some kind of public building by officers of a local temple or community, possibly a bridge over the Treia or a shrine. Purcell has suggested that the officials may be associated either with a *vicus* at Monte Gelato or with the settlement at Monte Caio to the north; but the interpretation of a *vicus* at Monte Gelato now seems less likely.

---

[54] No. 1 has been discussed previously by Reynolds (1988: 284-5) and nos. 2-5 by Purcell (1988a: 284-91). The complete text of no. 3 was first published by Gilliver (1990).

Fig. 132. Tombstone (inscription no. 1). *(KW)*

Fig. 133. Detail of inscription no. 1. *(KW)*

marble from a single slab that was originally 2.65 m long. Above this was another block with four roundels and sculpted heads of those commemorated (Claridge, this volume, cat. 6). Letters: l1 - 65 mm; l2 - 45 mm; l3 - 28 mm. The reading [Hi]lara is preferred to a shorter name, such as [C]lara, on the grounds of spacing. The inscription may be dated by letterforms and content to the early Imperial period. From the late Roman limekiln.

The four individuals mentioned are all freed slaves (*libertini*), and the monument as a whole is typical of those set up by groups of freedmen and freedwomen in the late Augustan and early Julio-Claudian period (cf. Kleiner 1977: cat. nos. 20, 48, 78; Frenz 1985: cat. nos. 52, 135; Claridge, this volume). The principal figure of the inscription is C. Valerius Faustus, the freedman of a C. Valerius; and [Hi]lara, whose patron was a woman of the *gens Aescionia*, is possibly his wife. The inscription does not clarify the relationships between the individuals commemorated, though the two other C. Valerii may be either *conlibertini* of Faustus or, perhaps more likely, freedmen of Faustus himself.

3. C•VALERIVS•C•L AESCIONIA• •L C•VALE-
    RIVS•C•L C•VALERIVS•C•L
    ZETVS [HI]LARA FAVSTVS HILARIO
    MERCATOR BOVARIVS MAG•AVG•VEIS

Figs 135 and 136. An inscription from a large tomb monument of fine-quality marble (cf. Claridge and Matthews, below). The whole inscription is on thirteen fragments of

Fig. 134. Inscription no. 2. *(KW)*

Faustus is described as being involved in the cattle trade, a fairly lucrative business,[55] and an official of the Imperial cult at Veii, 18 km to the south of Monte Gelato, probably at some time between *c.* 12 BC and AD 14.[56] The connection with Veii appears to be strengthened through the very rare *nomen* of the woman [Hi]lara. An Aescionius Capella was honoured under Augustus or Tiberius by the *municipes extramurani* and *Augustales* of Veii, and a link between the two Aescionii seems likely. Faustus therefore appears to have connections with Veii through the office he held and through the family of his wife's *patronus*. For further discussions of links between the site at Monte Gelato and Veii, see below.

4. [   ]IO FER[   ]
        DVLCISSIM[   ]
    [   ]ACHILL[   ]

Fig. 137. Inscription on three fragments of greyish white marble, possibly Proconnesian, with the remains of three lines, badly damaged in places by weathering. The letters of the first line cannot be established with certainty. Height of letters in two remaining lines: 72 mm. The letterforms suggest possibly a mid-first century AD date. SF 40, 92. Incorporated in later deposits in the baptistery.

The discovery of the third fragment of this inscription has proved Purcell's suggestion (1988a: 288-9) of the superlative form of *dulcis* in the second line, and the third refers to a name connected with the Greek ᾿Αχιλλευς. The inscription is clearly a funerary dedication, though it is not known whether Achill[was the deceased or the dedicator. The name is relatively common in Rome.

5. [   ]IS

Fig. 138. Inscription on a fragment of a strigillated sarcophagus in poor-quality coarse-crystalled greyish white marble, rapidly decomposing. SF 180. Incorporated into the structure of burial 2.

Only the letter S, 30 mm high, is visible on a smoothed panel, probably in the centre of one side. The previous letter may have been I. The sarcophagus probably dates to the late second or third century.

6. D [   ]
    V [   ]
    D[   ]

A roughly worked piece of volcanic tufo, with traces of a red painted text. B1. From the plough-soil over the church.

The D in line 1 is the only clearly visible letter and suggests that the inscription may have been a tombstone of the *D(is) M(anibus)* type. However, nothing further can be argued from the remaining fragments of text.

7. DIS   •   M
    HERENNIAE
    ]VIDI

Fig. 139. An inscription on a fairly rough block of local volcanic tufo with the first two lines and fragments of the third line surviving. (No number assigned.) Found built into the northwest corner of the baptistery, where it remains. Letters: l1 - 55 mm; l2 - 50 mm. A tombstone of the *Dis M(ani-*

[55] Cf. C. Caecilius Isidorus, also a freedman, who died in 8 BC, leaving 3,600 pairs of oxen, 257,000 other cattle and 60 million sesterces (Pliny, *Naturalis Historia* xxxiii. 135); Columella and Cato both stated that cattle farming was an extremely profitable enterprise (Columella, *De Re Rustica* vi. pref. 3-5; Cato, in Cicero, *De Officiis* ii. 89).

[56] Faustus is described as a *Magister Augustalis*, the only known holder of this office in Veii. All references to *Magistri Augustales* that can be dated are Augustan and they seem to have been replaced by the *Seviri Augustales* and *Augustales*. For the development of the different offices of the Imperial cult, see Taylor (1914).

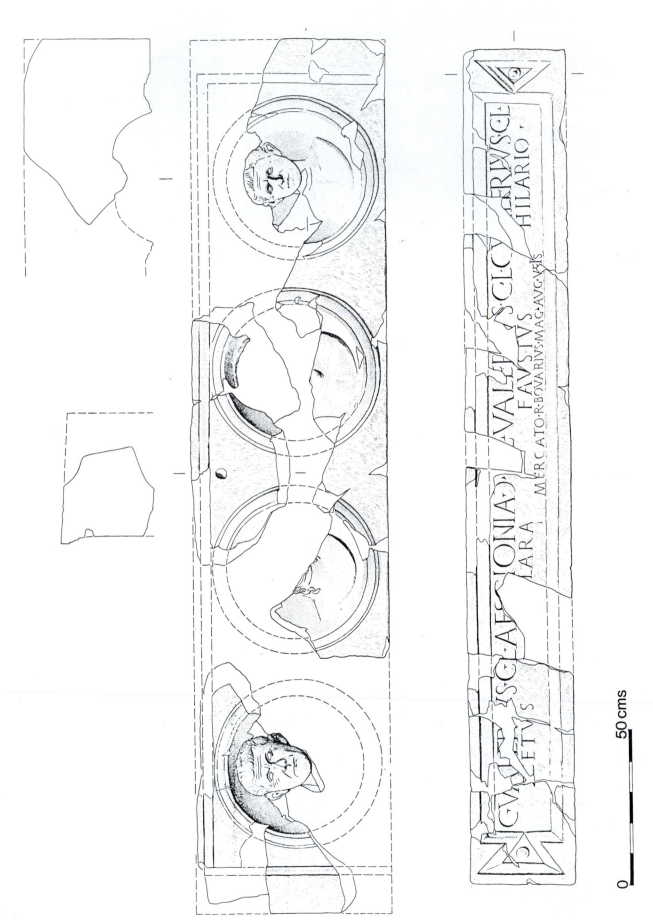

Fig. 135. The freed people tomb monument (inscription no. 3). (SA)

Fig. 137. Inscription no. 4. *(KW)*

bus) type, and the use of the word *Dis*, rather than its more usual abbreviation, *D*, suggests that the tombstone may be a fairly early example of this type. The letterforms and workmanship are also comparable to that of cat. 2 above, dated by Purcell (1988a: 286) to the early Imperial period.

The letters of the third line might be VIDI, possibly an Avidius or Helvidius, identifying the builder of the monument, perhaps the husband or son of the Herennia who is remembered. There would probably be room for a *praenomen* at the beginning of line 3, and a *cognomen* on line 4.

The workmanship is of low quality, shown by the poor letterforms, particularly the E and N in the middle of the name, and the letter spacing. This, together with the roughness of the block, suggests that the builder may have been of fairly low status.

The name Herennia is very common in both Rome and other towns in Italy, though particularly so around Tibur (for example, *CIL* XIV 3660, 3777, 4239). The tombstone of a Herennia Ianuaria was found at Casale Spezzamazze, between the Cassia and the Flaminia, but this probably

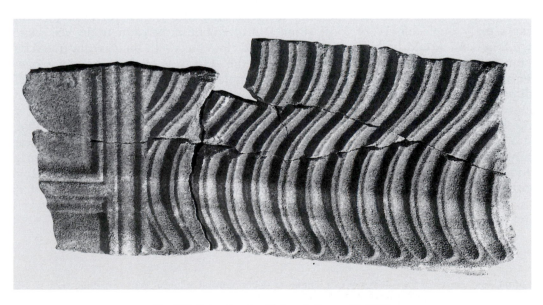

Fig. 138. Sarcophagus with inscription no. 5. *(KW)*

Fig. 139. The Herennia inscription (no. 6). *(KW)*

dates to the second century AD (Reynolds 1966: 56-67).[57] Reynolds noted that there may be a relationship between this woman and M. Herennius Picens, suffect consul of AD 1 and patron of the *municipium* of Veii (*CIL* XI 3797). In the light of the contents of cat. 3 above, a link between the Herennia of the Monte Gelato inscription and M. Herennius Picens seems quite possible. The dating of the inscription would certainly allow such a relationship with him or his family.

DISCUSSION

The original location of these inscriptions is by no means certain, and that of cat. 2 has been discussed elsewhere (Gilliver 1990: 195). Although it is conceivable that marble might have been brought into the site at Monte Gelato for reduction to lime, it seems unlikely that rough blocks of local stone such as cat. 1-2 and 6-7 would be brought in from a distance for building materials. A settlement is known to have existed at Monte Caio, a kilometre to the north of Monte Gelato, and it is possible that the inscriptions may have been set up there originally.[58] However, a road runs past the site at Monte Gelato and a mausoleum fronted on to it. This would certainly have been an appropriate place for the other funerary inscriptions, and this seems to be the most likely origin for them. Indeed, a Roman cemetery is now known some 200 m to the northwest (cf. Fig. 8).

The inscriptions dating to the early Imperial period, cat. 2, 3 and 7, are particularly interesting for a number of reasons. In the earlier publication of cat. 2 and 3, Purcell suggested (1988a: 291) that they might indicate a particular period of prosperity, and this is confirmed by the rich marble sculptures which are roughly contemporary.

Cat. 3 and 7 also suggest links between the settlement at Monte Gelato and the *municipium* of Veii, rather than the nearer *municipium* of Falerii. The cattle merchant, C. Valerius Faustus, was a member of the Imperial cult at Veii, whilst Aescionia, his wife (?), may well have been a freedwoman of the family of Aescionius Capella, a *duumvir* of the *municipium*. Cat. 7 also provides a possible link with the family of M. Herennius Picens, patron of Veii. The style of the large funerary monument, cat. 3, suggests links with the city of Rome, as does Faustus's involvement in the cattle trade. Veii is known to have had close links with the city, illustrated by the record of the *centumviri* of the *municipium* meeting in the Temple of Venus Genetrix in AD 26 (*CIL* XI 3805).

Unfortunately the inscriptions provide no clue as to the function of the site other than the possibility of local officials at work in cat. 2. The epigraphic record of the early Imperial period does, however, suggest the presence of persons of fairly low status, but probably linked with Veii and Rome through patronage and the cattle trade, and hints at the importance of the relationship between town and countryside at this time.

---

[57] A woman of the same name was joint dedicator of a tombstone to her husband Sulpicius Felix in Volsinii (*CIL* XI 2791), and a relationship between the two women is not impossible.

[58] For a tombstone of A. Petronius Urbanus from Monte Caio, see Tomassetti (1877: 263).

GRAFFITI (Fig. 140)[59]

Five buff-ware sherds with graffiti were recovered from the upper fill of the fish-pond. It is a context dating to the later second century AD and overlaid the deposit containing the 'stork-vase' with the long Greek inscription (below, Figs 239-42). The 'stork-vase' is an unusable waster, and must have been made on or near to the site. These graffiti are an additional pointer to the presence of Greek speakers at the Mola di Monte Gelato.

1. A small sherd with a deeply scored graffito.
   [...]ωκ[...]
   omega kappa
2. A sherd with a deeply scored graffito.
   ]A[
   alpha (or possibly LV[...])
3. Shoulder of a jar. The graffito may be read either as Greek or Latin.
   AL [...] or AI [...]
   In view of the context, R.S.O. Tomlin has suggested AI[ILIVS...], Ae[lius].
4. Small sherd from the shoulder of a small jar, apparently with one name written over another, possibly with some scratching out.
   [...] VFANI\[...]
5. Rim and shoulder of a jar.
   [...]EIAΣY[...]

MARBLE SCULPTURE, OBJECTS AND VENEER OF THE ROMAN PERIOD, by Amanda Claridge

1. **Statuette of Venus** (Fig. 141)
   Marble: medium-coarse crystalled translucent white.
   Dimensions: maximum preserved height, 0.404 m; width across shoulders 0.26 m; across nipples 0.14 m.
   Site ref.: MG89, L157, SF 529.
   Find-spot: from a rubble layer in the corridor south of the fish-pond, phase 3 (AD 350-550).

   The statuette was about two-thirds life-size. Only the upper torso as far as the navel survives. The head has broken away at the base of the neck, the left arm at the shoulder, the right arm just below the shoulder. The head originally turned slightly to the proper left. Two twisted locks of hair fell to the shoulders on either side. The right arm was bent at the elbow and crossed the chest just below the right breast, with the fingers of the hand extended to mask the lower half of the left breast. The stump of a strut of marble which once connected the forearm to the body, the tips of the third and fourth fingers and a trace of the thumb, are preserved. The left arm reached downwards over the left hip (where the scar of a connecting strut indicates its position). The weight of the body was apparently posed on the left leg.

   The basic elements are those of the well-known Capitoline Venus type (Rome, Musei Capitolini inv. no. 409;

LIMC 11, 1-2: 52, no. 409). However, the nature of the fracture across the abdomen suggests that the lower half of the Monte Gelato statuette was draped, in one of the variations on the Capitoline Venus theme (Di Vita 1955: 17 and 23, no. 24, pl. 10,2). Completely nude Venuses have usually fractured at or near the knees rather than higher up the body.

The workmanship is very good; all surfaces are carefully finished, the flesh smoothed with abrasives. The carving of the two twists of hair on the shoulders was pursued somewhat further on the left than on the right (an indication perhaps of the intended principal view): the channel between the locks on the left was deepened and the locks themselves set off from the flesh with the aid of a fine drill (diameter 2.5 mm) working a series of near vertical holes, subsequently trimmed and modified with a fine flat chisel. On the right, the detail remained as first drafted with the chisel.

2. **Statuette of a reclining nymph** (Fig. 142)
   Marble: fine crystalled, highly translucent, yellowish white, possibly Dokimeion.[60]
   Dimensions: maximum preserved length 0.705 m; height 0.195 m.
   Site ref.: MG 87, D76, SF 68.
   Find-spot: laid upside-down in a late Roman floor.

   The fragment comprises part of a two-thirds life-size reclining female figure, with a mantle draped over her hips and legs, arranged in elaborate folds around the bent left knee. With the exception of the tips of the first three toes of the right foot, both feet are intact. The carving is excellent, the use of the drill to deepen the folds and to emphasize surface detail on the folds being subsequently carefully pursued with fine flat chisel-work. All carved surfaces were smoothed to a light polish with rasps and abrasives.

   The figure type, presumably a nymph, is one much used for fountain figures in Rome and the West during the first three centuries AD (Kapossy 1969: 18), and compares particularly closely with an example in Copenhagen (Poulsen 1914: no. 400a, pl. VI), in the pose, in the arrangement of the drapery, and in dimensions.

   The underside of the figure presents an oblique, sawn surface with a dowel hole at the upper end (probably the cause of the fracture at this point). The area around the dowel hole has been lightly roughened with a pointed chisel. In other words, the surface seems to have been prepared for attachment to another block of marble, not simply the result of cutting up the sculpture for reuse in the floor in which it was found. If the figure was originally made in two (or more) pieces of marble, that would suggest a relatively early date, sometime before the end of the first century AD, when high-quality marble was apparently in short supply (Claridge 1988b). The style and workmanship are also indicative of the early Empire.

3. **Fragment of a small male head** (Fig. 143)
   Marble: medium crystalled white, degraded.
   Dimensions: maximum preserved height 0.145 m; width of eye 24 mm.
   Site ref.: MG90, M74, SF 683.

---

[59] I am most grateful to M.W.C. Hassall and R.S.O. Tomlin for their comments on photographs of these sherds (TWP).
[60] Analysis by Keith Matthews (British Museum Research Laboratory) indicated that it could be Proconnesian, Carrara or Dokimeion (see below).

Fig. 140. Graffiti (1:1). *(KW)*

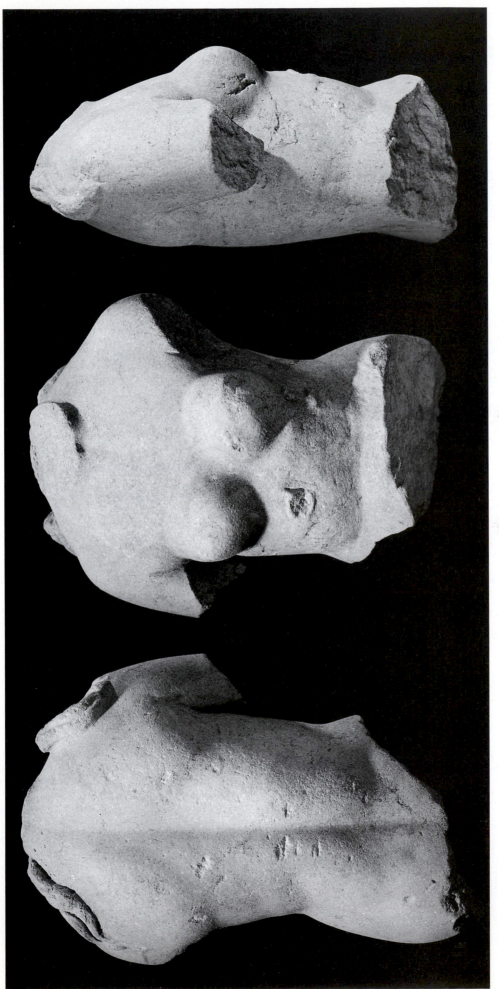

Fig. 141. Venus (cat. 1). *(KW)*

Fig. 142. Reclining nymph (cat. 2). *(KW)*

Find-spot: silty layer above Roman road, phase 5/6 (late ninth century +).

Battered and water-worn, the fragment consists of an oblique section of the upper left side of a head, including the left eye, about two-thirds lifesize. The hair is the only distinguishing feature, with long straggling curls over the brow and to the side, covering the ear. The curls extend only a short distance back from the face; behind, the narrower shape of the skull appears almost smooth. There is no sign of a fillet at the point where the curls end; it is possible that the smoothness indicates a Phrygian cap.

The head belongs to that indefinable category of idealized youth which sometimes denotes Apollo, Eros, the young Dionysos, or Narcissus, a Genius, Lar or an Ephebe. A Phrygian cap would suit Ganymede.

4. **Fragment of a large marble basin (*labrum*)** (Figs 144 and 145)

Marble: fine crystalled translucent white.

Dimensions: height 0.225 m; greatest preserved width 0.54 m.

Site ref.: MG89, L105, SF 533.

Find-spot: upper fill of fish-pond (later second century AD).

The original upper outer diameter of the basin was about 1.04 m. ($3\frac{1}{2}$ Roman feet). The edge of the rim was decorated with an egg-and-dart motif; the top of the rim bore a band of beads in high relief. The inside of the basin was plain and smoothly polished. The outside bore a whirling pattern of fluting, the flutes alternately convex (cabled) and concave in profile, terminating in hemispheres outlined with *tondini* and interspaced with darts. In the middle of the underside is a flat circular surface, dressed with a fine claw chisel, where the basin will have been mounted on a supporting pedestal.

Two fragmentary basins from the villa at Chiragan in southwest France had the same whirling pattern of fluting (but not cabled), and appear to have been the same size and shape (Joulin 1901: 85-6, pl. VII, nos. 81 and 82).[61] A basin in the Naples Museum, reputedly found at Pompeii (*Museo Borbonico*, III: pl. XLV), compares closely in size, shape and general type of decoration (its fluting is straight). It has two handles. A larger one, without handles and in *pavonazzetto* marble, was found near Rome in the 1790s (Amelung 1908: 30-1, no. 9, pl. 3). Such

Fig. 143. Small male head (cat. 3). *(KW)*

---

[61] From the 1826-30 excavations Joulin gave their diameter as 1.0 m and described the marble as grey '*bleu turquin*' from Italy. The shapes are difficult to determine from the photographs.

Fig. 144. Marble *labrum* (cat. 4). *(KW)*

basins could serve various functions, but are especially associated with the *caldaria* of bath-houses (Daremberg and Saglio 1877-1919: *s.v. Labrum*).

5. **Neck of a small marble crater** (Fig. 146)
Marble: fine crystalled white with faint grey flecks.
Dimensions: diameter (outer edge of rim) 0.34 m; maximum preserved height 0.225 m.
Site ref.: MG 89, L105, SF 547.
Find-spot: upper fill of fish-pond (later second century AD).

Recomposed from fifteen fragments, the neck is almost complete. The profile and proportions are those of a crater, broken at the point where the swelling of the bowl commenced.[62] Since the hollowing of the interior was almost vertical, the walls became extraordinarily thin towards the bottom (less than 50 mm in places). The start of a change in profile is just visible on the inside. On the outside, the stump of a tiny strut of marble presupposes a small loop handle parallel with the wall of the vase, of which there would have been two, springing from the bowl below. The missing bowl may have been decorated, but otherwise the vase was plain, with a simple rim and a highly polished surface. Its size and weight would permit a relatively tall and slender pedestal, perhaps like that on the vase from the peristyle of the Villa of San Marco at Stabiae (Fig. 147) (Jashemski 1979: 331, fig. 530).

6. **The relief from the tomb of the Valerii** (Figs 135, 136, 148, 149)
Marble: fine crystalled translucent off-white with faint grey patches. Stable isotope analysis (Matthews, below) indicates either Carrara or Dokimeion; visual appearance favours Carrara.
Overall dimensions: height 0.62 m; width *c.* 2.8 m; depth front to back 0.42 m. Tondi: outer diameter 0.52 m; width of frame 0.4 m; distance between centres of tondi 0.62 m. Heads: chin to top of brow – (Zetus) 0.18 m; (Hilario) 0.15 m.

Site refs: MG 87, C59, SF 135, 147 (Zetus), 151, 163; MG 88, C62, SF 17 (Hilario).
Find-spot: limekiln, fourth century AD.

Four individuals were represented by their portrait busts in high relief, each set off against a plain concave background within a circular frame, which is ornamented with a shallow convex moulding between two fillets. The surrounding field is dressed with a fine claw-chisel (five teeth, 13 mm wide). The whole was enclosed by an outer rectangular frame of single cyma recta moulding. The back of the block was left rough, worked with a pick-hammer; the underside was dressed flat with a medium claw (five teeth, 24 mm) and subsequently roughened with a pick, presumably to provide a key for cement. There are no clamps or dowel holes on any surviving part of the block. It is thus unlikely to have been placed directly on top of another block, which means that if, as seems reasonable to suppose, it and the inscription block found with it (Gilliver, this volume, cat. 3) belong together, set into the façade of a tomb, then a brick or masonry cornice probably ran between them.

According to the inscription, the two portrait heads which survive are those of C. Valerius Zetus, at the far left, and C. Valerius Hilario, to the far right. Zetus's head (Fig. 148) shows a middle-aged man with a hooked nose and jutting chin. Heavy lines furrow his forehead and deeply scored crow's-feet radiate from the outer corners of his eyes. The eyes are rather roughly cut, with upper and lower lids of equal weight, the upper overlapping the lower at the outer corner. The eyeball is flattened in the area of the pupil and the tear duct is marked with a small drill hole (diameter 2 mm). That the left eye is distinctly higher than the right is presumably an error on the part of the sculptor. The hair is shaped as a cap of short locks hugging the temples and rendered with shallow slightly curving grooves, using the edge of a flat chisel. The flesh surfaces are smoothed with abrasives.

Hilario's head (Fig. 149) is smaller and more finely featured but very similar in other respects, sharing the wrinkles, crow's-feet and profile (the chin especially). The

---

[62] Compare the profile drawings in Grassinger (1991).

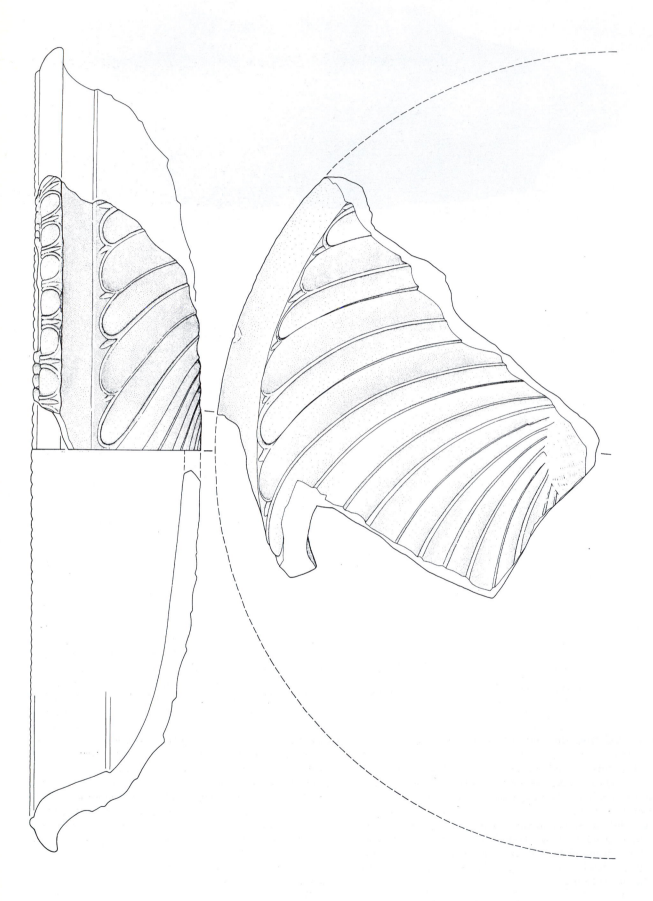

Fig. 145. Marble *labrum* (1:5). (SA)

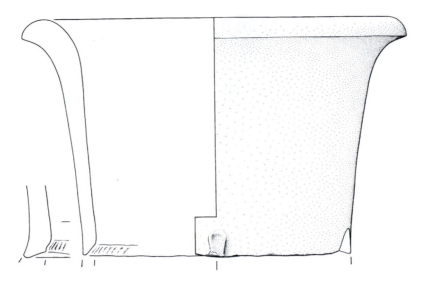

Fig. 146. Marble crater (cat. 5) (1:3). *(KW/SC)*

hair, worked with a fine flat chisel (4 mm wide), following a slightly bull-nosed chisel (8-9 mm wide), is only fully finished on the proper left side and over the brow, where it has a faint parting. Of the ears, the left is well worked, the right remains rough; the mouth and nostrils are chisel cut; the eyes have faint drill holes in their inner corners, the left one more strongly marked. There are possible traces of a rasp on the right cheek; for the rest the flesh is smoothed with abrasive.

The technique and the moderately 'Republican' portrait style, with its serious, rather down-at-mouth expression, close-cropped hair and sharply lined features, find numerous parallels among the freedmen grave reliefs of Rome, dating variously from the early Augustan to the Claudian period.[63] The size and shape of the male busts

and what little remains of Aescionia [Hi]lara's bust (centre left) are characteristically Tiberian or early Claudian. The loose corkscrew curls beside [Hi]lara's neck most closely resemble those found on portraits of Agrippina Major and Minor and some private individuals, probably dating from around AD 20-40 (for examples, see Zanker and Fittschen (1983: 5-6, no. 4, pls 4-5, Beilage 1-2, 3c-d) and Poulsen (1962: no. 35, pl. LV; no. 74, pl. CXXIX; no. 75, pl. CXXXI).[64]

The particular design of the relief as a whole has no precise equivalent among the reliefs from Rome but, like its sole companion from South Etruria (the monument of the Gessi found on the Via Cassia near Viterbo (Comstock and Vermeule 1976: 201, no. 319; Frenz 1985: 86, no. 14; Kockel 1993; J 1, pl. 68)), it was probably pro-

[63] Compare Kockel (1993), examples in Group I 4-6, I 12 (pls 63-5) and J 4 (pl. 71) early Augustan; L 5 (pl. 91a) mid-Augustan; L 8 (pl. 95a) mid-late Augustan; L 18 (pl. 102 c-d), L 23 (pl. 108) Tiberian?; M 5 (pl. 116 c-d, 117) Tiberian-Claudian.

[64] The comparison with portraits of Poppaea and consequently later dating which I allowed for in the preliminary report (Claridge 1988b: 294) was, on further reflection, not justified.

Fig. 147. Marble vase from Villa San Marco, Stabiae. *(AC)*

shell and the outer frame shaped as a wreath of laurel or oak, with rosettes or more extensive floral ornament in the spandrels; some are further embellished by being set within an architectural framework or held by erotes. The comparative simplicity of the Mola di Monte Gelato design could have been merely a measure of economy (less decoration naturally costing less to carve), but, even if only by default, it also gives a stronger impression of a series of portraits on shields hanging on a wall – the genuine *clipeatae imagines* of contemporary honorary, votive and aristocratic Roman funerary practice.[66]

7. The marble veneer

Four hundred and seventy-one loose fragments of marble revetment were retrieved from the excavations, scattered in 80 contexts, ranging in date from the late second century AD to the medieval period.

The largest single group (124 pieces) came from the upper fill of the fish-pond, L105, deposited in the later second century, and very possibly deriving from the nearby bath-house. The group consisted mainly of variegated grey/white marble mottled and veined with dark grey and black (*bardiglio fiorito*) from Carrara (ancient Luna), sawn into relatively thin slabs (6-13 mm), probably from floors or low vertical surfaces (such as dados or risers on steps); a smaller quantity of a paler *bardiglio* in rather thicker slabs (12-23 mm), some with rounded edges, which suggests the veneer of steps or ledges (for example, of pools); and seven fragments of plain greyish white Carrara of a thickness (50-3 mm) suitable for thresholds. There was also a piece of flat moulding which could come from a door-frame; six pieces of dark red limestone (*rosso antico*) quarter-round strip moulding; and three recognizable elements of an *opus sectile* panel or floor, their measurements compatible with each other: a rectangle (0.13 × >0.2 m) and an isosceles triangle (0.125 × 0.18 m) in the variegated grey/pink/flesh-red marble '*portasanta*' (from the island of Chios), and an isosceles triangle (0.09 × 0.125 m) in the black/white/red breccia *africano* (from Teos, western Turkey).

A predominance of monochrome greys and whites and a dearth of coloured marbles also characterize the rest of the finds, many of which could be further residue from the same source(s) as those represented in the fill of the fish-pond. In addition to quantities of thin *bardiglio* veneer and other Carrara veined and plain monochromes, and some thicker fragments in medium crystalled greyish white and white banded-with-grey of Proconnesian (Marmara) type and perhaps other eastern mediterranean marbles, the north cistern (also filled by *c.* AD 200), and the large room (A) and adjoining corridor, yielded several sizeable pieces of the green-and-white variegated *cipollino* (from Euboea) and fragments of a flesh-pink and white limestone breccia, apparently *breccia corallina* (from Bilecik, Turkey).

duced by a workshop in the city. As a type, not many Roman freedmen chose to have their portraits set in tondi and no two designs are alike. Kockel has catalogued eight, which he has dated from the early Augustan (20s BC) to the early Claudian period.[65] All are far more richly decorated – and more overtly funerary in character – than the Mola di Monte Gelato one, most having the field within the tondo fluted like a scallop

[65] (a) Boston, Museum of Fine Arts 1972.918. Comstock and Vermeule 1976: 205, no. 325; Kockel 1993: K4, 169, pl. 18b. Mid-late Augustan. (b) London, British Museum, Sc. 2275. Relief of the Antistii. Kockel 1993: 178, L 4, pl. 90B, 93d-e; Kleiner 1977: 207, no. 20; Frenz 1977: 178-9, no. J 5. (c) London, British Museum, acc. no. 1914.6-24.4. Kockel 1993: 203, M 9, pl. 118d; Walker 1985: 53-4, fig. 44. (d) Rome, Museo Nuovo, Palazzo dei Conservatori no. 2306. Kockel 1993: 164, J 16, pl. 78a. (e) Rome, Museo Nuovo, Palazzo dei Conservatori no. 2230. Relief of the Bennii. Three tondi in architectural frame. Kockel 1993: 191, L 21, pl. 106a-c, 107a-b. (f) Rome, Museo delle Terme, no inventory number (*MNR* I/7 part 2, 288-9, ix.49). Kockel 1993: 224, O 39, pl. 133e. (g) Formerly Lowther Castle. Kockel 1993: 216, O 5, pl. 128d. Tiberian or later. (h) Rome, Art market (in 1978). Kockel 1993: 231, O 72, pl. 138d.

The type occasionally recurs (for example, Dresden, Albertinum Hn 379 (Kockel 1993: 202, M 7, pl. 118c), Flavian or Trajanic). One other example, in the garden of the Palazzo Colonna in Rome (Kockel 1993: 170, K 5, pl. 85a), is a half-figure in a tondo, like the later medallion portraits on grave altars and sarcophagi. For further discussion, see Kockel (1993: 14 and 55).

[66] Winkes (1969) remains the standard work, but see also Vermeule (1965), Neumann (1988) and Smith (1990: 131).

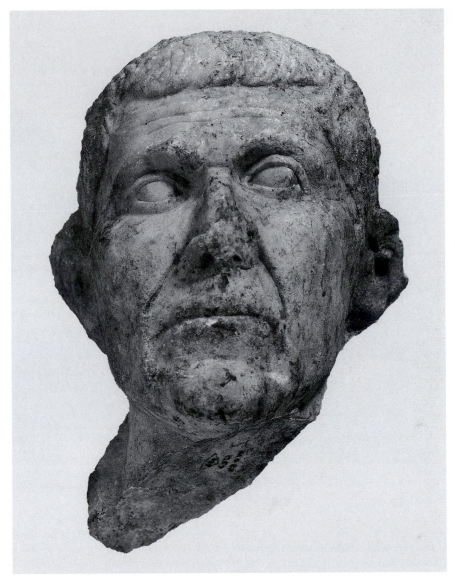

Fig. 148. Head of C. Valerius Zetus from the tomb monument (Figs 135 and 136). *(KW)*

STABLE ISOTOPE ANALYSIS OF THE MARBLE, by Keith Matthews[67]

Samples were submitted in 1987 from the heads of C. Valerius Zetus and Aescionia [Hi]lara from the tomb monument (cat. 6, above; it was not realized at the time that they belonged to a single monument). A sample from the nymph (cat. 2) was also provided. The marble of the tomb monument was described as being fine crystals, translucent and of a creamy white colour; this led to the suggestion that it may have been Pentelic. The marble used for the nymph was described as being fine crystalline, highly translucent, and of a yellowish white colour: it was suggested that the source may have been the Dokimeion quarries in Asia Minor.

EXPERIMENTAL PROCEDURE

The experimental procedure is based on the work of McCrea (1950), although it was not applied to the provenancing of classical white marble until the early 1970s (see for example, Craig and Craig (1972); Coleman and Walker (1979)).

The samples were supplied in the form of powder that had been obtained by drilling the sculptures. The sampling was undertaken by Amanda Claridge, then of the British School at Rome, following sampling instructions provided

[67] I am indebted to Professor Norman Herz of the University of Georgia, USA, for making his database of marble quarry analyses available. Also, thanks are due to Dr T.W. Potter for providing much detailed information about the history attached to these pieces, and to Amanda Claridge for the physical descriptions of the sculptures themselves and for taking the samples. Dr Susan Walker of the Department of Greek and Roman Antiquities of the British Museum has also provided much useful advice and information.

Fig. 149. Head of C. Valerius Hilario from the tomb monument (Figs 135 and 136). *(KW)*

by the British Museum Research Laboratory. From this powder, 10 mg was reacted with 100% orthophosphoric acid under vacuum. The carbon dioxide thus obtained was isotopically analysed using a VG micromass 602D mass-spectrometer. The isotopic ratio (δ) obtained is given in parts per mil (‰, that is, per thousand) relative to the PDB standard (Craig 1957), where

$$\delta = \frac{(Rsample - Rpdb) \times 1000 \ \text{‰}}{Rpdb}$$

and R= 13C/12C pr 180/160. The standard error on these measurements is typically ± 0.05 ‰.

RESULTS

The results are given in Table 51 and are also plotted graphically (Fig. 150) as the carbon isotope ratio δ 13C versus the oxygen isotope ratio δ 180. Also on the plot are the 90% ellipses (Leese 1988) of isotopic signatures obtained from quarry data very kindly made available by Professor Norman Herz of the University of Georgia, and supplemented by Carrara data from quarry samples measured by the British Museum Research Laboratory. The ellipses selected include those for some of the more important marble quarrying areas in antiquity, and for which data, albeit limited, are available.

The results (1 and 2) of the tomb monument can be seen to fall within the ellipses of Dokimeion and Carrara. It was suggested from the visual appearance of the marble that the Pentelic quarries were a possible source, but clearly this is not the case. However, it would seem to be difficult to resolve the origins further at this stage, and perhaps use of an alternative analytical technique such as NAA (see, for example, Mello, Monna and Oddone (1988)) might resolve the issue. On balance, the marble is more likely to be from Carrara, but this cannot be said to be certain.

Table 51. Isotopic analysis of the marble.

no.	description	reference no.	BMRL no.	δ 13 C ‰	δ 180 ‰
1	Head of Zetus	C59, SF 147	30786T	1.84	-2.62
2	Head of Aescionia	C59, SF 151	30787R	1.92	-2.53
3	Nymph	D76, SF 68	30785V	2.27	-2.27

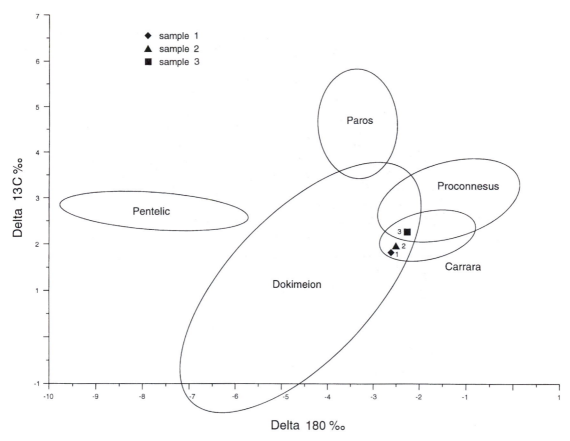

Fig. 150. Stable isotope analysis of the marble. *(KM)*

From the analysis of the sample from the nymph (3) it can be seen from the result that three different sources for the marble are indicated: Proconnesus, Carrara, and Dokimeion. It was suggested from the physical appearance that Dokimeion was the likely source: however, in view of the inconclusive nature of the isotopic result, further study is indicated, as suggested above.

THE EARLY MEDIEVAL SCULPTURE, by John Osborne

In early medieval Italy there were considerably fewer contexts in which sculpture could be employed than there had been in classical Antiquity. Virtually all the patronage of work in the medium of stone was commissioned either by or for the Christian Church, and in the pre-Romanesque period the possibilities for such activity were limited almost exclusively to the categories of church fixtures and furnishings: capitals and bases, choir and chancel screens, ciboria, altars, pulpits, tomb slabs and sarcophagi. This development had already taken place in late Antiquity, and from the first half of the sixth century there are splendid examples of the carver's art which survive in churches in Rome, Ravenna, Constantinople and elsewhere.

Another significant outburst of activity took place in the Italian peninsula and on the Dalmatian littoral during the period from roughly the mid-eighth to the mid-ninth centuries. Although initiated

under the Lombard monarchy, the phenomenon reached a peak during the reigns of Charlemagne and his immediate successors, and its comparative longevity is without question a direct consequence of the substantially increased wealth enjoyed by ecclesiastical institutions during the so-called Carolingian 'renaissance'. The sculpture which has survived from this period reveals its own very particular repertory of designs and motifs, very different from those of the age of the emperor Justinian. Patterns are primarily abstract and based on either geometric or vegetal forms, with the substantial use of interlaced and plaited designs, coupled with circles, spirals, rosettes, lilies, vines, crosses, and a wide variety of other ornamental devices, all of which may be found in abundance throughout the northern and central regions of the Italian peninsula as well as on the eastern shore of the Adriatic. While some of these motifs have their origins in earlier ecclesiastical sculpture, many reveal the substantial influence of a more general decorative vocabulary which has its roots in the arts of late Antiquity, for example in the designs of mosaic floor pavements, while others suggest links with the ornament to be found in contemporary manuscript illumination. The repertory of designs clearly transcended the specific medium employed. Animal figures are rare, and for the most part limited to creatures with a long tradition of symbolic significance in Christian art, for example peacocks or

mately derived from passages in the Book of Revelation which refer to Christ in this cryptic fashion (Book of Revelation 1.8, 21.6, 22.13). Its use carried on into the Middle Ages in a variety of media, including sculpture: for example the seventh- or eighth-century panels in the church of San Leonardo at Aquilea, near Lucca (*CSA* I: no. 1), and the cathedral at Amelia (*CSA* XII: no. 1). The concept of Christ as the sacrificial lamb of God ('Agnus Dei') may similarly be found throughout the New Testament and subsequent patristic literature, based on the words spoken by John the Baptist upon first seeing Jesus (John 1.29 '*Ecce agnus Dei, ecce qui tollit peccatum mundi*') and the subsequent vision of the apocalyptic lamb in the Book of Revelation. Lambs representing Christ, the apostles, and indeed Christians in general, were again a popular image in the visual arts from the earliest centuries of the faith, and one or more lambs holding crosses in their foreleg are not uncommon in early medieval Italian sculpture: for example, a seventh-century tombstone from San Vincenzo at Galliano (Cassanelli 1987: fig. 284), an eighth-century sarcophagus in Sant'Apollinare in Classe at Ravenna (*Corpus Ravenna* II: no. 59), and other eighth-century panels in Santa Maria Assunta at Gussago (*CSA* III: no. 201) and at Cividale (*CSA* X: nos. 340 and 353). In Rome itself, lambs bearing crosses appear on a plaque now in the Palazzo Senatorio on the Capitoline (*CSA* VII: no. 32) and the problematic reliquary altar in the church of Santa Maria del Priorato on the Aventine (*CSA* VII: 4 no. 33).

However, the combination of the two elements – the upright cross with apocalyptic letters, and the single lamb, or 'Agnus Dei', standing in front – is highly unusual, and seemingly without parallel in Italian sculpture of the Carolingian era. There are, however, related images which have survived in other media, for example a group of triumphal arch mosaics in Roman churches, in which the lamb and the cross are placed on a throne set between seven large candlesticks, following the text of the Book of Revelation. This occurs in the sixth-century church of Santi Cosma e Damiano and again, perhaps more significantly, on the triumphal arch of Santa Prassede, a project of Pope Paschal I (817-24). The issue is complicated by the fact that the depiction of Christ in the form of a lamb had been specifically prohibited in the years just prior to the onset of iconoclasm: by the 82nd canon of the Quinisext Council, held in Constantinople in 692 (for the text see Mango (1972: 139-40)). Although there had initially been strong Roman reaction against this decision, prompting Pope Sergius I to incorporate John the Baptist's words into the text of the mass (*Liber Pontificalis* I, 376), the image does disappear from Roman art throughout the course of the eighth century (see discussions of Nordhagen (1976: 165-6) and Davis-Weyer and Emerick (1984: 27-8)). If Nordhagen and Davis-Weyer and Emerick are correct in linking the revival of Agnus Dei imagery in Rome with the pontificate of Paschal I, then this may provide an important chronological indication for the production of the Mola di Monte Gelato relief. It seems likely that such an image would have occupied a position of importance in the decorations of the church, perhaps as an embellishment for the front of the altar, for which it would be both theologically and liturgically appropriate.

Also worthy of note is the small hole terminating the spiral form made by the lamb's tail. This rather unusual occurrence has a precise parallel in another piece from the site (cat. 7), presumably a product of the same sculptor or workshop.

2. **Fragment of a pilaster supporting an octagonal colonnette (probably from a chancel screen or iconostasis)** (Figs 153 and 154)
Site ref.: D29, SF 53; found built into the wall dividing the church from the baptistery (cf. Fig. 74). Marble (in two pieces). Pilaster: $0.36 \times 0.26 \times 0.14$ m. Colonnette: 0.2×0.13 m (diameter).

The principal face or front of the pilaster is decorated with one of the most characteristic and widely diffused designs from the period of the eighth and ninth centuries: two ribbons, each with two furrows or grooves, are arranged in a pattern of interlocking circles and diamond-shaped lozenges. (For the pattern, see discussions by Verzone (1945: 176-8 ('*cerchi intrecciati a rombi*'); and in *CSA* II: 17 ('*nastri bisolcati che formano cerchi annodati e intrecciati a losanghe*').) Excellent parallels may be found throughout the Italian peninsula: for example at Ventimiglia, Pavia, Venice, and Aquileia in the north (Verzone 1945: pl. lxii no. 105; Peroni 1975: no. 125; Kutzli 1974: pl. 2; *CSA* X: nos. 194, 275, 294), and closer at hand in pieces from Santa Maria Maggiore at Tuscania (*CSA* VIII: no. 366), San Saba in Rome (*CSA* VII: 4, no. 144c), and the abbey of San Pietro in Valle at Ferentillo (*CSA* II: nos. 29, 32-9).

The narrower side face bears the simple design of a single plaited ribbon set within a recessed field. Of the two carved faces, this is the less worn, with the result that the sharp triangular cuts (*Kerbschnitt*) of the two grooves in the ribbon are well-preserved. Once again, the design itself was widely popular, with good parallels in all regions, including Rome, where it appears for example on the portal of the San Zeno chapel in the church of Santa Prassede (*CSA* VII: 1, no. 90). A rather useful comparison may also be made to the ninth-century pilaster from San Pietro in Valle at Ferentillo, which similarly has the design of circles and lozenges on its main face (*CSA* II: no. 29).

In the smoothed but undecorated back face of the pilaster there is a vertical groove (width 50 mm, depth 20 mm) for the attachment of the adjoining section of the screen. A slightly larger groove in the left side (width 60 mm, depth 25 mm) similarly reveals where the adjoining section was inserted, and confirms that the pilaster was positioned at a corner. A small hole and shallow groove in the top suggest that something once was inserted in this face as well.

Screens of this type appear to have been widely popular in Rome in the early Middle Ages. An excellent and well-preserved example, probably still in its original configuration, survives to the north of the city, not far from Monte Gelato, in the church of San Leone at Capena (Matthiae 1952; *CSA* VIII: no. 180). Although the specific designs of the Capena iconostasis are different from those in question here, it is worth noting that the arch over the central opening is similarly supported by octagonal colonnettes of approximately the same size (*CSA* VII: nos. 192-3).

3. **Fragment of an octagonal colonnette** (not illustrated)
Site ref.: Sforzini 1983, Frag. 'A'; from deposits overlying the bath-house. Marble. 0.22×0.13 m (diameter).

The colonnette presumably belongs to the same screen as in cat. 2.

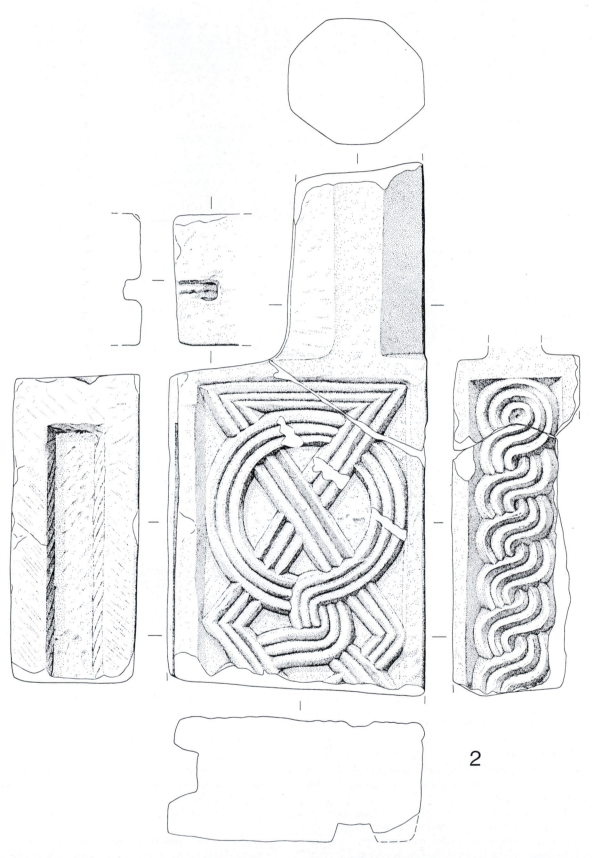

Fig. 153. The chancel screen or iconostasis (1:4). *(SA)*

2

Fig. 154. The chancel screen or iconostasis. *(KW)*

4. **Fragment of a pilaster or architrave** (Fig. 155)
   Site ref.: B1, SF 11; unstratified, over church. Marble.
   0.26 × 0.155 × 0.065 m.

   Although all four faces of the piece have been cut
   and smoothed, only one bears carved ornament: a
   design of two intertwined ribbons creating a pattern of
   interlocking circles. (For the design, see Verzone (1945:
   178- 9: '*doppio intreccio di cerchi alternati*').) The same pattern may also be found in cat. 5 and 6, which are presumably other fragments of the same piece. Good parallels may be found throughout the region north of

Rome, for example in the cathedral of Civita Castellana,
the church of Sant'Andrea at Ronciglione, and the
church of San Pietro at Tuscania, all assigned to the
ninth century (*CSA* VIII: nos. 59, 270, 390).

5. **Fragment of a pilaster or architrave** (Fig. 155)
   Site ref. D374, SF 351; built into the base of the second
   font (cf. Fig. 86). Marble. 0.2 × 0.155 × 0.065 m.

   See above, cat. 4. This section was clearly at one end, as
   is suggested both by the termination of the relief pattern
   and by the fact that the end is notched for attachment.

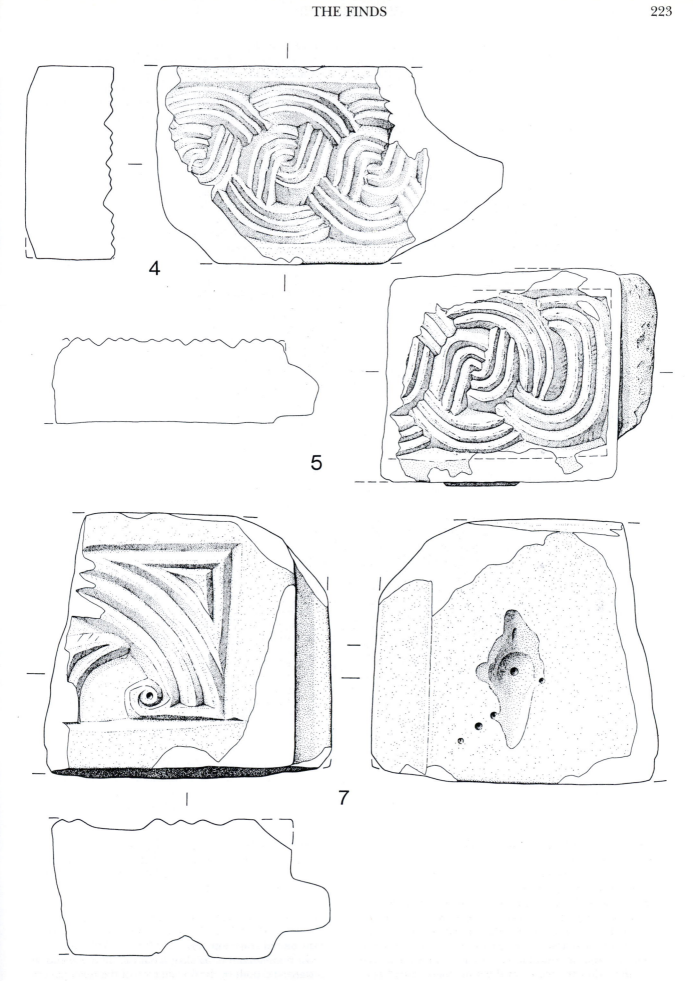

Fig. 155. Medieval sculpture (1:3). *(SA)*

6. **Fragment of a pilaster or architrave** (not illustrated)
   Site ref.: D301, SF 323; from a pit associated with a reconstruction of the font drainage system. Marble. 0.2 × 0.15 × 0.065 m.
      See above, cat. no. 4.

7. **Fragment from the end of an architrave or cornice (?)** (Fig. 155)
   Site ref.: D38, SF 94; found in the make-up for the latest baptistery floor. Marble. 0.215 × 0.19 × 0.105 m.
      The design on the one decorated face consists of a series of semicircles enclosing trilobate lilies. The semicircles have two grooves, and terminate with a curlicue spiral containing a pointed hole. While such holes are not entirely unprecedented in early medieval Italian sculpture (cf. *CSA* I: no. 35; VII: 2, no. 312), the practice is quite rare, and can perhaps here be regarded as a peculiarity or 'signature' of the sculptor or workshop concerned (cf. cat. 1). The fragment clearly comes from the end of the original piece, as it is notched for insertion. There is also a hole in the back face, perhaps for a metal clamp.

8. **Fragment from the end of an architrave or cornice (?)** (Fig. 156)
   Site ref.: D3, SF 41; found in the destruction deposit over the latest baptistery. Marble (in two pieces). 0.49 × 0.26 × 0.09 m.
      The design on the decorated face consists of a series of overlapping semicircles, each with a curlicue termination containing a pointed hole. In the triangular spaces created by the semicircles there are trilobate lilies. The pattern is thus rather similar to that of the preceding piece (cat. 7), although not identical, and the dimensions are clearly different. The holes in the spirals do, however, mark it as a product of the same sculptor or workshop. Patterns created by semicircles were popular in the Carolingian period for the decoration of horizontal elements such as architraves or cornices (for the design cf. Verzone (1945: 172-4: '*archetti intrecciati*')). A good parallel in Rome is provided by a late eighth-century cornice in the church of Santa Maria in Cosmedin (*CSA* VII: 3, no. 106), although this lacks the spiral terminations and floral additions. For the latter, compare the pattern of overlapping circles on a plaque from the Roman church of San Saba (*CSA* VII: 4, nos. 93-4).

9. **Fragment with design of concentric circles** (Fig. 156)
   Site ref.: A5, SF 1; from the fill over the bath-house, by the church. Marble. 0.23 × 0.16 × 0.12 m.
      A central pointed hole is enclosed in four outer concentric rings. This design is rare in the early Middle Ages, which generally preferred spirals to rings, but not without some parallels (cf. *CSA* I: nos. 32-3; VII: 3, no. 42; VIII: no. 389; *Seminario:* fig. 245). One end of the piece has a large groove (diameter 50 mm) for attachment.

10. **Fragment with design of plaited ribbon** (Fig. 156)
    Site ref.: Sforzini 1983, SF 387; from the fill over the bath-house. Marble. 0.19 × 0.085 × 0.095 m.
       All four sides of the piece are finished, but only one is decorated with a rather worn design of a single plaited ribbon, with holes at the centre of each section. There are good parallels throughout Italy, including an architrave from Trajan's Market in Rome (*CSA* VII: 2, no. 189).

11. **Fragment** (Fig. 157)
    Site ref.: D1, SF 158; from the plough-soil over the baptistery. Marble. 90 × 60 × 35 mm.
       The one worked side displays an outer border, and, in the recessed field, a circular line with two prominent holes on raised bases. It is possible that these form part of the decoration of the outer ring of a halo, comparable to those on depictions of the evangelist symbols at Cividale (*CSA* X: no. 332).

12. **Fragment with ribbon design** (not illustrated)
    Site ref.: D 319, SF 350; from the fill of the recut drain for the second font. Marble. 0.15 × 0.13 × 0.045 m.
       The one decorated face displays part of an outer border and an angular fragment of a ribbon design, perhaps from a lozenge. The pattern may have been similar to that on the main face of the pilaster (cat. 2), but the border widths are different, and thus this is not a fragment of the same piece.

13. **Decorated fragment** (Fig. 157)
    Site ref.: A12, SF 2; from the fill over the bath-house. Marble. 0.165 × 0.14 × 0.075 m.
       The one decorated face displays part of an outer border and what may be the curlicue termination of a ribbon design.

14. **Decorated fragment** (not illustrated)
    Site ref. B1; in the plough-soil over the church. Marble. 110 × 70 × 60 mm.
       One face has two strands of a ribbon design.

15. **Decorated fragment** (Fig. 157)
    Site ref.: B1, SF 877; from the plough-soil over the church. Marble. 130 × 50 × 50 mm.
       One face is decorated with two forms terminating in spirals, a design widely used for borders throughout Italy and Dalmatia, and ultimately deriving from late classical mosaic pavements. There are many parallels in Rome (cf. *CSA* VII: 1, no. 18; VII: 2, nos. 5, 46-8; VII: 3 nos. 122, 224, 231, 263; VII: 4, nos. 16-17, 45a, 235-7).

16. **Decorated fragment** (Fig. 157)
    Site ref.: C51, Special find no. 1; from the top fill over the limekiln. Marble. 120 × 65 × 50 mm.
       One face has part of a ribbon design.

17. **Decorated fragment** (Fig. 157)
    Site ref.: D219, SF 300; from the fill over the baptistery. Marble. 0.13 × 0.1 × 0.04 m.
       One face has part of a ribbon design.

18. **Decorated fragment** (Fig. 157)
    Site ref.: J4, SF 334; from the fill at the side of the paved road, and stratigraphically in a later position. Tufo block. 0.245 × 0.19 × 0.18 m.
       One face has remnants of an interlaced ribbon design.

19. **Decorated fragment** (Fig. 158)
    Site ref.: Sforzini C, SF 388; from the fill over the bath-house. Tufo block. 0.26 × 0.22 × 0.105 m.
       Interlace design.

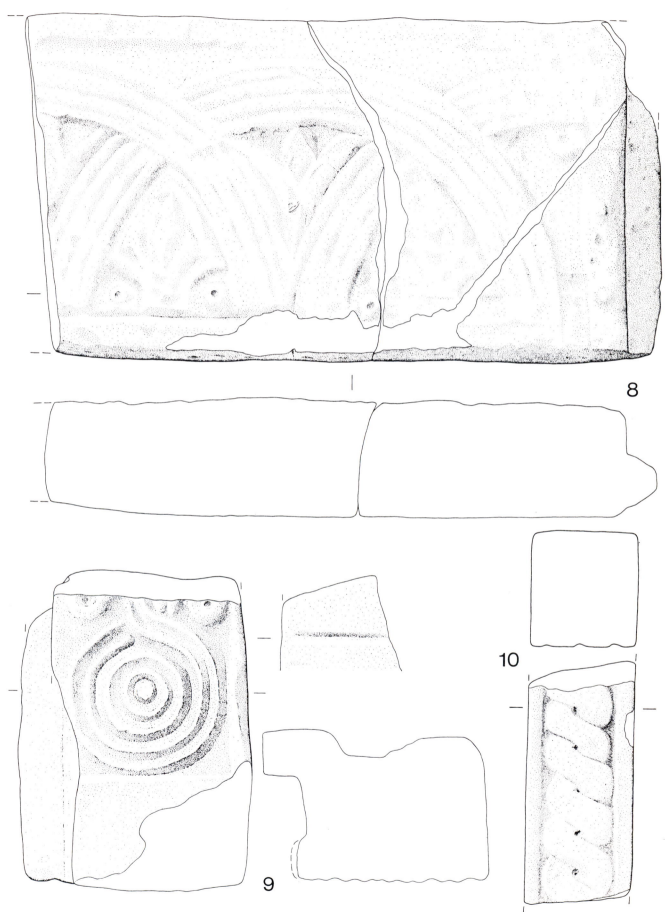

Fig. 156. Medieval sculpture (1:3). *(SA)*

some significant respects. Petrofabric 3 has no matrix calcite, implying a different clay source, and sanidine feldspar is the dominant inclusion, implying that the volcanic rocks of the source area were different. Petrofabric 4 also represents a different clay source, as its matrix is very silty and contains common mica. Volcanic inclusions are rare in this sample. Petrofabric 5 is characterized by the common occurrence of both sanidine and plagioclase feldspar.

Finally, Petrofabric 2 (hand specimen fabric E) is distinctive in its lack of volcanic inclusions and abundance of quartz. This fabric clearly originated in sedimentary deposits. Such deposits are rare in the region, and outcrop only where the rivers cut through the thick blanket of volcanic deposits to the underlying Pleistocene sediments. The nearest outcrop occurs at the modern tilery some 2.0 km down the river Treia, and a further outcrop occurs at Narce. The origin of this fabric could well be more distant, however.

WALL-PLASTER, by C.M. Gilliver

Painted wall-plaster was found in a large number of contexts in the main area of the site, but for the most part these pieces were very small, and in a very fragmentary condition. Two larger deposits were excavated, but these were also very fragmentary.

1. Panels of purple, yellow and red separated by narrow white borders c. 5-7 mm wide. From the late second-century fill of the cistern at the northern end of the site (L104, L143).
   The surviving decorative elements comprised green vegetation and flowers of yellow and white with green stems.
2. Quantities of wall-plaster in poor condition from the rubble of the late wall collapse east of the plunge bath (M23, Justinianic wall collapse).
   These panels had rather faded red, green and some darker colours, possibly black or purple, with some surviving fragments of green vegetation.

THE COINS, by Richard Hobbs

In total, 58 coins were recovered from the excavations. All except one were of bronze, and approximately half (31) were too worn to attribute to individual issuers. At least 46 coins were of the Roman period (from Trajan to Marcian), at least four were early Byzantine, one was Ostrogothic (cat. 57), and the latest coin was a ninth-century silver denarius of Pope Hadrian III. This coin, issued alongside those of Charles the Fat, is perhaps the rarest, with only around a thousand genuine papal coins known in total (Grierson and Blackburn 1986).

INTERPRETATION

Deliberate burial

Two coins were found in burial contexts, and hence were almost certainly deliberately placed. The first was a coin of Honorius (cat. 46), found in the mouth of a skeleton in an *a cappuccina* burial (no. 26). The second coin was a denarius of Pope Hadrian III (cat. 58), found in a child inhumation in the baptistery (no. 43). There was also a coin of Gratian (cat. 22) in the fill of burial no. 60, but this has been treated as a casual loss.

Casual losses

The contexts of the majority of the coins from the site are very likely to represent casual losses, as there is no evidence to suggest that any were part of a scattered hoard. The rates of coin loss varied over the history of the site, as shown in Table 52 (columns 2 and 3). By far the largest number of coins (over 60 per cent of the total) date to the late fourth and early fifth centuries AD. This fact has to be interpreted with caution, for a number of reasons.

Firstly, the coins of this date are generally smaller, lower value coins, and therefore more likely to be lost and not recovered. This contrasts with the second-century material, composed of larger module bronze asses and dupondii. The early Imperial material is therefore more significant in terms of intensity of occupation than mere numbers might suggest: taking into account their greater weight and value and their lower likelihood of being lost, even a few coins can be regarded as a significant group. In numismatic terms, the site may therefore have been occupied as intensively in the early Empire as in the later period.

Secondly, and more importantly, comparisons with data collected from Rome (Reece 1982), represented in Table 52 and Figure 167, show that a loss pattern of this nature is not unusual. In Rome too, the majority of coins found (over 80 per cent) dates to the late fourth and early fifth centuries AD. Loss in the second and third centuries AD, like Monte Gelato, is comparably low, with a sharp increase in period 6 (AD 350-400), a slight fall in period 7 (AD 400-50), and a significant fall in the subsequent periods (8 and 9) to levels comparable with the early Empire.

Therefore, despite Monte Gelato's firmly rural location, it does not appear to have been isolated from Rome and wider changes in coin circulation during the Empire, although with such a small sample observations can only be very general. At the very least, the coin evidence certainly supports the stratigraphic evidence which indicates a continuous occupation of the site during much of the Roman and into the Byzantine periods.

Table 52. Distribution of coins per period, comparing Monte Gelato and Rome.

Note: the periods were chosen because the bulk of the material was unable to be dated to more specific historical or numismatic phases. The methods used for comparing material from sites is fully explained by Reece (1987). Reece's data from Rome were a mixture of scattered hoards and stray losses from the Palatine area in the centre of Rome. Although a rather crude sample, the data are sufficient to establish a good comparative cross-section of coins lost throughout the Roman period and beyond.

period of issue	Monte Gelato – coins per period	Monte Gelato – coins per thousand	Rome – coins per period	Rome – coins per thousand
AD 100-150 (1)	1	17.86	73	12.28
AD 150-200 (2)	2	35.71	68	11.44
AD 200-250 (3)	1	17.86	45	7.57
AD 250-300 (4)	5	89.29	129	21.71
AD 300-350 (5)	3	53.57	417	70.18
AD 350-400 (6)	21	374.99	2,774	466.85
AD 400-450 (7)	12	214.29	2,224	374.28
AD 450-500 (8)	5	89.29	201	33.83
AD 500-550 (9)	6	107.14	11	1.85
total	56		5,942	

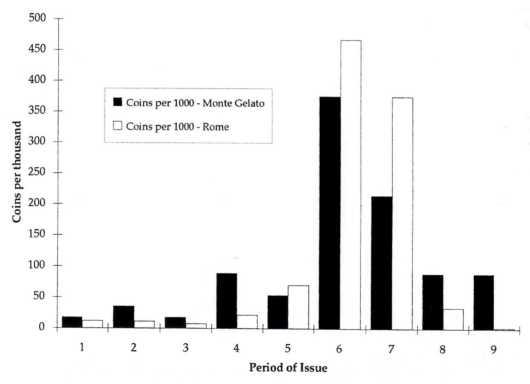

Fig. 167. A comparison of coin-loss between Rome and Monte Gelato. *(RH)*

CHRONOLOGICAL LIST OF SITE FINDS

1. Trajan (AD 98-117). Rome. AE as.
   obv. IMP CAES NERVA TRAIAN AVG GERM PM
   rev. TR POT COS III PP S C
   Weight: unknown.
   Cat. ref.: *BMC* 740.

Site ref. : MG86, B1, SF 7.
Find-spot: unstratified.

2. Marcus Aurelius (AD 159-60). Rome. AE dupondius.
   obv. AVRELIVS CAESAR AVG P II F
   rev. TR POT XIIII COS II SC
   Weight: 9.35 g.
   Cat. ref.: *RIC* 1355.

Site ref.: MG89, L101, SF 416.

Find-spot : hillwash.

3. Empress (Crispina?) (late second century AD). Mint uncertain. AE as.

obv. female bust r.

rev. Venus (?) seated l.

Weight: 18.06 g.

Cat. ref.: –.

Site ref.: MG90, S10, SF 705.

Find-spot: fill of rock-cut road, phase 2/3.

4. Trajan Decius (AD 249-50). Rome. AE sestertius.

obv. IMP C M TRAIANVS DECIVS AVG

rev. [DACIA FELIX] SC

Weight: 16.96 g.

Cat. ref.: *RIC* 114a.

Site ref.: MG89, M47, SF 563.

Find-spot: robbed north wall of bath-house, phase 3.

5. Claudius II (Divus) (AD 268-70). Rome. AE radiate.

obv. radiate bust r.

rev. CONSECRATIO eagle

Weight: 1.18 g.

Cat. ref.: – (barbarous).

Site ref.: MG89, M, SF 395.

Find-spot: unstratified.

6. Claudius II (Divus) (AD 268-70). Rome. AE radiate.

obv. radiate bust r.

rev. CONSECRATIO altar

Weight: 0.96 g.

Cat. ref.: – (barbarous).

Site ref.: MG89, L124, SF 415.

Find-spot: layer beneath paved road.

7. Diocletian (*c.* AD 298). Rome. AE radiate fraction.

obv. IMP DIOCLETIANVS AVG

rev. VOT XX in wreath

Weight: unknown.

Cat. ref.: *RIC* 86 (Δ).

Site ref.: MG86, B1, SF 15.

Find-spot: unstratified.

8. Uncertain (late third century AD). Mint uncertain. AE radiate.

obv. radiate bust r.

rev. illegible

Weight: 1.32 g.

Cat. ref.: –.

Site ref.: MG88, H01, SF 190.

Find-spot: unstratified.

9. Uncertain (late third century AD). Mint uncertain. AE radiate.

obv. radiate bust r.

rev. illegible

Weight : 0.39 g (fragment).

Cat. ref.: –.

Site ref.: MG88, D52, SF 319.

Find-spot: collapsed roof, end of phase 3.

10. Uncertain (?third-fourth centuries AD). Mint uncertain. AE.

obv. illegible

rev. illegible

Weight : unknown.

Cat. ref.: –.

Site ref.: MG86, A36, SF 35.

Find-spot: from the fill of the bath-house hypocaust, phase 3.

11. Constantine I (AD 326-37). Trier. AE folles.

obv. CONSTANTINVS AVG

rev. BEATA TRANQVILLITAS in ex., .PTR.

Weight: 3.22 g.

Cat. ref.: *RIC* 369.

Site ref.: MG90, M1, SF 666.

Find-spot: unstratifed.

12. House of Constantine (AD 330-5). Mint uncertain. AE folles.

obv. illegible

rev. GLORIA EXERCITVS (2 standards)

Weight: unknown.

Cat. ref.: –.

Site ref.: MG86, A35, SF 27.

Find-spot: from the fill marking the abandonment of the bath-house hypocaust, phase 3.

13. Constantius II (AD 353-8). Mint uncertain. AE 3.

obv. DN CONSTANTIVS PF AVG

rev. FEL TEMP REPARATIO (fallen horseman type)

Weight: unknown.

Cat. ref.: –.

Site ref.: MG86, A35, SF 26.

Find-spot: from the fill marking the abandonment of the bath-house hypocaust, phase 3.

14. Constantius II (AD 353-8). Mint uncertain. AE 3.

obv. DN CONSTANTIUS PF AVG

rev. FEL TEMP REPARATIO (fallen horseman type)

Weight: 1.67 g.

Cat. ref.: –.

Site ref.: MG88, E44, SF 265.

Find-spot: in the fill in the lobby, phase 3/4.

15. Constantius Gallus (AD 353-8). Mint uncertain. AE 3.

obv. bust r.

rev. FEL TEMP REPARATIO (fallen horseman type)

Weight: 1.95 g.

Cat. ref.: –.

Site ref.: MG88, E44, SF 277.

Find-spot: in the fill in the lobby, phase 3/4.

16. Julian II (AD 355-63). Mint uncertain. AE 3.

obv. DN FL CL IVLIANVS NOB CAES

rev. VOT X MVLT XX in wreath

Weight: 2.73 g.

Cat. ref.: –.

Site ref.: MG90, M119, SF 772.

Find-spot: in the fill of a slot cut into a late Roman floor, phase 3.

17. Constantius II (AD 358-61). Mint uncertain. AE 3.

obv. illegible

rev. SPES [REIPVBLICAE]

Weight: 1.37 g.

Cat. ref.: –.

Site ref.: MG89, M26, SF 452.

Find-spot: layer of silt, by the paved road, phase 3.

18. Valens (AD 364-78). Mint uncertain. AE 3.

obv. [DN V]ALEN-[S PF AVG]

rev. SECURITAS REIPVBLICAE

Weight: 1.84 g.

Cat. ref.: –.

Site ref.: MG90, M144, SF 837.

Find-spot: layer of silt, on a late Roman floor, phase 3.

19. House of Valentinian (AD 364-78). Mint uncertain. AE 3.

obv. bust r., pearl diadem

rev. [SECURITAS REIPVBLICAE]

Weight: 1.02 g (fragment).

Cat. ref.: –.

Site ref.: MG89, M26, SF 439.

Find-spot: layer of silt, by the paved road, phase 3.

20. House of Valentinian (AD 364-78). Mint uncertain. AE 3.

obv. bust r.

rev. ? [SECURITAS REIPVBLICAE]
Weight: 1.32 g.
Cat. ref.: –.
Site ref.: MG89, M38, SF 580.
Find-spot: rubble layer, with *opus reticulatum*, tile and silt, phase 3.

21. House of Valentinian (AD 364-78). Aquileia. AE 3.
obv. bust r.
rev. GLORIA ROMANORVM in ex., SMAQS
Weight: 2.11 g.
Cat. ref.: *RIC* 7 ff.
Site ref.: MG90, M97, SF 770.
Find-spot: layer of silt over a late Roman floor, phase 3.

22. Gratian (AD 367-83). Rome. AE 3.
obv. DN GRATIANVS PF AVG
rev. SECVRITAS REIPVBLICAE in ex., SM•RB
Weight: 1.92 g.
Cat. ref.: *RIC* 28b.
Site ref.: MG86, A34, SF 21.
Find-spot: from the fill of burial 60, phases 5-6.

23. Valentinian II (AD 375-8). Rome. AE 3.
obv. DN VALENTINIA-NVS IVN PF AVG
rev. SECVRITAS REIPVBLICAE
Weight: unknown.
Cat. ref.: *LRBC* II, 738 (T).
Site ref.: MG86, B32, SF 22.
Find-spot: level of the second church, phase 6.

24. Uncertain (late fourth century AD). Mint uncertain. AE 3.
obv. illegible
rev. Salus
Weight: 0.69 g.
Cat. ref.: –.
Site ref.: MG87, A41, SF 43.
Find-spot: unstratified.

25. Uncertain (?fourth century AD). Mint uncertain. AE.
obv. illegible
rev. illegible
Weight: 0.70 g.
Cat. ref.: –.
Site ref.: MG87, A42, SF 46.
Find-spot: unstratified.

26. Uncertain (?fourth century AD). Mint uncertain. AE.
obv. illegible
rev. illegible
Weight: 0.93 g.
Cat. ref.: –.
Site ref.: MG87, A42, SF 47.
Find-spot: unstratified.

27. Uncertain (?fourth century AD). Mint uncertain. AE.
obv. illegible
rev. illegible
Weight: 0.20 g (fragment).
Cat. ref.: –.
Site ref.: MG87, A42, SF 50.
Find-spot: unstratified.

28. Uncertain (?fourth century AD). Mint uncertain. AE.
obv. illegible
rev. ?Securitas
Weight: 0.69 g.
Cat. ref.: –.
Site ref.: MG87, D166, SF 157.
Find-spot: in possible beam slot, phase 3.

29. Uncertain (late Roman, ?fourth century AD). Mint uncertain. AE.
obv. illegible
rev. illegible

Weight: 0.79 g.
Cat. ref.: –.
Site ref.: MG88, D3, SF 205.
Find-spot: destruction level in baptistery, phase 7.

30. Uncertain (late Roman, ?fourth century AD). Mint uncertain. AE.
obv. illegible
rev. illegible
Weight: 0.47 g.
Cat. ref.: –.
Site ref.: MG88, D220, SF 246.
Find-spot: destruction level in baptistery, phase 7.

31. Uncertain (?fourth century AD). Mint uncertain. AE.
obv. illegible
rev. illegible
Weight: 0.80 g.
Cat. ref.: –.
Site ref.: MG89, L147, SF 462.
Find-spot: top fill of north cistern, phase 3.

32. Uncertain (?fourth century AD). Mint uncertain. AE.
obv. illegible
rev. illegible
Weight: 0.17 g (fragment).
Cat. ref.: –.
Site ref.: MG89, M38, SF 571.
Find-spot: rubble layer, phase 3.

33. Uncertain (?fourth century AD). Mint uncertain. AE.
obv. illegible
rev. illegible
Weight: 1.01 g.
Cat. ref.: –.
Site ref.: MG90, M97/37, SF 757.
Find-spot: silt over late Roman floor, phase 3.

34. Uncertain (?fourth-fifth centuries AD). Mint uncertain. AE.
obv. illegible
rev. illegible
Weight: 0.51 g (fragment).
Cat. ref.: –.
Site ref.: MG88, E42, SF 266.
Find-spot: on floor in the large room, phase 3.

35. Uncertain (?fourth-fifth centuries AD). Mint uncertain. AE.
obv. illegible
rev. illegible
Weight: 0.29 g (fragment).
Cat. ref.: –.
Site ref.: MG88, E106, SF 364.
Find-spot: on floor in the large room, phase 3.

36. Uncertain (?fourth-fifth centuries AD). Mint uncertain. AE.
obv. illegible
rev. illegible
Weight: 0.78 g.
Cat. ref.: –.
Site ref.: MG90, M94, SF 736.
Find-spot: rubble fill, phase 3.

37. Uncertain (?fourth-fifth centuries AD). Mint uncertain. AE.
obv. illegible
rev. illegible
Weight: 0.18 g (fragment).
Cat. ref.: –.
Site ref.: MG90, M103, SF 756.
Find-spot: debris from early medieval kiln, phase 5.

38. Uncertain (?fourth-fifth centuries AD). Mint uncertain. AE.

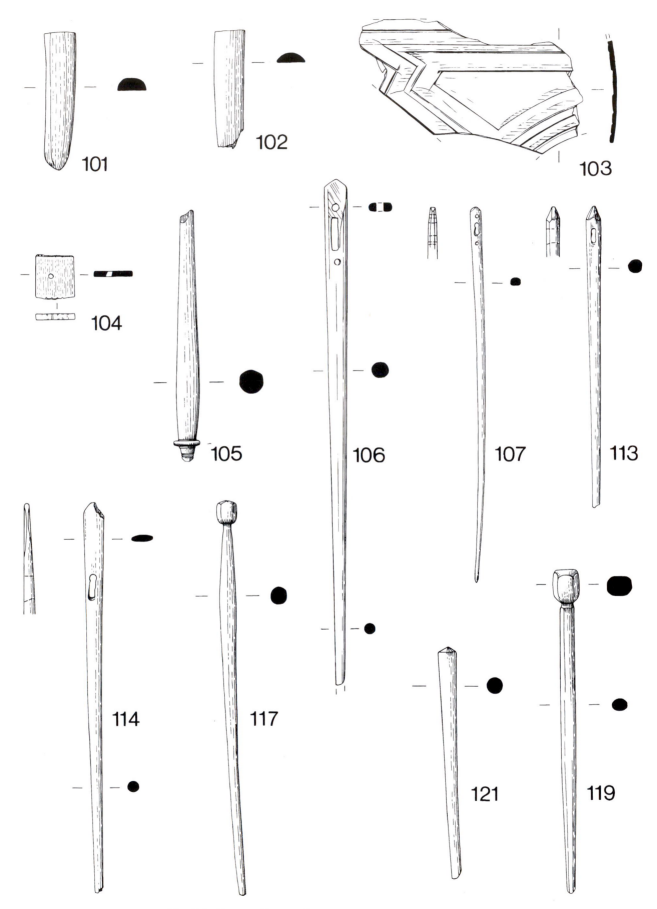

Fig. 175. Objects of bone. All 1:1 except 101 and 102 (1:2). *(SC/SA)*

pronounced ridge with two incised lines below it; cf. Wild 1970: pl. IIIb; MacGregor 1985: fig. 101, no. 3.
L. 63 mm; max. T. 7 mm. C/D1. Plough-soil.

106. Fig. 175. Large needle of circular section. The shank tapers from the flat pointed head which is pierced by three holes: a long rectangular hole with a small circular hole above and below. This arrangement of the eye is seen at Settefinestre: Famà 1985c: tav. 18, no. 6.
L. 131 mm; max. W. 6.5 mm; max. T. 4 mm; eyes: 8 × 2.5 mm; 2.5 mm; 2 mm. L105, SF 585. Fish-pond, later second century.

107. Fig. 175. Very fine needle with a slightly curved, oval-sectioned shank which narrows towards the pointed flat head. The point is well-shaped but flat. The head is pierced by two linked circular holes with a smaller circular hole above and below.
L. 96 mm; max. W. 3 mm; T. 2.5 mm; eyes: 3 × 1.5 mm; 1 mm; 1 mm. L165, SF 630. Fish-pond, early second century.

108. (Not illustrated.) Incomplete, oval-sectioned needle which tapers from the broken head. The arrangement of the eyes appears to have been similar to that described above: two linked circular holes and two separate holes.
L. 44 mm; max. W. 3 mm; max. T. 2.5 mm, eyes: 3 × 1.5 mm; 1mm. L165, SF 605. Fish-pond, early second century .

109. (Not illustrated.) Head of a needle which flattens to the rounded head. The elongated eye has been made by drilling a series of linked holes.
L. 20 mm; W. 5 mm; T. 2.5 mm; eye: 7 × 2 mm. L105, SF 506. Fish-pond, later second century.

110. (Not illustrated.) Incomplete needle of oval section with a pointed head. The eye has been formed by drilling two linked circular holes.
L. 48 mm; W. 3.5 mm; T. 3 mm; eye: 3 × 1.5 mm. L105, SF 520. Fish-pond, later second century.

111. (Not illustrated.) Needle with tapering, circular-sectioned shank and a conical head. The eye has been formed by drilling two linked circular holes.
L. 78.5 mm; T. 4 mm; eye: 3.5 × 2 mm. L165, SF 608. Fish-pond, early second century.

112. (Not illustrated.) Incomplete needle of tapering circular section. The pointed conical head has cancellous material left down one side which would have snagged on fine material, thus limiting its use. The eye has been formed by drilling two linked circular holes.
L. 39 mm; max. T. 3.5 mm; eye 3.5 × 2 mm. S10, SF 720. Phase 2/3, rock-cut road.

113. Fig. 175. Incomplete needle with a circular, slightly facetted shank, which tapers from the conical head. The eye has been made by drilling two linked circular holes.
L. 76.5 mm; max. T. 4 mm; eye: 3.5 × 1.5 mm. M104, SF 737. Phase 2.

114. Fig. 175. Incomplete needle of circular section which flattens and expands to a flat rounded head. The eye has been made by drilling a series of linked circular holes.
L. 101 mm; max. W. 5.5 mm; max. T. 3.5 mm; eye: 6.5 × 1.5 mm. L105, SF 539b. Fish-pond, later second century.

115. (Not illustrated.) Incomplete, large needle of circular section flattening at the head. The eye appears to have been rectangular.
L. 52 mm; W. 5 mm; T. 4 mm. SO4, SF 706a. Phases 2-3, rock-cut road.

116. (Not illustrated.) Incomplete pin with a globular, undercut head and a bulging, circular-sectioned shank. Cf. Francolise: Cotton and Métraux 1985: fig. 26, no. 2: c. 30 BC-AD 200.
L. 49 mm; max. T. 3.5 mm; D. of head 4.5 mm. L105, SF 531c. Fish-pond, later second century.

117. Fig. 175. Incomplete pin with a globular head, narrow neck and bulging, circular-sectioned shank.
L. 102 mm; T. 4 mm; D. of head 5 mm. L105, SF 405. Fish-pond, later second century.

118. (Not illustrated.) Incomplete pin with a roughly shaped, undercut, cylindrical head and a bulging, circular-sectioned shank.
L. 64 mm; T. of shank 3.25 mm; T. of head 4 mm. L105, SF 539a. Fish-pond, later second century.

119. Fig. 175. Pin of oval section with a narrow neck and a cylindrical head.
L. 83 mm; T. of shank 4 mm; W. of head 7 mm. SO3, SF 719. Phases 2-3, rock-cut road.

120. (Not illustrated.) Small pin with a circular-sectioned shank, conical head and flattened point.
L. 51 mm; T. 2 mm. L105, SF 531d. Fish-pond, later second century.

121. Fig. 175. Incomplete pin with a tapering, circular-sectioned shank and a shallow conical head.
L. 60 mm; T. 4.75 mm. L105, SF 653. Fish-pond, later second century.

122. (Not illustrated.) Small pin with a circular-sectioned shank and a rounded head.
L. 52 mm; T. 2 mm. L105, SF 506a. Fish-pond, later second century.

123. (Not illustrated.) Incomplete pin of circular section with a blunt head which has untrimmed cancellous material.
L. 70 mm; T. 4 mm. SO4, SF 752. Phases 2-3, rock-cut road.

124. (Not illustrated.) Circular-sectioned rod with a trimmed point. The shaping suggests that this has broken off a large pin and been reworked.
L. 49 mm; T. 2.5 mm. L105, SF 593. Fish-pond, later second century.

125. (Not illustrated.) Three fragments from a circular-sectioned pin.
Total L. 110 mm; T. 4.5 mm. L105, SF 579. Fish-pond, later second century.

126. (Not illustrated.) Oval-sectioned pin shank. Both ends are broken but one has snapped across a groove, making it unclear whether the piece was finished or had a grooved neck.
L. 47 mm; T. 4.5 mm. M172, SF 849. Phase 3.

127. (Not illustrated.) Circular-sectioned pin shank.
L. 20 mm; T. 4 mm. D3, SF 56. Phase 7.

128. (Not illustrated.) Bulging, circular-sectioned pin shank.
L. 52 mm; T. 3.5 mm. L105, SF 506b. Fish-pond, later second century.

129. (Not illustrated.) Tapered fragment of a circular-sectioned pin shank.
L. 24 mm; T. 2.5 mm. L105, SF 506d. Fish-pond, later second century.

130. (Not illustrated.) Fragment of a circular-sectioned pin shank. The tip is expanded to a rounded point.
L. 41 mm; T. 2.5 mm. L105, SF 531a. Fish-pond, later second century.

131. (Not illustrated.) Fragment of a tapered, circular-sectioned pin shank.
L. 78.5 mm; T. 3.5 mm. L105, SF 531b. Fish-pond, later second century.

Table 54. Iron nails from burial contexts.

burial context no.	small find no.	phase	no. of nails	length if complete (in millimetres) and additional comments
2 (C2)	103, 104	6	2	48
2 (C56)	109, 118-20	6	4	72, 66 The upper and lower shank of one nail have two different wood grain directions. From coffin corner?
2 (C58)	137-43, 148	6	8	56, 68 One T-headed
7 (C23)	66, 76, 83	6/7	3	38
8 (C46)	83, 87, 98, 101, 106, 108, 111, 115-17, 130, 161-70	6/7	16	69, 68, 70, 72
12 (B64)	32	5/6	1	
12 (B80)	34	5/6	15	97 The upper and lower shank of one nail have two different wood grain directions. From coffin corner?
17 (B73)	30	5/6	1	
37 (D229)	238	6	1	60
40 (D214)	212	6	1	
55 (D92)	102	6/7	1	
59 (D168)	-	6	2	
67 (D276)	275	5/6	1	
85 (L173)	642	6/7	1	206 Stud-headed
87 (E99)	321	3+	1	

Fig. 183. Fragment of glass chariot beaker (cat. 1). *(KW)*

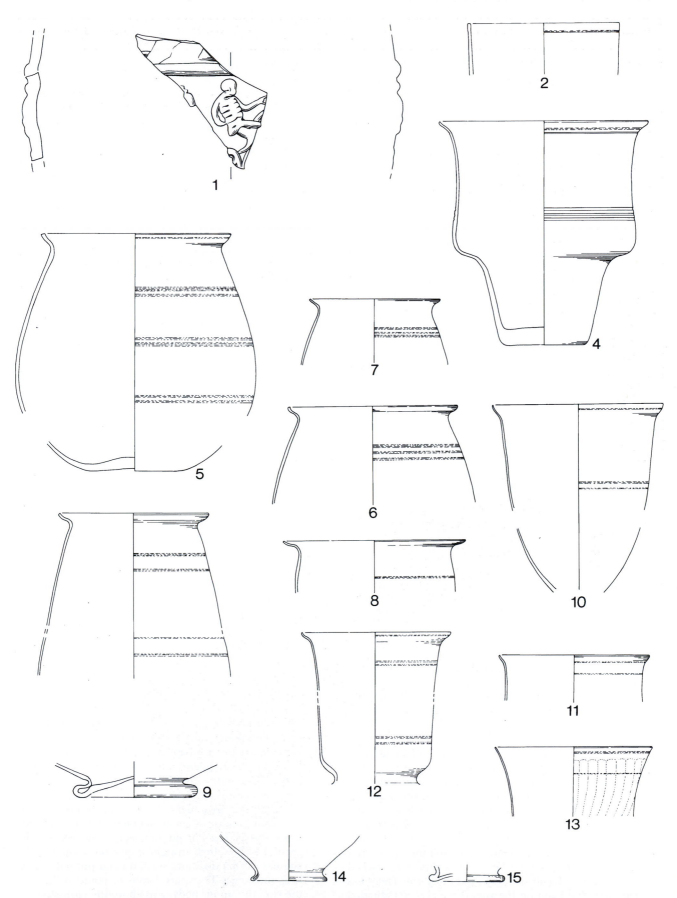

Fig. 184. Glass vessels. 1-2, first century AD; 4-15, late first to mid second centuries AD. All 1:2 except no.1 (1:1). *(SC/SA)*

Late first-mid second centuries AD

Colourless
Beakers and cups
Coloured trail decoration

3. (Not illustrated.) Seven fragments, three joining, from the body of an indented vessel. Colourless ground, opaque yellow trails; very little weathering; very small bubbles. The fragments are parts of the body, including the lower body above the base. The trails are not marvered flush with the surface.
Dim. (largest fragment) 28 × 20 mm; T. 0.75 mm. L165 and L184. Fish-pond, early second century.
Also:
(a) Two joining fragments. Dim. 17 × 9 mm; T. 0.65 mm. M172. Drain, phase 3.

Wheel-cut and abraded decoration

4. Fig. 184. Thirty-three fragments, many joining, of a carinated beaker. Greenish-colourless; small bubbles; outsplayed curved rim, edge cracked off and ground; straight, slightly concave upper body expanding out to curved carination; truncated conical lower body; slightly concave thick base. There are two horizontal wheel-cut lines at the junction of the rim and body, and three horizontal wheel-cut lines above the carination.
H. 118 mm; rim D. 110 mm; D. base 44 mm; T. 1.5-4+ mm. L184. Fish-pond, early second century.
Also:
(a) Fragment of the straight upper body of a biconical cup. There are single wheel-cut lines on the upper body and above the carination. Present H. 67 mm; T. 1 mm. L104. Phase 2.
(b) Two fragments of a form comparable to (a). There is a single abraded band above the carination. Present H. 61 mm; T. 0.7-1.5 mm. M172. Drain, phase 3.
(c) A fragment of a form comparable to (a). There is a single wheel-cut line on the upper body. Present H. 31 mm; T. 1.5 mm. D243. Phase 3.
(d) A fragment of a form comparable to (a). Pale greenish colourless. There is a single wheel-cut line on the upper body. Present H. 24.5 mm; T 1.5 mm. L146. Phase 2.

5. Fig. 184. One hundred and twenty-five fragments, many joining, of an ovoid beaker. Curved rim, edge cracked off and ground, convex body expanding out, lower body tapering in to concave base. There is an abraded band on the rim, two bands on the upper body, two bands above the maximum girth, and two bands on the lower body.
Present H. (rim fragment) 97 mm; rim D. 100 mm; T. 1-6 mm. L165 and L184. Fish-pond, early second century.
Also:
(a) Thirty-three fragments of the body and base of an ovoid (?) beaker/bowl. Small bubbles; outsplayed rim, edge missing; upper body convex expanding out; wide convex lower body tapering in to tubular pushed in base ring. There is a band of three abraded lines on the upper body. Dim. (largest fragment) 50 × 50 mm; T. 1-2.5 mm. L165.

6. Fig. 184. Eighteen fragments, some joining, of the rim and body of a convex beaker. Curved rim, edge cracked off and ground; convex body expanding out. There is a faint abraded band on the rim, three close-set abraded bands on the upper body, and two on the lower body.
Present H. (rim fragment) 54 mm; rim D. 90 mm; T. 1+ mm. L165. Fish-pond, early second century.

7. Fig. 184. Fragment of the rim of a beaker. Outsplayed slightly curved rim, edge cracked off and ground; convex upper body expanding out. A band of abraded lines was noted on the rim, and three bands on the upper body.
Present H. 34 mm; rim D. *c.* 90 mm; T. 1 mm. L105. Fish-pond, later second century.

8. Fig. 184. Fragment of the rim of a convex cup or beaker. Dull; small bubbles visible; outsplayed curved rim, edge cracked off and ground; convex upper body expanding out. There is a horizontal abraded band on the upper body.
Present H. 29 mm; rim D. 96 mm; T. 1 mm. S10. Rock-cut road, phases 2-3.

9. Fig. 184. Fifteen fragments of the rim, body and base of a carinated beaker. Greenish colourless; outsplayed curved rim, edge cracked off; slightly convex upper body expanding out to curved carination (mostly missing); wide convex lower body tapering in to tubular base ring and concave base with pointed central kick. There are two horizontal abraded lines on the upper body and two above the carination.
Present H. (rim) 86 mm, (base) 19 mm; rim D. 80 mm; D. of base 60 mm; T. 0.5-1.5+ mm. E179. Pit, phase 3.
Also:
(a) Fragment of the rim of a beaker. Outsplayed curved rim, edge cracked off, slightly convex body expanding out. Present H. 24 mm; rim D. 90 mm; T. 1 mm. E179. Pit, phase 3.

10. Fig. 184. Twelve fragments of the rim and body of a beaker. Thin glass; curved rim, edge cracked off and ground; straight upper body; convex lower body, curving in towards base (missing). An abraded line was noted on the rim and two on the body.
Present H. (rim fragment) 50 mm, (base fragment) *c.* 40 mm; rim D. 90 mm; T. 1.5 mm. E179. Pit, phase 3.

11. Fig. 184. Five fragments of the rim and body of a cylindrical beaker or cup. Small curved rim, edge cracked off and ground; straight side. There is a narrow horizontal abraded band at the base of the rim and also on the upper body.
Present H. 25 mm; rim D. 80 mm; T. 0.7+ mm. M172. Drain, phase 3.
Also:
(a) Two fragments of the body, concave side and carination of a beaker or cup. There is an abraded line above the carination. M172. Drain, phase 3.
(b) Fragment of the straight body of a beaker or cup. It has two abraded lines. L105. Fish-pond, later second century.
(c-o) Thirteen body fragments. Abraded bands were noted. L165. Fish-pond, early second century.
(p) Fifty-nine body and base fragments of (?) beakers or cups. These fragments had no abraded decoration. L165. Fish-pond, early second century.

12. Fig. 184. Thirteen fragments, some joining, from the rim, body and base of a conical carinated beaker. Pale greenish colourless; small bubbles; grey/black inclusions; outsplayed curved rim, edge cracked off and ground; thin-walled, straight upper body tapering in; angular carination above small tubular pushed in base ring (missing). There are bands of abraded lines on the rim, the upper body, and above the carination.
Present H. at least 85 mm (reconstructed by overlapping three fragments); rim D. *c.* 80 mm; T. 0.7-1.2 mm. L165. Fish-pond, early second century.

13. Fig. 184. Three fragments of the rim and body of a cylindrical beaker or cup. Very thin glass; slightly everted straight rim, edge cracked off and ground; straight side; faint vertical ribbing on body. There is an abraded band below the rim, and another on the upper body.
Present H. 39 mm; rim D. 84 mm; T 0.1+ mm. L165. Fish-pond, early second century.

14. Fig. 184. Three joining fragments of the lower body and base of a (?) beaker. Some small bubbles; lower edge of curved carination, straight lower body tapering in to small tubular base ring and thin domed base (mostly missing).
Present H. 25 mm; D. of base c. 40 mm; T. 0.5-1.5 mm. L165. Fish-pond, early second century.

15. Fig. 184. Fragment of the lower body and base of a (?) cup. Small bubbles; lower body tapering in to low outsplayed tubular base ring; domed base (centre missing).
Present H. 7 mm; D. of base 40 mm; T. 1 mm. S04. Rock-cut road, phases 2-3.

Abraded lines and indented decoration

16. Fig. 185. Twenty-five fragments of the rim, body and base of an indented beaker. Slight pale greenish tinge; some small bubbles; outsplayed curved rim, edge cracked off and ground. The tall straight side has four long oval indents extending from the upper body to above the concave base. There are abraded lines on the rim.
H. (reconstructed) c. 160 mm; rim D. 80 mm; D. of base 40 mm; T. 0.3-3.5 mm. L165. Fish-pond, early second century.

17. Fig. 185. Seventeen fragments of the rim, body and base of an indented beaker. Pale greenish tinge; outsplayed curved rim, edge cracked off and ground. The tall straight side has four long deep oval indents, extending from the upper body to above the concave base. There is an abraded band on the rim, and two bands on the upper body.
Present H. (rim) 46 mm, (base) 54 mm, (as reconstructed) 178 mm; rim D. 100 mm; D. of base 46 mm; T. 0.5-2.5+ mm. L165. Fish-pond, early second century.

18. (Not illustrated.) Body fragment of a beaker. Some small bubbles. The tall straight body has one narrow oval indent.
Present H. 50 mm; T. 0.5 mm. L184. Fish-pond, early second century.

Also:
– Two body fragments of indented vessels.
– Two body fragments.

Bowls and plates

19. Fig. 185. Rim fragment of a cylindrical bowl. Slightly incurved tubular rim, formed by folding edge up, out and down; vertical upper body.
Present H. 14 mm; rim D. c. 170 mm; T. 0.7 mm. L165. Fish-pond, early second century.

20. Fig. 185. Ten fragments of the rim, body and base of a shallow bowl or plate. Very pale greenish; small bubbles, aligned parallel to rim; very thin glass; small tubular rim, edge bent up, out and down; straight side tapering in to tubular base ring with figure-of-eight fold, flat base (centre missing).
H. 84 mm; rim D. 180 mm; D. of base c. 160 mm; T. 0.3-0.7 mm. L165. Fish-pond, early second century.

Jugs

21. Fig. 185. Seven fragments, some joining, of the rim, neck and handle of a jug with a pouring spout. Greenish colourless; small elongated bubbles; trefoil mouth, edge fire-rounded, elongated and raised pouring spout, end folded in, neck tapering in; upper handle attachment opposite pouring spout, vertical thumb rest with one pinched projection above rim; curved ribbon handle.
Present H. (excluding handle) c. 30 mm; present length (handle fragment) c. 38 mm; T. 1.5 mm. L165. Fish-pond, early second century.

22. Fig. 185. Fragment of the handle of a jug or bottle. Pale greenish colourless; lower attachment of thick broad ribbon handle; thin-walled body, broken edges of handle.
Present length 79 mm; T. (body) 0.5 mm. L165. Fish-pond, early second century.
Also (all fish-pond, early second century):
(a) Neck fragment of a jug or flask. Greenish colourless; very streaky weathering. L165.
(b) Neck fragment of a jug or flask. L165.
(c) Three ribbed body fragments. L165.

Blue-Green
Bowls

23. Fig. 185. Fragment of a tubular rim. Vertical rim, edge bent out and down, side tapering in.
Present H. 22 mm; rim D. 160 mm; T. 0.5 mm. P01. Temple-mausoleum, unstratified.

24. Fig. 185. Fragment of a high base ring, probably from a bowl or plate. Small bubbles; tall vertical tubular base ring.
Present H. 25 mm; T. 0.5 mm. L165. Fish-pond, early second century.
Also:
(a) Fragment of a high base ring, as cat. 24. Present H. 44 mm; T. 0.7 mm. L173. Burial no. 85, phase 6/7.
(b) Small fragment of a high base ring, as cat. 24. Present H. 10 mm; T. 0.5 mm. S03. Rock-cut road, phases 2-3.

25. Fig. 185. Fragment of the lower body and base of a (?) bowl. Wide lower body, tapering in to outsplayed tubular base ring, concave base (centre missing).
Present H. 11 mm; D. of base 54 mm; T. 1 mm. S10. Rock-cut road, phases 2-3.

Jugs

26. Fig. 185. Twenty-four fragments of the rim, handle, neck, body and base of a jug with a trefoil mouth. Flaring rim, edge rolled in and pinched to form pouring spout; cylindrical neck expanding out to wide convex shoulder and upper body; convex lower body tapering in to open base ring and concave base; rod handle applied to upper body and attached to rim edge opposite to spout; folded angular 'thumb rest' above rim.
Present H. (rim and handle) c. 105 mm, (base) 30 mm; D. of base 64 mm; T. 0.75-1.25 mm. E179. Pit, phase 3.

27. Fig. 185. Fragment of the handle of a small thin-walled jug. Small round bubbles in body, black streaks and elongated bubbles in handle; convex body, lower attachment of ribbon handle with two ribs; body broken to edges of handle.
Present H. 26.5 mm; T. (body) 0.2 mm. C/D 1. Unstratified.

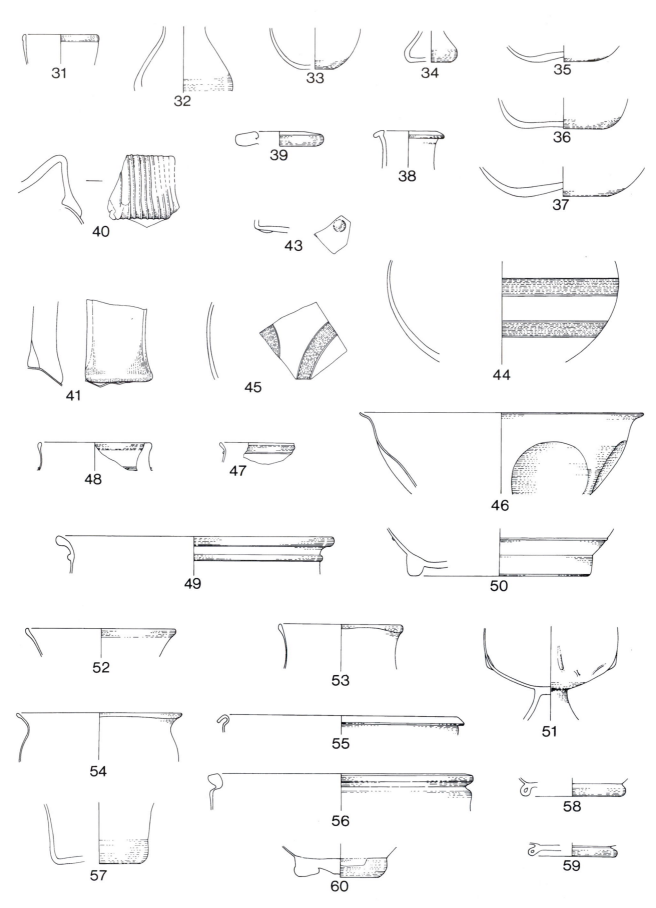

Fig. 186. Glass vessels. 31-43, late first to mid second centuries AD; 44-61, late second to early third centuries AD (1:2). *(SC)*

Also:
(a) Three body fragments, as cat. 44 and 45. There is a single horizontal abraded or wheel-cut line. S04. Rock-cut road, phases 2-3.

Wheel-cut and indented decoration
46. Fig. 186. Nineteen fragments, some joining, of the rim and body of a thin-walled, shallow indented bowl. Curved rim, edge cracked off and ground; convex body with at least seven indents. There is an abraded line on the rim.
Present H. 47 mm; rim D. 150 mm; T. 0.5 mm. M172/M38. Drain, phase 3; deposits of mid-sixth century.
Also:
(a) Nine body fragments with indents. L105. Fish-pond, later second century.

Trailed decoration
47. Fig. 186. Fragment of the rim of a cup or small bowl. Slightly out-bent rim, edge fire-rounded and thickened; convex upper body expanding out. There is an unmarvered horizontal trail below the rim.
Present H. 11 mm; rim D. c. 100 mm; T. 0.6+ mm. L105. Fish-pond, later second century.
48. Fig. 186. Fragment of the rim of a cup or beaker. Vertical rim, edge fire-rounded and thickened; upper body expanding out. There is a horizontal unmarvered trail on the upper body.
Present H. 15 mm; rim D. 60 mm; T. 0.5 mm. C/D1. Unstratified.
49. Fig. 186. Fragment of the rim and body of a bowl. Greenish colourless; small elongated bubbles aligned parallel to rim; outsplayed rim, edge fire-rounded and thickened; convex upper body. There is a horizontal unmarvered trail below the rim.
Present H. 20 mm; rim D. 146 mm; T. 1+ mm. (No reference.)
Also:
(a) Fragment of the rim and body of a bowl, as cat. 49. It has a horizontal unmarvered trail. M172. Drain, phase 3.
50. Fig. 186. Fragment of the body and base of a bowl. Greenish colourless; small circular bubbles; wide, slightly convex body tapering in, concave base (centre missing); thick trailed base ring. There is a horizontal unmarvered trail on the lower body.
Present H. 25 mm; D. of base 96 mm; T. 1.5 mm. L163. Phase 3.
Also:
(a) Small fragment of a concave base, with a thin trailed base ring. E11. North cistern.

Punched decoration
51. Fig. 186. Three joining fragments of the body and stemmed foot of a cup. Upper body almost cylindrical, carination, lower body slightly convex and tapering in; separately blown cylindrical stem and foot (edges missing); horizontal ring of small vertical pinched projections at carination.
Present H. c. 48 mm; T. (body) 0.5-1.5 mm. M38/S04. Deposits, mid-sixth century; rock-cut road, phases 2-3.
Also:
(a) Two fragments of a convex lower body, similar to cat. 51. M172. Drain, phase 3.

Undecorated
52. Fig. 186. Two fragments of the rim of a cylindrical cup. Slightly outsplayed rim, edge fire-rounded; straight upper body.
Present H. 17 mm; rim D. 80 mm; T. 1 mm. L105. Fish-pond, later second century.
53. Fig. 186. Three joining fragments of the rim of a cylindrical beaker. Very thin; rim edge fire-rounded and thickened; upper body tapering in slightly.
Present H. 25 mm; rim D. 66 mm; T. 0.1+ mm. M172. Drain, phase 3.
Also:
(a) Four fragments of the rim and body, as cat. 53. M172. Drain, phase 3.
(b) Fragment of a rim, as cat. 53. M125. Burial 79, phase 6.
(c) Four fragments of a rim, as cat. 53. S04. Rock-cut road, phases 2-3.
54. Fig. 186. Two joining fragments of the rim of a cup or bowl. Everted rim, edge fire-rounded and thickened; convex upper body expanding out.
Present H. 27 mm; rim D. 88 mm; T. 0.7+ mm. E179. Pit, phase 3.
Also:
(a) Fragment of a rim, as cat. 54. L138. Drain, phase 2.
55. Fig. 186. Fragment of the rim of a bowl or jar. Horizontal outsplayed rim, edge fire-rounded and thickened; convex body expanding out.
Present H. 8 mm; rim D. c. 130 mm; T. 1 mm. S04. Rock-cut road, phases 2-3.
56. Fig. 186. Two joining fragments of the rim of a cylindrical bowl. Pale greenish colourless; little visible weathering; small elongated bubbles aligned horizontally with rim; horizontal outsplayed rim, edge fire-rounded and very thick; small convex shoulder; vertical upper body.
Present H. 20 mm; rim D. 140 mm; T. 1 mm. S04. Rock-cut road, phases 2-3.
57. Fig. 186. Fragment of the lower body and base of a (?) beaker. Straight side, expanding out slightly above thick flat base.
Present H. 33 mm; D. of base 50 mm; T 1.7-3.5 mm. L105. Fish-pond, later second century.
Also:
(a) Fragment of a base, as cat. 57. A17. Phase 3.
(b) Fragment of a base, as cat. 57. S04. Rock-cut road, phases 2-3.
58. Fig. 186. Fragment of the base of a (?) small bowl. Convex lower body, tubular pushed in base ring.
Present H. 10 mm; D. of base 54 mm; T. 1-1.5 mm. L105. Fish-pond, later second century.
59. Fig. 186. Fragment of the base of a (?) small bowl. Wide lower body; outsplayed tubular base ring; slightly convex base (centre missing).
Present H. 7 mm; D. of base 46 mm; T. 1 mm. L147. North cistern, later second century.
Also:
(a) Fragment of a base, as cat. 59. Greenish colourless. S04. Rock-cut road, phases 2-3.
60. Fig. 186. Fragment of the base of a bowl. Convex side and base; trailed and flattened base ring.
Present H. 7 mm; D. of base c. 60 mm; T. 1.5+ mm. L105. Fish-pond, later second century.
61. (Not illustrated.) Fragment of the lower body and base of a (?) beaker. Very thin glass in body; slightly convex lower body; convex base with added disc and prominent pontil mark; thick trailed base ring, flattened on bottom surface.

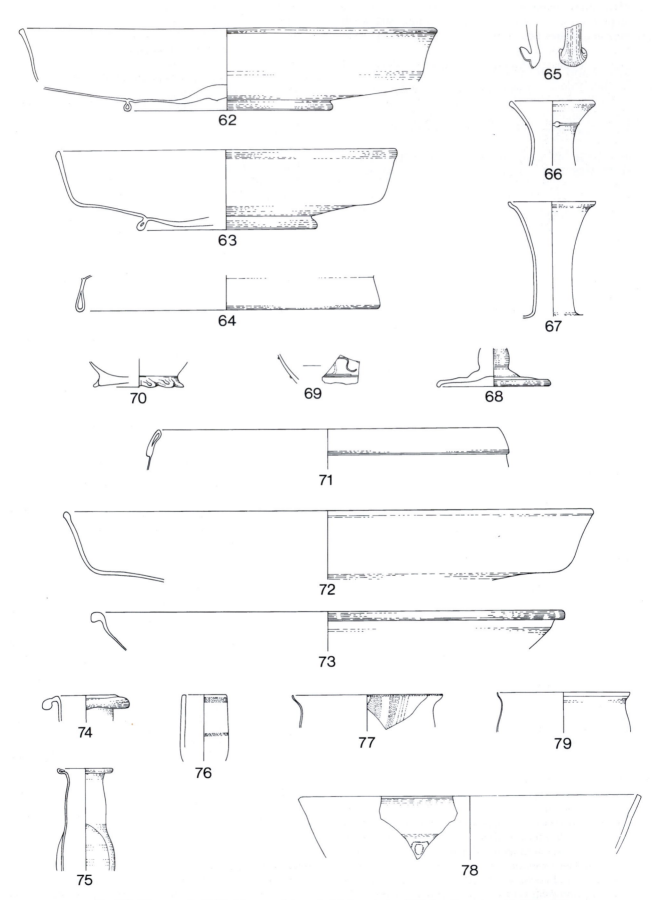

Fig. 187. Glass vessels. 62-75, late second to early third centuries; 76-9, fourth century AD (1:2). *(SC)*

Present H. 16 mm; D. of base *c.* 38 mm; T. 0.1+ mm. M172. Drain, phase 3.
Also:

(a) Fragment as cat. 60 and 61. Greenish colourless. M172. Drain, phase 3.

(b) Fragment as cat. 60 and 61. Greenish colourless. C/D1. Unstratified.

(c) Fragment as cat. 60 and 61. E11. North cistern, later second century.

(d) Fragment as cat. 60 and 61. Greenish colourless. S01. Rock-cut road, phases 2-3.

(e) Fragment as cat. 60 and 61. Greenish colourless. S12. Rock-cut road, phases 2-3.

62. Fig. 187. More than twenty fragments, many joining, of a shallow cylindrical bowl. Rim edge fire-rounded and thickened; upper body slightly concave, tapering inwards; rounded carination, wide flat lower body and base; tubular base ring; convex base; centre of base high and domed with pontil mark.
Present H. (rim fragment) 29 mm, (base fragment) 13 mm; rim D. 230 mm; D. of base 108 mm; T. 0.5-1 mm. L105. Fish-pond, later second century.

63. Fig. 187. More than thirty fragments, many joining, of a shallow cylindrical bowl. Rim edge fire rounded and thickened; straight upper body tapering inwards; rounded carination; wide slightly concave lower body; tubular base ring; convex base (centre missing).
Present H. (rim fragment) 33 mm, (base fragment) 12 mm; rim D. 180 mm; D. of base *c.* 96 mm; T 0.5-2.5 mm. L105. Fish-pond, later second century.
Also:

(a) Rim fragment, as cat. 62 and 63. Rim D. 170 mm. L105. Fish-pond, later second century.

(b) Rim fragment, as cat. 62 and 63. Rim D. 160 mm. L105. Fish-pond, later second century.

(c) Two rim fragments, as cat. 62 and 63. L146. Phase 2.

64. Fig. 187. Ten fragments of the high base ring of a bowl. Vertical folded base ring with tubular edge; small part of concave base.
Present H. 20 mm; D. of base *c.* 160 mm; T. 0.7-1 mm. L105. Fish-pond, later second century.
Also (fish-pond, later second century):

(a) Fragment of a base ring, as cat. 62-4. L105.

(b) Two fragments of a base, as cat. 62-4. L105.

Jugs
65. Fig. 187. Fragment of the handle and body of a (?) small jug. Thin-walled convex body; lower attachment of curved rod handle; broken edges of body neatly worked to edge of handle.
Present H. 23 mm. C/D1. Unstratified.

Flasks
66. Fig. 187. Fifteen fragments of the rim and neck of a flask. Outsplayed rim, edge fire-rounded and thickened; funnel mouth; narrow cylindrical neck. Horizontal unmarvered trail at junction of mouth and neck.
Present H. 35 mm; rim D. 46 mm; T. 1.25+ mm. L105. Fish-pond, later second century.

67. Fig. 187. Twenty-seven fragments, many joining, of the rim, neck and shoulder of a flask. Outsplayed curving rim, edge cracked off and ground; funnel mouth; cylindrical neck; shoulder expanding out.
Present H. *c.* 58 mm; rim D. *c.* 46 mm; T. 1.5 mm. L105. Fish-pond, later second century.

68. Fig. 187. Four fragments, two joining, of the stem and foot of a flask or cup. Solid globular stem; applied disc foot with fire-rounded edge.
Present H. *c.* 24 mm; D. of base *c.* 60 mm; T. foot 1.5+ mm. L105. Fish-pond, later second century.
Also:

(a) Three fragments of a stem and foot, as cat. 68. L105. Fish-pond, later second century.

(b) Fragment of a foot, as cat. 68. L173. Burial 85, phase 6/7.

(c) Fragment of a solid globular stem, as cat. 68. Reworked edges. E16. Phase 3.

Miscellaneous body and base fragments
69. Fig. 187. Fragment of body. Convex side. There is a horizontal unmarvered trail, and also curved meandering trail, which partially overlies the horizontal trail.
Dim. 18 × 19 mm; T. 1.25 mm. L105. Fish-pond, later second century.
Also:

(a) Twelve body fragments with horizontal trails. L105. Fish-pond, later second century.

(b) Three body fragments with horizontal trails. L147. North cistern, late second century.

70. Fig. 187. Fragment of a lower body and base. Convex side tapering in; thick concave base (pad added); six pinched points in ring at base edge.
Present H. 14 mm; D. of base *c.* 40 mm; T. 1.5 mm. PO1. Temple-mausoleum, unstratified.
Also:

(a) Fragment of a body and base, as cat. 70. It has two pinched points. M75. Phase 6.

Blue-green, greenish colourless and yellow-green
Bowls
71. Fig. 187. Fragment of the tubular rim of a bowl. Pale blue-green; little visible weathering; elongated bubbles aligned parallel to rim; slightly inturned rim, edge bent out and down to form narrow curved tube; straight upper body.
Present H. 24 mm; rim D. *c.* 190 mm; T. 1 mm. S04. Rock-cut road, phases 2-3.

72. Fig. 187. Two joining fragments of the rim and body of a large shallow bowl. Pale greenish; rim edge fire-rounded and thickened; straight upper body tapering in to rounded carination; flat lower body, tapering in to base ring (missing).
Present H. 33 mm; rim D. 280 mm; T. 1.5-2.5 mm. M172. Drain, phase 3.

73. Fig. 187. Fragment of the rim of a bowl. Pale yellow-green: outsplayed rim, edge fire-rounded and thickened; convex upper body tapering in.
Present H. 26 mm; rim D. *c.* 250 mm; T. 0.4-2 mm. L105. Fish-pond, later second century.
Also:

(a) Fragment of a wide concave base, with pontil mark, from a (?) bowl. Greenish colourless. S10. Rock-cut road, phases 2-3.

Jugs, flasks, unguent bottles
74. Fig. 187. Fragment of the rim and neck of a jug, flask or unguent bottle. Pale blue-green; horizontal folded rim, edge bent out, down and up; cylindrical neck.
Present H. 16 mm; rim D. 46 mm; T. 1 mm. L105. Fish-pond, later second century.

Also (both fish-pond, later second century):

(a) Two fragments of a large discoid unguent bottle. Greenish colourless. L105.

(b) Fragment of a small curved ribbon handle with edge ribs. Blue-green. L105.

75. Fig. 187. Two joining fragments of the rim, neck and body of an indented unguent bottle. Blue-green; small horizontal rim, edge rolled in and flattened; short neck; upper part of one (of four) indented sides. Present H. 56 mm; rim D. *c.* 30 mm; max. W. body 30 mm; T. 1+ mm. C/D1. Unstratified.

Fourth century

Strongly coloured

76. Fig. 187. Fragment of the rim and neck of a flask. Dark blue; small elongated bubbles aligned vertically; vertical rim, edge cracked off and ground; cylindrical neck, tapering in. There are horizontal bands of abraded lines at rim and on neck. Present H. 34 mm; rim D. 24 mm; T. 2-2.5 mm. S03. Rock-cut road, phases 2-3.

Colourless/greenish colourless

Beakers, bowls, cups

Coloured trail and abraded decoration

77. Fig. 187. Fragment of the rim of a cylindrical beaker or cup. Colourless ground, with opaque white marvered streaks; small bubbles; curved rim, edge cracked off and ground, almost straight upper body. There are slightly diagonal opaque white streaks marvered flush with the surface. A horizontal abraded band occurred on the rim. Present H. 19 mm; rim D. 80 mm; T. 0.6 mm. D5. Burial no. 93, phase 6.

Wheel-cut and abraded decoration

78. Fig. 187. Fragment of the rim of a cup or bowl. Greenish colourless; no bubbles visible; vertical, slightly curved rim, edge cracked off and ground; slightly convex side. Below the rim, there is a horizontal wheel-cut line and also a broad band of abraded lines; on the upper body, there is a horizontal band of abraded lines above a finely abraded circle (possibly the head of letter, such as B or P or R) and a small part of a horizontal motif, perhaps the serif from a second letter. Present H. 18 mm; rim D. 90 mm; T. 1 mm. C/D1. Unstratified.

79. Fig. 187. Fragment of the rim of a beaker or cup. Colourless; very thin; small bubbles; curved rim, edge cracked off and ground; slightly convex side expanding out. There is a narrow wheel-cut line on the rim. Present H. 21 mm; rim D. 70 mm; T. 0.3+ mm. A42. Unstratified.

80. Fig. 188. Two fragments of the rim and base of a conical beaker. Greenish colourless; very thin; many small bubbles; curved rim, edge cracked off and smoothed; upper body slightly convex; lower body straight, tapering to thick concave base. There is a broad horizontal band of abraded lines on the rim, and three bands on the upper and lower body. Present H. (rim) 34 mm, (base) 50 mm; rim D. 86 mm; D. of base 36 mm; T. 0.5-3.5 mm. A17. Phase 3.

Also:

(a) Fragment with a similar base. D. of base 36 mm. L149.

81. Fig. 188. Fragment of the rim of a beaker or bowl. Greenish colourless; small bubbles visible; curving rim, edge cracked off and smoothed; slightly convex upper body. There is a broad band of abraded lines on the rim. Present H. 21 mm; rim D. 72 mm; T. 0.5-1 mm. C46. Burial no. 8, phase 6/7?

Also:

(a) Fragment with a similar rim. Rim D. *c.* 100 mm. M38.

Abraded and indented decoration

82. (Not illustrated.) Fragment of the rim of a hemispherical or shallow indented bowl. Greenish colourless; small bubbles; small curved rim, edge cracked off and smoothed; convex side tapering in. There is a faint band of abraded lines on the rim, and slight evidence for an oval indent on the body. Present H. *c.* 25 mm; rim D. *c.* 120 mm; T. 0.6+ mm. D301. Pit, phase 6.

Undecorated

83. Fig. 188. Fragment of the rim of a bowl. Colourless; elongated bubbles aligned parallel to the rim; vertical wedge-shaped stepped rim, rounded top edge; straight side tapering in. Present H. 13 mm; rim D. *c.* 240 mm; T. 1-1.5 mm. L104. North cistern, top fill, phases 2-3.

Also:

(a) Fragment with a similar rim. S04. Rock-cut road, phases 2-3.

Flask or jug

Colourless trail decoration

84. Fig. 188. Fragment of a rim. Greenish colourless ground, translucent blue trail; very thin; bubbly; everted rim, edge fire-rounded, funnel mouth. There is a thick horizontal unmarvered trail below the rim. Present H. *c.* 12 mm; rim D. *c.* 70 mm; T. 1+ mm. C/D1. Unstratified.

Yellow-green

Bowls

Coloured blob and abraded decoration

85. Fig. 188. Fragment of the body of a (?) hemispherical bowl. Yellow-green ground, dark blue blob; bubbly; convex side. There are horizontal bands of abraded lines above and below the large circular unmarvered blob. Present H. *c.* 53 mm; T. 0.75-1.75 mm. L104. North cistern, top fill, phases 2-3.

Abraded decoration

86. Fig. 188. Fragment of the rim of a (?) hemispherical bowl. Many small bubbles; outsplayed curving rim, edge cracked off and left rough; slightly convex upper body. There is a horizontal band of abraded lines on the upper body. Present H. 33 mm; rim D. 100 mm; T. 1-1.5 mm. M104. Phases 5-6.

87. Fig. 188. Two joining fragments of the lower body and base of a bowl or beaker. Convex lower body tapering in; concave base. Present H. 12 mm; D. of base 30 mm; T. 1-1.5 mm. D52. Roof collapse, *c.* mid-sixth century.

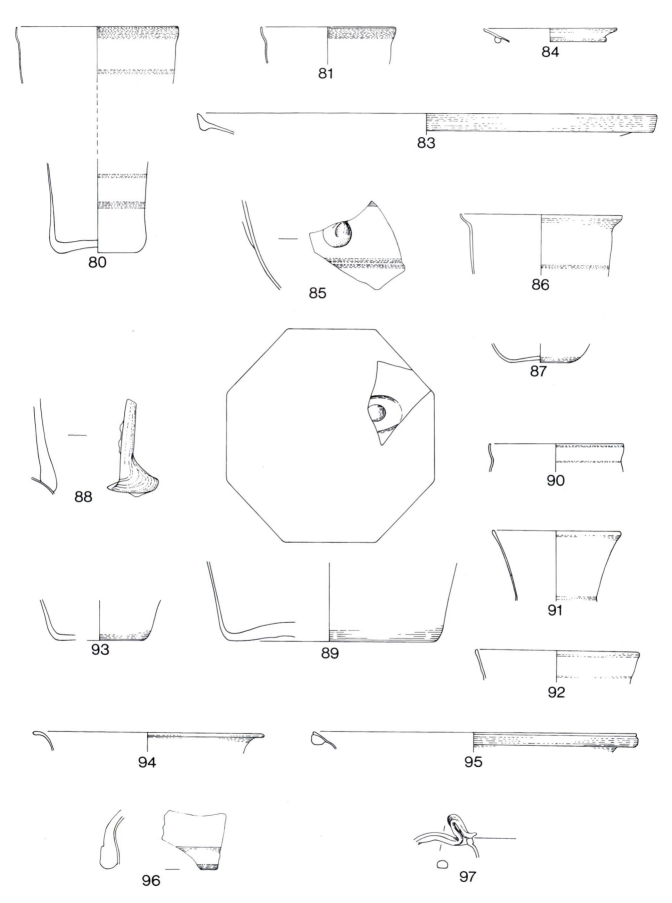

Fig. 188. Glass vessels, fourth century (1:2). *(SC)*

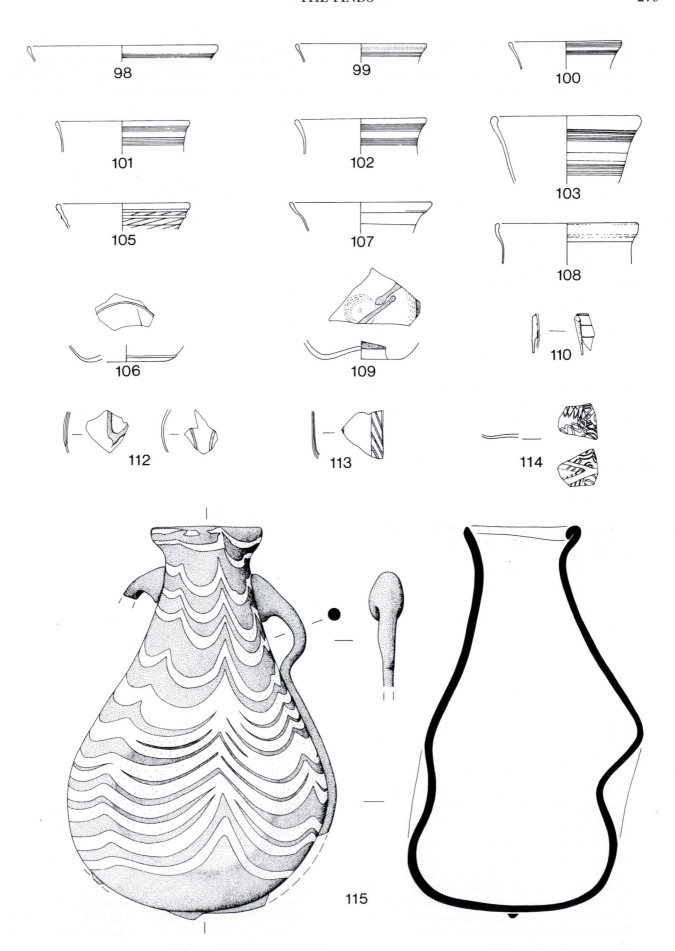

Fig. 189. Glass vessels, fifth century AD and later. All 1:2, except 115 (1:1). *(SC/SA)*

103. Fig. 189. Fragment of the rim of a conical cup or beaker. Pale green ground, opaque white trails; bubbly glass; slightly inturned rim, edge fire-rounded and thickened; straight upper body tapering in. There is a band of six close-set trails not marvered flush with the surface below the rim, a single trail on the upper body, and eight close-set trails on the middle of the body.
Present H. 37 mm; rim D. 80 mm; T. 0.7-1 mm. D94. Phase 6.

104. (Not illustrated.) Fragment of the rim of a (?) cup or beaker. Colourless ground, opaque white trail; dull, no weathering visible; slightly inturned rim, edge fire-rounded, thick. There is a trail on the rim which is not marvered flush.
Dim. 7 × 10.2 mm; T. 1 mm. D220. Phase 6.

105. Fig. 189. Fragment of the rim of a conical cup or beaker. Pale green ground, opaque white trails; optic-blown; fire-rounded and thickened rim; upper body tapering inwards. There is faint diagonal ribbing on the body. The band of four trails below the rim is not marvered flush.
Present H. 16 mm; rim D. c. 70 mm; T. 0.7-1 mm. M64. Phase 6.

106. Fig. 189. Fragment of the body and base of a cup. Pale green ground, opaque white trail; bubbly; convex side; concave base. The trail at the junction of the body and the base is not marvered flush.
Present H. 6 mm; T. 1-1.5 mm. B1. Unstratified.
Also:

(a) Colourless fragment of a straight body. The opaque white trail is not marvered flush. Dim. 18.5 × 9 mm; T. 0.25 mm. D57. Burial no. 39, phase 6/7.

(b) Fragment of a convex body. Blue-green. There are four widely spaced opaque white unmarvered trails. Dim. 20 × 22 mm; T. 0.8-1.5 mm. D 301. Pit, phase 7.

107. Fig. 189. Fragment of the rim of a (?) conical cup or beaker. Pale green ground, opaque yellow trails; everted rim, edge fire-rounded; straight upper body tapering in. Three widely spaced trails, now weathered, were probably not marvered flush.
Present H. 17 mm; rim D. 76 mm; T. 0.5-1 mm. M72. Burial no. 77, phase 6/7.

108. Fig. 189. Fragment of the rim of a (?) conical drinking cup. Blue-green ground, opaque yellow spiral trail; small oval bubbles aligned parallel to rim; fire-rounded and thickened rim, slightly inturned edge; straight side. The narrow horizontal trail on the upper body is not marvered flush.
Present H. 23 mm; rim D. 76 mm; T. 0.7-1.5 mm. A5. Unstratified.

109. Fig. 189. Fragment of the base of a (?) cup. Dark blue-green ground, opaque yellow trails; very bubbly; convex lower body; concave base; pontil mark. There is a broad horizontal marvered trail on the lower body, and two trail terminals on the base.
Present H. 8 mm; D. of base c. 35 mm at concavity; T. 1.5-2.5 mm. B36. Burial no. 10, phase 5/6.

110. Fig. 189. Three fragments of the convex body of a (?) cup. Dark blue-green ground, opaque yellow trails; parts of the side with widely spaced narrow unmarvered trails. One fragment has a vertical strip (perhaps an ornamental handle) applied to the trails.
Dim. (fragment with vertical strip) 18.5 × 11 mm; T. 1 mm. D107. Burial 24, phase 5.
Also:

(a) Fragment of a convex body. Dark blue-green; two opaque yellow trails. Dim. 12 × 9.5 mm; T. 0.4 mm. C/D1. Unstratified.

111. (Not illustrated.) Fragment of body. Greenish colourless ground; translucent dark red streaks marvered flush with surface; convex side above base.
Dim. 17.4 × 12.4 mm; T. 0.5-1.25 mm. B1. Unstratified.

112. Fig. 189. Six fragments, four joining, of body. Pale greenish colourless ground; translucent blue trails; convex side. There is a zig-zag unmarvered trail and a horizontal unmarvered trail.
Dim. (largest fragment) 22.5 × 16 mm; T. 0.3-0.7 mm. D273. Font sump, phase 6.

113. Fig. 189. Fragment of body. Colourless ground and colourless strips with diagonal opaque yellow marvered trails; straight side expanding out to curved carination; parts of two vertical strips applied to side.
Dim. 25.3 × 21.5 mm; T. 0.2-0.6 mm. B1. Unstratified.

114. Fig. 189. Fragment of a base. Greenish colourless ground; greenish colourless and opaque white twisted canes; small concave base; four canes applied to outside surface and marvered flush with surface, meeting at centre of base.
Dim. 20.3 × 19.0 mm; T. 1-1.5 mm. B36. Burial no. 10, phase 5/6.
Also (same burial):

(a) Small fragment of body. Dim. 10 × 7 mm; T. 0.25 mm. B36.

Flask
Coloured trail decoration

115. Figs 189 and 190. Indented flask with two handles, complete. Pale greenish colourless ground; opaque white feathered trails; rim slightly flared, edge rolled up, in and flattened; cylindrical neck expanding to globular body, with two uneven circular indents, producing flattened profile; very small concave base; spiral trail wound from lower body to rim, marvered flush with surface and manipulated into festoons; two thin vertical rod handles, applied below rim and attached to upper body, each with trail extending to base (much of trails now missing); pontil mark applied over the handle trails.
H. 100 mm; rim D. 31 mm; max. body D. 67 mm. D107. Burial no. 24, phase 5.

116. Fig. 191. Fragment of body. Greenish colourless ground; dark blue and greenish colourless trails; straight side; two thick v-shaped greenish colourless unmarvered trails above two similar dark blue trails.
Dim. 28 × 24 mm; T. 0.5+ mm. Z7. Castellaccio, twelfth-century deposit.

Yellowish colourless
Beakers and cups
Trailed decoration

117. Fig. 191. Fragment of the rim and upper body of a conical beaker. Yellowish colourless; rim edge fire-rounded and thickened; straight upper body tapering in. There are four unmarvered trails on the upper body.
Present H. 26 mm; rim D. c. 100 mm; T. 0.3-1 mm. B26. Burial no. 106, probably fifth century.

Undecorated

118. Fig. 191. Five fragments, two joining, of the rim and upper body of a (?) conical beaker or lamp. Yellowish

colourless; small elongated bubbles aligned parallel to rim; fire-rounded and thickened rim; straight side tapering in.
Present H. *c.* 40 mm; rim D. 88 mm; T. 0.5-1 mm. S03. Rock-cut road, phases 2-3.

119. Fig. 191. Fragment of the rim and upper body of a (?) conical beaker or lamp. Yellowish colourless. As cat. 118.
Present H. 15 mm; rim D. 86 mm; T. 0.3-0.7 mm. N30. Medieval cave, phases 5-6.

120. Fig. 191. Fragment of the rim and upper body of a (?) conical beaker or lamp. Yellowish colourless. As cat. 118.
Present H. 15 mm; rim D. 68 mm; T. 0.5-1 mm. D6. Phases 6-7.
Also:

(a) Fragment of a rim, as cat. 118-20. M64. Phase 6.
(b) Fragment of a rim, as cat. 118-20. B1. Unstratified.
(c) Fragment of a rim, as cat. 118-20. D218. Unstratified.
(d) Fragment of a rim, as cat. 118-20. A19. Phase 3+.
(e) Fragment of a rim, as cat. 118-20. B29. Phase 7.
(f) Fragment of a rim, as cat. 118-20. D266. Phase 3.
(g) Fragment of a rim, as cat. 118-20. A34. Burial no. 60, phase 6?
(h Fragment of a rim, as cat. 118-20. L101. Unstratified.

Yellow-green
Beakers, cups and lamps

121. Fig. 191. Fragment of the rim and body of a (?) cup. Everted rim, edge fire-rounded and thickened; convex side expanding out.
Present H. 18 mm; rim D. *c.* 80 mm; T. 0.5-1 mm. M106. Phase 6.

122. Fig. 191. Two fragments, rim and base, of a (?) conical beaker or lamp. Thin glass; rim slightly inturned, edge fire-rounded and thickened; upper body tapering in; straight lower body tapering to very small concave base; pontil mark.
Present H. (rim) 18 mm, (base) 27 mm; rim D. 74 mm; D. of base 10 mm; T. 0.3-2 mm. B80. Burial no. 12, phase 5/6.

123. Fig. 191. Fragment of the rim of a (?) conical beaker or lamp. Slightly everted rim, edge and upper body as cat. 122; distorted by heat.
Present H. 13 mm; rim D. *c.* 66 mm; T. 1 mm. A35. Phase 6.

124. Fig. 191. Fragment of the rim of a (?) conical beaker. Rim as cat. 122; upper body nearly vertical.
Present H. 25 mm; rim D. 76 mm; T. 0.2-1.2 mm. A5. Unstratified.

125. Fig. 191. Fragment of the rim of a (?) conical beaker. Slightly everted rim, edge fire-rounded and thickened; upper body nearly vertical.
Present H. 15 mm; rim D. 56 mm; T. 0.2-0.6 mm. A34. Burial no. 60, phase 6?

126. Fig. 191. Fragment of the rim of a (?) conical beaker. As cat. 125.
Present H. 12 mm; rim D. 70 mm; T. 0.5 mm. M38. Deposits, mid-sixth century.
Also:

(a) Fragment of a rim. A29. Phase 6.
(b) Fragment of a rim. M32. Phase 6.
(c) Fragment of a rim. M139. Phase 6.
(d) Fragment of a rim. B4. Burial 99, phase 6.
(e) Fragment of a rim. D6. Phase 6.
(f) Two fragments of rim. A21. Phase 6.

Fig. 190. Early medieval glass flask (cat.115). *(KW)*

(g) Two fragments of rim. A21. Phase 6.
(h) Fragment of a rim. M143. Phase 3.
(i) Fragment of a rim. A23. Burial no. 26, phase 5/6?
(j) Fragment of a rim. C/D1. Unstratified.

Blue-green and green-blue (peacock blue)
Beakers, cups and lamps

127. Fig. 191. Fragment of the rim of a (?) conical beaker or lamp. Pale blue-green; thin glass; rim edge fire rounded; upper body tapering in.
Present H. 16 mm; rim D. 90 mm; T. 0.7-1.5 mm. M64. Phase 6.
Also:

(a) Fragment of a rim. D218. Unstratified.
(b) Fragment of a rim. B8. Burial no. 18, phase 6/7.
(c) Fragment of a rim. M64. Phase 6.
(d) Fragment of a rim. B64. Burial no. 12, phase 5/6.
(e) Fragment of a rim. A35. Phase 6.

128. Fig. 191. Fragment of the rim of a (?) conical beaker or lamp. Deep green-blue (peacock blue); rim edge fire-rounded; upper body tapering in.
Present H. 15 mm; rim D. 76 mm; T. 1 mm. D244. Phase 6.

129. Fig. 191. Fragment of the rim of a (?) conical beaker or lamp. Deep green-blue (peacock blue); rim edge fire-rounded; upper body tapering in.
Present H. 25 mm; rim D. 70 mm; T. 0.5-1 mm. B26. Burial no. 106, probably fifth century.

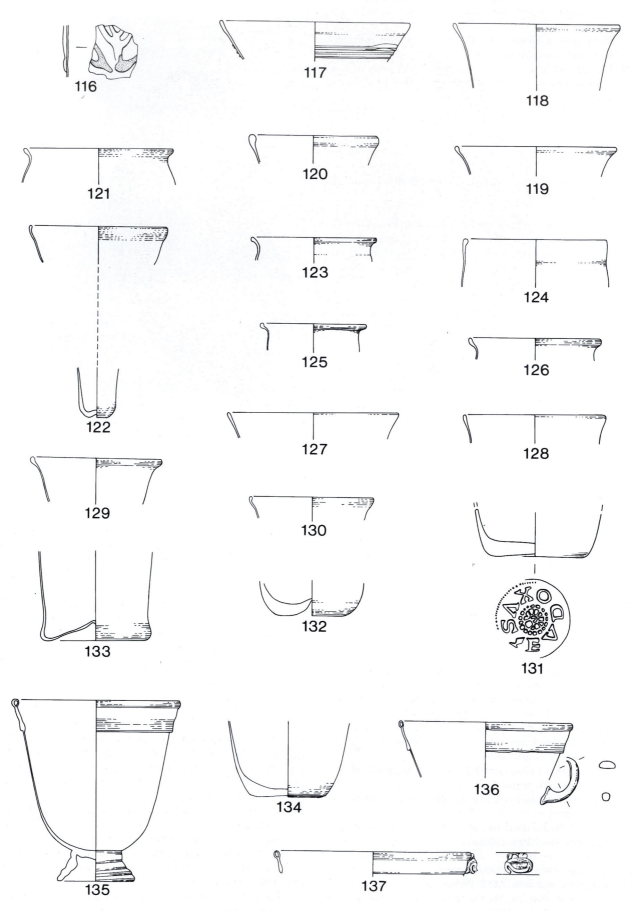

Fig. 191. Glass vessels, fifth century AD and later (1:2). *(SC)*

Fig. 192. Base stamped EUDOXUS (cat. 131). *(KW)*

Also:
(a) Fragment of a rim. B1. Unstratified.
(b) Fragment of a rim. J1. Unstratified.
(c) Fragment of a rim. E69. Phase 3.
(d) Fragment of body, with trail. M14. Phase 6.
(e) Fragment of body, with trail. M10. Phase 5.
(f) Fragment of body. D316. Phase 3.

Various colours
Beakers, bowls, cups and lamps
130. Fig. 191. Fragment of the rim of a (?) conical beaker or lamp. Greenish colourless; rim slightly inturned, edge fire-rounded; upper body tapering in.
Present H. 12 mm; rim D. 66 mm; T. 0.5+ mm. C46. Burial no. 8, phase 6/7?
Also:
(a) Fragment of a rim. C46. Burial no. 8, phase 6/7?
(b) Fragment of a rim. S03. Rock-cut road, phases 2-3.
(c) Fragment of a rim. M26. Phase 3.
(d) Fragment of a rim. M92. Phase 3.
131. Figs 191 and 192. Fragment of the lower body and base of a (?) conical beaker. Pale green; some small bubbles; straight lower body tapering in to thick concave base with impressed stamp. There is a rouletted ring enclosing E V D O X V S anticlockwise in a ring, with a leaf stop between S and E, and a rosette and ring of dots at the centre.
Present H. 25 mm; D. of base 48 mm; T. 2-9 mm. S04. Rock-cut road, phases 2-3.

132. Fig. 191. Fragment of the lower body and base of a (?) conical beaker. Pale green; some bubbles; straight lower body; concave base with central pointed kick.
Present H. 17 mm; D. of base 36 mm; T. 2.5-5.5 mm. H29. Unstratified.
133. Fig. 191. Fragment of the lower body and base of a (?) conical beaker. Greenish colourless; straight lower body expanding out above concave base with central pointed kick; pontil mark.
Present H. 45 mm; D. of base 54 mm; T. 1.5 mm. M23. Phase 3.
Also:
(a) Fragment of a similar base, also with a pontil mark. D. of base 32 mm. M136. Phase 3.
134. Fig. 191. Two joining fragments of the lower body and base of a (?) conical beaker. Colourless; straight side tapering in; thick slightly concave base; pontil mark.
Present H. 41 mm; D. of base 40 mm; T. 1-4.5+ mm. C/D1. Unstratified.
135. Fig. 191. Eighteen fragments, most joining, of a small footed bowl. Greenish colourless; vertical collar rim, tubular at top, formed by bending edge out and down; long convex body; applied conical base formed by twisting a trail four times round the bottom of the body; pontil mark.
H. 95 mm; rim D. 90 mm; D. of base 40 mm; T. 0.5-1.5+ mm. C51. Limekiln, early-mid fifth century.
Also:
(a) Fragment of a rim, as cat. 135. D317. Phase 6.

(b) Two fragments of rim. C46. Burial no. 8, phase 6/7?
(c) Fragment of a rim. B36. Burial no. 10, phase 5/6.
(d) Fragment of a rim, as cat. 135. D301. Phase 6.
136. Fig. 191. Three fragments of the rim, body and handle of a (?) small bowl or lamp. Pale yellowish colourless; very thin glass; vertical collar rim, tubular at top, formed by bending edge out and down; straight side tapering in; scar on outside of rim, probably from handle; one small vertical curved rod handle, not attached.
Present H. 33 mm; rim D. 92 mm; T. 0.24 mm. C51. Limekiln, early-mid fifth century.
137. Fig. 191. Fragment of the rim and handle of a (?) small bowl or lamp. Pale yellowish colourless; vertical collar rim, tubular at top, formed by bending edge out and down; handle attachment on outside of rim.
Present H. 13 mm; rim D. 104 mm. C1. Unstratified.
138. Fig. 193. Fragment of the rim of a (?) bowl or lamp. Yellowish colourless; vertical tubular rim, edge rolled out and down; straight side tapering in; handle scar on outside edge of rim.
Present H. 19 mm; rim D. 86 mm; T. 0.5+ mm. C46. Burial no. 8, phase 6/7?
139. Fig. 193. Fragment of the rim of a (?) bowl or lamp. Greenish colourless; tubular rim, edge rolled out and down; handle scar on outside edge of rim.
Present H. 6 mm; rim D. 82 mm; T. 0.5+ mm. C/D1. Unstratified.
140. Fig. 193. Fragment of the rim of a (?) bowl or lamp. Greenish colourless; tubular rim, edge rolled out and down; handle attachment on rim edge.
Present H. 8 mm; rim D. 106 mm; T. 0.5+ mm. B66. Phase 6.
Similar tubular rims:
(a) Fragment of a rim. Greenish colourless. D266. Phase 6.
(b) Fragment of a rim. Greenish colourless. D47. Phase 6.
(c) Fragment of a rim. Pale blue-green. D94. Phase 6.
(d) Fragment of a rim. Pale blue-green. B34. Phase 6.
(e) Fragment of a rim. Pale blue-green. D6. Phase 6.
(f) Fragment of a rim. Greenish colourless. B64. Burial no. 12, phase 5/6.
(g) Fragment of a rim. Greenish colourless. B80. Burial no. 12, phase 5/6.
(h) Fragment of a rim. Yellow-green. B34. Phase 6.
(i) Fragment of a rim. Deep green-blue (peacock blue). D4. Burial no. 95, phases 6-7.
141. Fig. 193. Fragment of the rim of a (?) small bowl or lamp. Yellowish colourless; fire rounded and thickened rim; side tapering in; handle scar on top of rim.
Present H. 14 mm; rim D. 80 mm; T. 0.5+ mm. A34. Burial no. 60, phase 6?
142. Fig. 193. Fragment of the handle and body of a (?) lamp. Yellowish colourless; conical body; lower attachment of vertical curved rod handle.
Present H. 50 mm; T. 0.5+ mm. C/D1. Unstratified.
143. Fig. 193. Fragment of the handle of a (?) lamp. Yellow-green; vertical rod handle, lower attachment flattened against body (missing).
Present H. 53.5 mm. M26. Phase 3.
144. Fig. 193. Fragment of the handle and body of a (?) lamp. Pale blue-green; little weathering; bubbly; convex side with horizontal unmarvered trails; lower attachment of small vertical angular rod handle.
Present H. 32 mm; T. 0.1+ mm. C/D1. Unstratified.
145. Fig. 193. Fragment of the handle and body of a (?) lamp. Pale blue-green; convex side; lower attachment of small vertical angular rod handle.

Present H. 27.5 mm; T. 0.1+ mm. C42. Phase 6.
Also:
(a) Fragment as cat. 144-5. Dark blue. C/D1. Unstratified.
(b) Fragment as cat. 144-5. Pale blue-green. C2. Burial no. 2, phases 5-6.
(c) Fragment as cat. 144-5. Pale blue-green. C47. Phase 6.
(d) Fragment, (?) as cat. 144-5. Pale blue-green. M86. Phase 6.
(e) Fragment, (?) as cat. 144-5. Pale blue-green. M132. Phase 3.
146. Fig. 193. Fragment of the lower body of a lamp. Pale green; narrow conical body terminating in convex base; pontil mark.
Present H. 37 mm; max. D. 21.5 mm; T. 0.5+ mm. B1. Unstratified.
147. Fig. 193. Fragment of the lower body of a lamp. Pale green. As cat. 146.
Present H. 33.5 mm; max. D. 22.5 mm; T. 0.7+ mm. B80. Burial no. 12, phase 5/6.
148. Fig. 193. Fragment of the lower body of a lamp. Pale green. As cat. 146.
Present H. 34.5 mm; max. D. 21 mm; T. 0.7 mm. C57. Burial no. 2, phases 5-6.
149. Fig. 193. Fragment of the lower body of a lamp. Pale blue-green. As cat. 146.
Present H. 40.5 mm; max. D. 17 mm; T. 0.7 mm. C42. Burial no. 2, phases 5-6.
Also:
(a) Fragment as cat. 146. Deep green-blue (peacock blue). C/D1. Unstratified.
(b) Fragment as cat. 146. Deep green-blue (peacock blue). B1. Unstratified.
(c) Fragment as cat. 146. Blue-green. M92. Phase 3.
150. Fig. 193. Two joining fragments of the lower body, stem and base, of a small cup. Pale greenish; thin glass; convex lower body tapering in, pinched into stem; folded into double layered base ring with tubular edge; base with high kick filling hollow stem.
Present H. 29 mm; D. of base 35 mm; T. 0.1+ mm. B49. Burial no. 11, phase 5/6.
151. Fig. 193. Fragment of the lower body, stem and base of a small cup. Yellowish colourless. As cat. 150.
Present H. 22 mm; D. of base 40 mm; T. 0.1+ mm. D6. Phase 6.
152. Fig. 193. Fragment of the lower body, stem and base of a small cup. Blue-green. As cat. 150.
Present H. 21 mm; D. of base 38 mm; T. 0.5+ mm. D6. Phase 6.
Also:
(a) Fragment as cat. 150-2. Yellowish colourless. M97. Phase 3.
(b) Fragment as cat. 150-2. Yellowish colourless. C/D1. Unstratified.
(c) Fragment as cat. 150-2. Yellowish colourless. D166. Phase 3.
(d) Fragment as cat. 150-2. Yellowish colourless. D92. Burial no. 55, phase 6-7.
(e) Fragment as cat. 150-2. Yellowish colourless. A34. Burial no. 60, phase 6?
(f) Fragment as cat. 150-2. Yellowish colourless. D48. Phase 3.
(g) Fragment as cat. 150-2. Yellowish colourless. D166. Phase 3.
(h) Fragment as cat. 150-2. Yellowish colourless. M74. Phase 6.
(i) Fragment as cat. 150-2. Yellowish colourless. B64. Burial no. 12, phase 5/6.

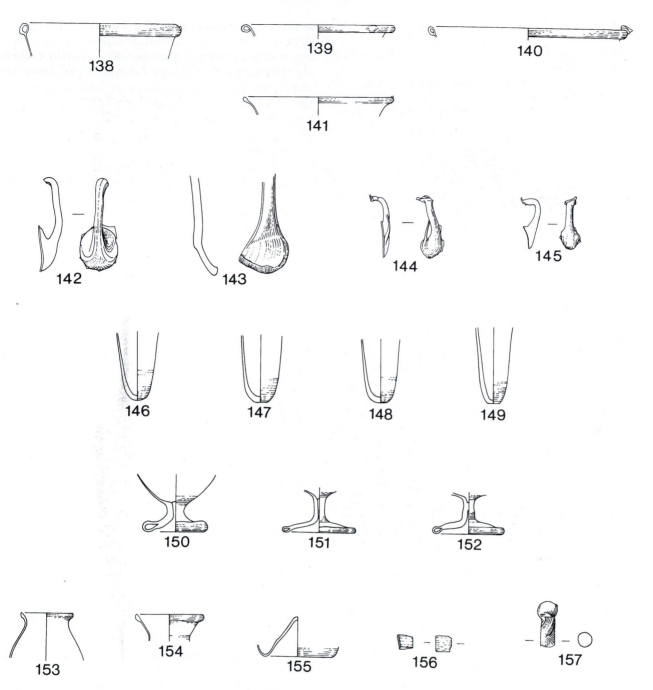

Fig. 193. Glass vessels, fifth century AD and later (1:2). *(SC)*

(j) Fragment as cat. 150-2. Yellowish colourless. M32. Phase 6.

(k) Fragment as cat. 150-2. Dark greenish. A34. Burial no. 60, phase 6?

153. Fig. 193. Fragment of the rim of a (?) flask or small jar. Greenish colourless; everted rim, edge fire-rounded; almost straight body expanding out.
Present H. 29 mm; rim D. 28 mm; T. 0.7+ mm. D273. Font sump, phase 6.

154. Fig. 193. Fragment of the rim of a (?) flask. Greenish colourless; thin glass; everted rim, edge fire-rounded; funnel mouth; top of narrow cylindrical neck; thick trail round outside edge of rim.
Present H. 13 mm; rim D. 36 mm; T. 0.1+ mm. B32. Burial no. 11, phase 5/6.

Also:

(a) Fragment of a rim, as cat. 154. Blue-green. B80. Burial no. 12, phase 5/6.

155. Fig. 193. Fragment of the high concave base of a (?) flask, bowl or lamp. Pale green; very bubbly; narrow straight lower body; small very high conical base with central kick; pontil mark.
Present H. 23 mm; D. of base *c.* 36 mm; T. 1 mm. C23. Burial no. 7, phase 6/7?

Also:

(a) Fragment of a base, as cat. 155. Greenish colourless. C/D1. Unstratified.

(b) Fragment of a base, as cat. 155. Deep green-blue (peacock blue). D273. Font sump, phase 6.

(c) Fragment of a base, as cat. 155. Pale green. D301.

Phase 6.
Also:
- Two fragments of body, with 'optic-blown' designs. Yel-lowish colourless.
- Two fragments of body, with horizontal unmarvered trails. Pale blue-green.
- Fragment of body, with meandering unmarvered trail. Pale blue-green.

Objects[68]
Tesserae
156. Fig. 193. Cube-shaped lump. No worn surfaces; semi-opaque dark blue.
8.7 × 8.9 × 7.8 mm. D33. Unstratified.
Also:
(a) Cube-shaped lump, as cat. 157. Semi-opaque dark blue. B64. Burial no. 12, phase 5/6.
(b) Cube-shaped lump, as cat. 157. Semi-opaque peacock blue. C/D1. Unstratified.

Pin-shaped rod
157. Fig. 193. Fragment of a rod with a globular terminal. Dark peacock blue; solid cylindrical shaft with slight anti-clockwise twist; globular end. There is a scar on the end, perhaps from a pontil.
Present length 23.5 mm; D. (rod) 8.5 mm. D81. Phase 6.

THE LAMPS, by D.M. Bailey

Some 127 lamps and fragments were found at this site and only two of them, cat. 62 and 63, were made outside Italy, apparently in Tunisia and Tri-politania respectively. All the others are central Ital-ian products and most were probably made in Rome or its immediate vicinity; the very late Roman or early medieval lamp, cat. 60, may have been made at the site itself, and cat. 61, of early medieval date, is of uncertain provenance but is probably local. Very few of these lamps were manu-factured before the end of the first century AD, the bulk of them being of the second century AD and the beginning of the third century. Most of these second- to third-century lamps came from a single source, the fish-pond, into which they were dumped in two main deposits: L105 and, below it, L165. Although L165 has, on the whole, earlier lamps than L105, there was a slight amount of mixing between the deposits, as there are joins of lamp fragments from both deposits – for example, cat. 4 and 5. The earliest lamp from the fish-pond is probably cat. 6, which could have been made as early as about AD 50, but more likely is as late as most of the lamps from the same deposit, Standard Italian Loeschcke 1919 type VIII lamps, produced between about AD 90 and 160 (cat. 12-24 include

many of these from L165). However, the upper deposit, L105, also included lamps of this type, together with a larger quantity of late Italian Loesch-cke 1919 type VIII lamps (amongst cat. 29-50) of about AD 150 to 225+, some of which type were found in the lower deposit, L165. The quantity of the recovered lamps thereafter drops dramatically, with one lamp only of fourth-century date (cat. 54), three lamps of about AD 375-450 (cat. 55-7), three lamps of the fifth or sixth century (cat. 58-9, 63), and two lamps of early medieval date, the seventh- to eighth-century cat. 60, and cat. 61, probably of the tenth century AD.

Cat. 1, a small fragment of a volute lamp with an incomplete shoulder form, could be the earliest lamp from the site, made probably between AD 40 and 100, but as the date-range of its type shows, it need not be any earlier than the end of the first century. It was residual in its late Roman find-spot in area E (the 'large room'): see Figure 12 for the areas of the site. Equally, cat. 2 and 3, although poss-ibly of a date well before AD 90 could well be later – cat. 2 came from the lower deposit in the fish-pond and cat. 3 from the early medieval pottery kiln, where it was residual.

Both the Loeschcke 1919 type V cat. lamps 4 and 5 are late forms of the type (Bailey 1980 type Civ) and are not earlier than AD 90 or later than AD 150; indeed, cat. 4, signed for the firm L. Munatius Adiectus, probably dates before AD 130. Each of the two lamps is made up from fragments that came from both major deposits in the fish-pond.

Central Italian Loeschcke 1919 type VIII lamps form the largest proportion of the lamps found (109 out of 127), and are divided almost equally between early forms, dating between about AD 50 and 160 (only two – cat. 6 and 7 – could be as early as AD 50; some 54 lamps are likely to be no earlier than AD 90), and the later forms, dating between about AD 150 and 225+ (53 examples).

The two lamps (cat. 6 and 7) of Bailey 1980 type Oii, with ovule decoration on their shoulders, are of a type made between AD 50 and 110; again nei-ther may have been made or deposited before AD 90. Cat. 6 came from the lower deposit in the fish-pond; cat. 7 was residual in a late Roman context on the lower terrace.

Cat. 8-10 are of the narrow-shouldered Bailey 1980 type Piii of Loeschcke 1919 type VIII and are likely to date between AD 90 and 140. Two of them, cat. 8 and 9, came from the lower level of the fish-pond, and cat. 10 was residual in a post-Roman deposit. Cat. 11 is close to the shape of Standard Italian Loeschcke 1919 type VIII lamps, but has a decorated shoulder. It came from the lower level of the fish-pond and probably dates between AD 90 and 150.

---

[68] See also, for a glass ring, beads and counters, Allason-Jones, this volume, nos. 136-43.

There are some 50 examples of Standard Italian Loeschcke 1919 type VIII lamps (Bailey 1980 type Pi): cat. 12-27 and uncatalogued fragments. Of these, five are of the later, shallow, form, probably dating to AD 140-80, and the remainder of the earlier, deeper form, of about AD 90-160. Four of the earlier versions are signed – LMADIEC (cat. 12), MVNTREPT (cat. 14), BASSA (cat. 18), GABMERC (cat. 24) -, and one (cat. 23) has a plain footprint stamp. Of the later standard form, one fragment (cat. 27) bears a stamp, probably of L. Fabricius Masculus, but perhaps of one of the other lamp-makers with the same nomen (*CIL* XV 6429-35). These lamps came from various sources on the site, but mostly from the fish-pond: part of cat. 13 came from the very lowest level (L184), but joins another sherd from the lower level L165, in which were also found cat. 12, 14, 16-17, 20-1, part of 23, 26 and sixteen uncatalogued fragments. From the higher level, L105, came cat. 19, 22, part of 23 (joining a sherd from the lower level) and nine uncatalogued fragments. Cat. 24-5 and two uncatalogued sherds came from the fill of the north cistern, which was probably constructed in the second century AD. An uncatalogued fragment came from below the *selce* road, another from a floor in area E and one from a post-hole, apparently of early Imperial date, also in area E. Cat. 27 was residual in a post-Roman deposit. From a trench across the rock-cut road, west of the main site, came cat. 15 and 18, and four uncatalogued sherds.

The 53 late Italian Loeschcke 1919 type VIII lamps cat. 28-50 (and uncatalogued fragments) are divided into several sections, but none is likely to be from before AD 140 (cat. 28), the bulk being later than AD 160; in most cases the shape of the lamps of this type continued to be made up to at least AD 225 and perhaps rather later. The makers' names include Passerius Augurinus (cat. 38), L. Fabricius Masculus (cat. 45) and L. Caecilius Saecularis (cat. 49); Fabricius was on the whole an earlier lamp-maker than were the other two, working sometime between AD 150 and 180, the others perhaps flourishing between about AD 180 and 225. Most of these late versions of Loeschcke 1919 type VIII lamps came from the fish-pond: cat. 29-30, 34-7, 39-42, 44-7, 49-50 and 24 uncatalogued sherds came from the later deposit, and cat. 28 and four uncatalogued fragments came from the earlier deposit (one of the last goes with a lamp fragment from the later level). Cat. 31, 43 and 48 came from the north cistern, that was probably filled in the late second century AD. An uncatalogued fragment came from a pit in area E, and cat. 32 from the rock-cut road to the west of the main site. Cat. 38 was found in a late Roman deposit in a drain in area M and was no doubt residual, as was cat. 33 from a post-Roman hillwash at the north of the site, and an uncatalogued sherd from the topsoil of a post-Roman terrace to the east of the main site. The central Italian *Firmalampe*, cat. 52, of Bailey

1980 type Nvi, is of the same date as the late Italian Loeschcke 1919 type VIII lamps above, about AD 160-225+, and came from the earlier level in the fish-pond. Roughly of the same date is the pine cone lamp cat. 53, but the lamp-stand/thymiaterion cat. 51 is probably somewhat earlier, roughly contemporary with the Standard Italian Loeschcke 1919 type VIII lamps. The former comes from post-Roman hillwash to the north of the site, and the latter from the very lowest fill of the fish-pond.

Of the later lamps from the site (of which there is nothing earlier than the fourth century) there is part of a very late form of Bailey 1980 type M, a wall-lamp of the fourth century AD (cat. 54), and also three of the copies of imported African red slip ware lamps of Hayes 1972 type I that were made in Rome about AD 375-450 (cat. 55-7). Two lamps (cat. 58-9), based upon imported African lamps of Hayes 1972 type II, are of the fifth century or perhaps well into the sixth century AD; they are probably of Italian manufacture. The wall-lamp, cat. 54, came from contemporary occupation deposits on the lower terrace. The Hayes 1972 type I lamps (Bailey 1980 type Si) came from late Roman silt in area H (cat. 56), from a post-Roman ash layer on the lower terrace (cat. 57), and from post-Roman silt in area L (cat. 55). The lamps of Hayes 1972 type II (Bailey 1980 type Siii) were found in late Roman to post-Roman fill/rubble in area E (cat. 59) and post-Roman rubble in area M (cat. 58).

Only the rear, with a large applied handle, remains of lamp cat. 60, which has a wide filling hole at the rear top. Enough survives to show that it had been made in a mould: the internal joint is very evident. I am informed by Paul Roberts that the fabric indicates that it was most probably made in the vicinity of Monte Gelato, and it seems to be a local version of a late Roman or early medieval shape stemming ultimately from Sicily (see Bailey (1988: 208-9)), but also made in southern Italy and probably at Rome. In shape it perhaps resembles a large version of the Sicilian Bailey 1988 Q 1872. The comparable local pottery fabric is of the seventh or eighth century, and the shape of the lamp would not argue against this; the lamp came from an orange-coloured fill in area M, of post-Roman date (cf. Fig. 63).

The wheelmade lamp cat. 61 is of post-Roman manufacture, made at some time in the early medieval period. It is one of a long-lived shape found throughout the Mediterranean and beyond – examples of the same basic form (flared bowl with a domed cover) have been found at Corinth (the earlier lamps of Broneer 1930 type XXXV: before the tenth century AD), at Cnidus, Sacidava in Romania, in eastern Anatolia, at Benghazi, and, with flared necks, at Carthage (for all these see Bailey 1988 Q 3343; add to the references given there Fulford and Peacock (1984: 240)): dates between the fourth century (probably too early) and the eleventh century have been suggested for these. In many cases, the smaller the dome, the later the lamp, as in the case of some Mameluke-period examples from Egypt and Jordan, of the thirteenth to fifteenth centuries, where the dome is merely a small cone in the centre ('Amr 1984: 208, fig. 2,4). A form shallower than ours found in some numbers at Palermo is dated between the ninth and twelfth centuries (Bonanno 1979: 357). Cat. 61 was found in a tenth-century deposit in area D and is probably of that date.

One of the two lamps that may be imports, cat. 62, is a very small fragment of nozzle with long decorative tongues underneath. The fabric could be Italian, and go with Bailey 1980 type Q lamps of about AD 150-225, but the tongues are found more often on African lamps like Bailey 1988 Q 1710-12. The raised edge of the area of the wick hole is not normally found on these Loeschcke 1919 type VIII lamps, either from Italy or Tunisia. Possibly this is a late central Italian *Firmalampe* of Loeschcke 1919 type X, but even here the curve out to the body indicates an unusually short nozzle. The fragment came from the fill of the north cistern. The other imported lamp, cat. 63, was perhaps made in Tripolitania during the fifth century AD: the form of the shoulder is rather different from most of these Tripolitanian lamps (Brants 1913 type XXIV, the source of which was first identified by Hayes (1972: 314-15); see also the discussion by and references in Bailey (1988: 204). Cat. 63 was found in post-Roman rubble in area M.

The discus scenes include: a figure of Victoria with a palm branch (cat. 16); an unidentified seated or enthroned figure, part of a larger scene (cat. 49); human heads surviving from lost figures (cat. 8 and 39), the former uncertain, the latter probably a woman; a dramatic mask of a slave, one of three on the discus (cat. 10). Animals are also depicted: a lion on cat. 5; a hare on cat. 4; a dog on a couch, perhaps the Sothic Dog of Isis on the Sacred Couch of Serapis; on cat. 46; the rear leg of an animal on cat. 56; a cock or peacock on cat. 55; two wing-tips, on cat. 18 and 20, the former perhaps of an eagle (or perhaps of Victoria), the latter perhaps of a gryphon; and a scallop shell, on cat. 13. Part of a larger scene, apparently with a tree on the left, is shown on cat. 26, and palm branches decorate cat. 15 and 28; rosettes adorn cat. 7, 30, 38 and 58. A crescent is shown on cat. 19. Very slight indications show that the discuses of cat. 21, 22, 37, 40, 43, 44 and 47 were decorated, the scenes of which have not been identified, although cat. 47 may have the foot of a couch-leg.

Several makers' names are found on the Monte Gelato lamps, all Italian and all are likely to have worked in the vicinity of Rome, if not at Rome itself. They range in date from late Flavian until Severan times:

BASSA (cat. 18). Bassus (*CIL* VIII 22644 48; X 8053 33; XIII 10001 66; XV 6337) made lamps of various

shapes at some time between late Flavian times and the early Antonine period (Bailey 1980: 91); Pavolini (1980b: tabella I) has dated Bassus's *Vogelkopflampen* between AD 130/40 and 160); there may have been more than one maker with this name.

LCAESAE (cat. 49). L. Caecilius Saecularis (*CIL* XX 4969 13; V 8114 17; VIII 22644 52; IX 6081 13; X 8053 41; XI 6699 39; XII 5682 17; XIII 10001 17; XV 6350) was a prolific and (as far as his figure-types were concerned) inventive lamp-maker, who worked during late Antonine and Severan times (Bailey 1980: 91-2; Pavolini 1980b: tabella I: AD 180/90 to the first decade of the third century).

LFABRICMAS (cat. 45). L. Fabricius Masculus (*CIL* II 6256; V 8114 46; VIII 22644 101; X 8053 74; XI 6699 78; XII 5682 40; XIII 10001 127; XV 6433): the dating given by me previously (Bailey 1980: 95) (late Flavian to early Antonine) may be too early, and Pavolini has suggested (1980b: tabella I) AD 150-80.

]FAB[(cat. 27). This may be from any one of the Fabricii, most probably Masculus as the last, but perhaps Aeuelpistus, Agat( ), Heraclides or Saturninus (*CIL* XV 6429-35; Bailey 1980: 94-5), all of whom worked during the Antonine period or a little earlier.

GABMERC (cat. 24). Gabinius Merc( ) (*CIL* VIII 22644 113; XI 6699 94; XIII 10001 142; XV 6460). Pavolini (1980b: tabella I) has dated his *Vogelkopflampen* to about AD 120/30-50.

LMADIEC (cat. 4 and 12). L. Munatius Adiectus (*CIL* V 8114 87; VIII 22644 219; X 8053 121; XI 6699 130; XII 5682 71; XIII 10001 216; XV 6560): a date in the late Flavian to Trajanic periods is probable (Bailey 1980: 98) or perhaps a little later (Pavolini 1980b: tabella I).

MVNTREPT (cat. 14). L. Munatius Threptus (*CIL* III 10184 33; V 8114 91; VIII 22644 10 and 226; X 8053 140; XI 6699 135; XII 5682 78; XIII 10001 218; XV 6565): late Flavian to early Antonine (Bailey 1980: 98).

PASAVGV (cat. 38). Passerius Augurinus (*CIL* III 12012 71; V 8114 105; IX 6081 54; X 8053 160; XI 6699 156; XIII 10001 247; XV 6610): late Antonine and probably well into the third century AD (Bailey 1980: 99).

The assemblage of lamps from Monte Gelato, a small rural site of no great importance, shows no surprises, except perhaps the early medieval lamp cat. 61, which I have not been able to parallel in Italy. There is nothing as early as the Augustan structures on the site, and the lamps indicate a main occupation and use between late Flavian times and the Severan period (or possibly the rubbish dumps of this period were found and others were not located). Very limited usage of pottery lamps occurred from the later fourth to the middle of the sixth century, glass lamps perhaps being employed to a greater extent; a locally made lamp of the seventh or eighth century was found, and a wheel-made lamp probably of the tenth century may also have been made in the vicinity of the site. Perhaps the most interesting aspect of these lamps is that the Roman Imperial examples, except for two possible African imports, were nearly all made at Rome or its immediate neighbourhood, and thus travelled by road the 34 km to the site. Several mechanisms for this travel can be envisaged: purchase at a local market or shop supplied from Rome; purchase at Rome by visiting locals; purchase at the site from travelling pedlars.

CATALOGUE

Central Italian volute lamps and early Loeschcke 1919 type VIII lamps

1. Fig. 194. Underbody and part of rim from a volute lamp. Shoulder form IIb, III or IV (for shoulder forms, see Loeschcke (1919: 25, fig. 2)). Buff clay; brown slip.
L. 24 mm. E138. c. AD 40-100.

2. Fig. 194. Right front part of a volute lamp, probably Broneer 1930 type XXI or perhaps Loeschcke 1919 type IV (Bailey 1980 type Diii or type Bii). Shoulder form IIIa. Buff clay; bright red slip.
L. 48 mm. L165. c. AD 70-100.

3. Fig. 194. Underbody from a volute lamp of Loeschcke 1919 type VIII. Orange clay; red slip.
L. 36 mm. E90. c. AD 40-120.

4. Figs 194 and 195. Fragmentary Loeschcke 1919 type V lamp (Bailey 1980 type Civ). Shoulder form VIIb. Air-hole. Discus: hare leaping to left. Raised circular base; LMADIE[C] incuse. Orange-buff clay; orange slip traces.
L. 91 mm; W. 68 mm. L105 and L165 (joined). c. AD 90-130.

5. Fig. 194. Right front part of a lamp similar to cat. 4. Shoulder form VIIa. Discus: lion to left. Orange-buff clay; orange slip traces.
L. 58 mm. L105 and L165 (joined). c. AD 90-150.

6. Fig. 194. Right front fragment with part of nozzle from Loeschcke 1919 type VIII lamp (Bailey 1980 type Oii). Shoulder form VIIIa, with impressed ovules. Air-hole. Plain discus. Buff clay; red slip.
L. 52 mm. L165, SF 655. c. AD 50-110.

7. Fig. 194. Shoulder and discus from Loeschcke 1919 Type VIII lamp (Bailey 1980 type Oii). Near shoulder-form VIIIb, with impressed ovules. Discus: rosette. Buff clay; red slip.
L. 24 mm. M144. c. AD 50-110.

8. Fig. 196. Rear right part of Loeschcke 1919 type VIII lamp (Bailey 1980 type Piii), with handle spring. Shoulder form VIIb. Discus: unclear – probably a human head. Buff clay; red slip.
L. 69 mm. L165. c. AD 90-140.

9. Fig. 196. Front right part of Loeschcke 1919 type VIII lamp (probably Bailey 1980 type Piii). Shoulder form VIIIb. Air-hole. Buff clay; red slip.
L. 54 mm. L165. c. AD 90-140.

10. Fig. 196. Discus from Loeschcke 1919 type VIII lamp (Bailey 1980 type Piii). Slave mask (one of three: cf. Bailey 1980 Q 1326); concentric circles round filling hole. Buff clay; red slip.
L. 24 mm. M167. c. AD 90-140.

11. Fig. 196. Shoulder from Loeschcke 1919 type VIII lamp (near standard form). Shoulder form VIIb, with impressed ovules. Buff clay; brown slip.
L. 32 mm. L165. c. AD 90-150.

Standard central Italian lamps of Loeschcke 1919 type VIII (Bailey 1980 type Pi)

12. Figs 195 and 196. Almost complete lamp. Shoulder form VIIa. Plain discus. Raised circular base; LMADIEC incuse. Buff clay; orange slip.
L. 95 mm; W. 66 mm. L165, SF 609. c. AD 90-130.

13. Fig. 196. Fragmentary, with non-joining sherd. Shoulder form VIIb. Discus: scallop shell. Air-hole. Raised circular base. Buff clay; purple-brown slip.
L. 87 mm. L165 and L184 (joined; + L184 non-joining). c. AD 90-160.

14. Figs 195 and 197. Fragmentary. Shoulder form VIIa. Plain discus. Raised circular base; MVNTREPT incuse. Buff clay; brown slip.
L. 96 mm. L165, SF 607 and SF 655 (joining). c. AD 90-160.

15. Fig. 197. Discus and shoulder sherd. Shoulder form VIIa. Discus: palm branch (one of two). Buff clay; red slip.
W. 27 mm. S10. c. AD 90-160.

16. Fig. 197. Rear right part with handle. Shoulder form VIIb. Discus: Victoria with palm branch. Raised circular base. Buff clay; red-brown slip.
L. 83 mm. L165, SF 631. c. AD 90-160.

17. Fig. 197. Rear part with handle. Shoulder form VIIIb. Plain discus. Orange-buff clay; orange slip traces.
W. 62 mm. L165, SF 622. c. AD 90-160.

18. Figs 195 and 197. Rear part with handle. Shoulder form VIIb. Discus: tip of wing. Raised circular base; BASSA incuse. Orange-buff clay; red to brown slip.
L. 81 mm, W. 70 mm. S4, SF 714. c. AD 100-60.

19. Fig. 198. Fragment of left side. Possibly Loeschcke 1919 type V. Shoulder form VIIb. Discus: crescent. Orange-buff clay; orange slip traces.
L. 56 mm. L105. c. AD 90-150.

20. Fig. 198. Rear part with handle. Shoulder form VIIb. Discus: wing of gryphon? Orange-buff clay; orange slip traces.
W. 38 mm. L165. c. AD 90-160.

21. Fig. 198. Rear left part with handle. Shoulder form VIIa. Discus: part of unidentified scene. Yellow-buff clay; purple-brown slip.
L. 52 mm. L165. c. AD 90-160.

22. Fig. 198. Handle sherd. Shoulder form VIIa. Discus: part of unidentified scene. Yellow-buff clay; purple-brown slip.
L. 44 mm. L105, SF 652. c. AD 90-160.

23. Fig. 198. Handle, underbody and base. Raised circular base; impressed plain footprint stamp. Buff clay; orange slip traces.
L. 98 mm. L105 and L165 (joining). c. AD 90-160.

24. Figs 195 and 198. Base sherd. Raised circular base; [GAB]MERC incuse. Buff clay; orange-brown slip.
W. 46 mm. L149. c. AD 100-60.

— Six nozzle and shoulder sherds. Shoulder forms VIIa (four examples) and VIIb (two examples). L105 (two examples, including SF 652), L149, L165 (two examples), S10.

— Five nozzle sherds. L105 (two examples), L143, L165, M104.

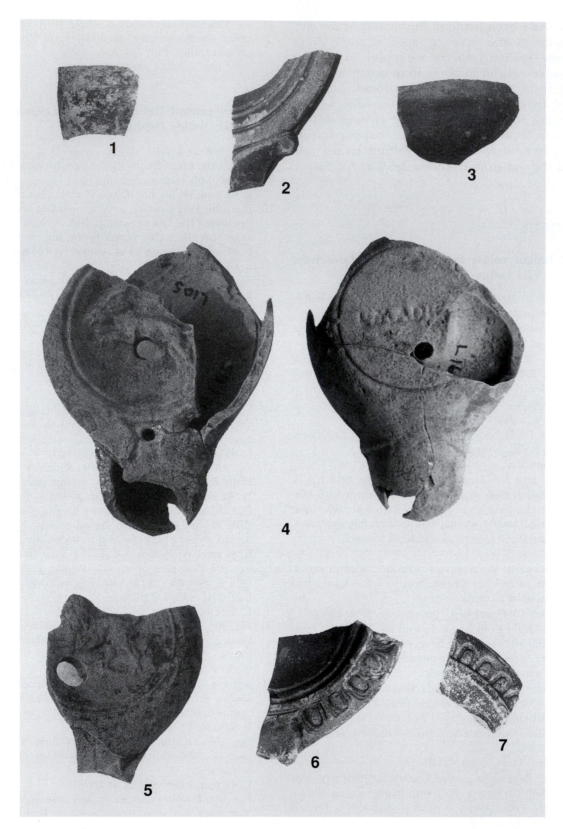

Fig. 194. Central Italian lamps. *(DB)*

– Eight shoulder and body sherds. Shoulder-forms VIIa (five examples) and VIIb (two examples). E42, E179, L105 (two examples), L165 (four examples).
– Four raised base sherds. L105 (two examples), L165 (two examples).
– Nine handle sherds. L105, L165 (five examples), S3, S4, S10.

Late standard central Italian lamps of Loeschcke 1919 type VIII (Bailey 1980 type Pi)

25. Fig. 198. Rear part with handle. Shoulder form VIIb. Raised circular base. Buff clay; orange-red slip traces. W. 62 mm. L143. *c.* AD 140-80.
26. Fig. 198. Rear left part with handle. Shoulder form

VIIb. Discus: uncertain; tree or floral on left. Buff clay; orange slip traces.
W. 64 mm. L165. *c.* AD 140-80.

27. Figs 195 and 198. Base sherd; [L].FAB[R ... incuse. Yellow-buff clay; thin orange slip, brown in places.
W. 26 mm. M167. *c.* AD 140-80.
– Body sherd. L165.
– Base sherd. L165.

Late central Italian Loeschcke 1919 type VIII lamps (Bailey 1980 type Qiii)

28. Fig. 198. Two non-joining sherds. Shoulder form VIIIa. Discus: radiating palm branches. Orange-buff clay; orange slip.
W. 46 mm and 50 mm. L165. *c.* AD 140-80.

Late central Italian Loeschcke 1919 type VIII lamps (Bailey 1980 type Qi)

29. Fig. 199. Fragment of the rear and right side, including handle and part of heart-shaped nozzle. Shoulder form VIIIb, vine tendrils in relief. Buff clay; thin orange slip.
L. 121 mm. L105, including SF 596. *c.* AD 170-225.
30. Fig. 199. Discus and shoulder. Shoulder form VIIIb, vine tendrils in relief. Discus: rosette. Orange-buff clay; thin orange slip.
L. 38 mm. L105. *c.* AD 170-225.
31. Fig. 199. Discus and shoulder sherd. Shoulder form VIIIb, vine tendrils in relief. Plain discus. Deep buff clay; no slip.
L. 43 mm. E11. *c.* AD 170-225.
32. Fig. 199. Shoulder fragment. Shoulder form VIIIb, vine tendrils in relief. Dark buff clay; no slip.
L. 28 mm. S4, SF 712. *c.* AD 170-225.
33. Fig. 199. Shoulder fragment. Shoulder form VIIIb, vine tendrils in relief. Orange clay; red slip.
L. 25 mm. L101. *c.* AD 170-225.
34. Fig. 199. Shoulder and discus. Shoulder form VIIIb, tendrils in relief, probably vine. Plain discus. Yellow-buff clay; thin orange slip.
W. 41 mm. L105. *c.* AD 170-225.
35. Fig. 199. Fragment of shoulder near nozzle. Shoulder form VIIIb, tendrils in relief. Air-hole. Yellow-buff clay; thin orange slip.
W. 30 mm. L105. *c.* AD 170-225.
36. Fig. 199. Nozzle and shoulder fragment. Heart-shaped nozzle. Buff clay; thin orange slip.
L. 32 mm. L105. *c.* AD 170-225.
37. Fig. 199. Shoulder fragment. Shoulder form VIIIb, two rows of ivy-leaves in relief. Small part of decorated discus. Dark buff clay; thin orange slip traces.
W. 24 mm. L105. *c.* AD 170-225.
– Three shoulder sherds from similar lamps, all with tips of relief leaves, and one with part of heart-shaped nozzle. L105.
– Two base sherds probably from this type of lamp. L105 and L165.

Late central Italian Loeschcke 1919 type VIII lamps (Bailey 1980 type Qiv)

38. Figs 195 and 200. Complete. Shoulder form VIIb, shoulder plain. Discus: rosette. Heart-shaped nozzle. Air-

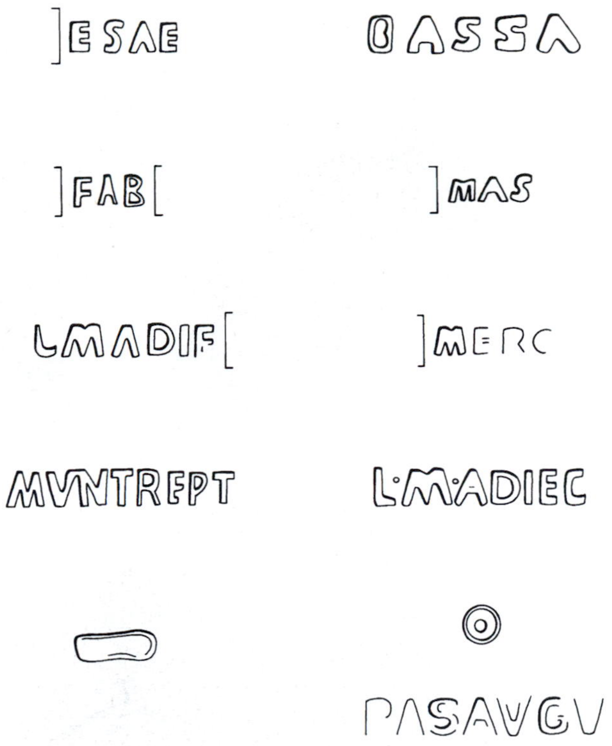

Fig. 195. Lamp stamps (1:1); the numbers refer to the catalogue entries. *(SC)*

hole. Base-ring: PASAVGV with ring-and-dot above and below, incuse. Buff clay; thin red slip.
L. 116 mm; W. 82 mm. M172, SF 862. *c.* AD 180-225.
39. Fig. 200. Handle and discus. Shoulder form VIIIb, shoulder apparently plain. Discus: head of woman to right. Dark buff clay; thin orange to dark brown slip.
L. 44 mm. L105. *c.* AD 160-225+.
40. Fig. 200. Discus sherd. Part of an uncertain scene, perhaps floral. Brown-buff clay; orange slip traces.
L. 32 mm. L105, SF 575. *c.* AD 160-225+.

Late central Italian Loeschcke 1919 type VIII lamps (Bailey 1980 type Qii)

41. Fig. 200. Rear right part, with handle. Near shoulder form VIIIb, impressed ovules. Discus apparently plain. Brown-buff clay; brown to dark brown slip.
L. 68 mm. L105. *c.* AD 160-225+.
42. Fig. 201. Two non-joining sherds: rear, with handle, and part of heart-shaped nozzle. Shoulder form VIIIb: wide shoulder with rows of raised points between ridges. Buff clay; thin orange slip traces.
L. 23 mm; W. 69 mm. L105. *c.* AD 160-225+.
43. Fig. 201. Discus sherd. Shoulder form VIIIb, rows of raised points? Discus: uncertain scene; two overlapping bow-shaped objects. Buff clay; thin red slip traces.
L. 28 mm. E11. *c.* AD 160-225+.
44. Fig. 201. Two non-joining sherds: rear left, with handle; part of underbody. Shoulder form VIIIb, band of incuse S-curves. Discus: uncertain pattern. Base-ring. Buff clay; red slip.
L. 45 mm; W. 54 mm. L105. *c.* AD 160-225+.
45. Figs 195 and 201. Part of base ring.]MAS. Buff-brown clay; thin red slip traces.
W. 24 mm. L105. *c.* AD 150-80.

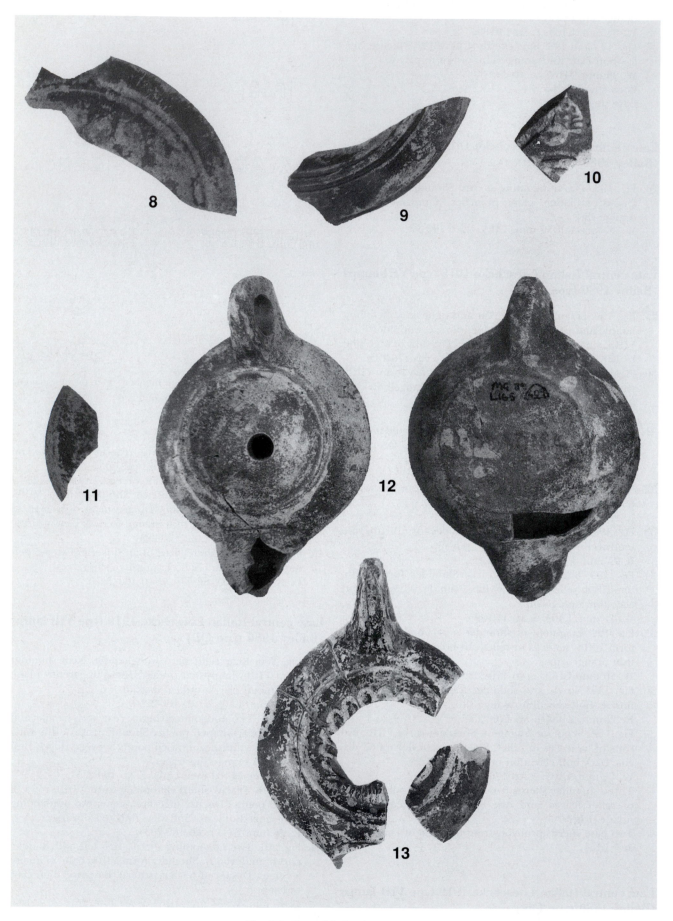

Fig. 196. Central Italian lamps. *(DB)*

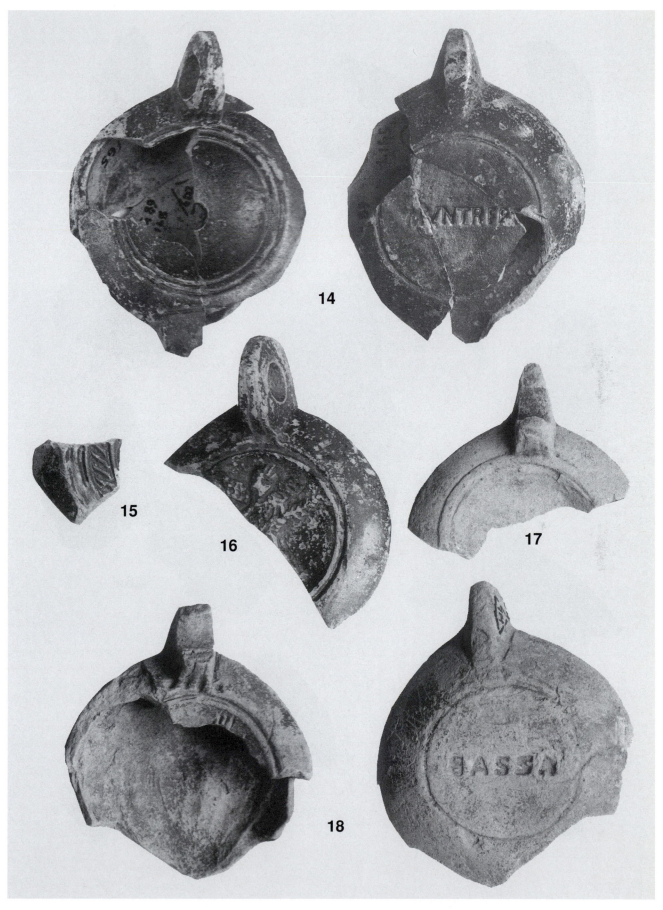

Fig. 197. Central Italian lamps. *(DB)*

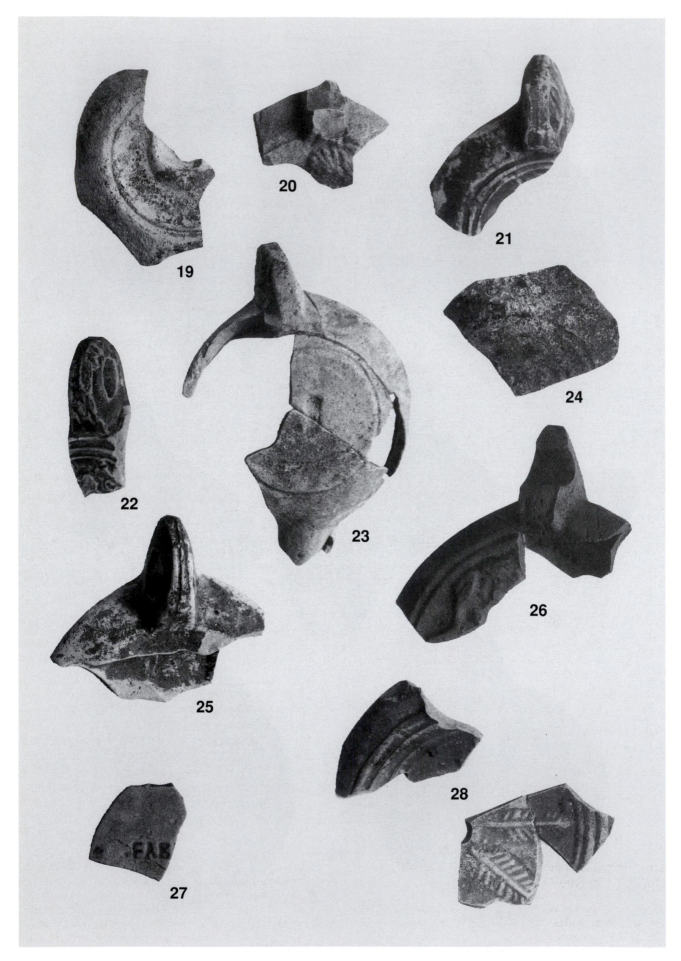

Fig. 198. Central Italian lamps. *(DB)*

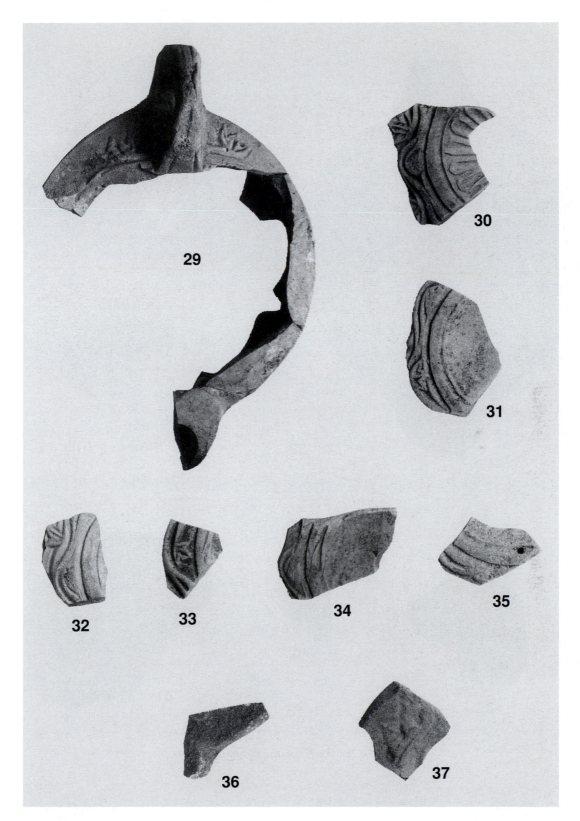

Fig. 199. Central Italian lamps. *(DB)*

Late central Italian Loeschcke 1919 type VIII lamps (Bailey 1980 type Qviii)

46. Fig. 201. Part of rear, with handle. Shoulder form VIIIb, impressed ovules. Discus: dog on couch (Sothic Dog?). Buff clay; thin red slip.
L. 58 mm. L105. *c.* AD 160-225+.

47. Fig. 201. Front right shoulder. Shoulder form VIIIb, impressed ovules. Discus: foot of couch? Yellow-buff clay; thin orange slip.
L. 41 mm. L105. *c.* AD 160-225+.

48. Fig. 202. Rear part, with handle. Shoulder form VIIIb?, myrtle-wreath in relief. Multiple base ring with row of raised points on inner ring and a pelta-shaped foot on outer ring. Buff clay; thin red slip.
W. 45 mm. L147. *c.* AD 160-225+.

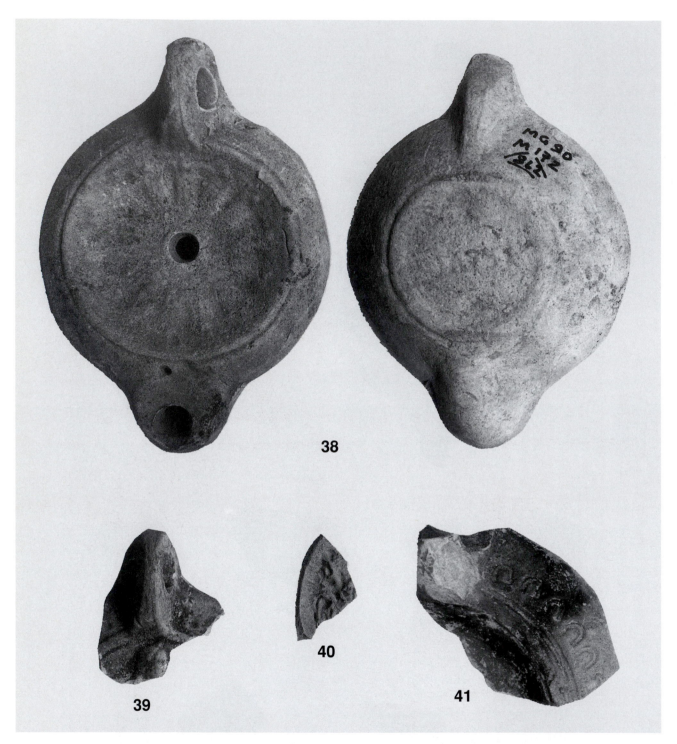

Fig. 200. Central Italian lamps. *(DB)*

Late central Italian Loeschcke 1919 type VIII lamps (Bailey 1980 type Qix)

49. Figs 195 and 202. Front left part. Shoulder form VIIIb, myrtle wreath in relief. Discus: uncertain scene – lower part of seated figure? to right at left, facing something on the right. Base ring: [LCA]ESAE incuse. Orange-buff clay; thin orange slip.
    L. 54 mm. L105, including SF 592. *c.* AD 180-225+.
50. Fig. 202. Shoulder sherd. Shoulder form VIIIb, impressed ivy-leaves between grooves. Buff clay; thin red slip.

L. 30 mm. L105. *c.* AD 160-225+.
– Twenty-five sherds from late central Italian Loeschcke 1919 type VIII lamps (Bailey 1980 type Q):
Four nozzle sherds. L105 (three examples, including SF 652), L165.
Five body sherds. E182, L105 (three examples), L165.
One raised base sherd. L105.
Five base ring sherds. L105 (there is also a sherd from L165 from the same lamp as one from L105).
Ten handle sherds. K101, L105 (nine examples).

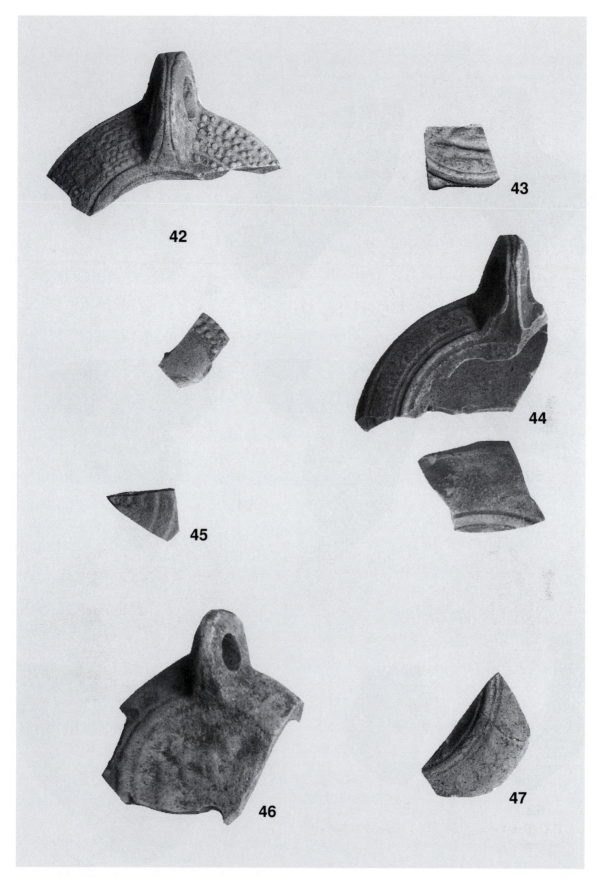

Fig. 201. Central Italian lamps. *(DB)*

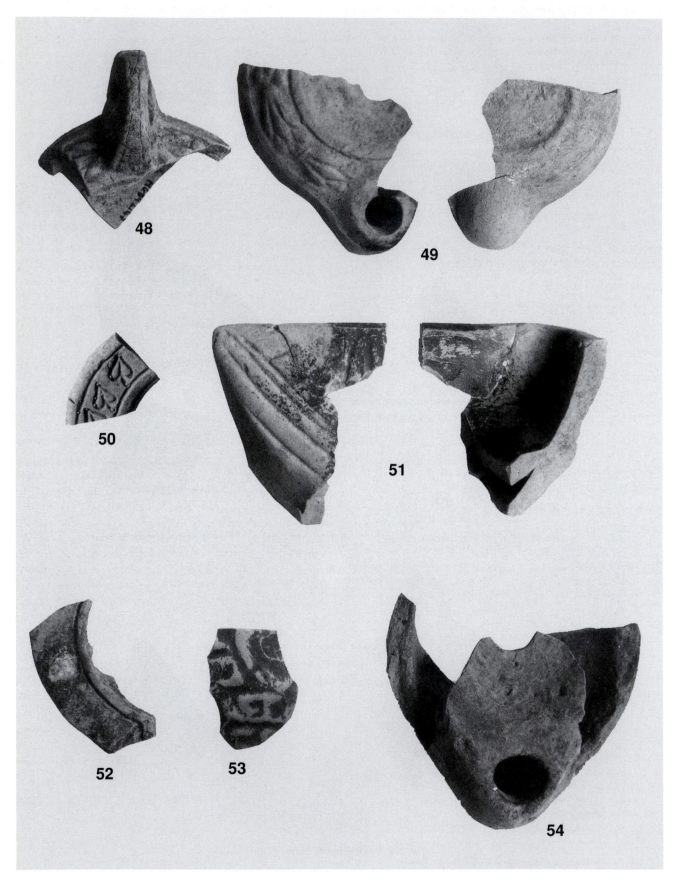

Fig. 202. Central Italian lamps. *(DB)*

Central Italian lamp-stand and thymiaterion

51. Fig. 202. Upper part of a combined incense-burner and lamp-stand. One face of the rectangular bowl decorated with impressed floral pattern. The base of the bowl is applied within the mould-made body. Indications of an applied lamp on plain side of bowl at right angles to the decorated face. Buff clay; orange slip traces.
H. 44 mm. L184. *c.* AD 100-60.

Central Italian *Firmalampe* of Loeschcke 1919 type X (Bailey 1980 type Nvi)

52. Fig. 202. Front left part. Shoulder form IX; lug broken away; incuse diagonal defining nozzle. Buff clay; orange slip.
L. 44 mm. L165. *c.* AD 160-225+.

Central Italian plastic lamp in form of a pine cone (early form of Bailey 1980 type T)

53. Fig. 202. Underbody and base ring. Buff clay; orange slip.
L. 36 mm. L101. *c.* AD 175-225.

Central Italian wall-lamp (very late form of Bailey 1980 type M)

54. Fig. 202. Front sherd with ill-defined nozzle, discus (plain) and base. Buff clay; no slip. Cf. Provoost 1976: 568, figure, type 3[B].
W. 65 mm. A17. Fourth century AD.

Central Italian lamps of Hayes 1972 type I (Bailey 1980 type Si)

55. Fig. 203. Rear part with unpierced handle. Devolved branch pattern on shoulder. Discus: head of cock or peacock. Deep orange clay; orange slip.
L. 42 mm. M32, SF 481. *c.* AD 375-450.
56. Fig. 203. Front left part. Series of impressed ring-and-dot patterns on shoulder. Discus: rear leg of animal (longitudinal on lamp). Orange-buff clay; orange slip.
L. 38 mm. H6. *c.* AD 375-450.
57. Fig. 203. Nozzle sherd. Deep orange clay; orange slip.
W. 34 mm. D104. *c.* AD 375-450.

Italian lamps of Hayes 1972 type II (Bailey 1980 type Siii)

58. Fig. 203. Top of lamp, with unpierced handle. Branch pattern within shoulder. Discus: rosette; rows of raised points on each side of nozzle-channel. Orange clay; orange slip.
L. 80 mm; W. 71 mm. M38, SF 548. *c.* AD 400-525.
59. Fig. 203. Left side. Curved and slanting relief lines within shoulder. Orange-pink to light brown clay; brown slip.
L. 92 mm. E16. *c.* AD 450-550.

Italian late Roman or early medieval lamp

60. Fig. 203. Rear of a mould-made, probably elongated, lamp with a substantial applied vertical band-handle. Low-placed carination. Buff clay; no slip.
W. 40 mm. M86. Seventh or eighth century AD?

Italian early medieval wheel-made lamp

61. Fig. 204. Fragmentary: most of rim lost. Wheel-made conical shape with inserted domed top and flaring rim. Large wick hole cut through top; central filling hole; applied bridge separating filling hole and wick hole. Unturned base. Coarse clay containing pieces of quartz, with brown surface and black core.
D. at rim 110 mm; H. 70 mm. D307, SF 656. *c.* tenth century AD.

Imported lamps

Tunisian? lamp of Loeschcke 1919 type VIII

62. Fig 205. Nozzle sherd. Raised rim round upper edge; elongated tongues on underside. Buff clay; red slip traces.
L. 24 mm. E11. *c.* AD 160-225+.

Tripolitanian? lamp, perhaps of Brants 1913 type XXIV

63. Fig. 205. Shoulder sherd with a plain sloping shoulder. Sunken top with joined spirals in relief. Deep orange clay; red slip.
L. 26 mm. M138. Fifth century AD.

THE ROMAN COMMERCIAL AMPHORAE, by Paul Arthur

Various fragments of commercial amphorae, all of Imperial date, were found during the excavations at Monte Gelato. Save for some scattered pieces, quantitatively insignificant and often not particularly well stratified, most came from the deposits found in the fish-pond. This contained two principal fills: L165, the lower deposit, dated to the early second century AD; and L105, the upper deposit, dated to the late second century AD. The whole fish-pond contained 1,495 amphora sherds, weighing a total of 144.100 kg. Some 798 fragments (61.850 kg) were recovered from the upper deposit and 697 (82.250 kg) from the lower deposit.

Of particular interest are the various amphorae that, on quantity and distribution, were, in the writer's view, of local origin. Some confirmation has come from thin-section analysis conducted by Dr David Williams (University of Southampton). The results of his work are included in this report both under the description of the sampled vessels, where his contribution is noted in double quote marks, and in an appendix at the end. The original recording reference number (P000) is given where applicable.

CATALOGUE OF TYPES

Italian

Dressel 2-4
1. Fig. 206. Hard, gritty orange fabric, with a self-coloured slip surface, occasional muscovite and small iron-oxide nodules. It looks Italian, though may not be from the Campano-Latian area. P106. L165.

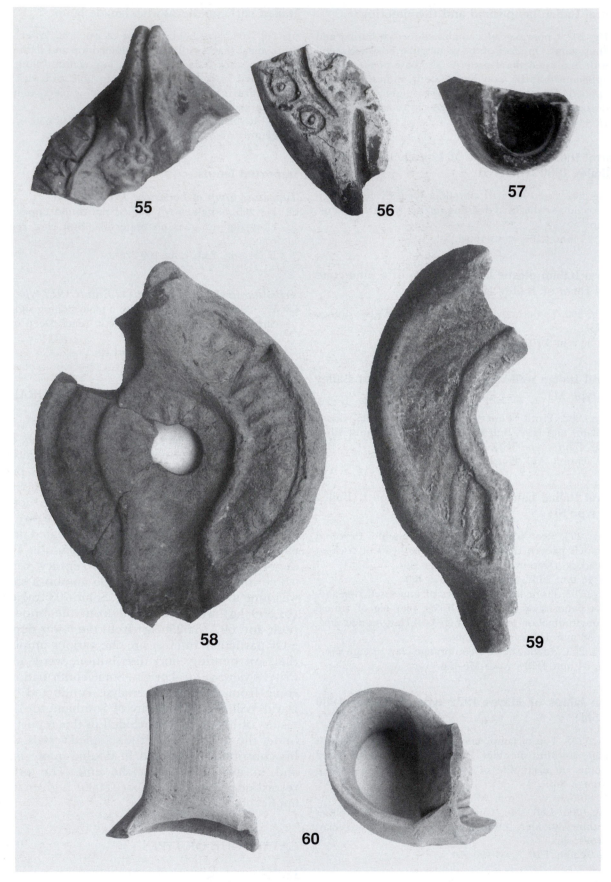

Fig. 203. Central Italian lamps. *(DB)*

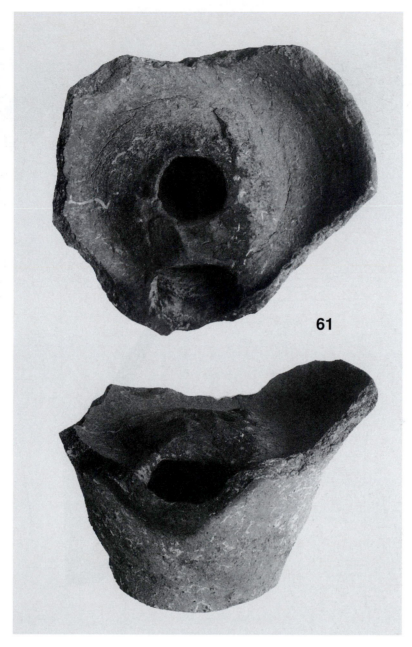

Fig. 204. Early medieval lamp. *(DB)*

2. (Not illustrated.) Hard, gritty orange-pink volcanic fabric with a cream exterior surface. Probably Campano-Latian. P104. L165.
3. Fig. 206. Light orange fabric with a pale brownish-cream exterior slip. Campano-Latian production. P111. L165.
4. Fig. 206. Medium hard cream-yellow (10YR 8/5) fabric with scattered dark specks, including volcanic glass. Probably a product of the area around Monte Gelato, as the fabric is similar to amphora type P105/169, discussed below. L105.
5. Fig. 206. As cat. 4 above. Soft (10YR 8/6) fabric with more inclusions than cat. 4. L105.

Type P105 (*Ostia* II, cat. no. 521/*Ostia* III, cat. nos. 369-70)

The amphorae here classed as type P105 would appear to be products of the general area in which Monte Gelato is sited. This is suggested by the quantity in which they have been found at the site and by their petrological characteristics. Furthermore, they are very similar to other amphorae found in great quantities in and around Rome. Though no intact examples have come to light during the excavations, the various fragments found suggest they are generally ovoid-bodied with ribbed handles, a small slightly everted rim and *omphalos* base. The fabric is generally quite fine and of a distinctive off-white/cream colour, though other, darker, hues exist. On morphology, the amphorae are not at all dissimilar to forms *Ostia* II, cat. no. 521/*Ostia* III, cat. nos. 369-70, or to Berenice mid-Roman amphora 13, to which they are clearly related. They are part of a tradition of central Italian amphorae now represented by a production site identified at Spello, in Umbria.

The identification of 'local' transport amphorae at Monte Gelato, probably both of Dressel's type 2-4 (above), and of the type illustrated here, is of great importance for an understanding of the somewhat problematic nature of the

Fig. 205. Imported lamps. *(DB)*

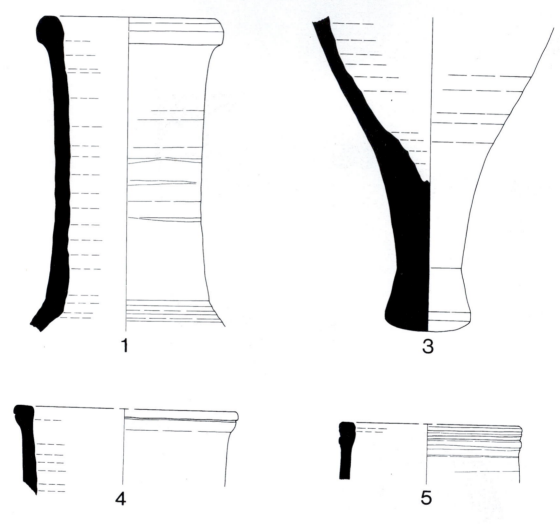

Fig. 206. Italian Dressel 2-4 amphorae (1:3). *(SC)*

Italian economy of the later first and second century AD. This will be discussed further below.

6.   Fig. 207. Hard yellow-beige fabric with abundant small calcareous and scattered red-brown inclusions (grog?: usually small but occasionally up to 7 mm), a little mica and an exterior beige slip. P105. L165.

7-11. Fig. 207. Local area production. L105.

12.   Fig. 207. Local amphora with traces of a Latin *titulus pictus* in red, on the shoulder, reading SEC.... Soft, cream-yellow fabric (10YR 8/3) with some scattered angular dark grey and reddish brown inclusions (<2 mm), a little biotite and perhaps occasional augite. Thin-section analysis indicates "a fairly fine-textured fabric containing a groundmass of silt-sized quartz grains, together with a few grains of sanidine, clino-

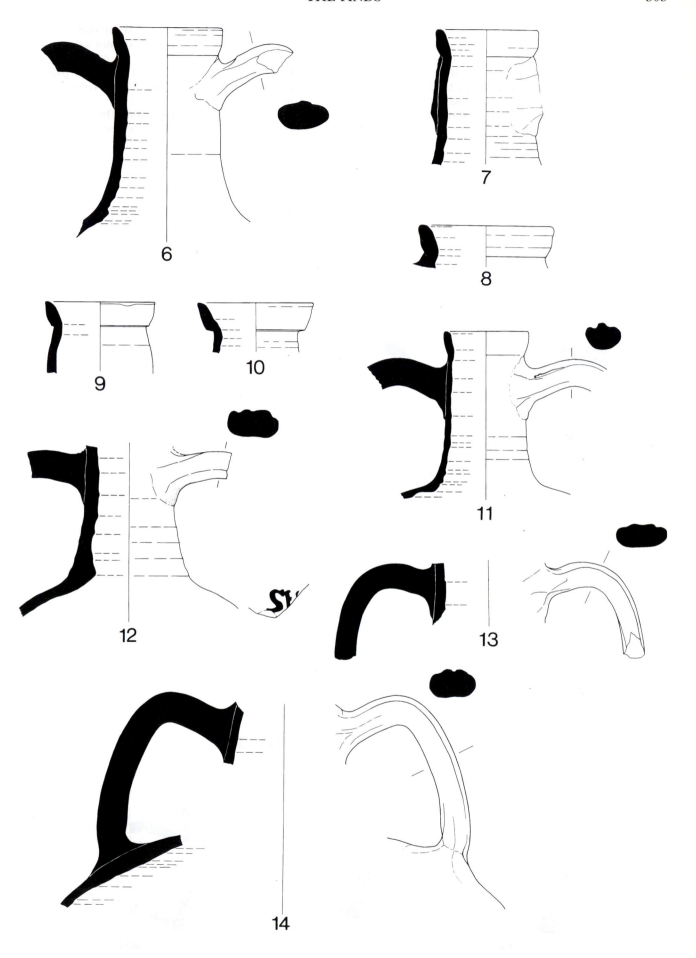

Fig. 207. Local P105 amphorae (1:3). *(SC)*

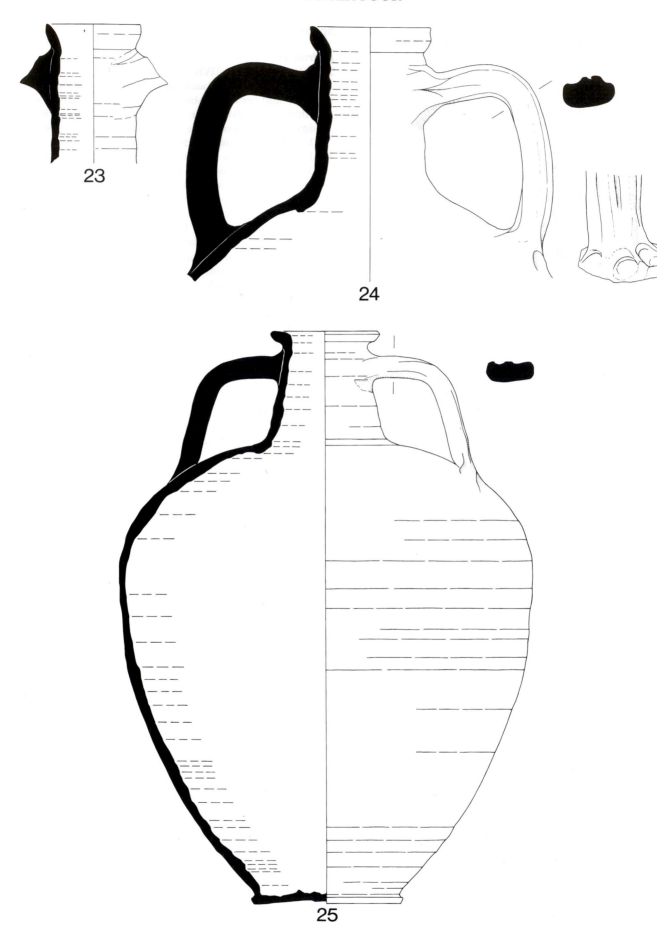

Fig. 209. Amphora types P23 (no. 23), P166 (no. 24) and P98 (no. 25) (1:3). *(SC)*

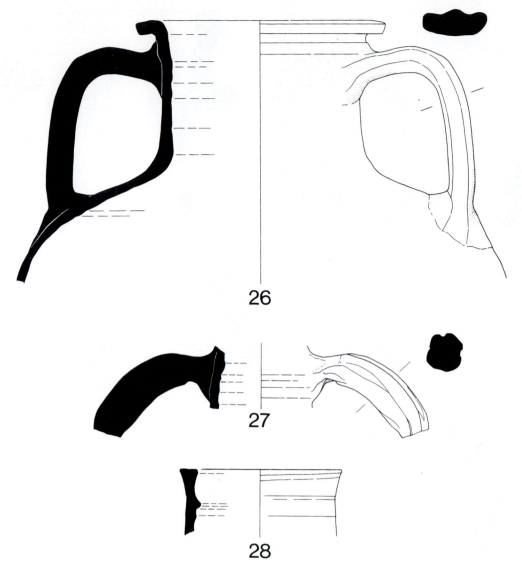

Fig. 210. Amphorae types P216 (no. 26), P235 (no. 27) and P28 (no. 28) (1:3). *(SC)*

stone inclusions and an overall cream-coloured exterior surface. See, in general, Laubenheimer (1985). P103. L165.

African (see also cat. 50, below)

40. Fig. 213. Small amphora or jug. Fine orange-pink fabric with abundant calcareous reaction rims and an off-white exterior slip which drips down the inside. The vessel appears to be from Tunisia, and the bulging neck is a feature common to that area: however, on fabric, it may possibly be from western Sicily, where ceramics of Imperial date are still little understood. P108. L165.
41. Fig. 213. Fabric is dark reddish grey towards the interior and orange towards the exterior, with a cream-coloured salt skin towards the top. North African. P110. L165.
42. Fig. 213. Orange-red fabric with abundant calcareous inclusions, minute quartz and occasional reaction rims. African. L165.

'Greek'

Koan

43. Fig. 214. Koan Dressel 2-4. Medium hard, fine, red-brown (2.5YR 6/6) fabric, with a thick greenish white (10YR 7.5/3) exterior skin, abundant minute mica and minute white calcareous inclusions. This virtually whole vessel accounts for 35 sherds and 4.300 kg in Table 55. The type has been discussed by Panella (1986: 617-19). P102. L165.
44. Fig. 214. Miniature Koan Dressel 2-4. Standard fabric, as above. P109. L165.

Agora G197

45. (Not illustrated.) An amphora type from the Meander valley of western Turkey. For the type see Panella (1986: 614, fig. 5 and note 7) and Peacock and Williams (1986: 188-90, class 45b). Only one body sherd was found. L105.

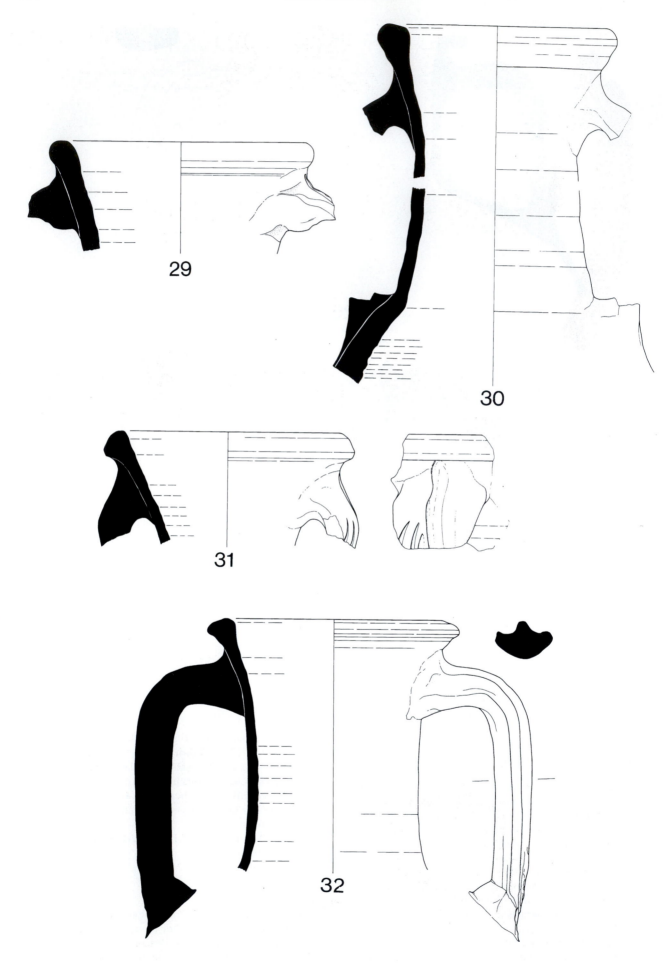

Fig. 211. Spanish Beltran IV amphorae (1:3). *(SC)*

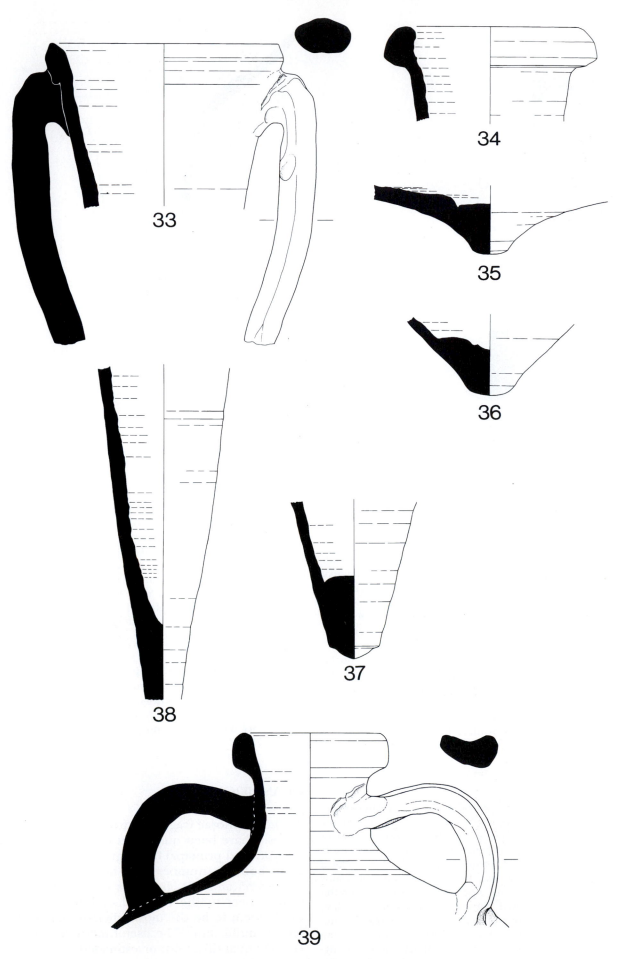

Fig. 212. Amphorae, various types. All 1:3, except 38 (1:6). *(SC)*

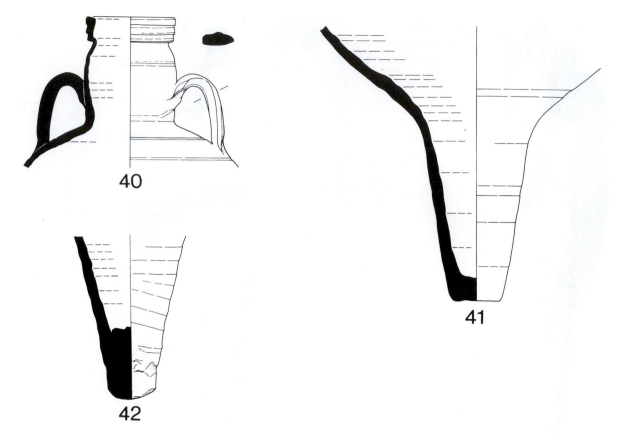

Fig. 213. African amphorae (1:3). *(SC)*

Uncertain eastern amphorae

46. Fig. 214. Unusual amphora. Highly micaceous (muscovite) dark reddish fabric (2.5YR 5.5/6), dirty grey-brown in handle section (5YR 5.5/3) and with a cream-brown exterior slip, with abundant small sub-angular calcareous inclusions (<1 mm). The general rim and neck type is represented by amphorae found in Aegean and Black Sea areas, though not associated with such a flattened handle; I have also seen similar fabrics in western Turkey. P239. L105.

47. Fig. 214. Ribbed shoulder from an amphora of probably eastern mediterranean origin. Hard pinkish red fabric (2.5YR 6/6) with abundant minute calcareous and brown inclusions, a little minute mica and a thick cream exterior slip. It probably dates no earlier than the fifth century, but is more likely to be sixth-century in date. P315. M144, fifth-sixth centuries AD.

Not identified

48. Fig. 214. Unusual amphora in a hard, orange-brown (2.5YR 6/5) fabric, yellow-brown (7.5YR 6.5/6) exterior slip, occasional minute calcareous inclusions, abundant minute dark inclusions and what appears to be volcanic glass. The vessel, in terms of its form, looks like a Levantine amphora, but apparent volcanic inclusions seemed to rule out such a possibility. For this reason the vessel was examined through thin-section, revealing "principal inclusions of grains of clinopyroxene, sanidine and quartz, together with flecks of mica and some fragments of volcanic rock". An Italian origin is suggested (cf. appendix). For a morphologically similar

vessel, perhaps of Eastern origin, see, for example, Panella (1968: 110, fig. XLI, no. 558, from Ostia). L165.

49. Fig. 214. Hard, reddish brown (2.5YR 5/6), slightly lighter self-coloured slip, scattered small white angular to rounded inclusions and very rare calcareous reaction rims. Uncertain provenance – possibly from the Aegean area, though the fabric does look somewhat similar to Tarraconensian examples. P112. L165.

Addendum (African)

50. Fig. 215. Spatheion. Upper part with knocked-off handles reused as a drainage pipe for the baptistery font. Produced in Tunisia, this piece is of a medium-sized vessel which is likely to be of later fourth- or fifth-century date. (I have not personally seen this piece.) P347. D317.

QUANTIFICATION

All the amphorae fragments from the two fish-pond deposits have been quantified under their respective types and principal fabric groups. This has been done both by number and by weight of sherds (Tables 55 and 56). In terms of cost-effectiveness with respect to the retrieval of information, this would seem to be the most efficient means of pottery quantification. The useful method of rim percentage quantification, or estimated vessel equivalents (EVES), was not adopted because of the relat-

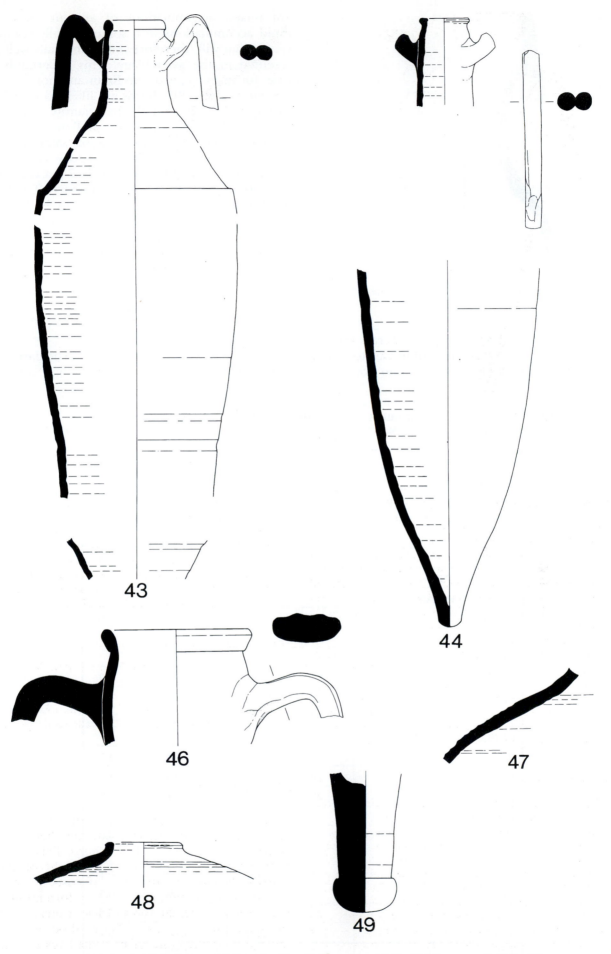

Fig. 214. Greek (43-4), Eastern (46-7) and unidentified amphora (48-9). All 1:3, except 43 (1:6). *(SC)*

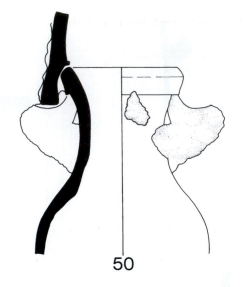

50

Fig. 215. Late Roman spatheion amphora (1:3). *(SC)*

ent mixed accumulations of ancient waste, but rapid accumulations with some virtually complete vessels that will, therefore, be abnormally well represented in the assemblage. This is certainly the case, for instance, with the Koan amphorae.

Some of the 1,495 sherds are likely to have been wrongly assigned, though the quantity of material studied will, for our purposes, swallow up a certain number of errors on the basis of 'safety in numbers'. The 'not identified' category is relatively high, ranging numerically from 28.7 per cent (context L165) to 46.9 per cent (context L105). When measured by weight, the proportion is, however, rather lower (11.8 per cent and 26.4 per cent respectively). Nevertheless, the more general trends should be clear enough with the present data.

ively low number of surviving rim sherds. Indeed, one of the drawbacks of the Monte Gelato assemblage is that the fish-pond deposits do not repres-

DISCUSSION

The Monte Gelato amphorae are particularly significant on two scores. Firstly, they have provided

Table 55. Quantification of all amphorae from context L165 (lower fish-pond deposit).
Note: the Dressel 2-4 category includes four fragments, presumed to be local, weighing 200 g (cf. cat. 4 and 5).

types	no.	%	weight (g)	%
ITALIAN				
Black sand Dr. 2-4 (Pompeian)	4	0.6	1,370	1.7
Campano-Latian Dr. 2-4	5	0.7	4,100	5.0
other Dressel 2-4	64	9.2	8,550	10.4
type P105	27	3.9	2,680	3.3
no. 25 (type P98)	59	8.5	4,300	5.2
NORTH AFRICAN				
Tunisian	65	9.3	5,770	7.0
no. 40	5	0.7	240	0.3
SPANISH				
Dressel 20	27	3.9	4,000	4.9
Beltran IVB	22	3.2	6,130	7.5
others	92	13.2	24,250	29.5
GREECE/ASIA MINOR				
Koan	35	5.0	4,300	5.2
Koan miniature	20	2.9	950	1.2
uncertain	43	6.2	2,600	3.2
GAULISH				
Dressel 30	29	4.2	3,280	4.0
NOT IDENTIFIED				
no. 48	1	0.1	100	0.1
no. 49	1	0.1	450	0.5
light fabrics	22	3.2	2,300	2.8
dark fabrics	176	25.3	6,880	8.4
TOTAL	697		82,250	

Table 56. Quantification of all amphorae from context L105 (upper fish-pond deposit).

types	no.	%	weight (g)	%
ITALIAN				
Dressel 2-4	9	1.1	1,550	2.5
miniature Dressel 2-4	1	0.1	150	0.2
type P105	280	35.0	22,120	35.8
no. 24 (type P166)	4	0.5	720	1.2
no. 26 (type P216)	5	0.6	1,550	2.5
NORTH AFRICAN				
Tunisian	10	1.2	1,170	1.9
Tripolitanian	6	0.8	550	0.9
SPANISH				
Beltran II	17	2.1	1,900	3.1
others	30	3.8	5,420	8.8
GREECE/ASIA MINOR				
Koan	50	6.3	9,000	14.6
Agora G197	1	0.1	20	0.03
no. 46 (type P239)	1	0.1	350	0.6
uncertain	1	0.1	50	0.1
GAULISH				
Dressel 30	9	1.1	1,000	1.6
NOT IDENTIFIED				
light fabrics	323	40.0	13,400	21.7
light fabrics (ribbed)	3	0.4	200	0.3
dark fabrics	48	6.0	2,700	4.4
TOTAL	798		61,850	

much needed archaeological evidence for the production of commercial amphorae, and thus for the production of surplus liquid agricultural products, from the hinterland of Rome. Secondly, they have further supplemented our knowledge of Roman exchange systems in both a crucial area and a crucial period. The second point will be examined first.

The continuity in use of wine amphorae from the island of Kos in the Dodecanese down to the end of the second century AD is interesting, though the various sherds from L105 may represent the remains of one long-lived vessel. Whether cat. 46 (type P239) could also be residual is difficult to say, though it does bear a superficial similarity to the early variant of the Eastern form Kapitan I, which appears in the second half of the second century (Panella 1986: 615-16). Alongside a minor quantity of Gaulish amphorae, the presence of Greek vessels suggests that inhabitants of Monte Gelato may have been discriminating enough to have required certain provincial wines from time to time. Alternatively, it may echo the evidence of graffiti from the same deposit, and the inscribed 'stork-vase', for the

presence of Greek-speakers on the site; they may well have preferred Greek wines.

There is a far greater variety of Spanish amphorae in the earlier deposit, though Beltran IVB (Lusitanian?) garum amphorae predominate. Unsurprisingly, there are many fewer in the deposit of the late second century. It may be remarked that there is a low overall presence of Dressel 20 oil amphorae from Baetica, although these are exceedingly common in Rome; this perhaps implies that there were good local sources for oil for Monte Gelato and other areas of the Roman Campagna, which could not, however, satisfy the demands of the *urbs*. A little oil seems also to have come from north Africa.

As regards Italian vessels, the standard early Imperial west-coast wine container, form Dressel 2-4, is well represented in context L165 and diminishes greatly in the later context L105. This is now a well-established pattern. The examples from L105 may be the latest products of the series, as such types were produced up to the beginning of the third century, at least in the Rome area (see, for example, Freed (1989)). However, the type was gradually

Table 57. Quantification of wine amphorae from context L165 (lower fish-pond deposit).

types	no.	%	weight (g)	%
Italian imports	73	32.2	14,020	50.4
type P105	27	11.9	2,680	9.6
Greece/Asia Minor	98	43.2	7,850	28.2
Gaulish	29	12.8	3,280	11.8
TOTAL	227		27,830	

Table 58. Quantification of wine amphorae from context L105 (upper fish-pond deposit).

types	no.	%	weight (g)	%
Italian imports	10	2.8	1,700	4.9
type P105 (+ P166)	284	79.8	22,840	65.3
Greece/Asia Minor	53	14.9	9,420	26.9
Gaulish	9	2.5	1,000	2.9
TOTAL	356		34,960	

being supplanted by new vessels, generally of reduced capacity, throughout western Italy, from the end of the first century.[69] This process may be seen at Monte Gelato, where local Dressel 2-4 vessels account for 0.3 per cent numerically against 3.9 per cent of type P105 in context L165, and 0 per cent against 35.1 per cent in context L105 (Tables 55 and 56; see also Tables 57 and 58 for the general trend).

The production of mid-Imperial local amphorae in the area of Monte Gelato is especially interesting as evidence for local self-sufficiency in wine at times when, it has been argued, much of Italy was suffering a chronic shortage of wine produced within the peninsula. Indeed, not only is self-sufficiency attested, but exportation, at least to the capital, is implied by the very manufacture of transport containers. Panella has already suggested (1989: 144) the possibility of production centres along the Tiber valley and, to judge from the various fabrics now identified at Monte Gelato, Porta Pia (pers. comm. R. Schinke), Fosso della Crescenza (Arthur 1983: 80) (this last with its distinctive foraminifera), and elsewhere, they were probably fairly numerous. However, large-scale seaborne shipment of these vessels is probably to be excluded, not only because of their general absence on overseas consumption sites, but also because of their ring base which, it seems, was especially manufactured for the purposes of land or, at best, river transport.

An examination of probable Rome-area transport containers in and around Rome, taking the percentages of such vessels against all identified wine amphorae, is summarized in Table 59. The Via Nova, Crypta Balbi and Via Sacra figures are taken from Ciotola et al. (1989), whilst the Ostia figures come from Panella (1989). The earliest examples of the form date to the mid-first century AD, both at Luni and Rome, though at that time it appears to have been of secondary importance to wines contained in amphorae of Dressel 2-4 form. The later first-century contexts show growing proportions of Rome-area vessels. These supplement the declining proportions of wine amphorae, in particular of form Dressel 2-4, arriving from other areas along the Tyrrhenian coast. By the mid-second century, Rome-area vessels rapidly increase in proportion, becoming the commonest wine amphora in the Rome area and remaining so for the entire second century and perhaps the early years of the third.[70] According to the Terme del Nuotatore evidence, a drastic slump *may* finally appear by late Severan or post-Severan times, though more information is needed, especially from third-century contexts. This pattern may seem, in part, to support Carandini's revised views on the Italian economy (1989: 519), which envisage a new phase of suburban villas coming to the fore no later than the reign of Marcus Aurelius, perhaps partly specializing in viticulture for a specifically Rome-oriented

---

[69] I had already suspected this over ten years ago: cf. Arthur 1983: no. 8. See, especially, Panella (1989).

[70] Whilst I disagree with Purcell's Imperial boom in Italian viticulture (Purcell 1985), I agree that the new, early Imperial, vineyards of Spain and Gaul did destroy it. Archaeology seems, evermore, to be adding shades of grey to what, at times, seem to be historical arguments posed in black and white.

Table 59. Percentages of probable Rome-area transport containers against all other amphorae in published contexts in and around Rome.

site	%	date range
Via Nova, Rome	2.0	AD 64
Terme del Nuotatore, Ostia	4.7	c. AD 70-90
Crypta Balbi, Rome	3.6	c. AD 80-90
Monte Gelato	11.9	early second century AD
Via Sacra, Rome	15.2	c. AD 110
Terme del Nuotatore, Ostia	2.9	c. AD 120-40
Meta Sudans, Rome	26.1	mid-second century AD
Terme del Nuotatore, Ostia	13.5	c. AD 160-80
Monte Gelato	79.8	late second century AD
Terme del Nuotatore, Ostia	2.4	c. AD 190-210
Terme del Nuotatore, Ostia	0	c. AD 230-50

market. Furthermore, field-survey evidence from Rome's northern hinterland does not suggest any great slump in rural occupation and farming until the third century.[71]

Some vessels that are similar to P105 seem to have been marketed outside the Rome area and, perhaps, even abroad, albeit on a limited scale. A kiln site producing similar forms of amphora has been unearthed at Spello in Umbria: this has led Panella to see the type as essentially a container for *hirtiola* or *irtiola*, a typical Umbrian wine known to both Columella and Pliny (Panella 1989: 146). A clearly related type was also produced at Santarcangelo di Romagna in the late first and second centuries (Stoppioni Piccoli 1983: tav. III, no. 12). In Italy the form has been recognized at Ostia, Bolsena, Settefinestre, Cosa, Luni, Cures Sabini, Pisa and elsewhere (Panella 1989: 144 and n. 18; Pasquinucci and Storti 1989: 114 (for Pisa)). If the type is also to be recognized in Riley's mid-Roman amphora 13, which has yet to be proven, then a distribution of the type and its variants outside Italy covers parts of ex-Yugoslavia, Greece, Libya, Crete, Tunisia and Malta (Riley 1979: 197; Hayes 1983: 144-5, type 7 (for Crete)). This would certainly allow for some reassessment of Italy's supposedly ailing economy in the second century.

The evidence from Porta Pia and, to a lesser extent, from Fosso della Crescenza, suggests not only that the type was produced in the hinterland of Rome, but that it continued to supply wine to the capital during at least part of the third century.[72]

The negative evidence from Ostia (Table 59) might suggest that it was no longer exported, even along the Italian coast. The next step clearly is to identify the various centres of production, both by fabric and by nuances of form, so as to be able to recognize respective chronologies and market areas, as well as to attempt the reduction of the frustrating unidentified categories.

Evidence for circulation of amphorae in late Imperial or post-Imperial times is slight, though whether this represents a lack of commodities imported from overseas or their arrival at the site after having been transferred to other, less fragile or local, containers is difficult to say. The small proportion of late Roman amphorae on rural sites in Italy is, none the less, quite frequently documented. Monte Gelato has yielded a number of unidentified ribbed amphora sherds from contexts M144 (cat. 47) and M164, associated with fourth- to early fifth-century African red slip ware, as well as north African spatheion rims from contexts M87, K102 and D317, again all fourth- or fifth-century in date.[73]

APPENDIX: A NOTE ON THE PETROLOGY OF SOME AMPHORAE FROM MONTE GELATO, by David Williams

Thin-section analysis of some amphorae suspected to be of local production showed that, to a greater or lesser extent, volcanic sand was present in each sample: for example, the potassic feldspar sandine, clinopyroxene, plagioclase and

---

[71] See, Potter (1979: 140-1), as well as the overall discussion on the chronology of villas and wine by Tchernia (1986: 264-71).

[72] The type, in a distinctive medium to dark reddish brown fabric, was also present at Via Gabina site G11 (pers. obs. 1976-7). For Porta Pia, see, now, Bird (1993: 82-96) and Schinke (1994: 117-22).

[73] I am grateful to Tim Potter for entrusting to me the study of the amphorae from the Monte Gelato excavations. Kate Gilliver kindly discussed the Roman tile fabrics from the Monte Gelato excavations and Robyn Schinke showed me the amphorae from the British School at Rome's excavations at Porta Pia, Rome, and shared her views on local amphora production. I am once again grateful to David Williams for having very rapidly provided me with thin-section analyses of selected pieces.

small pieces of volcanic rock. There are some differences amongst the various P105 sherds sampled that suggest that they were not all made at the same production centre. However, it is clear that these vessels certainly do not share the same fabric normally associated with the Berenice mid-Roman amphora 13 type-sample, which was found to contain little else but limestone, quartz and mica (Riley 1979; Peacock and Williams 1986: class 42). Instead, the volcanic nature of the inclusions present in the Monte Gelato sherds points to a likely origin somewhere in the Italian comagmatic region. A source fairly local to Monte Gelato would fit in with the petrology, that is the Rome volcanic province, including southern Etruria and northern Latium (Desio 1973), although somewhere else along the Italian volcanic tract is also a possibility.

THE ROMAN POTTERY, by Paul Roberts

INTRODUCTION

The catalogue and discussion below are intended to present a full account of the Roman pottery in circulation in the area of Monte Gelato between the early second and mid-sixth centuries AD. Given the very large quantity of pottery found, it was decided to concentrate on key contexts which yielded the most useful evidence. This selected material

was divided into the eight groups presented below, representing either single contexts or a group of contexts which seemed essentially contemporary. All datable fine-wares, irrespective of their find-spots, are listed in Table 60.

Examination of the material quickly revealed that the quantities of material representative of different periods vary considerably. The second to early third centuries are particularly well represented (Groups 1-3), as are the later fourth to mid-sixth centuries (Groups 5-8). Very little material, however, could be attributed with certainty to the mid-third to mid-fourth centuries (Group 4). Possible reasons for these fluctuations are discussed below.

In the primary recording of the Roman pottery from Monte Gelato, form and fabric series were established using Kenrick's (unpublished) system, originally designed for use with Romano-British pottery from excavations at Colchester. The system, with its standard notations for fabric, form, dimensions and weight, proved ideal for medium to large assemblages of Roman Imperial date. Ideally, full quantification of as much material as possible is desirable and necessary for meaningful comparison with material from other sites. However, the scarcity of large sealed groups resulted in the full

Fig. 216. Group of pottery from the lower fill of the fish-pond, early second century AD. *(KW)*

Fig. 217. Group of pottery from the upper fill of the fish-pond. Later second century AD. *(KW)*

quantification of only Groups 1 and 2 from the fish-pond (Figs 216 and 217).

Throughout the text relating to these groups, and in Table 61, a minimum number of vessels is used, obtained either by rim count, or by significant sherd count (SSC). This method of quantification involves, in addition to the counting of rim sherds, the counting of base and body sherds which form, fabric or finish indicate as not belonging to any rims already counted. SSC is generally most effective in quantifying fine-ware and table-ware vessels which are usually smaller, more distinctive and more easily reconstructable. However, it can also be helpful for coarse-ware vessels, particularly in smaller deposits such as Group 2, where recognition of constituent parts of individual vessels is more feasible. Given that SSC represents the nearest approximation to the minimum number of vessels, it should, I believe, be used wherever possible, with quantification by rim count (or weight) alone a useful, though less satisfactory, system.

DISCUSSION

The homogeneity of Group 1 (120s-30s AD) implies that it accumulated in a relatively short time, perhaps little more than a decade, while the diversity of material, from lamps and table-ware to amphorae, fine-wares and kiln wasters, suggests that it is fairly representative of many aspects of on-site activity. The quantity of material is considerable, particularly given the presence of other large near-contemporary deposits (Group 3 below). Together these reveal a very large-scale generation of refuse, and imply a high degree of economic activity on the site in the Hadrianic period. This is contemporary with the apparent boom in rural site density (and presumably general levels of population, as suggested by the results of the South Etruria survey (Potter 1979: 133)).

The fine-ware in Group 1 is predominantly Italian in origin (Italian sigillata and glazed ware), though it is interesting to note the first indications

Table 60. Fine-ware found at Monte Gelato.

KEY: B – base; BS – body sherd; P – profile; R – rim; unid. – unidentifiable.

form	date	fragments found	context
BLACK GLAZE			
unid.		3R, 1B	cistern (2R, 1B), S10 (1R)
ITALIAN SIGILLATA (forms and dates as in *Conspectus*)			
Consp. 3	*c.* AD 40-150	8R	L101 (1R), L165 (1R), S4 (4R), S10 (2R)
Consp. 7	mid-late Augustan	1R, 1BS	cistern
Consp. 21.3	first century AD	1R	L101
Consp. 33.3	first-early second centuries AD	1R	S4
Consp. 34.2	mid to late first century (+)	1P, 3R, 1BS	L105 (1R, 1BS), L165 (1P, 2R)
Consp. 36.2	Tiberian-late first century AD (+)	1R	L165
unid.		3R, 3B, 19BS	L101 (6BS), L165 (4BS), L184 (1R, 4BS), cistern (2R, 2BS), S4 (2B), S10 (1B, 3BS)
LATE ITALIAN SIGILLATA			
unid.		2R, 1BS	S3 (1R), S4 (1BS), S10 (1R)
EASTERN SIGILLATA B (forms as in Hayes (1985))			
Hayes 53	late first to mid second centuries AD	1R	cistern
Hayes 60	*c.* AD 100-50	1P	L165
Hayes 62	*c.* AD 80-120	1R, 1B	S4
unid.		1R	S4
GREEN-GLAZED WARE			
Martin 1992b: fig. 3	early second century AD	1R	L165
Martin 1992b: fig. 10	early second century AD	1BS	L165
conical beaker	early second century AD	1R	L165
open vessel	early second century AD	1R	S10
AFRICAN RED SLIP WARE (forms and dates as given by Hayes (1972; 1980))			
Fabric t.s.c. 'A'			
3A	late first to mid second centuries AD	3R	cistern, S4, S10
6B	mid to late second century AD	1P	cistern
6	second century AD	1R	S3
7	early to mid second century AD	1R	S3
8A	*c.* 110/20s-80s AD (+?)	1R	L105
8B	*c.* 160s-210/20s AD	1R	L105
9A	*c.* 110/20s-80s AD (+?)	3R	L105 (2R), S10 (1R)
9B	*c.* 160s-210/20s AD	2R	L105
8/9	second-early third centuries AD	1B	C59
7-10	second-early third centuries AD	1BS	L165
14A	early to mid second century AD	1P, 3R	L105 (1P, 1R), S3 (2R)
14B	mid to late second century AD (+?)	3R	C59, L101, S10
16	mid to late second century AD	1P	L105
27	*c.* AD 160-220	2R	S3
closed forms		3BS	L105 (1BS), cistern (2BS)
unid.		1R, 7B, 26BS	L105 (6B, 8BS), cistern (4BS), S3 (5BS), S4 (4BS), S10 (1B, 5BS)
Fabric t.s.c. 'A' – cooking-ware			
22	early to mid second century AD (+)	1R	L105
23A	early to mid second century AD (+)	1P, 5R	L105 (2R), L165 (1P, 2R), S4 (1R)
23B	mid second to early third centuries AD (+)	1P, 2R, 1BS	L105 (1P, 1BS), cistern (1R), S3 (1R)
23	second to third centuries AD (+)	1R, 3BS	L101 (1BS), S3 (2BS), S10 (1R)
182	mid second to mid third centuries AD (+)	1P, 2R	L105 (1P, 1R), S3 (1R)

form	date	fragments found	context
183/184	second to third centuries AD (+)	1R	L105
196	mid second to mid third centuries AD (+)	14R, 2B	L101 (3R, 2B), L105 (4R), cistern (2R), S3 (3R), S10 (1B, 5BS)
197	late second to mid third centuries AD (+)	11R, 4BS	L101 (1R), L105 (3R, 1BS), S3 (3BS), S4 (4R), S10 (3R)
Fabric t.s.c. 'C'			
35	late second to mid third centuries AD	1R	L105
50A	c. AD 230/40-325	2R	S3, S10
52B	c. 280/300 to late fourth century AD	1P	M87
53A	c. AD 350-430 (+)	1B	C1/D1
unid.		2BS	C59, S4
Fabric t.s.c. 'D'			
58	c. AD 290/300-75	1R	S4
61A	c. AD 325-80 (+)	1R	M74
61B	c. AD 380-440	3R	K101, L101, M164
67	c. AD 360-440	4R	K101, M79, M82, S4
92	early to mid fifth century AD	1R	M164
93A	c. AD 470-540	1P	D48
99A	late fifth century-c. AD 540	1R	C1/D1
stamp: Hayes type 4h	mid fourth to fifth centuries		M79
stamp: Hayes type 69b	mid fourth to fifth centuries		H1, L157
unid.		6BS	D45 (3BS), K101 (2BS), L101 (1BS)

Table 61. Quantification of Groups 1 and 2 (fish-pond).

	Group 1		Group 2	
class	vessels (by SSC)	% of total	vessels (by SSC)	% of total
FINE-WARE				
terra sigillata italica	10	5	2	1.5
eastern sigillata B2	1	0.5	-	-
green-glazed ware	3	1.5	-	-
African red slip ware	3	1.5	26	22.5
imports	**17**	**8.5**	**28**	**24.0**
colour-coated ware	40	20.0	41	35.5
table-ware	**57**	**28.5**	**69**	**59.5**
COARSE-WARE				
Pompeian red ware	-	-	5	4.5
dishes, bowls, cups	8	4.0	6	5.0
jars	61	31.0	18	15.5
cooking pots	57	28.5	3	2.5
flagons/jugs	12	6.0	11	9.5
miscellaneous	4	2.0	4	3.5
(lids)	(57)		(2)	
(bases)	(68)		(20)	
coarse-ware	**142**	**71.5**	**47**	**40.5**
TOTAL	199 vessels		116 vessels	

of the presence of African red slip ware (ARS), which is the predominant fine-ware in the later Group 2. This presence of ARS at such a relatively early stage in its import, together with the presence of glazed ware, now believed to have a northern Campanian or, more likely, a Roman source (Martin 1992b: 329), the large number of lamps of specifically Roman origin (Bailey, this volume), and Italian, Greek and Spanish amphorae (Arthur, this volume), indicates close economic ties with Rome. They serve as tangible markers for the important exchange of goods (much of which presumably has left no archaeological trace) between the site and Rome, either by direct purchase or by intermediate marketing systems.

The presence of kiln wasters (misfired vessels) of colour-coated ware and coarse-ware pieces in Group 1 strongly suggests, in addition, that the site also served as a centre of pottery manufacture. Much of this local/on-site production is very similar to pottery found in Rome, Ostia and the South Etruria survey, which suggests a ceramic community or koine, showing the strength of the economic and social ties which existed in the area. However, the vitality and individuality of the site's production is shown in particular in the variety of the colour-coated table-ware, most noticeably the 'stork-vase' (see below).

Pottery production at Monte Gelato seems to fit into the fourth of Peña's categories (Peña 1987: 441-4), namely manufacture linked to villas or other rural settlements, producing a diversified range of products aimed at the needs of the local market. Indeed, the range of pottery found at Monte Gelato is very comparable with that found on South Etruria sites 6 and 9, which Peña (1987: 444) has cited as typical of this mode of production.

Clearly, Monte Gelato in this period was only one of a (large?) number of rural sites producing domestic and/or architectural ceramics for local or medium-distance markets, perhaps in some cases exclusively for the sites themselves. Future analysis of fabrics may help to shed light on the nature of the mechanisms by which products were distributed over short and medium distances, an area still almost as under-researched as it was when discussed some fifteen years ago by Peacock (1982: 156).

The fine-wares in Group 2 (170s-90s AD) form an equally large or larger part of the deposit than was the case in Group 1, though the possibly different nature of Group 2 (discussed below) should be considered. With the exception of a small continued presence of Italian sigillata, ARS now dominated the markets which supplied the site, reflecting the increasing import of African products to Rome and indeed to Italy as a whole.

Colour-coated ware was still plentiful, though in a less idiosyncratic and smaller range of forms, suggesting that colour-coated ware was no longer manufactured on site. However, local production of transport amphorae seems to have increased substantially in this period (Arthur, this volume), and a production of so-called Pompeian red ware, perhaps of fairly local origin, appeared on local markets.

The coarse-ware may reveal other clues as to changes in the circumstances of the site and its markets. The general quality of coarse-ware in Group 2 is lower than that of Group 1, and the range of forms considerably reduced, some common forms of Group 1 disappearing altogether. Production of coarse-ware is not attested in Group 2, and this, together with the cessation of production of colour-coated ware, might indicate a decrease in the general level of economic activity on the site. The proportion of coarse-ware in Group 2 (40.5 per cent) is far lower than that of Group 1 (71.5 per cent), and this may indicate an alternative dumping site for food-preparation refuse; this in turn might suggest a restructuring of the site's main function areas.

In short, Group 2 seems to show considerable changes, both in the types of vessels used on the site and therefore, presumably, in the markets which supplied them. There might well have been a decrease in the number of manufacturing centres, as in the case of Monte Gelato itself, and this may reflect a decrease in demand. Peña (1987: 161) has suggested that the drop in the number of sites yielding ARS as opposed to Italian sigillata around some of his sites (for example, site 6) indicates a contraction of settlement, presumably the first signs of the much sharper contraction seen in the third century (below).

The period between the deposition of Group 2 (late second century) and that of Group 4 (mid-fourth century) is the least well represented in the ceramic record. Only two sherds of fine-ware representative of this period (ARS 50A – early version) were found (see Table 60), signalling a very sharp drop in imports to the site in comparison with the plentiful imports of the later second century. This paucity of evidence for the early third to mid-fourth centuries is also found in the lamps (Bailey, this volume), suggesting a period of sharply diminished economic activity on the site, very possibly its total abandonment, at some stage in the early third century. Such a situation seems to have persisted for at least a century, the only evidence of any activity being the presence of several coins (Hobbs, this volume); however, given the proven continuity in use of fourth-century coinage well into the fifth century, the evidence of the pottery and lamps may in this case be more reliable indicators.

A period of near or total abandonment of the site in the third and early fourth centuries finds parallels at other rural sites throughout the area of South Etruria (Peña 1987: 160 site 6; 211 site 9), while Potter (1979: 141-2) has spoken of 'massive' depopulation of the area. Elsewhere in Italy, at sites such as Settefinestre (Carandini 1985: 183-5), San Rocco (Cotton and Métraux 1985: 83) and Posto (Cotton 1979: 56) in Campania, Matrice in Molise (Roberts forthcoming) and San Giovanni di Ruoti in Basilicata (Freed 1982: 2) the same phenomenon seems to occur.

Altogether, the evidence suggests a period of decline or disruption in many areas of the Italian countryside, and/or a fundamental change in the methods of exploiting the land. Such major changes would clearly have had serious consequences for most elements of the settlement pattern, and this seems to have included marked changes at, and ultimately the abandonment of, the site of Monte Gelato itself.

Group 4, dating to the mid-fourth century, marks the reoccupation of the site and/or the resumption of detectable activity. The small sample, however, and the lack of contemporary deposits, strongly suggests that whatever the nature of the activity in this phase, it was on a very small scale (despite other indications, for example from the coins, to the contrary).

The group, though small, reveals considerable information on developments on the site and in the surrounding area. The reappearance of imported fine-ware (ARS) on the site, after an absence of a century or more, signals the site's return to participation in marketing networks. In the coarse-ware, forms and fabrics, some radically different from those of earlier deposits, suggest profound changes in the local ceramic tradition and/or in the sources of pottery for the site. This in turn suggests a period of considerable change, of which the abandonment of the site in the third century may have been a symptom.

Among the pottery in Group 5 (early to mid sixth century), the presence of ARS shows that the site's economic links with the markets around Rome were maintained, although the generally limited quantities of ARS reaching the site after the mid-fifth century should be noted (Table 60). The fabrics of the coarse-ware are consistent with those noted in Group 4 of well over a century earlier, suggesting a broad continuity of supply. The forms, however, are noticeably different, indicating the adoption of new types and not simply the development of those already existing. The new forms seen in Group 5 may represent the simplification not only of the forms themselves, but also, very importantly, the general range of forms available, a phenomenon seen elsewhere in Italy in the later Roman period (Roberts 1992: 421-2).

Group 6 (mid-sixth century+) contains no imported fine-ware, even as a fragmentary, residual element, thereby suggesting the continuing decline of imports seen from the mid-fifth century. It is significant that even a site so close to Rome as Monte Gelato could not always gain ready access to the fruits of international trade, assuming that the

inhabitants of the site still wished to obtain them. The coarse-ware of Group 6 is quite different from the other late Roman assemblages, with forms, especially the cooking pots, unparalleled elsewhere. Given the large number of generally late Roman contexts (later fourth to mid-sixth centuries) on the site, the unusual forms support the idea of a slightly later date for the assemblage, while the absence of parallels suggests a period of low levels of refuse generation. As with Group 4, this may be indicative of a relatively low level of economic activity on the site.

In the period covered by Group 7 contexts (late fourth to mid-sixth centuries (+?)) ARS represents the only international fine-ware import to the site. No trace was found of Phocaean red slip ware (unsurprising, perhaps, given its scarcity in Rome itself), or of 'Tiber red slip' recently isolated in late Roman levels at Rome (T. Peña, pers. comm.). ARS, whilst not as plentiful as in second-century contexts, is none the less present in some quantities, implying a healthy level of economic activity on the site and sustained contacts with local markets. Rome was clearly predominant amongst these, as can be seen by the similarity of coarse-ware types and regional fine-ware forms.

Coarse-wares from Group 7 contexts, despite their broad chronological range, present several important groupings of forms which seem to have a chronological significance. At this point it is interesting to note the absence of forms that are recognizably sub-Roman or post-Roman, until the appearance of identifiable late eighth-century forms (Patterson, this volume). This contrasts with the evidence from sites such as Casale San Donato (H. Patterson, pers. comm.) and Madonna del Passo near Rieti (pers. obs.) which have revealed sub-Roman wares and forms.

The vessels in Group 8 attest the late Antique phenomenon of on-site burials, common to many rural sites from the later Imperial period. The earlier piece cat. 186 (mid-later fifth century) finds parallels in its fabric and diagnostic features with elements of Groups 5 and 7, while the later vessel cat. 187 (mid-later sixth century), though lacking definite parallels in material found on the site, is none the less still recognizably in the Roman period ceramic tradition.

Work currently in progress in and around Rome, such as the analysis of coarse-wares from sixth- to eighth-century deposits at the Crypta Balbi, Rome (L. Saguì, pers. comm.), may eventually permit some of the Group 7 material to begin to bridge the gap between the mid-late sixth and late eighth centuries on the site. On present evidence, however, there seems to be a complete absence of such material. Given that Monte Gelato's proximity to Rome makes it unlikely that the site would at any stage have been completely aceramic, the evidence seems to suggest the complete cessation of occupation, or its reduction to a level undetectable in the

archaeological record, at some point in the mid-
later sixth century.

FABRICS

A fabric series was constructed by eye, with the aid
of a magnifier. While petrological and/or chemical
analysis would have been desirable (and is planned),
sufficient inclusions were visible to enable a satisfactory division into major fabric groups. This procedure was also adopted for fine-wares with the
exception of the ARS, where Lamboglia's categories, terra sigillata chiara (t.s.c.) 'A', 'C' and
'D' are used (Lamboglia 1950; 1958; 1963; see
Hayes (1972: 288)).

1. Soft clay with smooth/powdery feel and finely irregular fracture. Colour: orange (5YR 6/6; Munsell reddish yellow) to buff (10YR 8/4; Munsell very pale brown). Inclusions: very fine quartz, iron and silver mica (all infrequent).

2. Medium-hard clay with smooth/powdery feel and smooth fracture. Colour: orange (7.5YR 7/6; Munsell reddish yellow) to buff (10YR 8/3; Munsell very pale brown). Inclusions: medium to coarse iron (infrequent), fine silver mica, quartz and shiny black platelets (all very infrequent).

3. Soft clay with smooth/powdery feel and finely irregular fracture. Colour: off-white (2.5Y 8/3; Munsell not given) to buff (10YR 8/4; Munsell very pale brown). Inclusions: fine silver mica and lime (infrequent).

4. Medium-hard clay with smooth feel and smooth fracture. Colour: off-white (2.5Y 8/3; Munsell not given) to greenish buff (10Y 8/2; Munsell not given). Inclusions: fine gold mica, lime, iron and shiny black platelets (all infrequent).

5. Medium-hard clay with smooth feel and smooth fracture. Colour: orange (5YR 7/6; Munsell reddish yellow) to buff (10YR 8/4; Munsell very pale brown). Inclusions: fine-medium lime and fine iron (infrequent).

6. Soft clay with soapy feel and finely irregular fracture. Colour: light brown (7.5YR 7/6; Munsell reddish yellow). Inclusions: fine lime, silver mica and red particles (all infrequent).

7. Hard clay with smooth feel and finely irregular fracture. Colour: buff (10YR 7/4; Munsell very pale brown). Inclusions: coarse iron, medium lime, fine silver mica and quartz (all infrequent).

8. Very hard clay with smooth feel and hackly fracture. Colour: off-white (2.5Y 8/2; Munsell white). Inclusions: medium-coarse black particles (abundant) and medium red particles (frequent).

9. Hard clay with smooth feel and smooth fracture. Colour: buff (10YR 7/4; Munsell very pale brown). Inclusions: medium-coarse rounded brown and black particles (abundant), fine silver mica (frequent) and coarse lime (infrequent).

10. Medium-hard clay with smooth/powdery feel and smooth fracture. Colour: off-white (2.5Y 8/2; Munsell not given – 2.5Y 8/4; Munsell pale yellow). Inclusions: coarse quartz, medium-coarse shiny black platelets and silver mica (all infrequent).

11. Medium-hard clay with smooth feel and smooth fracture. Colour: orange (5YR 7/8; Munsell reddish yellow) to buff (10YR 8/4; Munsell very pale brown). Inclusions: fine to coarse quartz and iron, fine lime and black particles (all frequent), fine silver mica (infrequent).

12. Soft clay with soapy feel and smooth/finely irregular fracture. Colour: buff (10YR 8/4; Munsell very pale brown). Inclusions: fine quartz (infrequent).

13. Hard clay with smooth, occasionally pimply feel and finely irregular fracture. Colour: orange (5YR 7/8; Munsell reddish yellow) to brown (7.5YR 5/3; Munsell not given). Inclusions: coarse lime, medium-coarse iron, fine-medium quartz, fine silver mica and angular green particles (all frequent).

14. Hard clay with pimply feel and hackly fracture. Colour: orange (7.5YR 8/6; Munsell reddish yellow) to buff (10YR 8/4; Munsell very pale brown). Inclusions: fine to coarse black platelets and fine-medium quartz (frequent), coarse iron, fine silver mica and lime (infrequent).

15. Hard clay with slightly rough feel and hackly fracture. Colour: orange (5YR 6/6; Munsell reddish yellow) to brown (7.5YR 5/4; Munsell reddish brown). Inclusions: medium-coarse quartz, iron, shiny black platelets and gold mica (all abundant), angular green particles (infrequent).

16. Hard clay with smooth feel and finely irregular fracture. Colour: orange-red (2.5YR 6/6; Munsell light red). Inclusions: medium-coarse quartz, iron and silver mica (all abundant).

17. Hard clay with smooth feel and finely irregular fracture. Colour: light brown (7.5YR 7/4; Munsell pink) to orange (7.5YR 7/6; Munsell reddish yellow). Inclusions: medium-coarse rounded red particles (abundant).

18. Hard clay with smooth/pimply feel and hackly fracture. Colour: orange (2.5YR 5/6; Munsell red) to brown (7.5YR 6/4; Munsell light brown). Inclusions: medium-coarse quartz, fine to coarse gold mica and fine-medium iron (all abundant), coarse brown particles and fine silver mica (infrequent).

19. Very hard clay with pimply feel and finely irregular/hackly fracture. Colour: orange (5YR 6/8; Munsell reddish yellow) to brown (5YR 6/4; Munsell light reddish brown). Inclusions: fine-medium black particles (abundant), fine to coarse quartz, fine silver and gold mica (frequent).

20. Very hard clay with smooth feel and finely irregular fracture. Colour: red (2.5YR 7/4; Munsell not given) to brown (5YR 6/4; Munsell light reddish brown). Inclusions: medium quartz, iron and lime (infrequent), shiny black platelets and silver mica (very infrequent).

21. Hard clay with smooth feel and finely irregular/hackly fracture. Colour: brown (5YR 5/6; Munsell yellowish red). Inclusions: medium iron and fine to coarse white, red and black particles (all frequent).

22. Hard clay with smooth feel and finely irregular fracture. Colour: light brown (5YR 6/6; Munsell reddish yellow). Inclusions: fine quartz (abundant).

23. Hard clay with pimply feel and hackly fracture. Colour: red (5YR 6/6; Munsell reddish yellow) to purplish red (5YR 6/3; Munsell light reddish brown). Inclusions: fine to coarse quartz, gold mica and iron (all abundant), medium lime (infrequent).

24. Hard clay with pimply feel and hackly fracture. Colour: red (5YR 6/6; Munsell reddish yellow) to brown (7.5YR 4/4; Munsell dark brown). Inclusions: fine to coarse quartz and fine silver mica (abundant), medium-coarse iron (frequent).

25. Medium hard clay with rough feel and finely irregular fracture. Colour: brown (7.5YR 6/6; Munsell reddish yellow). Inclusions: fine silver mica and fine-medium quartz (abundant).

26. Hard clay with rough feel and finely irregular/hackly fracture. Colour: orange (5YR 7/8; Munsell reddish yellow) to brown (7.5YR 5/2; Munsell brown). Inclusions: fine to coarse quartz (abundant), fine gold mica and red and black particles (frequent).

27. Hard clay with smooth feel and hackly fracture. Colour: orange-brown (5YR 6/4; Munsell light reddish brown) to purplish brown (5YR 5/3; Munsell reddish brown). Inclusions: fine to coarse quartz, gold mica and iron (abundant), medium lime and shiny black platelets (frequent).

28. Very hard clay with smooth feel and hackly fracture. Colour: dark brown (7.5YR 5/4; Munsell brown). Inclusions: coarse quartz, fine to coarse gold mica, medium shiny black platelets, and medium-coarse iron (all abundant), medium lime (infrequent). An extremely dense fabric, with rough matrix.

Fine-wares

29. Hard clay with smooth feel and finely irregular fracture. Colour: buff (10YR 8/2; Munsell white). Inclusions: fine-medium black particles (frequent). Colour of glaze: interior = yellowish green (5Y 6/6; Munsell olive-yellow); exterior = bluish green (Munsell not given).

30. Hard clay with smooth, waxy feel and finely irregular fracture. Colour: orange (2.5YR 6/8; Munsell light red). Inclusions: fine-medium mica (frequent) and black particles (sparse). Reddish brown slip (2.5YR 6/6; Munsell light red).

31. Hard clay with smooth feel and finely irregular fracture. Colour: pink (2.5YR 7/6; Munsell not given). Inclusions: fine silver mica and lime (infrequent). Reddish brown slip (2.5YR 5/8; Munsell red), overall, semi-lustrous.

32. Very hard clay with smooth feel and smooth fracture. Colour: light red-brown (2.5YR 6/4; Munsell light reddish brown). Inclusions: fine silver mica and fine-medium red particles (infrequent). Reddish brown slip (2.5YR 5/8; Munsell red), overall, lustrous.

33. Hard clay with smooth feel and finely irregular fracture. Colour: pink (2.5YR 7/4; Munsell not given). Inclusions: fine silver mica (abundant). Dark reddish brown slip (2.5YR 4/6; Munsell red), overall, almost matt.

CATALOGUE

Throughout the catalogue the following structure has been used. After the general discussion of each group, the material from that group is divided up by ware and/or class, for example ARS, jars. Individual catalogue entries give, first, the catalogue number used for the identification of pieces in the catalogue and discussions, then a description of the form, with acknowledged nomenclature and dates (if known). Below this are the original recording reference number (P000), and details of dimensions and finish. In cases of multiple context groups (for example, Group 7) provenance is given. Below this, information is supplied on similar vessels from the same deposit and comparanda from other sites. All dates are AD unless specified otherwise.

Group 1 – L165 (lower fill of fish-pond) (Fig. 216)

Group 1, as well as being the largest single homogeneous deposit from the site, is also the earliest. Very small quantities of earlier fine-wares have been found on the site (Table 60), though all were from redeposited groups.

Group 1 comprises material from the lower fill of the fish-pond. Excluding amphorae, lamps and glass (see Arthur, Bailey and Price, this volume), remains of at least 199 vessels were found by SSC, ranging from table-ware to vessels for cooking and storage. A wide range of imported fine-wares is present, including Italian sigillata, glazed ware, Eastern sigillata B2 and ARS; these suggest a date for the deposit in the later first quarter of the second century (c.120s-30s), a dating broadly supported by the evidence of the amphorae, lamps and glass vessels.

Italian sigillata comprises the largest group of imported fine-ware in the deposit (form numbers used below are those of Ettlinger in the *Conspectus* (1990) (hereafter *Consp.* plus form number)). All the identifiable forms (*Consp.* 3.2 (cat. 3), 34.2 (cat. 4), 36.2 (cat. 1)) form a homogeneous group, with no necessarily residual forms, though *Consp.* 36.2 (cat. 1), might be a little earlier. *Consp.* 3.2 (cat. 3) and 34.2 (cat. 4), are among the commonest forms of the later phases of Italian sigillata production, throughout all production areas (*Consp.* 56 and 112). The stamps on cat. 4a-b indicate origins for these vessels in the area of Arezzo.

Glazed ware began arriving in Italy in the later first century BC, from workshops in the Near East and Asia Minor (Maccabruni 1987: 167-8). The area of Tarsus in northern Syria seems to have exported a range of drinking vessels, especially ring-handled skyphoi, which have been found on several Italian sites, including Rome, Pompeii, and, on the Adriatic coast, at Adria (Hochuli Guysel 1977: Abb. 35).

Production in Italy seems to have begun in the mid-first century AD, certainly in northern Italy around Aquileia (Maioli 1983: 113), and there is evidence for production beginning at around this time in Lazio and Campania (Celuzza 1985: 163-5). Soricelli (1988: 253) has gone further, suggesting Puteoli as a possible origin for the 'honey-coloured' jugs and beakers found in Pompeii and Herculaneum. It seems likely, however, that the majority of vessels found in Rome, Ostia (see parallels below) and at Santa Rufina (Cotton, Wheeler and Whitehouse 1991: fig. 91, nos. 9-11), to which the Monte Gelato pieces bear most resemblance in terms of form, fabric and glaze colour, had a different origin, very probably in or near Rome.

The quantities of glazed ware found on Italian sites are generally small, as for example at the extensive villa at Settefinestre, where fewer than a hundred sherds were found, as opposed to thousands of sherds of Italian sigillata. Although it is very possible that the most prized table-wares (for those with the ability to afford them) were of metal, glazed ware, with its unusual finish, clearly reminiscent of metal, in particular bronze, may well have been relatively highly prized. If so, then the presence of three examples in the deposit gives an impression of relative affluence, this being confirmed by other prestige items from the site. It also shows clearly the access that the owners of the site enjoyed to the marketing systems operating in and around Rome and neighbouring centres.

Eastern sigillata B originated in the area of the Meander valley, probably in or near Tralles (Hayes 1972: 9), and was produced from the later Augustan period. Earlier products (Eastern sigillata B1) were distributed mostly around the Aegean, while the later wares (B2), though of lesser quality, were distributed throughout the central and eastern Mediterranean. The most recent and comprehensive discussions of the ware have been by Hayes (1985: 49- 70) and Kenrick (1985: 245-56).

ARS began to arrive in Italy from north Africa during the last quarter of the first century AD. The earliest pieces of ARS are found in Pompeii (Hayes 1972: 190, 205 and 207), though the ware would presumably also have begun to penetrate the markets of Ostia and Rome at an early date. By the turn of the century ARS comprised a sizeable minority of fine-ware assemblages at Ostia (Martin 1992b: fig. 3).The forms present in Group 1 do not represent the earliest forms of ARS import, but rather the late Flavian/Hadrianic types, in particular the small version of 23A (cat. 9), that characterize the first major period of the ware's penetration of Italy.

Taking the imported fine-ware as a whole, the scale of its presence at Monte Gelato demonstrates the ease of access enjoyed by the inhabitants to a whole range of imported goods from local and regional markets.

Colour-coated or slipped ware, locally made vessels decorated by total or partial immersion in a slip or suspension of clay slurry, was the most common type of table-ware used in many regions of Italy throughout the early-mid Imperial period. Peña (1987: 210) has assembled the evidence for a gradual development in the use of colour-coating, from its original use on smaller thin-walled pieces, such as beakers, to its application on a much wider range of forms such as bowls and jugs. Large quantities of the ware have been found on sites such as Cratere Senga (Garcea, Miraglia and Soricelli 1985: 262-3), Posto (Cotton 1979: 136-9) and San Rocco (Cotton and Métraux 1985: 203-17) in Campania; Santa Rufina (Cotton, Wheeler and Whitehouse 1991: fig. 74) in South Etruria; Settefinestre (Camaiora 1985: 172 and tav. 45) in central Etruria; Torre Rebibbia (Staffa 1984: 116-19) north of Rome; and, further afield, Matrice (Roberts 1988: 96-101) in Molise.

The numerous colour-coated vessels found in Group 1 form the majority of table-wares in the deposit, far outnumbering imported sigillata and glazed ware. The wide variety of forms ranges from broad shallow dishes (cat. 11) to tall narrow beakers (cat. 28).

Shallow dishes (cat. 11-17) show considerable variety, with one (cat. 11) revealing the influence of sigillata, probably late sigillata Italica (*Consp.* 48) or Eastern sigillata (Hayes 1985: form 62A). Much more obvious is the influence of sigillata on one of the most common colour-coated vessels, the flanged cup/bowl cat. 18, identical to the Italian sigillata form *Consp.* 34. The presence in the deposit of genuine sigillata examples of the form suggests that the colour-coated imitations reflect the enterprise of the local potters and their ability to respond to the demands of their local markets, rather than any difficulty in acquiring the original products.

Small, carinated cup/bowls (cat. 19-20) form a small but significant subgroup, including cat. 19 with its flaring, well-formed rim. Cat. 20 appears to be a local version of the thin-walled ware form Mayet XLIII (Mayet 1975), widespread throughout the western Mediterranean in the first and early second centuries (see Lopez Mullor (1989: 409-11)). The broad, shallow carinated bowl, cat. 23, is a common form and was to become the predominant colour-coated form in later deposits on the site and elsewhere (Staffa 1984: tav. II-III). Cat. 25-7 also have parallels around Rome. Cat. 29 differs from other bowls in the deposit, with its unusually deep, broad body.

Drinking vessels or *pocula* are well-represented, in particular ovoid vessels such as cat. 26 and 27. Of particular interest is a tall, conical beaker cat. 28, a small version of the stork-vase (*pelargos?*), discussed below.

Of the forms of decoration applied to vessels before colour-coating, rouletting is the most common (for example on cat. 21-4 and 27-9), and with the exception of cat. 29 was fairly well and evenly applied. Applied 'petals' or 'scales' appear on two pieces (cat. 25 and 26), reflecting the frequent use of this motif on early Imperial table-wares, including thin-walled wares (Ricci 1985a: tav. CVII, nos. 14-17) and green glazed ware (as above cat. 6 and 7).

Almost without exception, the colour-coat of the vessels in Group 1 is thin (which explains its often poor state of preservation), dull and poorly applied, with frequent smears, dribbles and finger-marks. On all pieces the slip was applied overall, though its colour varies considerably between vessels and between different areas of the same vessel. This is presumably a result of chemical changes in the slip during firing, as is the occasionally metallic appearance of some pieces.

The bowls/dishes/cups comprise a limited range of bowls for preparation (cat. 32) and dishes for cooking and serving (cat. 33-5), all of a good standard of potting. Cat. 32, though of local fabric, seems to belong to a tradition of large, handled bowls found throughout the eastern and central Mediterranean during the first centuries BC and AD. Traces of direct contact with fire are present on cat. 33-5, indicating their probable use in on-hearth cooking.

Cat. 34 and 35 are in a fabric which, with its abundant volcanic inclusions, was probably an import from the volcanic areas of coastal Etruria or Campania. Cat. 34 seems part of the range of unslipped wares exported from these areas during the early Imperial period, while cat. 35, though of slightly unusual form, appears to be from the same workshops. Although these Tyrrhenian coast imports are present in the deposit, not a single sherd of Pompeian red ware, with its distinctive red finish, was found. This may indicate a decline in the output of the Pompeian red ware workshops, in which case the continuity of the unslipped wares is interesting.

The jars in the deposit divide into two main types; those with coarse fabrics and traces of burning, such as cat. 36 and 38, used for the preparation of food and liquids, and those with finer, levigated fabrics such as cat. 37 and 39, used presumably for storage and serving. Nearly all pieces are of a high potting standard, with even large, bulky vessels such as cat. 36a being evenly and (for coarse-ware) thinly walled.

Cat. 36a and 38a appear to have been used in on-hearth cooking or heating, the concentration of burning on the side opposite the handle indicating that the vessels were pushed directly into the flames or embers. Vessels from second-century deposits at Matrice (Roberts 1988: 112-13) and San Giacomo degli Schiavoni, Molise (Roberts 1993: 193) bear identical patterns of burning, suggesting their use in similar contexts. This method of slow, on-hearth cooking, using a terracotta pot (often the two-handled *pignatta*) can still be seen today in parts of Italy.

Cat. 37a, in a levigated fabric, with its wide mouth and double handles, was probably used for storage of foodstuffs, while cat. 39a, with its distinctive single round handle, may have been used for the short-term storage and serving of liquids.

In contrast to the general scarcity of parallels for the colour-coated vessels from the deposit, numerous comparanda have been found for the coarse-ware jars, in particular among the pottery found at Sutri (Duncan 1964). The robust cooking jar cat. 36 is very similar to Duncan's form

27, though with slightly heavier rim. Other close parallels include cat. 37 (Duncan's form 28), cat. 38 (Duncan's form 30), and cat. 39 (Duncan's form 31). As well as the local comparanda from Sutri, other parallels come from Ostia, and in particular from material found during the South Etruria field survey (Peña 1987). This implies either a broadly shared ceramic tradition in the manufacturing of pottery throughout South Etruria or a very extensive system of distribution, capable of bringing the products of a limited number of production centres to a very wide market. The latter model cannot be discounted, given the large numbers of imports which were in circulation; however, it seems likely that the bulk of the coarse-ware was produced by a number of centres broadly united by a ceramic koine. The idea of more diffuse production seems supported by evidence for manufacture at Monte Gelato. Three badly blistered and warped wasters of jars were found, similar to cat. 36a, 38a and 39a. Several other jars in the group, including cat. 36a, were heavily overfired. In view of this, and of the large numbers of very similar vessels present, it seems reasonable to propose a pottery workshop(s) at or near the site itself.

Nearly all the cooking pots found in the deposit are carinated, with broad overhanging rim and flat base (as cat. 43a). This type is commonly found in early to mid Imperial deposits throughout central and southern Italy, from Etruria (Dyson 1976: figs 42-3 and 56-7) to Campania (Cotton and Métraux 1985: figs 55-6) and Molise (Roberts 1992: figs 66 and 68). Burning on the exterior of rim and/or wall, as on cat. 43a-c, 45 and 48, indicates that they were used by being placed either directly on the hearth, or on a grille or tripod, as at the House of the Vettii, Pompeii. All of the cooking pots, even bulky pieces such as cat. 46-8, were well and evenly potted. With the exception of rims decorated with grooves (cat. 43 and 46) or cogged rouletting (cat. 43f), there were no examples of decoration. The cogging of cat. 43f suggests the piece belongs to the early-mid Imperial 'cogged ware' production, first noted by Threipland (1968) in the Ager Veientanus and Ager Faliscus, and noted elsewhere in Italy in first- and second-century contexts (Peña 1987: 211).

Cat. 43 is the most common type, extremely similar to Duncan's (1964) forms 20 and 23 from Sutri. The inclined rims of cat. 44 and 45 are quite unusual, as is the vertical handle under the rim of cat. 44, a feature unparalleled on other vessels from the site. The presence of large vessels such as cat. 46-8 implies the preparation and consumption of foodstuffs in some quantity, and may have implications for the size of the site's population. Cat. 46a-c, with their broad, rounded rims and distinctive deep grooves, are characteristic of the deposit, mirroring the situation on the South Etruria survey, where, on site 6, vessels similar to cat. 46 were the most common cooking pot form (Peña 1987: 166). Cat. 47 is unique, with its very deep, broad body. Cat. 48, with its distinctive triangular projection under the rim, and thickened inner edge, is fairly common in the deposit, this reflecting its popularity throughout much of central and northern Tyrrhenian Italy, from Ostia to Luni.

Cat. 49a-b, with their broad, shallow bodies, thickened rim and rounded base, are very different from the carinated pieces. The form may be related to pieces from Republican contexts near Sutri (Duncan 1965: form 24), where the carinated form seems to be absent until the early Imperial period, as at Cosa (Dyson 1976), where carinated pieces are absent from the 'Pottery Dump' (mid-late first century BC) but appear in '22 II' (mid-first century AD).

As with the jars, there is some evidence, in the form of kiln wasters, for local production; a near complete vessel similar to cat. 43a was found, very hard-fired and buckled into an elliptical form, while a sherd similar to cat. 46c was badly blistered and buckled, and cat. 47 was misshapen and hard-fired to the point of vitrification. Several other body sherds were found from unidentifiable cooking pots with similar firing defects.

The flagons/jugs of the deposit form a very homogeneous group, both in form and fabric. Cat. 50 may have had a broad flat base or a carinated base, leading to a ring foot as cat. 51 and 54. The two-handled flagon cat. 51 is the most common form in the group with the tall, broad neck and heavily-ribbed body also seen in cat. 52 and 54. Cat. 52 has a very unusual hollow rim and rounded handles in contrast to other handles in the group which have flattened, rectangular sections (cat. 50-2). Cat. 53 is the only jug in the group with a true pouring lip, though a drip groove was also seen on cat. 51. Several examples of cat. 54 are present, all with a thick ring foot and heavily ridged wall.

The similarity of the vessels in size and in shared diagnostic features suggests that all the flagons/jugs present in the deposit are the products of a small number of workshops, very probably only one. An example of cat. 51 was found in an underfired, crumbly fabric, implying a possibly local production centre, possibly on-site. Such production would have formed part of a shared tradition extending as far as Ostia.

Cat. 55 is widely known by the almost certainly erroneous term of 'amphora stopper'. Pavolini (1980a: 1009-12) has discussed the various interpretations of the vessel and its function, which are briefly as follows. Its use as an amphora stopper seems unlikely, given that plentiful amphorae retrieved intact from shipwrecks have as yet failed to yield a single example of the vessel used in connection with any closure device. They may conceivably have been used after the opening of the amphora, but again there is no archaeological evidence for this. Some, citing the frequent presence of the vessel in tombs, suggest that it was an unguentarium, or possibly a lamp. However, the crudeness of the vessel (and its porosity) seem to tell against these possibilities, especially given the presence of numerous colour-coated vessels and lamps of normal type in the deposit. Further suggestions include dice-cups (*frittili*), or drinking cups (*pocula*). Games involving dice were popular in the Roman world, but in surviving representations, for example from Pompeii (Ward-Perkins and Claridge 1976: no. 227), vessels such as cat. 55 are not represented. Its use as a drinking vessel would perhaps be difficult given its pointed base (damaged on cat. 55).

Cat. 56 is the only representative at Monte Gelato of a form often described as an '*incensario*' or incense-burner. Traces of burning restricted to the interior of the vessel could support such an identification, suggesting that it was used for the combustion of a commodity inside the vessel, rather than the heating of the commodity from outside. The form and decoration of the piece, and its uniformity on numerous sites of early Imperial date, suggest a specific function, but it is uncertain whether this was ritual or secular.

The large quantity of lids found, and the wide range of sizes, suggests that many of the vessels in the deposit would have been lidded. Only a small minority of the lids are in levigated fabrics, implying that the majority was used in cooking processes, on vessels such as jars and cooking pots. Cat. 57, with its triangular-sectioned rim, is by far the most common form of lid, and, as with certain jar (cat. 36)

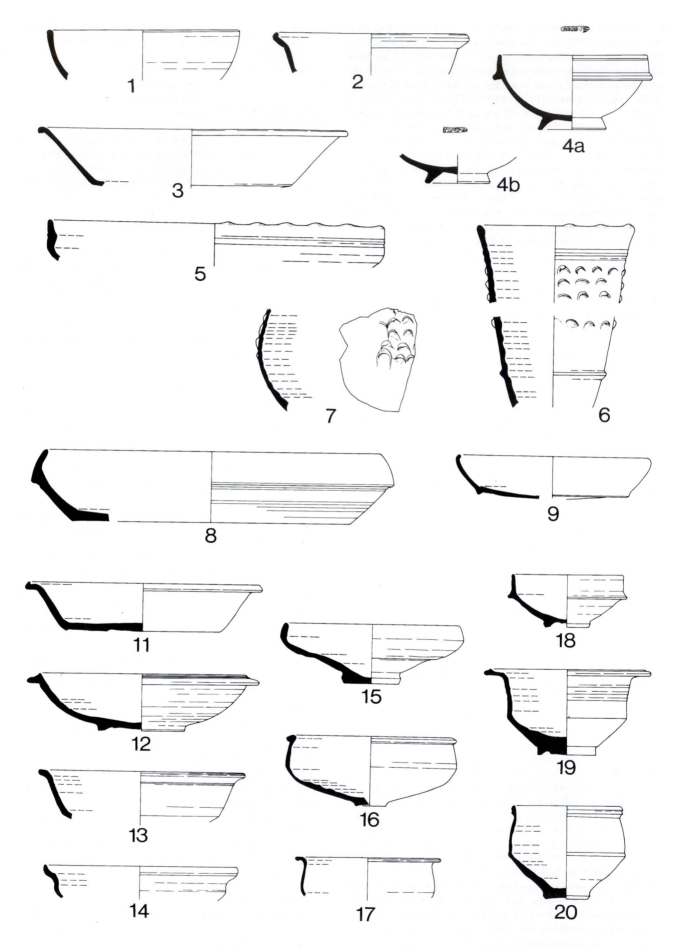

Fig. 218. Lower fish-pond: Italian sigillata (1-4), green glazed (5-7), Eastern sigillata B (8), African red slip ware (9-10), colour-coated (11-20) (1:3). *(SC)*

and cooking pot (cat. 48) types, seems to have enjoyed a very wide diffusion throughout South Etruria and Rome/Ostia. Cat. 60, illustrated here as a lid, but possibly also used as a dish, seems the only definite import. Its fabric is similar to, though a little more coarse and dark than, that of the imported cooking dishes cat. 34 and 35, and it may therefore share the same Tyrrhenian provenance. Hayes (1983: 108 and n. 31) has published examples of 'Italian baking lids' from Antonine levels at Knossos, and cited numerous parallels from the eastern Mediterranean. He has suggested an Etrurian or Campanian origin, with a possible concentration of exports in the earlier first century. The presence of examples in Group 1 (cat. 60) and Group 2 (cat. 95), however, both in a good state of preservation, suggest that export may have continued throughout, or re-started in, the early second century.

Italian sigillata

By SSC, the remains of ten vessels were found.
1. Fig. 218. Hemispherical cup. *Consp.* 36.2. Tiberian to late first century AD+.
   P4; rim D. 15 cm; fabric 32.
2. Fig. 218. Cup with straight wall and bevelled rim. *Consp.* not found.
   P2; rim D. 15 cm; fabric 31.
3. Fig. 218. Dish with sloping wall and bead rim. *Consp.* 3.2. Early/mid first to early second centuries AD.
   P3; rim D. 24 cm; fabric 31.
4. Figs 218 and 219. Hemispherical cup with short vertical rim and pronounced flange on wall. *Consp.* 34.2. Mid-first to early second centuries AD+.
   (a) P1; rim D. 11.5 cm; base D. 5 cm; H. 6 cm; fabric 32;
      CPRO *in planta pedis*
      C(LODIUS) PRO(CULUS) – Oxé and Comfort 1968: 158, nos. 452-4.
   (b) P5; base D. 5 cm; fabric 33;
      P.AV.PO. *in planta pedis*
      P.AV(ILLIUS) PO(?) – Oxé and Comfort 1968: 97, no. 219.
      Similar: one rim, rim D. 8 cm.

 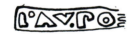

Fig. 219. Stamps on vessels 4a and 4b (x2). *(SC)*

Glazed ware

By SSC, the remains of three vessels were found.
5. Fig. 218. Dish with straight vertical upper wall and knobbed rim.
   P10; rim D. 26 cm; fabric 29.
   Cf. Ostia: Martin 1992b: fig. 3; Zevi and Carta 1987: fig. 109, nos. 82-3. Roselle: Michellucci 1985: tav. XIX, no. 27. Paphos (Cyprus): Hayes 1991: fig. XXII, no. 9.
6. Fig. 218. Beaker with tall conical body and knobbed rim. Four rows (surviving) of applied scale decoration. Above these, under rim, two rounded ridges; near base of vessel, a single, larger ridge.
   P8; rim D. 12 cm; fabric 29.
   Cf. Castelporziano: pers. obs. Rome: Carbonara and Messineo 1993: fig. 246, no. 1b (thin-walled ware).

7. Fig. 218. Closed vessel with rounded body. Three rows (surviving) of unevenly applied scale decoration.
   P11; fabric 29.
   Cf. Ostia: Martin 1992b: fig. 10.

Eastern sigillata B2

The remains of one vessel were found.
8. Fig. 218. Dish with broad, shallow body, straight wall and tall, inward curving rim. Hayes 60, second quarter of first to mid-second centuries.
   P6; rim D. 28 cm; base D. 22 cm; H. 5.5 cm; fabric 30.

African red slip ware (ARS)

By SSC, the remains of three vessels were found.
9. Fig. 218. Casserole with outward sloping wall and slightly rounded bottom, separated by a more or less pronounced ridge. Hayes 23A, early to mid second century.
   P7; rim D. 15 cm: base D. 12 cm; H. 3 cm; fabric t.s.c. 'A'.
   Similar: one rim, rim D. 16 cm.
10. (Not illustrated.) Sherd from wall of open vessel (cup/bowl) with traces of rouletting on exterior. Hayes 7-10, from *c.* 110s-80s.

Colour-coated ware

The remains of 48 vessels were found by SSC, including the unusual 'stork-vase', discussed in detail below (Murray, Parsons and Roberts, this volume).
Broadly, three main colour bands of slip were noted.
(a) Slip 1. Orange-red-brownish red (2.5YR 5/6-5/8; Munsell red, to 5YR 5/8-7/8; Munsell reddish yellow, to 7.5YR 7/8; Munsell yellow-orange).
(b) Slip 2. Brown (2.5YR 4/2; Munsell weak red, to 5YR 5/3; Munsell reddish brown, to 7.5YR 5/6; Munsell strong brown).
(c) Slip 3. Greenish brown (10YR 5/3; Munsell brown).
11. Fig. 218. Dish with broad, hooked rim, shallow body with straight wall and slightly raised foot.
    P13; rim D. 18.5 cm; base D. 12 cm; H. 3.5 cm; fabric 1; slip 1.
12. Fig. 218. Dish/bowl with flanged rim, rounded wall and ring foot.
    P19; rim D. 18 cm; base D. 6.5 cm; H. 4.5 cm; fabric 1; slip 1.
13. Fig. 218. Dish/bowl with narrow horizontal rim and carinated body.
    P27; rim D. 16 cm; fabric 1; slip 1.
14. Fig. 218. Dish/bowl with rounded, cupped rim and rounded body.
    P24; rim D. 15 cm; fabric 1; slip 2.
    Similar: two rim fragments, diameter not measurable.
15. Fig. 218. Dish with short, inturned rim, irregular rounded wall and solid bevelled foot.
    P22; rim D. 14 cm; base D. 4.5 cm; H. 4.5 cm; fabric 1; slip 1.
16. Fig. 218. Bowl with thickened, rounded rim, broad body with rounded wall and small ring foot.
    P26; rim D. 13 cm; base D. 2.5 cm; H. 5.5 cm; fabric 1; slip 1.
    Similar: four rim fragments, rim D. 10-12 cm.
    Cf. Rome: Carbonara and Messineo 1993: fig. 245, nos. 8a-d.
17. Fig. 218. Bowl with horizontal rim and broad body with rounded wall.
    P28; rim D. 11 cm; fabric 1; slip 1.

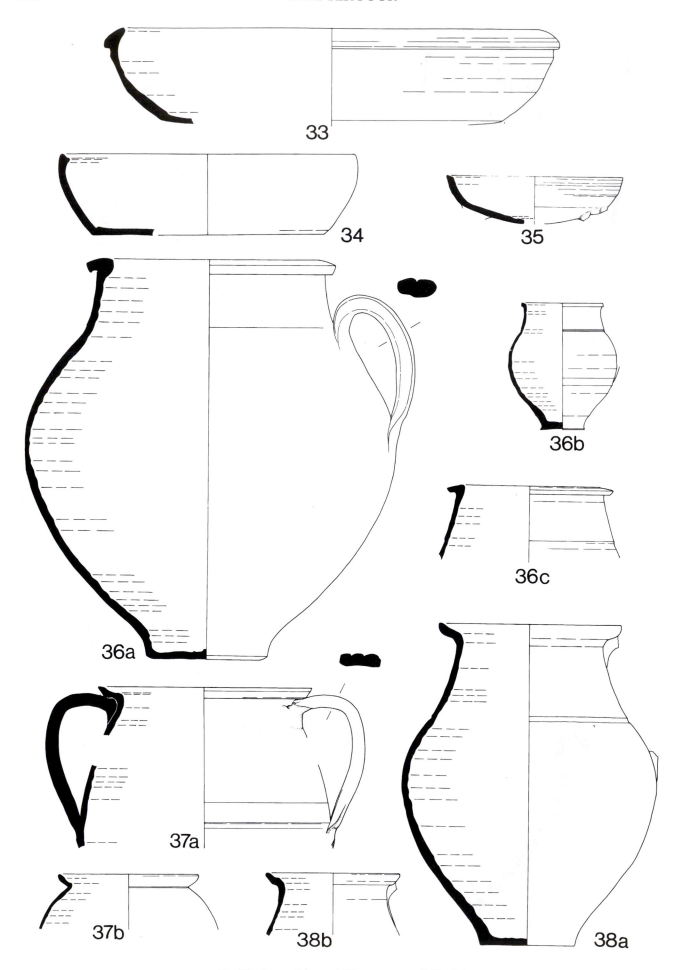

Fig. 221. Lower fish-pond fill: coarse-ware (1:3). *(SC)*

37. Fig. 221. Jar with everted rim, cupped on interior and rounded body. Two handles with broad rectangular section.
(a) P81; rim D. 17 cm; fabric 2.
Similar: three rim fragments, rim D. 17-21 cm.
Cf. Ostia: Zevi and Carta 1987: fig. 131, no. 274. South Etruria survey: Peña 1987: site 11, 618, no. 5.
(b) P70; rim D. 11 cm; fabric 13. Burnt on exterior of rim.
Cf. (a-b) Sutri: Duncan 1964: fig. 12, nos. 107-8 (Duncan's form 28).
38. Fig. 221. Jar with everted rim, ovoid body and flat base. Single handle.
(a) P67; rim D. 14 cm; base D. 7.5 cm; H. 25 cm; fabric 13. Burnt on exterior of wall and rim opposite handle.
Similar: fifteen rim fragments, rim D. 12-18 cm, including one waster; thirteen base fragments, base D. 5-7 cm.
Cf. South Etruria survey: Peña 1987: site 6, 600, no. 6.
(b) P68; rim D. 10.5 cm; fabric 13.
Similar: four rim fragments, rim D. 12-21 cm.
Cf. South Etruria survey: Peña 1987: site 9, 610, no. 2.
Cf. (a-b) Sutri: Duncan 1964: fig. 13, no. 112 (Duncan's form 30).
39. Fig. 222. Jar with horizontal rim, ovoid body and flat base. Single handle with round or rectangular section.
(a) Four grooves on exterior at shoulder.
P77; rim D. 10 cm; base D. 6 cm; H. 19.5 cm; fabric 2.
Similar: four rim fragments, rim D. 12-14 cm, including one waster; two base fragments, base D. 5 cm.
Cf. Sutri: Duncan 1964: fig. 13, no. 112 (Duncan's form 30).
(b) P79; rim D. 7 cm; fabric 2.
Similar: two rim fragments, rim D. 7 and 8 cm.
(c) (Not illustrated.) P65; rim D. 12 cm; base D. 7.5 cm; H. 25.5 cm; fabric 13. Warped, badly blistered on exterior.
40. Fig. 222. Jar with broad rim angled downwards, short neck and slightly rounded body.
P72; rim D. 18 cm; fabric 13. Burnt on exterior of rim and wall.
Cf. South Etruria survey: Peña 1987: site 1, 592, no. 9. Santa Rufina: Cotton, Wheeler and Whitehouse 1991: fig. 85, no. 13.
41. Fig. 222. Jar with everted, rounded rim and rounded body.
P71; rim D. 12 cm; fabric 13.
42. Fig. 222. Jar with everted rim and broad body.
P80; rim D. 15 cm; fabric 2.

Cooking pots

By rim count, 57 vessels were represented.
43. Fig. 222. Cooking pot with straight, broad rim, carinated body and flat base. Groove at outer edge of rim.
(a) P45; rim D. 20 cm; base D. 4.5 cm; H. 10 cm; fabric 13. Burnt on underside of base.
Similar: three rim fragments, rim D. 21-2 cm, including waster; 27 base fragments, base D. 4-7 cm.
Cf. Ostia: Zevi and Pohl 1970: fig. 86, no. 238.
(b) P44; rim D. 21 cm; fabric 13. Burnt on exterior of rim and upper and lower walls.
Similar: seventeen rim fragments, rim D. 20-8 cm.
(c) P56; rim D. 20 cm; fabric 13. Burnt on exterior of rim.
Cf. Ostia: Ostia III: tav. LIII, no. 435.
(d) P55; rim D. 19 cm; fabric 13.
Cf. Cosa: Dyson 1976: fig. 56, LS 17-19.
Cf. (a-d) Sutri: Duncan 1964: fig. 10, nos. 67-9 (Duncan's form 20).

(e) P53; rim D. 20 cm; fabric 13.
Similar: two rim fragments, diameter not measurable.
(f) (Not illustrated.) Two rows of rouletting on upper surface of rim.
P57; rim D. 26 cm; fabric 13.
Cf. Veientanus survey: Threipland 1968: 199, fig. 26, no. 2.
44. Fig. 222. Cooking pot with broad, thickened rim angled upwards. Vertical handle.
P54; rim D. 26 cm; fabric 14.
Similar: one rim fragment, rim D. 19 cm.
Cf. Ostia: Ostia I: tav. XIX, no. 391; Ostia II: tav. VIII, no. 14; Zevi and Pohl 1970: fig. 86, no. 471a.
45. Fig. 222. Cooking pot with thickened, flattened rim and shallow, carinated body with straight wall.
P40; rim D. 18 cm; fabric 13. Burnt on exterior of lower wall.
46. Figs 222-3. Cooking pot with broad, curved rim and deep carinated body with straight wall. Grooves/ridges on upper surface of rim.
(a) P43; rim D. 28.5 cm; fabric 13.
Similar: three rim fragments, rim D. 24-9 cm.
Cf. South Etruria survey: Peña 1987: site 1, 592, no. 1.
(b) P47; rim D. 26 cm; fabric 14.
Similar: seven rim fragments, rim D. 17-28 cm.
Cf. Cosa: Dyson 1976: fig. 54, LS4. Ostia: Ostia II: tav. XXVII, no. 478; Ostia III: tav. XXV, no. 138. Rome: Carbonara and Messineo 1993: fig. 248, no. 6. South Etruria survey: Peña 1987: site 13, 622, no. 4.
(c) P51; rim D. 25 cm; fabric 13.
Similar: four rim fragments, rim D. 23-6 cm, including waster.
Cf. Lugnano in Teverina: Monacchi 1990: fig. 13, no. 12. South Etruria survey: Peña 1987: site 6, 598, no. 10.
47. Fig. 223. Cooking pot with curved rim and deep body, widening towards base, with straight wall.
P48; rim D. 26.5 cm; fabric 13, almost vitrified. Waster.
Cf. South Etruria survey: Peña 1987: site 6, 598, no. 3.
48. Fig. 223. Cooking pot with broad rim, thickened and squared at junction with wall, triangular projection on underside of outer edge. Straight wall.
P46; rim D. 30 cm; fabric 13. Burnt on exterior of rim.
Similar: four rim fragments, rim D. 26-8 cm.
Cf. Gabii: Almagro-Gorbea 1982: fig. 2, no. 27. Lugnano in Teverina: Monacchi 1990: fig. 14, no. 18. Luni: Luni I: tav. 74, 12 CM2622/1; Luni II: tav. 196, 6 CS1740/1. Ostia: Pohl 1978: fig. 158, no. 223; fig. 110, no. 1601; Zevi and Carta 1987: fig. 131, no. 270b; Zevi and Pohl 1970: fig. 23, no. 8; fig. 30, no. 2; fig. 86, no. 232; fig. 117, no. 92. Rome: Cianfriglia et al. 1990: fig. 38, no. 306. South Etruria survey: Peña 1987: site 9, 610, no. 6.
49. Fig. 223. Cooking pot with heavy, rounded rim and broad shallow body with rounded base. Groove/ridge on upper part of rim.
(a) P39; rim D. 15 cm; H. 5 cm; fabric 13.
Cf. Rome: Carbonara and Messineo 1993: fig. 248, no. 6. Santa Rufina: Cotton, Wheeler and Whitehouse 1991: fig. 83, nos. 4 and 5.
(b) P38; rim D. 21 cm; fabric 13.
Cf. Cosa: Dyson 1976: fig. 55, LS12.

Flagons/jugs

By SSC, the remains of twelve vessels were found.
50. Fig. 223. Flagon with thickened, rounded rim, narrow neck and cylindrical body, widening towards base.

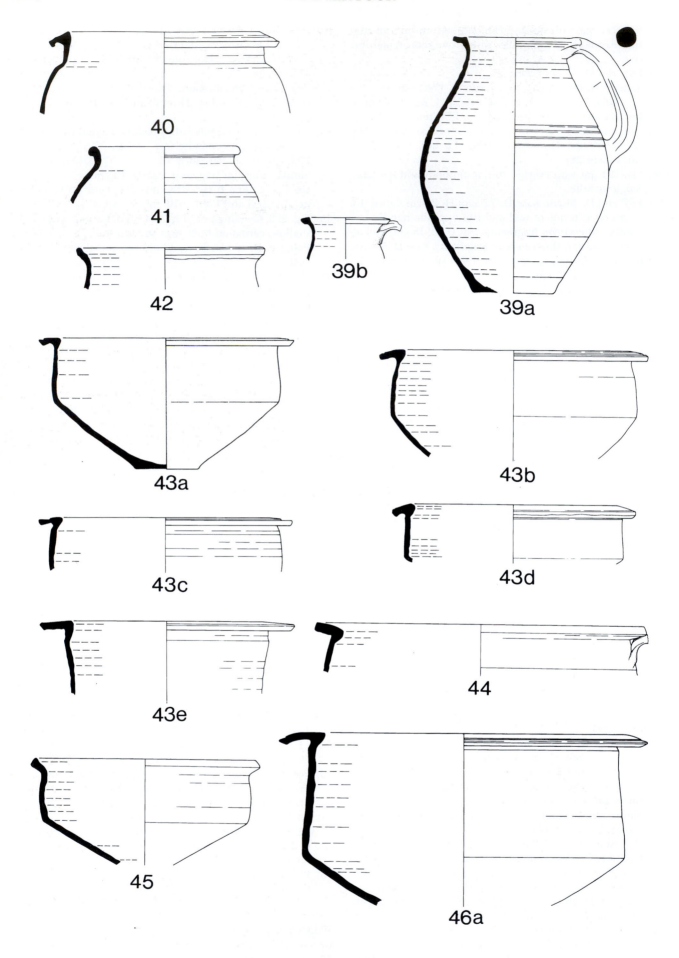

Fig. 222. Lower fish-pond fill: coarse-ware (1:3). *(SC)*

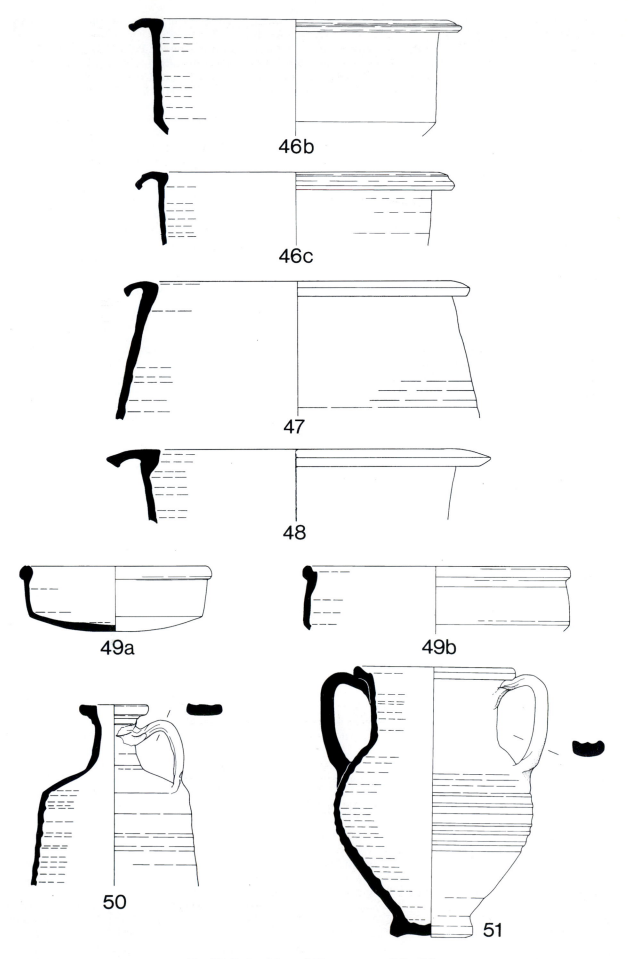

Fig. 223. Lower fish-pond fill: coarse-ware (1:3). *(SC)*

Single handle with rectangular section.
P88; rim D. 5.5 cm; fabric 2.

51. Fig. 223. Flagon with everted rim with broad groove on upper surface. Tall, broad neck and ovoid body with bevelled ring foot. Two handles with sub-oval section, bearing two deep broad grooves on upper surface. Series of ridges and grooves on body.
P82; rim D. 12.5 cm; base D. 6.5 cm; H. 21 cm; fabric 3.
Similar: two rim fragments, rim D. 15 and 16 cm, including one underfired; three base fragments, base D. 6.5 cm.

52. Fig. 224. Flagon with rounded, hollowed rim, tall narrow neck and rounded body. Two handles with rounded section.
P85; rim D. 6.5 cm; fabric 3.
Cf. Gabii: Almagro-Gorbea 1982: fig. 9, no. 141. Ostia: *Ostia* II: tav. XXI, no. 378; *Ostia* III: tav. XVII, no. 52.

53. Fig. 224. Jug with broad everted rim with pouring lip and broad groove on upper surface, tall narrow neck and broad body. Single handle with broad rectangular section and two shallow grooves on upper surface.
P86; rim D. 7.5 cm; fabric 3.
Similar: one rim fragment, rim D. 7 cm.
Cf. Gabii: Almagro-Gorbea 1982: fig. 8, no. 113. Ostia: Zevi and Pohl 1970: fig. 84, nos. 168-9, fig. 109, no. 622. Rome: Carbonara and Messineo 1993: fig. 249, no. 16.

54. Fig. 224. Flagon/jug with bevelled ring foot, rounded body and tall, narrow neck. Possibly the lower part of a vessel as cat. 52.
(a) P84; base D. 6.5 cm; fabric 3.
Similar: three base fragments, base D. 6-8 cm.
(b) P89; base D. 5 cm; fabric 2.

Miscellaneous

Remains of three vessels were found by SSC.

55. Fig. 224. 'Amphora stopper'. Vessel with broad, angular rim, tall narrow neck and rounded body.
P84; rim D. 6.5 cm; fabric 3.
Similar: one rim fragment, rim D. 5.5 cm; one base fragment.

56. Fig. 224. '*Incensario*'. Bowl with everted tripartite rim and carinated body.
P41; rim D. 24 cm; fabric 13.
Indented decoration on exterior of rim and carination.

Lids

By rim count, the remains of 57 lids were found.

57. Fig. 224. Lid with central knob, gently rounded body with ridged wall and everted rim with triangular-sectioned extremity.
(a) P92; rim D. 22 cm; H. 5 cm; fabric 13.
Similar: 32 rim fragments, rim D. 11-25 cm; fourteen knobs.
Cf. Ostia: *Ostia* II: tav. XXVIII, no. 516. *Ostia* III: tav. XXXIV, no. 244; tav. LIX, no. 521; Pohl 1978: fig. 147, no. 84; Zevi and Carta 1987: fig. 131, no. 254; Zevi and Pohl 1970: fig. 87, no. 274. Rome: Cianfriglia *et al.* 1990: fig 33, nos. 164 and 166; fig. 46, no. 606. Santa Rufina: Cotton, Wheeler and Whitehouse 1991: fig. 87, no. 2. South Etruria survey: Peña 1987: site 6, 604, nos. 2 and 6.
(b) P96; rim D. 20 cm; fabric 13.

58. Fig. 224. Lid with pinched knob, conical body and bevelled rim.
P93; rim D. 12 cm; H. 3.5 cm; fabric 13.

Similar: fourteen rim fragments, rim D. 10-19 cm; four knobs.
Cf. South Etruria survey: Peña 1987: site 6, 604, no. 1.

59. Fig. 224. Lid with raised, rounded knob and flat body with thickened, rounded rim.
P94; rim D. 13 cm; H. 1.5 cm; fabric 2.
Similar: six rim fragments, rim D. 15-26 cm.

60. Fig. 224. Lid/dish with flattened top, rounded wall and thickened, rounded rim.
P95; rim D. 23 cm; H. 2 cm; fabric 19.
Cf. Cosa: Dyson 1976: fig. 60, LS57.

Bases

Excluding bases which could be attributed to vessels similar to those above, remains of four bases were found.

61. Fig. 224. Base of closed storage vessel (for liquids?) with ring foot with central *omphalos* and straight wall.
P91; base D. 7.5 cm; fabric 2.
Similar: three base fragments, base D. 6-7 cm.

Group 2 – L105 (upper fill of fish-pond) (Fig. 217)

Group 2 comprises material from the upper fill of the fish-pond. Although some joins were found between Groups 1 and 2, the numbers involved are very small – two lamps (Bailey, this volume) and one colour-coated piece – and may indicate post-deposition processes. Excluding amphorae, lamps and glass, the remains of at least 116 vessels were found by SSC. Imported fine-wares, almost exclusively ARS suggest a date for the assemblage of the 170s-90s AD, a date substantiated by the lamps, amphorae and glass.

In contrast to Group 1, the fine-ware in Group 2 consists almost entirely of ARS: the only exception is a small group of Italian sigillata. It is noteworthy that Italian sigillata still constitutes approximately ten per cent of assemblages in Ostia in the later second century (Martin 1992b: fig. 5).

The probability that cat. 62 is residual seems lessened by its good state of preservation (over 80 per cent of the rim is preserved). In addition, the form *Consp.* 34 is one of the latest forms in Italian sigillata production and it is quite possible that examples would still have been in circulation in South Etruria in this period. The form, with its thick heavy wall and flanged rim, bears a close resemblance to Hayes form 3 in Çandarli ware (Hayes 1972: 320-1), though close examination of the fabric of the piece failed to reveal any large flakes of golden mica, one of the main distinguishing features of the ware (Hayes 1972: 316).

The assemblage of ARS from Group 2 seems homogeneous, with no piece necessarily residual or intrusive, and suggests a date for the deposit in the 170s-90s AD. Hayes 35 (cat. 69), though in fabric t.s.c. 'A'/'C' and dated by Hayes (1972) to the first half of the third century, is found in later second-century levels at Lambaesis (J.W. Hayes, pers. comm.), and does not therefore pose problems for the later second-century date proposed for Group 2.

The ARS is evenly divided between table-ware and cooking-ware. The table-ware includes Hayes 8A (cat. 63), 8B (cat. 64), 9A (cat. 65), 9B (cat. 66), 14A (cat. 67) and 16 (cat. 68), among the commonest ARS forms of this period. Less common are the closed form (cat. 70) and the deep bowl/dish Hayes 35 (cat. 69).

The ARS cooking-ware presents a range of casseroles, Hayes 23A (cat. 72), 23B (cat. 73), 183/4 (cat. 71) and 197 (cat. 74), and lids/dishes, Hayes 22 (cat. 75), 182 (cat. 76) and 196A (cat. 77). Hayes 23 is present in both the smaller version, also seen in Group 1 (cat. 9), and the larger vessel

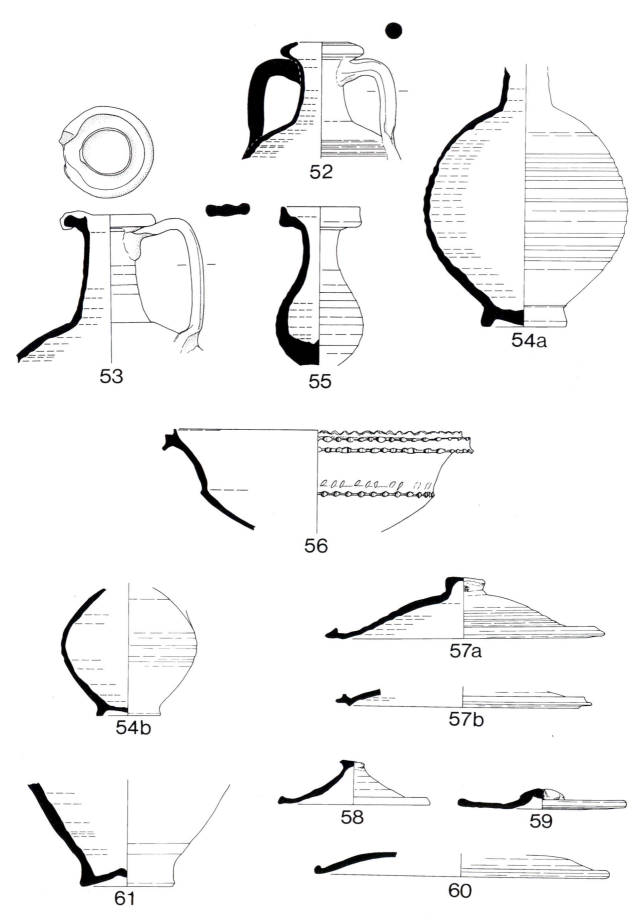

Fig. 224. Lower fish-pond fill: coarse-ware (1:3). *(SC)*

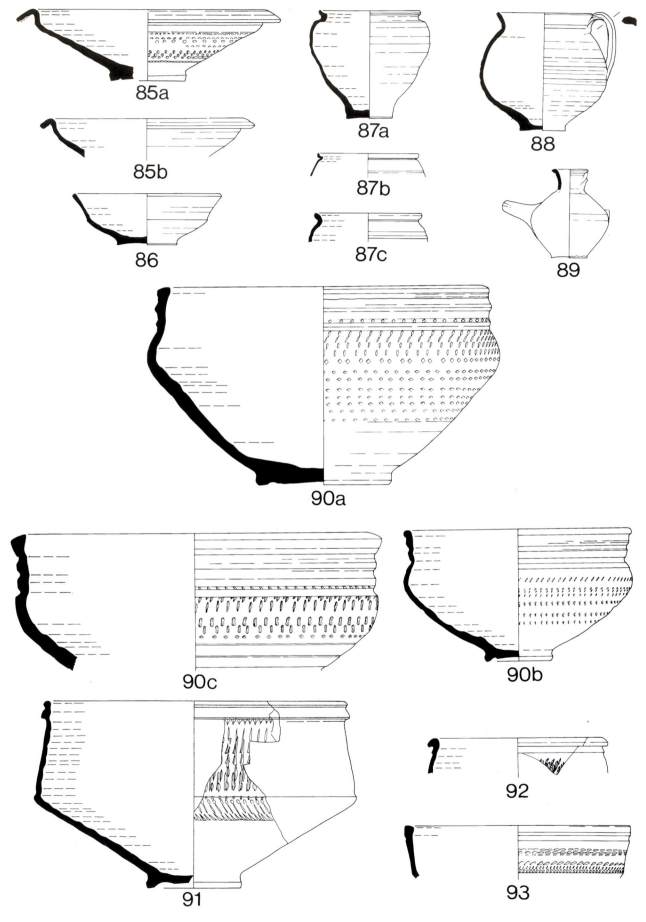

Fig. 226. Upper fish-pond fill: colour-coated (1:3). *(SC)*

86. Fig. 226. Cup/bowl with flaring carinated body and slightly hollowed flat base.
P137; rim D. 12 cm; base D. 4.5 cm; H. 4 cm; fabric 5; slip 1.
87. Fig. 226. Cup/beaker with small, cupped rim, irregular ovoid body tapering towards simple flat base.
(a) P153; rim D. 8 cm; base D. 3.5 cm; H. 8.5 cm; fabric 6; slip 4.
(b) P152; rim D. 8 cm; fabric 4; slip 1.
Similar: four rim fragments, rim D. 9-10 cm.
(c) P149; rim D. 9 cm; fabric 5; slip 4.
Similar: one rim fragment, rim D. 9 cm.
88. Fig. 226. '*Boccalino/urnetta a collarino*'. Cup/beaker with tall, everted rim underlined by rounded ridge or 'collar', spherical body and slightly hollowed flat base. Single handle with irregular section.
P144; rim D. 7.5 cm; base D. 3.5 cm; H. 9.5 cm; fabric 6; slip 1.
Similar: two rim fragments, rim D. 6 and 7 cm; thirteen base fragments, base D. 3-4 cm.
89. Fig. 226. Baby feeder? Closed vessel with narrow, beaded rim, tall narrow neck and spherical body with flat base. Long, narrow spout and single handle (missing).
P151; rim D. 3 cm; base D. 3 cm; H. 7 cm; fabric 4; slip 2.
90. Fig. 226. Large bowl with vertical/slightly everted thickened rim bearing two or three ridges and grooves on exterior, carinated body rounded at carination, with ring foot. Rouletted decoration on exterior.
(a) Thirteen bands of rouletting on exterior.
P158; rim D. 26.5 cm; base D. 11 cm; H. 16 cm; fabric 6; slip 1.
Similar: three rim fragments, rim D. 23-8 cm; one base fragment, base D. 11 cm.
(b) Six bands of rouletting on exterior.
P157; rim D. 18 cm; base D. 5.5 cm; H. 10 cm; fabric 4; slip 3.
Similar: six rim fragments, rim D. 16-19 cm.
(c) Five bands of rouletting on exterior.
P159; rim D. 29.5 cm; fabric 4; slip 1.
Similar: two rim fragments, rim D. 27 and 31 cm.
Cf. (a-c) Ostia: *Ostia* I: tav. XIII, nos. 281-3. Rome: Staffa 1984: 116, tav. II, nos. 46-50; tav. III, nos. 51-8; tav. IV, nos. 59-60. San Rocco: Cotton and Métraux 1985: fig. 47, no. 4. South Etruria survey: Peña 1987: site 6, 608, nos. 1 and 2; site 9, 614, no. 4; 616, nos. 8 and 9.
91. Fig. 226. Bowl with thickened, double beaded rim, carinated body with straight wall and bevelled ring foot. Numerous bands of rouletting on exterior.
P154; rim D. 24 cm; base D. 7.5 cm; H. 15 cm; slip 4.
Similar: one base fragment, base D. 8 cm.
92. Fig. 226. Bowl with thickened, rounded overhanging rim, underlined by ridges on exterior and rounded wall. Four bands (surviving) of rouletting on exterior.
P162; rim D. 14 cm; fabric 7; slip 2.
Similar: one rim fragment, rim D. 26 cm.
93. Fig. 226. Bowl with thickened, squared rim and carinated body with straight upper wall. Two bands (surviving) of multiple rouletting on exterior.
P161; rim D. 18 cm; fabric 6.

Pompeian red ware

By rim count, the remains of five vessels were found.
94. Fig. 227. Dish with curved wall and flat base. Ridge at base of wall.

(a) P223; rim D. 38 cm; base D. 32.5 cm; H. 5.5 cm; fabric 21.
Similar: three profiles, D. 33-4 cm.
(b) P202; rim D. 19 cm; base D.16 cm; H. 3 cm; fabric 22.

Bowls/dishes/cups

By SSC, the remains of six vessels were found.
95. Fig. 227. Dish/lid with thickened rounded rim, thick rounded wall and flat base.
P206; rim D. 36 cm; base D. 24 cm; H. 3 cm; fabric 19.
96. Fig. 227. Dish with thickened, rounded inturned rim, straight flaring wall and flat base.
P226; rim D. 36.5 cm; base D. 28.5 cm; H. 7 cm; fabric 18.
Very burnt on interior of base, exterior of wall and base.
Similar: one base fragment, base D. 24 cm.
Cf. Lugnano in Teverina: Monacchi 1990: fig. 15, nos. 29-30. Luni: *Luni* I: tav. 75, 19 CM1407; *Luni* II: tav. 269, nos. 17, 18 and 21.
97. Fig. 227. Bowl/basin with everted, thickened rim and carinated body, rounded at carination, with slightly rounded lower wall and bevelled ring foot.
P205; rim D. 26 cm; base D. 12 cm; H. 17 cm; fabric 4.
Similar: two base fragments, base D. 10 and 11 cm.
Cf. Ostia: Martin 1992b: fig. 2 (in glazed ware).

Jars

By SSC, the remains of eighteen vessels were found.
98. Fig. 227. Wide-mouthed jar with broad rim angled upwards and slightly rounded wall. Vertical handle(s) with sub-rectangular section, joining immediately below rim.
(a) P233; rim D. 24 cm; fabric 19.
(b) P234; rim D. 11 cm; fabric 20. Burnt on exterior of rim and wall.
Cf. (a-b) Rome: Quilici 1990: fig. 94, nos. 81 and 86.
99. Fig. 227. Jar with everted rim and carinated body with ridged wall and rounded base. Two vertical handles with rectangular section.
P150; rim D. 13 cm; H. *c.* 15 cm; fabric 5.
Cf. Ostia: *Ostia* III: tav. XIX, no. 80. Rome: Carbonara and Messineo 1993: fig. 247, no. 5.; Cianfriglia *et al.* 1990: fig. 46, no. 612.
100. Fig. 228. Jar with thickened, flattened rim, short broad neck and ovoid body with flat base.
(a) P229; rim D. 11 cm; base D. 4 cm; H. *c.* 13.5 cm; fabric 20. Burnt on exterior of wall.
Similar: one base fragment, base D. 4 cm.
(b) (Not illustrated.) P200; rim D. 13 cm; fabric 5.
Similar: nine rim fragments, rim D. 10-14 cm.
Cf. Rome: Carbonara and Messineo 1993: fig. 248, no. 12a.

Cooking pots

By SSC, remains of three vessels were found.
101. Fig. 228. Cooking pot with broad horizontal rim with hooked triangular projection on underside of rim.
P228; rim D. 26 cm; fabric 19.
Two grooves on exterior of wall.
Cf. Luni: *Luni* I: tav. 74, 12 CM2622/1. Ostia: *Ostia* I: tav. XIX, no. 399; *Ostia* III: tav. XVI, no. 49. Rome: Cianfriglia *et al.* 1990: fig. 45, no. 565; Quilici 1990: fig. 94, no. 84. South Etruria survey: Peña 1987: site 6, 598, no. 5.

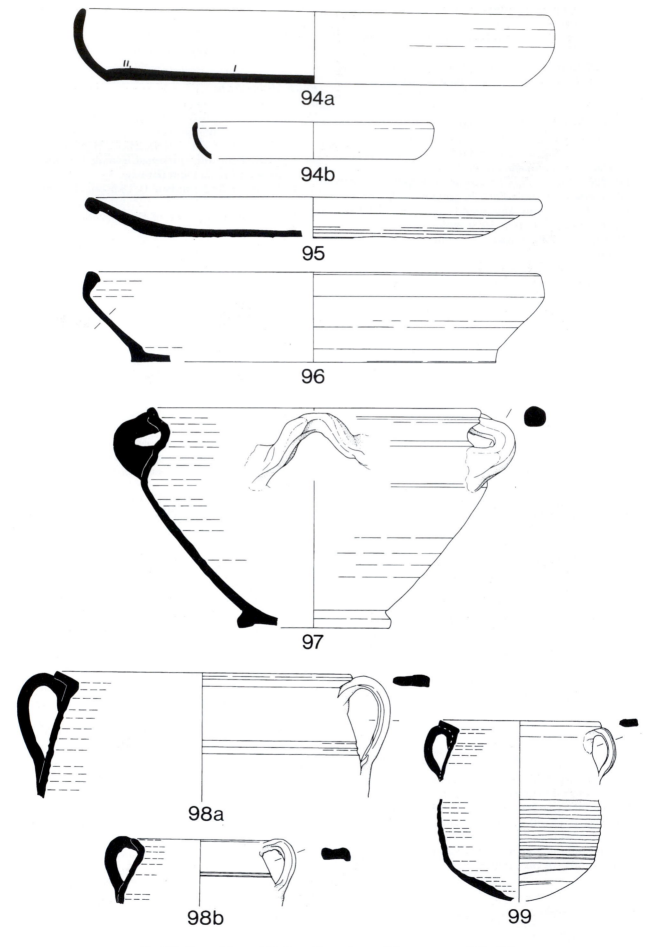

94a

94b

95

96

97

98a

98b

99

Fig. 227. Upper fish-pond fill: Pompeian red ware (94), coarse-ware (1:3). *(SC)*

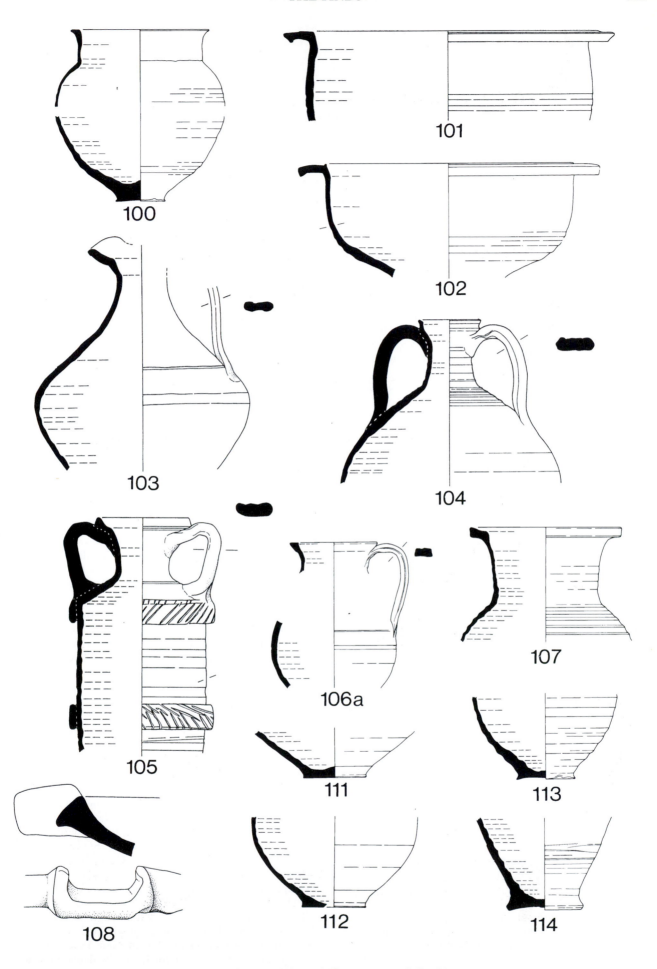

Fig. 228. Upper fish-pond fill: coarse-ware (1:3). *(SC)*

102. Fig. 228. Cooking pot with broad, gently curved rim, with small ridge at inner edge, and carinated body with rounded wall. Series of ridges at carination.
P227; rim D. 24 cm; fabric 18.
Similar: one body sherd, max. D. 20 cm.
Cf. Luni: *Luni* I: tav. 74, 11 CM1008. Santa Rufina: Cotton, Wheeler and Whitehouse 1991: fig. 84, no. 1.

Flagons/jugs
Remains of eleven vessels were found by rim count.
103. Fig. 228. Jug with trefoil rim, tall narrow neck and squat body with rounded wall. Single handle with irregular section.
P163; max. D. 17 cm; fabric 18.
104. Fig. 228. Flagon with everted, cupped rim, short narrow neck and spherical body. Two handles with rectangular section. Series of grooves at base of neck.
P215; rim D. 5 cm; fabric 5.
105. Fig. 228. Flagon with everted thickened rim, short narrow neck, angular shoulder and cylindrical body. Two handles with sub-oval section. Applied horizontal bands of clay at shoulder and on lower part of exterior, decorated with series of diagonal slashes.
P164; rim D. 8 cm; fabric 4.
106. Fig. 228. Flagon/jug with thickened bevelled rim, short wide neck and spherical body. Single handle with rectangular or barley sugar section.
(a) P211; rim D. 7 cm; fabric 7.
    Similar: five rim fragments, rim D. 7-9 cm.
(b) (Not illustrated.) P235; rim D. 8 cm; fabric 5.
107. Fig. 228. Flagon with thickened rectangular rim, tall broad neck and rounded body.
P209; rim D. 12 cm; fabric 5.

Miscellaneous
By SSC, the remains of four vessels were found.
108. Fig. 228. Mortarium with thickened triangular rim, rounded wall and broad pouring spout.
P168; rim D. *c.* 40 cm; fabric 8. Extremely weathered.
109. (Not illustrated.) Bucket with broad rim and straight wall, tapering to flat base. From above, mouth of vessel has oval section.
P224; max. D. 35 cm; fabric 5.
110. (Not illustrated.) 'Amphora stopper'. Vessel with broad angular rim, tall narrow neck and rounded body.
P208; rim D. 6 cm; fabric 5.
Similar: one base fragment.

Lids
By rim count, the remains of two lids were found similar to cat. 57 in Group 1. (Not illustrated.)

Bases
Excluding bases which could be attributed to vessels similar to those above, the remains of twenty bases were found.
111. Fig. 228. Flat base and straight, flaring wall.
P231; base D. 5 cm; fabric 19.
Similar: four base fragments, base D. 4-7 cm.
112. Fig. 228. Flat base and rounded wall.
P232; base D. 5 cm; fabric 18.
Similar: three base fragments, base D. 5-6 cm.
113. Fig. 228. Flat base and rounded, ridged wall.
P214; base D. 4.5 cm; fabric 5.
Similar: seven base fragments, base D. 5-6 cm.

114. Fig. 228. Bevelled ring foot, slightly concave, with steep, straight wall.
P213; base D. 6 cm; fabric 5.
Similar: two base fragments, base D. 6 and 7 cm.

Group 3 – mid to late second-/early third-century comparanda

Unlike previous groups, Group 3 does not constitute an individual deposit, but rather it amalgamates two contexts which seem to be broadly contemporary with Groups 1 or 2. One of these, S10, is from the lowest fill of the rock-cut road. The overwhelming majority of the fine-ware in S10 indicates a second- to early third-century date (Italian sigillata *Consp.* 3; late Italian sigillata; ARS Hayes 3A, 9A, 14B, 23, 196, 197 and 50A (thin early version)). It should be noted that very small quantities of earlier (first century) and later (fourth century) material are also present.

The other context comprises the fill of the north cistern, and contains fine-ware dating to the second or early third century (Eastern sigillata B Hayes 53; ARS 3A, 6B, 9B, 23B, 196, and an unidentified closed form) with some residual material (first centuries BC and AD), a piece of fourth-century glass and a fourth-century coin. The large majority of fine and coarse pottery found in these two contexts, however, mirrors those types found in Groups 1 and 2. Some pieces supplement these forms and are discussed below. (The provenance is given after the fabric notation.)

In addition to the fine-wares listed above, a new form of glazed ware, cat. 115, was noted in S10. Like the examples in Group 1, it seems to be of Italian, and specifically Roman, origin. Colour-coated ware is very common in the contexts which make up Group 3. In addition to numerous examples of types cat. 87 and 90, a large colour-coated cup/beaker, possibly a variant of the *boccalino a collarino*, was noted (cat. 118). Its distinctive, pinched handle is paralleled in Roman productions of glazed ware (Martin 1992b: figs 6, 7 and 9), and thin-walled ware (Carbonara and Messineo 1993: fig. 243, no. 4 and fig. 244, no. 1)

In the coarse-ware, many of the bowl/dish forms found in Groups 1 and 2 are repeated in Group 3, including the Campanian? forms cat. 34 and 95. The large bowl (cat. 119) reflects a tradition seen in Group 2 (cat. 97) which encompassed much of the central Mediterranean. The heavily knobbed rim of cat. 120 is unusual, as is the straight-walled body of cat. 121. The jars from Group 3 contexts add no recognizably new forms to those found in Groups 1 and 2: the majority is variants of the tall-necked, ovoid bodied jars (cat. 36 and 38).

All cooking pots from Group 3 contexts are carinated with a broad rim, the standard type found in Groups 1 and 2. Especially common are variants of types cat. 43, 46 and 48. Cat. 122, with its very thick flanged rim and heavy body, may well be contemporary with the later examples seen in Group 2 (cat. 101 and 102), though the body still retains a sharp carination. Cat. 123, with its finer, hooked rim, seems to be closer to the feel of pieces in Group 1.

Few flagons/jugs in Group 3 differ substantially from examples in Groups 1 and 2. Especially common are ribbed vessels (as cat. 51, 54 and 107). Cat. 124, however, was conspicuous, with its angular carination and unribbed body. Apart from several examples of the so-called amphora stopper (cat. 55), few unclassified forms were found. The large storage jar cat. 125 is noteworthy for its decoration, which recalls that of pre-Roman pottery.

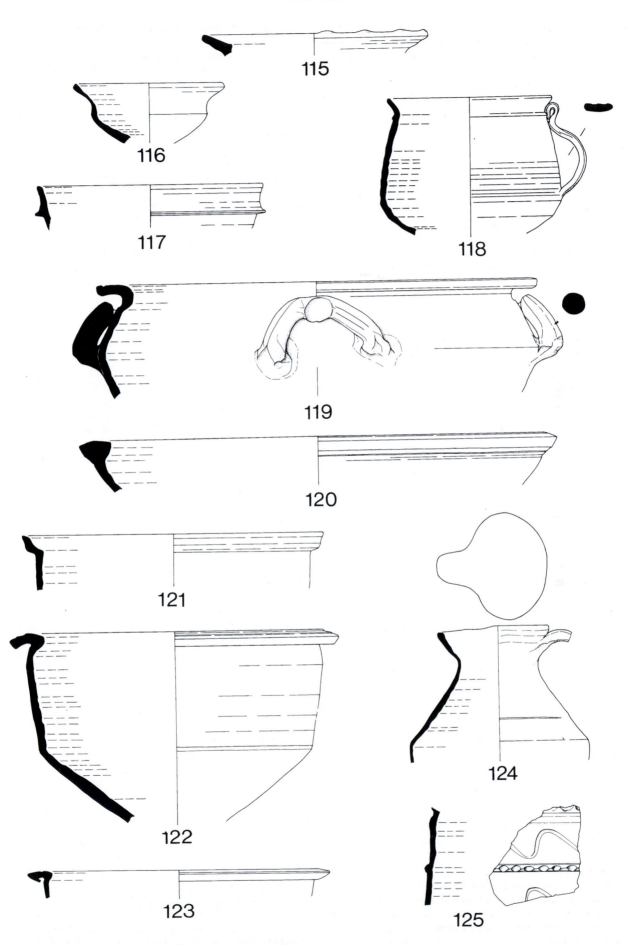

Fig. 229. Comparanda from groups of the mid to late second century: green glazed (115), colour-coated (116-18), coarse-ware (119-25) (1:3). *(SC)*

Green glazed ware

115. Fig. 229. Rim of an open vessel with broad knobbed rim angled upwards.
     P256; rim D. 18 cm; fabric 29. S10.
     Cf. Santa Rufina: Cotton, Wheeler and Whitehouse 1991: fig. 91, no. 10.

Colour-coated ware

116. Fig. 229. Cup/bowl with flaring, thickened rim and carinated body.
     P261; rim D. 12 cm; fabric 7. Cistern.
117. Fig. 229. Bowl with straight rim and small, stubby flange.
     P262; rim D. 18 cm; fabric 6. Cistern.
118. Fig. 229. Cup/beaker with everted rim underlined by ridge or 'collar', deep carinated body with rounded wall. Single 'pinched' handle with narrow sub-rectangular section. Series of shallow ridges/grooves above carination.
     P368; rim D.13 cm; fabric 4. Cistern.

Bowls/dishes/cups

119. Fig. 229. Bowl with broad horizontal rim and rounded wall. Single horizontal handle with round section pressed onto wall. Groove at outer edge of rim.
     P253; rim D. 35 cm; fabric 19. S10.
120. Fig. 229. Bowl with thickened, bevelled rim and rounded wall.
     P264; rim D. 38 cm; fabric 4. Cistern.
121. Fig. 229. Bowl with everted, angular rim cupped on interior, and straight, vertical wall.
     P265; rim D. 24 cm; fabric 8. Cistern.
     Cf. Santa Rufina: Cotton, Wheeler and Whitehouse 1991: fig. 83, no. 8.

Cooking pots

122. Fig. 229. Cooking pot with broad, curved rim, ridged on upper surface and carinated body with straight, thick walls.
     P266; rim D. 26 cm; fabric 18. Cistern.
     Cf. Santa Rufina: Cotton, Wheeler and Whitehouse 1991: fig. 84, no. 1.
123. Fig. 229. Cooking pot with horizontal rim, sharply hooked on underside and straight wall.
     P267; rim D. 24 cm; fabric 19. Cistern.
     Cf. Ostia: *Ostia* III: tav. XIX, no. 85. South Etruria survey: Peña 1987: site 6, 598, no. 9; site 9, 610, no. 7.

Flagons/jugs

124. Fig. 229. Trefoil jug with tall flaring rim and tall conical upper body. Single handle.
     P268; max. D. 9 cm; fabric 4. Cistern.

Miscellaneous

125. Fig. 229. Sherd from base of large closed vessel (storage jar?). Decoration consists of applied cordons bearing finger indentations, separating broad bands containing single incised wavy lines.
     P255; fabric 20. S10.
     Cf. South Etruria survey: Peña 1987: site 13, 624, no. 3.

Group 4 – fourth-century context (M87)

This small but significant group comprises the only recognizable sealed body of fourth-century material from the site. The ARS piece cat. 126 suggests a date for the group in the middle of the fourth century, an idea strengthened by the dissimilarity of the associated coarse-wares to earlier or later assemblages. The good state of preservation of the ARS bowl cat. 126 argues against its being residual. This seems reinforced by the absence of characteristic ARS forms such as Hayes 61B and 67, which are found in contexts of the third quarter of the fourth century and later (Table 60).

In the coarse-ware the forms seem to have developed from types found in earlier groups, though the degree of evolution has been considerable, as may be seen, for example, in the rims of jars and cooking pots. Many rim variants which were common in earlier periods disappear, and generally the impression is one of a smaller range of forms, often displaying a markedly reduced potting skill. The fabrics of the Group 4 pieces, which are uniformly heavier and coarser than those in earlier groups, contain volcanic inclusions which seem to rule out a very local manufacture, suggesting, instead, fairly distant centres of production.

The only diagnostic dish/bowl cat. 127 was similar in form to a piece from Group 2 (cat. 97) of over a century earlier. However, the grooves around the rim seem a late Roman feature (see also cat. 165 in Group 7). Jar forms seem to have simplified considerably in the later Empire, with plain, everted rims and oval bodies replacing the much broader range of types seen in Groups 1 and 2 (above).

All cooking pots found in Group 4 are still of the carinated casserole type, giving a useful *terminus post quem* for the appearance of the tub-shaped variety seen in Groups 5 (cat. 137-8) and 7 (cat. 170-4). However, the flanges of the Group 4 casseroles are much heavier than in previous periods, with thickened and ridged profiles, possibly the forerunners of later forms (Group 7, cat. 177-80).

African red slip ware

126. Fig. 230. Bowl with straight, steep wall, broad rim with flattened extremity and small, low ring foot. Hayes 52B (large variety), *c.* 280/300 to late fourth century. Appliqué on rim; seated animal (boar? lion?).
     P299; rim D. 21 cm; base D. 5.5 cm; H. 5.5 cm; fabric t.s.c. 'C'.

Dishes/bowls/cups

127. Fig. 230. Dish/bowl with upright, thickened rim and tapering body with straight wall. Three deep grooves on exterior of rim.
     P295; rim D. 30 cm; fabric 23.
     Cf. Ostia: *Ostia* IV: tav. LII, no. 419.

Jars

128. Fig. 230. Jar with tall everted rim and broad rounded body.
     P292; rim D. 12 cm; fabric 25.
129. Fig. 230. Jar with thickened everted rim and tall, narrow neck. One or more handles.
     P297; rim D. 10.5 cm; fabric 27.

Cooking pots

130. Fig. 230. Cooking pot with broad rim, thickened heavily on underside, and grooved upper surface.

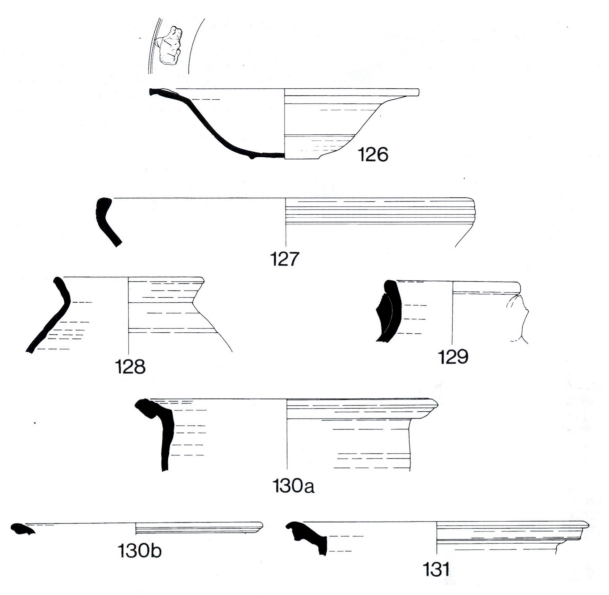

Fig. 230. Fourth-century group: African red slip ware (126), coarse-ware (127-31) (1:3). *(SC)*

(a) P293; rim D. 24 cm; fabric 23.

(b) P296; rim D. 20 cm; fabric 23.

131. Fig. 230. Cooking pot with broad rim, thickened and flattened with small hooked protrusion at extremity. P294; rim D. 24 cm; fabric 26.

Group 5 – 'Justinianic' contexts

Group 5 comprises material from two contexts (D48 and D52) associated with destruction levels, in particular roof collapse. Numerous joins between sherds from the two levels suggest that they were contemporary. Two coins of Justinian and one of Totila were found in D52, giving a *terminus post quem* of the mid-sixth century for the contexts. It seems likely, however, that the pottery is a little earlier – certainly the ARS piece cat. 132 should not long post-date the 520s. Indeed, the ARS bowl cat. 132 is one of the latest recognizable imports to the site.

With regard to the coarse-ware, it should be stressed that the typological developments of late Roman coarse pottery

in and around Rome are far from well-documented; future research will, it is hoped, sharpen the chronology of this and following groups (6, 7 and 8).

The coarse-ware shows uniformity of fabric with material from earlier contexts, but considerable differences in form. In the bowls the irregular body of cat. 133, and its apparent use in cooking, set it apart from vessels of similar size from earlier groups, as does the straight wall and heavily knobbed rim of cat. 134. Of the jars/flagons, cat. 135 is perhaps the 'local amphora' type more completely represented in Group 6 (cat. 146). Cat. 136 is distinctive for its minimal neck and rim.

Cooking pots are one of the more significant classes in Group 5, with the appearance of the tub-shaped cooking pot cat. 137a-b. This provides a useful *terminus ante quem* of the early sixth century for the introduction of tub-shaped form, a date that would fit with the presence of variants of the form in the Forum Cistern group at Cosa (Dyson 1976: FC20-21). Similarly, the complete absence from Group 5 of the carinated variety of cooking pot, standard in all earlier deposits, and one of the most characteristic forms of coarse-

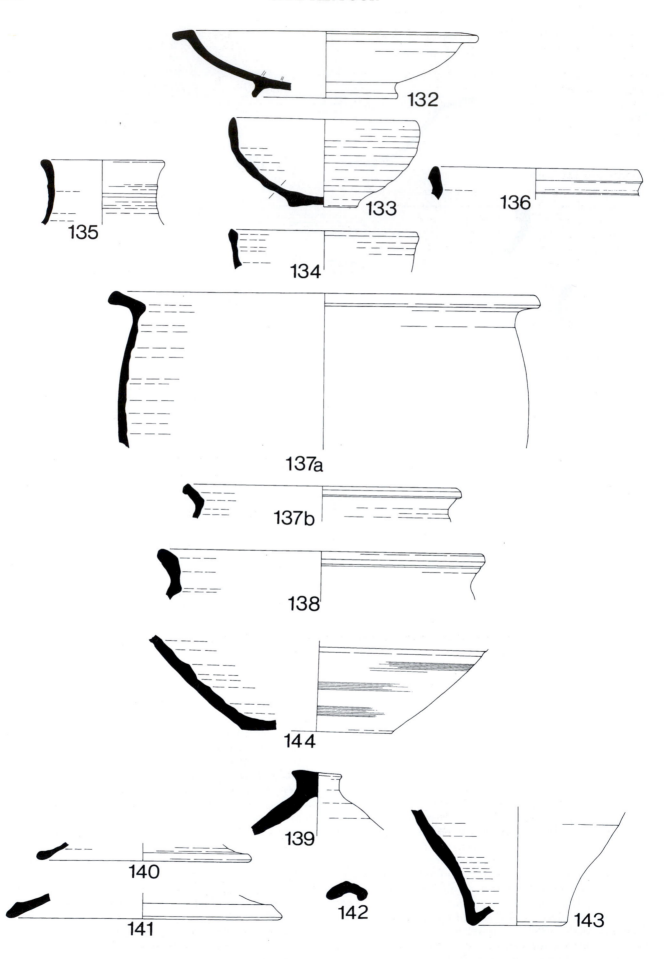

Fig. 231. Sixth-century contexts: African red slip ware (132), coarse-ware (133-43) (1:3). *(SC)*

ware in the Roman period in Italy, suggests wide-scale changes in the ceramic tradition.

The sharply folded handle cat. 142, quite unlike handles from earlier groups, seems to be a late Roman feature. A very similar piece (cat. 184) was found in another late Roman context (Group 7, below). The rilling (groups of fine grooves/striations) seen on cat. 144 also seems to be a standard late Roman technique.

African red slip ware
132. Fig. 231. Bowl with flat rim rounded on underside, broad shallow body with rounded wall and flaring ring foot. Hayes 93, late fifth to first quarter of sixth centuries AD.
P324; rim D. 24 cm; base D. 12 cm; H. 5 cm; fabric t.s.c. 'D'. D48.

Bowls/dishes/cups
133. Fig. 231. Bowl with vertical rim, irregular rounded wall and thick, flat base, slightly hollowed on underside. Numerous irregular ridges/grooves on exterior.
P317; rim D. 15 cm; base D. 5.5 cm; H. 6.5 cm; fabric 23. D52.
134. Fig. 231. Bowl with thickened, bevelled rim and vertical wall.
P329; rim D. 15 cm; fabric 23. D48.

Jars
135. Fig. 231. Jar/flagon with thickened, rounded rim and tall, broad neck.
P322; rim D. 10 cm; fabric 24. D52.
136. Fig. 231. Jar with small vertical rim and bevelled outer edge.
P319; rim D. 17 cm; fabric 24. D52.

Cooking pots
137. Fig. 231. Cooking pot with rectangular-sectioned rim, angled upwards, broad deep body with rounded wall and flat base.
(a) Bands of fine rilling on exterior.
P316; rim D. 34 cm; fabric 24. D52.
(b) P318; rim D. 22 cm; fabric 23. D52.
138. Fig. 231. Cooking pot with everted thickened rim, small rounded spur at base of rim on interior.
P328; rim D. 26 cm; fabric 26. D48.

Lids
139. Fig. 231. Knob of lid with conical body.
P327; knob D. 4 cm; fabric 27. D52.
140. Fig. 231. Lid with thickened, rounded rim and conical body.
P320; rim D. 17 cm; fabric 23. D52.
141. Fig. 231. Lid with thickened, triangular-sectioned rim.
P321; rim D. 22 cm; fabric 25. D52.

Miscellaneous
142. Fig. 231. Handle of closed form with rounded right-angled section.
P326; fabric 24. D52.

Bases
143. Fig. 231. Base of closed form (flagon/jug?) with rounded ring foot, central *omphalos* and rounded wall.
P323; base D. 8 cm; fabric 9. D52.
144. Fig. 231. Base with slightly rounded underside and straight wall.
P325; base D. 12 cm; fabric 27. D52.

Group 6 – context D86 (baptistery pit)

Group 6 comprises the material from a pit which, in terms of its stratigraphy, must post-date the contexts which make up Group 5. Given the dating of that group (early sixth century, probably pre-dating the 530s AD) and the slightly unusual nature of the material in Group 6, a date for the pottery (if not necessarily the date of its final deposition) in the mid-sixth century seems appropriate.

Cat. 145 with its heavy triangular rim, unique on the site, is the only dish/bowl found in the deposit. The jar/flagon cat. 146 may have been intended for short-distance transport as well as storage, in effect one of the last Roman amphora types seen on site. Ribbing as on cat. 146, when used on non-levigated pottery, seems almost exclusively a late Roman feature.

The jar (/cooking pot?) cat. 147 is unparalleled, and shows the advent of forms which blurred traditional distinctions. The body, with its wide mouth, is very unusual, while the base, burnished and noticeably convex, is solidly in the very late Antique tradition. Both cat. 146 and 147, however, are in the same heavy, volcanic fabric that was predominant on the site from the mid-fourth century, indicating some continuity of supply.

The cooking pots cat. 148 and 149 show some affinities with the tub-shaped form, though with considerable differences in the rim. I would suggest that they mark a development of the form into a hybrid jar/cooking pot such as cat. 147. The lids cat. 152a-b seem to share the same broad tradition.

Bowls/dishes/cups
145. Fig. 232. Bowl with squared rim, angled inwards and straight wall.
P340; rim D. 27 cm; fabric 27.

Jars
146. Fig. 232. Jar/flagon with thickened rounded rim, tall broad neck and ovoid body. Single handle. Deep, broad grooves on most of body.
P331; rim D. 12 cm; fabric 23.
147. Fig. 232. Jar/cooking pot with thickened, rounded rim, wide mouth, broad deep ovoid body and uneven, slightly rounded base.
P332; rim D. 27 cm; base D. 10.5 cm; H. 24 cm; fabric 23.

Cooking pots
148. Fig. 233. Cooking pot with thickened overhanging triangular rim and rounded carinated body, tapering towards flat base.
P335; rim D. 25 cm; base D. 10 cm; H. 19 cm; fabric 28.
Two uneven grooves below rim on exterior.
Cf. Santa Rufina: Cotton, Wheeler and Whitehouse 1991: fig. 86, no. 28.

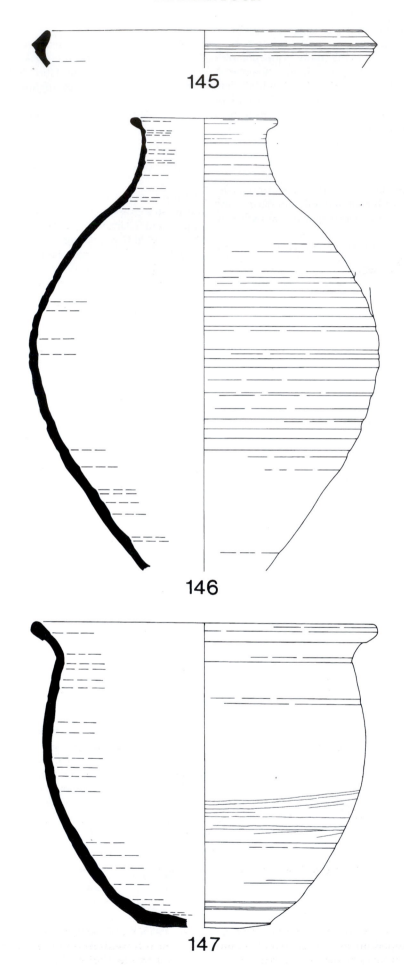

145

146

147

Fig. 232. Pit D86 (sixth century): coarse-ware (1:3). *(SC)*

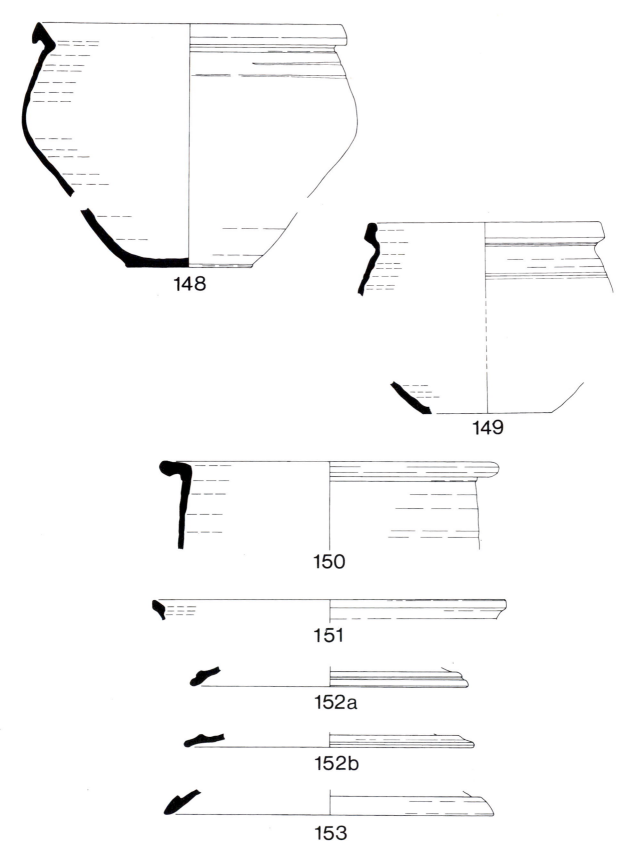

Fig. 233. Pit D86 (sixth century): coarse-ware (1:3). *(SC)*

149. Fig. 233. Cooking pot with offset right-angled-sec-
tioned rim with cupped interior, squat rounded body
and flat base. Two grooves below rim on exterior.
P336; rim D. 19 cm; base D. 10.5 cm; H. 15 cm; fabric 23.

150. Fig. 233. Cooking pot with thickened horizontal rim,
heavily rounded on underside and straight wall. Ridge
on exterior below rim.
P333; rim D. 27 cm; fabric 23.

172. Fig. 235. Cooking pot with rectangular-sectioned rim and rounded wall.
     P274; rim D. 20 cm; fabric 24. E69.
173. Fig. 235. Cooking pot with offset, rounded, thickened rim, cupped on interior and sharp ridge at base.
     P278; rim D. 22 cm; fabric 24. L157.
174. Fig. 235. Cooking pot with tall, everted, rounded rim, ridge at base of rim on interior.
     P305; rim D. 25 cm; fabric 24. K101.
175. Fig. 236. Cooking pot with broad curved rim and straight wall.
     P307; rim D. 34.5 cm; fabric 26. M74.
176. Fig. 236. Cooking pot with everted rim, thickened on underside.
     P286; rim D. 33 cm; fabric 26. M144.
177. Fig. 236. Cooking pot with everted thickened rim, rounded and overhanging on underside.
     P283; rim D. 26 cm; fabric 27. M138.
178. Fig. 236. Cooking pot with everted thickened rim with ridge on underside.
(a) P362; rim D. 26 cm; fabric 27. A12.
     Cf. Rieti field survey: pers. obs.
(b) P301; rim D. 24 cm; fabric 24. K103.
179. Fig. 236. Cooking pot with tall everted rim, hooked at extremity and cupped on interior. Outward flaring wall.
     P281; rim D. 20 cm; fabric 23. M143.
180. Fig. 236. Cooking pot with thickened everted triangular rim with curved/cupped upper surface and sharp ridge at base of exterior. Straight vertical wall.
(a) P400; rim D. 24 cm; fabric 27. M166.
     Cf. Rome: Staffa 1986: fig. 398, no. 194; fig. 399, nos. 201-2.
(b) P287; rim D. 27 cm; fabric 28. M144.
     Cf. Rome: Gianicolo, pers. obs.

Lids

181. Fig. 236. Lid with rounded, upturned rim. Rounded projection on upper surface.
     P304; rim D. 22 cm; fabric 25. K101.
     Cf. Santa Rufina: Cotton, Wheeler and Whitehouse 1991: fig. 87, no. 14.
182. Fig. 236. Lid with thickened round rim and conical body with thick rounded wall.
     P330; rim D. 24 cm; fabric 23. K102.

Miscellaneous

183. Fig. 236. Neck/spout of vessel with tall, thin neck and broad body.
     P300; rim D. 4 cm; fabric 23. M105.
     Single continuous spiral of cogged decoration around neck.
184. Fig. 236. Handle of closed vessel (jar/flagon) with right-angled section.
     P346; fabric 23. D247.
185. Fig. 236. Base of vessel (jar/cooking pot?) with slightly rounded underside and steep wall. Uneven burnishing on underside only.
     P348; base D. 11 cm; fabric 23. E160.

Group 8 – burials

Though the smallest of the eight groups presented here, Group 8 none the less is of considerable importance in the light that it sheds on developments in and around the site. Cat. 186 has been dated by Arthur (pers. comm.) to the mid-later fifth century, a date span with which I broadly agree, perhaps extending it into the early sixth century, given the similarities in fabric and form with pieces from Groups 5 and 6. On the basis of its profile alone the vessel would probably be seen as a drinking vessel. However, the presence of burning, if not caused by a ritual associated with the burial, seems to indicate that it was used in cooking. If so, it represents a form and size unparalleled in other cooking vessels from the site, and may be indicative of increasing changes in traditional vessel forms.

The context of cat. 187 has produced a calibrated radiocarbon date of AD 565-635, making it one of the latest identifiable pieces from the Roman period on the site. As a whole, the vessel, with regard to its diagnostic features, is still recognizably Roman, though it is interesting to note that its fabric, to the naked eye, has more in common with the levigated fabrics seen in the late eighth-century kiln deposit from the site (Patterson, this volume). However, as stated above, the piece appears to be a singleton, and there is no ceramic evidence for any occupation of the site on any noticeable scale between the late sixth and late eighth centuries.

The pottery vessels were retrieved intact from burial contexts. (The provenance is given after the fabric notation.)

186. Fig. 237. Jar with thickened, rounded rim, slightly concave on interior, tall narrow neck and dumpy body with flat base. Single handle with sub-rectangular section. Single groove at base of neck.
     P360; rim D. 5 cm; base D. 4.5 cm; H. 10.5 cm; fabric 23. B26; burial no. 106. Slightly burnt on underside of base and on wall near handle.

187. Figs 237 and 238. Jar with short, straight everted rim, short neck and broad rounded body. Single handle with oval section.
     P402; rim D. 8.5 cm; base D. 6 cm; H. 7.5 cm; fabric: light yellowish brown clay with black (volcanic?) inclusions. D168, burial no. 59.

THE STORK-VASE, by Oswyn Murray, Paul Roberts and Peter Parsons[74]

THE VESSEL (FIGS 239 AND 240), by Paul Roberts

Form

When reconstructed, the vessel proved to be a tall, narrow beaker with a low base and shallow ring foot. The tapering lower wall broadens at the approximate mid-point of the vessel to become almost cylindrical. The rim is thickened and folded-over with two protrusions of rounded section on the exterior. Two holes had been drilled or punched di-

---

[74] This is substantially the same text as printed in *Papers of the British School at Rome* 59 (1991); 177-95.

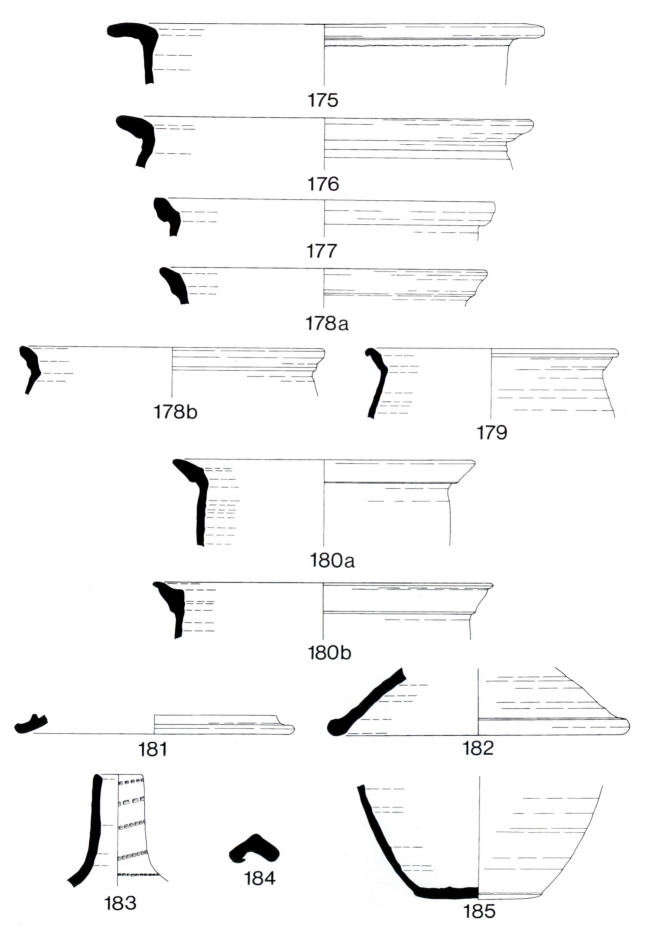

Fig. 236. Late Roman comparanda, various contexts: coarse-ware (1:3). *(SC)*

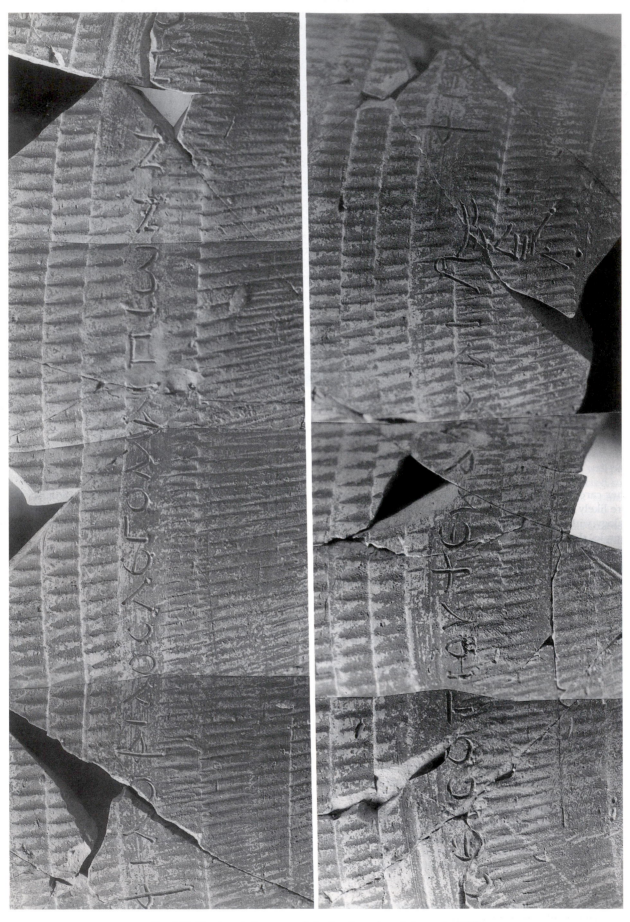

Fig. 242. The inscription around the 'stork-vase', and the stork. *(KW)*

The fabric, colour-coated finish, decoration and inscription of the 'stork-vase' imply strongly that it was a piece of table-ware, designed to be used for the consumption of a liquid. However, the size of the vessel raises some problems. With an estimated capacity of *c.* 1.25 litres, it held, when full, a far greater volume of liquid than the average cup or bowl. There is the possibility, therefore, that it was used either in the stage before drinking, for example in the mixing of wine and water, (though its tall, narrow form makes this less likely), or that it was intended to be used from one filling by more than one person.

The pair of holes below the rim suggest that the vase could have been suspended, either for display or storage. Vessels bearing suspension holes are not uncommon in pre-Roman and early Roman Italy.[78] Suspended vessels are also depicted in the stucco decoration of at least one Etruscan tomb.[79] If our vessel had ever been suspended for display, it would have been quite striking, and one of its presumably more significant features, the stork, could have faced outwards.

There must be some doubt, however, as to whether the vase was ever used in any capacity, since it is badly misfired. It was, in effect, a waster. The warping and fissures would have rendered the vase quite unusable for the consumption of liquids, and would have made it, at best, an ornamental piece. Indeed, the vessel's unusable state is very important, since it opens up the possibility of local manufacture (cf. further, Roberts, this volume).

THE INSCRIPTION, by Oswyn Murray

The most remarkable feature of the vessel is the inscription (Fig. 242), which runs around the body about two-thirds of the way down on a band apparently smoothed with the thumb after the decorative striations had been made. The inscription was incised before firing, and was carefully planned to fit the space available; beginning with the first word, it runs around the vase with a slight downward fall, ending up one decorative band (approximately 10 mm) lower than the starting point. The representation of the 'stork' is on this

lower level, and does not quite fill the remaining space. The bird was therefore drawn after the inscription, but not apparently as an infill or afterthought, since it is not centrally placed, but slightly nearer to the end of the line than to its beginning. Thus the writer seems to have planned both inscription and drawing together, after the decoration had been applied, and to have inscribed them in that order.

Φιλόφιλος λέγομαι · πιὼν ν[ο]ήσεις ὅτι
οὐ ψεύδομαι

I am called a friend of friends; when you drink you will understand that I do not deceive.

The script is not documentary, but an elegant literary or semi-literary hand. The inscription might loosely be described as rhythmic, though not metrical. It is divided into two equal cola of nine syllables; at the central point after πιών there is a small gap, and the initial N of the next word appears slightly larger, as if the writer wished to mark something – clearly not a pause in the sense, but perhaps the rhythmic centre of the line. The inscription as a whole gives the impression of a carefully designed and executed sentiment, created for its position and for the function of the vase by an author of some literary skill and sophistication.

Φιλόφιλος is in literary texts an unusual word, found primarily in philosophical discussions of Φιλία: for instance, Aristotle, *Ethica Nicomachea* viii. 1155a29-30: 'τοὺς γὰρ φιλοφί–λους ἐπαινοῦμεν, ἥ τε πολυφιλία δοκεῖ τῶν καλῶν ἕν τι εἶναι' ('for we praise those who love their friends, and it is thought to be a fine thing to have many friends').[80] But it is not a specialized philosophical word: it is found in Polybius (i. 14.4) and Philodemus (*peri Parrhesias* ed. Olivieri F 50, 85); and its formation is discussed by Eustathius (*ad Iliadem* i. 690). A number of funerary stelai from Egypt, mainly of Roman Imperial date, show that it was in common use along with other φίλος compounds as a laudatory epithet of the dead, being presumably especially appropriate to those who lacked close ties of kinship.[81] It is also found in astrological texts of the Imperial age, in contexts where φίλος compounds and virtues are listed.[82] In general these uses suggest a non-literary word especially appropriate to contexts involving a series of φίλος compounds, but rarer in isolation.

Otherwise the language is unexceptional, and the form of the sentiment shows a number of characteristics found in inscriptions on drinking vessels from a wide range of periods in the Graeco-Roman world. We may note the following.

[78] For example, chalices, dishes and bowls from Etruscan tombs at Cerveteri; see Bosio and Pugnetti (1984: 52, 58-9). For drinking vessels from Samnite tombs near Gildone in Molise, see Macchiarola (1989: 62, 66).

[79] The end wall of the 'Tomba dei Rilievi', Cerveteri, features, amongst other objects moulded in stucco, a kylix suspended by its handle and a large dish suspended seemingly by a cord or thong. A pilaster in the same tomb features another kylix and a large jug-like vessel (Moretti 1978: 24-5).

[80] See also Aristotle, *Ethica Nicomachea* viii. 1159a33-4; *Rhetorica* ii. 1381b27; 1389a35; *De virtutibus et vitiis* 1250b32; 35; 1251b35.

[81] Dain 1933: 174 (Ptolemaic); *SEG* 30 (1980) nos. 1764 and 1769 (= *Arch. Pap.* 5 (1913), 167 no. 20); 35 (1985), nos. 1657 and 1668; the popular nature of the context is shown by the occasional substitution of π for φ These examples show that Michael was certainly correct to emend φιλόσοφος to φιλόφιλος in Plutarch, *Consolatio ad Apollonium* 120a. φιλοφίλου also appears on a stele from Thera (? third-fourth centuries AD), where it is probably the usual funerary epithet of the deceased rather than a patronymic (registered among the *dubia* by Fraser and. Matthews (1987: *s.v.*); Mrs Matthews informs me that the archive holds a possible fragmentary example of the name: Φι]λοφίλου, *Inschriften von Ephesos* no. 20 B 22 (54-9 AD)).

[82] Vettius Valens, *Anthologiae* (ed. D. Pingree, 1986) i. 2.56; i. 19.19; i. 20.27; cf. appendix I pp. 387.4; 411.8; see also *Catalogus Codicum Astrologorum* vii.205.

– Π with the top projecting either side.
– Υ in the V-shape.

Most of the forms could be paralleled in such calligraphic scripts as the 'Roman Uncial' (exemplified in the Hawara Homer – Turner 1971: no. 13; 1987: no. 13). But here, of course, the execution is much less formal and consistent, and parallels for the overall effect lie within Turner's category of 'informal round hands' (Turner 1987: 21). It is especially interesting to compare two examples of script incised on wax, which palaeographers have dated to the same general period as the Monte Gelato vessel. Firstly, there is a tablet in Berlin which copies an epigram of Posidippus (Schubart 1911: no. 17): the beginning is in a script rather like ours, with literary pretensions though not fully controlled, the end degenerates rapidly into cursive. Secondly, a tablet in the British Library (Turner 1987: no. 4) gives a moral maxim in an elegant bilinear script, and two attempts to copy it, no doubt by a schoolboy. The Monte Gelato scribe comes much closer to the copperplate of the master than to the gawky, tottering efforts of the pupil.

Whoever inscribed the vessel, then, had a good model in mind, and did the work carefully. That has its interest in assessing the character of the estate and its employees. It has also a wider interest for the question, how far the Greek diaspora of the Empire maintained a cultural unity. Palaeographers debate whether different areas practised different sorts of script. For documentary hands there is indeed some evidence of local peculiarities (Turner 1987: 17). For literary hands, the evidence itself (apart from the Herculaneum Library) is minimal. The Monte Gelato text adds interestingly to that evidence, and speaks for uniformity: I can see nothing in the script that would be surprising in Graeco-Egyptian manuscripts of the same period.

THE EARLY MEDIEVAL AND MEDIEVAL POTTERY, by Helen Patterson

INTRODUCTION

The early medieval and medieval ceramic sequence from the main site at Monte Gelato dates from the late eighth century, with the rebuilding of the church of the *domusculta*, until the abandonment of the site around the late eleventh to early twelfth centuries. Although there is slight evidence to suggest that some frequentation of the site could have occurred in the transition phase between the late Roman and early medieval periods, there appears to be a virtual gap in the ceramic sequence between the latest identifiable deposits of the mid-sixth century and the late eighth century. The seventh-century ceramic types recently identified at the Crypta Balbi, Rome, for example, do not appear to be represented in the Monte Gelato

deposits. The only exception is one vessel of probable sixth- to mid-seventh-century date, recovered from a tomb (Roberts, cat. 187). Similar vessels have been found in cemeteries in central-southern Italy, and are generally dated on the basis of associated metalwork and coins to this period (Peduto 1984; Salvatore 1982; 1983): a later sixth- to seventh-century date for the Monte Gelato vessel is further supported by radiocarbon dating.

In general, the evidence from Monte Gelato in fact conforms with the picture emerging elsewhere in the Roman Campagna, where there is a hiatus in the ceramic sequence, and in many cases the settlement evidence, from sometime in the early sixth century until the late eighth century. From the late eighth century, contemporary with the ecclesiastical reorganization of the Campagna, we witness an economic revival, a characteristic element of which is the emergence of a distinctive local ceramic tradition whose wares are common to both the urban centre and rural sites.

The material from Monte Gelato is of particular interest, however, because of the discovery of a small pottery kiln and related kiln dumps. In operation from the first phase of the early medieval settlement, in the late eighth century, until the mid to late ninth century, the kiln produced a range of domestic pottery, probably including some with painted decoration, in a refined fabric. Despite the presence of sporadic wasters recorded from both Rome and sites such as Pianabella (Ostia Antica),[95] this is the first pottery kiln of early medieval date to be identified in the area of Rome. The vessel forms are identical or very similar to those in use in Rome and the Roman Campagna during this period: however, the analysis of the material from the Monte Gelato dumps offers us a valuable opportunity to study the ceramic evidence, the range of forms and their relative proportions, from a production site and therefore in terms of production rather than as a reflection of consumption patterns.

The ceramic sequence and the nature of the assemblage

The sample derives from a series of often mixed deposits. There are few independent dating elements and the pottery is largely dated on the basis of parallels with material from other excavations, in particular with that of the Crypta Balbi, Rome (Bonifay, Paroli and Picon 1986; Manacorda *et al.* 1986; Saguì and Paroli 1990; Cipriano *et al.* 1991; Ceci 1992; Paroli 1992a; Romei 1992), which has established a datable typological sequence for the early medieval and medieval wares which is supported and confirmed by other

---

[95] For example, in Rome wasters of forum ware have been recorded from excavations in the Roman forum and at the Crypta Balbi (Whitehouse 1980: 186; Romei 1992: 382-3), while a waster of a ninth-century amphora was recovered from the vaults of Santa Maria in Cosmedin (Giovenale 1927: pl. Xla; Mazzucato 1977: fig. 70; Whitehouse 1980: 139). Outside Rome, a waster of ninth-century forum ware was recovered from excavations at Pianabella (Ostia Antica) (Patterson 1992).

Table 62. Late eighth- to early ninth-century kiln dumps: percentages of ceramic classes based on the number of fragments (A) and on sherd weight (B).

TRENCH	domestic pottery		(of which wasters)		painted pottery		kitchen-ware		Roman residual	
	A	B	A	B	A	B	A	B	A	B
E	99.5	99.6	0.2	0.2	0	0	0.1	0.1	0.4	0.3
M	96.7	94.5	0.9	0.5	0.4	1.0	2.3	3.1	0.6	1.4
D	98.6	99.0	0.1	0.1	0.7	0.4	0.6	0.4	0.1	0.2

Table 63. Quantification of vessel forms by typological group from the kiln dumps.

form	group	rim count		EVEs (trenches D and M only)
		no. of rims	% of no. of rims	
closed	1a	155	66.8	621%
	1b	15	6.5	-
	2	20	8.6	63%
	3	6	2.6	12%
	4	30	13.0	13%
	5	1	0.4	3%
	TOTAL	227	97.9	734%
open	TOTAL	4	1.7	10%

excavations in Rome itself, its ports, and the Roman Campagna.

The stratigraphy relating to the early medieval and medieval occupation of the site appears to have been heavily disturbed. Few late eighth- and ninth-century deposits had remained in situ, because of later activity on the site, and the large ceramic deposits recovered from the tenth- to eleventh-century phases (in particular from areas D and M) include a significant and often overwhelming amount of residual domestic pottery, including some wasters. In fact, in most deposits domestic pottery represents over 70 per cent of the assemblage. Presumably the kiln dumps originally deposited during the late eighth and ninth centuries were, at a later stage, removed in order to clear certain areas; certainly in some cases they appear to have been used for levelling surfaces prior to laying down floors. This frequent redeposition of the dumps from the kiln also accounts for the fragmentary state of the pottery and the lack of reconstructable pieces.

Quantification

As noted above, one of the most interesting aspects of the pottery from Monte Gelato is that it permits us to examine the material from a production site. However, the fragmentary nature of the sample and the fact that the majority was not found in situ, but was redeposited at a later date, is problematic. In order to achieve a valid assessment of the range of wares produced, it was decided to include in the type series material from the redeposited kiln dumps which, on the basis of parallels elsewhere, can be securely dated to the late eighth to early ninth centuries. In terms of quantification and in particular an estimate of the relative proportions of the vessel types produced at the kiln site, three large deposits were selected. The first, contexts E9 and E36, are two of the few kiln deposits to be found in situ, comprising the fill of the kiln itself and a dump from the kiln (1,041 sherds: 15.975 kg). The two other sets of kiln dumps examined were both redeposited at a later date. The first comprises a series of tips from Trench M (contexts 2, 4, 7, 11, 12, 14, 17, 19, 20, 21) which contains solely diagnostic material of the late eighth and ninth centuries (2,992 sherds: 37.382 kg); and the second is a large deposit from Trench D (D219) which, although it includes sporadic material of the later tenth and eleventh centuries, is worthy of note simply for the quantity of material, the overwhelming majority of which is of late eighth- to ninth-century date (3,381 sherds: 65.154 kg).

Table 62 gives the relative proportions of the ceramic classes represented in the selected kiln dumps, based on both sherd count and weight. Table 63 gives the relative proportions of the domestic pottery types (according to typological group) on the basis of rim count and, for the larger deposits from Trenches M and D, using the estimated vessel equivalent or EVEs method, as developed by Orton

The kitchen-ware jars of the tenth century onwards are typical of those found in Rome and on sites in the Roman Campagna: they are limited to one main form, which undergoes a gradual evolution (see, for example, Ricci (1986: tavv. XI-XIII) and Patterson (1991: fig. 24, nos. 6-20)). This is a globular vessel with a flat base and two strap handles attached at the rim and extending to the widest point of the body. Unlike the domestic pottery, the bases of the kitchen-ware vessels are not wire-cut.

Testi or baking covers first appear in post-*domus-culta* contexts and comprise *c.* 50 per cent of the kitchen-ware assemblage. (For a description of the history and function of these vessels, see Cubberley, Lloyd and Roberts (1988) and Patterson (1991).) The fabric of the *testi* is noticeably coarser than that of the jars; this is a common phenomenon in both Roman and medieval assemblages (Ricci 1986: 537; Cubberley, Lloyd and Roberts 1988: 106; Patterson 1991: 122), and presumably was the result of a deliberate attempt by the potters to increase the refactory properties of the clay. They are generally wide-mouthed vessels with flaring walls; in terms of diameter, the *testi* fall into two main groups, the first, and by far the larger group, ranging from 30 to 35 cm, the second, from 19 to 25 cm. Of the *testi* present in these contexts, some chronological distinctions can be made on the basis of datable parallels elsewhere (see, for example, for the Crypta Balbi, Rome, Ricci (1986: tav. XI-XIII); for Santa Cornelia, Patterson (1991: fig. 25)). The examples with thick walls and thickened rims (cat. 116-19) are probably of the later ninth to tenth centuries, the fabric of these vessels being noticeably coarse. The *testi* with thinner walls and a more refined fabric (cat. 120-2) are probably of the late tenth to eleventh centuries, and have the beginnings of the downturned lip which characterizes the later examples of this form. The latest *testi* form has a prominent vertical lip (cat. 123): similar forms are dated both at Rome and at Santa Cornelia to the twelfth century.

One example of a *tegame* was recovered in phase 6 (cat. 124). At Rome this form is present in contexts of the tenth to early eleventh centuries (Ricci 1986: tav. XII, no. 4), but does not seem to have been common outside the urban centre; no examples were recorded from Santa Cornelia or Santa Rufina.

The majority of the kitchen-wares (93.5 per cent) throughout the early medieval and medieval periods are of one fabric (fabric 3), fired in oxidizing conditions. It ranges from red-brown to dark reddish grey in colour (Munsell 5YR 4/3 to 5YR 4/2), and is soft to medium fired, with a rough feel and hackly fracture; it contains numerous ill-sorted inclusions, characterized by large plates of biotite, visible on the surface of the vessels, some augite, large angular transparent inclusions, frequent small yellowish inclusions and flint. This fabric appears to correspond to Schuring's fabric 1

(Schuring 1987: fig. 1), which is typical of the kitchen-wares in Rome and in the Roman Campagna during the early medieval and medieval periods. From the later tenth or eleventh centuries, the fabric of both the jars and *testi* becomes more refined, and the walls of the vessels become correspondingly thinner. The second fabric (fabric 4), present in minimal quantities, was identified only in kitchen-wares of the late eighth and early ninth centuries. It is dark grey-brown (Munsell 5YR 3/1), hard fired, with a rough feel and sandy fracture, containing numerous small yellowish white inclusions and some muscovite.

FORUM WARE AND SPARSE GLAZED WARE

The pottery discussed here belongs to the early medieval and medieval production of glazed pottery characteristic of Rome and the surrounding area, known as *ceramica a vetrina pesante* (Mazzucato 1972) or forum ware (Whitehouse 1965) and sparse glazed ware. These are not two separate classes of pottery, but two successive phases of a tradition of glazed pottery production which underwent a gradual evolution. (For discussion of this class, see Bonifay, Paroli and Picon (1986), Paroli (1986; 1990; 1992a; 1992b) and Patterson (1991; 1993b).) The term forum ware is used here to refer specifically to the early medieval *ceramica a vetrina pesante* of Rome and the surrounding area, which forms a distinctive and homogenous group. Although its origin and chronology have been the subject of much debate, the sequence established by the Crypta Balbi excavations, and now supported by finds from other excavations, seem to have established an initial date for the production of forum ware in the late eighth century. Forum ware and later sparse glazed ware underwent a gradual evolution. One of the main characteristics of this production is the progressive diminution in the amount of glaze used and, by the late tenth to eleventh centuries, with the first examples of sparse glazed ware, the diminution of the surface area of the vessel to which the glaze was applied. Production of sparse glazed ware finally ceased during the early thirteenth century.

At Monte Gelato no diagnostic forms of forum ware and sparse glazed ware were recovered, and this class is poorly represented compared to other sites in the Roman Campagna. Forum ware of ninth-century date is extremely rare, consisting of only one fragment, which has the applied petal decoration characteristic of the forum ware of this date. From the late ninth to tenth centuries forum ware is more common, comprising 1.2 per cent of the material from the quantified deposits, and includes some examples with incised wavy line decoration. It is not until the late tenth to eleventh centuries, however, that glazed products are present in consistent, although small, quantities. These examples represent a transitional phase in the evolution from forum ware to sparse glazed ware, and are characterized by a thinnish glaze with occasional patches of the vessel left unglazed. By the late eleventh to early twelfth centuries the glazed pottery consists solely of sparse glazed ware, this comprising 2.0 per cent of the assemblage.

Two fabrics have been identified (fabrics 5 and 6). Fabric 5 is characteristic of the forum ware products of the ninth to tenth/early eleventh centuries. Fired in oxidizing conditions, the colour ranges from reddish yellow (Munsell 5YR 6/6) to reddish grey (5YR 5/2) to grey (5YR 5/1); it is hard fired with a rough feel and fairly hackly fracture, containing numerous small matt yellowish white inclusions, fine mica and some angular black inclusions. Petrological analysis of examples of forum ware/sparse glazed ware of the late tenth to early eleventh centuries placed the Monte Gelato fabric in the same petrological group (group 9g, containing volcanic and sedimentary inclusions) as that of examples from Rome and other sites in the Roman Campagna, such as Santa Cornelia, Scorano, and Lucus Feroniae. Fabric 6, characteristic of the sparse glazed ware of the later eleventh to twelfth centuries is more refined. It is reddish yellow in colour (Munsell 5YR 6/6 to 7.5YR 7/6), hard fired, with a smooth feel and smooth fracture containing occasional small white and large rounded red inclusions.

CONCLUSION

In recent years our understanding of the early medieval and medieval ceramics of Rome and the Roman Campagna has improved dramatically, giving some fundamental insights into social and economic developments during this period. The discovery of the kiln site at Monte Gelato is a further, important, contribution to this knowledge.

The pottery sequence at Monte Gelato in general follows the pattern emerging elsewhere in Rome and the Roman Campagna. The late eighth-/ninth-century production is characterized by the variety of forms and the richness of the decoration, although this is most strikingly reflected in the forum ware products of this period (see, for example, Romei (1992)). It is significant that it is also seen in an everyday product such as the domestic pottery and, to a certain extent, the kitchen-wares. At the same time, however, the modest level of standardization of the vessel forms and the fact that the same forms often occur in other ceramic classes is indicative of a fairly modest scale of production. Certainly in the case of the Monte Gelato kiln site, the evidence suggests that this was the case (see below).

Although the ceramic sequence of the later ninth to tenth centuries onwards at Monte Gelato is not particularly clear, because of the high proportion of residual material, one can nevertheless detect the same general trends noted from other sites in this area. From the later ninth to tenth centuries the ceramic products are characterized by the reduction in the range of forms. These are increasingly limited to a restricted number of standardized forms, specific to each ceramic class, coinciding with the increasing simplification and gradual disappearance of the decoration both on the domestic pottery and the forum ware products. There is also a notable decrease in the amount of glaze used; in addition, the fabrics become increasingly refined and the walls of the vessels thinner. After the richness of the late eighth/ninth centuries, these elements seem to reflect a streamlining of production, to a more industrial form in terms of a reduction of time, work and costs. This coincides with an increase in the amount of pottery in circulation, especially evident in the Roman Campagna (Patterson 1993b: 323-6).

At Monte Gelato, as elsewhere in the Roman Campagna, the renewed evidence for the circulation of pottery in the late eighth century coincides with the reorganization of the territory by the papacy, with the foundation of the *domuscultae* as a fundamental element. Monte Gelato, like Santa Cornelia, was almost certainly a *domusculta* centre, part of a programme of rational exploitation of the territory and of the provisioning of the people of Rome. From the time of their foundation they yield the same ceramic products as are found in Rome itself, clearly reflecting the renewed links between the urban capital and its territory. Furthermore, although these rural sites were very probably supplied in part by production centres in or near Rome, the discovery of the kiln site at Monte Gelato clearly shows that from the very beginning social and economic conditions existed which favoured and stimulated the development of local production centres in the Roman Campagna itself. The evidence also suggests that these centres were not only producing pottery for everyday use, as at Monte Gelato, but probably also a small amount of a luxury product such as forum ware.

Although no production centres of this ware have yet been identified, petrological analysis of forum ware indicates that, from the initial phase of production in the late eighth and ninth centuries, production centres existed in the Roman Campagna (Patterson 1992; 1993b: 322). The kiln site at Monte Gelato is, however, the only direct evidence we have so far of a rural production centre. It is impossible to say how typical the Monte Gelato kiln is of production sites of this period, although the products themselves are typical of the domestic pottery in use throughout this area during the late eighth and early ninth centuries. However, the small dimensions of the Monte Gelato production site, consisting of a single, small kiln, only 1.95 m in length, apparently without any associated working structures, and situated a few metres from the

15. Fig. 243. P526; rim D. 11 cm; fabric 1. D215. Phase 6.
16. Fig. 243. P508; rim D. 7.5 cm; fabric 1. D219, kiln dump. Phase 7.
17. Fig. 243. P519; rim D. 9 cm; fabric 1. E9, kiln dump. Phase 5.
18. Fig. 243. P511; rim D. 10 cm; fabric 1. M112. Phase 5.
19. Fig. 243. P633; rim D. 10.5 cm; fabric 1. M106. Phase 5.
20. Fig. 243. Cf. P526. M19. Phase 5.
    Cf. Crypta Balbi, Rome: Paroli 1992a: tav. 5, no. 41; Pianabella (Ostia Antica): Patterson 1993a: fig. 2, no. 22. Both are of the second half of the eighth century.
21. Fig. 243. P561; rim D. 9.5 cm; fabric 1. M11, kiln dump. Phase 6.
22. Fig. 243. P510; rim D. 11 cm; fabric 1. E9, fill of kiln. Phase 5.
    Cf. Crypta Balbi, Rome: Paroli 1992a: tav. 3, no. 9 (of the second half of the eighth century).
23. Fig. 243. P518; rim D. 10 cm; fabric 1. E9, fill of kiln. Phase 5.
24. Fig. 243. P548; rim D. 8 cm; fabric 1. E36, kiln dump. Phase 5.
25. Fig. 243. P557; rim D. 8.5 cm; fabric 1. M11, kiln dump. Phase 6.
    Cf. Santa Cornelia: Patterson 1991: fig. 26, no. 55 (of the late eighth to early ninth centuries).
26. Fig. 243. Cf. P602; rim D. 9 cm; fabric 1. M72. Phase 6/7.
    Cf. Crypta Balbi, Rome: Paroli 1992a: tav. 5, no. 37 and (with painted decoration) tav. 4, no. 12 (both of the second half of the eighth century).

Neck and shoulder fragments (cat. 27, 28) and handles (cat. 29-32) probably belonging to above vessels
27. Fig. 243. P703; fabric 1. M61, kiln dump. Phase 6.
28. Fig. 243. P705; fabric 1. D219, kiln dump. Phase 7.
29. Fig. 243. P721; fabric 1. M61, kiln dump. Phase 6.
30. Fig. 244. Cf. P532; fabric 1. E9, kiln dump. Phase 5.
31. Fig. 244. Cf. P531; fabric 1. E9, kiln dump. Phase 5.
32. Fig. 244. Cf. P533; fabric 1. E9, kiln dump. Phase 5.

Group 2. Jugs or two handled jars (anforette) *with tall flaring necks (cat. 33-40) (rims)*
33. Fig. 244. Cf. P520; rim D. 12 cm; fabric 1. D219, kiln dump. Phase 7.
34. Fig. 244. Cf. P656; rim D. 8 cm; fabric 1. M72. Phase 6/7.
35. Fig. 244. P517; rim D. 10 cm; fabric 1. E9, fill of kiln. Phase 5.
36. Fig. 244. P525; rim D. 10 cm; fabric 1. E36, kiln dump. Fabric 5.
37. Fig. 244. P559; rim D. 8 cm; fabric 1. M18, kiln dump. Fabric 6.
    Cf. Pianabella (Ostia Antica): Patterson 1993a: fig. 5, no. 46 (of the late eighth century); Santa Cornelia: Patterson 1991; fig. 26, no. 60 (of the early ninth century).
38. Fig. 244. P552; fabric 1. M2, kiln dump. Phase 6.
39. Fig. 244. P558; rim D. 9 cm; fabric 1. M11, kiln dump. Phase 6.
40. Fig. 244. P549; rim D. 8 cm; fabric 1. D219, kiln dump. Phase 7.

Group 3. Jug (?) rims with handle attached at rim (cat. 41-3)
41. Fig. 244. P644; rim D. *c.* 6 cm; fabric 1. P9. Phase 6.

42. Fig. 244. Cf. P527; rim D. *c.* 8 cm; fabric 1. E9, fill of kiln. Phase 5.
43. Fig. 244. P527; rim D. 10 cm; fabric 1. E36, kiln dump. Phase 5.

Group 4. Wide-mouthed jug or jar rims, possibly with tubular spouts (cat. 44-58)
44. Fig. 244. Cf. P515; rim D. 11.5 cm; fabric 1. M19. Phase 5.
45. Fig. 244. P649; rim D. 10 cm; fabric 1. P17. Phase 5.
46. Fig. 244. P524; rim D. 10 cm; fabric 1. E36, kiln dump. Phase 5.
    Cf. Crypta Balbi, Rome; Paroli 1992a: tav. 5, no. 20 (of the second half of the eighth century).
47. Fig. 244. P512; rim D. 10 cm; fabric 1. E36, kiln dump. Phase 5.
48. Fig. 244. P514; rim D. 12 cm; fabric 1. D219, kiln dump. Phase 7.
49. Fig. 244. P560; rim D. 15 cm; fabric 1. M11, kiln dump. Phase 6.
    Cf. Santa Cornelia: Patterson 1991: fig. 26, no. 37, 39, 42 (of the late eighth/early ninth centuries).
50. Fig. 244. P523; fabric 1. D219, kiln dump. Phase 7.
    Cf. Santa Cornelia: as cat. 49.
51. Fig. 244. P528; fabric 1. M11, kiln dump. Phase 6.
52. Fig. 244. P515; rim D. 12 cm; fabric 1. M11, kiln dump. Phase 6.
    Cf. Santa Cornelia: Patterson 1991: fig. 26, no. 37 (of the late eighth century).
53. Fig. 244. P516; rim D. 11 cm; fabric 1. E9, fill of kiln. Phase 5.
    Cf. Santa Cornelia: Patterson 1991: fig. 26, nos. 36 and 38.
54. Fig. 244. P622; fabric 1. M64. Phase 6.
55. Fig. 244. P538; fabric 1. E36, kiln dump. Phase 5.
56. Fig. 244. Cf. P598; fabric 1. M19. Phase 5.

Tubular spouts probably belonging to above vessels
57. Fig. 245. P546; fabric 1. D219, kiln dump. Phase 7.
58. Fig. 245. P629; fabric 1. M61, kiln dump. Phase 6.

Group 5. Jar with impressed decoration (cat. 59)
59. Fig. 245. P638; rim D. 15 cm; fabric 1. P16. Phase 5/6. There is impressed decoration along the rim, as cat. 84 and 93.
    Cf. Crypta Balbi, Rome: Paroli 1992a: 366-8, tav. 5, nos. 22-3 (of the second half of the eighth century).

Handles (cat. 60-8)
60. Fig. 245. P530; fabric 1. D219, kiln dump. Phase 7.
61. Fig. 245. P535; fabric 1. M61, kiln dump. Phase 6.
62. Fig. 245. P723; fabric 1. M95, kiln dump. Phase 5/6.
63. Fig. 245. P725; fabric 1. E9, fill of kiln. Phase 5.
64. Fig. 245. P726; fabric 1. E9, fill of kiln. Phase 5.
65. Fig. 245. P727; fabric 1. E9, fill of kiln. Phase 5.
66. Fig. 245. P567; fabric 1. M18, kiln dump. Phase 5/6.
67. Fig. 245. P729; fabric 1. M61, kiln dump. Phase 6.
68. Fig. 245. P728; fabric 1. E36, kiln dump. Phase 5.

Bases of closed vessels (cat. 69-75)
69. Fig. 245. P731; base D. 10 cm; fabric 1. E9, fill of kiln. Phase 5.
70. Fig. 245. P542; base D. 10 cm; fabric 1. D219, kiln dump. Phase 7.
71. Fig. 245. P635; base D. 10 cm; fabric 1. P16. Phase 5/6.

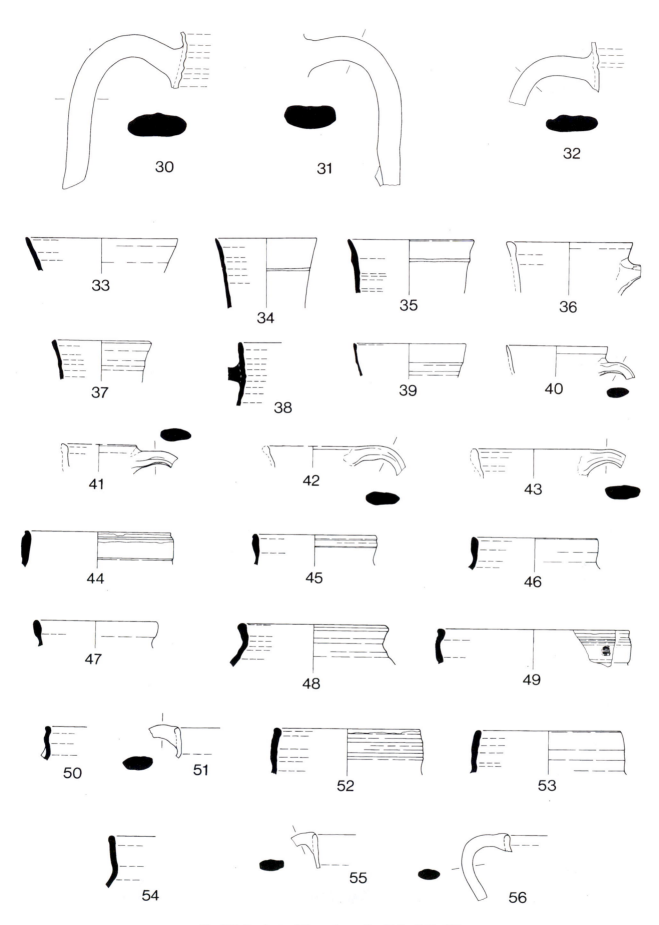

Fig. 244. Products of the early medieval kiln (1:3). *(SC)*

Table 65. Mammal, amphibian and reptile bones: fragment count by phase.

phase	1-2	3	4	5	6	7	Sub-total
ox (*Bos taurus*)	20	27	3	17	40	7	114
sheep/goat (*Ovis aries/Capra hircus*)	64	176	7	93	174	70	584
pig (*Sus scrofa*)	210	*280	19	121	273	76	979
horse (*Equus caballus*)	1	1	1	-	3	1	7
dog (*Canis familiaris*)	**231	5	-	3	-	-	239
cat (*Felis catus*)	-	-	-	-	-	1	1
red deer (*Cervus elaphus*)	1	-	-	-	1	-	2
fallow deer (*Cervus dama*)	-	2	-	1	1	-	4
roe deer (*Capreolus capreolus*)	-	1	-	-	-	-	1
hare (*Lepus europaeus*)	-	-	-	-	2	-	2
black rat (*Rattus rattus*)	-	1	-	-	3	4	8
edible dormouse (*Glis glis*)	5	-	-	-	-	-	5
water vole (*Arvicola terrestris*)	-	-	-	-	5	-	5
bank vole (*Clethrionomys glareolus*)	-	-	-	-	13	11	24
wood mouse (*Apodemus sylvaticus*)	-	3	-	-	5	-	8
mustelid	-	-	-	1	-	-	1
ribs: large (ox, horse size)	10	8	-	10	19	-	47
ribs: small (pig, sheep size)	81	113	24	118	314	76	726
ribs: very small (cat size or smaller)	53	8	-	2	10	9	82
vertebrae: large	1	9	2	9	14	3	38
vertebrae: small	42	47	5	31	119	27	271
long bone fragments: large	6	11	5	3	9	2	36
long bone fragments: small	129	131	29	102	285	72	748
other fragments: large	-	1	-	1	1	1	4
other fragments: small	39	32	1	26	54	9	161
unidentified small mammal size	19	1	-	4	10	4	38
toad (*Bufo* sp.)	7	1	-	1	1	4	14
tortoise (*Testudo* sp.)	-	1	-	-	-	3	4
SUB-TOTAL	919	859	96	543	1,356	380	4,153

* of which 141 bones were from a neonate skeleton; ** of which 142 bones were from an adult skeleton and 81 bones were from a juvenile skeleton

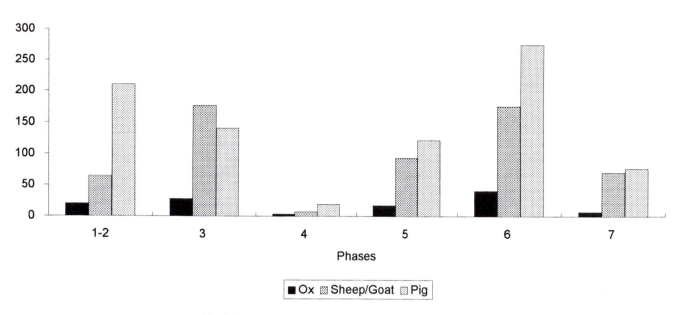

Fig. 249. Mammal bones: fragment count by phase. *(ACK)*

itely or probably eaten were deer (red, roe and fallow), hare and dormouse. The horse bones showed no evidence of having been butchered, so no positive conclusions can be drawn as to whether this species was exploited as a source of meat.)

As is readily apparent from Table 65 and Figure 249, pig bones were the most frequent in the fragment count in all phases (if the dog skeletons in phase 2 are excluded), and it therefore seems likely that cuts of pork were more frequently eaten than other meats. In phases 1-2, the proportion of pig to other bones was at its highest, forming *c.* 70 per cent of the total of the main meat sources (Table 66). This percentage declines sharply in phase 3 (late Roman) to *c.* 40 per cent (if the influence of the juvenile articulated

Table 66. Domestic species represented, (a) by fragment count (NISP) adjusted to count articulated skeletons as a nominal two bones each, (b) by percentage of the NISP for ox, sheep/goat and pig, (c) by minimum number of individuals (MNI), and (d) by NISP:MNI ratio.

phase	unit	ox	sheep/goat	pig	horse	dog	cat
1-2	NISP	20	64	210	1	12	-
	NISP%	6.8	21.8	71.4			
	MNI	1	3	5	1	3	-
	NISP:MNI	20:1	21:1	42:1			
3	NISP	27	176	141	1	5	-
	NISP%	7.8	51.2	41.0			
	MNI	1	11	5	1	1	-
	NISP:MNI	27:1	16:1	28:1			
5	NISP	17	93	121	-	3	-
	NISP%	7.3	40.2	52.3			
	MNI	1	5	3	-	1	-
	NISP:MNI	17:1	19:1	40:1			
6	NISP	40	174	273	3	-	-
	NISP%	8.2	35.7	56.0			
	MNI	1	9	8	1	-	-
	NISP:MNI	40:1	19:1	34:1			
7	NISP	7	70	76	1	-	1
	NISP%	4.6	45.8	49.7			
	MNI	1	4	3	1	-	1
	NISP:MNI	7:1	18:1	25:1			

Table 68. Fusion of epiphyses for pig and sheep/goat. The number fused (F) and not fused (NF) is given for each group of bones, together with the group's percentage fused (i.e. surviving to be older than the approximate ages given for each group). Adapted from Bull and Payne (1982) for pig, and Silver (1969) and Bullock and Rackham (1982) for sheep/goat.

	phase months	1-2 F-NF	%F	3 F-NF	%F	5 F-NF	%F	6 F-NF	%F	7 F-NF	%F
PIG											
scapula	7-11	5-2		3-3		4-0		14-2		3-2	
pelvis	7-11	2-3		5-0		2-1		6-2		-	
radius p	11	0-1	59	3-1	68	0-3	71	1-2	69	1-0	63
humerus d	11+	1-1		1-3		2-0		0-3		1-1	
phal II	11+	2-0		3-0		2-0		1-1		-	
tibia d	19-23	1-0		0-2		0-4		0-3		0-1	
metacarpal d	19-23	2-3		0-2		-		0-6		0-3	
metatarsal d	19-23	2-8	30	0-2	31	1-3	36	1-7	23	0-2	0
phal I	19-23	1-3		4-3		3-0		5-4		-	
calcaneum	31-5	0-3		0-2		-		1-3		0-2	
femur p	31-5	1-4		0-2		0-1		0-8		1-3	
humerus p	31-5+	-		0-3		0-2		0-3		0-1	
radius d	31-5+	0.4	7	0-2	7	0-3	0	0-2	7	-	8
ulna	31-5+	0-2		1-2		0-1		0-1		0-1	
femur d	31-5+	0-1		0-1		0-1		0-3		0-2	
tibia p	31-5+	-		0-2		0-4		1-6		0-2	
SHEEP/GOAT											
humerus d	<12	0-1		3-2		0-1		3-3		0-3	
radius p	<12	1-0		3-0		1-0		7-2		2-0	
scapula	12	2-1	70	5-2	68	5-1	82	7-2	76	4-1	64
pelvis	12	4-1		4-3		8-1		11-2		3-1	
phal I	14-35	-		7-3		4-0		4-0		2-1	
phal II	14-35	-		3-0		-		-		-	
tibia d	35	1-0	100	4-3	65	0-2	63	3-1	80	0-2	50
femur p	36	1-0		1-2		1-1		1-1		1-0	
metacarpal d	47	0-1		3-0		3-0		-		0-1	
metatarsal d	47	-		2-1		3-0		0-2		-	
femur d	48	0-1	0	1-3	62	0-1	86	1-1	50	1-0	25
tibia p	48	-		2-1		-		2-0		0-2	
calcaneum	48-60	-		4-0		-		1-0		-	
radius d	48-60	1-0	100	-	71	1-0	100	5-3	60	-	0
humerus p	48-60	1-0		1-2		1-0		0-1		0-1	

it may be the case that some of the males were in fact castrates. There appears to have been another phase of slaughtering when animals were aged two-three years, since only up to eight per cent of bones were fused in the 31-5+ months bone group. This would support the suggestion that nearly all largely adult-sized animals had been slaughtered by three years, leaving a minority, probably breeding sows, to continue into middle and old age.

Although all phases are roughly the same in their bone fusion data, phase 5 is slightly different in having fewer an-imals over two years (only a single jaw aged at four or more years: see below and Table 69), and fewer juveniles at one year or less. This implies a condensed period of slaughter at one to two years of age for the majority of pigs in this phase. The *domusculta* is the dominant element in this phase, for which there is literary evidence indicating that *domuscultae* in general reared pigs for the Rome meat supply (see discussion). The pattern hinted at for Monte Gelato may be one of well-organized slaughter of young but almost mature animals. They would have been in their prime, and have

Table 69. Summary of age at death from mandible tooth wear. Approximate ages for pig are from Bull and Payne (1982).

PIG	age							
phase	2 m	6-10 m	1 y (-)	1.5-1.75	2	2+	3+	4+
2	-	-	3	1	-	2	-	-
3	2	1	-	2	1	-	-	1
5	1	-	-	-	2	-	-	1
6	2	2	-	3	-	4	1	-
7	1	-	2	-	-	-	-	-
TOTAL	6	3	5	6	3	6	1	2
% of total	43.8			28.1		28.1		
% still alive at end of stage	56.2			28.1		0		

SHEEP/GOAT		
phase	no. of mandibles	tooth wear
2	3	all adult
3	10	8 adult; 1 with M3 coming into wear; 1 with M2 coming into wear
5	3	all adult
6	2	2 with M3 coming into wear
7	2	both adult

represented the best return in meat value for the investment in terms, for example, of feed and herding.

The overall pattern for all phases for pig is supported by the tooth wear evidence, despite the relatively low number of mandibles available (Table 69). If all phases are taken as one group, 56 per cent are older than one year, and 28 per cent are older than two years. Thus, *c.* 72 per cent of the pigs had been killed by two years of age, a figure in close agreement with the fusion data. Twenty-eight per cent of the mandibles are of animals of two years or older, including three (nine per cent) of adults aged three or more, again a figure which appears to conform with the fusion evidence. Most other sites in the region have generally similar slaughter patterns, seen for instance at Settefinestre (King 1985: figs 192-3), Ponte Nepesino (Clark 1984: 129) and other medieval sites such as Farfa abbey (Clark 1987b: fig. 5).

As far as sheep/goat is concerned, the fusion of epiphyses indicates that in phase 3, about two-thirds of the animals were still alive at four years of age, and this dominantly adult pattern continues in the medieval period, and indeed is accentuated in phase 5. Only in phase 7 does a more typical fall-off in survival with age occur, but the data from this phase are not very numerous (as is also the case for phase 1/2). The small number of surviving mandibles supports the generally adult pattern. Nearly all have adult dentition, with the youngest having the second permanent molar coming into wear (that is, *c.* one year). This is a pattern also seen at nearby Ponte Nepesino (Clark 1984: 129) and at the later medieval site of Tuscania (Barker 1973: 161, 164) and elsewhere (Clark 1987a: 13). It can be contrasted with a pattern of more juvenile slaughter seen, for instance, at the wealthy urban site of Palazzo Vitelleschi, Tarquinia (Clark 1987a: 13; Clark 1989: 225-6) and Farfa abbey (Clark 1987a: 14; 1987b: 186).

In general, the adult pattern is one that would be associated with a wool pattern of husbandry, in which the animals (except non-breeding males) are allowed to survive into adulthood in order to obtain the maximum yield of wool and other renewable products such as milk and cheese. Slaughter would occur when wool quality and milk yield started to diminish amongst the older animals. This type of husbandry implies the existence of flocks of sheep (and to a lesser extent goats) that would have been composed of animals of a variety of ages. Their grazing needs would have been relatively great, and thus it is likely that extensive sheep pasture would have been required, either locally, or within the framework of a transhumance system. Unfortunately the bone evidence alone cannot indicate directly whether transhumant agriculture was practised at Monte Gelato.

Ageing data for oxen yielded few positive indicators. In all phases, fused epiphyses and adult teeth were dominant, giving the impression of a small number of cattle raised into adulthood, presumably for purposes such as use in plough-teams and traction. Milk, meat and hides may also have been (secondary) motives for keeping cattle.

A factor affecting and reflecting animal husbandry practices is that of the health of the animals. The Monte Gelato assemblages include very few specimens indicating poor health amongst the domestic stock. A phase 2 sheep/goat adult mandible with very worn teeth has so-called 'cauliflower' roots, indicating minor abcessing of the cheek teeth. A similar condition occurs in a phase 3 example, and a phase 6 sheep/goat mandible has very worn adult premolars. Dental pathologies also occur in pig: a very worn phase 3 third mandibular molar has clear indications of caries, a phase 6 female adult canine has been broken during the animal's lifetime (and was subsequently worn down on the broken surface), and a phase 7 upper jaw has a slightly impacted third adult molar in the process of eruption. Virtually all the dental conditions noted above occur in adult or elderly individuals, as might be expected. Non-dental abnormalities are rare: a sheep/goat acetabulum (phase 5) has slight lipping, perhaps due to an arthropathy, and a pig- or sheep-sized rib has an exostosis joining it to its neighbour, perhaps in consequence of an injury. None of these conditions

Table 72. Bird bones.

species ↓ phase →	2	3	3/4	5	5/6	6	6/7	7
chicken (*Gallus gallus*)	28	23	5	1	10	50	4	2
chicken/duck size	5	6	-	2	5	19	1	4
domestic duck (*Anas platyrhyncos*)	-	1	-	-	-	-	-	-
duck species	-	1	-	-	-	-	-	-
domestic goose (*Anser anser*)	-	-	-	-	-	-	1	-
goose species	-	1	-	-	-	-	1	-
goose size	-	-	-	-	-	-	1	-
dove species (*Columba* sp.)	-	1	-	-	-	-	-	-
tawny owl (*Strix aluco*)	1	-	-	-	-	-	-	-
jay (*Garrulus glandarius*)	2	-	-	-	-	-	-	-
song thrush (*Turdus philomelos*)	1	-	-	-	-	-	-	-
blackbird (*Turdus merula*)	6	-	-	-	-	-	-	-
thrush species (*Turdus* sp.)	11	-	-	-	-	-	-	-
chaffinch (*Fringilla coelebs*)	1	-	-	-	-	-	-	-
finch species (*Fringillidae*)	1	-	-	-	-	-	-	-
unidentified bird	37	6	2	-	1	6	2	-
subtotals (total = 249)	93	39	7	3	16	75	10	6
% of total sample in each phase	37	16	3	1	7	30	4	2

Table 73. Chicken sex ratios.

phase	2	3	6
males	2	1	3
females	-	1	1

Table 74. Chicken age ratios.

phase	2	3	6
adults	63% (15)	95% (18)	76% (31)
juveniles	37% (9)	5% (1)	24% (10)

DISCUSSION

An examination of the distribution of the bird bones across the site indicates that they represent scattered domestic refuse. All the wild species from phase 2 came from the fish-pond fills, the jay and female tawny owl, particularly, indicating nearby woodland. Jays need well-secluded woodland with dense foliage in which to nest, and are never far from trees, while tawny owls nest in hollow trees (Peterson, Mountfort and Hollom 1979). The other birds from this deposit, such as thrush, blackbird and chaffinch, are commonly found in woods and gardens. The suggestion that there may have been an aviary (cf. Chapter Three) should here be noted.

The patterns from both the age and sex data for chickens suggest a distinct change in activity in the late Roman period. Young, tender birds almost disappear from the diet in this period (phase 3), although they are well-represented in second-century and in medieval contexts. Furthermore, medullary bone occurs only in phase 3. Eating an egg-laying hen instead of her future eggs implies a disregard for subsistence levels, and a waste of dietary resources, suggesting a certain degree of affluence.

THE FISH BONES, by Caroline Cartwright

A total of 26 fish bones was recovered from Roman and medieval contexts. Standard techniques of optical microscopy were used to assist the identification of the fish bones, in conjunction with comparisons made to reference collections of mediterranean fish taxa.

THE IDENTIFICATIONS

Phase 2 (second century)

– One vertebral centra of *Anguilla anguilla* (eel); two unidentifiable spine fragments.
  L165. Fish-pond, early second century.
– Three fragments of spine and two fragments of dentary of *Alosa* sp. (shad); six unidentifiable spine fragments.
  L105. Fish-pond, late second century.
– Two scombrid neural spines.
  S10. Rock-cut road.
– One scombrid neural spine fragment.
  L143. North cistern, late second century.

Table 75. Chicken bone measurements.

phase	context	sex	measurements				
CORACOID			GL	Lm	Bb	Bf	
2	L165		61.0	58.0	17.0	14.3	
3	D316		53.4	-	14.8	12.6	
3	D316		53.8	-	14.9	11.9	
6	D107		52.0	49.6	12.7	10.9	
6	D273		53.0	50.8	14.0	12.2	
6	D301		48.4	46.0	13.2	10.8	
6	D301		48.7	45.7	-	10.5	
SCAPULA			Dic				
2	L105		12.2				
2	L165		13.3				
3	M143		10.0				
6	D266		11.4				
6	D273		11.9				
6	D301		11.4				
HUMERUS			GL	Bp	SC	Bd	
2	L165		-	-	7.0	14.3	
3	M121		69.8	18.4	6.6	14.8	
3	M50		-	-	6.7	14.2	
3	M136		-	-	6.3	13.2	
6	A23		-	-	7.2	16.3	
6	D319		-	16.2	5.8	-	
RADIUS			GL	SC	Bd		
2	E11		64.2	2.9	6.4		
2	L165		64.8	2.9	6.7		
ULNA			GL	Dip	Bp	SC	Did
3	L162		73.0	13.6	9.6	4.4	10.0
6	D301		-	13.3	9.2	4.2	-
METACARPAL			GL	Bp	Did		
3	M146		35.9	12.3	6.9		
6	D107		34.6	-	6.7		
TIBIA			La	Dip	SC	Bd	Dd
2	L105		22.5	-	-	-	-
2	L105		-	-	-	12.6	13.2
3	M114		-	-	-	10.0	10.7
3	M136	F	-	19.5	-	-	-
6	D168		-	-	-	10.5	-
6	D301		-	-	-	10.8	11.7
6	D301		-	-	6.2	10.0	9.9
FEMUR			Bp	Dp	SC	Bd	Dd
3	M121		-	-	6.3	15.8	12.7
3	D48		16.3	10.4	-	-	
6	D107		15.3	10.2	6.3	-	-
6	D319		-	-	6.5	14.4	12.0
6	D301		15.1	9.7	6.1	-	-
METATARSAL			GL	Bp	SC	Bd	
2	L105	M	-	-	-	15.6	
2	L105	M	98.8	14.9	7.5	15.4	
3	D316	M	100.3	15.6	8.7	17.3	
6	M64	F	74.9	-	6.2	13.7	
6	D168	M	91.9	14.1	7.8	16.1	

Phase 3 (late Roman)

– One fragment of dentary of *Pagrus pagrus* (sea bream).
  E9. Occupation layer.

Phase 3/4 (late Roman)

– One fragment of dentary of *Diplodus* sp. (sea bream).
  E16. Rubble/occupation.

Phase 5 (early medieval)

– One neural spine fragment, possibly of a scombrid; one
  fragment of lateral scute of an *Acipenser sturio* (sturgeon).
  M121. Mortar dump.

Phase 6 (medieval)

– One vertebra from the herring family, Clupeidae, possibly
  from *Sardinia pilchardus* (sardine)
  B80. Burial no. 12.
– One urohyal of *Pagrus pagrus* (sea bream).
  D104. Ash layer.
– One fragmented haemal spine of *Pagrus pagrus* (sea
  bream).
  D282. Burial no. 46.
– One fragment of neural spine, possibly of a scombrid.
  D15. Burial no. 28.
– One fragment of lateral scute of *Acipenser sturio* (sturgeon).
  A4. Burial no. 26.

DISCUSSION

The second-century fill of the fish-pond yielded fourteen fragments of fish bone of which six pieces could be identified to taxon. *Anguilla anguilla* (eel) was present in the early second-century context of L165. Eels are present today in freshwater habitats and in surface marine waters around the atlantic and mediterranean coasts (Whitehead *et al.* 1989). Regular spawning migrations of eels take place from mid-atlantic waters into freshwater rivers, estuaries and brackish lagoons in Europe (Wheeler and Jones 1989; Whitehead *et al.* 1989). Elvers may spend a variable amount of time in the freshwater rivers (from five to twenty years); the maturing adults then migrate back to marine waters (Wheeler and Jones 1989). Substantial quantities of eel are often present as part of the fish-food refuse from secular and monastic medieval (and later) archaeological sites in Europe (Wheeler and Jones 1989; Van Neer 1994). It has been suggested that eels could be fished from lagoons or rivers, possibly using traps (Wheeler and Jones 1989). Although it is somewhat problematic to postulate that the river Treia (in whose valley Monte Gelato is situated) may have contained eel populations during the second century, it is not impossible that eels caught from freshwater locations could have been kept in a fish-pond for short periods prior to being con-

sumed. However, it should be noted that, on other archaeological grounds (cf. Chapter Three), there is good reason to suppose that they may have been kept as a decorative feature.

Alosa sp. (shad) was present in the late second-century fill (L105) of the fish-pond. *Alosa* spp. are anadromous (that is, they migrate from marine waters to spawn in fresh water), semi-anadromous or purely freshwater and range from pelagic marine, estuarine to (freshwater) river and lake environments (Wheeler and Jones 1989; Whitehead *et al.* 1989). *Alosa alosa* (Allis shad) has a present-day distribution in marine pelagic waters around the atlantic and western mediterranean coasts; it has a migratory spawning far up rivers (Whitehead *et al.* 1989). *Alosa fallax* (Twaite shad) displays a marine pelagic present-day distribution around the atlantic and mediterranean coasts; it penetrates a short distance up rivers to spawn and there are some entirely freshwater lacustrine (non-migratory) populations (Whitehead *et al.* 1989). At the present day, the Black Sea and Sea of Azov contain *Alosa caspia* and *A. pontica* anadromous and semi-anadromous populations (Whitehead *et al.* 1989). Wheeler and Jones (1989), amongst others, have noted the importance of migratory fish (particularly anadromous species) as a major (cyclic) food source for coastal and riverine prehistoric and early historic communities. LeGall's research (1994) on freshwater fish in the south of France has highlighted the importance of *Alosa* spp. (in particular, *Alosa alosa*, which may attain a maximum weight of 3 kg). Despite the fact that *Alosa alosa* is considered to be primarily an atlantic fish at the present day, during pre- and proto-historic periods the distribution and adaptation of anadromous migrators such as *Alosa alosa* is considered to be closely linked to thermotaxis which governs reproductive maturity; in consequence, distribution is not a simple matter to reconstruct (LeGall 1994). Whilst it may be suggested that prehistoric peoples tended to utilize those taxa which lived within the immediate environs of their site (LeGall 1994), the same suggestion cannot necessarily be made for the late second-century occupancy of Monte Gelato, where trade in exotic or foreign commodities (including fish) is feasible. The distribution of marine and freshwater *Alosa* spp. during the late second century in Italy can only be extrapolated from the present-day distribution described above, but it is clear that freshwater *Alosa* spp. could have been stored live on a temporary basis in a fish-pond prior to consumption.

Other second-century contexts yielded three fragments of scombrid neural spines. The Scombridae family comprises mainly epipelagic marine fish such as mackerel and tuna which have a wide present-day distribution in temperate and tropical seas (Collette and Nauen 1983; Wheeler and Jones 1989). In the Mediterranean, scombrid taxa such as *Euthynnus* spp. (tunny), *Auxis* sp. (bullet tuna),

Katsuwonus pelamis (skipjack tuna), *Sarda sarda* (Atlantic bonito), *Scomber* spp. (mackerel), *Thunnus* spp. (tuna) represent important food sources at the present day and in the archaeological record (Collette and Nauen 1983; Wheeler and Jones 1989; Whitehead *et al.* 1989).

Late Roman contexts produced two dentary fragments of sea bream: *Pagrus pagrus* and *Diplodus* sp. Both belong to the Sparidae family which frequents temperate and tropical coastal waters (Whitehead *et al.* 1989). These, too, have been important sources of food in the past and are still commercially exploited today (Wheeler and Jones 1989; Whitehead *et al.* 1989). There were insufficient sparid bones present to utilize any osteometric techniques (such as those used by Desse and Desse-Berset (1994) on Sparidae, Serranidae and Scombridae) for the evaluation of size reconstruction of fish present on the archaeological site.

A phase 5 context (M121) of the early medieval period produced one possibly scombrid neural spine fragment, and one fragment of lateral scute of *Acipenser sturio* (sturgeon). Although very rare at the present day, *Acipenser sturio* has a distribution on atlantic coasts (including the coasts of the Baltic and North Seas) and the northern coasts of the Mediterranean and of the Black Sea (Whitehead *et al.* 1989). *Acipenser sturio* is an anadromous fish which inhabits saline nearshore waters and frequently undertakes extensive sea migrations; river spawning takes place over spring and summer (Whitehead *et al.* 1989). Desse-Berset's documentation (1994) of numerous sturgeon bones at Arles (France), dating from the sixth century BC through to the second century BC, has provided an ideal opportunity not only for evaluating the role of the sturgeon as a prized source of caviar, but also for evaluating the value set on sturgeon *meat* as a luxury food. It is possible that the presence of sturgeon in two medieval contexts at Monte Gelato similarly reflects the high status of the sturgeon during the Middle Ages.

Other medieval contexts (phase 6) yielded fragmented remains of *Pagrus pagrus* (sea bream) and a vertebra from the Clupeidae family, possibly *Sardina pilchardus* (sardine). The presence of sardines, either preserved in brine or salt within amphorae or as hallec (plain salted fish), and garum (fish sauce) from Roman contexts in Europe has been well documented (for example, Wheeler and Locker 1985; Van Neer 1994). The possible sardine vertebra from a medieval grave could, however, simply be food refuse from freshly caught sardines, widely available in coastal pelagic waters of the Mediterranean (Whitehead *et al.* 1989). Two other medieval contexts, both from graves, produced a fragment of scombrid neural spine and another lateral scute fragment of *Acipenser sturio* (sturgeon).

As the overall quantity of fish bones from Monte Gelato is small, no estimations of (minimum) numbers of individuals of fish can be put forward, using techniques such as those described by Nichol and Wild (1984), Wheeler and Jones (1989) and Van Neer (1994).

THE CHARRED PLANT REMAINS, by John Giorgi

INTRODUCTION

During the excavations soil samples were systematically collected for the recovery of plant remains, to gain information on the range of plants cultivated, gathered, utilized or imported onto the site; on crop husbandry and processing activities; on the use of different areas of the site over time; and on the character of the settlement.

Sampling and processing methods

Soil conditions at the site limited the preservation of plant remains to charred material. Samples were recovered from potentially well-stratified and datable contexts from a wide range of features across the site. The fills of drains (eight samples), burials (five samples) and burnt layers (six samples) were the most frequently sampled features.

A total of 679.5 litres of sediment was collected, equivalent to just over ten litres a sample, although individual sample size was variable. Thus, large quantities were taken from potentially 'rich' contexts, for example, 37 litres from a Roman cistern, while smaller features containing less than ten litres of sediment were 100 per cent sampled.

The samples were processed on a Siraf flotation tank with mesh sizes of 0.5 mm and 1.0 mm for the recovery of the flot and residue respectively. The residues were dried and sorted for environmental and artefactual evidence.

Identification

The flots were dried and sorted for charred plant remains using a binocular microscope and the material was identified with the aid of modern seed reference material, charred archaeobotanical material and seed reference manuals, housed in laboratory facilities at the British School at Rome.

RESULTS

Twenty-five of the 67 samples produced charred plant remains from thirteen of the sampled zones. However, the quantity of material was very low, with a total of just 162 plant items or almost one seed for every 4.2 litres of processed soil. A low seed density of just one seed for every two litres of sediment was also recorded at the Roman villa site of Settefinestre, Tuscany (Jones 1985).

However, there was great variability between the size of individual assemblages. Thus, one sample from context D86 produced 70 seeds, equivalent to seven seeds per litre of soil, or just over 43 per cent of all the plant remains recovered from the site, while 21 of the 25 productive samples contained fewer than ten plant items. Plant remains were, nevertheless, recovered from virtually all the sampled periods of the site, although phases 3 and 5/6 produced the best results. The results are tabulated in Tables 76 and 77.

commentò l'epigrafe suddetta, per analogia con il *Patrimonium Appiae*, la cui menzione è chiaramente conservata nel testo mutilo dell'epigrafe, ritenne di completare la localizzazione dei suddetti tre *fundi* collocandoli, appunto, *in Patrimonio Tusciae*. Tuttavia, è solo con il pontificato di Gregorio II (715-31), che si ha una insindacabile attestazione di tale circoscrizione patrimoniale attraverso una serie di contratti di locazione regestati nella *Collectio Canonum* di Deusdedit. Il Patrimonio della Tuscia includeva allora tutto il territorio fra la riva destra del Tevere ed il mar Tirreno: infatti le attestazioni documentarie ci consentono di localizzare beni lungo gli assi delle vie Aurelia, Cornelia, Clodia e Flaminia. Molto probabilmente la attestazione di un *casalis* lungo la via Portuense, nel corso del pontificato di Onorio I, è da ascrivere al *Patrimonium Tusciae* anche se, come si è detto in precedenza, non lo si può affermare con certezza. Non tutte le pertinenze fondiarie di questo patrimonio sono localizzate in relazione agli assi viari: in molti casi il referente geografico è rappresentato da territori cittadini o, più semplicemente, distanze in miglia da Roma. Dalla documentazione dell'epoca di Gregorio II si evince l'esistenza di un nucleo di beni nel territorio di *Forum Clodii* ed un altro all'VIII miglio della via Clodia. Un unico *fundus* è noto al XIV miglio della via Flaminia: tuttavia, è da ritenere che in quest'area le pertinenze fondiarie della Chiesa Romana fossero di ben altro rilievo, se, come ha suggestivamente proposto la Bosman, la *domusculta* al XIV miglio *Patrimonio Tusciae* fondata da Papa Zaccaria (l'unica di cui si riporti la localizzazione all'interno di un *patrimonium*) è da collocare, appunto, al XIV miglio della Flaminia (Deusdedit, *Collectio Canonum* III: can. 118).[103] Il limite, verso l'esterno, del *patrimonium*, doveva necessariamente coincidere con il limite del ducato romano (Bavant 1979: 41-89; e, più recentemente, Sennis (1996: 36-9 e tav. XVII)). Successivamente, due documenti ci informano sulle pertinenze pontificie nell'area della Tuscia romana: un diploma dell'854 emesso da Leone IV in favore del monastero di San Martino presso San Pietro in Vaticano (Schiaparelli 1901: 432-7); un'altro del 906, emesso da Sergio III in favore del vescovo di *Selva Candida* (Marini 1805: papiro XXIV). Essi esorbitano dall'arco di tempo di cui ci occupiamo in questo paragrafo, ma ne esamineremo comunque il contenuto, poiché i beni in essi elencati rientrano nell'area dell'antico ducato bizantino di Roma, nel quale i pontefici detenevano possessi anche precedentemente alla metà dell'VIII secolo: pertanto i dati che da questi docu-menti si raccolgono possono essere indizi di concentrazioni proprietarie di data anteriore al IX secolo. Il diploma dell'854 presenta tuttavia vari problemi, che esamineremo rapidamente. La elencazione dei beni fondiari, innanzitutto, non concerne solo l'area della Tuscia romana, ma tocca anche alcune proprietà situate nel territorio di Velletri. Inoltre, l'ordine con cui queste proprietà appaiono nel documento sembra piuttosto casuale e non sistematicamente 'agganciato' alla geografia dei *patrimonia*. Dopo una serie di beni interni alla *nova civitas Leoniana*, appare un gruppo di *fundi ... omnes invicem quoerentes*, i quali sono localizzati fra il IV ed il V miglio della via Clodia, si registra una serie di quattro *fundi* e una *casa* la cui posizione è lungo la via Cornelia, a partire dalla *porta Sancti Petri Apostoli*, sino, almeno, a Boccea (Cecchelli Trinci 1980): è chiaro che queste entità fondiarie sono accomunate dal fatto di gravitare entro un'area prossima alla città. Ad esse segue la menzione di un gruppo consistente in una *massa*, un *fundus* e un monastero con altre proprietà annesse, situati a *Centumcellae*, ovvero Civitavecchia, e nei dintorni. Quindi entrano in scena le proprietà *in territorio Billiternensi* (= di Velletri), che avevamo preannunciato, composte da due *fundi*. Subito dopo si ritorna al V miglio della Clodia, con quattro *fundi* dei quali viene detto che sono *ex corpore suburbani patrimonii*: ma il testo è corrotto in questo punto e ci manca la parola decisiva, ossia il nome del *patrimonium*, così come non possiamo escludere che nel gruppo fosse compreso almeno un altro *fundus*. Si prosegue con un *fundus* sito nel *territorio Collinense*, quindi lungo la via Flaminia, all'altezza del XXV miglio,[104] e poi si conclude con sette *fundi ex corpore massae Vurianae*, allo stesso XXV miglio da Roma, che il documento sibillinamente dice *positos Urbe Vetere*. L'*Urbs Vetus* in questione non può certo essere Orvieto, che si trova ben più distante da Roma, e francamente non sapremmo proporre una soluzione definitiva e convincente al problema.[105] Quali conclusioni generali trarre da questo complesso documento? È chiaro che gran parte dei toponimi dovrebbe rientrare nel *Suburbanum Patrimonium Tusciae*, che analizzeremo qui di seguito: almeno tutti quelli al IV-V miglio della via Clodia, e quelli nel tratto iniziale della via Cornelia. Ma perché questa appartenenza è esplicitata solo nel caso del gruppo di quattro *fundi* siti al V miglio della Clodia e non per gli altri? E, perché, altrettanto, il riferimento al *patrimonium* manca per tutti gli altri beni fondiari elencati? Ci si potrebbe accontentare dell'idea che le lacune del testo abbiano proprio interessato quei

---

[103] È il *fundus Capanianus*, menzionato nel canone 119 del libro III della *Collectio Canonum* di Deusdedit (Bosman 1994).

[104] Il testo del documento è in realtà corrotto nel punto in cui viene espressa la distanza in miglia; l'integrazione con la indicazione del XXV miglio è ricavata dal fatto che a questa altezza della Flaminia si trovava, appunto, il *territorium Collinense*. Su di esso, nell'antichità classica, si veda Tomassetti ((1913 (1979): 355ss.); si tratta di una partizione territoriale che compare solo nei documenti medievali e che 'formava un triangolo irregolare con base sulla riva destra del Tevere, tra Santa Maria e Torrita, e il vertice presso Campagnano, incluso anche il Soratte; ... è da escludere che derivasse il suo nome dall'esistenza di un'antica città *Collina*' (Tomassetti 1913 (1979): 355-7).

[105] L'unico centro antico della zona è *Capena* (Potter 1985: 88-9; Cambi 1990).

passi che menzionavano i *patrimonia*: ma è chiaramente una soluzione che lascia più di qualche sospetto. Una risposta più articolata potrebbe essere cercata nel fatto che questo diploma contiene l'affiliazione al monastero di San Martino al Vaticano di altri quattro istituti religiosi dell'area prossima a San Pietro: i gruppi di possessi fondiari elencati (escluso quello stornato dal *patrimonium suburbanum*) sarebbero potuti originariamente appartenere proprio a quegli altri enti che venivano ora a ricadere sotto il controllo del monastero di San Martino. Questa ipotesi, tuttavia, si scontra con il fatto che la *pensio* annua richiesta al monastero di San Martino per il possesso perpetuo di questi beni doveva essere versata alle *rationes ecclesiasticae*, presupponendo quindi un passaggio, anche se momentaneo, all'interno della contabilità centrale della Chiesa Romana. La soluzione più credibile può forse contemplare ambedue le eventualità: e cioè che beni originariamente di alcuni enti siano stati 'travasati' nella contabilità centrale pontificia, senza essere aggregati ad alcun patrimonio, per poi essere distaccati in perpetuo in favore del monastero di San Martino, con l'aggiunta di *fundi* 'storicamente' propri del *Patrimonium Tusciae Suburbanum* (vedi oltre).

Il diploma del 906 è invece assai meno complicato, poiché tratta due grandi blocchi fondiari, due *massae*, la *Clodiana* e la *Cesana*, localizzate al XX miglio da Roma in territorio di Nepi e confinanti fra loro (cf. Radke 1981: 303-14). Nel territorio di Nepi erano posti anche i tre *fundi* superstiti dalla lapide di Sergio I in favore del *titulus* di Santa Susanna. La complessità del problema dell'identificazione dell'asse viario cui effettivamente alludono le fonti altomedievali quando si riferiscono alla via Clodia non consente conclusioni definitive, ma è da ritenere che la menzione del territorio di Nepi contempli piuttosto un riferimento alla via Cassia che non alla Clodia vera e propria, cosa che, del resto consentono di dedurre il toponimo stesso di *massa Cesana* e quello, ad essa interno, di *fundus Martinianus*.[106]

In conclusione, la documentazione di cui disponiamo ci consente di individuare con certezza i seguenti nuclei fondiari all'interno del *Patrimonium Tusciae*.

Sull'asse delle vie Cassia-Clodia:

(a) alcuni *fundi* sono attestati fra 715 e 731, all'VIII miglio della via Clodia: in assenza di un'indagine topografica più approfondita, non ce la sentiamo in alcun modo di andare al di là di una generica localizzazione fra La Giustiniana e La Storta;

(b) un gruppo di beni – il più cospicuo – intorno al lago di Bracciano, nel territorio di *Forum Clodii* (attestati fra 715 e 731) ed in quello che era allora considerato territorio di Nepi, vale a dire l'area compresa, all'incirca, fra Cesano e Monterosi; lo stesso territorio di Nepi è documentato per tre fondi, non localizzabili con maggiore precisione, al tempo di Sergio I;

(c) fra 599 e 638 è nominata due volte la *massa Gratiliana*, sita nel territorio di Blera: non viene esplicitamente attribuita al *Patrimonium Tusciae*, ma è chiaramente di proprietà della Chiesa Romana.

Lungo la fascia costiera:

(a) un *casalis* lungo la via Portuense, presso la chiesa dei Santi Abdon e Sennen, documentato fra 625 e 638, ma non esplicitamente attribuito al *Patrimonium Tusciae*;

(b) un *fundus* è noto al X miglio della via Aurelia fra 715 e 731;

(c) si giunge quindi nel territorio di Civitavecchia dove è attestata una *massa* nel periodo fra 625 e 638; si deve quindi attendere l'854 per vedere documentata un'altra *massa* nello stesso territorio, fra quelle attribuite al monastero di San Martino al Vaticano. Ambedue le *massae* non sono esplicitamente associate al patrimonio della Tuscia.

Lungo l'asse della via Flaminia:

(a) fra 625 e 638 vengono locati dalla Chiesa una serie di terreni fra la porta Flaminia e ponte Milvio: non sono esplicitamente associati al patrimonio;

(b) al XIV miglio della via si registra un *fundus* per il periodo 715-31, al quale potrebbero essere associati i beni che andarono a formare la elusiva *domusculta in XIV miliario patrimonio Tusciae*, costituita al tempo di Zaccaria;

(c) nell'854 appare un *fundus in territorio Collinense*: come tutti quelli del diploma in favore di San Martino al Vaticano, non è associabile con certezza al *Patrimonium Tusciae*;

(d) ancora all'854 e allo stesso documento, si riferiscono sette *fundi* da una *massa* sita a 25 miglia da Roma, nel territorio detto di *Urbs Vetus*, che corrisponde all'incirca all'area degli attuali Rignano Flaminio e Faleria.

Localizzazione incerta:

(a) una *massa Castelliana* locata al monastero di San Silvestro al Soratte fra 715 e 731 (Tomassetti 1884: 425-8).[107]

---

[106] Il *fundus Martinianus* richiama ovviamente il nome del lago di Martignano, che si trova ad est di quello di Bracciano; sulla *massa Cesana* e sui suoi dintorni, si veda Wickham (1978: 156-7). Tale *massa* sembra essersi conservata integra e caratterizzata essenzialmente da un'insediamento colonico sparso sino agli inizi del XII secolo, quando parte di essa fu distaccata dal patrimonio della diocesi di *Portus – Silva Candida*, in favore del monastero di San Paolo fuori le mura. Sulla connessione della *massa Cesana* con il territorio di Nepi in epoca altomedievale, si rinvengono utili informazioni in Penteriani e Penteriani Iacoangeli (1986: 35-76).
[107] Per la verità, il Tomassetti argomentava la sua ipotesi anche in funzione del fatto che il locatario della *massa Castelliana* era il monastero di San Silvestro al Soratte, in posizione contigua, quindi, a Civita Castellana.

zione sulla possibile esistenza di manodopera servi-
le all'interno delle terre pontificie laziali e anche in
aree assimilabili a quella romana per tradizioni gestionali della proprietà (come la Romagna, vedi Pasquali (1985)) le soluzioni ad analoghi quesiti re-
stano ancora piuttosto vaghe.

Per concludere, possiamo dire che il *Patrimonium
Tusciae* della Chiesa Romana (vale a dire, come
sembra, quello della cattedrale di Roma), mostra di
serbare al suo interno, almeno sino all'VIII secolo,
una struttura fondiaria forse non troppo modifica-
ta rispetto ai secoli della tarda antichità. Più plastica doveva essere l'articolazione interna dei patri-
moni fondiari di altri enti ecclesiastici ovvero di lai-
ci, ma va tenuto presente che la '*economic unit*' più
comune della proprietà terriera nel territorio romano, durante il IX secolo, continua ad essere ancora il *fundus*, anche grazie alla creazione di nuove
parcelle classificate in questo modo.[115] Un conser-
vatorismo lessicale, se così si può dire, che non ha
confronti in altre aree del Lazio (come la Tuscia
già longobarda e la Sabina), ove il *fundus* appare
nello stesso periodo come una realtà residuale, li-
mitata entro un numero di casi sempre decrescente.

Non tutto il territorio, però, come si è visto, era
suddiviso in *fundi*. E in alcuni casi (se vedano i *fundi invicem quoerentes* siti al IV-V miglio della via Clodia, menzionati nella concessione di Leone IV
dell'854, in favore di San Martino al Vaticano) essi
ci appaiono come delle vere e proprie 'isole' di terreni definiti in questo modo, circondati da entità
fondiarie di altro tipo (dei *casales*), ovvero da por-

zioni di terreno non delimitate (come le due *valles*
che confinano sul quarto lato con il suddetto gruppo di *fundi*).

Le lettura della documentazione sul Patrimonio
della Tuscia ci consente di immaginare un ordina-
mento del territorio che non ha conosciuto varia-
zioni strutturali di rilievo rispetto ai secoli dell'antichità tardiva, quanto piuttosto una semplificazio-
ne delle proprie componenti costitutive. I territori
cittadini, ad una certa distanza da Roma, continua-
no ad essere i referenti basilari per la localizzazione delle proprietà. Le superfici coltivate sono ge-
neralmente raggruppate in unità fondiarie dotate
di confini e nomi propri; l'insediamento rurale è
sparso all'interno di tali unità, che talora si mo-
strano dotate di propri luoghi di culto. La presenza di edifici in rovina, che in vari casi vengono
menzionati tra le caratteristiche interne di questo o
quel fondo, ci lasciano intravvedere i vuoti lasciati
dalla regressione demografica altomedievale, ma
anche l'incapacità – e forse il disinteresse – di prov-
vedere alla manutenzione dell'ingente patrimonio
edilizio rurale, ereditato dall'antichità, riducendo
al minimo indispensabile le strutture per l'abita-
zione e la produzione. Fenomeno che è stato del
resto ben testimoniato dal caso stesso di Monte Gelato, ove la fattoria tardoromana fu solo in minima
parte recuperata – e forse 'capita' – nella sua complessità planimetrica al momento delle ricostruzio-
ni del tardo VIII secolo, che pure videro la profu-
sione di notevoli risorse, ad esempio nella ricostru-
zione della chiesa.

---

[115] Analogo ragionamento vale per la *massa fundorum*, anch'essa prodotto della ristrutturazione fondiaria tardoantica. Ben testimoniata
nel territorio della Tuscia, la *massa*, in questo come in altri settori del suburbio romano mostra chiaramente di essere un agglomerato di
fundi cresciuto intorno a un *fundus* principale e eponimo, che forse era il cuore dei possedimenti di un *dominus* tardoantico (Vera 1995:
350-1).

Chapter Six

CONCLUSIONS

While necessarily repetitive of some of the arguments advanced in previous chapters, it will be as well to draw together the principal conclusions. It should be recognized that these are not cast in stone. Erroneous decipherment of the evidence in both the field and the study is a commonplace in archaeology, while mistakes and omissions in recording inevitably recur. Moreover, on a site as large as this, one can be certain that further investigation will bring modifications and additional perspectives. Although this is a 'final' report, its interim nature, as part of an ongoing programme of research by many archaeologists, requires emphasis. The perceived facts have been described as faithfully as possible; their interpretation is necessarily more provisional.

THE VILLA OF C. VALERIUS FAUSTUS (?)

Although the sherds found in field survey in the 1950s and 1960s indicated a Republican origin for the site, this was not supported by the results of the present excavations. The first buildings were laid out in the Augustan period, the choice of position no doubt influenced by the extraordinary beauty of the setting. The waterfalls, in particular, make this one of the most delightful places along the Treia valley, a point that will not have been lost upon an owner who was clearly conscious of the merits of ostentatious display. Moreover, the Mola di Monte Gelato has the additional advantage of easy accessibility via a good system of communications, not least by means of a country track (later to be paved), with the town of Veii, and with Rome itself. Thus, municipal obligations could be fulfilled easily, and the urban markets were likewise readily accessible, factors of enduring significance for much of the site's history.

The Augustan complex was indeed ornate. Although relatively little of its plan could be recovered, it was clearly provided with an imposing façade, embellished by some of the fine architectural elements found in the excavations. All was laid out in Roman feet, and within were gracious rooms, floored in mosaic and with painted wall-plaster; a courtyard with a pool and clumps of trees; and marble statuary (one from a nymphaeum) and other elements, such as a *labrum* from a fountain. There were probably ducks in the pool, to judge from the bones, as well as a small fish-pond, which provided a home for eels, very likely kept as pets (cf. Pliny, *Naturalis Historia* ix. 170-1) rather than for commercial purposes. Moreover, the bones also may indicate the existence of an aviary, with tawny owls, jays, chaffinches, thrushes and the like, perhaps penned in by nets in the trees in the courtyards. In short, the excavated evidence provides an extraordinary parallel for the features in the villa near Casinum, owned and described by Marcus Terentius Varro (116-27 BC); it is almost as though Monte Gelato was an 'off-the-peg' villa, based upon a reading of Varro (cf. Purcell 1988b: 196).

No *pars rustica* was discovered, although there would have been ample space for it; certainly, its existence cannot be ruled out without much more extensive investigation. The question of the identity of the owner may here be relevant. We earlier offered the very tentative suggestion that the tomb monument of the Valerii, which, from its size and preservation, was surely erected nearby, may record the name of the first owner, namely C. Valerius Faustus. As *magister* of the *Augustales* of Veii (a title likely to be of Augustan date), he would have been an important local official, and his profession, a cattle merchant, included some very rich people (Gilliver 1990; this volume). He is precisely the sort of *nouveau riche* who would have wished to construct for himself an elegant country residence – but conveniently close to Veii – and one can easily imagine him (or, more probably, one of his educated Greek slaves) consulting his edition of Varro's *Rerum rusticarum*. And certainly, as a *mercator bovarius*, we could expect him to have provided his villa with a *pars rustica*.

That much is, however, speculation. The links with Veii are nevertheless supported by the otherwise very rare *nomen* of his presumed wife, Aescionius, which is paralleled by that of a *duumvir* of Veii, Aescionius Capella, who was honoured by the *Augustales*; and by the tombstone of Herennia, who could have been connected with M. Herennius Picens, consul of AD 1 and patron of Veii. The pointers are, therefore, that in the main the early Imperial inhabitants of the Mola di Monte Gelato directed their attentions southward, towards Veii and Rome, rather than to local towns such as Nepi and Falerii Novi. Even so, the *Augustales* themselves were an important factor in promoting relations between Rome and the settlements in its hinterland, doubtless as a result of official encouragement. Colleges are known at Nepi (*CIL* XI 3200) and Falerii Novi (*CIL* XI 3083), and *seviri* are at-

noteworthy. We infer that, between the foundation of the *domusculta* and the abandonment of the site some three centuries later, *c.* AD 1100, the community became ever more parochial and conservative, isolated from the outside world. The recovery of but a single medieval coin, of AD 884-5, is perhaps symptomatic of this.

The abandonment of the pottery kiln, in the mid- (or possibly late) ninth century may mark the demise of the *domusculta* of *Capracorum* (itself not heard of in the documentary or epigraphic sources after AD 846). This is in line with the evidence from the estate-centre at Santa Cornelia (Christie and Daniels 1991: 187), and reflects a gradual diminution of papal authority at the hands of the Roman nobility (and, too, the impact of raids by the Arabs). At neither Santa Cornelia or Monte Gelato, however, is it possible to say much about events between the late ninth century and the beginning of the eleventh century. Although there is some pottery of this period at Monte Gelato, significant stratigraphical deposits were lacking, and only the sequence over the bath-house (Fig. 77) suggests unbroken occupation. On the other hand, many decorative elements in the church, including the very fine altar screen (if that is what is is) with the Agnus Dei, remained to be broken up *c.* AD 1000, and burials seem to have been made continuously: on balance, therefore, the indications are that the site remained in use over this time, albeit in a decaying state.

THE REBUILDING OF *c.* AD 1000, AND ITS DEMISE

There is unambiguous testimony to show that, in the late tenth or early eleventh century, the church was partly or wholly reconstructed; the baptistery was rebuilt on a much larger scale, with a rather grand font; and other rooms were added to the north of the baptistery, including an entrance. Although the work was relatively crude, and there is no surviving evidence for embellishment (which could, however, have been in perishable materials), the importance of the ecclesiastical complex would seem to have been strongly reaffirmed.

At first sight this is surprising, for it flies in the face of a rich vein of documentary sources, which shows that *incastellamento* in the Ager Faliscus was well under way by this time (Potter 1979: 164). The village adjacent to Mazzano, for example, is first heard of in AD 945 and Calcata, a little further down the Treia valley, in AD 974, and they were part of an extensive reorganization of the landscape. However, as Wickham (1979: 89) has pointed out, the term *fundus* commonly coexists with that of *castellum* in charters for the Ager Faliscus up to the twelfth century. Something of the late Antique arrangement of estates clearly survived well into

the Middle Ages, and the rebuilding of the complex at Monte Gelato may indeed reflect this.

If so, it was a short-lived revival. Around the beginning of the twelfth century the buildings were systematically demolished, and the materials carted away; even some of the post-holes for the scaffolding needed for this operation were identified in the baptistery. Occupation also ceased in the rock-cut cave and in the temple-tomb, and the impression is of a systematic and orderly evacuation. Indeed, some of the more important graves were emptied of the bones, and then reconstructed, which may well reflect the fact that the place was not forgotten. Burials continued to be made for a time, including those of children placed in graves cut into or across the demolished wall footings in the baptistery. Moreover, in the church a tufo block foundation was constructed, probably to support a wayside shrine or some other form of commemorative monument, such as a cross. Continued veneration of this long-lived focus of Christian worship and interment was clearly considered a matter of considerable consequence, hardly surprisingly in a small, close-knit rural community.

CASTELLACCIO: CASTRUM CAPRACORUM

That the population moved to the nearby castle site of Castellaccio (identifiable as *castrum Capracorum* from a bull of 1053) was, from the outset of our work, always seen as a likelihood. The juxtaposition of late Roman villas and medieval *castelli* is a striking feature of the Ager Faliscus, and a shift from one to the other has long seemed a probability (Potter 1975). While a view that this was the process that took place in the sixth-eighth centuries (Potter 1979: 165-7) is not supported by the present work, the occurrence in our trenches at Castellaccio of a little eleventh-century pottery and, overwhelmingly, of twelfth-century material, amply sustains this conclusion. Whether this was an enforced move (as the archaeological indications could well imply, given the signs of a reluctance to forget the site in the valley), or a voluntary decision to abandon an unprotectable location, is another matter. Perhaps the former is more likely, given the broader historical background (cf. Wickham 1979: 88-9).

The very limited scope of the excavations at Castellaccio (where heavy tree cover restricted trenching), allows few other conclusions. Unsurprising were the remains of a masonry curtain wall, with a building constructed behind it; nor the traces of timber structures, perhaps of the sort encountered at Ponte Nepesino (Cameron *et al.* 1984). More interesting were the signs from the animal bones that the stock economy had reverted to the rearing of sheep and goats, as in the late Roman period; once again, the traditional practices of the region since prehistoric times (Barker 1976), still current today, were being reasserted. No plant remains were recovered, but the present mill, itself likely to be of twelfth-century date, is surely testimony to the active cultivation of cereals. Even so, the dearth of refuse implies a relatively small community, and there is little evidence to show that Castellaccio was occupied much after the late thirteenth century. Indeed, the dearth of pottery other than sherds of the twelfth century suggests that a decline began soon after; a migration to Mazzano, which has traditionally included the Mola di Monte Gelato within its sphere of influence, is more than likely. Only the mill continued in use, exploiting its advantageous position on the river, and protected, it would seem, by militia based in an adjoining tower.

LATE MEDIEVAL AND POST-MEDIEVAL TIMES

Rome continued to exert a powerful influence in the region, whether through the Church or through noble families, for most of the later Middle Ages and post-medieval times. The Mola di Monte Gelato and Mazzano were both the property of the monastery of San Gregorio on the Coelian down to the early fourteenth century. Also Civita Castellana emerged as an important centre of papal power: this is symbolized by the construction of the monumental Porta Romana by Calixtus III (1455-8), and the papal fortress, started by Alexander VI (1492-1503) and completed by Sangallo the Elder for Julius II (1503-13). Likewise, Nepi was endowed with imposing fortifications by Duke Pier Luigi Farnese in 1540, and a papal aqueduct, built in 1727 (Tomassetti 1913 (1979): 150). The appearance of new road stations like Baccano and Settevene on the via Cassia, in the fifteenth-sixteenth centuries, further marks the re-establishment of papal authority. Some of the remoter medieval villages like Castel Porciano (Mallett and Whitehouse 1967) were abandoned, and many of the others demonstrate a conspicuous investment in new buildings from the sixteenth century onwards, Mazzano being but one example (Potter 1972). Indeed, in early post-medieval times, there was what seems to have been a significant spread of rural *casali*, perhaps indicating substantial changes in agrarian practices.

The continued importance of the mill in this period at the Mola di Monte Gelato is well documented (Fedeli, this volume). Yet, outside the major towns of the Ager Faliscus, and away from the main highways, one has the impression that a very ruralized existence, largely divorced from that of the city of Rome, persisted. This may well have become still more accentuated in the nineteenth century. Sadly, the journeys of George Dennis never took him to the area of Narce and Monte Gelato; but his evocative description of the view

from nearby Capena may well be apt: 'the bare swelling ground to the north with Soracte towering above: the snow-capt Apennines in the eastern horizon: the deep silence, the seclusion: the absence of human habitations (not even a shepherd's hut) within the sphere of vision, save the distant town of San Oreste .... compose a scene of more singular desolation than belongs to the site of any other Etruscan city in this district of the land' (Dennis 1878: I, 133). Similarly, the photographs of Thomas Ashby (1927; 1986), taken mainly in the first two decades of the twentieth century, depict an empty, desolate Campagna, despite the burgeoning of Rome at this time.

Even in the mid 1960s, when the writer first began to explore the Ager Faliscus, it seemed extraordinarily cut-off from Rome (Potter 1991). As a lengthy sojourn in Mazzano showed, considerations were above all parochial, and contact with Rome infrequent for many of the village populace. Equally, the region was seldom visited by outsiders, and tourism was non-existent. The Mola di Monte Gelato, then approached by a rutted *strada bianca*, was the preserve of local people, apart from visits from time to time by film and television crews. During the 1970s, however, as Rome dramatically expanded, this gradually began to change. With the construction of the Via Cassia *superstrada* (the Via Veientana) in the early 1980s, this part of the Campagna once again became much easier of access. The opening of the '*Parco suburbano della valle Treja*' in 1982 provided a further incentive for urban people to come to the area. Now the Mola is flooded with weekend visitors, new properties are rising everywhere, and the local dialect is almost submerged by a welter of non-regional and foreign tongues.

The story has therefore come full cycle. The city and its northern hinterland is once more fully integrated, as was the case in early Imperial times. The Latin, Greek and (probably) Faliscan, that will have been heard at the Mola in the first and second centuries AD, may have been replaced today by Italian, local and non-local, together with English, French, German and other languages; but the implication, namely of close links between the major international city of Rome and its *territorium*, is the same. Likewise, in the Carolingian era, a further period of prosperity in Rome (Delogu 1988), contacts were close. Only when Rome's power waned were these links reduced or severed, a matter put in sharp perspective by the results of the present investigation. In both late Roman and medieval times, considerations at the Mola became largely parochial; in the seventh and early to mid eighth centuries all contact was lost in what seems, at the Mola di Monte Gelato at any rate, to have been genuinely a Dark Age. We might with Krautheimer (1980: 93) recall that in Rome 'not a single building remains from the more than one hundred years between the construction of S. Agnese fuori

le mura (625-638) and that of S. Angelo in Pes-
chiera, 755'. To portray the settlements at the Mola
as in some respects a mirror of the history of the
city of Rome is assuredly to oversimplify: but to
deny a series of persistent echoes of the fortunes of
Rome, in this seemingly remote and rustic place in
the Roman Campagna, would indeed be perverse.
The waxing and waning of the city's power and
influence is, it would seem, writ large upon its adjacent landscape.

REFERENCES

Adams, J.P. (1984) *La construction romaine.* Paris.

Albarella, U. (1993) The fauna. In U. Albarella, V. Ceglia and P. Roberts, S. Giacomo degli Schiavoni (Molise): an early fifth century AD deposit of pottery and animal bones from central Adriatic Italy: 203-22, 226-30. *Papers of the British School at Rome* 61: 157-230.

Albarella, U. and Frezza, A. (n.d. a.) I reperti faunistici di GI 52. Unpublished bone report for P. Arthur, Naples.

Albarella, U. and Frezza, A. (n.d. b) I reperti faunistici di via San Paolo. Unpublished bone report for P. Arthur, Naples.

Allason-Jones, L. (1985) Bell-shaped studs? In M.C. Bishop (ed.), *The Production and Distribution of Roman Military Equipment* (BAR International Series 275): 95-108. Oxford.

Allason-Jones, L. (1989) Roman and native interaction in Northumberland. In V.A. Maxfield and M.J. Dobson (eds), *Roman Frontier Studies 1989*: 1-5. Exeter.

Allen, H.L. (1974) Excavations at Morgantina (Serra Orlando), 1970-1972: preliminary report XI. *American Journal of Archaeology* 78: 361-83.

Almagro-Gorbea, M.J. (1982) *El santuario de Juno en Gabii.* Rome.

Alvarez, W. (1972) The Treia valley north of Rome: volcanic stratigraphy, topographic evolution and geological influences on human settlement. *Geologica romana* 11: 153-76.

Alvarez, W. (1973) Ancient course of the Tiber River near Rome: an introduction to the Middle Pleistocene volcanic stratigraphy of central Italy. *Geological Society of America Bulletin* 84: 749-58.

Amelung, W. (1908) *Die Sculpturen des Vaticanischen Museums. Belvedere. Sala degli animali. Galleria delle statue. Sala de' busti. Gabinetto delle maschere. Loggia scoperta* II. Berlin.

'Amr, A.-J. (1984) Some Ayyubid pottery lamps from Rujm al-Kursi and other related Mamluke examples. *Berytus* 32: 201-10.

Andreolli, B. (1981) I prodotti alimentari nei contratti agrari toscani dell'alto medievo. *Archeologia medievale* 8: 117-26.

Andrews, D. (1978) Medieval masonry in northern Lazio: its development and uses for dating. In H. Blake, T.W. Potter and D. Whitehouse (eds), *Papers in Italian Archaeology* I. *The Lancaster Seminar* (BAR International Series 41): 391-412. Oxford.

Andrews, D. (1982) L'evoluzione della tecnica muraria nell'alto Lazio. *Biblioteca e società* 1-2: 3-16.

Annechino, M. (1982) Suppellettile fittile per uso agricolo in Pompeii e nell'agro vesuviano. In *La regione sotterrata dal Vesuvio* (*Atti del Convegno Internazionale (Naples)*): 753-73.

Arnason, H.H. (1936) Early Christian silver in North Italy and Gaul. *The Art Bulletin* 20 (3): 193-226.

Arthur, P. (1983) The pottery. In E. Fentress, S. Judson, T. Blagg, M. de Vos and P. Arthur, Excavations at Fosso della Crescenza, 1962: 78-96. *Papers of the British School at Rome* 51: 58-101.

Arthur, P. (1993) Early medieval amphorae, the duchy of Naples and the food supply of Rome. *Papers of the British School at Rome* 61: 231-44.

Arthur, P. and Whitehouse, D.B. (1982) La ceramica dell'Italia meridionale: produzione e mercato tra V e X secolo. *Archeologia medievale* 9: 39-46.

Arthur, P. and Whitehouse, D.B. (1983) Appunti sulla produzione laterizia nell'Italia centro-meridionale tra il VI e il XII secolo. *Archeologia medievale* 10: 525-37.

Arthur, P., Caggia, M.P., Ciongoli, G.P., Melissano, V., Patterson, H. and Roberts, P. (1992) Fornaci medievali ad Otranto. Nota preliminare. *Archeologia medievale* 19: 91-122.

Ascadi, G. and Nemeskeri J. (1970) *History of Human Life Span and Mortality.* Budapest.

Ashby, T. (1927) *The Roman Campagna in Classical Times* (1970 reprint). Tonbridge.

Ashby, T. (1986) *Thomas Ashby. Un archeologo fotografa la campagna romana tra '800 e '900.* Rome.

Auth, S.H. (1976) *Ancient Glass at the Newark Museum.* Newark, N.J.

Avagnina, M.E., Garibaldi, V. and Salterini, C. (1976-77) Strutture murarie degli edifici di Roma nel XII secolo. *Rivista dell'Istituto nazionale d'archeologia e storia dell'arte* 23-4: 242-7.

Bailey, D.M. (1980) *Catalogue of the Lamps in the British Museum* ii, *Roman Lamps made in Italy.* London.

Bailey, D.M. (1988) *Catalogue of the Lamps in the British Museum* iii, *Roman Provincial Lamps.* London.

Baker, P. and Clark, G. (1993) Archaeozoological evidence for medieval Italy: a critical review of the present state of research. *Archeologia medievale* 20: 45-77.

Balsdon, J.P.V.D. (1962) *Roman Women.* London.

Baradez, J. (1957) Nouvelles fouilles à Tipasa. Les fours à chaux des constructeurs de l'enceiente. *Libyca* 5: 277-94.

Barker, B.C.W. (1975) Relation of the alveolus to the cemeto-enamel junction following attritional wear in Aboriginal skulls. An enquiry into the normality of cementum exposure with ageing. *Journal of Periodontology* 46 (6): 357-63.

Barker, G.W.W. (1973) The economy of medieval Tuscania: the archaeological evidence. *Papers of the British School at Rome* 41: 155-77.

Barker, G.W.W. (1976) Animal husbandry at Narce. In T.W. Potter, *A Faliscan Town in South Etruria. Excavations at Narce 1966-71*: 295-307. London.

Barker, G.W.W. (1977) L'economia del bestiame a Luni. In A. Frova (ed.), *Scavi di Luni. Relazione delle campagne di scavo 1972-1973-1974*: 725-35. Rome.

Barker, G.W.W. (1982) The animal bones. In D.B. Whitehouse, G. Barker, R. Reece and D. Reese, The Schola Praeconum I: the coins, pottery, lamps and fauna: 81-91, 96-9. *Papers of the British School at Rome* 50: 53-101.

Barnish, S.J.B. (1987) Pigs, plebeians and potentes: Rome's economic hinterland *c.* 350-600 AD. *Papers of the British School at Rome* 55: 157-85.

Barnish, S.J.B. (1995) Christians and countrymen at San Vincenzo, *c.* AD 400-550. In R. Hodges (ed.), *San Vincenzo al Volturno 2: The 1980-86 Excavations Part II (Archaeological Monographs of the British School at Rome* 9): 131-7. London.

Baroni, E. (1980) *Guida botanica d'Italia.* Bologna.

Baruzzi, M. (1987) I reperti in ferro dello scavo di Villa Clelia (Imola). Note sull'attrezzatura agricola nell'altomedioevo. In R. Francovich (ed.), *Archeologia e storia del medioevo italiano (Studi NIS Archeologia* 3): 149-70. Rome.

Bass, G.F. and von Doorninck, F.H. (1982) *Yassi Ada.* Texas.

Bass, W.M. (1987) *Human Osteology: a Laboratory and Field Manual of the Human Skeleton* (third edition) (Missouri Archaeological Association Special Publications). Columbia.

Bavant, B. (1979) Le duché byzantin de Rome. Origine, durée et extension géographique. *Mélanges de l'Ecole Française de Rome. Moyen Âge et Temps Modernes* 91: 41-89.

Becatti, G. *et al.* (1970) *Mosaici antichi in Italia. Regione settima. Baccano: villa romana.* Rome.

Beltran Lloris, M. (1970) *Anforas romanas de España.* Zaragoza.

Berry, A.C. and Berry, R.J. (1967) Epigenetic variation in the human cranium. *Journal of Anatomy* 101: 361-79.

Bertelli, G., Guiglia Guidobaldi, A. and Rovigatti Spagnoletti Zeuli, P. (1976-77) Strutture murarie degli edifici di Roma nel XII secolo. *Rivista dell'Istituto nazionale d'archeologia e storia dell'arte* 23-4: 160-4.

Bertolini, O. (1947) Per la storia delle diaconie romane dalle origini alla fine del sec. VIII *Archivio della Società romana di storia patria* 70: 1-145.

Bianchi, L. (1989) Roma: tessuto urbano e tipologie monumentali. *Studi romani* 37: 104-15.

Bird, J. (1993) The 1969 excavations. In J. Bird, A. Claridge, O. Gilkes and D. Neal, Porta Pia: excavations and survey in an area of suburban Rome, Part I: 52-100. *Papers of the British School at Rome* 61: 51-113.

Birley, A. (1971) *Septimius Severus. The African Emperor.* London.

Blake, H. McK. (1983) Sepolture. *Archeologia medievale* 10: 175-97.

Blake, M.E. (1947) *Ancient Roman Construction in Italy from the Prehistoric Period to Augustus.* Washington.

Blake, M.E. and Bishop, D.T. (1973) *Roman Construction in Italy from Nerva through the Antonines.* Philadelphia.

BMC = H. Mattingly (1923-) *The Coins of Rome and the Roman Empire in the British Museum.* London.

Boardman, J. (1974) *Athenian Black Figure Vases.* London.

Boessneck, J. (1969) Osteological differences between sheep (*Ovis aries* Linné) and goat (*Capra hircus* Linné). In D. Brothwell and E. Higgs (eds), *Science in Archaeology* (second edition): 331-58. London.

Bonanno, M. (1979) Tipi e varietà di lucerne arabo-normanne rinvenute a Palermo. *Archeologia medievale* 6: 353-8.

Bonatti, E. (1970) Pollen sequence in the lake sediments. In G. Hutchinson (ed.), *Ianula – an Account of the History and Development of the Lago di Monterosi, Latium, Italy (Transactions of the American Philosophical Society* 40/4): 26-31.

Bond, F. (1908) *Fonts and Font Covers.* London.

Bonifay, M., Paroli, L. and Picon, M. (1986) Ceramiche a vetrina pesante scoperte a Roma e a Marsiglia: risultati delle prime analisi fisico-chimiche. *Archeologia medievale* 13: 79-95.

Bosio, B. and Pugnetti, A. (1984) (eds) *Gli etruschi di Cerveteri.* Modena.

Bosman, F. (1993) Viabilità ed insediamenti lungo la via Flaminia nell'alto medievo. In L. Paroli and P. Delogu (eds), *La storia economica di Roma nell'alto medioevo alla luce dei recenti scavi archeologici*: 295-308. Florence, All'Insegna del Giglio.

Bovini, G. (1960) L'impiego di tubi fittili nelle volte degli edifici a culto ravennati. *Felix Ravenna* (3rd series) 30: 78-99.

Brants, J. (1913) *Antieke Terra-Cotta Lampen uit het Rijksmuseum van Oudheden te Leiden.* Leiden.

Broneer, O. (1930) *Corinth IV, 2, Terracotta Lamps.* Cambridge, Mass.

Broneer, O. (1947) Investigations at Corinth, 1946-1947. *Hesperia* 16: 233-47.

Brothwell, D.R. (1972) *Digging up Bones* (second edition). London.

Brothwell, D.R. (1981) *Digging up Bones. The Excavation, Treatment and Study of Human Skeletal Remains* (third edition). London and Oxford.

Brown, T.S. (1984) *Gentlemen and Officers: Imperial Administration and Aristocratic Power in Roman Italy, 504-800.* London.

Bull, G. and Payne, S. (1982) Tooth eruption and epiphysial fusion in pigs and wild boar. In B. Wilson, C. Grigson and S. Payne (eds), *Ageing and Sexing Animal Bones from Archaeological Sites* (BAR British Series 109): 55-71. Oxford.

Bullock, D. and Rackham, J. (1982) Epiphysial fusion and tooth eruption of feral goats from Moffatdale, Dumfries and Galloway, Scotland. In B. Wilson, C. Grigson and S. Payne (eds), *Ageing and Sexing Animal Bones from Archaeological Sites* (BAR British Series 109): 73-80. Oxford.

Burnett, D., Clark, G. and Sutherland, S. (forthcoming) The animal bones from the Mura di Santo Stefano (Anguillara). In *Excavations at the Mura di Santo Stefano (Anguillara).*

Burzachechi, M. (1962) Oggetti parlanti nelle epigrafi greche. *Epigraphica* 24: 3-54.

Buxton, L.H.D. (1938) Platymeria and platycnemia. *Journal of Anatomy* 73: 31-6.

Camaiora, R. (1985) Suppellettile da mensa. Ceramica a parete sottili. In A. Ricci (ed.), *Settefinestre. Una villa schiavistica nell'Etruria romana. 2. La villa e i suoi reperti*: 166-73. Modena.

Cambi, F. (1990) *Paesaggi romani dell'Etruria meridionale.* Tesi di Dottorato di Ricerca in Archeologia, Università di Pisa, III Ciclo, 1987-1990.

Cameron, F., Clark, G., Jackson, R., Johns, C., Philpot, S., Potter, T., Shepherd, J., Stone, M. and Whitehouse, D. (1984) Il castello di Ponte Nepesino e il confine settentrionale del Ducato di Roma. *Archeologia medievale* 11: 63-147.

Cameron, J. (1934) *The Skeleton of British Neolithic Man.* London.

Capitulario Regum Francorum = A. Boretius (ed.) (1883) Capitularia Regum Francorum. In *Monu-menta Germaniae Historica, Legum Sectio II, Capitularia Regum Francorum I.* Hannover.

Cappelletto, R. (1983) *Recuperi Ammianei in Biondo Flavio.* Rome.

Carandini, A. (ed.) (1985) *Settefinestre. Una villa schiavistica nell'Etruria romana. 1* La villa nel suo insieme, 1** La villa nelle sue parti.* Modena.

Carandini, A. (1989) L'economia italica fra tarda repubblica e medio impero considerata dal punto di vista di una merce: il vino. In *Amphores romaines et historie économique, dix ans de recherche* (*Collection de l'Ecole Française de Rome* 114): 505-21.

Carandini, A. and Panella, C. (1981) The trading connections of Rome and central Italy in the late second and third centuries: the evidence of the Terme del Nuotatore excavations, Ostia. In A. King and M. Henig (eds), *The Roman West in the Third Century*: 487-503. Oxford.

Carbonara, A. and Messineo, G. (1993) La Celsa. Il complesso delle fornaci. *Bullettino della Commissione archeologica comunale di Roma* 91: 542-8.

Carroll-Spillecke, M. (ed.) (1992) *Der Garten von der Antike bis zum Mittelalter.* Mainz.

Cassanelli, R. (1987) Materiali lapidei a Milano in età longobarda. In C. Bertelli (ed.), *Milano, una capitale da Ambrogio ai Carolingi*: 238-57. Milan.

Castagnetti, A. (1980) Continuità e discontinuità nella terminologia e nella realtà organizzativa agraria: 'fundus' e 'casale' nei documenti ravennati altomedievali. In V. Fumagalli and G. Rossetti (eds), *Medioevo rurali*: 201-19. Bologna.

Cecchelli Trinci, M.M. (1980) La chiesa di S. Agata *in fundo Lardario* e il cimitero dei SS Processo e Martiniano. *Quaderni dell'Istituto di archeologia e storia antica dell'Università di Chieti* 1: 85-111.

Ceci, M. (1992) Note sulla circolazione delle lucerne a Roma nell'VIII secolo: i contesti della Crypta Balbi, con Appendice di H. Patterson. *Archeologia medievale* 19: 749-66.

Celuzza, M.G. (1985) La ceramica invetriata. In A. Ricci (ed.), *Settefinestre. Una villa schiavistica nell'Etruria romana. 2. La villa e i suoi reperti*: 163-6. Modena.

Cherkauer, D. (1976) Site K. The stratigraphy and chronology of the River Treia alluvial deposits. In T.W. Potter, *A Faliscan Town in South Etruria. Excavations at Narce 1966-71*: 106-20. London.

Chevallier, R. (1976) *Roman Roads.* London.

Christie, N. (1991a) Three South Etrurian churches – an overview. In N. Christie (ed.), *Three South Etrurian Churches: Santa Cornelia, Santa Rufina and San Liberato* (*Archaeological Monographs of the British School at Rome* 4): 353-9. London.

Llewellyn, P. (1983) *Rome in the Dark Ages* (second edition). London.

Llewellyn, P. (1991) The historical record: the bishopric of *Silva Candida* at S. Rufina. In N. Christie (ed.) (1991), *Three South Etrurian Churches: Santa Cornelia, Santa Rufina and San Liberato* (*Archaeological Monographs of the British School at Rome* 4): 214-23. London.

Lloyd-Morgan, G. (1981) *Description of the Collections in the Rijksmuseum G.M. Kam at Nijmegen. IX. The Mirrors.* Nijmegen.

Loeschcke, S. (1919) *Lampen aus Vindonissa.* Zürich.

Lopez Mullor, A. (1989) *Las ceramicas romanas de paredas finas en Cataluna.* Zaragoza.

Lovejoy, C.O., Burstein, A.H. and Heiple, K.G. (1976) The biomechanical analysis of bone strength: a method and its application to platycnemia. *American Journal of Physical Anthropology* 44: 489-506.

Lovejoy, C.O. Meindl, R.S. and Mensforth, R.P. (1985) Multifactorial determination of skeletal age at death; a method and blind tests of its accuracy. *American Journal of Physical Anthropology* 68: 1-14.

LRBC = R.A.G. Carson, P.V. Hill and J.P.C. Kent (1960) *Late Roman Bronze Coinage.* London.

Lugli, G. (1957) *La tecnica edilizia romana.* Rome.

Luni I = (1973) *Scavi di Luni I. Relazione preliminare della campagna di scavo 1970-1971.* Rome.

Luni II = (1977) *Scavi di Luni II. Relazione delle campagne di scavo 1972-1974.* Rome.

Lupu, N. (1937) La Villa dei Sette Bassi sulla Via Latina. *Ephemeris Dacoromana:* 117-88.

Maccabruni, C. (1987) Ceramica romana con invetriatura al piombo. In P. Lévêque and J-P. Morel (eds), *Ceramiques hellénistiques et romaines* II: 167-89. Paris.

Macchiarella, G. (1976) Note sulla scultura in marmo a Roma tra VIII e IX secolo. *Roma e l'età Carolingia:* 289-99. Rome.

Macchiarola, I. (1989) Il sepolcreto sannitico di Gildone. *Conoscenze* 5: 37-79.

MacDougall, E.B. and Jashemski, W.F. (1981) *Ancient Roman Gardens.* Dumbarton Oaks.

MacGregor, A. (1985) *Bone, Antler, Ivory and Horn.* London.

Maioli, M.G. (1983) La ceramica invetriata. In G. Bermond Montanari (ed.), *Ravenna e il porto di Classe. Vent'anni di ricerche archeologiche tra Ravenna e Classe:* 113-17. Imola.

Mallett, M. and Whitehouse, D.B. (1967) Castel Porciano: an abandoned medieval village of the Roman Campagna. *Papers of the British School at Rome* 35: 113-46.

Manacorda, D., Paroli, L., Molinari, A., Ricci, M. and Romei, D. (1986) La ceramica medioevale di Roma nella stratigrafia della Crypta Balbi. In *La ceramica medievale nel Mediterraneo occidentale* (*Atti del III Congresso Internazionale*): 511-44. Florence.

Manchester, K. (1983) *The Archaeology of Disease.* Bradford.

Mango, C. (1972) *The Art of the Byzantine Empire, 312-1453* (*Sources and Documents in the History of Art*). Englewood Cliffs.

Manning, W.H. (1966) A hoard of Romano-British ironwork from Brampton, Cumberland. *Transactions of the Cumberland and Westmorland Antiquarian and Archaeological Society* 66: 1-36.

Manning, W.H. (1983) The cauldron chains of Iron Age and Roman Britain. In B. Hartley and J. Wacher (eds), *Rome and her Northern Provinces:* 132-54. Gloucester.

Manning, W.H. (1985) *Catalogue of the Romano-British Iron Tools, Fittings and Weapons in the British Museum.* London.

Marabini Moevs, M.T. (1973) *The Roman Thin Walled Pottery from Cosa* (*Memoirs of the American Academy at Rome* 32). Rome.

Marazzi, F. (1988a) L'insediamento nel suburbio di Roma fra IV e VIII secolo. Considerazioni a 80 anni dai 'Wanderings in the Roman Campagna' di R. Lanciani. *Bollettino dell'Istituto storico italiano e archivio muratoriano* 94: 256-313.

Marazzi, F. (1988b) Inquadramentro storico del sito di Mola di Monte Gelato: suoi legami con le vicende dei possessi fondiari della Chiesa Romana nell'alto Medioevo. In T.W. Potter and A.C. King, Scavi alla Mola di Monte Gelato, presso Mazzano Romano, Etruria Meridionale: primo rapporto preliminare: 301-9. *Archeologia medievale* 15: 253-311.

Marazzi, F. (1991a) Il conflitto fra Leone III Isaurico e il papato fra il 725 e il 733, e il 'definitivo' inizio del medioevo a Roma: un'ipotesi in discussione. *Papers of the British School at Rome* 59: 231-57.

Marazzi, F. (1991b) *Il Patrimonium Sancti Petri da proprietà fondiaria a entità politica.* Thesis for a *Dottorato di Ricerca* in medieval history, *IV Ciclo,* University of Turin, 1988-91.

Marazzi, F. (1993) Roma, il Lazio, il Mediterraneo: relazioni fra economia e politica VII-IX secolo. In L. Paroli and P. Delogu (eds), *La storia economica di Roma nell'alto medioevo alla luce dei recenti scavi archeologici:* 267-85. Florence.

Marazzi, F. (1994a) Le 'città nuove' pontificie e l'insediamento laziale nel IX secolo. In R. Francovich and G. Noyé (eds), *La storia dell'alto medioevo italiano (VI-XI secolo) alla luce dell'archeologia*: 251-77. Florence.

Marazzi, F. (1994b) Proprietà fondiaria nel braccianese durante il primo medioevo (secoli VII-IX). In *Atti del convegno "Antichità tardoromane e altomedievali nel territorio di Bracciano"*: 299-314. Rome.

Marazzi, F. (in press) I "Patrimonia" laziali della chiesa romana tra IX secolo e inizi del X: strutture amministrative e prassi gestionali. *Nuova studi storici* 37.

Marazzi, F., Potter, T.W. and King, A.C. (1989) Mola di Monte Gelato (Mazzano Romano – VT): notizie preliminari sulle campagne di scavo 1986-1988 e considerazione sulle origini dell'incastellamento in Etruria meridionale alla luce dei nuovi dati archeologici. *Archeologia medievale* 16: 103-19.

Marini, G. (1805) *I papiri diplomatici*. Rome.

Martin, A. (1992a) Ceramica fine a Roma e Ostia tra la seconda metà del I e il II secolo. *Rei Cretariae* 31-2: 91-104.

Martin, A. (1992b) La ceramica invetriata romano: la testimonianza dell'area NE delle Terme del Nuotatore ad Ostia. In L. Paroli (ed.), *La ceramica invetriata tardoantica e altomedievale in Italia*: 323-9. Florence.

Martinori, E. (1930) *Via Cassia*. Rome.

Mastroroberto, M. (ed.) (1990) *Archeologia e botanica. Atti del Convegno di studi sul contributo della botanica alla conoscenza e alla conservazione delle aree archeologiche vesuviane*. Rome.

Matheson, S.B. (1980) *Ancient Glass in the Yale University Art Gallery*. Yale.

Matthiae, G. (1952) La iconostasi della chiesa di S. Leone a Capena. *Bollettino d'arte* ser. IV, no. 37: 293-9.

Mattias, P. and Ventriglia, U. (1968) *Carta geologica – regione vulcanica dei Monti Sabatini e Cimini*. Florence.

Mattias, P. and Ventriglia, U. (1970) La regione vulcanica dei Monti Sabatini e Cimini. *Memorie della Società di geologia italiana* 9: 331-84, maps.

Mayet, F. (1975) *Les céramiques à parois fines dans la peninsule Iberique*. Paris.

Mays, S.A. (1991a) *The Burials from the Whitefriars Friary Site, Buttermarket, Ipswich, Suffolk (Excavated 1986-1988) (Ancient Monuments Laboratory Report 17/91)*.

Mays, S.A. (1991b) *The Medieval Blackfriars from the Blackfriars Friary, Ipswich, Suffolk (Excavated 1983-1985) (Ancient Monuments Laboratory Report 16/91)*.

Mazza, M. (1986) Organizzazione produttiva e forza lavoro nell'agricultura romana di età imperiale. Premesse economiche del colonato tardoromano. In *La fatica dell'uomo. Schiavi e liberi nel mondo romano*: 119-94. Catania.

Mazzucato, O. (1972) *La ceramica a vetrina pesante*. Rome.

Mazzucato, O. (1977) *La ceramica laziale nell'altomedioevo*. Rome.

McCarthy, M.R. (1991) *Roman Waterlogged Remains at Castle Street, Carlisle*. Stroud.

McCrea, J.M. (1950) The isotopic chemistry of carbonates and a palaeotemperature scale. *Journal of Chemical Physics* 18: 849-57.

McKern, T.W. and Stewart, T.D. (1957) *Skeletal Age Changes in Young American Males (Technical Report for the Headquarters Quartermaster Research and Development Command (Natwick, Massachusetts))*.

McMinn, R.M.H. and Hutchings, R.T. (1977) *A Colour Atlas of Human Anatomy*. London.

Meates, G.W. (1987) *The Roman Villa at Lullingstone, Kent*. Maidstone.

Mello, E., Monna, D. and Oddone, M. (1988) Discriminating sources of Mediterranean marbles: a pattern recognition approach. *Archaeometry* 30 (1): 102-8.

MIB = W. Hahn (1973) *Moneta Imperii Byzantini* I. Vienna.

Michellucci, M. (1985) *Roselle. La domus dei mosaici*. Montepulciano.

Mielsch, H. (1987) *Die Römische Villa: Architektur und Lebensform*. Munich.

Migliario, E. (1992) Terminologia e organizzazione agraria tra tardo antico e alto medioevo: ancora su *fundus* e *casalis/casale*. *Athenaeum* 80 (2): 371-84.

Miles, A.E.W. (1978) Teeth as an indication of age in man. In P.M. Butler and K.A. Joysey (eds), *Development, Function and Evolution of Teeth*: 455-64. London.

Modzelewski, K. (1978) La transizione dall'antichità al feudalesimo. In R. Romano and C. Vivanti (eds), *Storia d'Italia 'Einaudi', Annali, 2, Dal feudalesimo al capitalismo*: 3-110. Turin.

Monacchi, D. (1990) Lugnano in Teverina (Terni). Loc. Poggio Gramignano. Saggi di scavo di una villa rustica romana. *Notizie degli scavi di antichità*: 5-36.

Montanari, M. (1989) Campagne e contadini nell'Italia bizantina (Esarcato e Pentapoli). *Mélanges de l'Ecole Française de Rome. Moyen Âge et Temps Modernes* 101 (2): 597-607.

Montanari, M. and Andreolli, B. (1983) *L'azienda curtense in Italia*. Bologna.

Moore, W.J. and Corbett, E. (1973) The distribution of dental caries. In *Ancient British Populations* (*Caries Research* 7): 139-53.

Moretti, M. (1978) *Cerveteri*. Novara.

Moretti, M. and Moretti, A.M.S. (1977) *La villa dei Volusii a Lucus Feroniae*. Rome.

Munzi, M. and Crifani, G. (1995) Considerazioni sugli insediamenti in area falisca. In N. Christie (ed.), *Papers of the Fifth Conference on Italian Archaeology*: 387-94. Oxford.

Murray, O., Parsons P., Potter, T.W. and Roberts, P. (1991) A 'stork-vase' from the Mola di Monte Gelato. *Papers of the British School at Rome* 59: 177-95.

Neumann, G. (1988) Ein späthellenistisches Tondo-Bildnis. *Athenische Mitteilungen* 103: 221-38.

Neville, R.C. (1856) Description of a remarkable deposit of Roman antiquities of iron, discovered at Great Chesterford, Essex, in 1854. *Archaeological Journal* 13: 1-13.

Nichol, R.K. and Wild, C.J. (1984) "Numbers of individuals" in faunal analysis: the decay of fish bone in archaeological sites. *Journal of Archaeological Science* 11: 35-51.

Nicholson, P.T. and Patterson, H. (1989) Ceramic technology in Upper Egypt: a study of pottery firing. *World Archaeology* 21 (1): 71-86.

Nordhagen, P.J. (1976) Un problema di carattere iconografico e tecnico a S. Prasede. *Roma e l'età Carolingia*: 159-66. Rome.

O'Connor, T.P. (1986) The garden dormouse *Eliomys quercinus* from Roman York. *Journal of Zoology* 210: 620-2.

Oliver, A. Jr (1980) *Ancient Glass in the Carnegie Museum of Natural History, Pittsburgh*. Pittsburgh.

Ortner, D.J. and Putschar, W.G.J. (1981) *Identification of Pathological Conditions in Human Skeletal Remains*. Smithsonian Institute.

Orton, C. (1975) Quantitative pottery studies: some progress, problems and prospects. *Science and Archaeology* 16: 30-5.

Orton, C. (1982) Computer simulation experiments to assess the performance of measures of quantities of pottery. *World Archaeology* 14 (1): 1-20.

Ostia I (1968) (*Studi Miscellanei* 13).

Ostia II (1970) (*Studi Miscellanei* 16).

Ostia III (1973) (*Studi Miscellanei* 21).

Ostia IV (1978) (*Studi Miscellanei* 23).

Oxé, A. and Comfort, H. (1968) *Corpus Vasorum Arretinorum*. Bonn.

Pallottino, M. (1937) Capena – resti di costruzioni romane e mediovali in località 'Montecanino'. *Notizie degli scavi di antichità*: 7-28.

Panella, C. (1968) Anfore. In *Ostia* I (*Studi Miscellanei* 13): 97-135.

Panella, C. (1973) Appunto su un gruppo di anfore della prima, media e tarda età imperiale (secoli I-IV). In *Ostia* III (*Studi Miscellanei* 21): 460-633.

Panella, C. (1986) Oriente ed occidente: considerazioni su alcune anfore "egee" di età imperiale a Ostia. In J.-Y. Empereur and Y. Garlan (eds), *Recherches sur les amphores grecques* (*BCH* Supp. XIII): 609-36.

Panella, C. (1989) Le anfore italiche del II secolo d.C. In *Amphores romaines et histoire économique, dix ans de recherche* (*Collection de l'Ecole Française de Rome* 114): 139-78.

Parker, A. (1977) Lusitanian amphoras. In *Méthodes classiques et méthodes formelles dans l'étude des amphores* (*Collection de l'Ecole Française de Rome* 32): 35-40.

Paroli, L. (1986) Ceramiche a vetrina pesante e macchie. In D. Manacorda, L. Paroli, A. Molinari, M. Ricci and D. Romei, La ceramica medioevale di Roma nella stratigrafia della Crypta Balbi: 516-20. In *La ceramica medievale nel Mediterraneo occidentale* (*Atti del III Congresso Internazionale*): 511-44. Florence.

Paroli, L. (1990) Ceramica a vetrina pesante altomedievale (Forum ware) e medievale (Sparse glazed). Altre invetriate tardo-antiche e altomedievale. In L. Saguì and L. Paroli (eds), *Archeologia urbana a Roma: il progetto della Crypta Balbi, 5. L'esedra della Crypta Balbi nel medioevo (XI-XV secolo)*: 314-56. Florence.

Paroli, L. (1991) I laterizi. In N. Christie (ed.), *Three South Etrurian Churches: Santa Cornelia, Santa Rufina and San Liberato* (*Archaeological Monographs of the British School at Rome* 4): 152-72. London.

Paroli, L. (1992a) Ceramiche invetriate da un contesto dell'VIII secolo della Crypta Balbi, Roma. In L. Paroli (ed.), *La ceramica invetriata tardoantica e altomedievale in Italia*: 351-7. Florence.

Paroli, L. (1992b) La ceramica invetriata tardo-antica e medievale nell'Italia centro-meridionale. In L. Paroli (ed.), *La ceramica invetriata tardoantica e altomedievale in Italia*: 33-61. Florence.

Paroli, L. (1993a) Ostia nella tarda antichità e nell'alto medioevo. In L. Paroli and P. Delogu (eds), *La storia economica di Roma nell'alto medioevo alla luce dei recenti scavi archeologici*: 153-65. Florence.

Paroli, L. (1993b) Porto (Fiumicino). Area II-2000. I. In L. Paroli and P. Delogu (eds), *La storia economica di Roma nell'alto medioevo alla luce dei recenti scavi archeologici*: 231-43. Florence.

Pasquali, G. (1985) I rapporti di lavoro: resistenze e cambiamenti nelle campagne romagnole del Medioevo. In B. Andreolli, V. Fumagalli and M. Montanari (eds), *Le campagne italiane prima e dopo il mille. Una società in trasformazione*: 69-94. Bologna.

Pasqui, A. and Cozza, A. (1894) Antichità del territorio Falisco esposte nel Museo Nazionale romano a Villa Giulia. *Monumenti antichi* 4.

Pasquinucci, M. and Storti, S. (1989) *Pisa antica. Scavi nel giardino dell'Arcivescovado*. Pontedera.

Patterson, H. (1991) Early medieval and medieval pottery. In N. Christie (ed.) (1991), *Three South Etrurian Churches: Santa Cornelia, Santa Rufina and San Liberato* (*Archaeological Monographs of the British School at Rome 4*): 120-36. London.

Patterson, H. (1992) La ceramica a vetrina pesante (Forum ware) e la ceramica a vetrina sparsa da alcuni siti nella Campagna romana. In D. Manacorda, L. Paroli, A. Molinari, M. Ricci and D. Romei, La ceramica medioevale di Roma nella stratigrafia della Crypta Balbi: 529-43. In *La ceramica medievale nel Mediterraneo occidentale* (*Atti del III Congresso Internazionale*): 511-44. Florence.

Patterson, H. (1993a) Pianabella (Ostia Antica). La ceramica altomedievale. In L. Paroli and P. Delogu (eds), *La storia economica di Roma nell'alto medioevo alla luce dei recenti scavi archeologici*: 219-31. Florence.

Patterson, H. (1993b) Un'aspetto dell'economia di Roma e della Campagna romana nell'altomedioevo: l'evidenza della ceramica. In L. Paroli and P. Delogu (eds), *La storia economica di Roma nell'alto medioevo alla luce dei recenti scavi archeologici*: 309-31. Florence.

Patterson, H. and Whitehouse, D. (1992) The medieval pottery from Otranto. In F. D'Andria and D. Whitehouse (eds), *Otranto: the Excavations of the British School, Vol. II. The Finds*: 87-196. Galatina.

Patterson, J.R. (1987) Crisis: what crisis? Rural change and urban development in Imperial Appennine Italy. *Papers of the British School at Rome* 55: 115-46.

Pavolini, C. (1980a) Appunti sui 'vasetti ovoidi e piriformi' di Ostia. *Melanges de l'Ecole Française de Rome. Antiquité* 92 (2): 993-1020.

Pavolini, C. (1980b) Una produzione italica di lucerne: le Vogelkopflampen ad ansa trasversale. *Bullettino della Commissione archeologica comunale di Roma* 85: 45-134.

Pavolini, C. (1982) *Itinerari ostiensi IV. Ostia, vita quotidiana II. L'edilizia – Le attività artigianali – Il commercio*. Rome.

Payne, S. (1990) Preliminary report on the animal bones from the Palatine East excavations, Rome, 1989-90. Unpublished bone report.

Peacock, D.P.S. (1977) *Pottery and Early Commerce*. London.

Peacock, D.P.S. (1982) *Pottery in the Roman World*. London.

Peacock, D.P.S. and Williams, D.F. (1986) *Amphorae and the Roman Economy*. London.

Peduto, P. (1984) *Villaggi fluviali nella pianura Pestana del secolo VI* (*Studi storici meridionali*). Salerno.

Peña, J.T. (1987) *Roman-period Ceramic Production in Etruria Tiberina: a Geographical and Compositional Study*. Unpublished Ph.D. thesis, University of Michigan.

Peña, J.T. (1990) Internal Red-Slip cookware (Pompeian Red Ware) from Cetamura del Chianti, Italy: mineralogical composition and provenience. *American Journal of Archaeology* 94: 647-61.

Penhallurick, R.D. (1986) *Tin in Antiquity*. London.

Pensabene, P. (1985) No. IV.3: tempietto tetrastilo di Torrenova (inv. no. 121509). In A. Giuliano (ed.), *Museo nazionale romano. Le sculture: I/8.I. Aule delle terme*: 170-7. Rome.

Penteriani, U and Penteriani Iacoangeli, M.P. (1986) *Nepi e il suo territorio nell'alto Medioevo*. Rome.

Peroni, A. (1975) *Pavia: Musei civici del castello visconteo*. Bologna.

Perrino, P. and Hammer K. (1982) *Triticum monococcum* L. and *Triticum dicoccum* Schubler (syn. of *T. dicoccon* Schrank) are still cultivated in Italy. *Genetic Agriculture* 36: 343-52.

Peters, W.J.T. (1963) *Landscape in Romano-Campanian Mural Painting*. Assen.

Peterson, R., Mountford, G. and Hollom, P.A.D. (1979) *A Field Guide to the Birds of Britain and Europe*. London.

Pettinau, B. (1984) No. XIII, 8: Acroterion. In A. Giuliano (ed.), *Museo nazionale romano. Le sculture: I/7.II. Giardino dei cinquecento*: 398-9. Rome.

Phenice, T.W. (1969) A newly developed visual method of sexing the os pubis. *American Journal of Physical Anthropology* 30: 297-302.

Picard, C. (1910) A propos de deux coupes du Vatican et d'un fragment du Musée Mircher. *Mélanges d'Archéologie et d'Histoire* 30: 99-116.

Picard, C. (1913) Questions de ceramique hellenistique. *Revue Archéologique* 22: 174-8.

Pietri, C. (1966) Le sénat, le peuple chrétien et les partis du cirque sous le pape Symmaque. *Mélanges de l'Ecole Française de Rome* 78: 123-39.

Pietri, C. (1976) *Roma Christiana* (*Bibliothèque de l'Ecole Française d'Athènes et de Rome* 224). Rome.

Pietri, C. (1978) Evergetisme et richesses ecclésiastiques dans l'Italie du IVe à la fin du Ve siècle. *Ktema* 3: 317-37.

Pietri, C. (1981) Aristocratie et societé clericale dans l'Italie chrétienne au temps de Odoacre et de Théodoric. *Mélanges de l'Ecole Française de Rome. Antiquité* 93 (1): 427-67.

Pohl, I. (1978) Piazzale delle Corporazioni. Portico ovest, saggi sotto i mosaici. *Notizie degli scavi di antichità*, supplement: 165-443.

Potter, T.W. (1972) Excavations in the medieval centre of Mazzano Romano. *Papers of the British School at Rome* 40: 135-45.

Potter, T.W. (1975) Recenti ricerche in Etruria meridionale: problemi della transizione dal tardo antico all'alto medievo. *Archeologia medievale* 2: 215-36.

Potter, T.W. (1976) *A Faliscan Town in South Etruria. Excavations at Narce 1966-71*. London.

Potter, T.W. (1979) *The Changing Landscape of South Etruria*. London.

Potter, T.W. (1985) *Storia del paesaggio dell'Etruria meridionale*. Rome.

Potter, T.W. (1991) Power, politics and territory in southern Etruria. In E. Herring, R. Whitehouse and J. Wilkins (eds), *Papers of the Fourth Conference of Italian Archaeology 2. The Archaeology of Power*. 173-84. London.

Potter, T.W. (1995) *Towns in Late Antiquity: Iol Caesarea and its Context*. Sheffield.

Potter, T.W. and Dunbabin, K.M. (1979) A Roman villa at Crocicchie, Via Clodia. *Papers of the British School at Rome* 47: 19-26.

Potter, T.W. and King, A.C. (1988) Scavi alla Mola di Monte Gelato, presso Mazzano Romano, Etruria Meridionale: primo rapporto preliminare. *Archeologia medievale* 15: 253-311.

Poulsen, F. (1914) *Tillaeg til Katalog over Ny Carlsberg Glyptoteks Antike Kunstwaerker*. Copenhagen.

Poulsen, V. (1962) *Les portraits romains* I. Copenhagen.

Prina Ricotti, E. (1988) Cibi e banchetti nell'antica Roma. *Archeo* 46: 52-97.

Provoost, A. (1976) Introduction et essai de typologie générale avec des détails concernant les lampes trouvées en Italie. *L'antiquité classique* 45: 5-39, 550-86.

Purcell, N. (1983) The *apparitores*: a study in social mobility. *Papers of the British School at Rome* 51: 125-73.

Purcell, N. (1985) Wine and wealth in ancient Italy. *Journal of Roman Studies* 75: 1-19.

Purcell, N. (1988a) Le inscrizioni. In T.W. Potter and A.C. King, Scavi alla Mola di Monte Gelato, presso Mazzano Romano, Etruria Meridionale: primo rapporto preliminare: 284-91. *Archeologia medievale* 15: 253-311.

Purcell, N. (1988b) Review of A. Carandini (ed.) (1985) *Settefinestre: una villa schiavistica nell'Etruria romana. Journal of Roman Studies* 78: 194-8.

Quilici Gigli, S. (ed.) (1990) *La Via Appia* (*Archeologia laziale* 10, 1). Rome.

Quilici, L. (1974) *Forma Italiae I.x. Collatia*. Rome.

Quilici, L. (1990) Via di S Paolo alla Regola – scavo e recupero di edifici antichi e medievali. *Notizie degli scavi di antichità*: 175-416.

Radke, G. (1981) *Viae publicae romanae*. Bologna.

Rahtz, P. (1977) Late Roman cemeteries and beyond. In R. Reece (ed.), *Burial in the Roman World* (*Council of British Archaeology Research Report* 22): 53-64. London, Council of British Archaeology.

Ramfjord, S.P., Kerr, D.A. and Ash, M.M. (1966) *World Workshop in Periodontics*. Ann Arbor, Michigan.

Rathbone, D.W. (1983) The slave mode of production in Italy. *Journal of Roman Studies* 73: 160-8.

Rebuffat, R. (1991) Vocabulaire thermal. Documents sur le bain romain. In *Les Thermes romains*: 1-34. Rome.

Reece, R. (1982) A collection of coins from the centre of Rome. *Papers of the British School at Rome* 50: 116-45.

Reece, R. (1984) The use of Roman coinage. *Oxford Journal of Archaeology* 3: 197-210.

Reece, R. (1987) *Coinage in Roman Britain*. London.

Reynolds, J.M. (1966) Inscriptions from south Etruria. *Papers of the British School at Rome* 34: 56-67.

Reynolds, J.M. (1988) Commento alle iscrizioni. In T.W. Potter and A.C. King, Scavi alla Mola di Monte Gelato, presso Mazzano Romano, Etruria Meridionale: primo rapporto preliminare: 284-5. *Archeologia medievale* 15: 253-311.

Reynolds, J.M. (1991) Inscriptions. In N. Christie (ed.), *Three South Etrurian Churches: Santa Cornelia, Santa Rufina and San Liberato* (*Archaeological Monographs of the British School at Rome* 4): 137-52, 301-7. London, British School at Rome.

RIC = *Roman Imperial Coinage*, vols III-IX.

Ricci, A. (1985a) Ceramica a pareti sottili. In G. Pugliese Carratelli (ed.), *Enciclopedia dell'arte antica classica e orientale – Atlante delle forme ceramiche* II.

Ceramica fine romana nel bacino mediterraneo (tardo ellenismo e primo impero): 231-357 + tavv. LXXVIII-CXIV. Rome.

Ricci, A. (ed.) (1985b) *Settefinestre. Una villa schiavistica nell'Etruria romana. 2. La villa e i suoi reperti.* Modena.

Ricci, M. (1986) Ceramica da fuoco. In D. Manacorda, L. Paroli, A. Molinari, M. Ricci and D. Romei, La ceramica medioevale di Roma nella stratigrafia della Crypta Balbi: 529-43. In *La ceramica medievale nel Mediterraneo occidentale (Atti del III Congresso Internazionale)*: 511-44. Florence.

Richter, G. (1915) *Greek, Etruscan and Roman Bronzes in the Metropolitan Museum of Art, New York.* New York.

Richter, G. (1926) *Ancient Furniture.* Oxford.

Rickman, G.E. (1980) *The Corn Supply of Ancient Rome.* Oxford.

Riley, J.A. (1979) The coarse pottery from Berenice. In J. Lloyd (ed.), *Excavations at Sidi Khrebish, Benghazi (Berenice)* II (Supplement to *Libya Antiqua* V): 91-467.

Ritchie, J.N.G. (1971) Iron finds from Dùn an Fheurain, Gallanach, Argyll. *Proceedings of the Society of Antiquaries of Scotland* 103: 100-12.

Roberts, P.C. (1988) *Pottery and Settlement in the Province of Molise during the Roman Imperial Period.* Unpublished M.Phil. thesis, Department of Ancient History, University of Sheffield.

Roberts, P.C. (1992) *The Late Roman Pottery of Adriatic Italy.* Unpublished Ph.D. thesis, University of Sheffield.

Roberts, P.C. (1993) The pottery from the cistern. In U. Albarella, V. Ceglia and P.C. Roberts, S. Giacomo degli Schiavoni (Molise): an early fifth century AD deposit of pottery and animal bones from central Adriatic Italy: 163-203. *Papers of the British School at Rome* 61: 157-230.

Roberts, P.C. (forthcoming) The Roman pottery. In J. Lloyd (ed.), *Excavations at the Roman villa at Matrice.*

Robinson, D. (1941) *Excavations at Olynthus* X. Baltimore.

Robinson, H.S. (1959) *Pottery of the Roman Period (Athenian Agora* V). Princeton.

Roes, A. (1963) *Bone and Antler Objects from the Frisian Terp-mounds.* Haarlem.

Rösler, W. (1995) Wine and truth in the Greek *symposion.* In O. Murray and M. Tecuşan (eds), *In Vino Veritas*: 106-12. London.

Rogers, J. and Waldron, T. (1989) Infections in palaeopathology; the basis of classification according to most probable cause. *Journal of Archaeological Science* 16: 611-25.

Rogers, J., Waldron, T., Dieppe P. and Waitt I. (1987) Arthropathies in palaeopathology; the basis of classification according to most probable cause. *Journal of Archaeological Science* 14: 179-83.

Romanini, A.M. (1971) Problemi di scultura e plastica altomedievali. *Artigianato e tecnica nella società dell'alto medioevo occidentale* (Spoleto): 425-67.

Romanini, A.M. (1991) Scultura nella "Langobardia Maior": questioni storiografiche. *Arte medievale* 5: 1-30.

Romei, D. (1986) Ceramica acroma depurata. In D. Manacorda, L. Paroli, A. Molinari, M. Ricci and D. Romei, La ceramica medioevale di Roma nella stratigrafia della Crypta Balbi: 523-9. In *La ceramica medievale nel Mediterraneo occidentale (Atti del III Congresso Internazionale)*: 511-44. Florence.

Romei, D. (1990) Ceramica acroma depurata II. In L. Saguì and L. Paroli (eds), *Archeologia urbana a Roma: il progetto della Crypta Balbi, 5. L'esedra della Crypta Balbi nel medioevo (XI-XV secolo)*: 264-87. Florence.

Romei, D. (1992) La ceramica a vetrina pesante altomedievale nella stratigrafia dell'esedra della Crypta Balbi. In L. Paroli (ed.), *La ceramica invetriata tardoantica e altomedievale in Italia*: 378-93. Florence.

Rösing, F.W. (1983) Sexing immature human skeletons. *Journal of Human Evolution* 12: 149-55.

Rossiter, J.J. (1978) *Roman Farm Buildings in Italy* (BAR International Series 52). Oxford.

Saguì, L. (1986) Crypta Balbi (Roma): lo scavo nell'esedra del monumento romano. Seconda relazione preliminare. *Archeologia medievale* 13: 345-55.

Saguì, L. (1991) Ceramica da fuoco. In M.T. Cipriano, L. Paroli, H. Patterson, L. Saguì and D. Whitehouse (1991), La documentazione ceramica dell'Italia centro-meridionale nell'alto medioevo: quadri regionali contesti campioni. In *A ceramica medieval no Mediterraneo ocidental (Atti del IV Congresso Internazionale)*: 102-5. Mertola.

Saguì, L. and Paroli, L. (eds) (1990) *Archeologia urbana a Roma: il progetto della Crypta Balbi, 5. L'esedra della Crypta Balbi nel medioevo (XI-XV secolo).* Florence.

Salter, M. (1984) Compilation of age of fusion data from twelve sources. Unpublished paper.

Salvatore, M. (1982) La ceramica altomedievale nell'Italia centromeridionale: stato e prospettive della ricerca. *Archeologia medievale* 9: 47-66.

Salvatore, M. (1983) La ceramica tardoromana e altomedievale in Basilicata alla luce delle recenti scoperte. In M. Gualtieri, M. Salvatore and A. Small (eds), *Lo scavo di S. Giovanni di Ruoti ed il periodo tardoantico in Basilicata*: 111-23. Bari.

Saunders, S.R. (1989) Nonmetric skeletal variation. In M.Y. Iscan and K.A.R. Kennedy (eds), *Reconstruction of Life from the Skeleton*: 95-108. New York.

Schiaparelli, L. (ed.) (1901) Il cartario di San Pietro in Vaticano. I parte. *Archivio della Società romana di storia patria* 24: 393-496.

Schinke, R. (1994) The amphorae. In O.J. Gilkes, S. Passigli and R. Schinke, Porta Pia: excavation and survey in an area of suburban Rome, Part 2: 117-22. *Papers of the British School at Rome* 62: 101-37.

Schour, I. and Massler, M. (1944) *Development of the Human Dentition* (second edition). Chicago.

Schubart, W. (1911) *Papyri Graecae Berolinenses*. Bonn.

Schuring, J.M. (1987) Supplementary note to the Roman, early medieval and medieval coarse kitchen wares from the San Sisto Vecchio in Rome. *Bullettin Antieke Beschaving* 61: 109-29.

SEG = Supplementum epigraphicum Graecum.

Seminario = (1976) Seminario sulla tecnica e il linguaggio della scultura a Roma tra VIII e IX secolo. Roma e l'età Carolingia: 267-88. Rome.

Sennis, A. (1996) Un territorio da ricomporre: il Lazio tra i secoli IV e XIV. In *Atlante storico-politico del Lazio*: 27-61. Rome/Bari.

Serafini, A. (1927) *Le torri campanarie del Lazio nel medioevo*. Rome.

Sereni, E. (1982) *Storia del paesaggio agrario italiano*. Bari.

Shelton, K. (1981) *The Esquiline Treasure*. London.

Silver, I.A. (1969) The ageing of the domestic animals. In D. Brothwell and E. Higgs (eds), *Science and Archaeology* (second edition): 283-302. London.

Siviero, R. (1954) *Gli ori e le ambri del Museo Nazionale di Napoli. Le Opera d'arte recuperate* II. Sansoni.

Small, A.M. and Buck, R.J. (1994) *The Excavations of San Giovanni di Ruoti 1. The Villas and their Environment*. Toronto.

Smith, R.R.R. (1990) Late Roman philosopher portraits from Aphrodisias. *Journal of Roman Studies* 80: 127-55.

Smith, W. (1865) *Dictionary of Greek and Roman Antiquities*. London.

Sölter, W. (1970) *Römische Kalkbrenner im Rheinland*. Düsseldorf.

Solin, H. (1982) *Die Griechischen Personnamen in Rom: ein Namenbuch*. Berlin.

Soricelli, G. (1988) Osservazioni intorno ad un cratere in ceramica invetriata a Pompeii. *Rivista di studi pompeiani* 2: 248-54.

Spurr, M.S. (1986) *Arable Cultivation in Roman Italy c. 200 B.C.-c. A.D. 100 (Society for the Promotion of Roman Studies, monograph 3)*. London.

Staffa, A.R. (1984) Villa romana presso la Torre di Rebibbia. *Bullettino della Commissione archeologica comunale di Roma* 89: 114-24.

Staffa, A.R. (1986) Località Rebibbia, via S Canizzaro. Un punto di sosta lungo la via Tiburtina fra l'età di Augusto e la tarda antichità (circ. V). *Bullettino della commissione archeologica comunale di Roma* 91 (2): 642-78.

Steele, D.G. (1983) The analysis of animal remains from two late Roman middens at San Giovanni di Ruoti. In M. Gualtieri, M. Salvatore and A. Small (eds), *Lo scavo di S. Giovanni di Ruoti ed il periodo tardoantico in Basilicata*: 75-84. Bari.

Steinbock, R.T. (1976) *Paleopathological Diagnosis and Interpretation; Bone Disease in Ancient Human Populations*. Springfield.

Stone, M. (1984) I laterizi. In F. Cameron, G. Clark, R. Jackson, C. Johns, S. Philpot, T. Potter, J. Shepherd, M. Stone and D. Whitehouse, Il castello di Ponte Nepesino e il confine settentrionale del Ducato di Roma: 108-21. *Archeologia medievale* 11: 63-147.

Stoppioni Piccoli, M.L. (1983) I materiali della fornace romana di Via della Resistenza, a Santarcangelo di Romagna. *Studi romagnoli* 34: 29-46.

Storz, S. (1994) *Tonröhren im antiken Gewölbebau*. Mainz.

Strong, D.E. (1953) Late Hadrianic architectural ornament in Rome. *Papers of the British School at Rome* 21: 118-51.

Strong, D.E. (1963) Some observations on early Roman Corinthian. *Journal of Roman Studies* 53: 73-84.

Strong, D.E. (1966) *Greek and Roman Gold and Silver Plate*. London.

Stuart-Macadam, P.L. (1989) Nutritional deficiency diseases; a survey of scurvy, rickets and iron deficiency anaemia. In M.Y. Iscan and K.A.R. Kennedy (eds), *Reconstruction of Life from the Skeleton*: 201-22. New York.

Sundick, R.I. (1978) Human skeletal growth and age determination. *Homo* 30: 297-333.

Svenbro, J. (1988) *Phrasikleia: Anthropologie de la lecture en Grèce ancienne*. Paris.

Swan, V.G. (1984) *The Pottery Kilns of Roman Britain.* London.

Tattersall, I. (1968) Dental palaeopathology of medieval Britain. *Journal of the History of Medicine* 23 (4): 380-8.

Taylor, L.R. (1914) Augustales, Seviri Augustales, and seviri: a chronological study. *Transactions and Proceedings of the American Philological Association* 45: 231-53.

Tchernia, A. (1986) *Le vin de l'Italie romaine: essai d'histoire économique d'après les amphores (Collection de l'Ecole Française de Rome* 261). Rome.

Thesing, R. (1977) *Die Grossentwicklung des Haushuhns in Vor- und Frühgeschichtlicher Zeit.* Dissertation der Universität München.

Thomas, R. and Wilson, A. (1994) Water supply for Roman farms in Latium and south Etruria. *Papers of the British School at Rome* 62: 139-96.

Thompson, D.W. (1936) *A Glossary of Greek Birds.* London.

Thompson, H.A. (1934) Two centuries of Hellenistic pottery. *Hesperia* 3: 311-480.

Threipland, L.M. (1968) Cogged ware. *Papers of the British School at Rome* 36: 199, figs 26 and 35.

Tomassetti, G. (1877) Mazzano. *Notizie degli scavi di antichità*: 262-3.

Tomassetti, G. (1882) Della campagna romana nel medioevo. *Archivio della Società romana di storia patria* 5: 67-156.

Tomassetti, G. (1883) Della campagna romana nel medio evo (cont.). *Archivio della Società romana di storia patria* 6: 173-222.

Tomassetti G. (1884) La campagna romana nel medioevo. *Archivio della Società romana di storia patria* 7: 183-258, 353-462.

Tomassetti G. (1910) *La campagna romana antica, medievale e moderna* I. Rome.

Tomassetti, G. (1913) *La campagna romana.* Rome.

Tomassetti, G. (1913 (1979)) *La campagna romana, antica, medioevale e moderna* 3 *(nuova edizione aggiornata a cura di L. Chiumenti e F. Bilancia).* Florence.

Tortorella, S. (1981) Ceramica africana. Ceramica da cucina. In G. Pugliese Carratelli, *Enciclopedia dell'arte antica classica e orientale. Atlante delle forme ceramiche. I. Ceramica fine romana nel bacino mediterraneo (medio e tardo impero)*: 208-27 + tavv. CIV-CIX. Rome.

Tosti, A. (1835) *Rilevazione dell'origine e i progressi dell'Ospizio Apostolico di S. Michele.* Rome.

Toubert, P. (1973) *Les structures du Latium médiéval: le Latium méridional et la Sabine du IX siècle à la fin du XII siècle (Bibliothèque des Ecoles Françaises d'Athènes et de Rome,* 221). Rome.

Toynbee, J.M.C. (1973) *Animals in Roman Life and Art.* London.

Tozzi, C. (1981) L'alimentazione nella Maremma medievale: due esempi di scavi. *Archeologia medievale* 8: 299-305.

Tran Tam Tinh (1988) *La casa dei cervi a Herculaneum.* Rome.

Trotter, M. and Glesser, G.C. (1952) Estimation of stature from long bones of American whites and negroes. *American Journal of Physical Anthropology* 10: 463-514.

Trotter, M. and Glesser, G.C. (1958) A re-evaluation of estimation of stature based on measurements of stature taken during life and long bones after death. *American Journal of Physical Anthropology* 16: 79-123.

Turner, E.G. (1971) *Greek Manuscripts of the Ancient World.* Oxford.

Turner, E.G. (1987) *Greek Manuscripts of the Ancient World* (second edition). London.

Ubelaker, D.H. (1978) *Human Skeletal Remains; Excavation, Analysis and Interpretation.* Taraxacum, Washington.

Ubelaker, D.H. (1989) *Human Skeletal Remains. Excavation, Analysis, Interpretation (Manuals on Archaeology* 2) (second edition). Taraxacum, Washington.

Van Essen, C.C. (1957) Reliefs décoratifs d'époque carolingienne à Rome. *Mededelingen van het Nederlands Historisch Instituut te Rome* 9: 84-113.

Van de Noort, R. and Whitehouse, D.B. (1992) Le mura di Santo Stefano and other medieval churches in south Etruria: the archaeological evidence. *Archeologia medievale* 19: 75-89.

Van Neer, W. (ed.) (1994) *Fish Exploitation in the Past (Proceedings of the seventh meeting of the ICAZ Fish Remains Working Group / Annales du Musée Royal de l'Afrique Centrale, Sciences Zoologiques* 274). Tervuren.

Vassy, A. (1934) Découverte de deux estampilles de plombiers romaine et estampilles du Musée de Vienne. *Rhodania* 16: 159-77.

Vera, D. (1986) Forme e funzioni della rendita fondaria nella tarda antichità. In A. Giardina (ed.), *Società romana e impero tardoantico* I: 367-447, 723-60. Rome/Bari.

Vera, D. (1995) Dalla "villa perfecta" alla villa di Palladio: sulle trasformazioni del sistema agrario in Italia fra principato e dominato. *Athenaeum* 83: 189-211, 331-56.

Vermeule, C.C. (1965) A Greek theme and its survivals: the ruler's shield (tondo image) in tomb and temple. *Proceedings of the American Philosophical Society* 107: 361-97.

Verzone, P. (1945) *L'arte preromanica in Liguria*. Turin.

Voza, G. (1989) I crolli nella villa romana di Patti Marina. In E. Guidoboni (ed.), *I terramoti prima del mille in Italia e nell'area mediterranea*: 496-501. Bologna.

Waldbaum, J.C. (1983) *Metalwork from Sardis: the Finds through 1974*. Cambridge, Mass.

Waldron, T. (1991) Rates for the job. Measures of disease frequency in palaeopathology. *International Journal of Osteoarchaeology* 1: 17-25.

Waldron, T. (forthcoming) The human bone from St Mary Graces (the Royal Mint), London.

Walker, S. (1985) *Memorials to the Roman Dead*. London.

Ward-Perkins, J.B. (1955) Notes on southern Etruria and the Ager Veientanus. *Papers of the British School at Rome* 23: 44-72.

Ward-Perkins, J.B. (1961) Veii. The historical topography of the ancient city. *Papers of the British School at Rome* 29: 1-123.

Ward-Perkins, J.B. (1970) Introduction to T. Ashby, *The Roman Campagna in Classical Times* (1970 reprint): v-x. Tonbridge.

Ward-Perkins, J.B. (1971) Quarries and stoneworking in the early middle ages: the heritage of the ancient world. In *Artigianato e tecnica nella società dell'Alto Medioevo occidentale*: 525-44. Spoleto.

Ward-Perkins, J.B. and Claridge, A. (1976) *Pompeii AD 79*. London.

Wells, C. (1982) The human burials. In A. McWhirr, L. Viner and C. Wells, *Romano-British Cemeteries at Cirencester*: 135-201. Cirencester.

West, B. (1982) Spur development: recognising caponised fowl in archaeological material. In B. Wilson, C. Grigson and S. Payne (eds), *Ageing and Sexing Animal Bones from Archaeological Sites* (BAR British Series 109): 255-61. Oxford.

West, B. (1985) Chicken legs revisited. *Circaea* 3 (1): 11-14.

Wheeler, A. and Jones, A.K.G. (1989) *Fishes*. Cambridge.

Wheeler, A. and Locker, A. (1985) The estimation of size in sardines (*Sardina pilchardus*) from amphorae in a wreck at Randello, Sicily. *Journal of Archaeological Science* 12: 97-100.

White, K.D. (1970) *Roman Farming*. London.

Whitehead, P.J.P., Bauchot, M-L., Hureau, J-C., Nielsen, J. and Tortonese, E. (1989) *Fishes of the North-eastern Atlantic and the Mediterranean* I-III. UNESCO.

Whitehouse, D.B. (1965) 'Forum ware' a distinctive type of early medieval glazed pottery from the Roman Campagna. *Medieval Archaeology* 9: 55-63.

Whitehouse, D.B. (1980) The medieval pottery from Santa Cornelia. *Papers of the British School at Rome* 48: 125-56.

Whitehouse, D.B. (1982) The pottery. In D.B. Whitehouse, G. Barker, R. Reece and D. Reese, The Schola Praeconum I: the coins, pottery, lamps and fauna: 56-80. *Papers of the British School at Rome* 50: 53-101.

Whitehouse, D.B. (1983) Ruoti, pottery and pigs. In M. Gualtieri, M. Salvatore and A. Small (eds), *Lo scavo di S. Giovanni di Ruoti ed il periodo tardoantico in Basilicata*: 107-9. Bari.

Whittaker, D.K., Griffiths, S., Robson, A., Rogers-Davies, P., Thomas, G. and Molleson, T. (1990) Continuing tooth eruption and alveolar crest height in an eighteenth century population from Spitalfields, East London. *Arch.Oral.Biol.* 35 (2): 81-5.

Wickham, C.J. (1978) Historical and topographical notes on early medieval south Etruria (part one). *Papers of the British School at Rome* 46: 132-79.

Wickham, C.J. (1979) Historical and topographical notes on early medieval south Etruria (part two). *Papers of the British School at Rome* 47: 66-95.

Wickham, C.J. (1981) *Early Medieval Italy. Central Power and Local Society, 400-1000*. London.

Wild, J.P. (1970) *Textile Manufacture in the North West Provinces*. Cambridge.

Wilson, R.J.A. (1992) Terracotta vaulting tubes (*tubi fittili*): on their origin and distribution. *Journal of Roman Archaeology* 5: 97-129.

Winkes, R. (1969) *Clipeata Imago. Studien zu einer Römischen Bildnisform*. Bonn.

Wolters, P. (1913) Eingeritzte Inschriften auf Vasen. *Mitteilungen des Deutschen Archäologischen Institute, Athenische Abteilung* 38: 193-202.

Woolf, G. (1990) Food, poverty and patronage: the signficance of the epigraphy of the Roman alimentary schemes in early Imperial Italy. *Papers of the British School at Rome* 58: 197-228.

Zanker, P. and Fittschen, K. (1983) *Katalog der Römischen Porträts in den Capitolinischen Museen und den anderen Kommunalen Sammlungen der Stadt Rom III: Kaiserinnen- und Prinzessinnenbildnisse Frauenporträts*. Mainz.

Zevi, F. and Carta, M. (1987) La taberna dell'Invidioso. *Notizie degli scavi di antichità*, supplement: 9-164.

Zevi, F. and Pohl, I. (1970) Ostia – saggi di scavo. *Notizie degli scavi di antichità*, supplement.

INDEX

compiled by Gillian Clark